# CHARLES I
## The Personal Monarch
### Second Edition

'It is hard to imagine a more balanced, fairer study than Charles Carlton's *Charles I: A Personal Monarch*. Faultlessly documented, yet unfolding as a primarily human story, it reveals him in every aspect, as king, husband, father, devout churchman, neither tyrant nor saint, until he becomes wholly known and understandable to us.'

*The Bookseller*

'This is a splendid biography... Professor Carlton deserves congratulations on this outstanding and fascinating book on the last ruling king of England.'

*Catholic Herald*

'The author shows an unusual degree of insight into the King's character, and excels in relating cause and effect.'

*Eastern Daily Press*

'His grasp of the political context is firm and confident. He is extremely good on both the artistic and the political dimensions of the royal court'

*The Scotsman*

Charles Carlton's biography of the 'monarch of the Civil Wars' was praised for its distinctive psychological portrait of Charles I when it was first published in 1983. Challenging conventional interpretations of the king, as well as questioning orthodox historical assumptions concerning the origins and development of the Civil Wars, the book quickly established itself as the definitive biography.

In the eleven years since *Charles I* was published an immense amount of new material on the king and his reign have emerged and yet no new biography has been written. Professor Carlton's second edition includes a substantial new preface which takes account of the new work. Addressing and analysing the furious historiographical debates which have surrounded the period, Carlton offers a fresh and lucid perspective. He has also thoroughly updated the text of the first edition.

# CHARLES I

## The Personal Monarch
## Second Edition

*Charles Carlton*

London and New York

First published 1983

Second edition published 1995
by Routledge
11 New Fetter Lane, London EC4P 4EE

Simultaneously published in the USA and Canada
by Routledge
29 West 35th Street, New York, NY 10001

The moral right of the author has been asserted
© 1983, 1995 Charles Carlton

Phototypeset in Garamond by Intype, London

Printed and bound in Great Britain by
Clays Ltd, St Ives, plc

*British Library Cataloguing in Publication Data*
A catalogue record for this book is available from the British Library

*Library of Congress Cataloging in Publication Data*
A catalogue record for this book has been requested
ISBN 0–415–12141–8
0–415–12565–0 (pbk)

For Caroline

# CONTENTS

# ILLUSTRATIONS

*Between pages 206 and 207*

1 Charles, Duke of York (St John's College, Cambridge)
2 Charles, Prince of Wales by Daniel Mytens (from the collection at Parham Park, Sussex)
3 Charles I and his family by Van Dyck (by gracious permission of Her Majesty, the Queen)
4 Charles I dining in public by Gerard Houckgeest (by gracious permission of Her Majesty, the Queen)
5 Charles I with Henrietta Maria and the Prince of Wales by Hendrick Gerritsz Pot (by gracious permission of Her Majesty, the Queen)
6 The Banqueting House ceiling by Rubens (Crown Copyright: reproduced by permission of the Department of the Environment)
7 'St George and the Dragon' by Rubens (by gracious permission of Her Majesty, the Queen)
8 'Charles I on horseback' by Van Dyck (courtesy of the Trustees of the National Portrait Gallery)
9 Peter Pett and the *Sovereign of the Seas* (National Maritime Museum, London)
10 Cartoon of Prince Rupert hiding in a bean field after the battle of Marston Moor from a contemporary satirical pamphlet (B. T. Batsford Ltd)
11 Charles I dictating to Sir Edward Walker (courtesy of the Trustees of the National Portrait Gallery)
12 Charles I in later life (by kind permission of Peter Walker Esq.)
13 Charles I from the frontispiece of *Eikon Basilike* (Mansell Collection)

# PREFACE
## 'That memorable scene'

The scene is so familiar that it runs the risk of becoming a cliché. That cold January afternoon in Whitehall, the black draped scaffold, the ring of soldiers, the short, dignified and frightened figure trying in vain to make himself heard as the raw east wind carried his words over the heads of the pikemen to be lost among the bare trees of St James's Park. The axe swings, the hooded executioner holds up the head as that of a traitor, the crowd moans, surging forward to dip their handkerchieves in the martyr's blood, before the roundhead cavalry roughly cleared the street, leaving only Andrew Marvell's lines to haunt the memory:

> That thence the Royal Actor born
> The Tragic Scaffold might adorn . . .
> He nothing common did or mean
> Upon that memorable scene:

In several ways Charles's death was the climax of his life. In martyrdom he won by losing, resolving many of the tensions – which he called 'disturbances' – that beset him for most of his days. His death gave his life a tragic dignity. In dying he showed grandeur in place of meanness, resolve instead of vacillation, honesty where duplicity had often been the norm. The dénouement of the final act, however, should not overshadow the rest of the play. In life, unlike the theatre, the finale is not known, the start and progress being barely comprehended. On one sense, our under-standing of Charles's passage through life must inevitably be warped by our knowledge of the way he left it. Thus whilst a biography may provide the emotional satisfaction of describing the most important task that we all have to do – the living of a single life – it has the disquiet of a detective novel in which the last chapter has to be read first.

This book was started longer ago than I care to remember in that seminary of creative ideas, the British Museum's coffee room, with a discussion about who in early modern British history needed a fresh biography. I would like to think that I have tried to satisfy such a need. Although grounded on the king's letters, this book contains no new evidence from some remote muniment room or miscatalogued bundle. I did not expect to find any. On the other hand, it does try to place the king's life in the context of recent interpretations of the period, or rather the lack thereof, since the syntheses that stressed social change or radical religion no longer hold the sway they once enjoyed, being yet to be replaced. If this work substantiates the axiom that each generation reinterprets the past in the light of its own experience I make no apology: we have seen how fragile are the bonds that unite a kingdom, how a great nation can, almost without thinking, get caught up with an entanglement abroad that nigh destroys it at home, and how long standing flaws of character can, within a short time, cause an incumbent to lose the highest of offices.

In recent years theories about human behaviour have developed that may be of use to a biographer. Disraeli's advice to 'Read no history; nothing but biography, for that is life without theory' has always been impossible because no one can describe a life without making theoretical assumptions about human behaviour.[1] For instance, some have interpreted 'Little Laud's' lack of stature as the key to understanding Archbishop Laud's aggravating personality and policies. Others have explained Charles's determination, or stubbornness as the reaction to a childhood weakness, which he forced himself to overcome by strenuous exercise, riding and hunting.[2] The trouble with such explanations is that they are frequently naive; unbacked by empirical evidence or experimentation they often fail to take into account the complexities of the human psyche, with its various parts working consciously or unconsciously against each other.

On the other hand the applications of modern social science theories of human behaviour to biography lack neither their dangers nor critics.[3] Psychoanalysis and psychology are essentially predictive methodologies. Thus the historian who applies them to the known outcomes of the past runs the risk of claiming the omnipotence of the punter who is allowed to place his bets after the race has been run. Inherent to this process is the danger of 'reductionism' – a form of psycho-biographical predestination as implacable as anything to come from Geneva.

Take, for instance, an incident Bishop Laud noted in his diary. In January 1623, twenty-six years and two days before he was executed, Charles was exceedingly merry at dinner, talking on a wide range of subjects, including the choice of a career. One thing he could never be, declared the 22–year-old prince, was a lawyer, because 'I cannot defend a bad, nor yield a good cause.'[4] Although uncannily prophetic Laud's story possesses an equally disturbing note of inevitability. While one may use it to explain Charles's later actions, it would be absurd to suggest that because Prince Charles announced that he could not compromise his principles, all of King Charles's parliaments had to end in confrontation, every concession he made had to be wrung from him like an impacted wisdom tooth, that he could never accept the constitutional monarchy of 1641, or that, after the civil war, at the bargaining table he could not grant the other side the gains they had won on the field of battle.

Thus the theoretical framework in which a biographer writes must allow his subject to both grow and yet remain consistent: our fates are not unalterably cast by the time of adolescence, weaning or even the moment of our births. To provide this element of flexibility, concepts such as socialization, modelling, social learning theory and the life cycle are useful. The latter is not a new idea. At Carisbrooke Charles may have read the passage in *As You Like It*, wherein Shakespeare talks of the seven ages through which man must proceed, each with its own tasks and challenges, its physical and mental conditions. Certainly on the scaffold Bishop Juxon talked to the king in such terms: 'There is but one stage more, which through turbulent yet it is a very short one.'[5] In addition to the idea of the stages through which a man must pass on the journey of life, recent work on social learning theory has examined the ways in which people deal with these, showing how an individual's reactions to an experience will be mainly influenced by his behaviour during the most recent similar experience, and second, by his expectations of his own and other people's behaviour. Yet far from reacting with Pavlovian simplicity (for most experiences are much more complex than the mere ringing of a bell, and reactions much more interesting than salivation), we continually undergo a reciprocal interaction, constantly learning from new experiences: as we meet them our expectations change and develop. None the less, research on learned helplessness and depression would suggest, once learned, a reaction is very hard to shed.[6]

Perhaps such ideas may seem far fetched: certainly they are not fully proven. Some might argue that such modern concepts cannot be applied back three centuries in time; and yet anthropologists have used them with telling effect to understand equally – if not more distant – non-Western primitive societies.[7] Others might oppose them on the grounds that as curative methodologies such theories do not work; yet, as far as a biographer is concerned, this objection is irrelevant, for his task is to understand his subject as thoroughly as possible, and not to alleviate his condition. When still more critics point out that the vast majority of historical figures lack sufficient surviving evidence to make a clinical judgment, they are uttering the obvious whilst they miss the point. The psycho-biographer is not interested in arriving at a clinical diagnosis. Thus it would be as unfair to hold him to the same exacting standards of proof as a clinician, as to insist, for instance, that a medieval demographic historian only comes to conclusions employing the same plethora of data as used by a modern census bureau, or an econometric historian be as rigorous in the use of his evidence as a forecaster for the government or modern corporation. If only because – thank goodness – he cannot recall his subject to Clio's couch, a psycho-biographer cannot be held to a higher standard of proof than any other sort of historian. After all he is essentially a historian, not a clinician. Unlike the latter he need not spend sleepless nights worrying that if his analysis is wrong his subject might commit suicide!

Yet criticisms of the use of new methodologies by historians and biographers are extremely valuable. They mean that the biographer cannot hide his assumptions about human behaviour – although for aesthetic reasons he may be allowed to bury his theoretical explanations and sources in the footnotes. They mean that he cannot take refuge in unspoken explanations of motivation, or theories that depend on hereditary or national characteristics. They remind us that human beings are extremely complex creatures, rarely comprehensible through simple generalizations about short archbishops or weak boy princes, often behaving in ways that defy mere 'common-sense' explanations. Take, for example, Charles's stutter. For nearly the whole of his life the king spoke with hesitation, his impediment making it hard for him to win support through public oratory or friends in private conversation. Was this impediment the result of the cord under his tongue which his father wanted to have cut when he was four or five? Or was it the symptom of some deep-seated neurosis, coming possibly from the fear of his father, rejection by his mother, or domination by an elder brother that haunted Charles for most of his life?

It is my final, and most pleasant duty to thank all who have helped me with this project. A senior fellowship from the Folger Shakespeare Library allowed me to spend a very enjoyable year in Washington, DC, doing the basic research on printed materials, which a summer fellowship at the Huntingdon Library enabled me to complete. Grants from the American Philosophical Society and the Faculty Research and Professional Development Fund of North Carolina State University helped me to spend several summers working in the archives in England, during one of which I enjoyed the hospitality of Clare Hall, Cambridge. Fellowships from the National Endowment for the Humanities permitted me to spend a month at the City University of New York studying psycho-history and an academic year (with plenty of time for writing) as a visiting fellow at the University of Wisconsin, Madison. The staffs of the following libraries were unfailingly helpful: Cambridge University Library, St John's College, Oxford, Sheffield Public Library, Memorial and Law Libraries of the University of Wisconsin, Madison, the Public Record Office, the Institute of Historical Research, the British Library, the Bodleian Library, Duke University Library, the University of North Carolina Library, Chapel Hill, and the D. H. Hill Library at North Carolina State University. For answering inquiries I am indebted to the Victoria and Albert Museum, the Virginia State Historical Society, the University of Chicago Library, and the Surrey Record Office.

I am much obliged to *British Heritage* for allowing me to use material mainly from Chapter IV. The president and fellows of Wolfson College, Cambridge, very kindly elected me a visiting fellow – an honour I cherish all the more for with it came the friendship and hospitality of all members of that most pleasant college.

My thanks and obligations to those who read drafts of this book, or let me pick their brains with a remarkable generosity, can never be properly recognized, particularly with an alphabetical list: Curt Bartol, Kate Bostock, Christopher Coleman, Esther Cope, Murray Edelman, Geoffrey Elton, Raghild Hatton, Lamar Hill, Joe Hobbs, Joel Hurstfield, Frank Larkin, Peter Loewenburg, David Lovejoy, Bruce Mazlish, Marlynn May, John Morrill, John Pocock, Conrad Russell, Don Scott, Joe Slavin, Bill Speck, Bob Tilman, Nicolas Tyacke, Andrew Wheatcroft, Bernard Wishy, and Fred Youngs – to you, and many more, are due my sincerest thanks; it has been your friendship and kindnesses that has made this the happiest of human endeavours. Finally to my family, who have quite literally crossed continents and oceans following my pursuit of the king, my appreciation can never be fully expressed, especially to my wife, Caroline. For several years she has had to live with two Charleses, without ever once becoming a Henrietta Maria.

# PREFACE TO THE SECOND EDITION

Since this life of Charles I was published eleven years ago a tremendous amount of new material on the king and his reign have appeared, and yet no new biography has been written. In contrast, during the decade before the first edition of this biography, five lives of the monarch saw the light of day.[1] So it now seems appropriate to publish a second edition updating the first by taking into account recent historiographic developments.

*Charles I: The Personal Monarch* has four main themes. First, it uses psychology, and psychoanalysis in particular, to look at the king's life, paying special attention to his childhood. Second, it enters the debate over the origins of the civil war, an argument so vigorous that Conrad Russell once described it as 'the favourite blood sport of English Historians'. I maintain that the king – more than anyone else – was to blame for the bloodiest war known to English history. In sum, Charles failed because of his own personal defects. Third, the biography posits that during the 1630s, the time of the so-called 'personal rule', Charles retreated to the world of his court only to emerge to introduce what Henrietta Maria described as 'that fatal book', the Scots liturgy. Finally, it suggests (not terribly originally), that the king's reign must be viewed within a British context.

Today there is a growing awareness of the British dimension of the wars that engulfed the three kingdoms, as well as the Principality of Wales, in the mid-seventeenth century. Scholars such as Conrad Russell, John Morrill, Nicholas Canny, Steve Ellis, David Stephenson, Maurice Lee and Peter Donald, have done a tremendous amount to make us aware of the British context of the period.[2] The denominator that the British Isles had in common was the monarch, and in Charles's case it was a pretty low one, whose initiatives stimulated similar reactions from different nations.

The aspect of this biography which received the most comment among reviewers was its use of psychology, psychoanalysis in particular. Interestingly enough, American reviewers welcomed the methodology, while suggesting that it was not taken far enough: English critics were horrified by this technique, suggesting that taking it anywhere was taking it too far. In the last decade, however, psychohistory has lost ground to social history.[3] None the less there is something to be said for this genre.

When asked to explain how Freud had helped him to understand the ancient Greeks, E. R. Dodds replied that 'He did help me to understand myself and other people a little better, but that is a benefit which I share with millions of others.'[4] The attraction of writing – and reading – biographies lies, I believe, in the way in which they help us to understand our fellow creatures, and thus ourselves. When used carefully psychobiography can take our comprehension of personality far further than simple 'common sense' explanations.

To give one example. A leading scholar of the king's reign has recently written: 'The product perhaps, of a dislocated youth and strict self discipline, Charles developed into a rather rigid personality.'[5] I am not quite certain what a dislocated youth is (I hope it's different from a dislocated hernia), but I do believe that using the phrase 'rigid personality', when we have such a rich and precise series of descriptive words to describe character, is rather like a twentieth-century physician employing a seventeenth-century term such as 'the bloody flux' to diagnose a modern problem. When writing about, say, law or economics, historians use the appropriate professional terms. Surely biographers should do no less when dealing with personality?

A biographer's first duty is to understand his or her subject and the environment in which they live. He or she must look at the subject's whole life, showing consistencies and development of character – something a short-term study cannot do. For instance, in his superb monograph *The Forced Loan*, Richard Cust writes that in May 1626 the French ambassador told Charles that if he did not stand up to the opposition, Europe would account him as inconsequential as the Doge of Venice.[6] If one examines Charles's life as a whole, the image of the Doge as an impotent figure of fun emerges as a powerful one. The king referred to it in one of the most insightful letters he ever wrote. 'So long as the covenant is in force,' he told the Duke of Hamilton on 11 June 1638, 'I am no more in Scotland than as a Duke of Venice. . . . I *will rather die* than yield to their *impertinent* and *damnable* demands.' To show the depth of his feelings Charles underlined his letter, one of only two occasions that he did so.

A biography can give short-term studies a degree of consistency. Again. let me borrow from Dr Cust, who says that in reacting to the opposition to the Forced Loan the king 'appeared to have been in the grip of something approaching paranoia.'[7] In his fine study *Charles I and the Road to Personal Rule* (1989), John Reeve makes the same point when describing Charles's proclamation of 4 March 1628 that castigated the Commons for locking the door in Black Rod's face, holding the speaker to the throne and passing the four resolutions against papism and Arminianism. In this proclamation the king divided the country into those – the few – who were against him and those – the silent majority – who supported their lawful sovereign.[8]

Both Reeve and Cust's conclusions – like those of Thomas Cogswell – would have been more convincing had they been fitted into the context of the king's life as a whole.[9] While human beings do change, their personalities remain remarkably consistent, modifying themselves, if at all, from one similar experience to the another. Charles hounded the leaders of the March 1629 Commons' fracas, letting Elliot die in the Tower. Nine years later he believed the Scots rebellion to be the work of a few agitators: the real issue, he maintained, being 'whether we be their king or not.'[10] In 1642 Charles blamed the Five Members for all of his problems with parliament, and in the pamphlets he published in the ensuing six months he personalized the conflict. Immediately after war broke out Charles found great psychological relief in the 'them and us' aspect of hostilities.

Charles was never comfortable with 'them', preferring to live with 'us'. After Buckingham's murder, he retreated to the world of his court, collecting paintings, falling in love with his wife and starting a family. In the last two decades or so, historians have paid much attention to royal courts, some seeing them, not parliament, as the place where the real politics struggle took place. This emphasis on courts, pioneered by David Starkey, stresses the importance of access to the king in an almost Namierite fashion, assuming that all connections are of equal weight.[11]

Perhaps this biography defines the king's court too narrowly, but as far as Charles I was concerned, it was the place where he felt at home – it was, if you like, his extended family, much as a rich aristocrat would have an extended family of relatives, retainers and servants.[12] If Charles's court was not, to quote Kevin Sharpe, 'a retreat from Reality, but rather a model for the reformed government of Church and State,'[13] then it was a model whose messages, projected mainly by art, were intended mainly for internal consumption. We may have taken masques too seriously: certainly they are pretty tedious pieces of entertainment, and had little impact outside Whitehall Palace. Even if dramatists did criticize the king, they did so with a delicacy that did not offend an ego as touchy as Charles I's. All of the king's playwrights (as well as his artists and poets) came to praise him, not bury him: a conclusion to which Prynne, Burton, and Bastwick would – had they had any left – have surely lent their ears.

Since the publication of this life of Charles I, most historians have seen the king as the villain of the piece, who was personally responsible for the disaster of the civil war. In part, this has been a reflection of the 'revisionists' who have emphasized personal, as opposed to impersonal forces (such as radical religion or the rise of the bourgeoisie), and see the collapse of royal government as a short-term phenomenon. Anyway, there is no doubt that in the last decade historians have been nigh unanimous about their criticism of Charles I. 'As a reigning monarch he was woefully inadequate,' writes John Reeve, 'at the very bottom he was an unsuccessful king because he was a weak man.'[14] In a television documentary Ronald Hutton called Charles 'the worst king we have had since the Middle Ages.' 'What happened to him in Scotland was his own doing,' concluded Maurice Lee, 'if ever a man brought ruin upon himself it was Charles Stewart.'[15]

The main exception to this rule has been Kevin Sharpe. There is no doubt that Dr Sharpe's contribution to our understanding of the period has been substantial. As a pioneering revisionist he has both posed and answered critical questions. No one has done more than Dr Sharpe to investigate the relationships between literature and politics in the first half of the seventeenth century.[16] His massive study *Charles I and the Personal Rule*, published by Yale University Press in 1992, is the culmination of two decade's work. It is a big book in every sense of the word. Weighing in at 983 pages, it fills many voids in our knowledge, particularly in foreign policy. But if it is good on the details of the personal rule, its interpretation of the personal ruler is unsatisfactory.

Dr Sharpe argues that Charles was a hardworking monarch. No one doubts that the king could display spurts of energy, such as when Buckingham was away fighting in Ré, or during the Prayer Book Rebellion. But until the 1640s Charles never demonstrated consistent day to day, month to month, year in and year out, hard work. His fingerprints – or rather his handwriting – cannot be found all over the written record. The king was rarely listed as being present at the privy council. The record shows that he attended only nine of the ninety-nine meetings held in 1630, the first full year of the personal rule.[17] Yet Dr Sharpe argues that the king personally used the council as the motor for a dynamic royal government and that he frequently chaired its meetings, directing its proceedings. The only reason why he is not registered as present is that the clerk did not bother to enter his name into the minutes.[18] I personally find this assertion as credible as suggesting that the President of the United States or Queen Elizabeth II could attend a function and no one would have recorded their presence.

Far from seeing Charles as lazy and his personal rule as reactive, Kevin Sharpe insists that 'We must instead place the king prominently at the center of government.'[19] This, of course, assumes that the government had both a centre and a consistent policy, as opposed to being departmentalized and reacting in an *ad hoc* fashion to such outside stimuli as the Draining of the Fens, the Fishing Company or the dismissal of the Earl of Menteith. The only times when Charles clearly initiated policies were the Forced Loan of 1626 and the Scots Prayer Book of 1637, and both enterprises were utter catastrophes.[20]

That is not to say that the king did nothing. To be sure, he annotated Secretary Coke's letters. Sir Thomas Herbert and Sir Philip Warwick were right when they say that the king worked hard, but they were referring to the period after the personal rule. Peter Donald correctly notes that the large numbers of letters Charles wrote to Hamilton in 1638–9 (as the personal rule was collapsing) is 'not typical.'[21] Charles's problem was that he had bursts of energy, taking up an idea, dropping it, and then rushing back to the fray to make a hasty decision. The Venetian ambassador noted that in the days after the crisis of 2 March 1629, the privy council met 'day and night, the king always being present.' Yet the following year he attended less than nine per cent of the council meetings. As Conrad Russell astutely observed, Charles 'suffered from energy.'[22] He combined occasional hyperactivity with a low attention span – a fatal mixture, far more dangerous than a blend of diligent plodding.

There is, of course, much to agree with in Dr Sharpe's massive study. He is, for instance, right to say that Charles was essentially a conservative who looked back to an ideal of parliament which predated the squabbles of the 1620s: but that these parliaments existed more in the king's imagination than in the reality of Westminster Hall. When Charles told the leaders of the 1629 Commons that he would not call another parliament until they 'shall come to a better understanding of us and themselves', he was not only insisting that they saw they error of their ways, but the rightness of his own.[23] Charles was less a Burkeian, even Thatcherite Conservative, than he was a reactionary, whose insecurity made him an authoritarian. Ultimately for Charles, character was destiny, and that is why this life of the king who ended his life on the scaffold is subtitled *The Personal Monarchy.*

# I

# THE DUKE 'FAR OUT OF ORDER'

Charles's entry into this world was far less noteworthy than the manner in which he left it. He was born shortly after midday on Wednesday, 19 November 1600, in Dunfermline castle, the second son and third surviving child of Anne of Denmark and James VI of Scotland. Although the birth was a difficult one, the midwife, Janet Kinlock, being amply rewarded for her services, the boy's father was not pacing anxiously up and down outside the delivery room, but was, instead, a day's ride away in Edinburgh supervising the distribution of the remains of the Gowrie brothers, who had been hung, drawn and quartered for treason. Even though Dunfermline was her favourite castle, the surrounding countryside reminding the queen of her native land, Charles's birth did not bring his mother and father closer together, their marriage having long since gone sour. No outburst of popular rejoicing welcomed the baby into this world, only the official three-gun salute from Edinburgh castle. No bonfires were lit in Edinburgh town, no Latin paeans came from the dons at St Andrews, not a dram recorded tippled to wet the bairn's head in the Highlands, not a kirk bell tolled. In fact the only man who bothered to record the exact moment of the baby's birth was an unknown astrologer, who fearing perhaps that the conjunction of the planets or else the expectations from a second son promised so little, did not bother to continue to cast Charles's fortune.[1]

On 23 December, five weeks after his birth, Charles was taken from Dunfermline to Holyrood Palace, Edinburgh, to be christened. For the first time in his life he became part of the spectacle that attends royalty. The Prince de Rohan carried the boy wrapped in a golden robe into the Chapel Royal, where the Bishop of Ross preached, exhorting all to obey the king as God's lieutenant upon earth. As the choir sang a psalm, the bishop baptized the boy, and Lord Lyons proclaimed his full style – Duke of Albany, Marquis of Ormonde, Earl of Ross and Lord Ardmonach. Canons roared, trumpets blared, as Dingwall Pursuivant shouted the new prince's titles out through a window to the crowd who waited below, excited less in expectation of learning Charles's correct style than in scrimmaging for the 100 marks that John Blinsele, another herald, tossed down.

1

The mob fought, the royal party withdrew for a banquet in the queen's rooms, and Charles was taken back to the daily routine of his nursery.[2]

This was to be his home for the next three years. His governess, Margaret Stewart, Lady Ochiltree, had overall charge of the baby; Jean Drummond was his wet nurse, and Marion Hepburn his 'rocker', whose special job was to lull him to sleep. Charles's nursery was well supplied. In 1602, James spent £33 5s on a fine coat and suit of French serge for his son. He paid his nurses well. In 1603 he granted Marion Hepburn £166 13s 4d a year with an additional £15 two years afterwards. When Charles became king he gave Lady Ochiltree a pension of 700 marks, being most annoyed to learn in 1634 that it had fallen in arrears.[3]

Whether he did so because he had fond memories of the fine job his governess had done one cannot say, for Charles was remarkably reticent about his past. But one may conclude that his nurses had a difficult task, for he was a weak and sickly infant. In an age deficient in medical knowledge and without even a rudimentary sense of public health, Anne was not unusual in losing five of her eight babies. Following weaning at the age of one, Charles suffered from rickets brought about by a poor diet consisting mainly of curds and whey, and lacking vitamin D, calcium, as well as a general lack of sunlight.[4] After examining Charles in June 1604, Dr Henry Atkins (later President of the Royal College of Physicians) wrote to James that the 'joints of his knees, hips and ankles being great and loose are not yet closed, and knot together, as it happens to many in their tender years.' To James's chief adviser Atkins was more blunt, telling Sir Robert Cecil, 'The Duke was far out of order.'[5]

Dr Atkins was writing to Charles's parents who were in England, Queen Elizabeth having fulfilled their greatest expectations by dying on 24 March 1603, making James the sixth of Scotland the first of England. He had waited long for the day when he would inherit what he called the 'promised land', secretly negotiating with Cecil to ensure a smooth succession. Indeed James was so anxious to confront the finest prospect that any Scot can face that he set out from Edinburgh on 3 April to travel the high road beckoning south to England alone. He left his family behind; Anne and his eldest children, Henry and Elizabeth, were to follow the next month, and baby Charles if and when he was strong enough to survive the journey.

The day before James left Edinburgh, he appointed his friend and Lord Chancellor, Alexander Seton, Lord Fyvie, his son's guardian. Although Fyvie appears to have had no influence on the boy, his task was as difficult as Lady Ochiltree's, with the additional complication of having Anne and James constantly pestering him about their son's health. To one of their anxious letters Seton replied in April 1604 that Charles was eating, drinking and using his natural functions like any normal child of his age, and a month later assured them that 'Duke Charles continues, praises be to God, in good health, good courage and lofty mind, although weak in body is beginning to speak some words. He is far better yet of his mind and tongue than of his body and feet.'[6]

So by the spring of 1604 Anne and James felt the son they had not seen for two years might be well enough to join them, and thus sent Dr Atkins to Scotland to examine the boy. Under the doctor's care – or at least according to the doctor's letters – the duke's health rapidly improved. From being 'out of order', the state in which Atkins claimed to have found him, Charles grew daily 'from one perfection to another'. At the age of three and a half he was able to walk the length of the great hall at Dunfermline castle unaided, and, in spite of a touch of fever, his doctor was sure that the benefits of being reunited with his family were well worth the risks of the journey: 'He often talks of going to London,' Atkins told the queen, 'and desires to see his gracious mother.'[7]

On 13 July Charles left Dunfermline for the kingdom where he was to spend most of the rest of his life. Two coaches and a dozen horses carried the royal party, which included Lord Seton and his sons, Dr Atkins, several nurses and servants and a small escort under the command of Sergeant Myners. The local gentry welcomed them to Berwick on 21 July from whence Atkins reported that the duke was in fine fettle, enjoying the trip greatly. The royal party passed the night of 8 August at the Earl of Shrewsbury's house at Workshop, Nottinghamshire, where Charles was introduced to the sport that was to become a passion, taking great delight in seeing a buck hunted and killed.[8] On 12 August the entourage resumed their leisurely pace south, arriving at Leicester on the 15th, where they passed the next couple of days, purloining the corporation's linen and plate, and consuming three gallons of its claret, two of its white wine and one and a half of the municipal sack.[9] Perhaps it was the liquid attraction of the journey rather than a concern not to over-tax the duke that made his retinue linger, for they took another six weeks to reach Easton Neston, near Towcester, where his parents met him to take their son the last seventy miles to Windsor castle.

Once Charles was safely lodged with his mother and father in early October, Fyvie's duties were done, and James discharged him as guardian to return to the Lord Chancellorship of Scotland, with his majesty's thanks for having so 'carefully and discreetly governed our son'.[10] Having pensioned off the rest of Charles's Scots servants, James's next problem was finding someone from England to take their place. According to Sir Robert Carey few wanted that dubious honour, because they were afraid that the child was so sickly that he might readily die in their charge. When James formally made Sir Robert's wife, Elizabeth, the boy's governess in February 1605 many felt the appointment a fitting reward for the man who two years before had opportunely ridden three days and nights to Edinburgh to be the first to tell his new sovereign that his old one was at long last dead.[11]

In fact the Careys were good guardians. Lady Carey cared for Charles with love and diligence, and thanks to her nurture the frail boy grew stronger every day. She managed to protect him from the more outrageous suggestions of his father who wanted to cut the cord underneath his tongue to help Charles speak, and put him in iron braces to force him to walk. Most important of all the Careys were able to provide the boy with a secure home founded on a happy marriage, for as Sir Robert recalled, he had chosen a wife 'more for the warmth than her wealth'. Later, David Price, one of the royal chaplains, and thus in a position to observe Lady Carey's care of the prince, wrote that it was excellent enough to 'deserve much respect of all good hearts'.[12] James certainly agreed: he gave Lady Carey a pension of £400 a year and, in 1622, made Sir Robert Baron Leppington. To pay Lady Carey's expenses in bringing up his son, James set aside lands worth £3015 15s 8d a year. Apparently this was not enough, for in October 1607 she complained that Charles was being inadequately fed and that his servants were grousing about their diets. So James ordered that she be paid a lump sum of £100, and that his son's allowance he increased by £50 to £650 a year. Even this was insufficient, for by November 1610 the annual cost of the boy's household (which had grown large and thirsty enough to drink forty gallons of beer a day) had risen to £2422 6s 11d.[13]

In analysing Charles's earliest years much attention has been paid to his poor health that often made him appear an unattractive child. At the age of three he refused to open his mouth to let Dr Atkins examine his teeth. A little later one observer remembered he was 'very wilful, somewhat inclining to perverseness of disposition', while another recalled that, 'If anyone crossed him he would hardly be stilled, crawling about on all fours in a most unseemly manner.'[14] It has been suggested that Charles tried to over-compensate for this early weakness by forcing himself to excel in rigorous sports, such as riding, hunting and running, which produced a sense of determination that in later life manifested itself as intransigence, or, if you prefer, resolution. While admittedly fascinating – even facile – such theories are both thin on evidence and as dangerous a set of speculations as wondering what effect being separated from his family at the crucially important age of three had on the boy. In addition Charles does not seem to have been as weak or in as poor health as some would have us believe. There is no doubt, of course, that he had rickets and found the reinforced boots that Edward Stuteville, the London bone-setter, made for him useful, but by the standards of the age he was not exceptionally fragile.[15] Charles's guardians could have exaggerated their ward's ill health not just as insurance in case he died under their care, but to emphasize their own services in the hope of being rewarded by a grateful father and generous monarch. Fyvie told James and Anne how well their son was doing after they had left the boy in his custody. On arriving in Scotland

Atkins first reported that the lad was in poor shape, and then how quickly he was improving. When two decades later Carey published his *Memoirs* our chief source for Charles's childhood, he may have stressed the boy's initial frailty and thus his wife's contribution to his nurture, in order to bolster the application he was making to the king for a sinecure to support them in their old age. If, as Carey asserts, Charles could not walk when his wife became his governess, it is strange that a year earlier Atkins should have seen him dance a galliard in the great hall in Dunfermline, and that in 1604 James should have spent 50 marks having his son taught fencing.[16]

As difficult, if not more so, than the physical problems facing the young Charles, were the psychological ones that involved trying to move between the fairly secure world of the Carey's household and the rather alien one of the court, which necessitated coming to terms with his father, mother, brother and sister. Of course, in these tasks his physical weaknesses were an impediment, as evidenced at his creation as Duke of York in January 1605. Throughout the ceremony, which James used to introduce his second son to English society, two nobles stood beside the boy to catch him, so it was widely believed, in case his legs gave way. In fact, Charles never fully understood what was going on, asking if he was about to be made king. The court attached little significance to the ceremony, squeezing it in as a prelude to the far more important annual Twelfth Night masque. Few Englishmen were impressed: one sardonically commented, 'so we have a Duke of York in title though not in substance.'[17] To give the title some meaning, and strengthen the recent link between the two nations, Sir Thomas Lake in 1604 suggested that the Duke of York be made King of Scotland, but Sir Edward Cole squashed the idea pronouncing it invalid in English law. The following year Patrick Tipper urged the duke be made Vice-Regent of Ireland, but once more the idea got no support, and Charles had to be content with an honorary captaincy in the King of France's bodyguard.

Charles was an unimpressive boy. His earliest portrait, painted when he was about five, shows a concerned child, with a remarkably high forehead, and an intense, almost manic stare (see Plate 1). His left hand clasps his gloves, his right is placed on his hip in a most awkward fashion as if he is far from at ease with himself and worried about his position within both his family and the realm.[18] And in both Charles counted for little: even the Guy Fawkes conspirators decided to kidnap him only as an afterthought to their main business.[19]

On Charles's arrival in England James reserved an apartment at Whitehall Palace for his use, and as the boy grew older insisted that he spend more time at court. In 1609, for instance, he was on the court's ration strength for sixty days.[20] Sometimes James would let his son entertain visiting dignitaries, once sending him with a harquebus over his shoulder to the antechamber, where the Venetian ambassador was waiting, to announce that he was a soldier reporting for duty in the republic's service, the incident (which was the closest that Charles ever came to espousing republicanism) becoming a standing 'in joke' for several years in the diplomatic correspondence between the two nations.[21] When Charles was eight his father took him to the menagerie at the Tower of London to see a bear condemned to death by being eaten by lions for mauling a child. The following year James let Charles take part in the celebrations for Henry's creation as Prince of Wales. As 'the chiefest of Neptune's servants', he danced prettily with twelve young girls in the antimasque before presenting his brother with a sword worth 20,000 crowns.[22] In 1611 Charles had to share his installation as a Knight of the Garter with the Earl of Arundel and Robert Carr, his father's favourite, whilst Henry reminded the audience that he was the heir by presiding as master of ceremonies.[23]

James's court was not a suitable place for a growing, shy boy of Charles's disposition. Its grossness and intrigue were so repellent that his older sister, Elizabeth, tried hard to stay away from it, and were so notorious that the court alienated many of the king's more sober subjects. For instance, the rich costumes that the queen and her ladies wore when they were painted up as blacks in the masque following Charles's creation as Duke of York, exposed so much of their breasts they they shocked many spectators. They were not, however, provocative enough to explain the frenzy that followed the dramatic presentation: as flunkeys carried in the post-masque banquet the audience charged, collapsing the tables and sending delicacies flying to be trampled under foot before a bite could be swallowed. The next year the behaviour at the reception for Anne's brother, Christian IV of Denmark, was just as bad: everyone from their majesties down got beastly drunk, including the ladies playing Faith, Hope and Charity, who had to be led off stage too 'sick and spewing' to say their lines.[24]

Charles must have found the coarseness of his father's court most distasteful, for on becoming king he immediately made his own the most decorous in Europe. But as a prince he had to live with – and in – his father's many motley mansions. Resigned to the crudity, he clammed up in the face of unpleasantness. This helped make him an intensely private man, who, faced with something or someone he neither liked nor could control, retreated to the security of his own court. But as a growing child he could not create such a refuge; like us all, he had to come to terms with the outside world.

In this difficult process, his mother was of little help. Anne had been born in Denmark on 12 December 1574. Bitterly disappointed she was not a son, her father ignored her as he incessantly migrated from one hunting lodge to another (just like her husband and son) and left her upbringing to her mother, Queen Sophie, and maternal grandfather, Ulric II of Micklenburg. They gave her a warm and loving childhood. She turned into an attractive women, whose future happiness seemed assured when in September 1589, three months before she was sixteen, she married James by proxy. A violent winter storm that drowned several sailors defeated her efforts to sail across the North Sea to join her husband: so she had to wait for him to come to Oslo, where they were married on 23 November. At first all was bliss. The couple spent five months with the bride's family before returning to Scotland in the spring of 1590. But soon after the birth of their first child, Henry, in 1594, their marriage soured, probably because James's basic homosexuality reasserted itself. Even though it remained malleable enough to allow the king to sire two more children (as well as ten miscarriages), he much preferred pretty young men. Worn out by her husband's sense of duty, and embittered by his preferences, the queen sought consolation in dramatics, Catholic piety, and the occasional bit of procuring to maintain some fickle link with her irascible husband. The poor woman was equally ineffectual at winning her subjects' affections. 'Good Lord,' declared one minister of the kirk, 'we must pray for the Queen for the fashion's sake, but we have no cause, for she will never do us any good.'[25]

Anne did not do her second son much good either. Although her concerns about his ill-health were genuine enough to send Dr Atkins to Scotland, and insist that he write back full and frequent reports on the boy's progress, and to select Lady Carey as his governess, she did not visit him very often, nor spend much time with him. According to one witness, albeit a hostile one, she used to call her son 'a fool and wilful'. If years afterwards she would sing the boy's praises to visiting ambassadors, and boast that Charles was her favorite child, the poor state of her relations with Henry and Elizabeth made the competition for that tide far from rigorous.[26] The lack of a satisfactory close relationship with his mother – or with a substitute mother, such as the proverbial English nanny – meant that in later life Charles found it hard to make friends, particularly with women, which added to his sense of shyness and insecurity, and deprived him of 'the feeling of a conqueror, that confidence of success that often induces real success,' that Freud called 'the legacy of a mother's favour.'[27]

In contrast to his mother his father had a positive – although far from beneficial effect – on the young Charles. Few British monarchs have had so derisive a press as James, whom Anthony Weldon profiled with unforgettable venom:[28]

he was of middling stature ... his eyes large ever rolling after any stranger that came into his presence insomuch as many for shame have left the room ... his beard was very thin, his tongue large for his mouth, which ever made him speak full in the mouth and made him drink very uncomely, as if eating his drink which came out into the cup at each side of his mouth, his skin was as soft as taffetta sarsnet, which felt so because he never washed his hands, only rubbing his finger ends slightly with the wet end of a napkin ... leaning on other men's shoulders ... his fingers ever ... fiddling about his codpiece.

What piquantly delicious malice! No wonder, more than any other source, Weldon has shaped posterity's view of King James. Yet Weldon was neither accurate, fair nor unbiased, for he bore the king a grudge. He had been dismissed from the Clerkship of the Green Wax, a cosy court billet, for writing 'A perfect Description of the Peoples and Country of Scotland', in which he described James's native land as 'too good for them that possess it, and too bad for others to be at charge to conquer it.'[29] Weldon's malice prejudiced his conclusions. Admittedly James was frequently a buffoon. In 1610, for example, he posted guards on the *Prince Royal* to stop saboteurs armed with augers creeping aboard at night to bore holes in the hull, so at the ship's launching the next day it would not sink with the royal party aboard.[30] Yet James's precautions, such as his stiletto-proof padded doublet, were usually as sensible as those of any modern head of state. After all his father had been murdered, the King of France assassinated, and he had survived at least three attempts on his life.

The most devastating part of Weldon's caricature is not that it portrays the king as an evil, greedy or indolent man, but as a ridiculous one. In contrast to his style the achievements of James's reign were many. From the turbulence of his mother's forced abdication and expulsion from Scotland, James brought law and order to his native land, calming the passions stirred by John Knox's reformation, playing the factious nobility off against each other with remarkable adroitness. After becoming King of England he ended a wasteful war with Spain that had dragged on for two generations, and kept his country out of the far more devastating Thirty Years War that ravaged the Continent. During his reign the colonization of Ulster and North America began, the Bible was translated into matchless English, and men such as Bacon, Coke, Jonson, Ralegh, Cecil and Shakespeare flourished. If James failed to resolve the great constitutional and religious issues of his time – that were perhaps neither as serious nor amenable to solution as posterity would have us believe – then at least he did not make the situation any worse.

Towards his father Charles was more ambivalent than most sons. His firm rejection of the style of his father's court at the first possible instance suggests that Charles basically accepted Weldon's view of the king, particularly as he knew James in middle age, when his excesses were at their worst. After bringing order to Scotland and peacefully inheriting the throne of England, James felt that he had achieved his life's goals, and could thus sit back and enjoy the spoils – playing favourites, eating and drinking excessively, and hunting each day becoming more senile and sillier. At the same time as feeling contempt towards such goings on, Charles tried desperately to win the notice and approval of the man he called 'the best king and father'. When James fell ill Charles wrote in his childish hand that he wished he was clever enough to discover a medicine that would make him better. Knowing his interest in education Charles wrote to the king about his Latin and French lessons, telling him that he was studying the divine right of monarchs, and how obedience to the king was, after the pursuit of goodness, the greatest wish of 'Your Majesty's dutiful son'.[31] Although such carefully penned letters reflected the editing of his tutors, Charles was naturally deferential to his parents, one observer describing his attitude to them as 'obsequious'.[32] While this adjective did not have then the perjorative implications that it conveys today, it was an effective way of disguising the dilemma of a lonely child trying hard to win the affection of an unhappy mother, and a father whom he both feared, loved, admired and yet of whom he did not approve.

Although James occasionally played and laughed with his youngest son, letting him into the presence chamber at the end of diplomatic audiences, he was not a good father. His own parents' marriage had been a disaster of the first order. Three months before James was born his father, Henry Stuart, Lord Darnley, had David Rizzio, his mother's secretary, murdered almost before her eyes, and then forced Mary, Queen of Scots, to gallop all night through a storm the twenty-five miles from Edinburgh to Dunbar. As a result Mary, who nearly lost her child, determined on revenge. Forming a liaison with the Earl of Bothwell, she pretended to be reconciled with Darnley, luring him to the Kirk of the Fields, a house outside Edinburgh, where he was found murdered, three months after James was born, following a mysterious explosion. Her elopement with Bothwell proved the final straw for Mary's Calvinist subjects: they forced her into an English exile, placing the infant James on the throne instead. A quarter of a century later James had to acquiesce to his mother's execution for plotting to supplant Queen Elizabeth.

Throughout his life James never overcame the doubts about his own paternity, suspecting (like Darnley) that David Rizzio was his real father: the humiliating thought that he was illegitimate – or as one wag cruelly put it, that the British Solomon was really the son of David – would drive him, even as a grown man, to tears. Normally, however, the epithet of the British Solomon was one he treasured, for James was a scholar of some note, and was profoundly interested in education. Once, following a tour of the Bodleian Library, he said that if he were not king he would like to be a don. He wrote texts for his children's education that became extremely popular, and ordered that Henry's household 'should rather imitate a College than a Court'.[33] In all, James much preferred the role of schoolmaster than that of father, in the belief that it enabled him to hide from his children the failings of which he was only too aware.

James found the protection afforded by distance especially comforting when dealing with his eldest child. A contemporary referred to Henry as 'the flower of the house, the glory of this country, and the admiration of all strangers'.[34] He was one of those Prince Charmings who are at their best when the going is good, being better remembered for their promise than performance. He was, in a sense, both the victim and the creature of the legend that others spun about him. Upright to the point of priggishness he fined all who swore in his presence. An obdurate Protestant, almost to the degree of rashness, he became so popular that he threatened his father.[35] It is no surprise that relations between the two mirrored those between another mythical prince, The Oedipus of Greek mythology, and his father, for the tensions between the king and impatient heir invariably exacerbate those usually found between father and son. Sometimes such tensions surfaced in public. Once while they were out hunting near Royston the king upbraided the prince for his lack of enthusiasm for the chase. Angrily Henry moved to strike his father with his cane, but before committing so heinous a deed, rode off, taking with him (much to James's chagrin) the majority of the hunting party.[36]

James used his second son to pressure his first. After lecturing Henry for his idleness, which he contrasted with Charles's diligence, the king once threatened to leave the crown to the latter.[37] Such taunts did nothing to improve relations between the two mismatched brothers. Henry did not like Charles, whom he used to tease without mercy. According to one version of the only surviving anecdote about the two, Charles, Henry and Archbishop Abbot were waiting in the presence chamber for James when the heir snatched off Abbot's square episcopal hat and put it on his nine-year-old brother's head saying that when he became king he would make him Archbishop of Canterbury since he was swot enough for the job, and, anyway, the long clerical robes would hide his ugly rickety legs. Charles was so upset that he threw the cap on the ground, stamped up and down on it, and had to be dragged away streaming tears. When Sir Robert Cecil suggested that Prince Henry give Charles a small, bronze statue of a horse, part of a collection sent him by the Duke of Florence, he sharply refused, 'No. No. I want everything for myself.'[38]

The duke tried hard to make his peace with Henry, who was not just his big brother but, as the court ceremonials and masques constantly reminded him, the heir, by using the same techniques as he had with his father. 'Most loving brother,' he wrote in 1611, 'I earnestly entreat you to ever keep me in your favour . . . I shall ever rest your highness's most loving brother.'[39] Uncertain and insecure, Charles accommodated himself almost to the point of grovelling. When Henry and his household switched from wearing French fashion to Italian, Charles and his servants immediately followed suit.[40] Whenever Henry did him a favour, such as lending him horses and hounds, Charles was pathetically grateful. 'So longing to see you,' he wrote, 'I kiss your hand and rest yours to command.' When neither gratitude, imitation nor humility worked, Charles tried bribery, attempting like many a threatened child to buy affection; 'Sweet, sweet brother,' wrote the ten-year-old boy, 'I will give anything that I have to you, both horses and my books and my pieces [guns] and my cross bows, or anything that you would have. Good brother, love me....'[41]

Such pleas did little good, for although Henry and Charles might sometimes ride or play golf together, Henry had little patience with his younger brother, much preferring the company of his sister Elizabeth. Anyway, all Charles's efforts came to nought in November 1612. Seven weeks earlier Henry had been reported ill, his poor complexion being attributed to a surfeit of fresh fruit. In early November he caught a chill after a strenuous game of tennis. Sir Thomas Mayerne, the royal family doctor (whose reputation as a physician far exceeded his ability to make his patients better) was called in, and prescribed bleeding. Other doctors applied freshly killed cocks and pigeons to draw the peccant humours from Henry's fevered body, and from the Tower Sir Walter Raleigh sent a secret elixir to save his patron's life. But all was to no avail. Henry died from typhoid fever at about eight in the evening of 6 November, asking for his sister. He left his brother, an awkward eleven year old, heir to a great legacy, and his people numb with grief. That night John Chamberlain, the London letter writer, noted 'the world here is much dismayed.'[42]

# II

# 'THE ILLUSTRIOUS HOPE OF GREAT BRITAIN'

Between the ages of ten and eleven Charles's life changed dramatically: first he left the security of Lady Carey's house, second his brother died, and third he rapidly won and then lost the friendship of his sister and brother-in-law. As a result the already insecure Charles returned to the rather bland existence he had known before: reading, studying, exercising, and doing little to attract attention, until his father's last favourite, George Villiers, rescued him in 1618, becoming the substitute for the elder brother he had lost six years before. And so were dashed the widespread hopes, expressed on Henry's death by poets such as Thomas Middleton that 'The High and Mighty Charles' would become 'the illustrious hope of Great Britain'.[1]

Few heirs to the English throne have been as widely and deeply mourned as Prince Henry. 'Our Rising Sun is set' eulogized the Earl of Dorset 'ere scarcely did he shine.'[2] Henry's body lay in state at St James's Palace for four weeks to allow the public plenty of time to pay their last respects and the king to collect enough money for the extravagant funeral that took place on 7 December. Over a thousand people walked in the mile-long cortège to Westminster Abbey to hear the Archbishop of Canterbury deliver a two-hour sermon, after which Henry was lowered into the ground whilst his chief servants broke their staves of office over the grave. Apart from the madman who ran naked through the mourners shouting that he was Henry's ghost, the ceremony was a dignified one that expressed the nation's profound sense of loss.[3] Within a few months no less than thirty-two poets, including John Donne, Sir Walter Ralegh, George Chapman, William Drummond, Lord Herbert, Thomas Campion, Thomas Heywood and Joshua Sylvester published eulogies. John Taylor tried to sum up the nation's grief in his dirge. 'Great Britain all is Black', while Henry King explained that mere words could never convey the world's dismay.[4]

Immediately after Henry's death, Charles fell ill and on his recovery had to bear the burden of being the chief mourner at the funeral. James refused to attend: other people's funerals reminded him of the inevitability

12

of his own, while Anne was too prostrate with grief (and the gout) to be able to go.

Now that Charles was the heir, he became, for a brief while, the object of much public speculation, particularly concerning the choice of a wife. Marie de Medici told the Duke of Bouillion, the French ambassador, whom she had originally sent to London to negotiate a marriage alliance with Henry, to shift his bargaining to Charles. Even though Bouillon and James got on well together, talks dragged on for three years without result, largely because the French were more interested in preventing an Anglo-Spanish marriage than making one with England.[5] Sir Henry Wotton, the diplomat, advocated an alliance with the Infant Maria of Savoy (another legacy from Henry), persuading her father, the duke, to send an ambassador to London to present Charles with a fine suit of Milanese armour. Rumours about Charles's marriage plans were rife, negotiations with Denmark, Lorraine, Spain and Tuscany being reported.[6] So for a few months after his brother's death, and for the first time in his life, Charles was worth gossiping about.

People had expectations of the heir: 'All men's eyes are upon you,' Sir Robert Dallington told him, 'men look upon your worthy brother in your princely self,' and hoped that Henry's ghost might take Charles by the hand to school him in all the royal virtues he had so fully displayed during his tragically short life.[7] Whether Dallington put too much trust in the efficacy of the supernatural, or was unduly optimistic, or else the public's expectations of the eleven-year-old Charles was unfairly high, one cannot say. Without doubt, however, all were to be disappointed. Dedications were a useful indication of public popularity. Poets, playwrights and hacks dedicated their work to celebrities in the hope that the prestige would rub off, and sell their works. In 1609 Charles received no dedications, one in 1610, two in 1611, and four in 1612, suggesting a gradual, though limited, growth of interest in the second son, particularly when compared to the eighteen dedications Henry received during the last year of his life, which were twice as many as James's. On Henry's death Charles received twenty dedications, compared to eight posthumous ones for his brother, even though several authors dedicated works to Charles whilst expressing the wish that they could have done so to Henry. The expectations the public had of Charles were not sustained, the dedications he received falling from thirteen in 1614 to six the following year.[8]

The second episode that helped shape Charles's adolescence opened in late October 1611, with the arrival in England of Frederick, the Elector Palatine to court Princess Elizabeth. The alliance had been fostered by Henry, whom Frederick, his junior by a couple of years, resembled in many ways, being just as popular, handsome and full of promise. Following the death of his father, Frederick IV, in 1610, he became Elector of the German Palatinate, one of the seven rulers who chose the Holy Roman

Emperor. His Palatinate was divided into two parts: the upper between the Danube and Bohemian forests, and the lower, a rich wine growing triangle astride the Rhine at Heidelberg, both being of great strategic importance. Frederick was a sensitive and affectionate seventeen-year-old, a good friend and mediocre enemy, 'whose virtues,' one commentator noted, 'exceeded his tender years.' There was no doubt that the virtue that most endeared him to the Londoners who cheered as he was first rowed up the Thames to woo Elizabeth was his staunch Protestantism.

Charles's lifelong friendship with Frederick started when he formally welcomed the Elector as he landed from his barge at Westminster Steps. Unlike his father and mother Frederick kept Charles company at Henry's funeral, walking in the cortège immediately behind him. Charles escorted Frederick to his betrothal with Elizabeth at the Banqueting Hall at Whitehall on 27 December, and the next month the two went for a boating trip up the Thames to Putney, Frederick calling Charles 'his dearest prince'.[9] Quickly the German managed to fill the void left by Henry's death. Perhaps Charles saw him as a substitute for the brother he had just lost: certainly the evening that Henry died James sent a messenger to the Palatine to tell Frederick that he would consider him his first born son, and, as if to symbolize the transfer of his affections, invested him with the same star and ribbon of the Garter that Henry had worn. Charles's role at the ceremony, held privately on 21 December, was that of a younger son: stooping he attached the Garter about Frederick's knee. The only member of the royal family whose friendship Frederick failed to win was Queen Anne, who told her daughter that in marrying the Palatine she, the best match in Christendom, was throwing herself away on a petty – and worse still – a Protestant German princeling.

Elizabeth ignored her mother since she had fallen in love with her suitor with an intensity unusual for normal seventeen-century marriages, and miraculously rare for diplomatic ones. Thus it was most fitting that they were wed on St Valentine's Day, 1613, with an extravagance so wild that at times it seemed that the court was desperately trying to spend money to exorcize its recent loss. The opening festivity, a sham naval battle on the Thames between the British and some 'Turks', ended with the victory of the former and the sacking of the infidel's 'castle' (built just by the Archbishop of Canterbury's Palace at Lambeth), and was followed by a firework display which was an exact copy of the one put on at Henry's creation as Prince of Wales but two years before.[10] The next day the couple wed in the Chapel Royal at Whitehall. Elizabeth wore a richly embroidered stain robe, and a gold crown ringed with pearls, under which her hair hung in the long traces symbolic of virginity. John Donne celebrated the union:[11]

A Bride before a good night could be said
should banish from her clothes into her bed . . .
He comes and passes through sphere and sphere,
First her sheets, then her arms, then everywhere.

Early the next morning James visited the newly weds in their bridal room to assure himself that every sphere had been fully vanquished.

Charles seemed to share the young couple's happiness. He was their constant and welcome companion. In early March he and Frederick left Elizabeth at Newmarket to visit Cambridge, where Charles delivered the traditional Latin speech full of the usual platitudes about how glad he was to be in so famous a university, and the dons and students responded with a dramatic presentation so boring that the royal visitors could hardly stay awake.[12]

For Charles the idyll of this new friendship came to an end in April when Frederick and Elizabeth had to return to Germany. In spite of suggestions that his sister should stay in England for a couple more years until Charles was strong enough to take over in case James died suddenly, she and her husband left London on 10 April, as the crowds lined the banks of the Thames and London Bridge to wave goodbye.[13] On the evening of 14 April, after spending the day inspecting the Royal Navy at Chatham, James and Anne tearfully kissed their daughter adieu, never to see her again. Charles lingered with his sister and brother-in-law for a week longer at Canterbury, until James curtly ordered him back to London to return to the dull routine of his household, as Elizabeth sailed away on the *Royal George* to the excitement of a new life.[14]

Just before he had to face the twin cries of his brother's death and the loss of his sister abroad, James had removed Charles from Lady Carey's secure household, and established him in one of his own. Even though this change was normal for a prince of his age, leaving Lady Carey separated him at a critical point from the care of the woman who had looked after him for as long as he could remember. Three men, two of them strangers, governed his new household: Sir Robert Carey was master of the robes, Sir Jasper Fullerton, surveyor general, and Sir Thomas Murray became Charles's tutor.[15] Although James increased Charles's privy pursue allowance by £400 per annum on Henry's death, and eventually granted him most of the late prince's lands, the king was determined to keep a tighter leash on his second son than he had on his first. As Peter Heylin, Charles's friend and biographer noted, 'Old Princes do not love to have their sons too active and tread too close upon their heels.'[16] Lest 'the popish faction' subvert him, James appointed two sober divines to supervise Charles's religious instruction.[17] Although he first insisted that Charles give up his own household and come to live with him at court, the king quickly discovered that the lad was too docile to need a close eye kept on him

15

and too much of a nuisance under foot at court. For example on 13 March Charles wrote to his father about some unspecified offence:[18]

> Sir:
> I cannot express the thanks I owe to so good a father, first in showing my faults so truly and then in forgiving so freely. Albeit I cannot love and honour your Majesty more than I did . . . I shall prosper no longer than I shall deserve to be called your Majesty's most humble and obedient son and servant.
> Charles

Since about that aspiration James had little doubt, three months later he allowed charles to return to his own household, to which he added Sir Robert Carr as the fourth governor.[19]

Sir Thomas Murray retained overall charge of Charles's education, which included the usual subjects: the Classics, French, Italian, arithmetic and theology. Murray supervised the prince's other tutors. Charles Guerolt taught the boy fencing, John Beauchesne the distinctively beautiful italic handwriting that he retained for the rest of his life, and John Norton supervised the library.[20] Under Murray's direction Charles attended sermons at least once a week, and copied pithy passages from Anglican divines, such as Lancelot Andrewes and Thomas Hooker, into commonplace books – which have, alas, been lost.[21] From the Camp of the Great Mogul Sir Thomas Roe, the British ambassador, sent detailed descriptions of India. From the Hague Dudley Carleton, another ambassador, dispatched coins and books to add to the collection Charles inherited from Henry. At the age of fifteen Charles started collecting pictures for himself, and as he grew older companies of actors, including Ben Jonson's, performed in his household.[22] Charles's knowledge of foreign affairs, particularly of the complex diplomacy of Germany and Italy, so impressed the Venetians that they assumed (quite wrongly), that he must be influential in shaping English policy in these areas.[23] Charles also enjoyed rigorous activities. Every morning when at St James's he used to run around the palace grounds. He tossed the pike, was a first-class shot, and practised long and hard in the tiltyard, being an excellent horseman who could subdue the most spirited of mounts. Thus James was right to reward Murray by making him the heir's secretary, for the education he gave Charles had enough learning to produce a cultivated man without the excesses of his father's pedantry.[24]

But the one thing that Murray did not give the boy was a secure, stable and supportive home. Indifferent to their charge's feelings, his guardians squabbled amongst each other, with Carey, Fullerton and Carr ganging up against Murray. Two years later James ignored Charles's objections to appoint Sir Arthur Ingram the prince's cofferer (treasurer), and when the post became vacant the following year offered it to Sir David Fowles, who, 'thinking too meanly of the palace, and valuing himself higher', sold it to Sir Henry Vane.[25] So snug a harbour for courtly greed as Charles's households did not come cheap: in 1617 Vane received £17,000 for its expenses from the prince's lands, which were so extensive that a list of them taken by Sir John Norden that summer covered some 140 closely written folios.[26]

The half dozen years of Charles's life following Henry's death were noteworthy mainly for their lack of note. For the heir to three thrones Charles's public life was particularly empty, especially when compared to those of his predecessors and posterity. On 19 April 1613 he was confirmed.[27] A year later he made his next appearance by riding with his father to open parliament.[28] In March of 1615 he and James visited Cambridge University, and in September, much to his father's concern that some weekend warrior might accidentally discharge his musket in the heir's direction, Charles inspected London's militia.[29] James was far happier to let his son stand in for him at the Garter service held each St George's Day at Windsor, but would not let him join him in his summer progress about southern England in 1616.[30] Although James created Charles Prince of Wales in November of that year the ceremony was rather lack-lustre. At the joust held in London Charles was not strong enough to put on an impressive display, so his opponents had to hold back lest they outshone the hero of the hour.[31] The following summer, in spite of Charles's request 'to let me see the County where I was born, and the customs of it,' James would not take him on his royal tour of Scotland, and although he made the boy a member of the council appointed to govern England in his absence, Charles played no part in its deliberations.[32]

What then can be made of the uneventfulness of this period of Charles's life, roughly from the ages of twelve to eighteen, when he seemed to withdraw into himself, shunning the limelight that Henry relished? One explanation is that this was a time of extended melancholia for the loss of his brother, sister and brother-in-law. Mourning is a painful process at which the mind must work until it has adjusted to the new reality. Generally an individual's ability to complete this task depends on his sense of self-identity.[33] In this respect Charles was poorly equipped, having suffered the loss when he was twelve, too young for a strong sense of self-identity to have developed, particularly after so bruising a childhood. The problem with this hypothesis, it must be admitted, is that it is essentially based on negative evidence: not what Charles did, but what he did not do, and presumably should have. Thus on its own it might not be worth advancing, but as a part of the pattern of a whole it is consistent, for we know that in later life, when faced with bereavements of similar magnitude (such as Buckingham's assassination, or Rupert's betrayal at Bristol), Charles responded in much the same way, by retreating into himself.

There is no doubt that Charles had just gone through a difficult period: leaving Lady Carey's nurture, Henry's sudden death, being brought back to court, a short-lived popularity dashed by unfulfilled hopes, an intimacy with Frederick and Elizabeth which was as short as it was sweet, and then back to his lonely childhood. All this took its toll, and created strains over and above the normal ones of growing up. But to whom could Charles turn for help? His sister was too far away, her letters assuring 'My only Dear Brother' of her 'dearest love' being of little practical assistance.[34] The memory of the brother, whom Charles came to love far more in death than he had in life, returned to haunt him. At Charles's installation as Prince of Wales the Bishop of Ely made the slip – surely a Freudian one – of praying for Prince Henry, and not Prince Charles, and several commentators concurred that the celebrations at both London and Ludlow were not a scratch on those held six years earlier. As we have seen Anne had little influence at court and scant interest in her son. Thus the only person left able to end the boy's bland and indifferent childhood was his father.

But James had problems enough of his own.

The origins of the king's homosexuality go back to his own equally lonely childhood.[35] James had known neither his mother nor father. His chief tutor, George Buchanan, was a Presbyterian scholar with all that ilk's reputed dourness, who constantly reminded James of his other's wickedness and her son's sins. At the age of thirteen, repressed, anxious and starved of affection, James met Esmé Stuart, a pretty young man a few years his senior just back from Paris with all the charm and sophistication that city can teach. A few months later a group of ultra-Protestant nobles forced Stuart into exile. Heartbroken James wrote:[36]

> And shall I like a bird or beast forget,
> For any storm that threatening heaven send
> The object sweet, where my heart is set
> For whom to serve my senses all I bend.

At the age of twenty-three, just before sailing to Norway to marry Anne, and without the slightest hint of irony, the king reassured the Scots privy council that he was not going for any carnal reasons: 'As to my nature, God is my witness, I could have abstained for longer.' Afterwards James used to boast that he had known no other woman but his wife.[37] Within a few years this 'knowledge' became rare, for their marriage quickly broke down. Some say it was because the king alienated his wife by insisting that the Earl of Mar bring up their first child. Yet the story is not very convincing; at that time no lady of the queen's standing would dream of rearing her offspring personally. Also Anne's interest in her other children, who were not liable to the Mar's tradition of guardianship, was limited. Most likely, soon after Henry's birth, James realized that marriage would not curb his true nature, and returned to his old ways. It may be that the Gowrie conspiracy of 1600, which James claimed was an assassination attempt, was, in fact, a botched homosexual encounter. After his accession to the English throne James's homosexuality became more blatant, particularly at court. 'The love the king showed,' Francis Osborne recalled, 'was as amorously conveyed, as if he had mistaken their own sex, and thought them ladies.' Aspiring favourites were primped so that James might fondle them, 'slobbering over them, and kissing them in so lascivious a mode in public' that Osborne, like many of His Majesty's subjects, shuddered to think what went on in private.[38]

As he grew older the focus of James's sexuality – like that of most heterosexuals – shifted from the physical to the emotional, from the role of lover to doting parent. He became the ageing roué, whose drunken bouts, maudlin outbursts, and frantic progressions from hunting lodge to hunting lodge was symptoms of a sexual drive repressed to allow him to play the role of the kindly father figure to his favourites and their families.[39] So long as his favourites continued to love their 'Dear Dad' – which was how James described himself – he generously rewarded them and their kin. He delighted in their marriages, since their wives were no threat and their children a source of pleasure to the ageing man who called himself their 'grandfather'. In short, his favourites were the king's Peter Pans; they could be naughty, then contrite, spoilt but still loving brats, in fact almost anything so long as they never grew up, and became independent. He was determined that his fledglings would never completely leave the nest even if it meant that the cuckoos ended up running the kingdom.

James's relations with Robert Carr illustrate the pattern of the middle-age homosexuality; Carr was a Scot, who as a page had run alongside the king's coach all the way from Edinburgh to London in 1603. His journey completed, he was dismissed from the royal service, and travelled in France, returning to court in 1607. Soon afterwards James noticed the youth when he was injured during a joust, and visited the boy, supervising his nurses, doctors and diet, whilst trying to teach him Latin. By the time Carr regained his health (he never learnt much Latin) he had become the king's new favourite.[40] One courtier reported that James believed that nothing was too good for his boy. On 23 December 1607 he knighted him, and made him Viscount Rochester the following March. The next year James gave Carr Sir Robert Cecil's seat on the privy council, and in 1612 created him Earl of Somerset. There seemed no favour beyond Carr's asking. When he fell in love with Frances Howard, the Earl of Essex's wife, the king bullied the bishops into granting an annulment, and (like the father of the bride) paid for their magnificent wedding on Boxing Day 1613, even selling lands worth £10,000 go give Frances what was, in effect, a dowry. James revelled in the new family he had created, finding the Carrs far more exciting than his own wife and child.[41]

At a theoretical level, at least, James had always been interested in his children's upbringing. For Henry's edification he wrote *Basilikon Doron*, a manual packed with sage advice. Study the scriptures, fear God, eschew fornication and adultery, choose a wife for her virtue not her looks nor her money, eat drink and dress in moderation, and always be courteous to others, counselled the king, who like many a schoolmaster seemed best at teaching those things he, himself, could not do. Again, with a characteristic not unknown in that profession, James failed to realize when he was being ridiculous, once advising his son to choose servants 'of good form and without blemish lest the people think that you have preferred them for the love of their vices.'[42] To salve his own sense of inadequacy James advanced the theory of the divine right of monarchs, almost as if he had received it straight from the Almighty himself. 'The state of monarchy is the supremest thing upon earth: for Kings are not only God's lieutenants upon earth, and sit upon God's throne, but even by God himself are called Gods.'[43] So James told the parliament of 1610 with whom he was trying to negotiate the Great Contract, the sort of earthly haggling with which the Almighty's lieutenants do not normally demean themselves.

At a practical level James's real feelings towards Charles were very different from those one might expect from the wise and divinely anointed British Solomon. At the same time as his son's lack of assertiveness irritated the king, that he was the heir, whose expectations waited upon his death, disturbed James deeply. He refused to give Charles any real responsibilities or influence. Only once did a petitioner make the mistake of seeking the prince's help. In 1616 Dr George Carleton begged Charles to ask his father to appoint him Bishop of Carlisle, but the post went to Robert Snowden, 'an obscure fellow' – at least Carleton thought. James resented any comparison between himself and his heir. When during a visit to Cambridge University in 1615 Francis Nethersole described Charles as 'Jacobissime Carole', and 'Jacobale', the king was most annoyed by these references to 'a very James-like-Charles', and 'a little James'.[44]

Charles's relations with his father operated simultaneously on two levels. His father's theoretical teaching helped shape his son's conscience.[45] And all his life Charles's conscience was a mighty force! It prevented him from making effective compromises in religious matters, such as the prayer book, the Anglican Church, Presbyterianism, bishops, or the divine right of kings. As a grown man Charles recalled of his father, 'Among all his cares in my education his chief was to settle me right in religion.'[46] Just before he died Charles told his own son 'of mine own conscience, which is dearer to me than a thousand kingdoms.'[47] From ministers, such as Robert Wilkinson, who preached to him and his father in 1615 that 'Kings are God's anointed . . . Kings are leaders to all other men,' and from James's own writings Charles learnt that monarchs were the lynch-pin of that great chain of being which linked planets and peoples, fathers and families, sovereign and subjects, in one harmonious cosmic order.[48]

However, if Charles accepted James as the sacred *pater patriae*, whom one day he would become, at the mundane level of coming to terms with him as the profane *pater familias* the prince's task was far from easy. As has been suggested Charles's impression of the king was similar to Anthony Weldon's. The timid and fastidious boy could not help noticing that, quite literally, his father was a dirty old man, with food stains down his doublet, drink dribbling out of the sides of his mouth, his manners loud, vulgar and often embarrassingly foolish.

Thus the milieu in which Charles confronted the always difficult years of adolescence was a far from healthy one. James was getting older, sillier and more senile. His son was still painfully withdrawn, and neglected. Even though Charles failed to become Great Britain's 'illustrious hope' he was, as James well knew, the heir to an ailing monarch. The different levels at which father and son viewed each other were fraught with the most dangerous potential. For example, Charles could have found the tensions he felt in trying to reconcile his father as *pater patriae* and *pater familias*, whose interest lay in families other than his own, so unbearable that he might, like Henry, have gone against the king by creating a reversionary interest around which opposition politicians could have grouped, and have indelibly altered the character of the reign. Indeed many at court wondered why he never did so, and how he ever managed to put up with his father; some thought him a milk-sop, scared of offending the king, others a machiavellian, carefully biding his time until he could enjoy the throne without any obligations to those who had helped him during the long days of waiting.[49] In fact, such speculations remained moot. For better or worse George Villiers resolved this unhealthy and dangerous dilemma, by leading Charles out of the wilderness of his childhood, bringing father and son together, and thus established a hegemony that would dominate Britain for the next decade at least.

# III

# 'BABY CHARLES', 'STEENIE' AND THEIR 'DEAR DAD'

Charles's lonely childhood ended during his late teens, when his father's last, and most influential favourite found him a place in the king's new surrogate family. James had always preferred his favourites to his own children, if only because he could disinherit them if their independence became intolerable. Thus when Carr trampled over the king's sensitivities, James discarded him in favour of George Villiers, whom in a sense he adopted, calling him his 'only son'. He was enchanted – no besotted – with the new favourite whom he nicknamed 'Steenie', purportedly because George had the same angelic visage as St Stephen. Only behind that pretty face lay a brain astute enough to win not only the old king's friendship but that of the heir as well, achieving 'a kind of wonder, making favour hereditary.'[1] George was as handsome and self-assured as Henry had been, yet instead of teasing the younger brother he shielded him from the conflicts with his father that are an inevitable part of coming of age. In sum, Steenie found 'Baby Charles' (the epithet that both he and the king used) a place in the cadet line of that particular family over which he ruled, and James reigned happy to call himself 'his sweet boy's Dear Dad'.

This process was crucial not just in Charles's personal development, but in the politics of early seventeenth-century England. Of the last seven or so years of James's reign, as the old monarch decayed, and in the first three of Charles's, when the new one lacked self-confidence, it would not be too great an exaggeration to say that in many ways Villiers ruled England. Without doubt the crown's policies during this period were very different from those of the preceding and following years. England became entangled in a series of aggressive and expensive foreign adventures that necessitated calling parliament to raise taxes. Because these adventures failed, and because Villier's initial attempts to use parliament to pressure the king backfired, during the 1620s the crown failed to get along with parliament, and thus tried to rule without it in the 1630s.

It was particularly droll that James first met the man who was to sign himself 'Your Majesty's humble slave and dog' whilst he dominated the last years of the reign, in the kennels of Apethorpe House, Northamptonshire. George Villiers came from a minor family of Leicestershire gentry, the second son of a second marriage. His mother sent him to France where he learnt the courtly arts of riding, dancing and fencing, adding style and finish to his considerable good looks and natural charm. On his return to England the rise in James's favour 'was so quick that it seemed rather a flight than a growth.' The king made him Master of the Horse and a viscount in 1616, Master of the Wardrobe and Earl of Buckingham in 1617, marquis in 1618 and ultimately duke in 1623. 'No man danced, no man runs or jumps better,' a contemporary observed sourly, 'indeed he jumped higher than any Englishman did in so short a time from private gentleman to dukedom.'[2]

The old favourite's fall helped the new one's rise. Carr became increasingly petulant, ignoring the king's warning not to bully him. 'You might lead me by the heart and not the nose,' James wrote to him in early 1615.[3] Carr took no notice, his wife having turned Peter Pan into one of the pirates. Frances Carr hated Sir Thomas Overbury, her husband's secretary and confidant, for having opposed their marriage. To get him out of the way she had the king offer Overbury an ambassadorship to some distant country, and when he turned it down, he was imprisoned in the Tower where she secretly poisoned him – the romantic say with tarts baked by her own fair hands, the prosaic with an enema of mercury. Anyway two years after Overbury died, apparently one more victim of England's premier prison, an apothecary's apprentice in Antwerp confessed from what he assumed was his death-bed that he had supplied Frances Carr with the poison. Eventually the Carrs were brought to trial, and condemned to death. Although, unlike their accomplices (including the apprentice) they were not hanged, their time in the royal favour was over.

Many strained to fill the vacancy. With the queen's help Archbishop Abbot, in a role unfamiliar to the Primate of all England, pimped for George Villiers and like most in that profession stressed his ware's physical allures: 'He had a very lovely complexion, he was the handsomest bodied man in England: his limbs were so well compacted.'[4] Following the failure of his marriage and the hurt inflicted by the Carr scandal, James was as ready to find someone new to love as were the various court factions to provide such an object. When he did find that person the king made no secret of his feelings, telling the privy council in a confession as remarkable for its unconscious frankness, as for its blasphemy, 'I, James, am neither God nor angel, but a man like any other. Therefore I act like a man and confess to loving those dear to me more than other men. You may be sure that I love the Earl of Buckingham. . . . Jesus Christ did the same and therefore I cannot be blamed. Christ had his John and I have my George.' Unlike John the Baptist, however, George, the favourite, had a homosexual relationship with his saviour: they first became intimate at Farnham in August 1615.[5] George listened to James, flattered James, bullied James, stroked James's ego, knowing to the last inch how far he could go, constantly smoothing the rough edges of a life that the king found increasingly bumpy. Towards the end of the 1618 Twelfth Night masque the king became obstreperous, barking, 'Why don't they dance? What did you make me come here for? Devil take you all! Dance!' George saved the day (as well as Charles's face, for he had sponsored the masque) by jumping to his feet and leading actors and audience in a merry dance that restored the king's good humour. Even Anne found Buckingham useful in dealing with her difficult husband. 'My Dear Dog,' wrote the queen, 'You do very well in lugging the sow's ear, and I do thank you for it.'[6]

In addition to his good looks, pleasing personality, and ability to pour oil on the troubled waters of old age, Buckingham was the entree to a whole new family over which James could play the patriarch. The king gave Buckingham's mother, brothers and brother-in-law titles of nobility, and helped him marry Lady Katherine Manners, the richest, if not the fairest heiress in England. 'Thy Dear Dog send thee his blessing this morning,' James wrote to them on their honeymoon, hoping that 'I may have sweet chamber boys to play with', and when they were born James let shrieking Buckingham brats race around his palace like 'rabbit conies about their burrows' – all antics he never tolerated from his real family.[7]

Initially there was no place for Charles in his father's new family. When he and Buckingham quarrelled James sided with the favourite. In 1616 Buckingham complained to the king that Charles had lost a ring that he had borrowed. James called for his son, and 'used such bitter language to him as forced his highness to shed tears', telling the lad not to return until he had found the ring – which Sir Robert Carey immediately discovered in the pocket of yesterday's breeches. Two months later, as James and Buckingham were strolling through the gardens at Greenwich Palace, Charles turned on a fountain hidden in a statue of Bacchus soaking the favourite. Seeing he was 'much offended', James boxed his son and heir's ears.[8] At first Buckingham had as little time for the boy as had Henry, treating appointments to the prince's household with an equal lack of regard for Charles's wishes.[9] He ignored the warnings of advisers: 'The Prince grows up fast to be a man,' Sir Francis Bacon told his patron in 1616, 'and if you (keeping that distance which is fit) do humbly interpose yourself in such a case, he will one day thank you for it.'[10] Two years later Buckingham's cavalier treatment of the prince went too far when, on 18 June 1618, he entertained the king at his country house in Wanstead, Essex, without bothering to invite Charles, who was spending the night less than a mile away. James 'took amiss'. So that evening Buckingham rode over to Charles's lodgings to apologize, blaming the incident on a steward who said that they did not have enough food to invite the prince's party. To make amends he presented him with furniture and fittings enough for two large rooms.[11] A week later, to placate James, Buckingham entertained him and Charles at a two-day entertainment so splendid that even in those days of gargantuan banquets it become known as 'The King's Feast'. The ploy worked. During the meal the king proposed a toast to Buckingham's noble house, which he declared he was determined 'to advance above all others whatsoever'.[12] For Charles, sitting with his father at the head table the message was quite clear – if he wanted to join the king's new family he must play second fiddle.

Charles accepted the offer avidly. Within two months he surrendered his reversion of the office of Lord High Admiral to his new friend (as he had over six years before to Henry) and by the end of 1618 was reported to be allowing Buckingham to handle 'all his business of importance'.[13] The favourite shielded the prince from the king's wrath. James asked Charles to persuade the queen not to leave her personal possessions to her Danish maid, and when at first he botched this admittedly delicate task was so angry that Charles had to ask Buckingham to intervene on his behalf. 'Tell him I am very sorry that I have done anything that might offend him,' wrote the heir, 'I will be content to have any penance inflicted upon me so he may forgive me. . . . I deserve to be punished,' and signed this letter to Buckingham, 'Your true, constant, loving friend, Charles Prince.' Like many a younger son he was using his 'big brother' to protect him from external threats, as well as an entry into a more exciting grown-up world. Furthermore Buckingham's good looks and suave self-confidence appealed to that mild homosexuality that is a normal part of adolescence.[14]

During March of 1619 two events cemented this new friendship between Charles, James and Buckingham.

On the second of the month Anne died. Charles's actions at her death betrayed his feeling towards her. Learning that she was dangerously ill he rushed to Hampton Court, and insisted on sleeping in the room next to hers. Just before she passed away he managed to persuade her to leave him, and not her Danish maid, Anna, all her personal estate worth £360,000. Even though it took James twelve weeks to raise enough money for his wife's funeral, most spectators agreed it was 'a tedious sight . . . a poor show'. The king refused to attend, deputizing his son to be chief mourner, a task, one observer recalled, Charles performed 'with a just measure of grief, without any affected sorrows'.[15] the queen's passing broke the last link with the king's old – and real – family, and as if to signify that a new generation had taken over James divided the property his wife left him between his son and his favourite.

Three weeks after Anne's death James fell so ill that he seemed about to follow her to the grave. Painfully he moved in slow stages to Royston, his favourite retreat in Hertfordshire, unable to sleep, and in excruciating pain from bladder stones, three of which he voided. His pulse was weak; ulcers covered his face and chin; he was racked with fever and suffered from diarrhoea. Convinced that the end was nigh he sent for his son and, as the favourite stood by, gave him 'a very religious and wise speech', telling him to protect the Church of England and its bishops, and to rely on sage counsellors, the wisest of whom was, without question, the Marquis of Buckingham. For eight more days the crisis raged, until in early April James recovered enough for a public service of thanksgiving to be held in St Paul's Cathedral.[16] This brush with death strengthened Buckingham's grip on Charles. Bishop Andrewes persuaded James from his sickbed to dismiss the prince's Scots servants and replace them with loyal Anglicans, most of whom Buckingham managed to select. At the same time James's illness reminded Charles that any day the heavy burden of kingship might suddenly be thrust upon him, and thus more than ever he needed the help and friendship of Buckingham.[17] In addition James's illness had intensified his feelings towards his favourite, while impressing Buckingham of the need to make his hegemony hereditary. Thus it is not surprising that when Buckingham became seriously ill in June, Charles and James constantly visited the patient, who was reported 'as great a favourite with the prince as with his father'.[18]

So by the summer of 1619 the triumvirate that was to govern England for the next six years had been formed. James was now *pater familias*, Buckingham the king's first minister, and Charles the liaison, who forwarded the favourite's letters and reported back the king's reaction.[19] The three supported each other emotionally, each having a role to play and needs to be satisfied. This does not, of course, mean that their relationship was a placid one in which nothing changed: such would be unusual in any family, particularly one so artificial as theirs. Again, as in most families, the tensions were often fought out over petty issues: arguments over dress, hunts and tilts recollected, wagers made, games played, races run. We know, for instance, that in 1620 Charles bet Buckingham a banquet over a tennis match (he lost), and a little later which of two footmen could run the faster (again he lost).[20] However, the vast majority of such incidents, while significant as part of a pattern to an analyst (or even a novelist), were considered too trivial to record by contemporaries who preferred instead to set down events such as parliamentary sessions or diplomatic negotiations, which they believed more worthy of their pens. Therefore the surviving record necessitates taking well-documented episodes, such as the parliaments of 1621 and 1624, the negotiations over the Spanish marriage, and (the theme that runs through them all) the attempt to recover the Palatine, to see what light they shed on the development of Charles's personality as a young man and adult, and his changing relations with his father and best friend.

Of the prince's part in the rather ridiculous surrogate dynastic feuding of his father's court, the general public remained blissfully ignorant. All they saw was a very young man growing in vigour, his childhood frailties overcome, showing off his military prowess in the tiltyard. By charging on horseback at full speed in full armour to snatch a ring from a gibbet with his spear, Charles could demonstrate his martial skills without the discomfort and danger that attends real war. The government staged grand tilting displays to impress ambassadors, and thus their masters, as well as the people. For instance, the king and all the officers of state, as well as several scribes to ensure that not a jot of Charles's valour escaped the attention of pamphlet readers, attended the great tilt put on in the yard at Whitehall on 20 June 1620. At noon, as six trumpeters dressed in green velvet with gold and silver threads blew their loudest, and cannon reverberated all along the Thames from Denmark House, Charles entered the tiltyard. He was alone. Mounted on a powerful white horse, decked in splendid plumes, and wearing a suit of the finest armour inlaid with gold and silver, the heir graciously received the crowd's plaudits before tilting with the scions of the aristocracy and according to one of the official scribes, 'distinguished himself to the great joy of the people'.[21] One reason why the audience cheered with such enthusiasm at the exhibition, the like of which, another scribe recorded, had not been seen for many a day in England, was that they hoped that very soon the prince would be fighting in earnest. Charles shared their aspirations, because he badly wanted to lead a Protestant crusade to restore his sister and brother-in-law to their German Palatinate.

Seven years earlier Frederick and Elizabeth had left England with all the hope and happiness of any young couple setting off to make a life together. Their journey up the Rhine was that round of entertainments which may sometimes bore modern readers, but which contemporaries lapped up so impatiently that some gossip sheets described events before they had taken place so as to scoop the competition. In June Frederick eventually brought his bride back to Heidelberg, his capital city and their new home. To celebrate his success in returning with so great a prize as the King of England's only daughter, he rode in triumph about the palace yard dressed as Jason bringing back the Golden Fleece.[22] Had Frederick's classical education been more rigorous, he might have chosen an analogy that was not so unhappily prophetic, for the Jason of Greek myth ended up being hounded by Furies who sowed snakes in his hair. The first few years of his marriage were, however, very happy. Frederick and Elizabeth had their first son, Henry, in 1614, their second, Charles Louis, in 1617, and their first daughter, Elizabeth, the following year. They spent wildly on an ambitious building programme, and extravagant entertainments, being determined to make their mark on the world.

That Frederick did in 1619, bringing their idyll to an end. In May the Protestant nobility of Bohemia expelled the Catholic Archduke Frederick of Styria from the throne to which they had recently elected him, and threw the imperial emissaries, Slavata and Martinitz, out of a third floor window of Hradschin castle, Prague – both Catholics and Protestants taking the emissaries' survival by happening to land in a dung heap as a sign that the Almighty favoured their particular brand of Christianity. The Bohemian nobles went on to offer the throne to Frederick, who accepted it, so he later explained, on the dictates of some inner voice that many believed was more likely that of his wife than his Maker. Frederick soon discovered that the nobility were not prepared to give him much military support, and as having a Protestant as ruler of Bohemia upset the delicate balance of central Europe, he also found himself at war with the Hapsburgs.

A Spanish army under Ambrogio Spinola invaded the Palatinate, and in November 1621 troops of the Catholic League, under Count Tilly, routed Bohemian forces at the Battle of the White Mountain, forcing Frederick and Elizabeth to flee into exile in Holland. On accepting the Bohemian throne Frederick had explained that he did so 'to prevent the effusion of much blood and the wasting of many lands.'[23] He could not have been more wrong, for he triggered off the devastating Thirty Years War which was to ravage Europe for a generation, and even though England did not really become a belligerent, preoccupied Charles for much of the rest of his life.

Charles welcomed Frederick's acceptance of the crown of Bohemia: 'I am very glad to know that my brother is of so ripe a judgement, and so forward an inclination to the good of Christendom as to become king,' he wrote in 1619.[24] As Frederick's fortunes waned Charles's anxieties waxed. 'I have nothing to do at present but to think of the affairs of Bohemia,' he told the Spanish agent in January 1620. 'For some days I have been hearing, reading and studying the arguments of the Bohemians, and they appear to be very strong.' Elizabeth's desperate pleas for help to the brother she loved 'more than all the world' increased his concern, prompting him to head a list of contributors for the restoration of the Palatine with a £10,000 pledge.[25]

As England's St George Charles volunteered to lead a crusade across Europe to slay the papist dragon and rescue a Protestant queen, a fantasy that remained current for a quarter of a century, as Rubens's painting of 'St George and the Dragon' suggests (see Plate 7). Built on the brief but intense friendship with Frederick and Elizabeth when he was eleven, this fantasy enabled Charles to elaborate on the grandiose self-image of martial valour propagated by the carefully contrived displays on the tiltyard, and gave him the certainty of a mission that banished the doubts and loneliness of the past few years.[26] In sum, Charles had found a cause – a common enough thing for any adolescent.

As the concept of adolescence has been successfully applied to geographically diverse societies, it may surely be applied to chronologically distant ones too. After all, the tasks of adolescence – achieving biological and social maturity – are nigh universal.[27]

As far as we know physically Charles matured late, even by the standards of the seventeenth century when boys did not develop as early as today. When the prince was nearly sixteen the Venetian secretary reported it would be at least two or three years before he was capable of marriage. Later that year Charles was troubled with 'the green sickness', a form of anaemia common among girls at puberty.[28] During the summer of 1618 gossip linked him romantically with Anne, the daughter of Sir Bassingbourne Gawdy, a Norfolk gentleman, whom he and James twice visited, and some lines of love poetry, notable for their lack of emotion, were attributed to Charles. Yet, in truth, the Gawdy affair was more the product of the smoke of gossip that seems to attend every Prince of Wales than the fire of Charles's loins, for a couple of years later the Spanish ambassador noted that he had not 'yet anything to do with love affairs'. Indeed Charles was so reticent in this regard that it was widely reported that he was 'sterile'.[29]

James did nothing to help his son making him play second fiddle to Buckingham. The only responsibilities he gave the heir were trivial ones, such as presiding over the Garter ceremony, auditing the accounts of his Scottish estates, and supervising the Barons of Nova Scotia.[30] Thus Charles's adolescence was unduly prolonged, with the expected psychological consequences: friends became hard to make, homosexual tendencies more pronounced, and heterosexual ones often superficial and romanticized.[31] In consequence Charles developed the 'submissive, feminine and narcissistic self-sufficiency' that is often found among those whose adolescence has been over-extended.[32]

Towards James, the impediment to adult maturity, Charles felt highly ambivalent. While he wanted to become his own man, he was afraid of offending his father by standing up to him. For example, he qualified his enthusiastic offer to go and fight for the Palatinate, and alluded to both his *pater patriae* and *pater familias* by saying that he would only go 'if the king, my father, would give me leave.' As one diplomat noted, 'before his father he always aims at suppressing his own feelings.'[33] Thus Buckingham provided a way out of this impasse. Charles could please his father by making friends with the king's favourite, and then use the favourite first to protect him from his father, and then later to oppose him. Thus he employed a substitute elder brother to resolve an oedipal conflict, and the king's dearest subject to produce that contradiction in terms, a loyal opposition.[34]

This process may be best traced in the conflict over the Palatinate, which came to a head during the parliament of 1621.

Unlike his son and many of his people, James did not want to go to war over the Palatinate. He was by nature a pacific – some said cowardly – man, who thought that Frederick had been foolish to accept the Bohemian throne in the first place, and was now using England 'to pull the apple out of the fire for his own eating'.[35] On the other hand, his daughter's desperate pleas for help disturbed the king, who was under great pressure from all sides to do something. Courtiers and pamphlet writers urged James to draw his sword in the Protestant cause. One broadsheet even called upon the ghosts of Elizabeth I, Henry VIII, and Sir Walter Ralegh, to plead the Palatine's case, while a solitary figure dressed all in black stood outside the court gates praying for Frederick and the confusion of his enemies for a whole year, after which he committed suicide.[36] Fearful that England's entry into a war might have a similar end, or simply not knowing what to do, James did next to nothing. In 1619 he sent James Hay to the Continent on a peace mission that cost £30,000 and produced only Protestant complaints that the money could have been better spent on military aid. On learning that the Bohemian forces had been devastated at the Battle of the White Mountain, and that his daughter and her husband had been forced into exile, all the king could do was to refuse to hunt, ban court entertainments, and shut himself in his room.[37] Such feebleness disgusted foreign ambassadors; 'King James throws the affairs of Bohemia into confusion in every way, and says one thing and sometimes another,' complained the French, while the Venetians compared the frequency with which the king changed his mind to the fickleness of the English weather.[38] At home the public's unhappiness was so intense that it forced the calling of parliament in 1621.

The 1621 parliament should not be viewed with the clarity of Whiggish hindsight as one more episode in a century's long conflict between king and people that eventually produced parliamentary democracy, but as a power struggle within the surrogate royal family that got out of control.[39] Initially Buckingham rejected Sir Francis Bacon's advice to urge the king to call a parliament, but when he recognized that after the Battle of the White Mountain the pressure for one was insurmountable he tried to co-opt the country's jingoism by allying himself with the heir and many in the House of Commons against the king. Through this initial success, and then by losing control of the Commons which threatened to run rogue, Buckingham helped shape Charles's attitudes to that fatal body.

When Charles rode with his father on 20 January 1621 to the state opening he had his first real exposure to parliament, having been too young to have been much influenced by the 'addled parliament' of 1614. Now he was a young man of twenty, with a seat in the House of Lords, where he was treated by the nation's political leaders as a person of note and potential. He listened attentively to his father's speech from the throne, a well-received request for the passage of taxes to recover Frederick's patrimony and England's honour. Charles was an assiduous freshman member of the Upper House, attending sixty-three of its eighty-nine sessions. He sat on a number of committees, including one on the Mompesson case, another on the establishment of an academy to educate aristocrats' children, and soon won a reputation for diligence and doing his homework. Charles enjoyed it all, often laughing at Sir Edward Coke's anecdotes.[40] In return parliament used him to liaise with the king. In February the Marquis of Dorset asked Charles to present his father at a meeting of the privy council with a copy of the petition that the Lords had passed on 19 February complaining about the excessive creation of new peers, and was highly embarrassed to discover during the meeting itself that the prince denied ever having agreed to do any such thing.[41] Charles's next two liaison missions went off far more smoothly. On 26 March, as the spokesman for a parliamentary committee, he gave the king a speech so replete with Latin and Greek tags that his father had proudly to admit that not even he could appreciate every classical nuance.[42] Three months later, on 3 June, he was one of the dozen members of a deputation from both houses that waited on James at Greenwich to discuss whether parliament should be adjourned or prolonged, and all there agreed that Charles played his part 'very gracefully'.[43] His performance in the last, and most important, scene did not get such enthusiastic reviews. Six months later, by presenting his father with a copy of the Commons' remonstrance of 3 December that did not contain the conciliatory clauses, he exacerbated the deteriorating relations between king and parliament.[44]

The Commons had replied to James's request for subsidies by voting only two and then passing, on 10 February, a petition that the punitive laws against English Catholics be more strictly enforced. Nine days later they ordered the arrest of Sir Giles Mompesson, the notorious monopolist. When he managed to avoid their sergeants, by slipping out of a window and escaping to the Continent, they were outraged. Charles shared their feelings, being reported 'very forward against' Sir Giles.[45] Had he realized the dangers of the monopolist's prosecution he might not have been so enthusiastic, for Sir Giles was a relative of Buckingham, who was an even greater monopolist than the hapless fugitive. The Mompesson case raised the flood-gates, unleashing a wave of complaints that went far beyond an attack on some distant kin of the king's favourite. For instance, it prompted one gentleman to scribble a doggerel verse that started by criticizing all monopolists, and ending by attacking the very fabric of royal order, the hierarchy of bishops:[46]

> With scripture divine they play false and loose
> And turn holy writ into capon and goose.

Worse politically – though perhaps not poetically – was the revival of impeachment, a medieval instrument last employed in 1459, that was used against Sir Francis Bacon. On 3 May the Commons voted to impeach the Lord Chancellor, who rather than stand trial by his peers, pleaded guilty to corruption, being sentenced to loss of office, a £46,000 fine, and imprisonment during the royal pleasure. In this disgraceful episode Charles had little part except to plead that the fallen Lord Chancellor not be stripped of his peerage, for which Bacon was obsequiously grateful.[47] 'Swim with the tide,' Bishop Williams advised Buckingham, 'and you will not be drowned.'[48]

Yet the parliamentary tide proved to have so nasty a rip that it threatened to pull Buckingham under, and by late March the favourite was urging the king to dissolve parliament. To prevent this, and to discredit Buckingham, his enemies in the Lords dragged up his treatment of Sir Henry Yelverton, whom he had dismissed from the Attorney Generalship and imprisoned in the Tower for granting the City of London a charter that was supposedly too generous. On 30 April, during an examination in the Upper House, Yelverton vituperatively attacked Buckingham as Mompesson's unscrupulous master, who refused to do what the king told him, being as rotten as any of Edward II's advisers. Stung by the not wholly inappropriate comparison of his father to the most notorious homosexual to sit on the English throne (and, perhaps, mindful of the excruciatingly appropriate fashion in which he had been murdered) Charles leapt to his feet, demanding Yelverton to be silenced. Two days later he insisted that the former Attorney General be allowed to say no more in his defence, but be severely punished without delay.[49] As the tide continued to turn, Buckingham managed to persuade James in June to adjourn parliament until November. When it reassembled on 20 November all that the king's desperate requests for a speedy vote of taxes to relieve Frederick produced was a long and acrimonious debate on foreign policy.

As Buckingham lost control of parliament, Charles's attitude to it changed. Although in the excitement of his first few months as a member of the Lords he was not as keen to dissolve parliament as was his friend, by May he was becoming disillusioned. On 7 May he tried to reprove the Commons for attempting to have Edward Floyd, a Catholic barrister, mutilated for publicly celebrating the imperial victory at White Mountain, and at the end of the month angered several members of parliament by telling them not to trespass on the royal prerogative by pushing the king too hard to sign several pieces of legislation that they favoured.[50] During the second session, when it was apparent that all the summer recess had done was widen the breach between the favourite and his opponents in the Commons, Charles's sentiments shifted drastically. Eight days after parliament reassembled he wrote:[51]

> I would not wholly discount them: therefore my opinion is that the king should grant them a session at this time, but with all I should have him command them not to speak of Spain, whether it be of that war or my marriage.

But on 3 December the Commons not merely spoke of the prince's marriage and a Spanish war, but passed a remonstrance deploring the worsening situation in Germany, and the growing influence of papist recusants at home and of Spain abroad. Charles's initial reaction was, none the less, remarkably mild.[52] 'The Commons this day have been a little unruly but I hope that it will turn for the best, for before they rose they began to be ashamed of it,' he told Buckingham, and continued, 'Yet I could wish that the king would send down a commission that (if need were), such seditious fellows might be made an example to others.' Instead of the sharp punishment of the ringleaders that – like the arrest of the Five Members twenty years later – Charles was sure would bring the rest of the Commons, like naughty school boys, back to their senses, James immediately wrote to the Speaker forbidding any more discussion on foreign policy. When the Commons refused both the king's order, and the prince's advice to cool things, Charles complained to his father that 'his marriage was constantly prostituted in the Lower House.' On 3 January 1622 James sent for the Commons' journal to publicly rip out the pages on which the clerk had written the 3 December remonstrance, and packed parliament off home.[53] So, even if the Palatinate were not relieved one jot, and the Protestant crisis in central Europe remained as bad, perhaps worse than ever, and papists grew daily more impudent at home, the triumvirate of 'Baby Charles', 'Steenie' and their 'Dear Dad' had been saved. It had been saved at a price, the terrible cost of which was to become only too apparent as Charles grew older.

# IV

# 'THE VOYAGE OF THE KNIGHTS OF ADVENTURE'

On Monday, 17 February 1623, two horsemen rode the thirty-five miles from the king's hunting lodge at Royston to the Marquis of Buckingham's country house, New Hall in Essex. Early the next morning they cantered south to the Gravesend ferry. Their mien was, to say the least, suspicious. They carried pistols, wore false beards (which tended to slip around their faces), called each other 'John' and 'Thomas Smith', and having no small change tipped the ferryman a·silver 20–shilling piece. After pocketing this fare, equal to a couple of months' wages, the ingrate immediately alerted the authorities, suspecting that the 'Smiths' were off to the Continent to fight a duel.[1] Outside Rochester, going up the steep hill with its splendid views back across the River Medway, Tom and John Smith came across Sir Henry Mainwaring who was escorting Ferdinand de Boiscot, the new ambassador from the Archduchess of Flanders, to London. Their appearance prompted Sir Henry to send a messenger after them, but the two horsemen galloped off across the fields to Canterbury.[2] There the mayor tried to arrest them so the taller horseman had to pull down his beard and identify himself as the Marquis of Buckingham, who, with his assistant, was off to Dover to pay a surprise inspection on the fleet. The dozen miles from Canterbury to Dover were without incident. At the port they met Sir Francis Cottington and Endymion Porter whom they had sent ahead to arrange transportation, and were recognized by Jasper Fowler, a sharp-eyed immigration official, whom Charles ordered to close the harbour for a couple of days, and his mouth even longer, because he and Buckingham were off to Madrid to woo the King of Spain's sister. Their departure was so secret that not even the Secretary of State knew about it. A few days later when Secretary Conway did find out, in his astonishment he called their mission 'the voyage of the Knights of Adventure'.[3]

The origins of a marriage alliance between England and Spain go back to 1604, when the Treaty of London ended a generation's fighting. John Digby, the diplomat, first proposed a union between Henry and the Infanta, the King of Spain's daughter, in 1608. The arrival of Don Diego Sarmiento de Acuna, later Count Gondomar, in London in 1613, and

Digby's return the following year as British ambassador to Madrid revived the scheme, though this time with Charles as the prospective groom. Negotiations dragged on for five years, until Gondomar had to return home empty handed in 1618.[4] The obstacles to a treaty were immense. For one thing the parties were too young; for another the Spanish, while naturally willing to help their fellow Catholics in England and even to work to return England to the Roman fold, were more interested in stringing London along to prevent an Anglo-French alliance than consummating an Anglo-Spanish one.[5] Opinion in England was more openly divided. James wanted to wed his son to Catholic Spain to balance his daughter's marriage to a leading German Protestant. After the loss of the Palatinate, Charles and Buckingham easily convinced themselves that in return for a marriage alliance with his daughter the King of Spain would be only too happy to use his infantry, reputedly the finest in the world, to restore a Protestant to a strategically important part of central Europe. The blatant sectarian hatreds of most Englishmen saved them from such delusions. Few believed James's assurances that he had no intention of ameliorating the harsh penal laws against Catholics, agreeing instead with John Pym, the radical member of parliament, that if you gave a papist an inch he would take a mile, exterminating 'all contrary religions' along the way. In a sermon attacking the proposed mixed marriage between Charles and the Infanta, one London minister voiced the widely held view that the two faiths were unalterably incompatible by using as his text, 'Thou shalt not plough with an ox and an ass.'[6]

Both England and Spain were poorly served by their ambassadors, who having, as Digby and Charles 'laboured so long and suffered so much' to conclude a treaty, allowed their personal commitment to outrun their nations' interests.[7] Gondomar had more influence with the English king than with his own. He and James quickly became friends. The ambassador started audiences with a joke or two. They went out hunting together, both washing their hands in the warm blood of the slain beast claiming that it relieved the aches of old age. James lent Gondomar Nonesuch Palace, spent more time closeted with him than with the privy council, and even allowed him to purge Charles's household of those who opposed the Spanish marriage.[8] In spite of such intimacy and favour, Gondomar remained remarkably poorly informed about the reality of religious life in England, once reporting home that James 'was well inclined towards the mass' and could restore the link between Canterbury and Rome as easily as Henry VIII had broken it. 'Everything here depends solely on the king's will,' he wrote to Madrid in 1617, 'he has sufficient authority to introduce the sect of Turks or Moors if he pleases.'[9]

Like Gondomar, Digby had more influence in London than Madrid. He was constantly out-witted by the Spanish, who would show him one set of diplomatic instructions while sending a second secret set countermanding the first; he never understood the nuances of Spanish politics and public opinion, nor the extent of Spain's decline – which probably explains why he was such an ardent admirer of that country. On his return to Madrid in 1622 he did all he could to persuade Charles to marry the Infanta, writing to the prince how highly the Spanish court regarded him, and how attractive a woman the Infanta was: 'She has fine hair and complexion, of a middling stature, being of late well grown, she hath the fairest hands I ever saw, she is very straight and well bodied and a likely lady to make you happy', the ambassador rhapsodized, 'and I never heard of so much good in any creature.' Digby did not fail to mention the Infanta's other allures: by marrying the King of Spain's sister Charles would not only gain 'the greatest portion that was ever given in Christendom', but restore Frederick and Elizabeth to the Palatinate without 'inconvenience and difficulties'.[10] Such expectations were, in truth, unrealistic for as a contemporary pamphlet pointed out, hoping to use Catholic Spain to restore a Protestant ruler was like trying to get 'honey of the bee without danger of being stung'.[11]

That the Anglo-Spanish negotiations were founded on a bed of sand, and when made to bear some weight collapsed, would not normally have mattered. They were not the first (nor the last) to be built on mutual misconception, over-eager emissaries, hostile public opinion and divided counsels. Yet the crucial difference between these marriage negotiations and most others was that in 1623 the English principals went in person to do their own wooing.

In his *History* the Earl of Clarendon (who came to know Charles well two decades later) argued that the trip to Spain was all Buckingham's idea. The favourite persuaded Charles to go to Madrid by reminding him of the dangers of having others choose and court the woman with whom he was to spend the rest of his life: by riding personally to Madrid Charles would so convincingly prove his love that the Infanta must succumb to his gallantry, and Philip IV would cut through petty details to seal their union. At Buckingham's instigation, Charles first raised the possibility of the trip with his father in January 1623. On his knees he told James that he wanted to go in person to Madrid to fetch his bride. When James asked Buckingham for his views the favourite replied that to refuse so slight a request on so important a matter as his son's happiness might jeopardize Charles's love for his father. Blackmail worked. James approved. The next day that strange combination of vacillation and shrewdness that were the king's chief protections reasserted themselves. Tearfully James told Buckingham and Charles that they must not leave him: it would not be safe in Madrid, the Spanish would continually increase their demands, their absence 'would break his heart'. Charles and Buckingham furiously berated the king. The prince said that if the king broke his word then he would never marry; the favourite added that if James went back on his word his promises would be forever worthless. In the hope of gaining an ally James called in Sir Francis Cottington, an experienced diplomat and counsellor. 'Baby Charles and Steenie have a great mind to go by post into Spain to fetch the Infanta', he said, and asked 'what think you of the journey?' Cottington was dumbfounded, eventually managing to reply that such a mission would undo years of careful diplomacy, and deliver the prince as hostage to any demands the Spanish might care to make. He dared not contemplate what might happen if James were to die with his heir abroad. Buckingham attacked Cottington. The king was not interested in his view as to the wisdom of the trip, but merely wanted to know what was the best route to take. Even though James demurred, trying to protect his honest adviser, in the end he gave way agreeing to let Charles and Buckingham go. 'The whole intrigue', Clarendon concluded, 'was conceived by the Duke.'[12]

In leaving the kingdom, however, Buckingham was taking so huge a political risk of losing control of the king as well as his favour that the Venetian ambassador dismissed the rumour that he and Charles were going to Madrid as 'incredible'.[13] On the other hand if he refused to accompany the heir who had displayed a degree of initiative so uncharacteristic that not even Clarendon could credit it, the favourite would run the even greater risk of letting the reversionary interest slip through his fingers. For the first time in his life Charles was prepared to defy his father, and even his best friend, for quite simply – and quite naturally for a young man of twenty-two – the prince was in love.

He did not fall into that blissful state of misery without a struggle. At first, influenced by several of his Scots servants Charles opposed the alliance, but by the spring of 1617 after Gondomar had them purged from his household, his attitude to the project was reported as one of increasing 'towardliness'. In a pro-Spanish gesture he persuaded his mother not to go and see Sir Walter Ralegh off on his voyage to the Spanish Main. Once Buckingham took personal charge of negotiations, Charles's interest in them grew. He would often walk his friend to the garden where the discussions with Gondomar took place.[14] If the attacks on the marriage during the 1621 parliament greatly strengthened his commitment to the proposal (perhaps because he wanted to punish the Commons for their lack of deference) Digby's second ambassadorship to Madrid certainly consolidated it. Digby left in March 1622 carrying personal letters from James and Charles to Philip IV expressing the hope that the alliance would be concluded as soon as possible. To this end the ambassador sent back descriptions of the Infanta's financial, physical and diplomatic attractions so enticing that James elevated him Earl of Bristol, and Charles made an astounding proposal. 'The Prince has offered to me in strict confidence and secrecy,' Gondomar wrote to his master in May 1622, 'that if upon my arrival in Spain, I should advise him to come and place himself in your

Majesty's hands at your disposition, he would do it and come to Madrid *incognito* with two servants.'

After Charles carried out his promise and rode to Madrid in disguise with a few servants, there was no doubt in the king's mind whose idea it was all along: James told several diplomats and courtiers that it was his son's entirely. One of the king's confidants reported to a friend that the decision was 'so much urged by the Prince himself' because he was 'animated by the example of his predecessors'.[15] Had not his father brought a bride back from Oslo and his brother-in-law one from Westminster, so why should he not do the same from Madrid?

Few shared Charles's romantic notions. When they learnt of his departure for Madrid both the Venetian and French ambassadors paid special messengers to take the news to their governments. In the Hague the intelligence 'caused great consternation', in Venice it was 'as momentous as unexpected', from Savoy the duke was reported 'almost confused . . . at this impudent step', while it was recorded that the people of Florence 'never cease expressing their astonishment'.[16] English public opinion was equally surprised. 'I see wise men much troubled,' wrote Dudley Carleton, while Robert Carey remembered 'a great hubbub in our court and all England beside'.[17] To try and stop gossip and quieten fears James – in a manner reminiscent of his predecessor, Canute – ordered the court to cease tattling about the trip. He even considered issuing a proclamation that all doubts about its wisdom be vanquished, but had to settle for having prayers said in every church the following Sunday for Charles's and Buckingham's safe return. 'Where philosophy fails,' one cynic noted, 'faith must begin.'[18]

Such doubts and cares did not trouble the Knights of Adventure during their ride across Europe. Early on the morning of 19 February the two sailed from Dover, both being sick on the six-hour voyage to Boulogne, where they met their bodyguards, headed by Sir Richard Graham. The spent the rest of the day cantering along icy roads to Montreuil where they passed the night, riding on the morrow to Breteuil. Outside Paris the royal party met some German travellers who, having recently been to Newmarket, thought they recognized the prince and favourite, but Graham persuaded them they were mistaken. The incident may have made Charles and Buckingham more cautious, for when they arrived in Paris they bought themselves new – and presumably better fitting – wigs. They did the usual sights, and with the help of a Monsieur Proes went twice to court, seeing Louis XIII and the Queen Mother at dinner, and Queen Anne, Henrietta Maria, and their ladies rehearsing a masque. Glimpsing Queen Anne made Charles long even more to see her sister, the Infanta Maria; his first sight of Henrietta Maria, the French princess he was to marry and eventually come to love dearly, having no recorded effect on him at all.[19] After Louis discovered a few days later that Charles and Buckingham had been snooping about his court he was so furious that he even considered having them arrested, and James had to send Lord Carlisle to Paris to placate him.[20] On the advice of Lord Herbert, the English ambassador, the royal party had left Paris before dawn on 23 February, riding via Estaims and Orleans to Blois. In Bordeaux they all bought riding coats of the same colour. Outside Bayonne, where inns were few and far between, and the season being Lent meat was unavailable, Graham suggested that like the rivers of his native Scots borders they rustle some goats. 'Why Richard,' Charles chided, 'do you think that you may practise here your old tricks again?' He insisted instead on paying the goat keeper. Buckingham chased a kid which Charles shot with his pistol, and they barbecued it over an open fire, before galloping across the border to elude the French frontier officials.[21]

What splendid fun it all was! As Charles and Buckingham wrote to James:[22]

> We are now in Spain, free from harm of falls, in as perfect health as when we parted, and undiscovered by any Monsieur. We met Gresley, a post [royal messenger], beyond Bayonne. We saucily opened your letters, and found nothing in that or any other which we could understand without a cipher that made us regret our journey.

So on rode James's saucy lads. In an inn at St Augustine, a village ten miles north of Madrid, Charles became involved in an incident that said more for his patriotism than his discretion. He and a couple of Spanish soldiers became involved in a debate over the respective virtues of English and Spanish ladies that nearly altered the course of British history. The Spaniards later admitted that they were about to draw their swords and challenge Charles and Buckingham to a duel, the result of which might have been fatal to the prince and favourite, as a few days before they had foolishly left their bodyguards, Cottington, Graham and Porter behind so as to reach Madrid without delay.[23]

The two arrived outside the British ambassador's house at about five in the evening of Friday, 7 March, having ridden the 600 miles from Paris in twelve days. Simon Digby spotted them lurking outside, and let them in by a back door to his uncle's study, where he was working on some papers. When they revealed themselves the ambassador was, as one aide recalled, 'in a kind of astonishment', and, like a good civil servant, immediately dashed off a dispatch to his master.[24]

Bristol was not the only man in Madrid to be amazed to learn of Charles's and Buckingham's arrival. The next day on hearing a rumour to that effect, Gondomar hurried to Bristol's house to be assured it was so. He immediately went to inform Count Olivares. 'What brought you here at this hour looking as pleased as if you had the King of England in Madrid?' Philip IV's chief minister asked Gondomar, who had to admit that if he did not have the king, he at least had the next best thing – his son.[25] After he had informed Philip IV, Olivares went to the embassy to welcome Charles, and, showing the prince even more deference than he would his own sovereign, promised to arrange a meeting with the Infanta at the earliest possible moment. Although gossip reported that Philip was 'much transported with joy' to learn that Charles was in Madrid, in truth the prince's arrival had caught the Spanish off-balance. They could not, of course, send him home empty handed, but neither could they let the Infanta go at a discount. Thus the Spanish continued what they had been doing so well for over a decade: in public they were all hospitality, playing on Charles's emotions and Buckingham's vanity, while in private they were tough bargainers who played for time.

Charles first saw his lady-love less than forty-eight hours after he arrived in Madrid. On the afternoon of Sunday, 9 March, he, Buckingham, Bristol and Sir Walter Aston (Bristol's assistant), were riding in a carriage in the Prado where, by a carefully contrived accident, they happened to pass by a coach carrying the Spanish royal family. Charles interpreted the Infanta's blushes (surely of embarrassment) as the first flushes of maidenly ardour, and was ecstatic that evening when he and Philip first met. The following day Philip sent Olivares and Gondomar to wait on Charles, and on Tuesday evening the king and prince strolled in the gardens of the Casa del Campo, a small house outside the city. All that week Philip was the model host. He and Charles hawked and shot game together; he arranged for a company of comedians to amuse Charles; he sent the prince two horses, with the request that he select the better, and Charles, with equal grace, chose the worse.

Spanish courtesy reached its apogee on Sunday, 16 March, with Charles's formal entry into Madrid. In anticipation Philip had pardoned some 300 convicts, as well as all the English and Scots slaves in his galleys. The streets of Madrid were richly decorated, some having been even swept for the great occasion. After dining at St Jeronimo's monastery, just outside the city, Charles and Philip rode into the capital. Over them twelve gentlemen carried a costly canopy; before them trumpeters blew, drummers beat and soldiers marched; behind them Buckingham, Olivares and ambassadors-extraordinary rode. At the palace the queen welcomed the prince, and conducted him to his suite, where she had laid out many 'sumptuous and curious' presents. That evening there was a firework display, and, to demonstrate his people's happiness, Philip ordered a candle lit in every window in Madrid. The Spanish cheered the prince 'beyond admiration', because their priests told them he had come to convert to Catholicism, and that lighting candles would ensure God would answer their prayers.[26] The glow from Madrid, however, cast a distinct shadow in London, where many feared that Charles was about to desert the Protestant cause and the

Palatine. 'God send them all well and quietly home,' prayed Sir Charles Montague, voicing a sentiment so widespread that even James agreed.[27]

Charles, however, was too besotted with love to notice apprehensions of others. 'The Prince hath taken such a liking to his mistress,' Endymion Porter wrote to his wife, 'that now he loves her.' Buckingham agreed: 'Baby Charles is so touched by the heart that he confessed that all he ever saw is nothing to her.' Both seemed to have been touched in the head as well when, soon after arriving in Spain, they swallowed Olivares's suggestion that if the pope refused a dispensation letting Charles take the Infanta as his wife, then Philip, overwhelmed by the gallantry of their gallop to Madrid, would let him have her as his mistress.[28]

Once the bait was taken, with Buckingham and Charles safely lodged in the royal palace away from Bristol's influence, and the last candle was gutted, the real business of completing a marriage treaty remained as ethereal as Philip's firework display. Charles had arrived; the rockets had burst; the negotiations had been strengthened by no more than a few charred sticks and a whiff of gunpowder, while the obstacles to their successful conclusion were as immense as ever. Not only had Charles, Buckingham and Philip to agree, but the pope, James, Olivares and even the Infanta (all of whom had different objectives and objections) had to give their consent. Initially Charles and Buckingham found the smell of burnt gunpowder a heady aperitif for the start of talks. Buckingham was confident that the charm which had won him the favour of an English monarch would readily win him that of a Spanish king, and produce success where the professionals had failed. Thus he excluded Bristol from the negotiations, once even asking him to leave the coach in which he and Philip were having a discussion.[29] On 18 March Charles and Buckingham wrote home that they had high hopes of getting a papel dispensation, and a week later that negotiations were so close to success that James should immediately dispatch the fleet to bring them and the Infanta back. Two days afterwards they concluded that 'we never saw the business in better way than now it is,' and on 4 April that agreement was due within a couple of days. Back home the government shared their optimism. Only 'the desperately envious or vile almanac makers arguing from conjunctions of planets now talk of delay,' boasted secretary Conway.[30]

But the first round was to go to the 'vile almanac makers'. On 22 April Olivares announced that the pope had granted a dispensation, though with increased conditions: the Infanta was to educate her children as Catholics until the age of twelve, not ten as had been previously agreed, and that her chapel in London was to be open to all. Charles and Buckingham realized that it would be difficult, if not impossible, to get James to concede these terms, having just received his warning, 'I am not a monsieur that can shift his religion as easily as he can shift his shirt when he cometh from Tennis.' By 25 April the two were talking about going home and leaving Bristol to continue the negotiations. Yet within four days Spanish pressure overcame Charles's resolve, for on 29 April he wrote to James begging for a *carte blanche*, 'agreeing to do whatsoever I shall promise in your name.'[31]

The first cracks in the British position started to appear during the late spring of 1623 and by the early summer negotiations underwent a fundamental shift. Realizing that the Spanish were toying with him, Buckingham withdrew while Charles, infatuated with the Infanta, pressed on, taking personal control of negotiations and using Bristol to make ever more extravagant concessions. Both Charles and Buckingham kept their split a secret, since an open rupture would have weakened their position in Spain, damaged their relations with James, and would later be a painful reminder of a disagreement best forgotten. Yet the consequence of this split disturbed English politics for at least half a decade: after Charles's bid for independence ended disastrously he returned home a prodigal. In failure he grew more dependent on Buckingham and in compensation he blamed the ambassador who had helped him try to be his own man.

The arrival of the pope's dispensation in April 1623 precipitated the split, putting all parties in a quandary. Charles was upset because he might not be able to marry the Infanta. Donna Maria was unhappy because she still feared that he might. Buckingham knew full well that parliament would never repeal the laws that discriminated against recusants. The Spanish were equally disturbed, because the pope, whom they had secretly urged to refuse a dispensation, issued one on the grounds that his obligation was to succour England's Catholics rather than further Madrid's intrigues. Once their original plans had collapsed, all Philip and Olivares could do was to try and divide the prince and the favourite. So when in early May Buckingham threatened to go home Olivares promptly agreed that he should do so: Charles should stay behind in Spain to (eventually) marry the Infanta while he and James persuaded parliament to repeal the recusancy laws. Fully aware of the grave dangers of leaving the heir of a monarch who might die any day alone and abroad, a hostage in Madrid, where he was already under intense pressure from priests such as Father Zacaria di Salazza to convert, Buckingham straightway backed down. The vulgar believed that he was forced to do so because of thwarted lust rather than inept politicizing. According to a widely accepted story negotiations between him and Olivares broke off because the duke made a pass at Lady Olivares, who sent in her stead to the remote and dark rendezvous that he suggested 'a notorious stew bird'.[32] Apart from the fact that Buckingham never displayed the physical symptoms one might expect from such an encounter, later letters between him and the Spanish minister suggest that the tale was a salacious fabrication.[33] In face Buckingham determined to return home because, as he told the Venetians, he was 'furious' and 'disgusted' with the Spanish for continually increasing their terms. He did not, however, mention the two significant items a messenger had just brought him from London. First that James had created him a duke, an almost unprecedented honour, which clearly signified that the king's affection was strong enough to survive a foreign policy set-back, and second that the marriage had become so unpopular at home that a defeat in Madrid might well produce a triumph in London.[34]

Charles may not have been so well informed; certainly he was far less sanguine. Because the idea of coming to Madrid had been his, so too, he believed, would be the blame for the venture's failure. He had already spent most of the £30,000 in gold and letters of credit he had brought with him across France on wooing the Infanta with costly presents, sumptuous entertainments, and a retinue of servants which seemed to grow bigger, and more fractious and costly everyday. 'You must be as sparing as you can in your spending,' James begged him after he asked for a new tilting pavilion to be shipped to Madrid, because his old one of green and yellow would not go with his servants' latest livery of tawny velvet.[35] James was right to bewail, 'God knows how my coffers are already drained,' for he had spent much on entertaining the Spanish ambassadors in London, had started building a Catholic chapel for the Infanta at St James's Palace, and had commissioned a squadron of ships costing £300 a week to bring her back to England, decorating her cabin on the *Prince* 'as if it were about to receive some Goddess.'[36] Thus having put his father to all this expense Charles did not want, like some silly Sir Andrew Aguecheek, to be left a penniless figure of fun deserted by the woman he loved.[37] 'I have seen the Prince have his Eyes unmoveably fixed upon the Infanta,' James Howell reported, 'he watcheth her as a cat doth a mouse.'[38]

Having taking personal charge from Buckingham, Charles was not content with mere feline stares of devotion. Sure that deeds would speak louder than any gallant's tears, early one June morning he and Endymion Porter went to the Casa del Campo, where the Infanta usually took the air. With Porter's help Charles climbed the wall surrounding the garden, leapt down, and advanced towards his lady-love, who responded by running in the opposite direction, shrieking for her virtue and for her chaperon, an elderly marquis, who implored Charles to leave by a side door.[39] When one observer realized that the duke had no part in this hare-brained plot, and that Charles was in charge, he noted: 'the Spanish are now masters of this game.'[40] The position paper that Charles wrote for himself in mid-summer 1623 suggests that he really had no idea what to do next, each of his five drafts becoming increasingly confused.[41] Meanwhile James kept on imploring him and the duke to come home. 'I care for Match, nor nothing,' the king wrote on 14 June, 'so I may once more have you in my arms again: God Grant it, God grant it, God grant it, amen, amen, amen.' Charles reportedly read this letter 'with a sad countenance', and it may well have temporarily stiffened his resolve for he started to complain of

Spanish intransigence.[42] On 6 July Philip announced that September was the earliest the marriage could possibly take place, and that the Infanta would have to remain in Spain until the following March at least. All thought that Charles would find these new conditions unacceptable but the next morning, to Philip's surprise and Olivares's annoyance, Charles accepted them. No matter how hard the Spanish tried to throw the game, Charles insisted on booting the ball through the English goal, and to ensure that it remained safely there had James and the privy council swear on 20 July to honour both the public and private conditions of the Spanish marriage contract.[43] Spanish successes did not deter Madrid's quest for failure. Once more they increased their conditions, and once more Charles swallowed them. On 25 July he swore in a secret pact to repeal the recusancy laws within three years, let his children be educated as Catholics to the age of twelve, and allow the Infanta to choose her own advisers.[44]

After signing this agreement even Charles started to have second thoughts, writing to his father on 29 July, 'We are very confident when we see your Majesty to give you a very good satisfaction for all we have done.' However, what really prompted doubts in Charles's mind were the Spanish demands concerning the Palatinate. On 12 August Olivares proposed that Charles's nephew, Prince Frederick Henry, marry the emperor's daughter and be brought up a Hapsburg. In a moment of candour Olivares admitted that his Most Catholic Majesty would never fight the Hapsburgs to restore Germany's leading Protestant prince to the Palatinate.[45] A few days later the French ambassador further strained Charles's pro-Spanish sentiments by letting him know that all along the Spanish had been intercepting and reading his mail.[46] So it is not surprising that Charles was in a belligerent mood when he went to see Philip in the third week of August. He told the Spanish king that speed was of the essence: a fleet was waiting to take him home, his father was getting older and weaker every day, and as heir he could not remain abroad indefinitely. Philip called Charles's bluff, and taking his poorly camouflaged threats as a gentlemanly farewell, started to discuss the arrangements for the prince's departure.[47] The king had checkmated the Knights of Adventure.

Philip wanted to be rid of his English visitors, as much as most of them wished to be away from Spain. They found it hot, dirty, expensive and (the most damning adjective in the English tourist's vocabulary) foreign. Sir Richard Wynne complained of having nothing to do 'but play at cards'. They made no attempt to hide their distaste: one servant declared that he had never believed in the papist doctrine of purgatory until he had seen Madrid. In the heat of mid-August Anglo-Spanish enmity burst into a riot when a Catholic priest tried to convert a dying English page boy, and Sir Edmund Verney struck the Jesuit, starting a fight between the local populace and Charles's retinue.[48]

Before leaving Madrid Charles went twice to the monastery of Descalzas to say goodbye to the Infanta, and to promise once more to keep the conditions he had accepted on 25 July. His formal departure from the city took place on 30 August.[49] Charles and Philip exchanged magnificent gifts, including eighteen Spanish wildcats, and a diamond encrusted sword and pistol. Escorted by the grandees of Spain they rode to the Escorial. On 2 September, just outside the palace, they took their leave, Philip explaining that he could not accompany Charles to the coast as his wife was expecting a baby. Nevertheless in the field where they embraced goodbye he did raise a pillar engraved with a long Latin inscription to commemorate the prince's visit.[50]

Charles's party took ten days to ride the 200 miles to Santander, where an English squadron was waiting. At Segovia they admired the churches and local architecture. At Valladolid the university welcomed them 'with signs of joy and gladness', and Charles inspected paintings by Raphael and Michelangelo. Passing through Cuirone Charles visited a nun, one Luisa, who told him that regardless of the political consequences one day he would become a Catholic.[51] Sister Luisa (whom the Spanish Inquisition later burnt as a witch and impostor) did not understand what was going on in Charles's mind. The day after he left he sent a letter to the Spanish king promising to do his utmost to obtain a marriage treaty, and another letter to Bristol ordering him not to deliver, without his express permission, the marriage proxy he had left behind, because he was still concerned that the Infanta might carry out her long standing threat to become a nun rather than marry a heretic, leaving him, wrote Charles, 'a rash headed fool'.[52] As they rode side by side for the coast Buckingham played on Charles's fears, by harping on the dons' duplicity, especially over the Palatinate, and by sowing tares in the fertile soil of the prince's anger and humiliation. One of Charles's first acts after boarding ship off Santander was to write to Elizabeth saying that he wanted to be revenged on the Spanish.[53]

The Royal Navy squadron had left England on 24 August, a fair wind bringing the ten vessels to Santander in five days. The decision of their admiral, the Earl of Rutland, to anchor outside the harbour beyond the range of Spanish cannon nearly cost Charles his life.[54] As he was being rowed out to the flagship, the *Prince*, anchored three miles offshore, a sudden storm threatened to blow his pinnace out to sea, where he might have been lost in the dark had not Sir Sackville Trevor, captain of the *Defiance*, sent out a line buoyed with casks each with a lantern on top to catch his boat. Charles spent the night on the *Defiance* before transferring to the flagship, where on 13 September he entertained his Spanish escort.

Four days later the English fleet set sail for home. On 26 September, off the Scilly Isles, they came across a fight between some Dutch merchant men and Dunkirk pirates, which Charles tried, without success, to mediate. Three days later, with a storm impending, Charles and Buckingham landed at St Mary's, staying four more days in the Scilly Isles before a fair wind enabled them to start the last lap of their journey home. The *Prince* dropped anchor off Spithead early on 5 October, and at eight that morning Charles and Buckingham landed at Portsmouth Steps.

Every mile of their ride to London was a triumph. Indeed (with the possible exception of Mr Chamberlain's return from Munich) no English emissaries have been welcomed home after a débâcle abroad more enthusiastically than were the prince and duke. According to Clarendon the scenes of rejoicing were 'the loudest and most universal over the whole kingdom that the nation had ever been acquainted with.' Charles and Buckingham passed the night of 5 October at Viscount Annandale's house outside Guildford, entering London at breakfast-time the next day. The capital went wild. The church wardens of Wandsworth spent 3s 4d on ringing the parish bells, while those at Lambeth lavished with 12 shillings worth of campanology that became so impassioned that a little later they had to buy new bell ropes. In the streets, merchants spread tables of food and drink and the crowds, stimulated by their generosity and unmindful of the rain, hijacked wagon loads of timber to make bonfires.[55] The privy council pardoned a cartload of felons on their way to be hanged at Tyburn. St Paul's Cathedral held a special service of thanksgiving. Poetasters dashed off dreadful doggerel.[56] At Oxford the dons composed a book of Latin paeans, while at Cambridge – ever the more practical university – they decreed extra rations for the undergraduates.[57]

Charles and Buckingham did not linger in London to view the festivities, but after a bite and a drink rode on to Royston. James was delighted to learn that they were safely back in England, giving Mungay Murray, the messenger, a 200 mark pension for being the first to bring him the news.[58] The reunion of Steenie, Baby Charles and Dear Dad was unrestrained. They hugged and kissed, and for four hours were closeted in the king's private chamber, from which peals of laughter could be heard. When the king emerged he declared that he was truly content with all his son and favourite had done. That evening Bishop Laud wrote in his diary that the nation's reaction was 'The greatest expression of joy by all sorts of people that I ever saw.'[59] All were relieved that the rumours that Charles had been shipwrecked off Ireland, or that he had ordered the squadron to return home without him were untrue. They were overjoyed that the heir was back safely in England.[60] Without his papist bride and with his mission a failure, Charles was a great success. Of course, Charles's wooing of the King of Spain's sister never had a chance of success for, as Cervantes observed, 'you can't be a knight errant if you don't have a horse.'[61]

But on 6 October 1623 everyone cheered, and no one cared.

# V

# 'THE YOUNG FOLKS SHALL HAVE THEIR WORLD'

After the cheering stopped Charles's problems continued. Disappointed in love he needed a scapegoat. He could never admit that he had acted with besotted silliness over the Infanta, or that she, the object of his love, or that Buckingham, the friend who had rescued him from the mess in Madrid, were to blame. Gradually his resentment at being jilted convinced him that the Spanish in general, and Lord Bristol in particular, must be punished. James still wanted a Spanish marriage, while Buckingham urged a French one and war with the dons. So during the last quarter of 1623 Charles wavered, until by the end of the year the aggrieved lover won, and he sided with his best friend against his father. Buckingham, as senior partner, and Charles opened marriage negotiations with Paris, made James call parliament to use the popular dislike of Spain to force the King and the privy council to accept a war. When this did not work they sent an expeditionary force under Count Mansfeld to recover the Palatinate. Throughout the eighteen months between Charles's and Buckingham's return from Madrid to the king's death in March 1625, James was under intense pressure to fight Spain, and although he refused to formally go to war, England returned to the Elizabethan tradition of undeclared hostilities. In effect, the king had lost control of his kingdom. Less than a month after their arrival home the Earl of Kellie had prophesied that 'It may well come that the young folks shall have their world.'[1] The rump of James's reign proved the earl right.

For the first couple of weeks after Charles's and Buckingham's return 'welcome home' was the court's only business. James regained his frantic urge to travel: within the fortnight he, the heir and favourite had progressed from Royston to Hinchingbrooke, back to Royston, to Theobalds and then London.[2] 'The prince's return hath proved an excellent medicine for the king,' wrote Secretary Conway, who added that now everything was so back to normal that 'no man would judge there to have been an hour absence among them.'[3]

In one respect, at least, things had changed. For the first time Charles and Buckingham were hero-worshipped. Plaudits, such as Coke's blasphemous

47

description of Buckingham as 'Our Saviour', may have encouraged the duke's vigorous anti-Spanish policies, which over the next few months he pursued with consummate skill. By June 1623, while still in Madrid, Buckingham had realized that the Spanish were not serious in their negotiations, and on the way home to England had played on Charles's ever growing resentment at having been fooled. The duke also knew that Charles was committed to the recovery of the Palatinate (a goal the Spanish ultimately would not support), and that as the king got older the heir's wishes would become more important.

The journey to Spain had made Charles seem more mature. He had grown a beard, and become 'so fine a gentleman', one letter-writer told a friend, 'that some felt that previously he had been hiding his virtues.' In one regard, however, Charles was still the same: he vacillated. On one hand he wanted to teach the perfidious Spanish a lesson and to support the duke, his friend, and Elizabeth, his sister. On the other, Charles was afraid of crossing his father who wanted the negotiations with Madrid to continue. In opposing James he was opposing both *pater patriae* and *pater familias*, and Charles's guilt and anxiety in doing so were intensified by James's waning health. 'His Majesty has been very ill,' one observer wrote in early November 1623, 'both of his gout, and I think, as many others do, of his mind.'[4] James was deeply worried about the Palatinate, declaring on several occasions that he 'liked not to marry his son with a portion of his daughter's tears,' and yet in October he wrote to Bristol that he wanted a Spanish marriage treaty signed by Christmas.[5] Charles was far less enthusiastic, for as Secretary Conway put it, the prince desired the Infanta 'before all women, yet not before all other considerations.' So on 8 October Charles wrote to Philip promising to do all he could to hasten the marriage.[6] However, two days later he treated the Marquis de la Inojosa and Don Carlos Coloma, the Spanish ambassadors to the Court of St James, with marked coldness when they visited Royston. Charles, none the less, was far more courteous than the duke who was so rude to the emissaries that James ordered him to give a banquet in their honour at York House; which he did the next month to the tune of £300.[7]

Inojosa and Coloma almost certainly did not enjoy their expensive apology. Apart from having to sit through a long masque – the main theme of which was how glad the people of England were that Charles was back home – the ambassadors found their own government's protestations of enthusiasm for the marriage being treated with increasing scepticism. Stories from Madrid that the Infanta was avidly learning English and putting the finishing touches to a trousseau so magnificent that three litters, four coaches and 180 mules had been collected to carry it to the coast, did nothing to placate Buckingham.[8] On 31 October he counter-attacked, calling a select group of privy councillors together to tell them what had really happened in Spain.[9]

Charles, who was present at the cabal, felt the duke's pressure more than his father's. Early in November he, James and Buckingham had a long private meeting with Inojosa and Coloma, from which those outside heard shouting. Probably the English were demanding that no marriage be made until Spain had signed an alliance to restore the Palatine, while the Spanish countered that such diplomatic niceties had best be settled after young love had run its course. One of the young lovers, however, was becoming ever less inclined to complete the race. On 14 November Charles once again ordered Bristol not to deliver the proxy without explicit permission, and just to make sure the ambassador got the message sent another similar letter the next day. In late November Charles was threatening 'to remember' all who advocated a Spanish marriage.[10] It was perhaps appropriate that on New Year's Eve Charles chose to attend Fletcher's play, *The Wandering Lover*, for by the end of 1623 he had decided to leave his old love and go looking for a new one.

The repercussions of Charles's change of heart quickly became apparent. On 20 December the king issued writs summoning a new parliament, and ten days later recalled Bristol from Madrid.[11] The Spanish ambassadors were very concerned. On 11 January 1624 they offered to send the Infanta to England in March, surrender the Lower Palatinate in August and work for the recovery of the Upper Palatinate – conditions that a few months before would have led to an agreement. During the last week in January the privy council was in constant session considering the Spanish proposals. Even though Charles, who chaired the meetings, and Buckingham, who tightly restricted access to the king, vigorously advocated a war with Spain, they only managed to persuade James Hay and Sir Edward Conway. Four councillors, Richmond, Hamilton, Pembroke and Belfast stayed neutral, while five, Bishop Williams, Lionel Cranfield, Thomas Howard, Sir Richard Weston and Sir George Calvert, remained loyal to the king's pacific policies. Buckingham was livid, taking his defeat as a personal insult, and, as Williams recalled, strode up and down the council chamber 'as a hen that hath lost her brood.'[12]

Thwarted by the privy council, Charles and Buckingham tried to bypass the normal political processes by going outside the court and using parliament, where they knew they could count on a strong anti-Spanish sentiment. First they tried to mend political fences and influence elections. Charles had Lord Saye and Sele restored to favour, and patched up Buckingham's squabbles with Williams and Pembroke – the latter controlled some twenty seats. The prince nominated candidates for a number of constituencies, including all the Cornish boroughs, but in the end only 10 out of 489 MPs owed their election to his influence – a surprisingly low figure considering that he was the popular heir to an ailing monarch.

Unlike his son and favourite, James did not know what he wanted from the parliament of 1624. His confusion was obvious on 19 February in the

49

speech he made from the throne at the state opening, when he asked both Houses to give him their 'free and faithful counsels in the matter I propose, of which you have heard, the Match of my son.' Two days later Mr Speaker delivered the Commons' response. After the long and flowery set of compliments he told the king that the Lower House wanted monopolies curbed and recusants punished.[13] Charles and Buckingham tried to regain the initiative and divert the Commons from a full scale assault on the royal prerogative by attacking the Spanish. On 24 February the duke gave the Lords his version of the negotiations in Madrid, from which (not surprisingly) Charles emerged the hero. When it seemed that the Spanish would hold the heir hostage the prince courageously wrote to his father 'never to think upon him any longer as a son, but reflect on the good of his sister and the safety of his own kingdoms.' That he had never written any such letter did not make Charles hesitate – even for a moment – from agreeing with his friend and with the opinion of the audience that he had carried himself 'with a great deal of judgement and discretion', or from urging a committee of both houses to vote taxes for an immediate war with Spain.[14]

Stung by this distorted version of events, in late February the Spanish ambassadors told the king that if any Spaniard treated his monarch as Buckingham did James, his life would be forfeit, and demanded that parliament investigate the favourite's actions. This was a blunder of the first order, since both Houses naturally sided with an English duke against the emissaries of papist Spain. In the Lords Bishop Williams, who a couple of months earlier had opposed the duke in the privy council, volunteered to discard his surplice and gird on a sword; in the Commons some proposed paying off all the duke's debts, and Sir Edward Coke declared that the very thought of war with Spain 'made him feel seven years younger.'[15]

Adding public insult to parliamentary rout on 16 March Charles refused to accept a present from the Spanish ambassadors of three cart-loads of delicacies, ordering Cottington to give the bacon, olives, capons, melons, figs and fruit to the poor.[16] Nine days later James announced the end of negotiations with Spain. The public reaction was deep and delicious. Londoners rang church bells and lit bonfires – the largest opposite the Spanish embassy. 'All the world upside down,' commented Sir Cavalero Maycote to Lord Zouch, adding that although the king 'be inclined to peace and quiet, yet . . . he is content to pass over a power and will of war to his son, the prince.'[17]

At this point, as Sir Robert Cotton nicely put it, the Spanish ambassadors 'miscarried themselves'.[18] At an audience with the king on 29 March Inojosa managed to distract Charles's and Buckingham's attention while Coloma slipped James a note urgently requesting a private interview. It was arranged for All Fools Day. The Earl of Kellie conducted Carondelet, the third Spanish ambassador, to James's privy chamber, and stood guard outside as the ambassador alleged that Buckingham was using parliament to depose the king to some country house where he might hunt, but never rule again, and put Charles on the throne. Two days later Father Maestro repeated these charges, and on 19 April told James that the duke was planning to replace the House of Stuart with that of Villiers.[19] Charles discovered the intrigue through Bishop Williams, the prelate whose skill in trimming far outweighed his theology or pastoral concerns. Because he was becoming increasingly worried by his earlier opposition to the duke's bellicose policies, he took Charles aside at the House of Lords on 5 April to tell him of a Spanish plot, the details of which he had obtained from Carondelet's mistress, a prostitute from Mark Lane. 'Though the devil make her a sinner,' Williams sanctimoniously explained, 'I may make good use of her sins.' 'Yes,' Charles mischievously asked, 'but did you deal in her wares?' Williams denied as much as ever seeing her face – as well he might, a childhood accident having rendered the wily bishop incapable of the pleasures of Mark Lane.[20] Armed with William's information, Charles and Buckingham ambushed the ambassadors. Initially James seemed to believe the Spanish story; in late April he refused to let the duke ride in his carriage, and the snub so stung Buckingham that he had to retire to Wallingford House, prostrate with grief. Charles wrote urging him to answer the 'malicious accusations of the Spanish ambassadors', and assured the duke that 'you can incur no danger in this . . . for I cannot think any man is so mad as to call his own head in question by making a lie against you, when all the world knows me to be your true friend.'[21] Under such pressure the privy council exonerated the duke, and James restored him to the royal favour. In May, realizing that the game was lost, the Spanish ambassadors tried to leave for home. James stopped them, and when in late June he eventually let them go, they had to take passage in a common merchant ship.

By adopting an anti-Spanish policy, and provoking Madrid's ambassadors into over-reacting, Charles and Buckingham won great popularity, which they translated into parliamentary votes to destroy the minister who was their most powerful enemy. As a London apprentice, Lionel Cranfield had started a successful business career by marrying his master's daughter. James brought him from the City into government to restore his ailing finances, at which the merchant was at first most successful, saving the king £37,000 a year in household and wardrobe expenses alone. Such economies won Cranfield the Earldom of Middlesex and many enemies, while his opposition on financial grounds to war with Spain brought him Charles's hatred. When Cranfield advised the prince to subordinate his own inclinations to the national interest, Charles was deeply offended, telling the jumped-up apprentice lad to leave questions of honour to gentlemen.[22] Charles played a leading role in Cranfield's impeachment which started on 7 May 1624, in spite of a half-hearted attempt by James to save his minister. Because Buckingham was ill Charles supervised the prosecution – or rather did a little whipping-in once the duke had let the hounds go for the earl. When Cranfield petitioned for a recess after the trial's first day throughout which he had stood for eight hours at the bar of the House, Charles thought the earl's request a cheap ploy to win time, and had it rejected.[23] After five days of hearings the Lords found Cranfield guilty of bribery, and sentenced him to lose all his offices, be fined £50,000 and imprisoned in the Tower during the king's pleasure. Having broken the Spanish alliance and the minister who continued to urge it, Charles boasted to James Hay in Paris, 'all things go well here.'[24]

Charles's service in the parliament of 1624 did much to enhance his popularity. He attended the Lords regularly, served on a committee to investigate stocks of munitions and acquitted himself well in debates. 'The prince gains daily reputation, glory and good will from parliament,' the French ambassador wrote home.[25]

From the parliament of 1624 Charles gained something else. When he and Buckingham impeached Cranfield, James warned them that they were setting a dangerous precedent. 'You are a fool,' he told the duke, 'You are making a rod with which you will be scourged yourself.' To Charles James added, 'he would live to have his bellyful of parliaments.'[26] The king was right. The prince and duke were setting a fatal precedent, not just by reviving the medieval instrument of impeachment, but, more significantly, by employing parliament in an unusual and destructive way against the crown.

With hindsight it is tempting to see the constitutional motif of the first part of the seventeenth century as king versus parliament, as absolutism against law and representative government. Some have argued that the struggle between king and parliament was the product of the rising political aspirations of a gentry class, that following the dissolution of the monasteries in the 1530s had grown in wealth, and whose increasingly radical Protestant faith widened the void between them and the crown. At the same time the crown had lost the initiative in handling parliamentary business, and because it was selling off more and more of its land, came to be increasingly dependent on parliament for money for the daily running of the kingdom.

Such a state of confrontation in early modern parliamentary history was an unusual one. It developed only in moments of deep crisis such as 1641, 1688 or 1776, or over short-lived, yet intensely felt issues, such as Mary Tudor's attempt to restore monastic lands or the monopolies debate of Elizabeth's reign. Most of the time, however, parliament was neither the chief political arena nor the main protagonist. The vast majority of those men who went to Westminster did so to gain or confirm local prestige, win local battles, obtain local legislation, and support their sovereign's ministers. Those men who wanted to be national politicians and wield national power might well sit in parliament and take part in its debates, manipulating its proceedings, but they fought their main battles outside the House of Commons and within the court. During most of the Tudor period these court-based politicians joined or created factions (usually two), that struggled for the monarch's favour and thus the control of national policy. Since an able monarch played each off against the other, neither obtained a monopoly of power. Still, if one faction managed to exclude the other from court, a dangerous political situation ensued. For instance, when Robert Cecil persuaded Elizabeth I in 1600 to divest the Earl of Essex of the sweet wine monopoly, his last pork-barrel of rewards for his followers, Essex had to find a new power base outside the court. He tried to do so in Ireland and failed; attempted a coup in London, failed again, and lost his head. The execution of the Earl of Essex in 1601 was the prelude to a fundamental change in English politics that became apparent after the failure of the great contract debates in 1610, Cecil's death two years later and the subsequent rise of Robert Carr. Both James and Charles were politically faithful; having room in their affections for but one favourite at a time they created a monopoly of power that national politicians had either to join, or wander forever in a political Sinai. Ironically it was more a Pharaoh, than a Moses, who showed the way out of the desert. To circumvent James, Buckingham went outside the realm of court politics to parliament, were he made use of the deep-rooted, almost Elizabethan, hatred of Spain, while ignoring the equally firm distaste for voting money for a war. So by the time Charles became king, the duke had used false sign-posts to blaze a trail that led not to the promised land but to the parliamentary conflicts of the first three years of his friend's reign. 'It is very strange to see the prince go on so in applauding all or the most part of their [i.e. parliament's] doings,' observed Kellie in May, 1624, 'I assure you many think that he shall never recover again [when he shall] come to the crown ... which I pray God may not be so long as I shall live.'[27]

While Kellie's fears about the vicious political undertow he sensed were valid, during the summer of 1624 Charles was content to ride the crest of the wave. The coldest winter in living memory was, thank heavens, over; Buckingham's health restored; negotiations with Paris underway; those with Madrid broken; and his father's advisers cowed. All that remained to settle was the fate of the man whom the prince had come to blame as the architect of the Spanish alliance.

As soon as he learned that Charles and Buckingham were to leave Madrid without the Infanta, ambassador Bristol realized that he was in serious political trouble. In mid-August 1623 he sent James and Bishop Williams letters vigorously defending his conduct. After the departure of the prince and duke, Bristol ignored the contradictory instructions from London by going along with the Spanish assumption that one day a treaty would be signed. When in late November James wrote that a marriage was inexorably linked to the recovery of the Palatinate Bristol realized that 'all was dashed in pieces', and started making gestures of reconciliation towards the duke, while continuing right up to the very day he took his formal farewell of Philip IV to work for a marriage.[28] The dismissed ambassador took his time returning home, arriving in England in mid-May 1624 when anti-Spanish feeling was running at its peak. Although he was initially confined to his London house, James sent him 'gracious messages' that probably encouraged Bristol to write three very respectful letters to Charles asking what he 'would have me do so I may not err.' Charles wanted Bristol to confess that he alone was to blame for the débâcle in Madrid, where he had even urged the prince to convert to Rome. But, as he told Buckingham, the ambassador 'will by no means accept my counsels'.[29] Charles's treatment of Bristol contrasted markedly with that accorded the other Bristol ambassador to Madrid, Sir Walter Aston. The day after he had returned to Royston Charles sent a handwritten note addressed to 'Honest Watt' asking him to keep an eye on his senior colleague. Although in early November Aston went along with Bristol's suggestion that they deliver the proxy if a papal dispensation arrived, by the next month Aston was securely in Charles's and Buckingham's camp. When Aston confessed that he had been in error in co-signing Bristol's dispatches, Charles reassured him he would be held blameless.[30]

To a degree Charles sought a French wife on the rebound after failing to find a Spanish one. Even before he had sailed from Santander feelers had been sent to Paris, and in February 1624 Henry Rich, Baron Kensington, arrived there to start negotiations. These Rich conducted with more enthusiasm that discretion. Immediately on arriving in Paris he wrote home that the French wanted a marriage so badly that they would not press hard for the relief of recusants, and told Charles that Henrietta Maria was 'a Lady of much Loveliness and Sweetness to deserve your affections as any creature under Heaven can do.' Next – perhaps to put himself in the state of mind proper for a prince's wooer – Rich started an affair with Madame de Chevreuse.[31] Such devotion to his cause did not reassure Charles, who in early May sent James Hay, Earl of Carlisle, an experienced diplomat, to join Rich in Paris.

At first Charles was far less anxious to marry the King of France's daughter than he had been the King of Spain's. Having swallowed Digby's glowing descriptions of the Infanta he was sceptical of Rich's hosannas of the fifteen-year-old Henrietta Maria as 'the sweetest creature in France. Her growth is very little short of her age; and her wisdom infinitely beyond it.' The arrival of her portrait had no apparent effect on Charles, who in June was telling courtiers that he had little hope of concluding an alliance with France, and was thinking of looking elsewhere for a bride.[32] On 13 August, having received Richelieu's proposal that all recusancy laws be suspended, Charles wrote to Carlisle that he should 'dally no more', but come home if the French persisted in their outrageous demands. To Rich Charles was even more direct: 'The Monsieurs have played you so scurvy a trick that if it were not for the respect I have for the person of Madam, I would care not a fart for their friendship.'[33]

Charles's diplomatic flatulence did not last for long. Both Rich and Carlisle immediately wrote soothing letters saying that things were not as bad as he supposed. Gradually Charles came to realize how much he needed the alliance, having burnt his boats in Madrid. He wrote to Carlisle in October that if negotiations with the French failed, 'then Spain will laugh at us both.'[34] Fear of the Spanish weakened Charles's resolve against the French demands. When in early October James suggested reviving the negotiations for the Infanta, Charles adamantly objected, personally berating his father into dropping the idea: the Infanta was anathema, the Spanish had humiliated him, the Palatinate must be recovered, and every day a French treaty was more essential, since parliament was due to reassemble in November and might investigate his handling of foreign policy if a marriage were not a *fait accompli* by then.

Charles met his deadline by surrendering his goals. On 10 November England and France signed a treaty in Paris. It allowed Henrietta Maria, her children and servants to practise their religion freely, have a chapel in London open to the public and serviced by one bishop and twenty-eight priests, and to educate her children as Catholics until they were thirteen. It also permitted the King of France to select the queen's servants and advisers, and finally granted recusants complete toleration. There was no mention of a military alliance to save the Palatinate: only a secret codicil in which Charles swore to give recusants 'the utmost freedom'.[35]

The celebrations in England following the announcement of the treaty were more dutiful than delirious. Many so detested the Spanish that a liaison with anyone else was cause for satisfaction. James ordered that bonfires be lit in London; church bells rung, the organ in St Paul's played 'on their loudest pipes' for two hours, and the cannon in the Tower to fire salutes. To all this John Chamberlain ruefully hoped, 'God grant it may prove worth all this noise.'[36]

For Charles the immediate worth of the marriage treaty was having French help to recover the Palatinate. Yet Louis XIII had signed no definite commitments, having made only some vague promises, the ethereality of which became obvious during the Mansfeld expedition.

Count Ernest von Mansfeld was a German mercenary – one of those freebooters who did so much to make the Thirty Years War such a bloody affair, by being as ready to ravage the side that hired him as plunder the enemy. On arriving in London in April 1624 to discuss plans for an expedition to regain the Palatinate he was most cordially welcomed. Charles personally conducted him to St James's Palace where, in a clear signal to Madrid, he was lodged in the rooms originally prepared for the

Infanta. The next month Mansfeld left for the Continent, returning to England in November to raise troops. The army he collected was a sorry lot. While many Englishmen were willing to cheer, light bonfires, and even ring church bells for the Protestant cause, few wanted to die for it, the Commons' reluctance to vote taxes for the war accurately reflecting their constituents' views. Rather than be pressed one man hacked off a finger, another gouged out his eyes, a third hung and a fourth drowned himself. Some conscripts deserted, others mutinied and all behaved abominably. They were badly led, scantily provisioned, unpaid, underclothed, and poorly armed, short on swords and muskets, with many having only cudgels, which, one colonel complained, they used to beat up their officers.[37] During December, as the expeditionary force assembled in Dover, Charles and Buckingham tried desperately to persuade the French to let it land at Calais and march across country to the Lower Palatinate. They failed. So on 31 January 1625 Mansfeld had to sail from Dover (much to the relief of the mayor and citizens) without any clear idea where he was going. After spending several days off Flushing the fleet landed near Breda. Because they had a few days' rations, and little money to buy food, disaster was inevitable. 'We die like dogs,' wrote one commander from his regimental headquarters, a pigsty (the previous tenant having been eaten) 'and in the face of an enemy we could not suffer as we now do. We have bread and beer but no cheese. The burghers will scant deliver anything out of doubt of true payment.'[38] As spring melted the cold and snows of the Rhine Delta, so disappeared a British army.

The Mansfeld expedition was the first of a series of military disasters with which Charles and Buckingham were associated. Like the later ones it was poorly planned, badly equipped, reluctantly manned and incompetently led. It was sent out at the wrong season of the year, on an impossible mission. Yet unlike the later débâcles there was no major political crisis after the Mansfeld expedition. Perhaps the pressed men were riff-raff, whom their towns and villages were only too pleased to be rid of. Certainly their loss in no way tarnished Charles's reputation.

During the last six months of his life James declined rapidly in both mind and body. 'Make a new marriage,' he implored Buckingham, adding, 'for God's sake love me as I only live in the world for your sake.' He suffered from acute pains in his right elbow and knee, whilst a walk in the park would tire him so much that the 58-year-old monarch had to spend the rest of the day snoozing in a chair.[39] And, as the old king slept, others – from ambassadors to artists – wondered what the new one would be like.

'He is either an extraordinary man,' the French ambassador wrote of Charles to Richelieu, 'or his talents are very mean.'[40] Sir Thomas Wentworth was equally unsuccessful in trying to make sense of the heir's enigmatic personality. After writing several paragraphs attempting to do so he was forced to conclude a letter to his friend Christopher Wandesford, 'Well the hearts of princes are unsearchable, unfit objects for country swains to contemplate in.'[41]

One profession whose trade forces them to contemplate other men's hearts are portrait painters. Charles's earliest portraits (see for instance, Plate 2) show a beardless young man, with a large face whose long and rather wide chin set against cropped bunched hair, seem to give the impression of belonging to an older and more care-ridden man. The penetrating eyes, which in middle age suggest some tragic sense of destiny, in youth have a touch of manic intensity. Somehow the large heavily starched ruffs – as compared to later ones of delicate lace contoured to the shoulders – make the prince's face seem sullen and ordinary. His body gives the impression of awkwardness: Charles stands poorly, with neither a comfortable nor a heroic pose, not knowing where to place his hands, and having no better notion what to do with his legs. Portraits are, of course, a very subjective insight into the inner man, yet the early ones of Charles do suggest some intense inner tension, something so deeply repressed that artists – though perhaps not country swains – could not help but notice it.

The adult sense of self-identity that Charles had managed to develop by the end of James's life had been produced with much psychological labour and cost. At last Charles had learned to stand up to his father, particularly over the choice of a wife. When in the autumn of 1624, James suggested reopening talks with Spain, 'I made deal plainly with the king,' Charles wrote to Carlisle, 'telling him I would never match with Spain, and so instructed him to find a fit match for me. Though he was a little angry at first at it, yet afterwards he allowed our opinion to be reason [i.e. right] which before he had rejected.'[42] To overcome the uncertainties of adolescence, Charles found in Frederick both a surrogate elder brother and a cause that remained with him for the rest of his life, which he was able to use to oppose his father. To enhance his own independence from James he became increasingly dependent on Buckingham, who was another, and far more potent substitute for Henry. Admittedly in Spain Charles attempted to break away from Buckingham, but when his first real wooing of a woman ended in disaster, he tried to make Bristol the scapegoat, and returned to the hegemony of the man whom he called his 'Sweet Heart' – the very same appellation he was to use to his wife.[43] Charles would have certainly have been as shocked and surprised (though he would have tried hard not to show it) at any suggestion of impropriety in his feelings towards Buckingham, as he would at the idea he had opposed the king, his father. As he saw it, he had learned to obey the king and even if the lesson had been painful, the end product was pleasant. Thus when he obtained authority he insisted that others must yield just as he had. So, for instance, on returning from Spain he protected Jasper Fowler from the Warden of the Cinque Ports and knighted him, forgave Yelverton and even made him a judge after he abjectly apologized, hounded Bristol for not doing so, whilst rewarding Aston once he admitted to a fault that had never been his.[44]

Charles was a highly controlled young man. Outwardly he remained calm, rarely venturing his own opinion, 'his self-restraint causing amazement'.[45] Inwardly Charles seethed, his stutter being probably the symptom of some boiling subterranean rage.[46] He ate in moderation, eschewed spirits, drank his wine diluted with water, and did not like 'sauces or artifices to please the palate or raise the lust'.[47] His jibe to Williams about the delights of Mark Lane, or his effluvial comments about the French were out of character since normally his language was so chaste that he blushed 'like a modest maiden' at manly talk.[48] Charles took no mistresses, which for a prince was surprising: few women attempted his bed, which for the heir was astounding. When Charles let himself go (albeit in a highly romanticized fashion) with the Infanta he made a fool of himself. Having been burnt once, he was coldly restrained towards Henrietta Maria.

After an interview with the prince the Venetian ambassador sensed this inner tension, caused basically by Charles's relations with James. 'The coldness of his nature even in actions becoming his youth is not, perhaps, a good sign,' Valaresso wrote home, adding a vague note of hope: 'However, it is not difficult for the young to change, and kings whose characters have been repressed, possibly by an unfortunate education, sometimes burst forth into great and generous natures.'[49] Of course, only James's death and the prince's accession could give the ambassador's optimism the chance of proving itself and allow King Charles I the opportunity of displaying a great and generous nature, the repressions of an unfortunate childhood not-withstanding.

# VI

# 'OUR ONLY LAWFUL, LINEAL AND RIGHTFUL LIEGE LORD'

At noon on Sunday, 27 March 1625 James I died. Mentally and physically he had been declining for years. The evening after he heard of the death of his friend, the Marquis of Hamilton, James complained of feeling ill. His servants assured him that there was nothing seriously wrong and by the following Saturday he seemed a lot better. Within a couple of days he relapsed, and on Thursday Bishop Williams gave him the last rites. Then, according to one story, the dying king called Charles to charge him to take care of Elizabeth and her family.[1] Since the royal doctors seemed unable to do anything Buckingham insisted that James take a potion mixed by his own medical man, a general practitioner from Essex, but the only effect this prescription had was to start a rumour that the duke had poisoned him.[2] The king's death was a relief for the whole kingdom. James was old, pathetic and boring: Charles was young, seemed energetic and exciting, promising, like all new administrations, a better future. Thus the news of his accession was greeted everywhere with enthusiasm; the only ones, John Rous noted in his diary, who refused to take part in the celebrations were the papists. At Cambridge, despite a cloudburst during the ceremony proclaiming the new king, 'the joy of the people,' an observer noted, 'devoured their mourning.' One broadsheet hailed the new king as 'Great Britain's Charlemagne', and the crowds cheered as on Sunday evening outside Theobalds and throughout London heralds proclaimed Charles I 'Our only lawful, lineal and rightful liege Lord.'[3]

In a sense the heralds were proclaiming the wrong man for in the three years after James's death (just as in the half dozen ones before) the Duke of Buckingham in many ways ruled England, making the period from Charles's accession to Buckingham's assassination a whole. Working with the king, Buckingham pushed England into war, first with Spain and then France, and into military expeditions to try and loot Cadiz, occupy the Isle of Ré off the French coast, and relieve the Huguenots in La Rochelle. To pay for these ventures Buckingham had to call parliament only to feel the stick, with which he had tried to goad the old king, flaying his own shoulders. To save his friend Charles dissolved parliament, adding fuel to

59

a constitutional crisis. The favourite's influence even affected the new king's marriage. Charles was a faithful man having room for but one person at a time in his affections, and if that place were filled by a surrogate elder brother then there was no space left for a wife. The failure of his marriage helped push Charles into a war with France, which in turn further worsened relations between the King of England and his French wife. In the next three years these themes were, to varying degrees, played out, sometimes in a cyclical fashion. Thus to see the period as being delineated by Charles's first three parliaments is to read one's history backwards from the viewpoint of the Grand Remonstrance and the civil war. If in the first three years of his reign there were any milestones for Charles, they were not his parliaments, but the military expeditions that made those parliaments necessary.

Immediately after James's death Charles was most concerned for Buckingham's well-being – the duke being far more upset by the king's passing than his son. Charles tried to console his friend, assuring him that 'though he had lost one master he had gained another, and that to grieve more would show want of confidence in him.' George spent the first night of the new reign with Charles in his chamber, and the next day they rode to London together sharing a coach as equals. They stayed at St James's Palace in adjacent apartments. On 1 April Buckingham was so ill that he had to be carried about in a sedan chair, and when Charles emerged from seclusion two days later to hear the Sunday sermon he was reported as 'looking very pale', while John Donne preached on the text, 'If the foundations be destroyed what can the righteous do.'⁴

The new king's first duty was to bury the old king. At the first meeting of his privy council, held a couple of hours after James's death, Charles was advised that it would take at least forty days to raise the money for his father's funeral. So James had to be embalmed. First the doctors removed his organs. They found the heart large but soft, his liver good, one kidney fine, the other with two stones, his lungs black, and a skull so hard that it had to be opened with a chisel and so full that the brains spilled out.

Black lungs, a large soft heart and an overcrowded brain! Somehow it seemed typical of James. Equally so was his funeral. On 4 April James's body left Theobalds, perhaps his favourite palace, for the last time. Escorted by a motley rabble of some 3,600 people, the black draped coach carried his body to Denmark House to lie in state for a month. The funeral took place on 7 May. As chief mourner, dressed in a long black hooded robe, Charles walked in the mammoth procession of several thousand mourners to Westminster Abbey, where Bishop Williams preached a witty and learned sermon, marred only by a passing reference to Moses's stutter. Overall the funeral was a glorious shambles. 'I never saw anything worse performed for the order of it,' concluded one spectator, while another thought that 'all was performed with great magnificence, but the order was very confused and disorderly.'[5] James was buried as he had lived.

Charles's first acts as king reflected his distaste for his father's lack of decorum. On 31 March he ordered the privy council to clear away the rogues, vagabonds, beggars and whores who hung about the gates to the court. He insisted that courtiers stop entering his chambers pell-mell, but each rank come only at its proper time and in its proper order. Charles rose early, appointed hours for prayer, meals, business and exercise, attended sermons regularly and drew up a set of rules for court etiquette that he claimed were based on those of Queen Elizabeth I. To control the crowds of sick who hobbled or were carried to the court in the desperate hope of being cured by the royal touch Charles issued a proclamation that they were to come only at Easter and Michaelmas, bringing with them a certificate from their minister that the king, God's anointed, had not touched them before.[6]

Charles's new broom wanted not to just to tidy up the sick and sweep away the layabouts, but to get a grip on the government by establishing investigating committees. On 9 April the king commissioned Buckingham, Ley, Conway and Brooke to review foreign policy; they were to pay special attention to relations with Spain, the proposed French alliance, to consider ways to recover the Palatinate (especially with Dutch help), and lastly to review the militia and navy. Five days later the king appointed a council of war of fifteen, including Conway, Buckingham, Cecil and Ley to investigate the state of the nation's defences 'and all other matters concerning war'. On 23 April Charles set up a third committee that included Ley, Weston, Coventry and the judges of common pleas to prevent fraud in the collection of customs and subsidies, and a few days later the king established a surprisingly high-powered commission that included Buckingham, Ley, Pembroke, Conway and Brooke to see if squabbles within the East India Company had hampered trade with Russia.[7] The significance of these committees does not lie in the work that they did. In fact none ever issued a formal report and apparently all were without much effect. They do, however, shed light on the new king's concept of power: like the centurion in the Bible he believed he could get things done simply by ordering them done, not realizing that without constant prodding commissions issued under the great seal were no more than pretty documents. To make a political system go even divine right monarchs must labour incessantly. For Charles's reign the records contain no vast collection of papers of great innovators such as those of Thomas Cromwell or the Cecils, showing the government every day of the year goading, cajoling, terrifying or rewarding knights, bishops, rooks and especially pawns to make the game work. Far from initiating policies, the records reveal a government responding to pressures or situations, with the king usually endorsing his ministers' decisions, and acting as a sorter referring items to the relevant department. If in the first few weeks of his reign Charles showed neither the wit nor energy to play the game, he did reveal that his favourite piece, the Duke of Buckingham, had long since checkmated the king. While Charles relied on Lord Treasurer Ley, whom he appointed to three of the four committees, and had a special trust in his Lord Chamberlain, William Herbert, the Earl of Pembroke, and Sir Henry Vane, Buckingham dominated secular matters.[8] In ecclesiastical affairs a new force immediately emerged. On 9 April William Laud, bishop of the minor Welsh diocese of St Davids, handed Buckingham a list of prominent churchmen, with 'O' for orthodox and 'P' for Puritan written beside each name.[9]

Little is known about the formation of Charles's early religious beliefs. Who shaped them, and how they were shaped is a matter for speculation. Lord Fyvie, his first guardian, and Queen Anne were both crypto-Catholics, but the former was too early an influence, and the latter too distant a figure to have much effect on Charles's faith. The Careys were restrained Anglicans, while Charles's tutor, Sir Thomas Murray, was accused of Puritanism. Prince Henry and Princess Elizabeth were ardent Protestants, much hotter in their faith than their father, a careful – even timid – moderate. While James abhorred the excesses of Scots Presbyterianism which, he said, 'agreeth as well with a monarch as God with the devil,' he eschewed the right wing of the Anglican church, appointing the moderate Calvinist George Abbot, Archbishop of Canterbury, instead of the distinguished preacher Lancelot Andrewes.

Charles's religious preferences developed late. When he was seventeen they were uncertain enough to allow Robert Abbot, the archbishop's brother (and thus privy to the prince's devotions) to dedicate his polemic against Arminianism to the prince. By 1623, however, Charles's faith was more sure. After his return from Madrid four Arminian bishops, Wren, Andrewes, Laud and Neile, met secretly to discuss how to ensure the heir was favourable to their point of view. Wren recalled that Neile, Charles's chaplain, assured them their fears were groundless; the heir was far more sympathetic to Arminianism than his father.[10]

A confession of faith Charles almost certainly wrote in January 1626 proved Neile correct; in it the king revealed himself as a staunch Arminian, albeit intrigued by Rome.[11] 'I am a Catholic Christian,' Charles began conventionally enough. While revering saints and the Blessed Virgin Mary, he rejected their efficacy as intermediaries between God and man, and spurned private masses, transubstantiation, the adoration of images, purgatory, and indulgences as 'new fangles' from Rome. While accepting the pope's rights as a temporal ruler, he thought that his claims of infallibility were patently absurd. For Charles the attractions of Arminianism were more aesthetic and political than theological. He had little interest in the competing dogmas of salvation through grace or good work, finding instead emotional reassurance in the beauty of Arminian worship and the deference of Arminian worshippers. Through the 1626 confession Charles drew a fine, yet very distinct line between his faith and that of Rome. The problem was that many of his subjects, convinced that 'an arminian is the spawn of a papist', saw it as a blur.

Arminianism got its name from the theologian, Jacobus Arminius, whom the Puritan Simonds D'Ewes described as 'flashy divine of Leyden, Holland'.[12] In England Arminianism was a reaction against the determinist logic of Calvinism that had dominated Anglicanism during the reigns of James and Elizabeth. During his father's last two parliaments Charles seemed to go along with Buckingham's flirtations with Puritan members. Indeed in early 1625 J. Prideaux, the regius professor of Theology at Oxford, dedicated a book of anti-Arminian sermons to Prince Charles. Soon after coming to the throne, Charles found the duke's shift to the Arminian faction more palatable. Perhaps Buckingham did so to please the new king or because of Laud's increasing influence as his spiritual adviser. Most likely the cause of this change is to be found in parliament. Now James was dead the duke no longer needed Puritan allies in the Commons to pressure the king. Since these members were trying to use parliament to stop what they saw as an Arminian counter-reformation, coming from the universities and being master-minded by Bishop Neile, they inevitably came into conflict with the crown. Thus political considerations reinforced the king's emotional and aesthetic preferences for Arminianism. Anyway king and favourite wasted no time in publicly declaring their religious commitments: in July 1625 Charles appointed Richard Montagu, a leading Arminian polemicist, his chaplain, and the following February promised John Cosin, the Arminian Archdeacon of East Riding, 'the patronage of our cause'.[13] Over the years Charles made good his promise until the followers of Leiden's 'flashy divine' won a stranglehold on the Church of England.

In the early summer of the first year of his reign Charles was far more concerned with an immediate issue, his marriage to Henrietta Maria, which took place by proxy at Notre Dame, Paris, on May Day 1625. Once more the broadsheet readers of England eagerly lapped up the latest doings of the 'royals'. Louis XIII, 'looking like the glorious sun outshining the other stars', escorted his sister Henrietta Maria to the cathedral. The bride wore a wedding dress of gold and silver cloth decked with diamonds and precious stones, embroidered with fleurs-de-lis, and at the great west door of Notre Dame she was wed with the Duke of Chevreuse acting as Charles's proxy. Since Chevreuse was a Huguenot he waited outside the cathedral for two hours as the French royal family took nuptial mass, and afterwards all returned to the Archbishop of Paris's palace for a wedding breakfast 'of unmeasured splendour'.[14]

For nearly a month Henrietta Maria, now styled 'Queen of England', delayed joining the husband she had never seen. First Louis XIII was ill in bed, next the spring thaw flooded the roads north to the Channel. Eventually she left Paris on 22 May, her brother riding with her as far as Compiègne. On 12 June at about eight in the morning she boarded the *Prince* at Boulogne, and escorted by a flotilla of twenty other English vessels sailed to Dover. At eight that evening, as the flotilla fired off twelve lasts of gunpowder in a hundred gun salute, tired, apprehensive, and a little seasick, Henrietta Maria landed in England to spend an uncomfortable night in Dover Castle.

Although Charles had been anticipating his bride's arrival for many weeks he was not waiting at the quay to greet her. In April he had ordered the privy council to see the roads in Kent were smoothed for his wife's carriage, and that the gentry, mayors and militia of the county turn out to welcome their new queen.[15] He left London in early June, spending nights at Rochester and Canterbury before reaching Dover. On the fourth he dined aboard the *Prince*, which was anchored in Dover Roads, and that evening, as a Channel gale blew up, walked along the beach alone in his thoughts, occasionally looking up towards France. Thereupon he rode back to Lord Wotton's house in Canterbury where the court spent its 'days in conversation and nights in dancing'.

Very early on the morning of 13 June Charles heard that his wife was at last in England, and galloped to Dover, arriving at the castle at about ten. He and Henrietta Maria first met at the foot of some stairs. She knelt to kiss his hand, he bade her rise, embraced her, and kissed her profusely. 'Sir,' she said, 'I have come to this country for Your Majesty to use and command.' The two retired to a private room for about an hour, and then lunched on pheasant and venison which Charles carved for his wife, who ate in spite of her confessor's reminders that it was the fast of St John the Baptist. Then the king and queen rode together to Canterbury. Outside the city, at Barham Down, the quality of Kent met them and escorted them to Lord Wotton's mansion where they spent their first night, Charles having previously bolted every door and window to the wedding chamber. The newly-weds spent the next night at Cobham, before boarding a barge at Gravesend for their formal entry into London to the roar of cannon from the Tower, cheers from its citizens and rain from its notorious weather.[16]

London's weather seemed to reflect the state of its sovereign's marriage. Less than four days after Henrietta Maria's arrival in England the Venetian ambassador reported growing dissatisfaction on both sides: the French were unhappy at being excluded from English affairs and at not having received the naval support they were promised; the English were disturbed at the lack of French help for the recovery of the Palatinate. During her first week in London Henrietta Maria was not seen in public: it was said she was indisposed. Next week she and Charles had their first major public row. Charles ordered several English Catholics admitted to her household; in retaliation the queen dismissed all her Protestant servants. Within six weeks the two had parted company, Charles going to a small house near Woking and Henrietta to his grand palace at Nonsuch.[17] The reasons for the rapid deterioration of their marriage are not hard to find, being the product of personality and politics.

Apparently their wedding night was not a great success. Both were proud, uncompromising, repressed, unyielding virgins, having all the qualities that make excellent monks or nuns but inept honeymooners. The next morning the queen was described as 'moribund', and, a little later as 'not well at ease', and if the king was reported as 'very jocund', this was surely the result of a successful conquest rather than a tactful and considerate consummation. The day after his wedding night Charles took time to write a formal and very restrained letter to his brother-in-law, Louis XIII, thanking him for his wedding gifts, and saying nothing about his wife.[18] More significantly the rapid collapse of the marriage and their separation within six weeks suggest that neither developed an insatiable appetite for the delights of the flesh.

Mentally and physically Henrietta Maria was not ripe for marriage. Four days before she met Charles, Toby Mathew, her interpreter, wrote from Boulogne that, 'She sits already upon the skirts of womanhood.' Not yet sixteen, in an age when girls matured three or four years later than today, she had a small slight figure, large eyes, projecting teeth and bony wrists. She had been born in November 1609, losing her father, Henry IV, to an assassin when she was six months old, and had been closely brought up by a governess in a country château. Her education was as limited as any seventeenth-century girl's: later she confessed her ignorance of English history a grave disadvantage, matched only by her initial awkwardness with the English tongue. She had been living in England for seventeen years before she wrote her first letter in its language.

To immaturity and ignorance Henrietta Maria added a foul temper – for which the English were prepared to forgive her – and a Catholic sense of mission – which they could never pardon. 'The queen, however little of stature,' wrote the Cambridge don, Joseph Mead, in July 1625, 'is of spirit and vigour of more than ordinary resolution. With one frown, divers of us being at Whitehall to see her at dinner, and the room some what overheated with the fire and the company, she drove us out of the chamber. I suppose none but a queen could have cast such a scowl.'[19] Henrietta Maria had not come to England to woo her husband or his subjects. In granting her a dispensation to marry a heretic the pope told her that she was to become a second Bertha, the Frankish princess whose marriage to Ethelbert, King of Kent, a millennium before, had paved the way for St Augustine's conversion of England. Henrietta Maria spent the night before her proxy wedding in a convent in the Faubourg St Jacques being constantly reminded that she was to become the protector of England's Catholics; such was Marie de Medici's last message to her daughter.[20] Just in case Henrietta Maria forget Mama's wise words she brought with her to England an entourage of twenty-eight priests led by the Bishop of Mende, all as anxious to protect their mistress as save her new subject's soul for Rome. In mid-July, immediately before she and Charles first parted, Henrietta Maria asked him to intervene to protect Catholics. Whether her request helped prompt their separation one cannot tell, but certainly it did nothing to help recusants, to whom Charles's policies from now on became determined in part, at least, by the state of his marriage. On 1 May, the day of his proxy wedding, the king told Lord Keeper Williams not to prosecute Catholics so long as they behaved themselves moderately and obeyed the law. Yet by the end of 1625 Charles was ordering recusants' houses searched for arms, their weapons confiscated, and 'strict proceedings' taken against all 'open and professed papists'.[21]

Just as the protection of recusants, one of the chief political goals of the marriage, failed, so too did the other – England's hope for French help against Spain to recover the Palatinate. As the new queen was being rowed up the Thames into London the crowds on the bank sang:[22]

> Spain's Infanta shall stand by,
> Wringing her hands, and this shall say,
> I do repent! Too Late!

But it was Henrietta Maria who was too late. Her marriage did nothing to save the remnants of Mansfeld's expedition; one of whose officers wrote from Holland the next day that 'if it were not for dead horses and cats our army would perish.'[23]

The marriage might have made a better start had the couple been surrounded by people who wanted it to succeed. However, the queen's French advisers were intransigent, while Buckingham assumed that Charles's affections for his wife could increase only at the expense of his feelings towards his best friend. When the queen's entourage first arrived in Dover on the evening of 12 June they were depressed at the paucity of their reception: they were put up at Dover castle, a dank, dismal place, had to walk into town for food and drink, and then trudge back in the dark up the cliffs to their cheerless lodgings. Almost immediately they started to squabble with the English over petty matters, elbowing each other with genteel ferocity to see who entered which coach first. The queen's confessors advised uncompromising Catholicism, and encouraged her dislike of all things English, questioning her, so at least many of her subjects believed, about everything her husband did in bed. The English returned French animosity with compound interest, considering them an insufferable bunch; the men arrogant, the women painted harridans.

Buckingham very quickly realized the influence of the queen's French household, and on the ride from Dover to Canterbury, before the match had been even consummated, insisted that Madam St Georges leave the royal coach to make room for his half-sister, the Countess of Denbigh. In late June Charles appointed a commission consisting of Buckingham, Arundel, Pembroke and Conway to talk to the French ambassador about the introduction of English ladies into the queen's household, and early the next month Buckingham demanded that Henrietta Maria appoint his wife, sister and niece ladies of the bedchamber. When she refused, he personally rebuked the queen, and sent a messenger to the French ambassador who delivered the duke's protest with such vehemence that the ambassador threatened to throw the emissary out of the window. Once the favourite warned Henrietta Maria that 'there had been queens in England who had lost their heads.' Rebuffed in his attempts to control the queen through her household, Buckingham listened sympathetically to the king's complaints that 'the Monsieurs' were destroying his marriage.[24]

As relations with his wife and his wife's country floundered, Charles (rather like a man planning to build another floor to his house as he complained about the rapid spread of dry rot in the basement) was preparing for a war with Spain. In April the king ordered Buckingham, in his capacity as Lord High Admiral, to issue letters of marque permitting privateers to attack ships belonging to Spanish subjects resident in the Low Countries, and rode out to Blackwell to inspect some forty merchant vessels drafted into the navy.[25] A paper written at this time reflected Charles's thinking on foreign policy.[26] He adopted the traditional English view of the need for a balance of power in Europe arguing that the Palatinate must be recovered to curb the appetite of Spain which 'is on such an increase that if it is not presently stopped it will overrun all.' Few of Charles's subjects would have disagreed with such sentiments, many of them having just bought the current ballad with its chorus:[27]

> The true religion to maintain,
> Come let us to the wars again.

But going to the wars meant money, and money meant going to parliament.

In spite of warnings on his accession from the whole privy council that the kingdom's finances were in a desperate state, Charles was determined on an immediate parliament, and had to be reminded that the old writs his father had signed were no longer valid, and new ones must be sent out. Lord Keeper Williams – the prelate blessed with the sharpest hindsight of his day – remembered that he had advised the king to postpone calling parliament until his friends had time to ensure the election of trustworthy candidates. But the king would brook no delay. 'It is high time to have subsidies granted for the maintaining of the war with Spain,' Charles replied, 'and the fleet must go forth for that purpose this summer.'[28]

To such sentiments the overriding majority of those elected (with little interference from the crown) to Charles's first parliament would have given a resounding 'hear! hear!' Yet very quickly relations between them and Charles deteriorated into discord and animosity.

In retrospect, at least, the origins of this rift were discernible at the opening session of parliament, when on 18 June Charles started his speech from the throne by excusing his lack of eloquence, and his inability 'to spend much time in words'. He expected parliament to continue the policies that they had advocated during his father's reign. After all they had encouraged the break with Madrid, and must now vote taxes to fight Spain. Finally he denied rumours put out by those he called 'malicious men', that he was not 'so true a keeper and maintainer of true religion as I profess.'[29] Charles's stutter made him a poor public speaker so it is unlikely that his speech made a powerful impression. Anyway, after talking briefly, he handed over to Lord Keeper Williams who explained at greater length the government's need for subsidies to fight Spain and regain the Palatinate. Thereupon the crown lost the initiative. No privy councillor rose to tell the House how much money was needed and how it was to be spent, since they really did not know the answer to the first question and their master felt the second trespassed on his prerogative. So they let the Commons discuss the highly divisive topic of the spread of popery for twelve days before returning to the issue of taxation; the Commons voted only two subsidies worth £160,000 which was hopelessly insufficient to meet the crown's extraordinary expenses of about half a million pounds. Under the impression that they had done what Charles had required of them, three-quarters of the members went home, scared of the plague which was killing four or five thousand a week in London. Only the rump was left in Westminster to vote the king tonnage and poundage for a year, and not, as was usual for life, and as they were anxious to seek the sanctuary of their country estates Charles ordered a recess on 4 July asking parliament to reassemble on 1 August in plague-free Oxford.[30]

Though shorter, the second parliamentary session was equally as sharp. The adjournment to Oxford did nothing to reduce tensions, since the plague was firmly entrenched there by the time parliament reassembled. At the opening meeting Charles once more reminded both Houses sitting in Christ Church of their obligation to vote further taxes for a Spanish war and the Palatinate. While he was sincerely grateful for the two subsidies already voted that they were insufficient to send a fleet into battle. Again Charles's minister elaborated on his opening address, telling parliament that the crown now needed £800,000, and, as before, the Commons turned their attention to religious matters, sending Charles a petition protesting against his recent pardon of a dozen Jesuits and requesting the rigorous enforcements of all recusancy laws. Even though Charles seemed to respond to this petition sympathetically, taxes were not forthcoming, and on 10 August Sir Richard Weston delivered a message from the king that he still desperately needed money to send the fleet to sea before the autumn gales, and the plague reached Portsmouth. If they voted taxes, Charles promised on 'that royal word which he had never yet broken, nor given cause to mistrust' to call a parliament in the winter to consider their grievances, and so demanded 'a speedy answer'.[31] When none was forthcoming, and thus by implication (in Charles's mind at least) his royal word had been doubted, and when some of the Commons started questioning Buckingham's abilities, the king dissolved parliament.[32]

Charles's first parliament set an unhappy – a fatal – precedent. In the last four years of James's reign he and Buckingham had tried to use parliament against the king. Once Charles succeeded to the throne he found others using it to the same end, and the deterioration of relations between crown and Commons was as rapid as it was intense. On 16 July the Earl of Kellie wrote to his friend Mar, 'You cannot believe the alteration that is in the opinion of the world touching his Majesty.'[33] Who then was responsible for this shift? Who, in other words, fired the first shot in the constitutional struggle that led to civil war?

Of the answers to these questions Charles had no doubt. In his speeches and letters he made it clear that he believed parliament had wanted a war with Spain and they must now pay for it. Charles's interpretations of the bellicosity of the last two parliaments of his father's reign, however, glossed over the fact that he and the duke had tried to use them to push the king into war: the initiative to fight Spain had not come from the House of Commons. Charles furthermore felt that the Commons had thrown down the gauntlet by voting tonnage and poundage for a year and not life, as they had for all his predecessors back to Henry VI. Yet it has been recently suggested that this vote was not intended as a frontal assault on the prerogative, since with only a fourth of the members present it could hardly have been sustained when the plague abated, but was simply the means of postponing discussion on an issue, that had just gained widespread constitutional implications, until the whole house reassembled.[34] The king never understood this point. As far as he was concerned parliament had doubted his royal word, and, as he told them 'his condition would be miserable if he could not command and be obeyed.'[35]

Charles's behaviour during his first parliament must be seen in context of the collapse of his marriage. Indeed he was miserable with Henrietta Maria because he could not command her and be obeyed. His determination to impose his will on parliament may have been intensified by the need to compensate for not being able to do so with his wife. After the first session he and Henrietta Maria parted; during the second they were back together in Woodstock, uneasy in each other's company, and fearful of the plague.

The plague undoubtedly contributed to the tensions of Charles's first parliament. During 1625 the bills of mortality reported 35,428 dead in

London alone, with as many as 5,000 being buried a week. People dropped dead in the streets. At the service of deliverance held at St Clement Dane's in August three of the four priests fell ill and died, the surviving minister being a notorious drunkard. Such fickleness made the plague especially terrifying. Victims succumbed without warning and without hope, dying after a few hours of excruciating pain.[36] Plague forced the court, privy council and parliament to flee London, and the hint of a sick seamstress or soldier would send the royal household once more scurrying for a new refuge.

Members of parliament were as frightened of the plague as was the king. In addition they resented having to be recalled to Oxford in August, the most dangerous month for infection, and being away from their estates during harvest time. Some even suggested that it was all a ploy on Buckingham's part to wear them down until they voted taxes.

Many more members, however, were deeply concerned about recusancy, and saw Charles as leaning towards Rome. After all he favoured Arminians, had a Catholic wife, and his actions towards papists were hardly consistent: on 1 May, the day of his proxy marriage, Charles ordered the recusancy laws no longer be enforced; in July he promised to apply them; and in August privately told the French ambassador what many Puritans suspected – that all this was a sop towards parliament.

If any single issue caused the breakdown of Charles's first parliament it was recusancy – an emotional subject at the best of times, made even more divisive by both the plague, parliamentary attacks on Arminianism, and Charles's psychological need to compensate for the break-down of his marriage. Only later did the conflict between king and parliament become seen in constitutional terms, making relevant the question of who was the aggressor over tonnage and poundage. Still, if the causes of the failure of Charles's first parliament are open to debate, the immediate effect is not – the government desperately needed money. Buckingham suggested using Henrietta Maria's dowry and a forced loan to equip a squadron to capture the Spanish treasure fleet, so that when the expedition returned triumphantly laden down to the gunwales with gold and silver the constitutional niceties and religious hatreds would be forgotten in counting the loot.

The dissolution of Charles's first parliament increased (if that were possible) Buckingham's influence. On several occasions he boasted to Bishop Mende, the queen's confessor, that 'The King would place the defence of him, the duke, before his own interests.'[37] This was no idle bombast intended to cow Henrietta Maria, for when in mid-August Charles called the privy council to Woodstock to tell them he was dissolving parliament to protect his servants, Buckingham fell to his knees begging him to continue the session: he would be able to defend himself; his conscience was clear. Invariably Buckingham knelt to his monarch only when he was absolutely sure that his requests would never be met; raising his friend by the hand, Charles assured him that he was completely happy with his service.[38]

At the Woodstock meeting of the privy council only Abbot and Williams questioned the king's decision to dissolve parliament. Although Archbishop of Canterbury Abbot was merely a cipher, having lost influence after killing a gamekeeper in a hunting accident in 1621. Williams's loss of power was more recent. After siding with James's pro-Spanish policies in 1624 the Lord Keeper managed to restore himself to Charles's favour by betraying the attempt of the Spanish ambassadors to get James to drop Buckingham. In March 1625 Charles failed to heed Williams's advice to delay calling parliament, and now the Lord Keeper was about to pay the price for being right. His influence rapidly eroded in the first six months of the new reign, especially as Charles came to depend for ecclesiastical advice on Laud, a man who was so tenacious an enemy of Williams that he even dreamed of hating him.[39] In May, Williams unsuccessfully protested against the king's instruction to pay Secretary of State Conway £2,000 a year from the Court of Wards. As Lord Treasurer, James Ley might have objected to this unusual transaction, especially as a couple of months before he had warned of the dangers of financial extravagance. But Ley quickly learnt which way the political winds were blowing, and, if he required a weather vane, he need only note that while Charles asked Williams to expound on his opening speech to the first session of parliament, Conway and Coke did so at the second. So it is not surprising that during that last session of the 1625 parliament Williams moved into what amounted to virtual opposition to the government of which he was still technically Lord Keeper, and even less surprising that on 23 October Charles ordered him to surrender his great seal of office to Sir John Suckling, Comptroller of the Household.[40]

The price that Charles paid for Buckingham's victory over the duke's rivals was the defeat of the king's request for parliamentary taxation. Thus in September, Charles had to issue demands for a forced loan, justifying his action by arguing that the nation was in grave peril. As if to underline the point, he ordered the militia put in good order, explaining that 'the present doubtful and dangerous times require more than ordinary care for the protection of that happy peace that hath so long continued in our kingdom.' Charles claimed that he had ample precedent in demanding a forced loan, telling the lord lieutenants of each county to send the privy council lists of all who could lend and how much. Contributions should be paid within twelve days of assessment, the crown to repay them within a further eighteen months. All persons of quality who refused to contribute should be bound over to appear before the privy council, while lesser folk should be summarily drafted into the armed forces.[41]

The forced loan was intended to pay for one of the most inglorious chapters in the history of British arms – the Cadiz expedition. The assembly of this force was the usual saga of order, counter-order and disorder. Conscripts went unclothed, unfed, unpaid and unwilling. Of the force's commanders one observer noted, 'their zeal does not rise to the needs of such a great expedition,' Buckingham having chosen them more for loyalty than leadership.[42] Passing over Sir Robert Mansell, a veteran seaman, as admiral the duke selected Sir Edward Cecil, Lord Wimbledon, a soldier whose mediocre military experience was compensated for by an excellent record of devotion to Buckingham. The second-in-command, the Earl of Essex, had some experience was a soldier in the Dutch service, while the only qualification his assistant, Lord Denbigh, possessed was that of being married to Buckingham's half-sister. Just before it sailed Wimbledon summed up the expedition's weaknesses – and unconsciously his own – when he wrote to the king that a force never had left England 'so full of wants and defects'.[43]

One of the greatest defects aboard the fleet were the orders Charles and Buckingham issued. Though they failed to designate a target, the fleet lacked the great advantage of surprise since long before it sailed Cadiz was widely bruited as its destination.[44] Buckingham's orders contained much concerning the daily affairs of the fleet: discipline must be maintained, account books kept, fire precautions taken, and the Spanish generally harassed. Charles's instructions were a little more specific. The object of the expedition was 'the protection and restitution of our dear Brother and Sister,' the king wrote, without explaining how the seizure of a port on the southwest coast of Spain could regain territory in central Europe. Wimbledon must attack 'any rich town that without any great hazard you may take,' and then, Charles added, almost as an afterthought, he should capture the treasure fleet from the Americas, bearing in mind all the time how much the whole expedition had cost his master.[45]

While Charles and Buckingham may be faulted for issuing ambiguous orders their achievement in raising so large a force without parliamentary help was a remarkable one. In addition to a Dutch squadron of twenty-two vessels, plus another twenty-five guarding their flank off Dunkirk, the English contribution consisted of twelve Royal Navy ships and seventy-three armed merchantmen, carrying a total of 5,952 sailors and 10,448 soldiers. For a country such as England with a population of about $4\frac{1}{2}$ million, raising a fleet of eighty-five ships and 16,399 men was a massive effort.[46] Spain, with a population three times larger than England, and the gold and silver of the New World, managed to collect 132 vessels with 30,000 men for its Armada in 1588. But unlike the Armada, the Cadiz expedition was not intended to launch an invasion: it was to sack, harass and capture, and for these ends was too large, sacrificing quality to quantity, speed to delay, and elan to chaos.

Charles was most interested in the fleet's progress. In late August Henrietta Maria rejoined her husband in Beaulieu, where he had been hunting in the New Forest, she having been at the Earl of Southampton's house at Tichfield. In the second week of September Charles rode to Portsmouth, leaving his wife behind, so short of ready cash he had hardly money to pay for provisions on the way. He and Buckingham, who had just arrived from London, inspected several ships and reviewed the soldiers on Roborough Down, where the king knighted a half-dozen captains, and wished the officers and men God-speed.[47]

After being forced back once by storms the fleet eventually left Portsmouth on 8 October. On 20 October the ships hove to for a council of war that decided – as everyone knew they would – to attack Cadiz. If the English hoped to emulate Drake's famous raid they started off in an infamous manner, bombarding the harbour defences at Puntal on 22 October with a distinct lack of determination, many ships remaining far off shore, beyond the range of Spanish cannon fire, unconcerned that the enemy were in an equally safe position. Two days later 2,000 soldiers landed on the beach four miles south of Puntal. They marched across the dunes on a hot day without water until just before reaching Puntal they came across the main wine warehouse for the Spanish navy. 'No words of exhortation, or blows of correction would restrain them,' an officer wrote, 'but breaking with violence into the rooms where the wines were, crying that they were King Charles's men and fought for him, caring for no man else, they claimed all the wine their own . . . till in effect the whole army, except the commanders, were drunken and in common confusion.' It is unlikely that King Charles was touched by such enthusiastic professions of loyalty from his men, which prompted the defenders of Puntal to sally out to attack the English, driving those capable of staggering for the boats. 'I must confess,' reported Wimbledon, of the debauch, 'that it put me to some trouble and care,' but pathetically he added, by way of an excuse, that even when sober his men 'were incapable of order'.[48]

After evacuating Cadiz, Wimbledon procrastinated, earning the nickname 'sitstill'.[49] Half-heartedly he attempted to patrol the Spanish coast, just missing the treasure fleet which had taken a more southerly route than usual, before, on 14 November, rotten food, weather, water and ships forced him to run for home. Many men were lost to gales and disease. Morale fell. 'I can say I think that there was never any army went out, continued and returned with so much disorder as this,' Lord Delaware wrote aboard the *St George*, 'and our actions have been according, for we have done nothing like soldiers.' Sir William St Leger was even more depressed, writing from his ship to Buckingham, 'I am never so much ashamed that I wish I may never live to see my Sovereign, nor your Excellency's face again.'[50] But unlike many of his comrades, St Leger lived to see his monarch and master's face once more, only to discover that their smiles were magnanimous compared to the reaction of most of his compatriots to the débâcle at Cadiz.

# VII

# 'A SHAMEFUL RETURN'

The only things about which the survivors of the Cadiz expedition need not have worried in the winter of 1625, as they made it back to the harbours of England, or were swept west against the Irish coast, were the reactions of the king or the duke. Far from being dispirited, or even pausing a while to see if they might learn any lessons from the catastrophe, Charles and Buckingham praised the fleet's leaders and started planning another expedition. To pay for such an offensive they needed money, and had thus to call parliament, whose members were neither so forgiving nor so charitable. Instead the Commons tried to impeach Buckingham, whom they regarded as the architect of all England's woes, and once more the king (who, if not chief designer, was at least senior partner) dissolved parliament to save his friend. The two did not, however, dissolve their plans to attack Ré, the island a few miles off the French fortress of La Rochelle where Louis XIII was besieging Huguenot rebels: but this time, just to make sure of success, Buckingham was to lead the attack in person. In the two years between the Cadiz expedition and that to Ré Charles's marriage continued to deteriorate: Henrietta Maria was indifferent to English Protestant sensibilities: Charles had little consideration for his young wife's misery, and the queen's advisers went on encouraging their mistress's obdurance. Buckingham, meanwhile, benefited from the failure of his friend's marriage. Eventually Charles and Henrietta Maria's rows climaxed in the expulsion of her French servants and though Louis XIII sent an ambassador to try and patch things up, gradually England and France drifted into open hostilities. Thus in many ways the second two years of Charles's reign were a continuation of the opening stage, with a failed marriage, a failed parliament and a failed military adventure. Indeed John Rous could have been looking forward as well as back, when he wrote in his diary that the aftermath of the Cadiz expedition was a 'shameful return'.[1]

About a third of the fleet was lost to battle, gales, disease, incompetence and neglect. On one ship there were not enough men left to row the longboat: on another too few to man the pumps.[2] When they reached port, or were washed up on the shores of the West Country or Ireland, having broached their last barrels of putrid meat and algae-green water, the condition of the survivors was pitiful. In a single day a dozen of them dropped dead in the streets of Plymouth. In the spring plague carried away fifty or sixty more a week.[3] After the numb relief of having actually made it home alive wore off, many survivors became bitter: some mutinied, others sought to blame their leaders. St Leger (the officer, who off Cadiz wondered how he could ever face his monarch again) castigated the expedition's council of war, and the leadership – or lack thereof – of Lord Wimbledon. One diarist concluded that those responsible for the débâcle 'are worthy of the halter'.[4]

Rather than placing nooses about their necks Charles and Buckingham hung accolades. The king graciously welcomed Lord Wimbledon home, confirming him as a viscount, and creating him Lord Lieutenant of Surrey. Even when Wimbledon admitted that the attack had not been a complete success, the only benefit he could see coming from it being the training of officers, the king did not waver in his support, continuing to protect the commander from the complaints of his subordinates. Although Wimbledon was lacking in leadership and military skills (or even common sense) he did have the inestimable advantage, frequently denied more talented generals, of serving a master who could not admit that he was wrong. Had Joseph Mead, the newsletter writer, realized, as did Charles, that the best way of denying failure is to reward its perpetrator, he would never have told a friend, 'Would you have believed that the general of our late fleet hath gotten the better of all the colonels and sea captains about the miscarriage?'[5]

Charles had hoped that the successful attack on Cadiz and the capture of the Spanish treasure fleet would silence parliamentary opposition, consolidate his rule and start his reign with a triumph. Instead his coronation, which took place on 2 February 1626 was a muted affair. The plague had postponed the ceremony for almost a year. There had been talk of crowning the king in October, but since the infection lingered in London until the New Year, the earliest the ceremony could safely be held was February. Charles appointed a committee to establish the correct form for the service, and debarred Bishop Williams, who was Dean of Westminster as well as Bishop of Lincoln, from coming to Westminster Abbey, ordering Bishop Laud to take his place. Even though Charles could forbid Williams to attend the coronation, he could not make his wife come. He hoped that she would do so, including her in the coronation proclamation he issued on 17 January. Henrietta Maria refused to take part, insisting on the impossible demand that her confessor, the Catholic Bishop Mende, rather than the Anglican Archbishop of Canterbury, place the crown of England upon her head.[6]

So it was alone that Charles had to board the barge at Whitehall Steps at nine in the morning of 2 February, 'a very bright sun-shining day', to be rowed the few hundred yards to Westminster.[7] He entered the great hall where the Archbishop of Canterbury, George Abbot, showed him the symbols of office: swords, spurs, cups, plate, sceptre and crowns. At ten the king walked in procession to the west door of the abbey, and Abbot introduced him to the congregation:

> I have come to present unto you your king, King Charles, to whom the crown of his ancestors and predecessors is now devolved by lineal right, and he himself come hither to be settled in that throne, which God and his birth have appointed for him. And therefore I desire you, by general acclamation, to testify your content and willingness thereunto.

Unhappily many of the congregation could not hear the archbishop, while others expected him to go on for a little longer, so an embarrassing silence met his appeal for general applause until Lord Arundel prompted the congregation with shouts of 'God save King Charles!' Charles sat on his throne just below the altar, while the nobility paid homage, and Bishop Senhouse of Carlisle preached a sermon on the text, 'Be faithful unto death and I will give you the crown of life.' Abbot administered the oath, which Charles took, kissing the Bible, and the choir sang 'Come Holy Ghost, our souls inspire and lighten with celestial fire.' Then two bishops said the litany. For the climax of the service Charles's sumptuous robes were removed to reveal clothes of white satin, as if to symbolize his marriage to the people of England. Abbot anointed the king's shoulders, head, arms and breast with the sacramental oil, invested him with the robes of St Edward the Confessor and the royal sword and spurs. After taking communion, with Abbot administering the bread and Laud the wine, the six-hour ceremony was over, and Charles changed into a suit of red and black velvet to be quietly rowed back to Whitehall.

The coronation was a ceremony that meant much to Charles, a man who set great store on ritual. He had the sacramental oil made up to his own special formula (which has been used ever since) of orange flowers, roses, cinnamon, jasmin, sesame, musk and civet. He appointed a committee of bishops to determine the correct form for the service. Throughout his life Charles saw things in ceremonial, or symbolic, terms. With the oil God had anointed him king, making sinners as well as traitors of all who opposed his divinely sanctioned rule. His coronation was a sacrament as inviolable as marriage: he that God hath placed on the throne of England let no man put asunder. In his coronation oath Charles promised to 'grant and keep and by his oath confirm to the people of England the laws and customs to them granted by the kings of England ... and to the clergy ... agreeable to the prerogative and the ancient customs of the realm.' The proviso about the prerogative made this oath especially acceptable for Charles, as did its promises 'to keep peace and Godly agreement', and 'cause law, justice and discretion to mercy and truth to be executed.'[8] Thus he believed that breaking his coronation oath was literally 'damnable', jeopardizing his immortal soul. Charles felt the burdens of his office to be onerous ones, which he shared with Buckingham, and – albeit less intimately – with the Almighty. As he mounted the steps to the podium in Westminster Hall the duke offered Charles his hand, but the king declined saying, 'I have as much needs to assist you as you have to assist me,' and, contrary to the expected order, the king then helped up his favourite subject.[9]

For most of his people Charles's coronation was not a day of jubilation. The plague had prevented the traditional parade through the city to the abbey, and afterwards there was neither a banquet nor a masque. Indeed the atmosphere at Whitehall must have been strained for it was not until a week later that the king and queen started to speak to each other again, and the effects of Buckingham's jest that if the king could not control his wife how then could he expect to control parliament must have been felt for even longer.[10]

The parliament of 1626 was to prove the duke only too right. Three days after his coronation Charles opened the session, and again Henrietta Maria refused to attend the ceremony, deigning to look out of the window to see the royal procession ride past to Westminster.[11] Charles made little preparation for his second parliament. Perhaps mindful of the complaints that James had inflated honours with excessive creations at his coronation Charles promoted existing peers from within the ranks of the aristocracy, instead of inducting new men into the House of Lords who were friendly to him and Buckingham. In a short opening speech Charles told both Houses 'I mean to show what I should speak in actions,' and then let Laud set the tone with a sermon, based on the text 'Jerusalem is builded as a city that is compact together.' He made a strong plea for the nation to unite behind the king: 'never fear him, for God is with him. He will not depart from God's service nor from the honourable care for his people, nor from wise managing of his treasure.'[12]

Laud's sermon had little effect. The king's request for taxes to pay for the 'great crisis in Christendom' that threatened England met with the familiar parliamentary demand for redress of grievances. It was all bickering as usual until Sir John Eliot, member for Newport in Cornwall, dropped a bombshell. Buckingham and Eliot had once been good friends, travelling the Continent together as young men. Buckingham had Eliot appointed vice-admiral for Devon, and very recently Eliot had defended the duke in public. However, the return of the survivors of the Cadiz expedition turned the member for Newport against his patron. Having read Glanville's *Voyage to Cadiz* in manuscript Elliot knew every detail of that sorry expedition's history. He had seen the survivors land in Devon, their emaciated corpses befouling the streets of Plymouth, and when he told the duke of their sad state noted no response save plans to launch yet another military escapade. So on 10 February Eliot exploded: 'Our honour is ruined, our ships are sunk, our men perished,' he told the Commons, 'not by the sword, not by the enemy, not by chance, but . . . by those we trust.'

Initially the effects of Eliot's tirade were surprisingly muted. On 7 March John Chamberlain wrote, 'Our parliament talks much but doth little.'[13] Three days later the crown repeated its request for taxes saying that the money was desperately needed, and that afterwards it would consider – but not necessarily redress – parliament's grievances. The Commons responded that they wanted redress before voting money. Thus on 15 March Charles slightly modified his position by offering if necessary to recall parliament to consider grievances once taxes had been passed, while sternly reminding the Commons not to criticize his servants. The latter edict had no effect on Eliot, who on 27 March once more attacked the duke as the man responsible for the nation's current calamities. This time others joined in. Two days later Charles summoned the Commons and through Sir Edward Conway threatened to dissolve parliament if money was not forthcoming in three days. The Commons, Conway added, were to blame for the present crisis since their way 'is not a way to deal with a king'. The Commons did not, however, bow to this threat, which the king failed to carry out. April was a relatively quiet month, with both sides seemingly bracing themselves for the showdown in which the radicals tried to use parliament to impeach Buckingham, the crown to punish Bristol, and Bristol to clear his name. Thus – as in 1621 and 1624 – in 1626 the traditional model of king versus parliament was an oversimplification since all parties were trying to employ parliament to further their own political ends and punish their enemies.

The origins of Bristol's trial go back three years to Charles and Buckingham's trip to Madrid. On learning of James's death, Bristol had sent the new king a letter of condolence in which he expressed a wish to end their disagreements. Through Sir Kenelm Digby, Charles replied that he would be happy to do so if Bristol admitted that his advice in Madrid and attacks on Buckingham had been wrong. The earl demurred, and Charles told him not to attend the 1625 parliament or coronation. When in early 1626 Bristol wrote to the king once again that he be allowed to take his seat in the Lords, Charles refused, accusing Bristol of urging him to convert to Rome whilst in Madrid. Bristol responded to this new – and very dangerous – charge by offering to come to London to stand trial, adding that he still hoped that 'this unfortunate business may be passed over'.[14] Charles rejected the olive branch telling the earl that, 'he finds himself nothing satisfied therewith,' and wanted 'a direct answer without circumlocution'. Ever since Bristol's return from Madrid Charles had tried to keep him away from the centre of power in London; thus he had Lord Keeper Conway attach to Bristol's summons to parliament, which he issued under the Great Seal, a note not to attend. The earl replied that since writs under the Great Seal obviously had precedence over notes from the Lord Keeper, he was obliged to take his seat in the Upper House. By forcing this confrontation Bristol ensured his own trial for treason by his peers. It opened in the Lords in the first week of May, persuading Charles to keep parliament in session long after his chances of being voted taxes had evaporated. It gave each side time enough to present their version of what had transpired in Madrid, and the duke's enemies an opportunity to impeach Buckingham.[15]

On 1 May, the Commons voted articles of impeachment against the duke, charging him on five main counts: he had purchased the wardenship of the Cinque Ports, failed to protect English shipping, seized French vessels, extorted £10,000 from the East India Company, and given Louis XIII British naval support.[16] In one sense the charges were as false and trivial as those Charles and Buckingham had used to destroy Cranfield. In another sense they were far more lethal, for while James had quickly disowned Cranfield, Charles immediately rallied to the duke's defence, writing to the Speaker of the Commons that at least one of the five indictments 'toucheth as far upon himself as the duke'. So when Buckingham's trial opened on 9 May Charles insisted on standing, symbolically at least, beside his friend in the dock. But Charles had neither the patience nor perseverance to stay there long. After two days of hearings, hardly time enough for the Lords to consider the charges in any great depth, Charles counter-attacked. Accompanied by all the great officers of state, Buckingham, Weston, Dorset, Carlisle, Holland and Conway, he was rowed from Whitehall to the House of Lords where he ordered the arrest and close confinement of parliament's two leading trouble-makers, Sir John Eliot and Dudley Digges.[17] Eliot had compared Buckingham to Sejanus, and thus Charles, by implication, to that most notorious Roman Emperor Tiberius. Digges had argued that according to English law the sovereign could not order 'ill events', and his servants could be punished for carrying them out even on his orders. While Eliot's allusions were grossly impertinent, and Digges's claims clearly revolutionary, as members of parliament they were immune from arrest during sessions. Their colleagues vigorously protested against this serious breach of privilege, forcing the king to release the pair within a few days.

Although the session was to continue for another six weeks the chances of any agreement between the king and Commons had been lost, and relations between each side steadily deteriorated, especially after the election of Buckingham as Chancellor of Cambridge University. On the death of the Earl of Suffolk on 29 May Charles nominated his friend to this prestigious post. After a short but very bitter academic dog-fight, in which both sides literally mobilized the sick and lame, the masters of arts elected Buckingham.[18] Whether Charles intended his nomination of Buckingham as Chancellor of Cambridge University in the midst of an impeachment trial as an attempt to tighten up university discipline, or as a gesture of contempt towards parliament is debatable though the latter was in keeping with his character. It was, for instance, similar to his appointment of the Arminian Richard Montagu as his chaplain the previous year. The king was worried about the state of discipline at the university, having written six months before in response to a parliamentary complaint to the old chancellor about this matter.[19] Thus Charles (who was always far less concerned about parliamentary crises than historians feel he should have been) may have chosen Buckingham to get a grip on affairs at Cambridge, rather than slap the Commons in the face. Many members of parliament were sure that they knew Charles's real reasons, and 'greatly moved', started to draft a letter to the king protesting about irregularities in Buckingham's election. Hearing these preparations Charles told the Commons on 6 June to stop: the elections had been properly carried out and anyway the authority to investigate a corporation established by royal charter, rather than an act of parliament, lay with the crown not the Commons. So the next day the Lower House, which had clearly exceeded its authority, had to back down. Instead of graciously accepting their apology, or even letting the matter quietly drop, Charles immediately sent them another crowing letter rubbing his victory home.[20]

The king was in no mood for magnanimity. On 9 June he sent the Commons his 'last and final admonition' for money: if they did not vote taxes he would collect them on his own. Once more they replied by demanding the duke's dismissal.[21] On 14 June a deputation of peers went to see the king asking if parliament could sit a couple of more days to clear up some minor details of business. 'Not a minute,' Charles replied, and early the next morning he dissolved his second parliament, ordering the Earl of Bristol to the Tower.[22]

Parliamentary sessions were in a sense the floodlights of early seventeenth-century politics, illuminating the darkness for the cameras to see and history record. Thus it is easy to assume that when the house was not meeting, and when parliamentary journals, newsletters and diaries were not so abundant, politics did not go on, factions did not fight, decisions were not made. Once parliament assembled the floodlights lit up recording the scene in much greater detail for historians. At the same time, like those brilliant television night lights, parliamentary sessions attracted attention, increased tensions and generally exacerbated the situation. Thanks to the scholarship of several distinguished historians and their students a tremendous amount of work has been done on early seventeenth-century parliaments. In taking the limelight parliament has perhaps gained an exaggerated importance, that has been enhanced by its eventual emergence as the dominant force in British politics. Historians love a winner. Today, however, as parliament seems to be conceding centre stage to other institutions, such as trades unions or the EU, it may become apparent that it held a similarly less exalted position in the early seventeenth century. Charles certainly never saw parliament as the most important institution in his realm nor his problems essentially as struggles between the crown and parliament. At first, as prince, he and Buckingham had used parliament to pressure the king. With his usual deference to medieval institutions Charles saw parliament as the proper arena in which he should get things done. When he became king and parliament failed to do those things, he blamed a few trouble-makers, and resolved to rule without it. After all, Charles, like many of his subjects, saw parliament as a venerable body no longer vigorous, and not as the wave of the future that must be vanquished to make the world of the seventeenth century safe for absolute monarchs. Indeed Charles was as poor a tyrant as he was a clairvoyant. He was surprisingly unconcerned by parliamentary sessions. In early May 1626, for instance, at the height of the attempts to impeach the Duke of Buckingham, Charles was deeply involved with military matters, appointing a council of war of leading privy councillors to review the nation's defences, and ordering the weapons and armour at the Tower made serviceable.[23]

It would, of course, be incorrect to assume that just because in the 1620s Charles was not as involved with parliamentary matters as we think he should have been, that the king was indifferent to them. Soon after the collapse of the 1626 parliament he published *A Declaration of the True Causes which moved his Majestie to assemble and dissolve the last two meetings of Parliament* that sheds light on his actions and attitudes. Since there are no drafts of this printed declaration it is impossible to say how much of it, if any, was written by the king. The absence of the parenthetical clauses that were very typical of Charles's style, suggests that someone else, perhaps Conway or Laud, wrote the first draft, but as the king always carefully vetted such pronouncements and the ideas in the declaration agree with views expressed in his letters and speeches, it is safe to assume that it faithfully represented his opinions.

The declaration explained that while a king was obliged to account to God alone for his actions, Charles had most magnanimously decided to inform his subjects so as to allay their doubts and fears. To the king's opponents such a justification might seem condescending, but to Charles it was a gesture that was both gracious and at the same time put him in something of a dilemma since as a king he was answerable to God alone, and by explaining his actions to his subjects he was going against this hierarchical chain of command. So he tried to turn what could be interpreted as *lèse majesté* into a gesture of generosity. The declaration went on to point out that when Charles came to the throne he called parliament to vote taxes for a war with Spain that the members had urged, and for which they were thus obliged to pay. All this was only partially true since the initiative for a Spanish war had to a large extent come from Charles and Buckingham, and there were clear signs that parliament was opposed to voting taxes for an expensive war that they could not direct. Charles's explanation for the dissolution of the 1625 parliament was completely erroneous. He claimed that he had done so to save parliament from the plague, rather than save the duke from parliament. After glossing over the loss of the Cadiz expedition Charles said that he had called the 1626 parliament to preserve true religion and the nation's interests, but very quickly it was taken over 'by violent and ill advised passions of a few members', who 'for private and personal ends' tried to impeach Buckingham.

Charles could not understand those who opposed him, seeing them as no more than a small conspiracy of evil, selfish men. His concept of opposition operated at a number of levels, conscious and unconscious, frequently independent of each other, and varying according to the polemical demands of the moment and psychological needs of the king.

The most studied of these levels has been the constitutional. If English history is seen as the story of the growth of parliamentary democracy then any remark with constitutional implications becomes of prime importance, and if one studies parliament, where constitutional statements are more likely to be found, then such remarks gain an exaggerated significance as signposts on the road of Whiggish progress. Charles made several such statements to the parliament of 1626. For instance on 29 May he scolded the Commons, 'Remember that Parliaments are altogether in my power for their calling, sitting and dissolution: therefore as I find the fruits of them good or evil they are to continue or not to be.'[24]

At the second, pragmatic, level Charles justified his stand against those who opposed him in parliament in a note written a few days after the declaration.[25] He observed that 'great disturbances both in church and state have ensued out of small beginnings, when the seeds of contention were not timely prevented'. Thus opposition to the crown, while not yet a great disturbance (and here Charles is reassuring himself that he is still a popular monarch) was none the less dangerous in what it might lead to. Therefore, the king went on to argue that he must teach the handful of troublemakers a lesson 'that so by the exemplary punishment of some few who by lenity and mercy cannot be won, all others may be warned and take heed'. In other words Charles was trying to turn the coercion of a few into an act of kindness towards many.

The psychological process known as 'projection' may be helpful in explaining the third, and most basic, way in which Charles handled the problem of opposition. Projection consists of accusing the other side of acts or thoughts of which the plaintiff, consciously or unconsciously, feels guilty: for instance a latent homosexual may be convinced that the world is about to be taken over by homosexuals. Charles believed that Buckingham's impeachment was the work of 'violent and ill advised persons' working for 'private and personal ends'. Yet surely his own prosecution of Lord Bristol was prompted by similar motives. He hounded Bristol not because the ambassador was a political threat but because he, unlike Sir Walter Aston, would not submit, as Charles had had to submit to his own father.[26] Again opponents frequently claimed that Charles was trying to become an absolute monarch who, like the kings of France, would rule untrammelled by parliament: as Sir Robert Phelips reminded the Commons in 1625, 'we are the last monarchy in Christendom that yet retain our ancient rights and privileges.'[27] On 12 May 1626, the day after the arrest of Eliot and Digges, the king had Dudley Carleton (the minister whom Charles once said 'ever brought me my own sense in my own words') present the crown's case to the Commons:[28]

> In all Christian kingdoms you know that parliaments were in use anciently until the monarchs begin to know their own strength: and seeing the turbulent spirit of their parliaments at length they, by little and little, began to stand upon their prerogatives, and at last over-threw the parliaments throughout Christendom except here only with us.

In other words it was the other side not himself, Charles projected, who was to be blamed for pushing England towards absolutism.

No matter who was to blame for the failure of Charles's second parliament one thing was sure in June 1626 – the king needed money, and he needed it badly. Charles had to support the British regiments in Danish service on the Continent, who by the spring of the following year required 3,600 replacements, as well as maintain the survivors of the Cadiz expedition – the latter being so ill-kept and badly paid that they mutinied with monotonous regularity.[29] Once when the duke was at a meeting of the privy council 150 sailors attacked their Lord Admiral's coach, destroying it completely. In December a mob of matelots marched on the court, bran-dishing cudgels and demanding arrears of pay. Charles's order that they return to their ships on pain of death probably had less effect in stilling the strikers than a loan hastily negotiated with some city merchants. After-wards the king considered the whole incident so serious that he appointed a commission that included Buckingham, Wimbledon, Coke, Weston, Cotton, Penington and Phineas Pett. 'Much doing was about it,' the latter concluded in his *Autobiography*, 'but in the end it touched so far upon some great personages that it was let fall.'[30]

Even before the king formally dissolved parliament the privy council had been considering ways of raising money without its help. They ordered the attorney general to review the customs, and to imprison all who refused to pay the higher rates until they complied. The king also established a commission, that included Coke, Marlborough and Weston, to investigate ways of raising more money and cutting expenses. He sold or pawned many of the crown jewels and melted down 50,000 ounces of plate, as well as leasing the sugar customs at a large premium.[31]

The most effective way of raising money was the forced loan. As in the previous year the king wrote to the lord lieutenants of England and Wales asking them to send him the names of people in their counties who might lend and how much. From these returns the privy council made lists which the Earl of Worcester, as Lord Privy Seal, used to send out demands. Though the aristocracy were traditionally exempted from the forced loan, Charles wrote to every peer that he expected them to make a generous gift. To reassure any of his people who feared that by subscribing to the second forced loan in two years they might be starting a precedent, Charles issued a proclamation in which he blamed 'certain evil disposed persons under pretext of the common law' for opposing the loan, and explained that he had to have the money, since 'necessity has no law'. It was the duty of all true subjects, he argued, 'to be a law unto themselves' by contributing to the crown.[32]

It is easy to exaggerate the degree of opposition to the forced loan. Those who paid up made little impact on the records, unlike Sir Moulton Lambert, a delinquent who was forced to appear before the privy council to grovel that he was 'verie sorie', or the five knights who argued that Magna Carta forbade their imprisonment for refusing to lend, or Sir George Gateby, who declared 'I will be master of mine own purse and I will not part with a penny.' Most people were like the mayor and aldermen of Thetford who wrote to Conway that they 'were all very willing to yield'.[33] After all when British troops were risking their lives in France, and Algiers and Dunkirk pirates were ravaging Britain's coasts carrying thousands of men and girls into heathen slavery, it seemed obvious necessity should know no law. Towards the end of 1626 loans started to pour into the exchequer which had money enough to pay £200,000 for the Ré expedition and £30,000 for British regiments on the Continent. By November the forced loan had produced nearly £¼ million. Necessity had indeed proved most bountiful: 'Money being more readily furnished,' Charles admitted, 'than I could have expected in these needy times.'[34]

Throughout the whole of his second parliament Charles was under intense pressure because of the failure of his marriage. He had recognized his marital problems in a letter written to Buckingham as early as November 1625, in which he blamed the queen's French servants for alienating her from him, and considered sending them home. Although he was afraid of Marie de Medici's reaction – having a mother-in-law more formidable than most – he asked Buckingham what he thought of the idea.[35] The duke probably dissuaded him from taking such a drastic step, but did nothing to suggest that the problem lay anywhere but in the queen's household. As with parliament so with his wife, Charles blamed a small group of trouble-makers for his problems, never suspecting for a moment that he could be in the slightest fault. He forgot that he had tried to use the privy council to change the queen's ladies-in-waiting (who were after all her friends) and that he cancelled a Christmas pastoral Henrietta Maria and her ladies had been rehearsing for months.[36] On the other hand Henrietta Maria was just as bad: she refused to attend both the coronation and the state opening of parliament. The two squabbled over trifles: once the French ambassador had to be called in to settle an argument over whether or not it was raining! As a peacemaker M. de Blainville was not blessed. In retaliation for his wife's Catholicism Charles stationed officers outside the ambassador's chapel in London to take the names of all English subjects attending mass. One Sunday in February 1626 de Blainville's servants set upon the constables with drawn swords, wounding one in the face and another in the leg. Prompted more by xenophobia than an innate respect for law and order, the London mob joined in, and the brawl ended with de Blainville and Bishop Neile of Durham screaming insults at each other. Normally Charles would have written to the lord mayor demanding the rioters be severely punished; instead he sent Louis XIII a letter complaining that de Blainville and his servants were coming between husband and wife.[37]

During the parliamentary sessions of 1626 relations between Charles and Henrietta Maria remained calm, though frigid. Soon after Charles dissolved parliament Henrietta Maria and her confessors made a pilgrimage to Tyburn to pray, it was widely reported, for the souls of the Catholic martyrs executed there. Even if the queen was too naive to realize the provocative symbolism of this act, her advisers and husband did. Charles again blamed a third party, writing that it was all Bishop Mende's fault for 'presuming on her sweet nature'.[38]

Since their next row took place in bed Charles had no third party present to blame. He explained what happened at length in what must have been a very painful letter for such a shy and reserved man as Charles to compose. His words are worth quoting in full because he never again wrote so intimately about his wife.[39]

> One night when I was in bed she put a paper in my hand telling me it was a list of those she desired to be of the Revenue [i.e. administer her jointure]. I took it and said I would read it next morning, but withall told her that by agreement with France I had the naming of them. She said that they were both English and French in the note. I replied those English I thought fit to serve her I would confirm, but for the French it was impossible for them to serve her in that nature. Then she said that all those in the paper had Breviates [recommendations] from her mother and herself, and that she would admit no other. Then I said that it was neither her mother's power nor hers to admit without my leave and, if she stood upon that, whomsoever

she recommended should not come in. Then she bade me plainly to take my lands to myself, for if she had no power to put in who she would in those places, she would have neither lands nor house of me, but bade me give her what I thought fit in pension. I bade her then remember to whom she spoke, and told her that she ought not to use me so. Then she fell in a great passionate discourse, how she was most miserable in having no power to place her servants, and that business succeeded the worse for her recommendation, which when I offered to answer she would not so much as hear me. Then she went on saying that she was not of that quality to be used so ill.

A few days later Charles and Henrietta Maria had a most damaging quarrel. When he asked her to accept the Marchioness of Hamilton (Buckingham's niece), the Countess of Denbigh (Buckingham's sister), and the Countess of Carlisle (Buckingham's mistress), as ladies in her household she replied that since the king was her master she would have to do what she was told, but she could never trust these ladies. So Charles dropped the idea – which anyway was partly a ploy by Buckingham to try and introduce the Countess of Carlisle into the king's bed. A few days later Henrietta Maria gave her husband a list of people she wanted in her employ. Without reading the names Charles tossed it aside, declaring that he was going to be master in his own house. Henrietta Maria retorted that all she wanted was the same authority over her servants as his mother Queen Anne had enjoyed. Charles replied that his mother was a completely different woman than she was. Henrietta Maria agreed that there certainly was a great distinction between the daughter of a French king and one of Denmark. Charles stormed out saying that as the youngest daughter she was of no consequence.[40]

As a result of this quarrel Charles decided to get rid of the queen's French advisers, and in preparation for the inevitable diplomatic storm sent Sir Dudley Carleton as ambassador extraordinary to Paris, shutting the channel ports behind the emissary to ensure that Carleton could tell Louis XIII his side of the story first.[41] On 1 August, after a meeting of the privy council, Charles sent for the queen. She refused to come, pleading a toothache. With the whole privy council in tow, Charles marched to her chambers to find her servants 'unreverently dancing and cavorting in her presence'. He stopped the party, and told Henrietta Maria that he was sending her servants back to France 'for the good of herself and the nation'. The queen was stunned, unable to answer for several moments. Then she lost control, smashing windows in the chamber with her bare hands. Bishop Mende, who was Cardinal Richelieu's nephew, intervened protesting that to expel them was contrary to the marriage treaty, and, anyway as an ambassador he could only be recalled by his king. Without arguing any further Charles ordered the Yeomen of the Guard to clear out the French using force if necessary. 'The women howled and lamented, as if they were going to an execution,' but they went, spending the night in Denmark House.[42] The next day Charles called them together and told them, 'I have decided to possess my wife, which was not allowed me when she was surrounded by you.' The queen's servants, their families and minions left London on 7 August in a caravan of some thirty carriages and fifty carts. So anxious was the king to see the last of them that he paid them the £31,000 they claimed they were owed in back wages, and forbade their arrest for any reason including debts. Apart from the London merchants, whom the French owed £6,662, most Englishmen endorsed Charles's parting wish – 'the Devil go with them.'[43]

Nevertheless the spirit that had bedevilled Charles's marriage remained. Immediately after the dismissal of the queen's retinue she and Charles went to Nonsuch Palace, about ten miles south of London, where initially they where reported 'very jocund together.' Charles insisted on the introduction of English ladies into his wife's service, and although several observers claimed he treated her with 'the most tender solicitude', she was still desperately unhappy, being allowed to speak only in the presence of her English ladies. Henrietta Maria became most depressed; the quarrels between her and the king continued; Charles ran off to go stag hunting; his misery, the Marquis of Dorset reported, was greater than ever.[44]

Such quarrels are usually solved by counselling, perhaps by a priest or close friend, or even by recourse to a mistress. However, Charles's best friend had a vested interest in maintaining the split, while as Lady Carlisle's frustrated plans suggest, he was too religious – or perhaps not sexed enough – to find solace in adultery. When dynastic marriages crash, and neither counselling nor courtesans can suffice, then diplomats, and after them soldiers must step in.

Hearing of the expulsion of the queen's servants Louis XIII decided to send an ambassador to London to try and patch things up. He chose François de Bassompiere, a trusted adviser whose collection of 6,000 love letters presumably established his credentials to handle matters of the heart. Bassompiere landed in England in late September, being refused the courtesies usually extended visiting ambassadors. Soon after his arrival in the capital Buckingham paid the ambassador a private visit in which he complained bitterly about the queen's French servants, adding that he had come without the king's knowledge, and please not to tell Charles – a claim that Bassompiere quite rightly disbelieved. The next day, 8 October, the ambassador and the duke had an announced meeting, and on 11 October Bassompiere went to Hampton Court for a brief conference with the king. Negotiations immediately stalled, with Charles demanding that Bassompiere send home his chaplain, Father Sancy, who had been Henrietta Maria's confessor: the ambassador refused and three days later Charles backed down. On 15 October the king and ambassador had a private audience in the gallery at Hampton Court. Bassompiere remembered that Charles was in 'a great passion', treating him 'with great rudeness'. 'Why do you not execute your commission at once,' the king demanded, 'and declare war?' 'I am not a herald to declare war,' Bassompiere retorted, 'but a marshal of France to make it when declared.' At this point Buckingham rushed into the gallery, threw himself between Charles and Bassompiere, and, in a gesture as dramatic as it was contrived, announced, 'I am come to keep the peace between you two.'

Backstage more significant parts were being played. A commission was set up to work out the diplomatic differences, while in several long private conversations with the queen, Bassompiere told her more or less not to be so silly. As a result Charles and Henrietta Maria tried to make things up, oscillating between public displays of affection and animosity. Towards the end of November the English and French reached agreement. Buckingham had decided that such was advisable, perhaps because he feared the foreign policy repercussions of a continuing deterioration of the king's marriage, or because, as the Venetian ambassador Contarini (who played the role of honest broker in the discussions) put it, 'to suit his interests without any reason but that of self will.' According to the agreement Henrietta Maria was to be allowed one bishop, six priests, her chapel at St James's, six ladies of her bedchamber, a chamberlain, secretary, physician – in all some forty to fifty French servants. The English agreed to release some seventy recusants from prison into exile, and the French to pay the balance of the queen's dowry. After the conditions were announced Charles let it be known that he had consented to them only for his wife's sake: he cared not a jot for the French. His reservations did not, however, prevent him from attending the magnificent banquet Buckingham gave on 4 November to celebrate the agreement. Later that month Bassompiere left for home, and after four attempts to cross the storm-plagued Channel reached Paris only to find that his rival, Cardinal Richelieu, had persuaded Louis XIII to disavow the terms that he had so skilfully worked out: diplomatic relations between England and France had declined too precipitously to make any new marital agreement relevant or possible.[45]

When he first heard of the trouble between Charles and Henrietta Maria, Cardinal Richelieu, Louis XIII's chief adviser, was very angry. 'We made that alliance,' he said, 'expecting to marry England to France, more than to marry individuals.' On the English side the breakdown of the marriage between the individuals helped produce that between nations, since it made Charles more dependent on Buckingham, who was determined to pursue his anti-French policies. Why Buckingham wanted to go to war with France is difficult to explain. According to one story – incredible about anyone but the duke – he did so because Queen Anne had rebuffed his advances whilst he was on a mission to France in 1625. More likely he wanted to capitalize on Charles's resentment at the refusal of the French to allow the Mansfeld expedition to land in Calais and march across land to recover the Palatinate. Anyway the two sides slipped, unthinkingly and in small stages, towards hostilities. In May 1626 Charles formed a small council of war. That summer each side seized the other's ships and nationals in their own territory. On 12 July Charles wrote to Louis that the seizures were entirely the fault of the French, the English merely responding to their aggression, and demanded the release of all British subjects and ships.[46] Charles offered nothing in return except, perhaps, a letter which he wrote a couple of days later assuring the French king of his 'fraternal affections'.[47] Not surprisingly Anglo-French relations continued to worsen. In August the French detained all English citizens living in Calais in retaliation for the expulsion of the queen's servants, and the next month they stone-walled Sir Dudley Carleton, the king's ambassador extraordinary to Paris.[48] In December Louis rejected Bassompiere's settlement, and Charles wrote that an attack on France had higher priority than the recovery of the Palatinate, which, as he told Frederick in April 1627, he could now restore only by peaceful means.[49]

At the end of April Charles ordered Buckingham, as Lord Admiral, to start issuing letters of marque for privateers to attack the French so starting one of the most successful, yet neglected, phases of the English war against that country. 'Hardly a day passes', one diplomat wrote home in June 1627, 'that privateers do not bring French prizes into English ports.' In the first two weeks of that month alone the crown received £10,000 from their sale.[50]

Prizes captured by both privateers and Captain Penington's royal naval squadron, together with receipts from the forced loan made the attack on the Isle of Ré possible. There were the usual problems in assembling the expedition, ballad singers describing the drafts marching to their rendezvous at Portsmouth.[51]

> With an old motley coat and a malmsey nose,
> With an old jerkin that's out at the elbows,
> And with an old pair of boots drawn on without hose,
> Stuffed with rags instead of toes.

The officers moaned about the quality of their soldiers and their propensity to mutiny, the sergeant major at Portsmouth having to reject as unfit for service 120 of the 200 conscripts from Hampshire.[52] Still, compared to the Mansfeld or Cadiz expeditions, the problems of assembling that to Ré were remarkably mild, especially since, as those who have taken part in such activities will readily admit, most military operations are always something of an organized shambles. Buckingham's abilities did much to facilitate the assembling of the fleet, the third expedition to be dispatched from England in two years without parliamentary aid. While this time the duke did not repeat the mistake of sending too large a force, he and

Charles once again failed to define their objectives clearly. What was the point of establishing an English base off the coast of France? While it might possibly stimulate an anti-French alliance abroad, rally public support at home, and hamper France's growing naval strength, it could do little to directly restore the Palatinate, which anyway was no longer England's first foreign policy goal.[53]

During the summer of 1627, Charles was involved with the immediate problem of getting the fleet ready for sea. On 15 May Buckingham gave him and the queen a farewell feast at York House, followed by a masque in which the duke appeared pursued by Envy, and then a pack of howling dogs, symbolic of the rabble's baying. In the finale Fame and Truth came on centre stage leaving the audience in no doubt as to Charles and Buckingham's opinion of all who questioned the wisdom of the attack on Ré and the certainty of its success.[54]

On 3 June Charles arrived in Portsmouth to inspect the troops, staying at Sir Daniel Norton's house. On 11 June he reviewed the fleet. After examining Portsmouth's defences, which he found in disorder, he went aboard the *Victory* (moored a few hundred yards from where her namesake is docked today) to sail to Stokes Bay. Lunch aboard the *Victory* was a very pleasant gathering with several captains, the Lord Chamberlain, Lord Steward, the Earl of Rutland, Monsieur de Sobise (the Huguenot leader) and Lords Carlisle and Denbigh. Archie, the king's fool, was at his funniest, the duke's musicians played gracefully, while through the great stern windows the calm waters of Spithead and the low green Hampshire coast provided a splendid backdrop. After lunch the king inspected Captain Penington's squadron, going over the watch-keeping bills, asking why some vessels still lacked captains, before viewing *Warspite, Repulse* and *Vanguard*. In the early evening he was rowed ashore to review the soldiers on Broom Down.[55]

When Buckingham joined Charles in Portsmouth on 13 June the tour of inspection continued. They dined together on the *Triumph*, presumably off the ship's own tableware, since the hamper carrying the royal plate was accidentally dropped into the sea whilst being loaded aboard. Charles did not appear to mind. Every detail of the preparations fascinated him: none seemed too trivial to escape the king's attention. He ordered defective muskets changed, and personally went through every purser's books, as if he were a regimental sergeant major, or quartermaster, rather than the commander-in-chief.

Under the command of the Duke of Buckingham the fleet of 100 ships carrying 6,000 infantry and 1,000 cavalry set sail on 27 June. They rendezvoused off the Isle of Ré on 10 July, and on the afternoon of 12 July, with Buckingham in the van, 2,000 troops waded ashore, marching inland. On 17 July they started the siege of the main French stronghold at St Martin's, a task that was to occupy the army's attentions for the next 100 days.

Buckingham was everywhere: in the trenches, inspecting guns, observing the fall of shot, dodging snipers and even assassins, praising the officers, encouraging the men, and, through the letters and pamphlets that his friends back home published, ensuring that not a jot of his virtues as 'a noble general' escaped either the public or the king's attention.[56] Although Buckingham could be faulted in neither his personal courage nor his public relations, in the initial attack he made the fatal mistake of allowing the small outposts of La Pree, on the eastern side of Ré astride the lines of communication to the mainland, to remain in French hands. Gradually the English managed to wear down the defenders of St Martin's, but on the night of 28 September, when the garrison was reduced to a couple of days food, the French managed to break the blockade and slip in a month's supplies. The besiegers became the besieged. 'Our army grows everyday weaker,' Sir Edward Conway wrote to his father, the Secretary of State, 'our victuals waste, our purses are empty, ammunition consumed, winter grows.'[57] On 27 October the English made a last desperate effort to take St Martin's. It failed. The scaling ladders were 5 feet shorter than the wall of the fort at which they had been staring for the past three months. Two days later 2,000 French sailed out of La Pree falling on the English flank with great effect.[58] The English now had to withdraw, and, thanks to Buckingham's poor sitting of the rearguard, the French turned the retreat into a rout. The English set sail in early November, leaving behind forty regimental or company colours on what the London wags had now christened 'the Isle of Rue'.[59]

Unlike the Mansfeld or Cadiz expeditions, that to Ré had a great effect on Charles, largely because the duke was away leaving him the responsibility for dispatching supplies, and the opportunity to improve relations with his wife.

Even if in late 1626 Louis had accepted Bassompiere's agreement it is unlikely that Charles's marriage would have improved. As it was it continued to deteriorate. Charles complained that his wife's letters were dry and ceremonious, and answered them in like vein. On being asked by Lady Carlisle when the queen might be back from taking the waters in Wellingborough he replied, 'I will expect no certainty of women's determinations.'[60] In their separate summer progresses through St Albans, Theobalds, Ampthill, Woodstock, Wellingborough and Beaulieu the two saw very little of each other. Henrietta Maria was, quite naturally, upset by her husband's preparations to wage war against her brother, while Charles found her demands for pocket money when the fleet needed every penny exceedingly annoying.[61]

However, once Buckingham was away in France things changed. On 13 August Charles added an unusual postscript to a letter to the duke. 'I cannot omit to tell you that you that my wife and I were never better together: she . . . showing herself so loving of me, by her discretion on all occasions, that it makes all wonder and esteem of her.'[62] A few days later it was reported that Charles had written to Henrietta Maria that he regretted having to make war against her country, but explained that he must protect England's honour. She replied that while she shared his sorrow, she wished his venture the best, since she was now more concerned with his affairs than those of anyone else.[63]

With Buckingham in France the administrative burden of supporting the expedition fell mainly on Charles. As George Goring noted the king 'knit himself up close to the business'. In September alone Charles attended four meetings of the privy council, and threatened personally to examine every one of the forced loan commissioners' accounts to see how well they had met their assessments. He even ordered Roche Forest in Somerset cut down and sold.[64] So single-minded was the king to ensure that the soldiers in Ré got supplies, that other business went by the board. Charles postponed important foreign policy issues, such as those concerning Denmark, until the duke's return, or else sent the papers to Ré for his decision. Yet he did not hesitate, or delay, as far as reinforcements were concerned, constantly urging Lord Treasurer Marlborough and the Chancellor of the Exchequer, Weston, to 'diligently labour for the effecting of all things that are in my charge'. Ten days later he told them that 'these delays make me impatient almost beyond patience'.

Charles had no time for anyone who did not whole-heartedly support the Ré expedition. When the crew of the (aptly named) *Return* refused to deliver their cargo of 100 troops to Ré and put back into Plymouth, the king ordered the privy council to see that they were strictly punished: anyone hampering the war effort, he declared, 'deserves to make their end at Tyburn'.[65]

One of the reasons for Charles's determination was the feeling that the men at the front were depending on him in a crucially important struggle. He told the Earl of Salisbury that he was engaged in a desperate fight which involved not just his honour but the safety and security of the realm. In July Buckingham wrote to Conway, who immediately passed the letter on to the king, 'I am confident that his Majesty will not let us want.' By 19 September the duke sounded bitter; by describing his army as 'men neglected and forgotten in England', he prompted Charles to explain how 'much grieved and unhappy' he was that supplies had been delayed.[66] Sir William Beecher arrived in Ré with thirty-six days of supplies and replacements on 25 September, three days before the French were able to resupply St Martin's, and Charles even managed to send further food and ordnance in October. The truth of the matter was that the king had done a first-rate job in supporting the Ré expedition having sent enough supplies to maintain the army until Christmas.[67] The English were beaten not because they lacked support from home, but because of Buckingham's failure to take La Pree and prevent the relief of St Martin's. Yet Charles blamed himself for the defeat of the Ré expedition, and the duke did nothing to dispel him of this fiction, since it increased Charles's dependence on his friend and the king's own lack of self-confidence. Once again the lessons of defeat passed unlearned, and the old cycle of calling parliament, attacks on the duke, dissolution to save the king's friend, another forced loan and military failure seemed destined to repeat itself. John Rous realized the only escape from this impasse was unthinkable. 'What would a false heart rather see than,' he asked his diary, 'an insurrection?'[68]

# VIII

# TO 'TAKE THAT SLIME AWAY'

The scene was a depressingly familiar one: the survivors of a defeated expeditionary force limping home, ships leaking, short of food, clothes in rags, morale shattered, with no facilities to receive them. At Plymouth sailors stole soldiers' weapons to pawn for food, and a great storm drove sixteen ships from their anchorage on to the shore, dismasting the *Nonsuch*. Of the 8,000 men Buckingham had taken to Ré only 3,000 returned, and of the survivors, 1,600 had to be carried ashore too sick or wounded to walk.[1]

The reaction to the return of the Ré expedition was equally familiar. The public was outraged. Charles stood by the duke, the king and Buckingham decided on further military escapades, parliament had to be called. Rather than vote taxes the Commons attacked the duke. To save his friend Charles prorogued parliament, and together they prepared another expedition. The wheel of misfortune seemed to be turning as before. However, this time there was a difference: during the summer of 1628 events seemed to reach boiling point, almost as if the Duke of Buckingham was driving the nation to hysteria. A desperate poetaster wrote:[2]

> And now, Just God! I humbly pray
> That thou wilt take that slime away
> That keeps my Sovereign's eyes from viewing
> The things that will be our undoing.

Although God did not take 'that slime away', John Felton – whom many believed was His agent – did.

The public response to the defeat on Ré bordered between humiliation and mockery. One letter called the campaign 'the greatest and shamefulest overthrow the English have received since we lost Normandy.'[3] John Rous reported that the news of the defeat 'made much muttering', and caused so 'much suspicion' that the Jesuits and Spanish would use it as an excuse to stop England helping the German Protestants; he prophesied that 'the slaughter at Ré will breed but evil blood.' Even so loyal a poet as William Drummond shared in the general disgust, asking:[4]

95

Charles, would you quiet your foes, have better luck
Send forth some Drakes, and keep home the Duke.

But there were no 'Drakes', only Buckingham, back home again as firmly entrenched in the royal favour as ever.

According to Secretary Conway, Charles took the news of the reverse on Ré with 'the wisdom, courage and constancy of a great king'.[5] He immediately accepted responsibility for the defeat declaring that Buckingham was blameless. 'You have had honour, all the shame must light upon us here remaining at home,' he wrote to his friend, adding in another letter, 'since our misfortune has been not to send you supplies in time, that all honest men cannot but say you have done past expectation and (if a man may say it), beyond possibility.'[6] Here Charles was indulging in a form of self-deception that belies the wisdom of a great king. By declaring that all honest men must applaud Buckingham's actions, Charles was not just calling himself honest, but those who disagreed with him dishonest. Secondly, by adopting the explanation that the results of the Ré expedition were 'better than we had cause to expect or had devised', the king and his government managed to deceive few people other than themselves.[7]

After leaving Ré Buckingham carried on as if nothing untoward had happened. The only person to warn him of the dangers of his actions was his mother, who wrote of the great chasm that was developing between her son and the English people. He was 'so little regarded at home', his mother warned, that 'every man groans under the burden'.[8] Rather than take his mother's advice that 'this is not the way', Buckingham preferred to listen to sycophants like the Earl of Exeter who called his actions 'miraculous', and the Earl of Manchester who reassured him that 'no captain general in the world could play his part better.'[9]

Whatever his creatures might say, the views of Buckingham's creator were decisive. In early November Charles sent a gentleman of the bedchamber in his own coach with 'some comfortable message', and a diamond bracelet to Portsmouth to welcome the duke home. When Buckingham arrived back in London the whole court, in a vast procession of horses and some seventy coaches, rode out to greet him. The only person who did not know how to handle the situation was Henrietta Maria, who pleading some vague indisposition, retreated to bed. Charles received his friend with profuse affection, and spent the first night alone with him in the royal bedchamber discussing the campaign.[10]

The campaign that most concerned Buckingham was to ensure that the rout on Ré did not precipitate his political defeat at home; in this battle he displayed far more skill than he had as a general. Just as his clients, such as Conway, realized that they must stick by the duke to save their own skins, so Buckingham understood that he must praise his officers most generously to forestall the recriminations that so often follow military disaster.[11] Stories of his soldiers' heroism, and, perhaps a thwarted desire for military glory that not even hours of hunting or tilting could satisfy, made Charles feel even worse about his own failure to send supplies. While Buckingham had been in Ré Charles had often seemed unprepared and unsure of himself, appearing on stage, noted one diplomat, as it were without a script.[12] On his return Buckingham did nothing to bolster the king's self-confidence. Rather he cleverly managed to enhance Charles's sense of guilt, while at the same time letting him appear resolute. It was the king, not Buckingham, who begged his dearest friend 'to bear these misfortunes with that courage that thou has shown in all these actions'.[13] Buckingham played on Charles's fears. When the idea of calling parliament was mooted, the duke twice went down on his knees to beg the king not to reject the idea solely to protect him: if they deemed him worthy of death Charles should not spare him. Like all of the duke's requests to his monarch delivered from a kneeling position, this should be treated with great caution, especially as Buckingham was exaggerating the dangers of calling parliament: so far no Stuart parliament had demanded death as a punishment for impeachment, dismissal from office being the worst fate the duke could possibly suffer.[14]

With the king's favour Buckingham was safe. As Charles demonstrated in the letter he wrote him just before Buckingham's return to England giving him a free hand in planning future attacks on the French, there was no chance that the duke would lose this precious commodity. The two agreed that Calais was a suitable target, and in December Charles turned down an opportunity to open peace talks with Paris.[15] Instead he spent his days with the privy council trying to find ways to raise money to continue the war. On 29 December they ordered that a fleet of 100 ships be assembled at an estimated cost of £71,453, and that every lord lieutenant ensure that his country's militia be trained twice or thrice a month. So concerned was the king to improve the militia that he ordered that not even the gentlemen of the court be excused drills, and announced that he intended to review the cavalry on Hounslow Heath in the spring. On 28 February 1628 Charles appointed yet another council of war of admirals and generals to work out future plans.[16]

In his commission to the council of war the king included an injunction to continually consider 'the good husbandry of our treasure'. As usual the crown was desperately short of money. It had to pay arrears in wages, ship repair and supply bills of over £100,000, as well as having future military commitments to the tune of nearly £300,000. So Charles commissioned several senior ministers to 'consider all the best and speediest ways you can for raising money'.[17] As usual they never reported. Equally unproductive was Conway's suggestion that the king establish a 'Loyal Association' of persons especially devoted to the monarchy, who in return for contributions, would be allowed to wear the king's colours and get the best seats at public events.[18] The king, however, preferred tried and trusted ways. Through a very complicated land deal he obtained £120,000 from the City of London and resorted to a forced loan that produced nearly £200,000.[19] All this was still not enough, and Charles had to call his third parliament.

In spite of Sir John Hippisley's warnings that it was vital that his friends be returned, Buckingham did next to nothing to pack the 1628 parliament. At Westminster, a constituency whose broad franchise made it an excellent index of public opinion, a brewer and a grocer, both of whom had opposed the forced loan, defeated Sir Robert Pye, one of the duke's allies. 'It is to be feared,' wrote Joseph Mead, 'because such patriots are chosen everywhere, the parliament will not last above eight days.'[20] Some, indeed, suspected that Charles and Buckingham intended such a precipitous end: if the Commons did not immediately vote taxes they would dissolve them, blaming a 'do-nothing' parliament for foot-dragging in a national emergency.[21]

The tone Charles used when he opened parliament on 17 March showed that he was in no mood to compromise. 'These times are for action,' he told both Houses. He wanted money, not 'tedious consultations'. With a master stroke of tactlessness, that might well have been intended as a gesture of conciliation, Charles assured parliament to 'take not this as threatening, for I scorn to threaten any but my equals.'[22]

Initially parliament responded favourably to the king's overtures, especially when he stepped up the prosecution of recusants. He ordered officers stationed outside the queen's chapel and that of the French ambassador to arrest English subjects attending Catholic services, that rigorous steps be taken to stop mass being said secretly in prisons, and issued a proclamation for the arrest of the Bishop of Chalcedon, leader of the clandestine Jesuit mission to England.[23] After the king promised to enforce the recusancy laws with special vigour and hear the Commons' grievances 'with a pious and princely ear', the Commons voted five subsidies. Charles was delighted to hear the news, and promised in future to work most closely with parliament. He asked by how many votes the subsidies had passed. 'By one voice' was the reply, which greatly distressed the king until someone explained that far from winning by a single vote the resolution had been unanimous. Charles wept with joy, declaring that he was ready to grant all the Commons' demands – except those touching billeting.[24]

Billeting was an extremely sensitive subject. With the failure of three military ventures and frantic preparations for a fourth under way, the enforced lodging of troops on householders had become a grievous problem. All, from the owners of grand houses to cottages, had to billet and feed guests, about whom the government was inundated with complaints. In the Isle of Wight one Highland regiment was reported guilty of 'murders, rapes, robberies, burglaries, getting of bastards', of whom at least seventy had been acknowledged. In Canterbury troops ransacked shops for food and clothing. From Maldon, in Essex, the villagers complained that the Irish soldiers billeted on them 'command in our houses as if they were our lords, and we their slaves'.[25] In Buckinghamshire Lieutenant Sandelands threatened to cut off Richard Briscoe's head if he refused to lodge one of his soldiers, and when Sir William Fleetwood, the local justice of the peace, arrested Captain Read, Sandeland's superior, the rest of the company stormed Aylesbury jail to release their commanding officer. Far from being sympathetic to the civilians, who were trying to maintain law and order, the privy council ordered Briscoe and Fleetwood's arrest.[26]

The stormy issue of billeting, replete with such tales and complaints, worsened relations between Charles and his parliament. Eight days after he had wept with joy to hear of their vote of subsidies, Charles warned the Commons 'to take heed that you force him not to make an unpleasing end to that which hath been so happily begun.'[27] However, in the Commons, a group of members led by Sir Thomas Wentworth, a Yorkshire gentleman, broadened their attack to the point where it seemed to the king that his prerogative was in jeopardy. So on 2 May Charles reminded the Commons that whilst he would rule according to the laws they must not trespass on 'that sovereignty and prerogative which God hath put into his hands for our good'. They must instead take immediate action since 'the affairs of the kingdom and Christendom . . . cannot endure long debate or delay.'[28] Ten days later Charles repeated this theme to the House of Lords, adding that whilst he could never surrender his right to imprison subjects without trial 'without overthrow of sovereignty' he would do so with the utmost moderation. By declaring he was willing 'to satisfy all moderate minds', Charles implied that all whose minds remain unsatisfied must be immoderate.[29]

The success or failure of military ventures determined the state of relations between Charles and his first three parliaments much more than the evolution of long-term constitutional ideas or social changes. In the spring of 1628 military failure exacerbated the issue of billeting, while the pathetic performance of the Denbigh expedition brought about a parliamentary crisis.

Save for the overwhelming reason that he was Buckingham's brother-in-law, there was not the slightest cause to appoint William Feilding, Earl of Denbigh, admiral of the fleet sent to relieve La Rochelle. During the Cadiz expedition Denbigh had proved his military incompetence as amply as he demonstrated his loyalty to the duke in the recriminations afterwards. In late April 1628 his fleet left Plymouth, arriving on 1 May off La Rochelle, where the French had stretched a long chain, buoyed with huge logs, across the harbour mouth. After spending several stormy days blockading the port the weather cleared sufficiently to allow two captains to try and blow up the chain, but the charge went off prematurely, killing one and persuading Denbigh to scurry home the next day.

Charles was furious. He had told Denbigh not to quit since he (quite rightly) believed that a resolute attack could relieve the Huguenots in La Rochelle. 'The floating chain', wrote one who personally inspected it, 'can never stop anyone determined on going in, any more than a spider's web can stop eagles.' On Denbigh's return Charles sent Coke to Plymouth to investigate the admiral's conduct, while Buckingham tried to make Edward Clarke, a subordinate commander, scapegoat for his brother-in-law's failure.[30]

Such recriminations were becoming increasingly irrelevant in the face of the resentment that was welling up in parliament, where pressure was growing for the passage of a statement of grievances, known as the Petition of Right. The petition prohibited 'any gift, loan, benevolence or tax, without common consent by act of parliament', imprisonment without cause, proceedings by martial law contrary to the law of the land, and the billeting of troops in private houses. At the start of the parliamentary session Charles seemed inclined to accept the petition. His messages to parliament of 4 and 28 April gave the impression that he believed it merely confirmed liberties already granted. But in a third message of 2 May his tone appreciably hardened. Perhaps the crown realized that it would be months, if at all, before it actually received the five subsidies that parliament had promised, and which its armed forces desperately needed. Otherwise the king's ministers, or, as is more likely, Charles himself had fallen into the fatal trap of personalizing the issue, by telling parliament, 'You will find as much security in his Majesty's royal word and power as in the strength of any law you can make.'[31]

This warning did nothing to dissuade the Lords and Commons from passing the petition, nor did it reassure them they were indeed enacting a law. Thus when on 2 June the king accepted the petition by saying that he 'willeth that right to be done according to the laws and customs of the realm', many members were deeply dissatisfied. The petition was designed to redress grievous and immediate problems. Billeting, as we have seen, was a burden on all. The judges' recent decision in the Five Knights case that *Habeas Corpus* did not apply to some gentlemen arrested for refusing to pay the forced loan was of special concern to members of parliament. In addition some did not trust the king. They feared that when he no longer needed parliamentary taxes he would use the omission of traditional Norman-French assent, 'Soit droit fait come est desire: let it be as it is wished,' to welch on his promises. The correct form of assent for a private act was particularly important to ensure that the petition was accepted as a statute with the binding force of law, and not, as some feared, merely as guidance for the king's judges.

Immediately a storm swept parliament, becoming a hurricane two days later when Charles informed both Houses that he would accept the petition 'without further change'. Sir Edward Coke called this 'the greater violation' of the law 'that ever was'. A second message on 5 June prompted a full scale attack on the favourite. 'I think the Duke of Buckingham is the cause of all our miseries.' Eliot denounced. 'That man is the grievance of grievances.'[32] So to save his friend, and under unprecedented pressure from the Lords, at noon on 7 June Charles suddenly gave way. Four hours later he accepted the petition in the time-honoured fashion, and then, as he was leaving the chamber fired a parting shot: 'if this parliament have not a happy conclusion the sin is yours. I am free from it.'[33]

Quite simply Charles was a bad loser. He had neither the grace nor the inner strength of, say, a Queen Elizabeth, who in 1601 was able to turn her defeat over monopolies into her 'Golden Speech', which, if it did not have the members of the Commons eating out of her hand, at least persuaded a goodly number of them to kiss it. Charles must have found the celebrations that greeted the Petition of Right particularly galling. They were the wildest that London had seen since his return from Madrid. 'I am almost dead for joy,' exulted Coke.[34] Historians have been nearly as enthusiastic, one calling the petition 'the beginning, not the end of revolution', while many others have ranked it with Magna Carta. But the petition – like Magna Carta – lacked an effective means of enforcement. Because the judges were inclined to interpret it most narrowly, it had little immediate impact. Charles had scant intention of carrying out the petition's promises in good faith. Even before he assented to the petition, he wrote to the judges to be assured that doing so would not jeopardize his right to imprison without cause. On 5 June, three days after his English assent, and two days before the Norman-French one, after a six-hour meeting of the privy council, the king came close to dissolving parliament. On the next day, whilst sending parliament a conciliatory message Charles wrote Buckingham a secret letter about billeting that suggested that he was not going to surrender this prerogative. Afterwards he tried to have the petition printed in such a way as to minimize its significance.[35]

Throughout the period of the struggle over the petition, day to day events affected Charles far more than any long term constitutional considerations. He and his advisers interpreted the violent attack on Buckingham as pressure to obtain the petition, and thus assented only to relieve his friend. In fact their interpretation was incorrect, and so when a resolution was introduced into the Commons on 11 June calling for more rigorous enforcement of the recusancy laws, and attacking Arminianism and Buckingham, Charles felt he had been betrayed. He responded by declaring that he was 'fully satisfied of the innocency of the duke', and on 17 June after the Commons had formally presented their complaints to the crown, Charles publicly gave his friend his hand to kiss and reproved the House for meddling in matters of state: 'I am sure that I know more about them than you, and find you know less about them than I thought.'[36] The prorogation of parliament nine days later to 20 October came as no surprise. In a fighting speech Charles told parliament that even though 'I owe no account of mine actions but to God alone,' he would most graciously explain his decision. As far as the Petition of Right was concerned Charles elaborated on the ruling about imprisonment without cause that he had obtained from the judges before assenting to the petition, arguing that 'I have granted no new, but only confirmed ancient liberties.' Thus he could not tolerate any attack on his ancient liberty to collect the customs duties, tonnage and poundage, nor let anyone 'touch upon my prerogative'. Finally Charles reminded parliament of the constitutional reality that they could not 'make or declare a law without my consent'.[37]

The first session of the 1628 parliament settled nothing. It merely added fuel to the flames which, as the members returned home, seemed to spread across the land. Far from capitalizing on the widespread reaction that the Commons had gone too far in insisting on the petition, Charles fanned the flames.[38] He pardoned Dr Roger Mainwaring, whom the Commons had fined for preaching before Charles that the king could collect taxes without parliamentary approval, and gave the priest the living of Stanford Rivers in Essex, and made Richard Montagu, a notorious exponent of the most extreme views of divine right, Bishop of Chichester, and offered to pay the expenses of anyone the Commons imprisoned.[39]

So throughout the summer of 1628 the kingdom seemed to seethe. Everywhere portents of crisis could be found.

In London on the evening of Friday, 13 June a group of thugs spotted Dr Lambe, Buckingham's physician, walking home from the theatre. They started to stone him. Lambe ran. The mob, rapidly growing larger and more vicious, chased the unfortunate doctor, and although four constables tried to save Lambe, the crowd beat him to death, screaming that they wished they could do the same to the devil, and not just his disciple. 'Let Charles and George do what they can,' a doggerel verse warned, 'Yet George shall die like Dr Lambe.'[40]

The most outrageous rumours swept the land: Buckingham was trying to recruit German mercenaries as a personal bodyguard; with his own hands he had murdered the king; he and a cabal of Scots and Jesuits (an unlikely combination) plotted to three o'clock each morning; through his uncle, a cardinal, Buckingham was in daily communication with the pope; Dr Lambe had brewed his master an aphrodisiac with which he could seduce every woman in the realm; the duke had a nose bleed so copious that not even the Lord Keeper's mace placed on the back of his neck could stem it; his portrait in the high commission chamber had fallen from the wall; his father's ghost appeared thrice in Windsor castle to warn of the dangers of the duke's policies. In Loughor, Carmarthenshire, a couple of robbers managed to confuse the *posse* pursuing them and start a minor riot, by spreading the rumour that the duke had poisoned the king. The records are full of such incidents, symptoms of the general tension that John Rous summed up in his diary: 'Our king's proceedings have caused men's minds to be incensed, to rave and project.'[41]

Apart from ordering that Lambe's murderers be apprehended and punished, Charles seemed oblivious of events.[42] For instance on the day after the attack on Lambe, as the king and Buckingham were playing bowls, the duke put his hat on in his sovereign's presence. Outraged, one Wilson, a Scot, snatched it off saying, 'You must not stand with your hat on before my king.' Buckingham moved to kick Wilson, but Charles held out a hand saying, 'Let him, George, he is either mad or a fool.'[43]

Seeming to dismiss all who opposed their policies as insane or idiots, Charles and Buckingham continued their preparations to relieve the Huguenots. The king declared that he was 'quite determined to make a second attempt on La Rochelle', and in May ordered the press gangs to sweep the Thames and Medway 'without sparing any'.[44] Secretary Coke did a splendid job in licking the survivors of Ré back into shape, quelling at least two mutinies, and by late June assembling a fleet of about 100 ships with 4,000 men.[45] On 17 July Charles set out for Portsmouth leaving Buckingham behind in London to clear up some unfinished business. Five days later from his headquarters in Southwick, a village seven miles from Portsmouth, and admirably suited to supervise an invasion of France (General Eisenhower later chose it as his headquarters for D-Day) Charles wrote to Buckingham that the fleet was ready – all that was needed was the duke and a fair wind.[46] When neither was forthcoming, Charles spent the first two weeks of August hunting in the New Forest, returning to Southwick to meet the duke on 17 August. He was most anxious to see his friend again. Sir John Oglander remembered seeing Charles spend an whole hour looking out of his chamber window across the downs waiting for his friend to arrive.[47]

Oglander also noted that Buckingham was 'bravely attended'. He was not, however, well protected, particularly for one who was as hated as he was powerful. Great men naturally expect threats on their lives, especially when their policies fail. In 1626 there had been a report that some of the London militia intended to shoot the duke as he reviewed them. After his return from Ré rumours of assassination plots became rife.[48] Yet not even Lambe's murder persuaded the duke to take precautions: he scorned wearing a jacket of chain mail, denying he was in any danger.

On 23 August 1628, Buckingham took breakfast at Captain Mason's house on Portsmouth High Street – a few yards from the public house that now bears his name. After finishing his meal, he came downstairs to ride to Southwick to tell Charles of a report (later proved false) that La Rochelle had fallen. Standing in the crowd at the bottom of the stairs was

John Felton, a deranged army officer, who felt that Buckingham had wrongfully denied him promotion to captain. Felton shoved through the throng of lords, officers and servants and plunged a dagger, that he had just bought for 10 pence, through Buckingham's chest. The duke pulled the knife out from between his ribs, tried to draw his sword, staggered forward a couple of paces, and, with blood streaming from his nose, mouth and wound, collapsed dead across a table. People milled around shouting, some trying to revive the corpse, others out to hunt and kill the assassin. Eyewitness accounts vary. Some say people screamed, 'Where is the murderer? Where is the murderer?' and Felton, who had merged back into the crowd, announced, 'I am the man. Here I am.' Others remember that the crowd blamed one of Richelieu's secret agents, shouting 'A Frenchman! A Frenchman!' and Felton, assuming that they were calling his name, or else indignant that a foreigner might get credit for so noble a deed, admitted 'I am the man.' Captain Stamford, Buckingham's body-guard, and a professional wrestler, tried to run Felton through with his rapier. Felton might have been lynched had not Sir Dudley Carleton hustled him off to the safety of the governor's house.[49]

Messengers were sent to tell the duke's wife and best friend that he was dead. Kate Buckingham fainted. Charles, who was at prayers when he was whispered the news, signalled for the service to be completed, before retiring to his room, where he remained secluded for two days, without comfort or company, food or friends, hope or help.

For a decade Buckingham had dominated Britain's politics and her kings. With great finesse he had managed to transfer his influence from James to Charles. In order to maintain his hold on Charles he had encouraged an unusually aggressive – and unsuccessful – foreign policy that necessitated the calling of three parliaments. Buckingham exploited Charles's lack of self-confidence and energy, taking advantage of the failure of his marriage and the king's need for someone on whom he could lean in the uncertain world of politics. Ironically Buckingham never appreciated the strength of his hold on Charles, his own sense of insecurity driving the duke on to rasher and more dangerous ventures. As Archbishop Abbot, the fallen prelate (whose eye for politicians was sharper than for gamekeepers), observed, Buckingham 'feared his own shadow and desperately ventured upon many things for his own preservation'.[50]

Charles inherited Buckingham from his father, accepting the role of the surrogate younger brother. First Buckingham used Charles's sense of submission to authority in general and his father in particular, to make him a pseudo-sibling, and then intensified his control over Charles by manipulating the young man's desire to establish his own sense of identity and become independent of his father. At first Buckingham's hegemony was incomplete. Charles initiated the trip to Spain, where for a brief period he tried to be his own master. However, the débâcle in Madrid restored the duke's influence, necessitated Bristol's destruction, and made Charles want a war with Spain, which he saw as a stepping stone for the recovery of the Palatinate. Over the Palatinate the two main themes of Charles's childhood came together – loyalty to his sister and her cause, and dependence on the elder brother who, when alive, had so badly neglected him. Indeed by allowing Buckingham to fight for the restitution of the Palatinate, Charles saw himself as being a much better king and father than James had been. Charles married Henrietta Maria to get French help for his sister, and when it was not forthcoming Charles (as usual seeking a scapegoat) went to war with France blaming that country for the failure of Mansfeld's expedition.[51]

Throughout their foreign adventures Charles and Buckingham were in remarkable accord. 'As for answer to your letter,' the king wrote to the duke in February 1628, 'not differing with you in opinion (as I do but seldom) it is needless to make any.'[52] The hint of a tiff would send ambassadors and letter-writers to their pens in a tizzy, only to be calmed a little later by some splendid banquet or public embrace. Charles was often readier to punish his friend's enemies than Buckingham was himself, as he seemed to lack his sovereign's vindictiveness. The king constantly believed that he was being attacked by some third party – the Spanish, the queen's servants, a few wilful members of parliament, the French, the envy of the masses, all were grist for his fears and explanations for his troubles. Like most psychological devices they contain a degree of ambivalence. Charles wanted to accept his father's authority and at the same time be independent of James. So his habit of blaming some third party for his troubles became both a comforting excuse, as well as a source of concern. 'They' attacked Buckingham. If Charles accepted that 'their' attacks had any validity he would be making 'them' appear more powerful. Thus he had to insist that the arguments of 'those' who did not agree with him were worthless in order to make his enemies seem less threatening, and, concurrently endorse the correctness of his choice of Buckingham as his favourite. After the defeat on Ré the king wrote to Buckingham, 'every day I find new reasons to confirm me in being your loving, faithful, constant friend, Charles R.'[53]

The roots of Charles's dependence lay in his personal insecurity. He found friendship and loyalty hard to give and even harder to give up. In March 1626, for instance, the Earl of Totnes suggested in a private interview with the king that in return for a vote of taxes Charles let parliament imprison the council of war, of which Totnes was a member, as scapegoats for the failure of the Cadiz expedition. 'Let them do what they list, you shall not go to the Tower,' Charles replied, 'it is not you they aim at, but it is me upon whom they make inquisition; and for subsidies that would not hinder it. Gold may be brought too dear, and I thank you for your offer.'[54] Perhaps Charles's interpretation of the objectives of those who opposed his policies was correct. Certainly many members of parliament would have welcomed a scapegoat or two, since that would have allowed them to claim they were opposing the policies of the crown's misguided ministers and not the sovereign himself. However, the loyalty Charles gave to ministers such as Buckingham, Wimbledon, Totnes or Carleton, prevented him from reversing unpopular policies, removed a shield between the crown and public outrage, and denied the king the opportunity to blame others for his own failures. As the attacks on his favourite grew, so did Charles's commitment to Buckingham. On 19 June 1628, six days after Lambe's murder and whilst rumours spread fast and furious, Charles and Buckingham inspected the fleet at Deptford. Turning to the ships, the king said in a loud voice that all could hear, 'George, there are some that wish that these and thou might both perish. But care not for them. We will both perish together if thou dost.'[55]

Just as Charles formed myths about his opponents, so they held misconceptions about him which Buckingham helped perpetuate. These misconceptions were the product of the age-old dilemma faced by all Englishmen until the eighteenth-century development of the idea of a loyal opposition: that disagreeing with the crown bordered on treason. So Charles's opponents had to argue that his policies were really the work of evil advisers. Even Sir John Eliot accepted this myth, declaring in his famous 'grievance of grievances' attack on Buckingham that 'till the king be informed thereof we shall never get out with honour.'

One simple fact helped the duke dominate Charles. Buckingham was prepared to work hard at the business of government, while Charles was lazy. Occasionally the king could display bursts of energy especially with regard to trivial matters. He personally examined the lists of New Year's presents given and received.[56] Usually, however, the king could not be bothered with the daily business of the realm, as the surviving state papers indicate. During the first eighteen months of his reign, Charles attended only four privy council meetings. Secretaries of state constantly complained that he was too busy hunting or playing tennis to sign papers. When in a memo dated January 1627, Secretary Conway summarized seventeen items of business that needed the king's attention, Charles's response was hardly dynamic: he referred the first back to Conway, appointed a committee to consider the second, told Conway to take up the third with Buckingham and the fourth with Weston, and did nothing about the last thirteen items.[57] When Charles took decisive actions on his own, as in Madrid or whilst Buckingham was away on Ré, afterwards he felt that his efforts had ended in failure. Unlike Henry VIII, Elizabeth I, or even James I, Charles did not understand that making the political process work demands hard work, day in and day out, with scrupulous attention to detail. They, like Charles I, all believed in divine right, but unlike him were prepared to give the Almighty more than the occasional helping hand.

Charles's feelings towards the duke were so intense that the question might now be asked – as it was at the time – whether their relationship was a homosexual one.[58] Of course, the answer depends on what one means by 'homosexual'. In legal terms, where an act of buggery was the sole criterion, Charles and Buckingham were completely innocent of any crime. In psychological terms the judgment has to be more complex. Charles was not a highly sexed man; he had no mistresses – not even the beautiful, experienced, and very affectionate Lady Carlisle, whom Buckingham dangled before him after the collapse of his marriage. On the other hand, Charles's emotional needs for love, reassurance and someone on whom he could lean were intense. Like his father he found a home within the Villiers family, taking great pleasure, for example, in the birth of his friend's first son who was christened Charles. All the same, the king's relations with Buckingham went far beyond those of a doting honorary uncle, further even than those normal between the deepest of male friends, for they satisfied, as far as possible, Charles's libidinal drives, which were essentially emotional rather than physical. Thus Charles's feelings towards the duke precluded any deep relationship with anyone else – especially a woman. In Spain he had deserted his friend for the Infanta. On being rejected by her he returned to the security of a male relationship. Buckingham's presence prevented the king from developing any deep involvement with his wife, whilst the duke's removal by Felton enabled Charles to transfer his emotional ties to Henrietta Maria.

Just as Buckingham monopolized the king's emotions, so he dominated English politics. As Archbishop Abbot shrewdly observed the duke 'could endure no man that would not depend on him'.[59] Buckingham destroyed Bacon, Cranfield and Williams, creating a monopoly of power about the king for himself and his clients. One such client, Sir James Bagg, used to sign himself 'Buckingham's personal slave', while another, Edward Conway, told his benefactor that 'it is impossible for me ... to forget who made me.'[60] The duke used carrots as well as sticks to control his faction. He had Conway elevated to be Viscount Killultagh, and when, in the summer of 1628, Dudley Carleton raised fundamental questions about the duke's foreign policy, Buckingham flattered him, by saying that he was considering major revisions that needed the ambassador's considerable diplomatic skills.[61] Even after the reverses on Ré the duke's faction realized that they had to stick by him, being too closely identified with Buckingham to survive his fall.

Buckingham's monopoly of power about the crown meant that Charles was offered no policy options. He had no choices, and wanted none since choice implied uncertainty. This is not to say that Charles did not affect policy. Indeed in major items his wishes were paramount. However, he never consciously sat down to make choices from options, but rather drifted into issues without considering their consequences. Buckingham helped Charles towards the goals into which he slid by shielding him from the uncertainty – even chaos – implied by choice, something which, as the king's insistence of courtly decorum suggests, was utterly repugnant to his nature.

Charles's sense of decorum and authority, more than any other trait of his personality, accounted for his failure to get on with his first three parliaments. Charles was an authoritarian because he had neither the taste nor the energy for the hard work of deals, threats and stroking that consensus politics demands. Similarly Buckingham was an authoritarian because his position depended on winning and keeping one man's support: to survive Buckingham did not need popular approval. So, neither king nor duke bothered much about parliamentary elections. In truth to do so, to buy votes, to build up a faction of the king's friends in the Commons, or to create one in the Lords, and to use privy councillors to manage debates, would have recognized the legitimacy of parliament's claims to trespass on what Charles regarded as his prerogative.

In much the same way Charles did not view the politics of his reign in terms of parties. He did not, for instance, deliberately build up an 'Arminian party' in parliament or throughout the land, by rewarding leading exponents of that ideology, but merely preferred those people whom he liked, who (as with us all) tended to be those who agreed with him. To think of the politics of his reign, particularly before 1640, in party terms is as confusing as the use of such labels as 'Puritan' or even 'Arminian'. For one thing Charles never acted with the political foresight that historical hindsight has often granted him: for another to support parties would have been utterly repugnant given the seventeenth-century concept of politics with its emphasis on consensus. Thus within such a framework concession for Charles was as intellectually difficult as it was psychologically distasteful. Even when he gave something away he pretended he had in truth done nothing of the sort. After he assented to the Petition of Right, Charles convinced himself that he had not yet really conceded anything new but merely recognized rights his subjects already enjoyed. So while it may appear in retrospect that Buckingham made Charles's first three parliaments end in failure, at the time the king felt that it was his concept of prerogative government that had triumphed.

Similarly the consequences of the breakdown between king and parliament were not as serious at the time as hindsight might suggest. Parliament was one of many stages – perhaps not the most important, though certainly the most obvious – in which politics during the 1620s were played. The court still functioned, within their counties men struggled for power, using the crown to help themselves up and push their enemies down. In times of stress parliament ceased to be so important in the local based politics that involved most of the political nation. Private bills were the first to fall by the wayside; the last being national statutes wanted by the crown.[62]

Even when Charles failed to get his subsidy bills through the House, he and Buckingham still managed to raise enough money for their military adventures. Their military plans followed the traditional British strategy of attacking the enemy by sea with small amphibious forces, and subsidizing a Continental power to do most of the fighting on land. Parliament's refusal to vote taxes meant that the second half of this strategy went by the board. So if for lack of English gold Christian IV of Denmark was beaten at the Battle of Lutter, Britain at least was spared the horrors of being dragged into the Thirty Years War.

Buckingham certainly had all the talents: good looks, charm, grace, wit, the ability to manipulate kings, and work hard. What he lacked was luck: if the Cadiz expedition had lingered for two more days they would have met the treasure fleet from the Americas; if Denbigh had been a little more determined; if Buckingham had been able to attack La Rochelle in the summer when the tides had weakened the boom, or in October after storms had washed it away; if the French relief of St Martin's had been delayed for a couple more days, or if Felton's 10-penny dagger had not hit in exactly the right place at exactly the right angle, Charles's reign might have been very different.

It was not to be. Carried by colonels and captains, Buckingham's body left Portsmouth on 28 August. His funeral took place on 18 September. With only a hundred mourners the cortège walked from Wallingford House to Westminster Abbey. The city's trained bands, backs to the procession, arms at the ready, lined London's deserted streets. Six men carried the coffin, which was in fact empty, the duke having been secretly buried the night before lest the crowd attack the cortège to rip his corpse apart. Empty streets, an empty coffin, an empty administration – such were the final indignities for the man who more than anyone else influenced the first half of Charles's life and who so justly deserved James Shirley's epitaph:[63]

> Here lies the best and worst of fate,
> Two kings' delight, the people's hate.

# IX

# 'SOVEREIGNTY MAINTAINED ABOVE ALL'

Buckingham's sudden murder was both a terrible shock for Charles and a turning point in his reign. He heard the news at morning prayer at Southwick, but rather then stopping divine service to give vent to his anguish, he signalled to the minister to continue. Only after the office had been fully observed, and he settled the most urgent matters, did the king retire to his chamber to collapse in a paroxysm of grief. When, days later, he reappeared he tried to continue the duke's policies, perhaps as a tribute to his dead friend, for he was deeply hurt by the ensuing public jubilation. Following the ignominious defeat of the fleet that Buckingham would have led to La Rochelle, relations between Charles and parliament continued to deteriorate. They reached a crisis on 2 March 1629 when the Commons defied the king's order to adjourn by forcibly holding the speaker in his throne so they could pass an intemperate motion condemning Arminians, papists, and all who paid taxes that they had not voted. In reaction Charles dissolved parliament, and tried to rule without them.

The transition from Buckingham hegemony to personal rule was a rapid one. It owed more to precipitous decisions, miscalculations and misunderstandings than any carefully thought out long term design on Charles's part to become an absolute monarch. Yet throughout it all Charles's aims were both sure and simple, being perhaps best summoned up by the Earl of Banbury. 'Because things between the king and his people be gotten to extremities,' he wrote to Secretary Carleton in October 1629, 'I wish sovereignty maintained above all.'[1]

After the priest had finished matins on 23 August 1628 the king first ordered Kate Buckingham removed from Portsmouth to some safe place in case the duke's murder was the start of a wider plot. Next he summoned the privy council to wait upon him at Southwick, and ordered all ports closed so no ship could leave England carrying the conspirators or damaging rumours abroad. Finally Charles commanded that the Dutch ships, that had been waiting in Portsmouth for the La Rochelle expedition to leave, be prevented from returning home.[2] Less than an hour after learning of his friend's death Charles decided that the attack he would have led must go on, and that the crime might well be part of some evil conspiracy.

After Charles came out of his room a couple of days later his chief concerns were investigating his friend's murder and planning his funeral.

On 28 August he ordered that no honour due Buckingham be omitted: on land his body must at all times be borne by colonels; at sea captains should fire the salute proper for a Lord Admiral.[3] But Charles, who had already restrained his initial grief by waiting impassively for the end of morning service, was denied the further chance of mourning his friend with an elaborate state funeral, or by building him a grandiloquent memorial. When he suggested spending £10,000 on burying the duke, Lord Treasurer Weston demurred that the rabble might break up the ceremony, and anyway the money would be better spent on a more permanent memorial. Afterwards Weston torpedoed the latter proposal by pointing out that the king could hardly raise a monument to a duke, until he had erected one to his father. So Buckingham was buried at his own expense, unattended by his friend and sovereign. The only memorials left to him today are the ornate tomb his family paid for in Westminster Abbey, and the Portsmouth pub that bears his name a few yards from where he died.[4]

As usual following the assassination of a prominent figure Buckingham's murder engendered rumours of conspiracies. Charles immediately appointed a commission of Weston, Dorset, Pembroke and Carlisle, to investigate them, eagerly studying their reports. He learned how Felton's health was drunk in the Ship Inn, Dover, and order an example made of James Farrell, an Irishman, for declaring in Canterbury that ten thousand Englishmen wished the king as dead as the duke. He directed that Gilbert Andrews be closely confined on suspicion of knowing something about the crime, and that John Gill and William Chillingworth be similarly held for toasting Felton, and jesting that without Buckingham all Charles was fit for was standing like some silly apprentice lad outside a shop in Cheapside, asking the passing world 'What do you lack?' The Court of Star Chamber dealt harshly with John Savage, a lunatic, who claimed to have been Felton's accomplice, ordering him whipped, nailed by his ears to the pillory, pulled free, his nostrils slit, and his cheeks branded – as a result of which the poor simpleton died.[5]

In spite of the government's excessive concern with the faintest false lead, Charles's main interest remained Felton. He ordered Lord Chief Justice Richardson to examine the accused's mother, brother, sister and friends, appointed a commission to interrogate the prisoner, and sent his personal chaplain, Dr Brian Duppa, to talk to him in the Tower. Ironically, and it seems without being tortured, Felton displayed the apologetic humility that Charles demanded from those who offended him. Dr Duppa reported back to the king that the prisoner fell to his knees in gratitude for his sovereign's concern for his soul, profusely confessed his guilt, and begged to be allowed to do public penance in sackcloth and ashes. When a few days later Lord Dorset told Felton that 'it is the king's pleasure you should be put to the torture,' he replied with a faith in his monarch's magnanimity that must surely have tried his sovereign's patience: 'I do not believe, my lord, that is the king's pleasure, for he is a just and gracious prince,' threatening if racked 'to accuse you, my Lord of Dorset, and none but yourself.' Felton in fact was never tortured; he produced copious confessions with obliging regularity.[6] He was tried in November, suffering the following month the terrible fate of traitors – hanging, castration, drawing and quartering. Throughout his ordeal he was one of the few of the king's subjects to express remorse for the duke's death. 'Live ever Felton, thou has turned to dust,' one street balladeer wished him at his execution, 'treason, ambition, murder, pride and lust.'[7]

The virtually unanimous joy at his best friend's death wounded Charles deeply. In London the citizens openly drank Felton's health 'with great joy'. In Bedfordshire the celebrations were 'almost universal'. From the presses came doggerel warning the devil:

> Lucifer, thou must resign thy crown,
> for thou shall see a Duke who will put thee down.

Across the land Felton was hailed as a hero for slaying Britain's Goliath. 'God bless thee, little David,' shouted one crone as Felton was being marched to the Tower, where his cell became a place of pilgrimage for admiring crowds.[8]

Understandably all this drove one more wedge between the king and his people. According to Sir Dudley Carleton, who was with Charles through most of this crisis, it affected his mind 'very much'. The king could not understand the popular venom.[9] Rather than vilifying the duke they should revere him as 'a martyr' whose 'bloody assassination' was 'a common loss'.[10] The failure of the La Rochelle expedition was a suitable postscript to the duke's adventurous foreign policy, the end of which meant that wars abroad no longer dominated domestic politics, forcing the calling of parliaments. After Buckingham's passing new politicians and policies came to the fore, even though none grew as dominant as before. While Charles set the broad outlines of policy – sometimes by accident, often by reacting to a short-term event – he was no longer as involved in the stuff of government. Instead he turned away. Leaving much to others he retreated to his court where gradually (and much to his surprise) he found consolation in the love of his wife.

Buckingham had always been an impediment to Charles and Henrietta Maria's marital happiness. A month before his death the Venetian ambassador reported that Henrietta Maria begged her husband for the trifling sum of £2 for a destitute young Frenchwoman. Asked for whom the alms were intended she replied, 'I, Sire, am the penniless pauper.' This 'piqued the king greatly', but Contarini consoled himself, 'the French always give themselves airs.'[11] Yet, as the ambassador had to admit, a few weeks later the queen was beginning to show a little more tact, being able to intervene with her husband to arrange an audience for him. When she heard the news of the duke's death she behaved with even greater astuteness, rushing to console the widow, and, after he emerged from isolation, her husband. Six weeks later Lucy Carlisle wrote that one could not wish to find a happier couple. When Henrietta Maria caught a fever, believed by some to be a mild attack of smallpox, and became weak from bleeding, Charles was constantly by her side.[12] The next month Thomas Cary wrote: 'You would find our master and mistress at such a degree of kindness as you would imagine him wooer again, and her gladder to receive his caresses than he to make them'.[13] Charles put on displays of jousting before his lady, who could not sleep when he had to go to Theobalds for a few days, sighing for his return.[14] At about this time they conceived their first child, which the romantically inclined may see as the fruit of their new-found love, and the more prosaic as the product of the nineteen-year-old queen's much delayed physical maturity. Anyway, the baby helped bring the two closer, Charles displaying the touching solicitude of the first-time father. When the following May the child was miscarried, being born feet first, he told the doctors to save his wife at all costs even though it meant that they might not be able to have any more children.[15] 'The only dispute that now exists between us,' Charles wrote his mother-in-law, 'is that of conquering each other by affection.'[16]

The improvement in their marriage did not take place over-night nor without incident. In early September 1628 the queen and her French servants (who, like the late duke, believed that any betterment in their mistress's marriage could only take place at the expense of their own influence) boorishly barged through the guard-house at Tichfield where an Anglican chaplain was trying to preach to the queen's Protestant retainers. The latter had no doubt who was to blame when a couple of days afterwards someone fired a barrel-load of buckshot at the preacher. Another silly squabble erupted a little later at supper. As John Hacket, the king's chaplain, tried to say grace, the queen's confessor shoved him aside. Hacket pushed back, but before their elbowing could degenerate into fisticuffs, Charles angrily started eating the unblessed food, and at the end of the meal, with his wife in tow, stormed out to his chamber.[17]

The duke's death stiffened Charles's determination to launch the naval expedition to La Rochelle. Perhaps he envisaged a successful attack, and the liberation of the city's Protestant garrison as a memorial to his friend, more glorious than the one Weston had not allowed him to build. On 24 August Secretary Conway told Laud that the king intended sending the fleet into battle under the command of Robert Bertie, Earl of Lindsey, and the bishop was to see the prayers were said for its success in every church throughout the land.[18]

In view of Lindsey's abilities as a leader, the king's recourse to the Almighty was particularly necessary and especially unproductive. Even though the expedition had been ready to sail since the middle of July, when summer gales had swept away the harbour boom leaving La Rochelle open for relief, by early September when the French had repaired and strengthened the boom, Charles had still to prod Lindsey into action. On 3 September he told the admiral how displeased he was that his ships were still swinging at anchor in harbour, and ordered all officers back on board by nine the next morning.[19] Three hours later he arrived in Portsmouth and gave the troops 'a gracious speech', promising their arrears in pay, to which some heckled demanding Felton's pardon. In spite of the king's fine words, fine promises and a fine wind, Lindsey's fleet remained at anchor for three more days until 6 September, when with words and promises forgotten, and wind almost gone, they set sail to make a tardy passage across the Bay of Biscay.[20]

After a brush with four Dunkirk pirates, the fleet of 100 ships carrying 5,000 men arrived off La Rochelle on 10 September. They waited five days before making a half-hearted sally on the boom and coastal batteries, during which the English lost six men, the French about forty. The next day's attack was even less vigorous, for even though the English launched fire ships, all of which missed, not a single life was lost on either side. Lindsey withdrew six miles to sea, returning on 13 September to make his last futile assault on La Rochelle. A week later, as the anchored English armada watched through their telescopes, the 4,000 survivors of La Rochelle's 15,000 strong garrison surrendered, the city's horses, dogs, cats and most of its rats, all eaten. On 1 November Lindsey set sail for home braving the winter gales that two days afterwards once more smashed the harbour boom.[21]

Charles's initial reaction to the shambles at La Rochelle was very different to that of previous military disasters – perhaps because Buckingham was not involved. When in the middle of October he received a very pessimistic dispatch from Lindsey, Charles called the privy council for urgent discussions, and the next day commanded the admiral that La Rochelle must be saved, even if it meant heavy British casualties – the honour of the nation and the distress of the church demanded no less. On Lindsey's return to England Charles told him to come to court immediately. Yet the admiral's disgrace, if it was one, did not last for long. In spite of highly critical reports from junior officers that 'his councils of war were rather tumults than councils, when everyone spoke and nothing was done,' the king was more inclined to blame the captains than the commander, and within a couple of years had made Lindsey a Knight of the Bath and a privy councillor.[22]

In one regard, however, Charles's reaction to the failure at La Rochelle was different to those at Cadiz and Ré. He did not order the survivors to remain with the colours, but immediately demobilized them, paying them off with money or promissory notes, and issued a proclamation on 15 November that they were to return to their homes directly without begging. Even though Charles told the Huguenot leader, Rohan, that he would never abandon the Protestant cause, the king's 'never' did not last long. In January 1629 he sent Rohan a letter dismissing the loss of La Rochelle as 'the fortune of war'.[23]

Buckingham's death sent many scrambling for the fruits of office. Lord Salisbury hoped to become Master of the Horse. The Earls of Sussex and Holland both vied to be made Constable of Windsor.[24] The panic among the late duke's clients was especially frantic. Sir John Hippisley sought the Keepership of Bushey Park for life, while, more accommodatingly, Sir James Bagg wrote that he would take away sinecure going, no matter how humble.[25] Even Bishop Williams, banished in disgrace to Lincoln, tried his luck, requesting the Stewardship of Westminster, a suit that so outraged the king that he had Conway write expressing his extreme displeasure.[26] Every attempt to loot Buckingham's political estate angered Charles. 'Let not the duke's enemies seek to catch at any of his offices,' he warned, 'for they will find themselves deceived.' When Sir Ralph Clare and Sir William Crofts (who had attacked Buckingham in the last parliament) tried, they were expelled from court.[27] On the other hand, Charles was gracious to those such as Cambridge University who approached him with sufficient deference asking whom they might appoint to replace their late chancellor.[28]

Dislike it as he might, Charles could not stop the upheaval that inevitably followed the death of the man who had dominated politics for a decade. By the end of the year he let Archbishop Abbot back into the privy council, and restored Arundel to favour, personally showing the earl around his art collection.[29] But their return was more apparent than real. Arundel's influence remained confined to diplomatic missions that were as splendid as they were empty, while Laud, although recently promoted Bishop of London, was treated as if he were already Primate of All England.[30]

The minister who benefited the most from Buckingham's passing was Richard Weston. As Chancellor of the Exchequer he and the favourite had been enemies for years, because he opposed the heavy costs of the duke's military adventures. Buckingham delayed Weston's promotion to the Lord Treasurership until July 1628 – an elevation that some mistook as a sign that the king was losing confidence in the favourite. Immediately on assuming office Weston sent the Lord Admiral a memorandum protesting in the strongest terms about the cost of the La Rochelle fleet. The two seemed certain for a showdown, which Weston must have surely lost.[31] But as it was, Felton not only saved Weston's career, but advanced it rapidly. The Lord Treasurer's influence waxed so fast that he persuaded

Charles to appoint Sir Thomas Wentworth Lord President of the North, make Dudley Carleton Secretary of State, and Conway President of the Council. Four months after Buckingham's death an ambassador wrote home that Weston had grown so powerful that 'no one dares oppose him'.[32]

Considering that, on Buckingham's death, the king declared that he intended to handle his business by himself, ruling without a chief minister and letting no man inherit the Duke's influence. Weston's spectacular rise was particularly ironic, though perhaps obscured by the fact that it took place during months of political confusion, intensified by the prospect of a parliamentary session. Immediately after the duke's removal Charles displayed uncharacteristic vigour, responding to petitions, personally drafting many letters, even reviewing drafts of city charters. In mid-September it was said that the king had done more work in a fortnight than the duke had in a quarter.[33] But Charles sowed his energies in stony ground: lacking roots to survive the winter they withered away. The king appointed commissions to deal with such matters as the admiralty, prize disputes, and diplomatic affairs, and left more and more business to the bi- or tri-weekly meetings of the privy council, which he attended but once a month.[34] By Christmas Charles was his usual indolent self: Sir David Murray noted there was 'no great change' for 'the ghost doth yet walk'.[35]

Murray was writing on 22 December to Carlisle to persuade him to return from the British embassy in The Hague to try and counter Weston's growing influence, because like many others he was deeply worried by the prospect of the parliament due to meet in three and a half weeks time.

This session had in fact already been delayed. Less than a month after the duke's murder Charles told the privy council that he intended postponing the reopening of parliament from 20 October to 20 January 1629. In spite of objections that this would dissipate the good will created by the duke's removal (an argument hardly calculated to appeal to the distraught monarch) the next day, 1 October, Charles issued a proclamation putting his decision into effect.[36] He had little love for parliament, especially the Commons, whose Petition of Right he blamed for his friend's death. He had read Felton's confession that 'nothing but the remonstrance', motivated him and that George Willoughby, a scrivener from Holborn, admitted selling Felton a copy of it, which he had sewn into the brim of his hat so if he were taken dead no one could doubt his motives.[37] In addition to being virtually accessories to murder, Charles saw many members of parliament as bent on destroying the whole fabric of society, tearing apart that great chain of being which as a young man he had come so painfully to accept, and thus so ardently to espouse.

A sad pressage to the danger to this land
When lower strive to get the upper hand,

When Prince and Peers to Peasants must obey,
When laymen must their teachers teach the way.

Thus wrote Richard Corbet. Charles surely agreed with these sentiments
for a year later he made the poet Bishop of Oxford.[38]

As the day for the opening of parliament approached the government
started to consider tactics, particularly with regard to the critical issue of
tonnage and poundage. Of the king's minister Weston, more than any
other, welcomed a parliament, confident that it would confirm the crown's
prerogative to collect the customs and duties, something Charles had continued to do after June 1628, notwithstanding the strictures of the Petition
of Right. Naturally some citizens objected, citing the petition as grounds
for their refusal to pay. In September one delinquent, Richard Chamberlain,
a London merchant, even told the privy council that Muslim traders in
Turkey were better treated than Christian merchants in England: for this
impertinence, which bordered on blasphemy, he was imprisoned at the
king's pleasure. Chamberlain's outburst may have persuaded the king to
delay calling parliament to give himself time to counter such opposition,
build up support and plan tactics. On 27 November he told the privy
council that he anticipated that the Commons would attack the growing
power of recusants and Arminians, and that he was willing to concede by
purging the former from office and appointing a commission to investigate
the latter. In contrast to this realistic piece of contingency planning, Charles
adopted a rigid stance on the other important issue of tonnage and poundage. Those privy councillors who were also members of parliament were
to rush through a bill granting the king the right to collect the duties for
life. They were to stop all debate on the issue; and, if that did not work,
then the king would simply announce that he would permit no further
discussion. A fortnight later, as a part of his counciliatory tactics, the king
issued a proclamation ordering the arrest of Richard Smith, Bishop of
Chalcedon, and underground leader of England's Catholics.[39] In addition
he suppressed Richard Montagu's extreme polemic, *An Appeal to Caesar*.
Even so, these concessions were not enough: some tried to have Carlisle
recalled from The Hague to counter Weston; others believed that nothing
but 'the greatest dexterity and display of magnanimity' could placate the
Commons' 'peccant humours'. Yet Charles did not seem to worry that his
concessions had won little ground, announcing in December that he would
ride in person to Westminster on 20 January to open parliament.[40]

The opening session took place in an atmosphere of such cordiality that
Charles's self-confidence seemed well founded. 'Yesterday the parliament
met,' wrote Carleton to Carlise (who was still stuck in Holland) 'and by
the good appearance of both houses, and a quiet and peaceable beginning,
we promise ourselves a very happy proceeding.'[41] There were, of course,
thorns in this bed of roses. A few members raised the matter of tonnage

and poundage – a briar that no matter how hard the government pruned, seemed to grow back again quickly. John Selden, the distinguished jurist, brought up the case of Savage, the lunatic, who had died from the brutal punishment ordered by Star Chamber. Once more the crown seemed to be losing the initiative. So on 24 January Charles felt that he had to call both the Lords and Commons to the Banqueting Hall at Whitehall to explain that he had not collected tonnage and poundage on the strength of the prerogative alone, but during an emergency as a gift. He was confident that his loving people lacked 'time, not the will', to formally vote the duties. He was sure that they would now pass them so that 'this session, beginning with confidence one towards another ... may end with a perfect good understanding.'[42] His 'honeyed words' went down very well. As they left the Banqueting Hall several members remarked what a difference the duke's death had made.[43] The king's performance was especially remarkable for he had just heard that his nephew, Henry, the Prince Palatine and heir to his brother-in-law's lost lands, had been drowned in a boating accident in Holland. Two days later Charles followed up his Banqueting Hall speech by sending the speaker a request that the Commons pass tonnage and poundage as soon as possible.

At this juncture Charles's plans, so carefully contrived the previous December, fell apart. Not unexpectedly when Secretary Coke introduced the bill legitimizing tonnage and poundage, Francis Rous, a leading radical, countered with a vehement attack on Arminianism. Instead of falling back on the agreed tactic of offering to purge papists and investigate Arminians, Charles did not budge an inch. Thus he lost control of the Commons, who spent the next two weeks debating the state of religion, after which they passed a resolution endorsing the Elizabethan settlement and pet-itioned the king to proclaim a national day of prayer and fasting 'to almighty God for the preservation of His true religion'. Charles, less convinced than the Commons that God was in fact an Englishman who regularly attended His parish church to hear long sermons on the dangers of popery, agreed to this request with well-publicized reluctance, urging them to forsake empty gestures and vote taxes. The Lower House did not take the king's advice until 19 February, when they debated tonnage and poundage. Unfortunately the recent imprisonment for refusing to pay these duties of John Rolle, a London merchant – who was also a member of parliament, and thus, many of his colleagues protested, was privileged from arrest – made the tax issue even more divisive. The Commons called the customs men who arrested Rolle to the bar of the House. Three days later Charles defended his officers' actions by sending Coke to tell the Com-mons that they acted on his instructions. To underscore the point later that day he ordered all customs officers to rigorously collect the duties and throw any who refused to pay into jail 'till they conform themselves'.[44]

Here Charles made his second mistake. Instead of sacrificing a minion or two, he turned a molehill into a mountain without the resources to win in the Commons. While he may have been determined to protect loyal servants, no matter how humble, and resented the Commons' attack in the prerogative, he had in fact already decided on a show-down. On 15 February, four days before the customs men appeared at the bar, he told the privy council that he was going to collect every tax and duty that his father had enjoyed.[45] Admittedly a determined stand on the tax issue was part of the tactics the government agreed on just before Christmas, yet the king refused to implement the second part of the same scheme, religious concessions, that might have gained enough votes to win the first. Why Charles did so is hard to fathom. Perhaps the answer lies in his deep-rooted antipathy to concessions, or else he lost interest in domestic affairs. In late February he sent Sir Thomas and Sir Henry Vane on separate missions to the Continent, and formed a council of ministers to consider future military options and the state of the nation's defences.[46] The king's order of 25 February, that parliament be adjourned to 2 March, seems to support the latter explanation.

Certainly Charles hoped time would allow passions to cool, for, as the Venetian ambassador noted, the debate on religion and taxes 'generates very great rancour, and there is a great fear of a rupture.'[47] On 2 March, the king told parliament to adjourn for yet another week, probably to let tempers cool still more. If this was his intention it had the opposite effect. Already irritated by the expense and bother of having to wait in London for weeks, the Commons received news of another delay as they were about to reassemble. They exploded. Several members greeted the Speaker's announcement that it was His Majesty's pleasure that the House be adjourned until 9 March with shouts of 'No! No!' Others, mainly court dependents, got up to leave, as did the Speaker, whom Denzil Holles and Benjamin Valentine forcibly held struggling in his chair so debate could continue. Sir John Eliot introduced a sweeping resolution condemning papists and Arminians, as well as all who had paid or collected tonnage and poundage. After a vicious attack on Weston – during all of which the Speaker was desperately trying to rise, and royal messengers were hammering against the chamber's locked doors, the key having been secretly pocketed – the Commons passed Eliot's motion. Finally the doors burst open to let the members – some proud, others frightened, and most convinced that they had gone beyond the point of no return – leave for home, before closing for what very quickly seemed to be for ever.[48] As far as Charles was concerned the events of 2 March were not so much a turning point as the last straw. Public opinion seemed to agree with the king. Even Simonds D'Ewes, the radical Protestant member of parliament, called 2 March 'the most gloomy, sad and most dismal day for England that happened in five hundred years last past,' blaming it all on 'diverse fiery spirits in the House of Commons'.[49]

Immediately after the fracas the privy council met in long and hard debate, with the king in constant attendance. They were divided. Lord Keeper Coventry, and the Earl of Manchester, Lord Privy Seal, urged moderation. Weston, the Commons' *bête noire*, advanced strong measures, convinced the House's outrageous behaviour was not just the work of a few desperate subversives, but was the prelude to revolution. By 4 March Charles endorsed Weston's uncompromising stance. Since at the time the king was particularly concerned about the Palatinate this may have reflected a desire to oppose appeasement at home as well as abroad. It was widely rumoured that he intended expelling Coventry and Manchester from the privy council. That evening the king arrested the leaders of the parliamentary opposition, and two days later ordered the imprisonment of the merchants who were suing for the restoration of goods seized for the non-payment of tonnage and poundage.[50]

Charles made his most dramatic move on 10 March, when, dressed in his fullest regalia, he rode to the House of Lords. He told the peers he had never addressed them on 'so unpleasant an occasion'. None the less he thanked their lordships for their support. He explained that 'the seditious carriage' of certain members of the Commons had forced him to dissolve parliament, and that he was determined to punish 'those vipers', so 'his loving and faithful nobility' could continue to enjoy his 'favour and protection'.[51] Charles omitted the customary courtesy of inviting the Lower House to the upper chamber to hear his oration because he wanted to demonstrate that his quarrel was with the Commons and not his loyal peers. So the members of the Lower House – be they vipers or virtuous – had to read the crown's case in the proclamation the government rushed into print that evening, and that quickly ran to three editions. It began by explaining that although 'princes are not bound to give account of their actions but to God alone,' His Majesty was most graciously going to do so.[52] He reviewed the deplorable record of the past parliament, explaining that its failure was largely responsible for 'the miserably effected estate of those parts of the reformed religion in Germany, France and other parts of Christendom'. The Petition of Right did not apply to tonnage and poundage, which had been voted to all monarchs for the past 184 years. During the second parliamentary session 'some malevolent person, like emperics and lewd artists', tried to expand the House's jurisdiction by summoning the sheriffs of London and customs officers to the bar, and on 2 March they 'most contemptuously disobeyed' his orders to adjourn for a week. Thus he had no alternative but dissolve parliament. In future, Charles promised, he would continue to 'maintain the ancient and just rights and liberties of our subjects', as well as the established religion. He would encourage trade, and with the help of both Almighty God and 'all wise and discreet men' bring England to unprecedented peace, prosperity and happiness.

The underlying theme of the king's declaration was that a conspiracy of a few 'ill-effected persons' has caused all England's problems. Throughout his life Charles found conspiracies comforting explanations for his difficulties, and satisfyingly simple grounds for their solution. Almost by definition conspirators were bad men, which implied that those against whom they plotted must be good ones, and the mass of the people were at best fundamentally loyal, or at worst unwittingly duped. But once the rotten apples were removed, be they through the impeachment of Lord Bristol, or (a decade later) the arrest of the Five Members, all would soon be well again. Thus Charles went to great lengths to punish the eleven men he believed responsible for the 2 March fracas. He took extraordinary pains in drawing up the charges on which they were arraigned before the privy council on 18 March. Attorney General Heath wrote the first draft after long consultations with the king, who reviewed it and the seven further drafts, two of which he sent to the judges for their comments, before he was satisfied with the indictment. Charles was convinced his case was rock solid. 'Can any Privilege of the house warrant a tumultuous proceeding?' he annotated the charges in his own hand.[53]

Over the next two months most of the accused recanted and were released. But John Eliot remained obdurate on his cell in the Tower, where he died three years later.[54] Charles's famous (or infamous) retort that Eliot's body should not be returned for burial in his beloved Cornwall, but in the parish where he died, has been taken as a sign of vindictiveness so mean that it extended to the grave. Yet Charles blamed Eliot for another grave – Buckingham's. Eliot, who had once been the duke's friend and protégé, had repaid his patron's generosity by passing the Petition of Right – the trigger to Felton's insane deed. Charles believed Eliot to be a 'man desperate in mind and fortune', who compounded his offence by trying to turn his just imprisonment into a martyrdom, and by refusing to admit the slightest wrongdoing: in Eliot lurked the danger of a kindred spirit.

But rather than face the threat to his sovereignty that Eliot represented, Charles was far happier to withdraw. As one diplomat noted after watching him ride home on 10 March, having just explained to the House of Lords why he had dissolved his third parliament in less than four years, the king seemed 'in good spirits, as if he had freed himself from the yoke'.[55]

# X

# A FAMILY AT 'FULL PEACE AND TRANQUILLITY'

After the failure of his first three parliaments and the murder of the Duke of Buckingham, Charles spent most of his time and energies involved in the world of his court. Such a move should not be surprising, for he was merely repeating his behaviour after the previous major bereavements in his life, Prince Henry's death and Princess Elizabeth's departure for Germany, when he withdrew to the security of the humdrum routine of life within his own household.

Charles's court was not, of course, a new institution. Even before he became king he had a court of sorts, which grew larger and more significant as his father's health waned. All kings have courts, though in many ways they are extensions of the ruler's own family: the place where he can feel at home, manipulating the courtiers' activities and environment to reflect his fantasies, aspirations, anxieties and policies.

While most of those outside the royal favour (who in the early seventeenth century were often described as 'the country') thought of all the king's adherents as 'the court', in fact this description was far too broad. Certainly Charles drew a line between his social and governmental life, and the people who played a part in each. Thus the Master of Revels was a member of the court, while the privy council was part of the government, even though both might have offices in Whitehall Palace. Similarly Archbishop Laud or Lord Treasurer Weston were royal ministers, just as much as the Earl of Carlisle or the Marquis of Hamilton were essentially courtiers. However such distinctions were not always obvious; Charles employed Hamilton on missions abroad, and asked Laud to christen his children. In the 1630s, when Henrietta Maria and her court faction tried to influence foreign policy, the lines of demarcation became particularly blurred. Yet as far as Charles was concerned the distinction between courtiers and ministers remained a valid and reasonable one. It was not just a parameter within which he operated, but one about which his ministers frequently complained.

A court can be a public place, in which most of the action occurs with the curtains open: spectacle and show teach the audience their monarch's virtues; poets celebrate them; playwrights praise them; painters adorn them; and sculptors preserve them in perpetuity. In such a court great matters of state may be debated at the banqueting table; political factions founded on real issues may clash during the minuet, with the choice of a partner for the quadrille becoming perhaps the sign for the selection of an ally in a bloody war. The first Queen Elizabeth had such a court. In it everything seemed open for public view – except what was going on in the monarch's mind. In contrast Charles's court was a private place, where, paradoxically, just as the openness of Elizabeth's preserved her enigmatic secrets, so the closedness of Charles's revealed much about the king's innermost being. In essence, Charles's court was a controllable place: he could decide whom to admit and whom to exclude, which painter to commission, and which dramatists to patronize. In these decisions he selected those things that pleased him, for it was its controllability, that key attribute, which made the court a reflection of the king's most basic desires. Within the court Charles played out his family life. He did not bring up his children in the usual give and take of the daily domestic round, but in the structured world of the court where contact between child and parents (for instance as in arranging the sitting for a family group by Van Dyck, see Plate 3) was in effect an occasion. Again, much of his marriage was lived out in the world of the court: even his squabbles in bed with his wife became grist for diplomatic dispatches, and, surely, well-bred titters. Even the king's meals were taken in court, being served in public with so much ceremony and deference that Charles hardly ever ate warm food (see Plate 4).

All this does not mean that the court was completely separated from the world outside. The boundaries between the two were far from watertight. For instance, Charles carried over his concern for courtly decorum and modes of language into every parish in the land by allowing Robert Lesley, a courtier and gentleman of the bedchamber, to fine all 'loose and wicked persons', who swore contrary to statute 21 of James I.[1] None the less the court remained isolated from the mainstream, which for Charles was one of its chief attractions, because it made the court the comfortable centre of his being. If his wife's confessors and confidants played political games that were sometimes irritating, though more often amusing, at least they were not going to stage another 2 March, or question his divinely anointed authority. Charles envisaged the court as a household, a little common-wealth, in which every member knew his proper place, all working together for the general good under his benign leadership. Indeed, if his court was at peace, so too must be the country. As John Webster had put it in *The Duchess of Malfi*:[2]

> In seeking to reduce both State and People
> To a fix'd Order, their judicious King
> Begins at home.

And if half a decade after Charles dismissed his third turbulent parliament, someone had asked a member of the court how well the king had managed to achieve his goals, the courtier might reply (as Sir John Goring did to Secretary Coke in 1633) 'Never was there private family more at full peace and tranquillity than in this glorious kingdom, for we hear not of the least disorder therein from one end thereof to the other.'[3]

Foreigners agreed. After Rubens first came to England as an envoy working for the King of Spain, and was presented to Charles at Greenwich Palace, he wrote home, 'All the leading nobles here live on a most sumptuous scale and spend more lavishly. . . . Splendour and liberality are the first considerations of this court.' The painter was most impressed by the quality of life. 'In this place I find none of the crudeness that one might expect from a place so remote from Italian elegance.'[4]

A vast warren of servants supported this upstairs world of elegance. The household below stairs provided basic services, such as food, drink, laundry, cleaning, heat and light, which the chamber delivered with the appropriate decorum. That the former had a little over 300 members, and the latter was twice as large suggests the relative importance given to style as opposed to substance. The wardrobe looked after the royal family's clothes. Fifty-eight gentlemen pensioners stood in ceremonial attendance on the king, though they do not seem to have the influence on Charles as they had on his predecessors. There were 210 yeomen warders to provide the king's bodyguard, while 263 members of the royal stables supported his incessant hunting and travelling. The queen had 172 servants in her own household, and by the end of the 1630s 200 more worked in those of the royal children. In all the household employed between 1,8000 and 2,600 people; with their dependants they would amount to the population of a town almost the size of Exeter or Norwich.[5]

Supporting what was in effect the seventh or eighth largest community in the realm was extremely expensive. For instance, in 1630, the daily ration allowance for the king alone was £25 5s 4d which would have kept 1,962 people for one year. Since Charles stayed slim one must assume that the victuals intended for the royal palate lined his servants' bellies, as well as their purses.[6] In all the cost of the royal household was immense. Between 1631 and 1635 it averaged £260,000 a year, or some 40 per cent of the king's total income, much of the money being wasted or embezzled.[7] These expenditures would have been even larger had not by long standing tradition the crown been able to requisition horses and wagons and supplies, paying for them at well below the market price. Naturally this privilege, known as purveyance, did as little to endear the monarchy to those who were forced to subsidize its extravagances as it did to win the support of those uninvited to sup at the royal trough. Efforts to control waste were mostly ineffective because too many other people had a vested interest in enjoying His Majesty's largesse, particularly Her Majesty. Henrietta Maria strenuously opposed any attempt to curb her own or her friends' extravagances. 'We have no resolution of anything,' Sir Thomas Edmondes, Treasurer of the Household, complained in 1633 after much talk about the need for reform and economy, 'but from day to day the same is deferred to the continual raising of our charge.'[8]

Another reason why the costs of the court were so great was that the king had to support a number of royal residences. The largest – and most ramshackle – was at Whitehall. Spreading over some twenty acres, its fifty-three buildings and courtyards, which ranged from Inigo Jones's Banqueting Hall to the Small Beer Buttery, were built in a confused variety of styles, few of which impressed visitors from abroad. Through this hodge-podge ran a public thoroughfare, that was bridged by the King Street and Holbein Gates connecting the two parts of the palace. The northern part contained facilities to keep the court amused and healthy. As a young man Charles had ridden in the tiltyard, and he and his brother had played real tennis in the adjacent court with its sagging rope for a net, and gallery walls and roof on to which unreturnable balls might be lobbed. If rain prevented Charles and his friends from playing bowls – a game of which he became particularly fond as he grew older – on the greens adjacent in St James's Park, then they could come indoors and play in the palace's alley. Nearby, a few steps down a narrow lane, was the cockpit where they enjoyed private dramatic performances. The eastern section of the larger part of the palace south of the street was devoted to the below stairs department – kitchens, baker, cider house, coal yard and surveyor's office, with the stables at the palace's farthest limits in case the wind shift away from its prevailing westerly direction. Adding to the fragrance (which the court normally donated to the City of London) were the numerous shops, mainly fish stands, that squatters had built about the palace walls.[9] At the opposite west end were the king's own private apartments, grouped around a courtyard known as the Preaching Place because of the stone pulpit in its middle. On the south side of the courtyard was the guard house where the yeomen warders stood duty, and to its left the presence chamber, in which Charles received foreign dignitaries. In the southwest corner were the king's withdrawing room, privy chamber and bedroom, and on the west side the privy gallery along which privy councillors might stroll, enjoying the views of the formal private gardens that stretched almost to Westminster Hall, whenever meetings in the adjacent council chambers became too tedious. On the northern side of the Preaching Place as the gem of Whitehall, the Banqueting Hall designed in the new Palladian style by Inigo Jones, the finest and most modern building in the palace, perhaps the land, where Charles staged the court's most important occasions.[10]

Whitehall Palace was built on the north bank of the Thames between Westminster, where the law courts and parliament sat, and the City of London, centre of the nation's trade and wealth. From the queen's apartments, built just south of the king's, could be seen barges carrying wool to the Spanish Netherlands, or importing exotic luxuries from every corner of a rapidly growing world. Along the palace's northern wall Welsh drovers herded their sheep and cattle on the last mile of the long trail to be slaughtered at Smithfield to feed London's rapidly growing population. From Whitehall Steps a wherry might be hired to quickly carry one across the river to Lambeth, where Archbishop Laud had his palace, or, for a few pennies more, less than a mile farther downstream to the stews and play-houses of the south bank, where bawds and bards could ply their trades outside London's city limits. In many respects Whitehall Palace stood at the hub of the kingdom.

Charles had other palaces in both London and the rest of his realm. He could walk across the part to St James's Palace, built by Henry VIII, and the residence of the heir to the throne. Henrietta Maria had her private Roman Catholic chapel there, even though Somerset, or Denmark, House, situated on the north bank about a mile downstream from Whitehall, was her formal residence. The latter was also used for state funerals and to house visiting dignitaries. Twenty miles downstream lay Greenwich Palace, another of the queen's official residences, with superb sculpture gardens set before rolling parklands that dramatically rose to the hill where Charles's son was to build England's first observatory. From Greenwich Palace thousands of ships, large and small, could be seen sailing up and down the Thames, a reminder of England's growing seaborne might. Perhaps it was this sight that had made Greenwich one of Queen Elizabeth's favourite residences. By Charles's reign the palace had become so dilapi-dated that it had to be pulled down and replaced by the gem of a house that Inigo Jones built for the queen. Half a dozen miles upstream, in the opposite direction from London to Greenwich, was Richmond Palace, with its fantastic onion-shaped towers, and then an hour or so barge ride father on lay Hampton Court, the extravagant folly of the hapless Cardinal Wolsey. It would take the rowers at least half a day more to reach the royal castle and palace at Windsor, started by William the Conqueror, and now home of Charles's favourite order of chivalry, the Knights of the Garter. Although as a young man he and Buckingham had often swum on summer evenings in the Thames between the castle and the college that Henry VI had founded for the education of poor but deserving boys at Eton, during the 1630s the king spent little time at Windsor. He was even more negligent of Nonsuch, a decaying pile much favoured by the Tudors, a day's ride south of the capital, preferring to hunt on the other side of the Thames. If Charles left London after breakfast he could, even with time off to chase a stag or two, be in Theobalds, the palace originally built by Sir Robert Cecil in Hertfordshire, by supper time, and by noon the next day arrive at Royston, his father's favourite hunting retreat, set at the foot of some rolling hills that provided some of the best sport in

England. Northeast from Royston, across some flat country (known appropriately enough as Six Mile Bottom) the king could hunt his way to Newmarket, which, with Oatlands, in Surrey, he probably considered his most comfortable private home, for he spent as much time in each as he could.

If Charles grew tired of his own houses, he could always visit those of his subjects. In the summer of 1634, for instance, he spent six weeks hunting in Leicestershire, Northamptonshire and Huntingdonshire, staying at Hinchingbrooke two days, Althorp five, Belvoir four, and then across the valley to Holdenby for three and Castle Ashby for four more. From 4–19 August Charles and Henrietta Maria forsook their pleasures to pay a state visit to Nottingham. The corporation spent £200, a third of their annual revenue, on the occasion, cleaning the streets, painting and generally doing up buildings. Their efforts were more cosmetic than structural: the house they chose to store the royal wardrobe collapsed under the weight of the king's and queen's clothes.[11] Far grander (and much safer) was the entertainment the Earl of Newcastle gave when Charles and Henrietta visited his seat, Bolsover Castle, in Derbyshire. It was said to have cost £10,000 and been attended by gentry from all over the north of England.[12]

Charles's court – or at least part of it – was in constant motion from one hunting lodge to another, from university to palace, to magnate's stately home, and then, as likely or not, back to a hunting lodge. The court's perambulations in 1637, of which only the highlights can be mentioned, were fairly typical. It saw the New Year in at Whitehall, and then moved to Greenwich to avoid the plague. On 17 March the queen was in St James's Palace where she had her third daughter, Anne. By May she was back at Greenwich, again to avoid the plague that thrived in the capital's noxious air. Charles was off in the country hunting, Henrietta Marie again pregnant being unable to accompany her husband on his usual summer progress. In June Charles was at Theobalds, back to Greenwich to see his wife in early July, and then away again to Havering and Oatlands. He returned to London for a wedding on 13 August, and rode via Oatlands for a few days hunting in the New Forest, before coming back to Oatlands. September saw him at Hampton Court and Greenwich. Over a period of three months Charles moved house twenty-seven times, staying at each an average of three days. He spent the first week of October in Windsor, where he presided over the Garter ceremony, before sailing to Deptford to launch the *Sovereign of the Seas*, and then back to Hampton Court for a while before returning to Whitehall for the Christmas season.

Such journeying was usual: it was expected of the monarch. From time immemorial English kings had been virtual nomads, travelling throughout their domains. But for Charles there was a difference. Unlike, say, Queen Elizabeth, who used her progresses to show herself to her people and so win their loyalty, Charles hated such publicity stunts. His official visits became rarer and rarer. As he travelled the king devoted an increasing amount of his time to private pursuits, such as hunting. The royal party seemed to pass over the land like a swarm of locusts in pursuit of game, moving on once an area had been swept clean, going from house to house, palace to hunting lodge, with the minimum of display. When the king made an official visit the results were mixed: the Mayor of Northampton had to fine four aldermen £2 apiece for refusing to attend the 1637 state visit.

Hunting was the king's chief recreation, providing a restrained and unemotional man with a headstrong emotional outlet. Charles was a fine judge of horseflesh, an accomplished, though uncharacteristically reckless, rider. Once, for instance, he rode at full tilt into a bog, the green sward of which he mistook for a firm verdant meadow, and though he nearly drowned, borrowed some dry clothes from a courtier to continue the chase. Ambassadors and ministers frequently complained that they could not talk to the king because he was out hunting. Nothing got in the way of his love of the chase. He ordered enclosures at Godminster pulled down, and rabbit conies at Newmarket filled in lest they break his horses' legs and their riders' necks.[13]

Compared to the hurly-burly of the hunt, life at Charles's court was remarkably decorous. One of his first acts on becoming king had been to banish 'the fools and bawds, mimics and catamites' that frequented his father's palaces. This edict reassured Lucy Hutchinson, a hostile witness, that the new king was 'temperate, chaste and serious'. Charles went on to appoint a committee of leading peers to examine court etiquette. In March 1629 they recommended that the court – already the most formal in Europe – become even more so, particularly in the ceremony to be observed at the entrance and exit of the king and queen.[14] To ensure that all about the sovereign behaved with the proper respect and dignity, the court's regulations were to be read to them at least twice a year. The knight marshal was to see that no tippling houses, shacks or tents were erected alongside the palace walls, and to arrest all 'rogues, beggars, idle and loose people' in the vicinity. Such large, opulent and chaotic establishments as the king's residences naturally attracted criminals. As a deterrent the knight marshal was to hang those arrested and condemned by the special Court of the Royal Palaces outside the main gate. To protect the king's person porters controlled access to the court. No one was to come in carrying 'pistols, daggers, cudgels, or other unfit weapons', the regulations declared and all admitted were to wear the 'gowns or fit habits answerable to their degrees'. By eight each morning the gentlemen ushers were to inspect the presence chamber to see that it was 'clean and sweet'. By nine the servants should have cleaned the royal apartments, and the gentlemen pensioners, carrying their axes 'clean and bright', be standing by to attend the king in his chamber. By ten the carvers, cupbearers and waiters must be ready to serve the king's dinner, which, like most of Charles's meals, was a state ceremony so important in the crown's public relations that Charles even had it painted (see Plate 4). Waiters presented the king dishes on bended knee, Charles being the only monarch in Europe who insisted on such obeisance. And so the regulations proceeded, appointing each hour of the king's day at court. No one was to appear in his presence booted or spurred. No one, except barons, privy councillors or gentlemen of the bedchamber, was to come into the king's private rooms, and all were to keep their proper stations decreed by rank as the sovereign entered of left the royal chapel.

As these regulations demonstrated, the king was the centre of the court. He was, to borrow Louis XIV's famous phrase, the sun around which courtiers, though not the country, revolved. When the sun set the court lost its light and warmth. It is 'a dull and dead place here', one courtier wrote, 'when both the king and queen are absent and on progress.'[15]

For Charles and Henrietta the dull and dead times were when they were parted. The court was the place where they played out the public role of their marriage, the special nature of which gave the court much of its particular character.

Buckingham's death had helped improve relations between the two, as had the ending of the war with France, which was in effect a consequence of the duke's demise. A year later in August 1629, and two months after the signing of a peace with Paris, Charles signified that his relations with his wife had improve by granting her several parks and manors, including Oatlands, Greenwich, Holbeach, Holdenby, Grantham and Boston. The following June he ordered that she have the same rights to wardships and appointing vicars to church livings as his mother had enjoyed.[16] Since their first major quarrel, months after their marriage, involved her insulting his mother's status, the significance of this gesture goes beyond mere dowry details.

When, half a decade earlier, Henrietta Maria first crossed the Channel she was an immature Catholic Frenchwoman with little love for Protestant England. Her mother, her confessor and her pope had charged her with looking after her new Catholic subjects. That her husband was fighting her brother to support a bunch of heretical rebels was particularly galling. With the surrender of La Rochelle, however, an obstacle between the king and queen disappeared. Over the years Henrietta Maria, slowly at first, and then with some grace, became more English, gradually developing a fluency for the language, and falling out of sympathy for her old country. When in 1631 her brother, Louis XIII, once again forced her mother, Marie de Medici, into exile Henrietta Maria was very angry, vowing 'to be altogether independent of France'. As a result she became increasingly dependent on her husband. In 1629 she had cut short a visit to Tunbridge Wells to rush back to see Charles; she missed him.[17] When he was away in Scotland in 1633 for his coronation, she was reported 'sad in extremity', and there was little, her friends bemoaned, they could do to cheer her.[18] Three years later when the queen heard that Rochester Carr, a lunatic, had escaped from confinement in Lincolnshire, and was on his way to London gabbling that he was going to kill the king, she fainted; even after Carr had been reported captured she insisted in rushing to see that her husband was all right.[19] Years afterwards, as a widow exiled in France, Henrietta recalled the 1630s as the best years of her life: 'I was the happiest and most fortunate of queens, for not only has I every pleasure the heart could desire; I had a husband who adored me.'[20]

With that simplicity that complicated men so often have, Charles needed someone to love; someone on whom he could depend. His grandmother, Mary Queen of Scots, had such a need, as did his father, James I. After the duke's assassination Charles transferred these aspirations to his wife. The switch, however, posed a new problem. The parsimony of Charles and Henrietta Maria's sexual habits was fairly well recognized at the time. Not a whiff of scandal surrounded the king; the only vice John Milton ever managed to attribute to him being reading too much Shakespeare! Charles personally recoiled from such earthy virile types as Ben Jonson, censoring the least risqué passage from court masques and plays. If the king had affairs (and throughout English history there have always been many beautiful women ready to help their sovereign in this service) his puritan critics (with whom monarchs have been equally generously endowed) would surely have mentioned the fact, for as one early biographer wrote defending Charles's virtues, 'curiosity opens the closets and bedchambers of princes'. Henrietta Maria was equally above reproach. Her confessor, the best of all possible sources, reported that he was convinced that an impure thought had never crossed Her Majesty's mind.[21]

How then were these two restrained people to deal with the physical side of a marriage that produced nine children, and whose emotional depth and intensity waxed daily?

If the poetry and plays the king and queen patronized, and the culture of their court are any indication, then Charles and Henrietta Maria tried to resolve this dilemma through the artifice of courtly, or platonic, love. 'There is a love called Platonic Love that much sways there,' wrote James Howell in 1634. 'It is a love abstracted from all corporal, gross impressions and ideas of mind, not in any carnal fruction.' In his *Platonic Elegy* Thomas Randolph defined this love in poetic terms:[22]

> When essence meets with essence and souls join
> In mutual knots, that's the true nuptial twine.

In psychological terms courtly love has been defined as the repression of the id's physical side, and the compensatory exaggeration of its emotional basis. Courtly love is a non-adult, almost pre-adolescent stage in emotional development. Its practitioners find it hard to accept the transformation of the opposite sex from the pure loving, chaste and all-knowing parent, to that of the carnal, lusty, fallible, and dependent lover. Since the desired sexual object reminds them of the parent, they unconsciously punish their repressed incestuous drives, revelling in the hopelessness of their love. In sum, courtly love is based on an infantile fantasy rooted in the unconscious that is pitched into the reality of human sexuality. Like a film projected on to a screen it turns the reality of that screen, the wall, and even the whole cinema, into a new reality founded on its fantasies.[23]

As we have seen Charles's relations with his mother were distant, while those with his father were at first remote, and then became strained, being defined in terms of his friendship with James's favourite. When Charles first allowed his heterosexual lusts – or what he mistook for lust – free rein, the result has been a humiliating fiasco: the Infanta threatened to enter the chaste world of a nunnery rather than his bed.

Henrietta Maria's development had been equally strained. At her birth her father Henry IV announced that he would have given 100,000 crowns to the poor had she been a boy. Even so he was fond of his baby daughter, delighting in playing with her. His assassination when she was six months old meant that Henrietta Maria never really knew her father, and, as she grew up, no man ever became a substitute. Nannies and nuns raised her in a country château, with her father's legitimate and illegitimate children. The Carmelites gave her the limited education that she regretted in later life. She was seven when her brother Louis XIII had her mother's cronies and advisers murdered and her mother banished. She was eleven when she would have been betrothed to the Comte de Soissons had he, and her mother, not tried to raise a rebellion against her brother. She was a gawky girl of fifteen when she married Charles, being utterly incapable, in or out of bed, of pleasing a difficult husband.

In a court such as Charles and Henrietta Maria's, platonic love had advantages other than subduing 'the sensuous school of lust' that, according to Ben Jonson was fit 'for mere cattle and not men'. By repressing sex, so often a disruptive force, it brought order and stability to a court full of attractive, charming and frequently headstrong young men and women, many of whom were away from the restraints of their wives and families. 'So Love,' Jonson explained, 'emergent out of *Chaos* brought the world to light.'[24] Based on the French traditions of her father's and her brother's retinue, courtly love allowed the queen to surround herself with handsome young males without scandal. Indeed, as Thomas Carew, who was perhaps Charles's favourite poet, argued their love for the queen would strengthen the bonds of their own marriages and families, and thus those of society as a whole:[25]

> Thy sacred love shows us the path
> Of modesty and constant faith

Which makes the rude male satisfied
With one fair female by his side.

Thus courtly lovers might woo the queen without the necessity of trying
to seduce her, allowing her to reign over a party of admirers. Just as Queen
Elizabeth employed the ardours of her courtly lovers, such as Raleigh, and
even Burghley, to help a woman rule in a man's world, so Henrietta Maria
used her gallants to try and influence the king's policies. That she did so
to benefit Catholics was nicely appropriate, for through the use of the
adoration of the Blessed Virgin Mary to influence the Almighty they were,
in a sense, familiar with many of the emotions and techniques of courtly
love.[26] So courtly love forced the queen's suitors, like siblings, to compete
for the attention of a woman, who was not a mistress bestowing her
physical favours, but the mother figure – perfect and good, both kind and
cruel, sometimes a demanding figure of authority, other times a comfortable
source of solace, and always the person upon whom the courtly lover had,
so long as he wanted to play the game and enjoy its rewards, to depend.
In the ethos of courtly love then, the lady's husband was not the deceived
(and thus despised) cuckold but the respected, stern father-figure.

This role as mother-and-father figures was one that Charles and Henrietta Maria acted out with varying degrees of success. They did so within
their court, with their family, and to a much lesser extent towards their
people as a whole.

Charles and Henrietta Maria literally became expectant parents in about
November 1628 when they conceived their first child. Unfortunately the
following May, having been frightened by a couple of large dogs fighting
in her presence, Henrietta Maria miscarried. But twelve months later, at
about one in the afternoon on 29 May 1630 she gave birth to a healthy
son, the future Charles II. His father was genuinely delighted, though he
tried to do his best to hide his joy.[27] He rode in state to St Paul's cathedral
for a formal service of thanksgiving, gave the City of London £100 to
relieve plague victims, and ordered the privy council to drop charges
against the Earls of Bedford, Clare, and Somerset, as well as Sir Robert
Cotton, John Selden and Oliver St John.[28] All agreed that the bright star
that appeared over London at the baby's birth was an auspicious omen.
The child too could not have had a grander christening. Laud performed
the office on 27 June with the Duke and Duchess of Lennox and the
Marquis of Hamilton standing proxy for the infant's godparents, Frederick,
the Elector Palatine, Marie de Medici and Louis XIII.

The political and religious implications of having an heir to the throne
quickly became apparent. As soon as his son was born Charles told the
Capuchin Fathers that he did not want them to baptize the boy: notwithstanding the provisions of his marriage treaty, this was to be Laud's responsibility.[29] When Charles did try and fulfil part of the treaty by appointing

a Catholic, Lady Roxburgh, the heir's governess, his ministers objected, forcing him to engage Lady Dorset, a Protestant, instead. Having an heir to ensure the continuity of his line did much to strengthen the king politically. 'Welcome blest babe, whom God they father sent,' wrote Richard Corbet, the royalist Bishop of Oxford, 'to make him rich without a parliament!'[30]

At regular intervals Henrietta Maria continued to make her husband even richer. She had Mary in 1631, James in 1933, Elizabeth in 1635, Anne in 1637, Henry in 1639, Henrietta in 1644, and a second stillborn, Katherine.[31] To this growing brood Charles and Henrietta were distant figures, who like all kings and queens, had others to raise their offspring. Pot's portrait shows Charles standing woodenly at the other end of a long table, away from his wife and infant heir (see Plate 5). A child, as in Houckgeest's painting of the king and queen dining in public (see Plate 4), might be allowed to sit at table with them, but did so at a distance, displaying a reserve that exceeded even that of the parents. Better still, Charles hung the very charming group portrait of his children by Van Dyck above his breakfast table at Whitehall, where they could be easily seen without the possibility of being heard. While the king and queen gave their children none of the obvious traumas that James or Henry IV had inflicted on them, they were not particularly effective as parents. Charles II became a roué, whose two dozen bastards suggests that he did not inherit his parents' penchant for the platonic. In addition, he reacted against his father in other ways. Charles's execution and his own exile convinced him of the necessity for compromise and conciliation, of hiding his cards, playing his Catholic ace (or deuce) only on his deathbed. Paradoxically, Charles I had the opposite effect on his second son. Despising what he regarded as his father's weakness in treating with rebels (for James II was to young to remember much about the halcyon 1630s) he became even more inflexible, and so lost his throne in 1688. Thus the effect that Charles and Henrietta Maria had on their elder children came basically not from the part they played as parents during the years of the personal monarchy, as much as from the defeat and tribulations of the civil war.

Immediately after Buckingham's murder Charles took charge of the Villiers family. He made them several generous bequests, paid off Kate's debts, and brought George's children up with his own. The second Duke of Buckingham became an intimate friend of his eldest son.[32]

In much the same spirit Charles almost adopted Frederick's and Elizabeth's family during the exile in Holland, paying a most generous allowance for their support, which for instance totalled £18,000 in 1629.[33] On hearing of Frederick's death in 1632 Charles wrote to his nephews: 'I am truly sorry that I have lost more than you, for your have only changed your father, since I will not occupy the place of the deceased; but I have irreparably lost a brother.'[34] It was perhaps typical of Charles to write trying to console others by arguing that his bereavement was far greater than their own. But the letter did not seem to upset his nephews – who anyway were so dependent on English support that they could not afford the luxury of such an emotion. In 1635 Prince Charles Louis came to England to seek the king's help to restore his lost inheritance. As the embodiment of the Protestant cause – something for which most Englishmen were prepared to cheer ardently, even die, though not to be taxed – the prince was warmly welcomed. As he sailed into Dover harbour one navy gun crew were so transported with enthusiasm that they forgot to remove the ball from their cannon, and thus fired a salute that killed four men on the prince's ship, including two a couple of paces from him. In spite of the Prince Elector's pleas for help, this incident was the only time that British forces ever fired lived ammunition of his behalf, for Charles could not afford to send regular troops to intervene in the Thirty Years War. True, he did what he could. He wrote to Cardinal Richelieu supporting the suit of Prince Rupert, the Elector's younger brother, to marry the Duke of Rohan's daughter.[35] But without calling parliament to vote taxes the king's efforts could never amount to very much, and so in 1637 Charles Louis and Rupert returned home to The Hague empty handed.

Match-making was a familiar role for the king, who saw himself as a surrogate father. In 1636 he wrote to the Earl of Pembroke, who had just lost his wife, urging him to marry Dorothy Savage, one of the queen's maids of honour, and three years later to Lord Cork that his son should consummate his marriage to Lady Stafford's daughter before going to Europe on the Grand Tour, rather than merely going through the wedding ceremony.[36] Occasionally the king's suggestions did not have the intended effect. His letter on behalf of Sir John Suckling's suit of Sir Henry Willoughby's daughter so upset that young lady that she had another suitor, Sir John Digby, beat up Suckling, much to the amusement of the London gossips. Usually, however, Charles's requests were taken far more seriously. When he wrote to the recently widowed Lord Bath recommending the ubiquious Dorothy Savage, the earl had to get his friend Carlisle to explain to the king that he had no desire to remarry, and, even if he had, he could not afford to do so, having to find dowries for his many daughters.[37]

As well as serving as match-makers for their aristocratic dependants at court, Charles and Henrietta Maria acted *in loco parentis* for their servants. This role was normal: books of household government at the time likened the relationship between parents and children to that between master and servants. When some Dunkirk pirates captured Geoffrey Hudson, the queen's dwarf and pet, she was so distraught that one unfeeling courtier explained that the abduction had caused 'more upset at court than if they had lost a fleet'.[38] Charles took an especial interest in his servants' welfare. Normally he passed petitions addressed to him to the appropriate minister without recommendation, but those from servants, including the retired, he usually endorsed in their favour. As an extension of his paternal role in dealing with petitions Charles acted on behalf of poor widows, tried to settle family disputes, and sided with the elderly and infirm.

In sum the court was important in Charles's life as the sphere that, more than any other, he could control. Conversely the price that courtiers paid for the security their sovereign enjoyed was a high degree of insecurity. As Bishop Williams observed after being dismissed from office. 'A cashiered courtier is an Almanack of the Last Year, remembered by nothing but the Great Eclipse.'[39]

Just as the king's political influence decreased the further one moves from court, so did his ability to play the role of *pater patriae*, one in which he felt comfortable. This role contrasted with the other model of authority that may be found in Tudor and Stuart kingship, that of the negotiator, who searched for compromises, balancing and playing off one side against the other, dispensing rewards and punishments when necessary. Even though this model was alien to contemporary political theories about the divine right of monarchy, it was one that Elizabeth, Charles II and even James I employed with varying degrees of success. In contrast, Charles I saw himself as a judge to whom people came for the resolution of their problems. Like a father, or Solomon in the *Book of Kings*, Charles settled his children's disputes fairly but firmly. Thus he saw those who rejected his decisions as wilful and wicked children, who must be punished for their own, and everyone else's good. Within the court this model of the king as the parental judge worked fairly well. After all courtiers were as children in their dependence on him and like maturing adolescents they might rebel against parental platonic strictures by developing a forbidden and hidden cult of erotic poetry and love. But on the surface at least they had to dance whatever tune the king paid for. This does not mean that the court was some sort of tyrannical kindergarten, whose shallow foundations rested on the fear of losing the monarch's favour, with all the concomitant rewards of prestige, honour and profit. Originally the seed may have been planted in shallow ground, yet the fact remains that once the civil war was started, and the court was no longer the place where 'Tournies, Masques, Theatre', recalled Thomas Carew, filled 'Our Halcyon Days', courtiers stayed remarkably loyal to their master and mistress.[40] Indeed the myth of the dashing cavalier going gaily to the wars did much to sustain the king's most ardent followers, most of whom had never known the reality of court life in the days of peace.

During the 1630s the court was in many respects an isolated place that knew little and cared even less about the rest of the country. That is not to say that nothing happened at court. On the contrary it had an extensive and thriving political life that revolved mainly about the queen and her Catholic faith. Although court factions occasionally affected outside events, more often they were affected by them, and most often by their own internal conflicts each with the others. No wonder Secretary Conway bemoaned that 'The sands of the River Loire are not more changeable than the friendships of this court.'[41]

That Conway chose to compare the shifting map of court factions to a French river is not surprising, for the sea into which those changing friendships flowed was a French queen, who could be as stormy as the Bay of Biscay. Two main groups of what might be called 'the queen's set' may be charted. The first consisted of courtiers, secular figures, such as Goring, Montagu, Northumberland, Jermyn, Percy and Holland, whose influence depended on their charm and style. 'He was a very handsome man,' Clarendon recalled of Holland, Henrietta's mentor, and one of the most influential members of her set, 'of a lovely and winning presence and gentle conversation by which he got so easy an admission to the court.'[42] Gregorio Panzani, the papal agent to Henrietta Maria, described the style of the second group of the queen's set in a letter he wrote to his superior, Cardinal Francesco Barberini, the pope's nephew, wherein he defined the qualities his successor must have. The man must be fluent in English, delight in perfume, beautiful clothes, lively discourse, and, while being able to win the confidences of the queen and her ladies, through whom he should conduct negotiations with the king, do so without gaining a reputation for the least lasciviousness or lightness.[43] The second half of the queen's set were priests, celibate men, who could readily play the game of courtly love, while appealing to the queen's Catholic zeal.

Henrietta Maria had come to England in 1625 in a frame of mind more appropriate for a missionary than a bride. Ironically, not until the problem of her French servants was solved, Buckingham was removed, peace signed with France, and she fulfilled her role as a bride, could she start to achieve her goals as a missionary. Following the Anglo-French peace treaty, a mission of twelve Capuchins led by Father Leonard came to London to serve the queen. She lodged them near Somerset House, and within a couple of days they had settled in so well that they were able to claim the conversion of a Puritan, who had originally come to scoff. Their virtues of simple piety and worldly charm were, so the Capuchins believed, especially effective in enlightening English Protestants suckled on the myth of the papal anti-Christ and his devilish lieutenants. In fact, the Capuchins deceived themselves about the nature of their qualities, which were those of worldly piety and simple charm, and about the effect they had on the English people. They convinced themselves that Charles was about to undo the Reformation and return England, Scotland and Wales to Rome, that his subjects paid no taxes, and most Englishmen were really quite fond of the pope.[44] As evidence for the latter, the fathers cited the three cheers that the construction workers gave at the laying of the corner stone for the queen's Catholic chapel at St James's, apparently without considering that Her Majesty's most generous *pour boire* of 6,000 francs might have done something to slacken the men's usual Protestant sensibilities.

Most of the queen's Catholic entourage spent more of their time fighting each other than they did trying to return England to Rome. Within the clerical faction there were two groups, of which the queen generally favoured the Roman one, led by Gregorio Panzani, the papal envoy. He wanted to appoint a bishop for England, a step that the other group, consisting of Benedictines and Jesuits, opposed. They were mainly Englishmen, who had borne the heat and burden of the Elizabethan persecutions, often to the extreme of martyrdom, and considered the creation of a bishop as an attack by a bunch of pampered late-comers on their authority. They even called Panzani Richelieu's lackey. In retaliation the Italian borrowed that most heinous calumny from England's rabid anti-Catholics, accusing the Benedictines and Jesuits of wanting another Gunpowder Plot.[45] A disagreement over foreign policy further widened the gap between the queen's Catholic friends and the traditional leaders of England's recusants. Since Mary Tudor's time, if not Catherine of Aragon's, recusants had looked to Madrid for succour, an aspiration that greatly annoyed the French queen, who once remarked that most of them 'would think little of Heaven itself, unless they got it at the hands of Spain.'[46] When Henrietta Maria tried to use her Catholic friends in England to support her native land, she ended up by uniting England's traditional anti-papism with its centuries-old hatred of France, to produce antipathy so intense that in 1635 one Londoner threw a dead cat covered in dung into the French ambassador's coach.[47]

In spite of fights with each other, and their obvious unpopularity with the country, the court's Catholics did manage to make several conversions that to most Protestants were as spectacular as they were disturbing. Women were especially susceptible to the Roman siren. After Lady Maltravers and Lady Katherine Howard converted one courtier sadly noted, 'Our great women fall away every day.'[48] These conversions were the most pointed of several issues over which the queen and her set clashed with the king's ministers. Even though Weston had a Catholic wife and daughter (and converted on his death bed) Henrietta Maria neither liked nor trusted the Lord Treasurer. She blamed him for many of her husband's anti-Catholic policies, including the enforcement of the laws that forbade Englishmen from attending mass at her chapel. When the sergeants posted outside the chapel arrested Maria Aubert, wife of the queen's surgeon, as she tried to enter, dragging her off with such force that the pregnant woman lost her child, Henrietta Maria was outraged, holding Weston personally responsible.[49] Poor Weston was not really to blame; he was only enforcing policies at the king's command. But this was a fact that quite naturally neither Henrietta Maria nor Charles could admit to each other. On the other hand, it was no secret that Weston was responsible for the policy that upset her more than any other: the two fell out because the queen spent with far greater ease and pleasure than that with which the Lord Treasurer was able to collect. Weston's awkward style, his general lack of charm and manners, further irritated Henrietta Maria. 'He had not that application and submission and reverence for the queen, as might have been expected from his wisdom and breeding,' recalled Clarendon, 'and often crossed her pretences and desires with more rudeness than was natural with him.'[50] Feeling ill at ease with the queen's sophisticated and witty set, the Lord Treasurer appeared brusque and gauche.

So too did Archbishop Laud. He was equally lacking in the courtly graces, having neither the knack nor the inclination to cultivate Henrietta Maria. Possessing the king's favour he felt no need of the queen's. And even if he had tried to cultivate it, Laud would most likely have failed, for he was, as Simonds D'Ewes observed, 'a little low, red faced man, of mean parentage'.[51] Although considerations of birth and looks greatly influenced Henrietta Maria – who once wrote off Sir Thomas Wentworth because he had ugly hands – she and Laud fell out over far more important issues. Notwithstanding his enemies' allegations that he was cryto-Catholic, there were, in fact, few in England as obdurate in their opposition to Rome as Laud. He, for instance, persuaded Charles to issue a proclamation reminding those who continued to proselytize for the Catholic faith of the rigorous penalties the law prescribed.[52]

In addition the queen quarrelled with both Laud and Weston over foreign policy. The Lord Treasurer, and his successor, Bishop Juxon, Laud's friend and protégé, knew that so long as the king wished to rule without parliament, England could not afford a war with Spain, something the queen greatly wanted in order to help her native France. Thus she allied herself and her set, with those Hispanophobe radicals who had attacked Weston so vehemently in the fracas of 2 March, and accused Laud of being a fellow traveller with Rome.[53] Such strange bedfellows as a papist queen and radical Protestants complicated Charles's political relations with his wife and her set. Yet in all their dealings one fact was crucial: first and foremost the set's leader was the woman that Charles loved with an ever increasing dependence, a sign of which may be seen in the growing number of orders he issued for the release of imprisoned recusants 'at the instance of our dearest consort the Queen'.[54] None the less Charles and his ministers, most of whom operated outside the court, came into conflict with the queen and her set over vitally important issues of foreign policy, financial matters and religion. On the other hand, the king liked his wife's friends: he hunted with them, he acted in masques with them, dined, danced, drank and conversed with them, enjoying their company as they fought with each other for his favour, and the influence that they thought that it brought.

Charles was not, of course, a Catholic. Even though the religious confession attributed to him when he was a young man of twenty-six showed that he accepted many Catholic teachings, such a reverence of the saints and the Blessed Virgin Mary, the line that he drew between himself and Rome was a distinct and precise one: it had to be, because it was so narrow.[55] Charles charted the borders of his religious beliefs with microscopic precision. As he told one of his wife's French maids in 1638, 'I also am a Catholic'. The important point was that he was not a *Roman* Catholic.[56] In Charles's mind the precision of his religious definitions confirmed the Protestant purity of his own beliefs, granting him that personal and political toleration of Catholics that only sectarian certainty can bestow. This contrasts with Laud, who on one occasion recorded in his diary that he dreamt of becoming a Catholic, and thus, not so certain in his Anglicanism as Charles, was less tolerant of Rome than the king. On the other hand, many of Charles's subjects, viewing the parameters of his faith from a distance, could not distinguish the niceties of the distinctions that he made. They saw the outward show of liturgy and ceremonial, that Charles enjoyed and encouraged, and that Laud described as 'the beauty of holiness', as no better than appeasing papist superstitions. On the other hand, the theological beliefs that Charles expressed in a prayer that he started to write (though never finished) in February 1632 were soundly Protestant. He began by thanking God 'for keeping me this day', and prayed that he would 'keep me this night', He confessed his unworthiness having been 'in sin conceived and born, and that ever since I have lived in iniquity.'[57] Ironically few Puritans would have had much trouble endorsing the rather prosaic sentiments of the king's prayer. While they would, doubtless, have strenuously disagreed with his regrets that the break with Rome had taken place, and his belief that 'too much time is spent in controversies ... I would rather study were devoted to reunion,' they would with equal fervour have endorsed his distaste for papist practices such as the bowing to the cross and genuflecting at the statue of the Virgin that he remembered seeing in Spain. Certainly such Puritans would have said a loud 'amen' to the assertion Charles made in a letter to the Lord Mayor of London that 'more and greater works of Piety and Charity have been done in this kingdom since the reformation, than when Popery was at its Highest.'[58] For all but the last years of his life, Charles's religion was more a matter of dogma than deeply felt faith. This does not mean that Charles's attachment to the Anglican church was shallow. Far from it – the king went to war to impose his prayer book on the Scots. But religion was more than mere personal faith. It incorporated cosmic views on such matters as the proper relationship between church and state, governor and governed, order and hierarchy, in which Charles believed as firmly as he did the spiritual tenets of the Church of England. Only when civil war swept all of them away did his faith take on the intensity of a martyr's.

In spite of the king's Protestantism, which was as sure to him, and those that stood near him, as it was suspect to the many who analysed it at a distance, Charles found the faith of the queen, and her friends, rather reassuring. Although they were not members of the Church of England, they never questioned his divinely ordained right to rule England and her church. Although in theory they owed allegiance to a foreign potentate, and refused to take an oath of allegiance to Charles, their ultimate loyalty to the king was never in doubt. In this regard even that foreign potentate, the pope, was most cooperative: for example, he quickly scotched an attempt to canonize Father Henry Garnet, the Jesuit executed for his involvement in the Gunpowder Plot.[59]

Most important of all Charles liked the style of the Catholics who surrounded his wife. He was, for instance, especially fond of Father George Con, Panzani's successor as papal agent. The younger son of a Scots noble, Con was witty, a good conversationalist, and highly charming. He knew how to make himself agreeable. When he was presented to the queen on his arrival in England in 1636, he gave her a cross, a present from the pope, that she immediately hung about her neck. To the king he gave paintings and sculptures, and would talk intelligently about the works of leading European artists for hours. Court society wooed him. The Earl of Northumberland entertained him royally. At Oxford Hamilton gave him a guided tour of the Bodleian Library. Even Laud showed him the new quadrangle at St John's, where he hosted a banquet in the envoy's honour. Yet Con's influence over the king remained social rather than political or religious. He might persuade Charles to free a recusant or two, restore mass paraphernalia confiscated in Norwich, or the patrimony of an heir who had gone over to Rome, but Con never had a chance of achieving his chief goal, the conversion of the king and his kingdom. Like their Puritan enemies – and erstwhile allies – the queen and her set grossly exaggerated the influence Rome had over Charles, his ministers and the policies of his government. Basically Charles was content to let his wife and her friends play their games, so long as they did not cause trouble. 'Be cautious,' he warned Panzani, 'and above all things not to intermeddle in state affairs.'[60] Thus Charles opposed the appointment of a Catholic bishop for England because he viewed it as an attack on the authority of his own Anglican episcopacy. Whenever the crowd of recusants who heard mass at the queen's or ambassadors' chapels became large enough to create a public nuisance, he posted sergeants at the gates to stop them entering until the problem shrank to more manageable proportions. Whenever conversions at court became a public scandal, Charles took action. In 1635 he banished Walter Montague, son of the Earl of Manchester, for going over to Rome, and two years later, after a number of dramatic defections, issued a proclamation reminding Catholics that their missionary activities were highly illegal. At Laud's urging Charles even threatened to expel Con if conversions continued.[61]

The king was more concerned about his Catholic subjects' loyalty than their faith, trying hard to devise an oath of allegiance to the crown that they could take without jeopardizing their souls. So long as he behaved in public with decorum, Charles, like Queen Elizabeth, demanded no window into any papist's soul, being ready to grant *de facto* toleration in matters concerning the next world in return for obedience in this. But most of his subjects were not as tolerant of Catholics as was their monarch: they wanted to apply rigorously the penal laws on recusants in the country; he had no wish to hound his Catholic friends at court. This contradiction did not pass unnoticed. To the charge that he was a secret papist, John Hulton, alderman of Appleby, Westmorland, replied that since 'the king himself had a wife a Recusant', why then could he not be one?[62] In May 1629 Nathaniel Barnard, lecturer at St Sepulchre's Church, London, made the same point, though with less deference, by asking the congregation to pray God to 'open the eyes of the Queen Majesty, that she may see Jesus Christ, that she had wounded with her infidelity, Superstition and Idolatry.'[63]

Perhaps the best-known radical Protestant critic of the queen was the London barrister, William Prynne, whose diatribe, *Histriomastrix*, attacked not just her faith, but the social tone that she set at court. For such impudence Star Chamber sentenced him to be imprisoned for life, to be fined £5,000, to have both his ears cropped, and to lose his Oxford degree. With the possible expectation of the latter, their sentence was not just part of the barbarity for which Star Chamber was becoming synonymous, but a reflex because Prynne had just touched on a very sensitive nerve. It was in the court's social activities – its plays, masques, poetry, dramatic presentations, and picture collecting – that his wife and her set had the most contact with, and thus influence on, the king.

Without doubt Charles was the finest art collector ever to sit on the English throne – or for that matter, possibly on the throne of any other western kingdom. His patronage of painting, Sir Henry Wotton rightly told him, was 'the most splendid of all your entertainments'.[64] The king's tastes were exquisite, his commission first rate, his acquisitions excelled in their comprehension. While none of the few daubs he personally painted under Van Dyck's tutelage has (fortunately for both their reputations) survived, Charles had the artist's eye for detail. He could tell which part of a picture the master had done and which was by a pupil. Often he would spend hours visiting artists in their studios, watching them draw, and suggesting a new line, or colour tone with such skill that even the greatest painters had to admit he enhanced the harmony of their work.[65]

Charles's interest in art went back to his earliest days.[66] At eleven he inherited from Henry a collection that was particularly strong in paintings by Venetian artists, a school of which he became very fond. In 1615 he commissioned three works by the English artist Isaac Oliver, and two years later his mother left him her collection of 161 paintings. Charles was fortunate to come of age when, for the first time, a number of English connoisseurs were discovering and collecting the works of European masters.[67] The first and greatest of them, Thomas Howard, Earl of Arundel, who had a collection of some 779 paintings influenced the young prince, as did Buckingham (whose collection of some 331 works, including twenty-eight by Rubens, owed, one suspects more to a love of status, than of art) and Sir Henry Wotton the diplomat, who travelled extensively in Italy.[68] So by the time Charles was twenty he was knowledgeable enough to return the 'Judith and Holofernes' he had commissioned from Rubens, because he could tell it was largely the work of an apprentice. The master was so impressed (and perhaps even embarrassed) by the prince's acumen, that he admitted it was a 'terrible' picture, and promised another 'entirely of my own hand'.[69]

During his trip to Madrid Charles was exposed to the Spanish school of art. He visited the royal collection, attended auctions, purchasing several Titians, and bid for Leonardo da Vinci's notebooks. He admired the former's 'Venus of the Prado' so avidly that Philip IV gave it to him, and when he could not afford Correggio's 'Holy Family' the Spanish monarch was equally generous.

Without doubt Charles's greatest coup as a collector was the acquisition in 1628 of the works that the dukes of Mantua had accumulated over the past century and a half, which included some of the best paintings executed by Raphael, Titian, Correggio and Mantegna. 'So wonderful and glorious a collection the like will never again be met with,' wrote Daniel Nys, 'they are truly worthy of so great a king as his Majesty.' Two years later, using Rubens as an intermediary, Charles brought the Raphael cartoons that now hang in the Victoria and Albert Museum. In 1634 he purchased a fourth part of the collection of the Venetian Bartolomeo della Nova, his share being determined by the roll of a dice.[70] An inventory of the king's paintings taken by their keeper, Abraham Van der Dort, four years later lists some 546 works in Whitehall Palace alone. By his death, according to one estimate, the royal collection had grown to some 1,760 paintings.[71] In addition Charles possessed an extensive hoard of ancient coins and medals, mostly inherited from his brother, as well as a large number of sculptures, including some 210 pieces in Greenwich Palace and its gardens. Charles owned a small library of 1,200 books, nearly all of which his predecessors left him. During the 1630s, however, he tended to value them less for their contents than their bindings, delighting in the exquisite work done by craftsmen such as Nicholas Ferrar and the Anglican community at Little Gidding.[72]

To acquire so large and fine a collection of *objets d'art*, Charles patronized many artists, and employed dozens of agents, including diplomats. In the Netherlands Dudley Carleton and Balthazar Gerbier acted for the king, as did Wotton, Nicholas Lanier and Daniel Nys in Italy, Sir William

Hamilton in Rome, the Marquis of Hamilton in Germany, and Michael de la Croix and Henry Stone in Spain. Aware of the king's love of art, foreign governments and English ministers presented him with paintings. When the famous Italian sculptor Bernini could not come to England to do a bust of the king, Van Dyck painted the famous three-profiled portrait of him, from which the Italian might work. The list of artists that Charles patronized was a long and distinguished one, ranging from foreign masters such as Rubens and Van Dyck, to lesser known native craftsmen such as William Dobson, whom the king called 'the English Tintoretto'. For the king Cornelius Polenburg painted miniatures, Nicholas Lanier engraved, Christian Van Vianen etched silver plate, and Francis Fanelli made metal castings. Charles's tastes in art were wide, the only serious gap in his collection being of the early Renaissance. Artistic innovation did not upset the otherwise conservative monarch, who made Wenceslaus Hollar his drawing master so he could develop his *avant-garde* style of topographical illustrations.

Charles spent considerable sums of money on art: the Mantua collection cost £18,280, the Nova purchases £800, the Rubens ceiling £3,000. The total value of his collection in seventeenth-century terms is impossible to estimate, and at today's prices staggering to contemplate. When parliament ordered most of it sold in 1649, reserving the choicest pieces for the rulers of the new republic, the paintings fetched £31,913 and the sculptures another £17,990.[73] Yet Charles was a thrifty collector, paying good prices for his acquisitions; for instance, in 1638 he lowered Van Dyck's bill for some twenty-four works, reducing the price of 'Le Roi a la chasse' from £200 to £100. In spite of – or perhaps because of – the king's exquisite tastes, careful management, unequalled judgment and diligent pursuit and patronage of excellence, his collecting upset many. One critic even accused him of 'squandering away millions of pounds on old rotten pictures and broken nosed marbles'.[74]

Diplomats and courtiers took a very different view, trying to turn the king's love of art to their own advantage. Frequently those of his ministers who were outside the court circle, played upon this very court-centred interest by commissioning artists to make him presents. Weston had Van Dyck paint a 'Madonna and Child' to give the king at New Year 1630. Laud paid Hubert le Sueur £400 in 1634 to cast life-size statues of Charles and Henrietta, and two years later placed busts of the two at either end of his new quad at St John's.[75] Foreign potentates took advantage of the king's susceptibilities. Cardinal Barberini once remarked that he would 'not hesitate to rob Rome of her most valuable ornaments, if in exchange we might be so happy as to have the King of England's name amongst those princes who submit to the Apostolic See.'[76] Presents of art always pleased the king. Immediately after one consignment from the pope arrived in London in January 1637, Charles collected Henrietta Maria, the Earls of Holland and Pembroke and Inigo Jones, to rush and open the packaging cases. He and Inigo used candles to examine the brushwork in detail; covering the labels they challenged each other to guess a work's creator by its style.[77] Barberini had also arranged for Bernini to carve Charles's bust from Van Dyck's portrait. The results so enthralled its subject that when he first saw it he removed a ring from his finger, ordered it sent to the artist, saying that it must 'crown the hand that made so fine a work', and promptly made arrangements for him to do another bust of his wife.[78] Remembering how enamoured of art Charles had been as a young man in Madrid, Philip IV selected Rubens as his emissary to discuss peace in 1629; a wise choice, for the painter and Charles got on famously, and a treaty was quickly signed.

During the 1630s picture collecting was, quite simply, Charles's chief preoccupation. It not only took up much of his time, energies and enthusiasm, but as his hobby betrayed some of the most fundamental aspects of his aspirations and personality. His ability to assemble one of the world's greatest art collections demonstrates that he was a man of energy and judgment. Essentially he did so on his own, without the assistance of a curator to choose what his employer paid for. Van der Dort, Keeper of the King's Pictures, was more a cataloguer than a connoisseur on whom Charles relied for advice. The king collected by personal contact. He did not write long letters, or compile exhaustive catalogues of what he wanted, but preferred instead to operate through face-to-face contacts, friends and diplomatic networks. Typically, Charles did not create any institutions to advance art or organize it more effectively. In sum, collecting was the hobby he enjoyed at a time when he had neither the need, nor the inclination, to spend much energy governing England. Unlike most men, a king cannot chose his career: Charles was born to it. But he could choose his hobby, and (like most of us) this choice revealed more about him than his job.

If Freud is correct, collecting is a way by which a person may escape from reality to a fantasy world that allows 'full play for his erotic and ambitious wishes'. In addition those with strong authoritarian personalities frequently display an interest in collecting.[79] For Charles collecting had another psychological satisfaction. Just as fine art must, by definition, be in harmony, so through the patronage of fine art might the king bring harmony to his realm, appointing each rank and order in its proper regimented place. Edmund Waller, a court poet, noted of the king:[80]

> He, Like Amphion, makes those quarries leap
> In fair figures from a confused heap.
> For in his heart of regiment is found
> A power like that of harmony in sound.

Thus it is not surprising that Charles was fond of music, with its regular rhythm, space and lack of discord, where a single note out of tune can ruin the whole piece. Wotton told Charles that his patronage of 'music grows ever day more harmonious and accurate' – an interesting choice of epithets that reflected a love of precision and order. Giovanni Coperario, taught Charles as a young man to play the viola so well that some thought that he could have performed professionally had he not become a king. On becoming king, he made his old teacher composer in ordinary to the crown, a post to which the Italian, Alfonso Ferrabosco, and then his son, succeeded, while Nicholas Lanier became master of the king's music.[81]

One way of discovering more exactly how Charles's love of the arts reflected his personality is to look at the paintings he chose to hang in his most private rooms, as well as the ones he commissioned, or bought, or of which became fond enough to display in prominent positions. At Whitehall Charles hung a portrait of himself surrounded by those of Roman emperors, as if to say his lineage and fame was equal to theirs.[82] For the walls of his own bedroom Charles selected ten pictures, five of which were of members of his own family: Van Dyck's 'Henrietta Maria', life-size portraits of Frederick and Elizabeth, both by Honthorst, another of their children by Polenburg, and the fifth being Myten's portrait of Prince Henry. The sixth painting was almost family, a group of Buckingham with his wife and children. The next three, Correggio's 'Mary Magdalen' and paintings of 'The Virgin and Child' by Permensius and Raphael had obvious religious connotations. Indeed with the exception of the last picture, 'Nine Naked Muses', by Perino del Vago, the works that Charles chose for his bedroom were what one might expect.[83]

One of the most famous, and certainly the largest set of paintings that Charles commissioned, were those that Rubens did on the ceiling of the Banqueting Hall at Whitehall (see Plate 6).[84] The central panel, 'The Apotheosis of James I', shows Charles's father ascending into Heaven. It lauds not just the old king, but all kings, as divine-like beings who go straight to paradise. Another of the painting's panels celebrates James as the peacemaker, and so by implication Charles praises his own pacific policies. In the third panel James is shown as linking the crowns of England and Scotland after centuries of hostility. Indeed the whole building, climaxed by its remarkable ceiling, is a celebration of kingship, its focus being the throne under a canopy of state, where the monarch sat for the great ceremonial moments of his reign. The building's Baroque style, with its associations of foreign absolutism, linked Stuart kingship in many people's minds to the counter-Reformation.

Of course, one can go too far in trying to assess the significance of Inigo Jones's great building – or, for that matter, of any piece of art. After all it was designed for Charles's father, and Rubens's ceiling paintings are open to a number of interpretations. Court art was not supposed to present the subject 'warts and all'. The fact that on his arrival in England Prince

Charles Louis was unable to recognize his aunt from her portraits, should be taken as a warning not to take court art too literally. Yet over his lifetime the totality of Charles's patronage of art does have common themes, and may, with care, be used to shed light on his character. From his youth his choice of art had been significant. In Madrid he had been greatly smitten by Titian's 'Venus of the Prado', a work calculated to appeal to a love-sick boy. The painter depicted a naked, but chaste, Venus. Behind her a young huntsman chases a stag. Before her stands a Satyr, symbol of temptation. Above her Cupid flies, bow in hand, his arrow poised (Charles might well surmise) to slay the Satyr and unite the huntsman and Venus in true love. After all, was not the world of courtly love a place where temptation is slain and Venus reigns?

The power of perfect love and harmony was a theme of the 'St George and the Dragon' (see Plate 7) that Rubens painted in the 1630s during the heyday of the courtly love cult.[85] He portrayed Charles as England's patron saint, who had just rescued a maiden (that bears an uncanny resemblance to Henrietta Maria) and slain the dragon of war, bringing to the realm all the benefits of peace, as depicted by the pastoral background of the Thames and the buildings of a royal palace, which contrast strikingly with the carnage of corpses, symbolic of the Thirty Years War, that litter the foreground. Charles liked this painting greatly, giving the artist a diamond ring, a jewelled hatband and the sword with which he knighted him. Apart from showing his wife as a maiden, who in the finest traditions of courtly love fantasy must be rescued from a fate worse than death, the painting glorified the king's pacific policies, even though they were not of his choosing, having been forced upon him by the failure of Buckingham's military adventures and his own attempts to work with parliament. In the world of art, at least, St George was happy enough to make a virtue of necessity.

Rubens's greatest pupil, Van Dyck, painted 'Charles I on horseback', (see Plate 8). It was perhaps the most significant of the king's many portraits. The theme was a familiar one. Le Sueur cast an equestrian statue of the king for Whitehall Palace (it now stands at Trafalgar Square) being ordered to make the short monarch appear at least six feet tall.[86] Emperor Charles V had himself immortalized in a similar pose, and in 1633 Van Dyck painted the king riding through a triumphal arch like some hero from classical times. Three or four years later, Van Dyck executed his second equestrian portrait, 'Charles I on horseback', a masterpiece that evokes many complicated illusions and images: Charles is shown not just as the divinely anointed prince, but the emperor who accepts no man-made limits to his authority. He is not just the warrior poised for war, but the knight ready to ply the long sword that rests across his horse's flank in the service of justice, true religion and true love. At the same time this man of action is a thoughtful, sensitive creature – in sum the philosopher king, the perfect knight, always ready for anything, the complete master of everything he surveys. An intellectual description and analysis of the painting, or even the close examination of a reproduction, fails however to fully convey its real power. Charles I on horseback' is a very large painting that tends to make the viewer forget that at five feet four inches, the king was a short man even by the standards of his own time. Today the painting hangs at the end of an alcove in the National Gallery in London, dominating the whole area in a way that forces the crowds that walk through the gallery to look back over their shoulders even as they examine the other paintings. Hung in its original setting the work's power must have been even more domineering. Charles set it at the end of the long gallery at Hampton Court, placing it at the apex of his collection, sparing no effort to enhance the emotional effect and majesty of what, in every respect but one, was a self-portrait. The painting appealed to Charles not just because it was a work of genius, and he was a collector of such works, but because it was remarkably reassuring. One look at it it would banish all self-doubt, silence Puritan clamours or parliamentary agitation, stroking His Majesty's ego by telling him that all was well in the world – or, at least, in his world, the world of the court.

Painting and sculpture were not the only art forms that reflected Charles's personality and hopes. His patronage of poetry, plays and masques did so, though not in as direct a fashion, because in these art forms the relationship between patron and writer was neither so intense nor deliberate; their works are not collectable in the same way as paintings; and, anyway, Charles knew less about them that the plastic arts.

During the first fifteen years of Charles reign some 401 dramatic performances were staged at court, including 25 masques and 368 plays. The king invited companies of professional actors to stage their current repertoire in his private theatre.[87] His favourite playwrights were by far Francis Beaumont and John Fletcher, whom he once gave £40 as a sign of his regard. He also enjoyed Shakespeare (though not as avidly as the partisans of both would have us believe), and liked the works of Ludowick Carlell, Sir William D'Avenant and Ben Jonson.[88] Over the objections of English actors Charles patronized French players and by letting them perform at court on the sabbath (when they were unable to appear before the paying public) upset many of his more Protestant subjects.[89] The king and queen also enjoyed a play or two when they visited the universities. At Oxford in 1636 they laughed at the antics of Melancholio (a Puritan character much like Malvolio) in William Strode's *Passions Calmed*, and the next day sat through two more plays at St John's and Christ Church. In theatrical presentations Oxford always managed to beat its rival in the Fens. During a visit to Cambridge in 1632 Charles found Peter Hausted's *The Rival Friends* so long and tedious that he complained to Dr Betts, the vice-chancellor. The poor fellow (who was already depressed about some other matter) was so upset that he hung himself that Easter morn.[90]

In reality Charles was neither so harsh, not so discerning a drama critic as Dr Betts's drastic response would suggest, especially when compared to the king's exceptionally fine taste in the plastic arts. During his reign the English theatre declined. Perhaps after the Everest of the Shakespearean stage it could go no higher: certainly the attention the court gave to the masque, an essentially ephemeral and transient art form very different from the theatre with its concerns for the real world, did little to help. Sir Francis Bacon dismissed masques as 'but toys'. Inigo Jones, who made a good living from their production, admitted they were 'nothing else but pictures with Light and Motion.'[91] They were right. Of the major art forms developed on the western stage in the last half millenium the masque has had the least appeal to posterity. Part opera, part ballet, part drama, today the masque is neither sung, danced, nor played. The fact that the masque has been without lasting artistic significance does not mean that it is equally devoid of value as an indication of both the court's culture, and the king's personality and wishes.

Although masques first become popular during Elizabeth's reign, her parsimony hampered their development, for the queen much preferred others to produce and pay for them. James I had no such scruples: rather he delighted in shelling out large amounts of money for sumptuous presentations that occupied the attentions of his wife and her ladies, while glorifying himself.[92] Thus as the piper changed, so did the tune that masques played. In Elizabethan performances the sovereign appeared as an aloof figure. In James's masques the monarch comes down to centre stage: around him the action, but it the marriage of his daughter, the doings of the gods, or the escapades of comic Irishmen, revolved. During James's reign the court developed the tradition of holding a grand masque every Twelfth Night to mark the end of the Christmas season. As a young man, Charles frequently took part in these performances, including that for 1618, Jonson's *Pleasure Reconciled to Virtue*.

Horatio Busino, the Venetian ambassador's chaplain, remembered the occasion well. He arrived at Whitehall Palace at about four in the afternoon: the audience were crowded into a large hall that had boxes for the nobility on the sides, a stage at one end, and in the centre the royal throne under its state canopy. The hall was packed with some 600 people, all extravagantly dressed and bejewelled. Two hours later, at six o'clock the king entered, and the show began. In the first act a fat Bacchus, sitting on a cart drawn by four men sang a song, then twelve men dressed in barrels appeared, followed by a dozen boys disguised as frogs, who did a grotesque dance with each other. Mercury came on stage to make a speech praising the king. A guitar player, attended by a high priest wearing red robes, sang a number of Italian songs badly enough to upset Busino. And so on it went until the finale when Charles made his entrance as the star; he led a dozen knights wearing black masks with feathers on their heads, who danced in a pyramid formation, with the prince at the apex, and performed a number of dances from various countries. It all sounds a confused and tedious mish-mash. James certainly found it so, for in the last act he started barracking his displeasure, and the show was only saved when Buckingham leapt forward to lead the performers. Then the audience and players danced together – the world of the court and the theatre becoming as one.[93]

Masques were expensive affairs. *Pleasure Reconciled to Virtue* that Busino described was followed by a sumptuous banquet that lasted to two-thirty in the morning. Charles's three costumes alone cost £249 16s 11d. During the 1630s the court spent about £14,500 on some eleven masques.[94] Thus only large and rich corporations, such as the Crown of the Inns of Court, could afford to stage them. Being too expensive for the commercial stage masques did not need to respond to the dictates of the market place. Freed from having to please a mass audience, those who paid for masques could please themselves, and the exclusive few whom they invited to attend. By employing 'in' jokes, and making so many allusions to classical mythology (special cribs were printed for courtiers with a little Latin and a lot of ambition) masques tried to appeal to a small sophisticated elite. As Jonson explained, their object was to 'declare themselves to the sharp and learned', while the rabble merely 'did gaze, said it was fine, and were satisfied'.[95]

As the court became more isolated, as royal progresses became less public appearances and more hunting safaris, as public occasions, such as the Garter procession through the streets of London became a private service in the Chapel Royal at Windsor, so the exclusive nature of the masque grew more significant. When people start talking only to themselves, then their words begin to have greater meaning for themselves. Even the architecture of the masque was significant. When Inigo Jones built the Whitehall Banqueting Hall, which, until the Rubens paintings were hung on the ceiling, was used for all major masques, he introduced the Palladian style into England. Yet so isolated was the court from the cultural mainstream, this new style did not influence the houses that magnates or gentry built for themselves for another century.[96]

It was Jones's erstwhile collaborator, Ben Jonson, who wrote that masques were 'the mirror of man's life'.[97] However, in truth, they did not so much mirror mankind's life as the life of one man, for as Roy Strong has argued 'the masque is for the monarch, and about the monarch.'[98] Even it scenery underscored this conclusion. The masque introduced perspectives to the English stage with all lines culminating at the point where the king sat. Thus everyone else in the audience sat slightly out of focus: the greater their distance from the monarch the more their visual disharmony.

Through their focus on the king masques emphasized a number of themes. First they stressed the perfection of Charles's and Henrietta Maria's love, underlining the already familiar concept of courtly love. Frequently masques depicted the king as a classical god: as Neptune, tamer of the elements, or Pan, the life-giving sun. In Thomas Carew's *Coelum Britanicum*, presented to the court on Shrove Tuesday 1634, Charles even managed to convert several classical deities to Christianity (banishing the recalcitrant to America). As the divine-right monarch he acted almost as if he were a Christian god himself. With their adoration of the sovereign, and their emphasis on the benefits of the law and order that he bestowed, masques came close to the concept of the 'beauty of holiness', that Laud and Charles tried to establish in the Anglican church. Inigo Jones implied as much when he explained that he had designed the queen's beautiful costumes for *Tempe Restored* (1632), 'so that the corporal beauty . . . may draw us to the contemplation of the soul.'[99]

Naturally masques trumpeted the government's policies, for, as Jonson wrote, they were 'the Spectacles of State'. In *Coelum Britannicum* a character sums up the benefits of the personal rule: monopolises curbed, tobacco smoking purged, taverns shut down, pornography stamped out, the countryside revitalized, homosexuality driven from the land. 'In brief,' he concluded, 'the whole state of the Hierach a total reformation.' According to Sir William D'Avenant's *Temple of Love* Charles's government was so popular that he ruled as much by example as by power. Only once (and then obliquely) did a masque ever dare criticize the personal monarchy. In *The Triumph of Peace* the Inns of Court produced in 1633 to apologize for the libels of one of their members, William Prynne, a comedian appeared carrying a carrot and a capon; he explained that he was trying to obtain a monopoly to raise the latter solely on a diet of the former. Even though the king and queen laughed heartily at the thought of night-fighting chickens, just in case the joke had gone too far, the good lawyers promptly assured the royal party that they had dedicated their presentation:

> To you, Great King and Queen, whose
> Smile doth scatter blessings through this isle.

Masques mostly portrayed a world of sweetness and light. Opposition to the crown was rarely mentioned, and then easily explained away. For instance, in the masque that was put on at Richmond in Prince Charles's name in 1636, a group of humble yokels tried to get in to see the king and queen in order to present them with some baked pumpkins, tokens of their simple yet sincere love. But a supercilious court flunkey shooed them away as too lowly for their majesties presence. The message was simple: the court was telling itself that ship-money agitators, religiouss rabble rousers, parliamentary prattlers and constitutional carpers notwithstanding, the silent majority of the real people of England loved Charles and Henrietta Maria.

As the court grew more isolated a pastoral theme developed in its masques. The countryside, which had once been a wild place of terrible beasts contrasted with the order and harmony of the city, now became a pastoral heaven. Perhaps as Charles's court (like Louis XVI's) became more alienated from the urban centres of discontent the countryside became an idealized retreat. Certainly Gerrit Honthorst echoed this fantasy by painting Henrietta Maria as a shepherdess, as did Charles, who issued a number of proclamations ordering the gentry to leave London and return to their country estates.[100] During the 1630s a second theme emerged in the masque. As the crown recognized it could no longer afford to play a part in European affairs, and as Gustavus Adolphus became the hero of many Protestant Englishmen (news of his deeds constantly filling their letters and diaries), masques started to stress the blessings of peace and the peacemaker, themes that Rubens reflected in many of his paintings.

The last masque that Charles's court ever put on was, perhaps, the best example of the message that this genre tried to propogate. The court staged Sir William D'Avenant's *Salmacida Spolia* on Twelfth Night, 1640. At the time the king's Scots policy was in tatters, his army routed, his personal rule crumbling.[101] It opens by alluding to these problems with Discord, a Fury, raising a storm over England:

> And I do stir the humours that increase
> In thy full body, overgrown with peace.

In other words, if there were any problems in England, they resulted from the over-munificence of Charles's rule: because the king had given the English people an excess of his bounties, their appetite had sickened and was about to die. A number of figures attempt to still the Fury – fantastically dressed courtiers, jealous Dutchmen, mad lords, invisible ladies, ancient Hibernians – all try but to no avail, until in the last act Charles comes down from his golden throne, as Henrietta Maria descends from heaven in an ingeniously contrived mechanical cloud, that symbolically blocks out the picture of the City of London painted on the background scenery. They hold hands. They calm the Fury. And, as the royal couple, players and audience dance together in perfect concord, the 'Chorus of the Beloved People' sing the paean:

> All that are harsh, all that are rude
> Are by your harmony subdued.
> Yet so unto obedience wrought
> As if not forced to it but taught.

So the stage at Whitehall became the centre of Charles's kingdom, and the masques in which he acted, the pictures he collected, the painters he commissioned, the poets he favoured, the plays he chose to watch – in sum the whole culture of his court – became the most accurate expression of his personality.[102]

# XI

# 'HIS OWN DIRECTION AND COMMANDMENT'

On 22 February 1629 Charles heard that the Commons had called some of his customs officers to the bar of their House to question them about levying tonnage and poundage. Immediately the king summoned the privy council to tell them that the collectors had acted 'by his own direction and commandment'.[1] As usual Charles reacted to rather than initiated policies. In much the same way three days later he dissolved parliament in reaction to the Commons' outrageous behaviour on 2 March, and not as part of a carefully contrived scheme to become an absolute monarch. Charles believed he had no alternative: his precipitous style of rule being such that he rarely left himself options.

Thus it might be useful to see, as a result of this sudden decision, to what extent Charles actually directed and commanded England during the next eight years until the outbreak of the Scots Rebellion, and how he viewed the problems his government faced. In attempting to do so we are, however, hampered in two respects. A convincing modern history of the royal government of these years (which for convenience sake may be called the 1630s) is still to be written.[2] The thirties have inevitably been seen in terms of the turmoil of the forties, first by parliamentarians searching in the so-called 'eleven years tyranny' for reasons to explain, or justify, their attempts to limit the powers of the crown, and then by historians searching in the peace of one decade for the causes of the turmoil of the next.

All may read events backwards.

In many respects England's government returned to a more normal pattern during this time. Of course, come what may, the bulk of a government's business, responding to problems sent up to it, remains the same. For instance, Charles I's government was just as keen as Henry VIII's had been to investigate reports of treasonable words, even if they invariably turned out to be the prattlings of drunkards.[3] A comparison of proclamations shows that Charles's government was concerned with the same sort of subjects as James's had been.[4]

After Buckingham's death politics were no longer monopolized by a favourite with the ambition and power to move and shape major events (as opposed to reacting to a host of minor ones). During the 1630s ministers competed for the king's attention, and he left them to handle their areas of responsibility. Having an essentially tidy mind, which preferred order in government as much as in art, Charles departmentalized business, seeing policy not as something that must be shaped as it evolved, but more a matter of placing incoming items in the appropriate pigeon hole. In essence he viewed his government's activities not over time, but within the short term according to categories.

His government did, of course, change during the personal rule: Weston died in 1635; Laud and Juxon increased their influence in secular matters; the government grew more unpopular, with bishops becoming the focus for discontentment; interest shifted to foreign policy, and then back again to domestic affairs. But before 1637 these changes were subtle and hidden. Thus a chronological description of the king's government might not only exaggerate the king's control of affairs, and emphasize change at the expense of continuity, but give the government more form, cohesion, indeed more energy, than it actually possessed.

For example, in the first six years after 1631 the crown issued half the number of proclamations than it had in the previous six years. Private letters and diaries confirm the impression that during the personal rule not all that much happened. People were interested in scandals, such as the trial of Lord Audley for buggery and rape – and many God-fearing Protestants reached the appropriate conclusions from his accomplices's scaffold confessions that they had not gone in for this sort of thing until His Lordship had exposed them to popery. Others were worried by events on the Continent, being more concerned at the death of Gustavus Adolphus, Sweden's king, than the possible demise of England's parliament. Ardent parliamentarians had to find other activities. Simonds D'Ewes retreated to his study. John Pym became involved in privateering.

In one respect Charles's government did depart from the normal pattern. Although parliament was still more an occasion than a regular intrinsic part of the constitution, especially during times of peace (as demonstrated by the years from 1610 to 1621 which saw only the Addled Parliament of 1614), the king's determination to rule without parliament was a new factor, if only because it limited his choices.

Eight days after the fracas of 2 March Charles issued a proclamation explaining why he had dissolved parliament. While he defended his past actions, he said nothing about his future intentions until a second proclamation, published a fortnight later, declared that he did not intend calling parliament again until the people 'come to a better understanding of Us'. Most of the king's ministers supported this hard line. Weston, the man rising fastest in the royal favour, was very obdurate, largely because he feared another parliament would impeach him. The only people close to the king who pressed for the election of a fourth parliament were the adherents of Elizabeth of Bohemia, who believed that only the Commons could vote enough money to restore her family to the Palatinate. One of her leading advocates, Francis Nethersole, told Charles that a parliament 'is genuinely and passionately longed for'. Soon afterwards Charles sent him to the Tower. The dispatches of the Venetian ambassadors trace the king's growing intransigence against parliament: in May 1629 he told the ambassador that 'whosoever speaks to him about parliament shall be his enemy'; in 1631 that 'on no account' would he ever again call parliament; in 1633 that he was 'more opposed to it than ever'; and in 1635 that he would 'do anything to avoid having another parliament'.[5] In coming to this resolve the behaviour of the leaders of the Commons, especially Eliot, greatly influenced Charles, who took a personal interest in their interrogations, conditions of confinement and the nuances of their apologies.[6] Six years later, in a letter to Wentworth about the Dublin parliament – a pretty tame tabby compared to Westminster's – Charles revealed that the punishment of the ringleaders, including Eliot's lonely death in the Tower, had done nothing to lessen his enmity. Parliaments, he wrote:[7]

> are of the nature of cats, they ever grow cussed with age, so that if you will have good with them, put them off handsomely when they come to any age, for young ones are ever most tractable: and, in earnest, you will find nothing more conduce to the beginning of a new than the well ending of a former parliament.

In spite, or perhaps because of, the fact that Charles had no intention of calling a fourth parliament if he could possibly help it, the king was very sensitive to suggestions that such was his resolve. In 1629, for example, he was outraged to find a memorandum (later discovered a forgery) in Sir Robert Cotton's library purporting to advise the crown on how he might abolish parliament altogether, and at the same time increase his revenues. Nine years later Charles personally censored from Massinger's play *The King and Subject* the lines, 'We'll raise supplies what way we please . . . acknowledging no laws.'[8]

In deciding to send parliament packing in March 1629 Charles acted impulsively. Very soon, however, the king's reflex became a permanent policy to rule as long and as best he might on his own.

Was such a policy viable? Did it have a fair chance of succeeding? Could Charles and his successors reasonably expect to rule without ever again calling a parliament? The answer to these questions depended on how well Charles and his government were able to fill the void created by the absence of parliament. Traditionally the chief role of parliament has been seen in financial terms – in the power of the purse. In fact during the 1630s through the revival of old, and the development of new ways of raising revenue the government was able to get along without parliamentary taxes fairly well. Of course, they could not afford to wage an aggressive foreign policy, but given time they might have turned ship money into the land taxes of the eighteenth century, enabling them to fight popular wars. Indeed this was the key issue, for whether or not he depended on parliamentary taxes or some absolutist form of raising revenue, no monarch could fight a sustained war without the support of his subjects.

The failure of Charles's government to create mechanisms to replace those lost by the absence of parliament was as serious, if not more serious, in areas other than finances. When parliament met, it was a safety valve where the dissatisfied could let off steam; and when it eventually met in 1640, the head of steam had built up to a dangerous pressure. Local worthies strove to be elected to the Commons more as a recognition of their status within their counties than to influence England's affairs. Parliament was a national body for solving local problems: it determined who was the local 'top dog', and not who would be the king's first minister. When it no longer met, and these functions were lost, Charles failed to put anything in their place. Neither Charles nor his ministers had any need to do so. For one thing they were reluctant, even to the point of lethargy, to innovate. For another the crown was content to count on its subjects' centuries-old habits of obedience. His Majesty's government might coerce, bully, threaten and punish, becoming all the time less popular, yet apart from a couple of riots in the Forest of Dean and in East Anglia, there were no violent protests against the government's policies in England. No one even tried to assassinate the king; the narrowest escape he had was in 1635 when the crew of the inappropriately named ship, the *Safety*, forgot to remove the ball from a cannon before firing a salute as they sailed past Greenwich Palace.[9] Men continued to obey the government, some out of fear, most from habit. After all there was no alternative to the king. Or if there was, it was so unacceptable that Bishop Williams (who had no cause to love the personal rule) prayed, 'God send those men more wit who living in a monarchy rely on a democracy.'[10]

Two personal considerations influenced Charles's views of his government. First he had broad policy goals: to rule without parliament, maintain his own personal prerogatives and dignity as sovereign, help his sister abroad and his church at home. Second – and far more important in the day-to-day running of affairs – the king did not wish to work very hard, preferring to spend his energies on the world of the court. Thus he reacted in every area but one – the church. Before 1637 opposition to Charles's (and Laud's) English church policies was not widespread, becoming serious only after their Scots ecclesiastical reforms collapsed with the attempt to introduce a new prayer book.

Sometimes Charles displayed the occasional burst of energy. While signing a routine letter, one of thousands written in his name, to St Catherine's Hall, Cambridge, he noted the clerk had omitted to insert the recipient's name and address, so did so in his own hand. He personally went through the lists of presents given and received at New Year (without apparently noting the ominous sign that each time it included fewer peers). In 1635 Charles checked the arithmetic of the accounts presented supporting Lionel Cranfield's petition that he commute the balance due on the fine levied at his impeachment.[11] But such clerical interventions were noteworthy only for their rareness and a pettifogging concern for trivia. The king seldom bothered himself with the tens of thousands of petitions addressed to the crown. He might read some, and then act as a postman who sorted them to the appropriate minister, whose recommendations he invariably accepted. This was a serious omission, for though it meant that the king spent enough time at his papers to satisfy himself that he was doing his duty (and in this regard he was an easy man to please), it deprived him of both a detailed knowledge of his subjects' concerns, as well as the gratitude of a host of satisfied petitioners. For instance, in a typical bundle of some seventy petitions, selected at random from the papers of Attorney General Bankes, Charles perused a dozen at the most. In not a single instance did he initiate action.[12] Charles's lack of input and dependence on his ministers upset officials. Sir Henry Cary, Lord Falkland, who as Lord Deputy of Ireland was away from the centre of power, complained that the king 'seldom reads' papers, leaving decisions to his secretaries of state.[13] Charles's impact on broader policy matters was almost as slight. In January 1636 Secretary of State Windebank sent him a list of items that urgently required the king's attention, ranging from diplomatic decisions to the naturalization of denizens. The king's annotations betrayed that he was neither interested in, nor knowledgeable about, these subjects. His most frequent comment was 'Do it if you find it suit my service.'[14] Charles's reading of diplomatic dispatches was equally cursory: often he would only skim the Secretary of State's covering letter that summarized the enclosed ambassadorial reports, because, as he once confessed to Windebank, 'I have not the patience to read them all.'[15] Charles was as indolent in dealing with his 'out' correspondence as he was with his 'in', admitting on several occasions to his good friend Hamilton, 'you know that I am lazy enough in writing.'[16] Thus it seems reasonable to conclude that compared to any other Tudor and Stuart monarch a higher proportion of acts done in Charles's name were done either without his knowledge or initiative. If this were not the case it seems hard to explain why of the approximately two thousand letters that were sent to Scotland between 1625 and 1635 in the king's name not a single one was written in his hand, and only one annotated. True he could have dictated this correspondence or written drafts (since lost) from which fair copies were made; but had Charles done so, surely he would not have displayed such abysmal ignorance when handling the Scots Rebellion.[17]

Charles did not work at winning his subjects' loyalty. He preferred the pleasure of hunting from county to county to the tedium of state visits, with long addresses from petty worthies. Charles upset the Scots by continually putting off going to Edinburgh to be crowned. Thus his knowledge of the Celtic lands he ruled was second-hand; before the war he went to Scotland but once, and to Ireland and Wales never, his travels being confined to a small area in England two or three days' ride from London. Perhaps he kept his distance from his subjects because he was a shy man who was embarrassed by a stutter, or else because he was afraid that if he let them come too close they might discern things in himself that even he preferred not to see. As Bishop Williams observed, Charles expected loyalty knowing 'not the art to please,' treating people with little grace.[18] In 1633 the Earl of Suffolk pleaded with the king to let him retain the office of Captain of the Band of Pensioners to pay off his debts. 'What care I for your debts,' Charles retorted. 'You must look to them. If you surrender your office I will reward you to your content. If otherwise I will have the place and be disengaged of my promise.' And, an observer recalled, as 'His Majesty shook very much,' Charles concluded, 'Where is your Obedience?' When Charles sided with an obscure country priest in a quarrel with the Earl of Arundel over a rectory, the aristocrat ruefully observed, 'It is an ill dog that is not worth whistling.' On the outbreak of the civil war Arundel went abroad, depriving Charles of his considerable support. The king expected obedience. When given, as he told the Earl of Suffolk, it would be rewarded – though not so much as a condition of the gift but as a recognition for surrender. Even though it might be against his best political interests Charles favoured those who yielded obedience because he found such a surrender personally satisfying. He saw himself as the judge, who delivered his verdicts fairly and without passion, always on the merits of the case, even if it were not in the crown's advantage. Thus when his subjects surrendered, he could be a surprisingly fair man, and when they refused, an exceedingly vindictive one.

In addition to this sense of fairness Charles's indolence and lack of interest in routine government suggest (his authoritarian instincts notwithstanding) that he was not trying to create an absolutism similar to that developing on the Continent. Far from it; the personal monarchy was more an attempt to return to the old style of politics that had no domineering favourite, but factions that fought each other for the king's favour. After Buckingham's death two such groups emerged. One centred around Weston, which included the Earls of Holland, Carlisle and Arundel, Sir Francis Cottington, Sir Henry Vane and the two Secretaries of State, Coke and Windebank. The other faction consisted of Archbishop Laud, Lord Deputy Wentworth and Lord Keeper Coventry. Even though the former had stronger court connections, no major differences in policy divided the two groups. The lines between them were loosely drawn and frequently crossed, as in 1634, when Carlisle and Holland joined forces with Laud and Coventry to persuade the king to dismiss Weston for selling crown lands at very low prices. They failed because the king trusted (and needed) his Lord Treasurer, and was convinced that the accusations were too trivial to warrant so drastic a punishment. Following Weston's death a year later, Charles tried to play the two sides off against each other. Instead of awarding the treasurership to either Cottington or Juxon, he appointed a commission that included representatives from both groups to run the treasury. Since this compromise quickly proved unworkable, the next year Charles elevated Juxon, Laud's man, to the post. While this might suggest that the archbishop's influence was becoming paramount, Laud was, on the other hand, unable to persuade the king to let his friend and ally, Wentworth, return from Ireland. The archbishop recognized the limits of his power, constantly complaining to Wentworth of the sloth and ignorance of 'Lady Mora,' the Latin word for 'delay' they used for those with whom they did not agree. It would be wrong, however, to assume that there were two distinct factions among the king's ministers, with alternative political programmes. 'Thorough' and 'Lady Mora' were more symptoms of the frustration that friends often vent in private letters than the reality of public policy. Laud never understood that after Buckingham's death Charles refused to let any single individual completely dominate his government, for the duke's hegemony depended on a very special relationship that could never be replicated. As befitted a man with a tidy mind, Charles worked through the privy council, issued proclamations, briefed the judges before they set out to ride their circuits throughout the land, and, in general, departmentalized his administration.

The privy council was the executive committee that had governed England for over a century. It usually sat twice a week, on Wednesday and Friday evenings. Four of its standing committees (on trade, Ireland, ordnance, and plantations) met weekly, while the fifty (on foreign affairs) convened whenever the king ordered, perhaps because he occasionally attended and its members were especially influential. High officers of state, such as the Archbishop of Canterbury and the Lord Treasurer, were automatically members of the privy council, as were ministers the king particularly trusted. Although the council's formal membership grew during Charles's reign to between thirty and forty, in reality a small inner clique dominated its proceedings. In 1636, for example, Arundel, Juxon, Coke and Windebank were members of all five standing committees, Laud and Cottington of four, Dorset of three, and nine other men of one apiece.[19]

During his hegemony Buckingham had often by-passed the council. In the 1630s it regained its influence, with the number of orders it sent justices of the peace increasing greatly. Sometimes it lacked a sense of proportion. In November 1633 it appointed the Earls of Suffolk and Kellie, the Archbishop of Canterbury, the Lord Treasurer, and the Lord Keeper to an *ad hoc* committee to investigate a threat on the king's life made by an emotionally disturbed child of six.[20] Most of the time it dealt with more substantial matters. The problem was that Charles did not let it use consensus to solve routine business, but left that task to individual ministers operating within their own departments. This meant that although the solutions that each minister pursued might well have been just as good as those of the privy council as a whole, their enforcement lacked the weight of the council's authority. To compound the problem Charles chaired council meetings only in moments of crisis, or when some particular item of business caught his fancy: on average he attended their bi-weekly session once a month, and (apart from foreign affairs) hardly ever went to the sub-committees.

Charles left the government's business to ministers. Until his death in 1635 Weston handled financial matters. Of the two Secretaries of State Sir Dudley Carleton, Lord Dorchester, dealt with foreign affairs, and Sir John Coke was responsible for those at home – anticipating a division formally reached in 1782. Charles came to depend on Carleton, a hard-working diplomat who, as the king said, 'Ever brought me my own sense in my own words.' Having spent years as an ambassador in foreign countries Carleton was as ignorant about affairs at home as he was knowledgeable about those abroad, which was a special disadvantage when domestic issues were becoming more crucial. According to Clarendon, Coke's 'cardinal perfection was industry, and his most eminent infirmity covetousness'. The last part of this jibe was unfair, the first true, for even Laud had to admit that 'the old man was exceedingly diligent.'[21] After Carleton's death in 1632, and replacement by Sir Francis Windebank, Coke's influence waned. He was never informed about the secret negotiations with Spain, and as he grew older left much of the hard work to his Puritan secretary, George Weckerline.

That religion permeated Charles's government is not surprising, for it dominated seventeenth-century Englishmen's whole being in a way which we today find hard to fully appreciate. Although religion is crucial for an understanding of Charles's life, the faith for which he died in 1649 was very different from that in which he lived in the 1630s. The latter was far less intense: it was more a cultural, aesthetic, even administrative credo, than the mystical beliefs for which he gave his life. Those traits of his personality that we are inclined to explain in psychological terms he saw in religious ones. That religion, more than anything else, determined the sides that fought the civil war is undeniable. Yet the religious enthusiasm that has been assigned to the king's opponents by calling them Puritans may with equal validity be attributed to Charles. He was a devout Anglican, punctual – even punctilious – in his observances. He was a promoter of strict ceremonies, a discerning judge of sermons, being especially fond of those of Lancelot Andrewes and John Donne. Recognizing the power of the pulpit was (as he told his son) greater in peacetime than that of the sword, he ordered that no 'men of ill deposition towards the present State' should be allowed to preach the assize sermons.[22] In Charles's mind there was little difference between the judgement of God, as symbolized by the preaching of His Word, and that of the king, whose judges immediately after the sermon opened the assize to dispense his justice. Like Caesar, Charles was convinced that he should render unto God, and unto God alone. Eighteen months after becoming king he first published his views of the proper relationship between church and state in a circular letter to all bishops:[23]

> We have observed that the Church and State are so nearly united and knit together that though they may seem two Bodies, yet indeed in some relation they may be accounted but as one.... This nearness makes the Church call in the help of the State to succour and support her ... and ... the State call on for the service of the Church both to reach that duty which her members know not, and to exhort them to, and encourage them in that duty they know.

Because Charles consistently believed that the church and state must work intimately together, it is no accident that his relationship with his *de facto* minister for religious affairs was both a long and a close one, often making it impossible to tell which of them initiated a specific policy. Charles relied on Laud more than any other churchman. A protégé of Buckingham, Laud's rise in the royal favour was nearly as rapid. The king made him Bishop of Bath and Wells in 1626, of London in 1628, and in 1633 on the death of the incumbent, George Abbot, fulfilled the promise made seven years before, by creating Laud Archbishop of Canterbury. For a long time Abbot had recognized that Laud had eclipsed him, bitterly noting in 1627 that 'all the keys of England hang at his girdle.'[24]

William Laud had been born in Reading, a Berkshire market town, in 1573, the son of a prosperous clothier who held every municipal office but mayor. After a sickly childhood, he went to St John's College, Oxford, on the closed scholarship that Sir John White, the college's founder, endowed for the pupils of Reading Grammar School. At Oxford he had a brilliant career that culminated in his elevation, after a notoriously corrupt campaign, as president of his college. Laud was the 'scholarship boy' made good. He had the academic's relish for feuding, and the pedant's penchant for details. He was both proud and sensitive about his lowly start. Sometimes the archbishop intervened with the king on behalf of his home town, helping Reading obtain its 1636 charter, and raised money to build the majestic quadrangle at St John's that still bears his name.[25] At other times Laud let his humble origins make him seem rude and curt, almost to the point of spite, as if he felt that the low-born resented how far he had come, as much as the high-born scorned whence he had started. His contemporaries sensed that his shortness was the key to his choleric disposition, nicknaming him 'Little Laud'. One radical young priest, just down from the university, remembered that when he asked the archbishop to reconsider the ban on his preaching, Laud refused, becoming very agitated 'as though blood would have gushed out of his face'.[26] Laud was a public man in the sense that he had no private life. The only forms of exercise he took were callisthenics, whirling books, like Indian clubs, in the privacy of his study; once he did so with such vigour and with so weighty a tome (the title of which, alas, has been lost) that he ruptured himself. Laud never married, and unlike his Catholic rivals, such as Father Con, could not charm the ladies. His diary shows he suppressed his sexual desires: one night he dreamt of sleeping with Buckingham.[27]

Laud was a peppery little man, with a fine eye for the finest detail. Nothing seemed too small to escape the Primate of All England's censure. He wrote to the Warden of All Souls that the fellows' hair was too long, and to the college authorities at Cambridge that the undergraduates were wearing luridly coloured socks. He did not deliver these pretty rebukes with the tact or light touch that would have made them more palatable, but used the same strident tones for hairy dons or gaudy students as the most obdurate Puritans reserved for adulterers or actors. No matter how trivial the issue, Laud was convinced that the purity of his motives excused the harshness of his manner. Like his monarch he could not comprehend how any decent man could possibly question the immaculacy of his position, and thus did not deign to court support. While he agreed with his opponents that the Church of England was in bad shape, everyone being able to cite dozens of abuses (such as the incumbent at Stratford-upon-Avon, who kept pigs and chickens in the parish church), Laud effected no longterm solutions.[28] To be sure, his reforms at Oxford University might have produced a generation of first-rate ministers who could have revitalized the Church of England had the civil war not intervened. Yet, even had there been no war, and had Laud's educational reforms worked, they would have done little to help the Church of England for its strength lay in what he considered its weakness – the wide theological roof under which Protestants, from Calvinists to Arminians, might find shelter. In an age when toleration could not come from the intellectual consensus that men should be allowed to worship their Maker as they pleased, but was possible only as a result of an inefficiency that left people alone, effective reform was a contradiction in terms. It was also beyond Laud's limited abilities. He was 'a little urchin', Lambert Osbaldeston, a Westminster schoolmaster, quite rightly observed, 'the little meddling hocus-pocus'.

Two examples may illustrate how Laud, and his master, 'infused', as Thomas Fuller put it, 'more vinegar than oil' into religious affairs.[29]

In October 1633 Charles reissued his father's *Book of Sports* which declared that after Sunday Church people were free to enjoy healthy recreations such as dancing, archery, and (in moderation) church ales.[30]

Although some opposed such Sabbath breaking, for most people it was the only day that they had for recreation. Admittedly the church ales could degenerate into drunken brawls, but again they were one of the few releases working folk had from the daily grind. Yet Charles's reasonable edict failed to win the support of those most likely to benefit from it largely because he republished the *Book of Sports* to support Laud (who was having a dispute over jurisdiction with Lord Chief Justice Richardson concerning an injunction against church ales the judge had issued while riding circuit in Somerset) and not as part of a much welcomed social reform. To compound the mistake Charles did not allow those ministers who opposed the *Book of Sports* to duck the issue, but ordered all clergy to read his proclamation from their pulpits. Several refused, and lost their livings. One compromised by reading both the proclamation and the ten commandments, and then telling his flock, 'You have heard the commandments of God and Man, obey which you please.'[31]

Two years later, in 1636, Laud insisted that as archbishop he was entitled to inspect the universities. The vice-chancellor and heads of colleges at Cambridge protested that he had no such right, and, after an extended and acrimonious correspondence, the case went before the king, who decided in Laud's favour.[32] Yet, having alienated some very powerful men, Laud never found the time to exercise the right he had bought at so high a political price.

Laud's basic problem was that he saw only the trees (perhaps, only the twigs), believing that if they were healthy then the rest of the forest must be too. He dealt in symbolic details. If men worshipped God with the altar in the correct place, the prayer book opened at the right page, the service read in the proper order and the priest wearing the appropriate vestments, then true religion would automatically follow, and the Anglican church be ordered with the decorum fitting for the faith closest to Christ's original teachings. 'Unity cannot long continue in the church,' he argued, 'when uniformity is shot out at the Church door.'[33] In sum, Laud would have made a good non-commissioned officer, inspecting the troops to see that their belts and surplices were blancoed, their boots and Bibles spit-and-polished, making lists, bawling out trouble-makers, sure that if the details were perfect then the war would be won. And because Charles basically agreed with these assumptions, he chose as major general of his church militant a man more suited to be its sergeant major.

The line between the king's authority and initiative and Laud's is hard to draw. When Laud first became primate in 1633 he frequently told correspondents that he had referred church matters to the king, but within a couple of years he hardly ever mentioned having done so, passing decisions on his own authority. Details of such matters as the right of Protestant foreigners resident in England to worship in their own churches, Charles was content to leave to his archbishop. 'Put me at mind of this at some convenient time when I am at Council,' the king annotated, 'and I shall redress it.' As we have seen with the Cambridge case, the king invariably sided with Laud in jurisdictional disputes. He rejected the the 1636 petition from the Dean and Chapter of St Paul's to be excluded from the archbishop's annual inspection by explaining that he was 'resolved for the settlement of peace and the good order of the church, that no place without special grounds of privileges shall be exempt.'[34] The king's annotations of the annual reports that Laud wrote from those the bishops sent him, reveal that Charles knew little, and cared less, about the detailed problems facing the church at the local level, being content to leave their solution to Laud, who was only too willing to oblige. Thus in order to get Laud off their backs, and to show what a good job they were doing in licking their dioceses into shape, bishops tended to report fewer problems, until by January 1640 – less than a year before an all-out assault on episcopacy – they were mostly telling Charles that 'everything is well' with his church.[35]

On larger issues, such as clerical preferments, however, Charles tended to make the decisions. As Laud had to confess to Elizabeth of Bohemia, he could not persuade her brother to appoint her candidate, Dean Hassal, Bishop of Norwich, because the king would only promote men known to him, and had thus chosen the dean of his chapel, Matthew Wren.[36] In his dealings with the king, Laud remained remarkably insecure for a man who enjoyed so much power, having nightmares that he had lost the royal favour. The archbishop need not have worried. He and Charles were in basic agreement not just about theology and the proper relationship between church and state, but, as important, in the significance they attached to symbolic issues. The king applauded the archbishop's insistence that the altar must be placed at the east end of the church, and was not just a table on which parishioners could put their hats and under which their dogs could play and, Laud complained, 'piss'. In 1633 the king announced at a privy council meeting that the parishioners of St Gregory's, London, must move their altar back from the middle to the end of their church, declaring 'his dislike of all innovations'.[37]

Charles was particularly concerned about the fabric of church buildings. In 1629 he ordered all bishops to inspect every church within their dioceses, and repair those that needed it. Characteristically the king neither offered to, nor suggested, who might pay the cost.[38] The letter the king sent to the dean and chapter of Peterborough in 1633 was little more specific: it told them to use £319 from the leases of the manors of Caistor and Sutton to repair the cathedral. Since Laud drafted the letter, it seems likely that the initiative came from the archbishop, as did that for a similar letter sent in Charles's name a couple of years later, ordering the demolition of several shacks built too close to Canterbury Cathedral.[39]

There can be no question, however, who was behind the campaign to restore St Paul's. Indeed up until the outbreak of the Scots Rebellion, this project took up more of Charles's time and energy than any other matter pertaining to the church. Without doubt London's cathedral was in a mess. Lightning had damaged the roof and spire in 1561. The nave had become a clearing house for businessmen, a hiring hall for casual labour, a shortcut for Smithfield porters, carrying freshly slaughtered carcasses, a playground for children, and the place where gossips and the writers of newsletters picked up tit-bits and exchanged rumours. In sum St Paul's was a convenience for the public – in one case literally so, for in 1634 one Lucett, a yeoman from Warwickshire, was brought before the Court of High Commission, charged with moving his bowels within the cathedral. In his defence he explained that he had done so in a dark corner, out of the necessity of age, and anyway did not realize that he had done anything wrong. Even in those less fastidious days Lucett was lucky to get off with a 40 shilling fine, especially as Charles had just issued a set of regulations, that were posted conspicuously throughout the cathedral, on the proper behaviour therein.[40]

In addition to improving the decorum to be observed inside St Paul's, Charles was anxious to repair the fabric without. In 1620 James first issued a commission to raise money for this purpose, but it was quickly forgotten as the war with Spain occupied the public's attention and purses. The £2,000 Sir Paul Pender left the following year to repair St Paul's was a mere drop in the bucket, and the building remained in so deplorable a state that on becoming king Charles called it 'a national scandal'. In 1631 he commissioned fifty of the most important men in the land, including Laud, Weston, Wentworth, Cottington, Heath, Noy and Windebank, to raise money for repairs, and wrote personal letters urging prominent people 'to make a speedy and plentiful collection'.[41] Since neither scheme worked, in December 1633, Charles sent commissioners to every county soliciting donations, and to set an example gave £1,000, pledging £500 pa for the next three years.[42] This time the results were so gratifying that in April 1634 he promised to sell crown lands to pay for restoring the cathedral's west end.

Those who would not do their bit received shrift from the king. They were, he wrote, 'ill affected persons', who spread 'false and scandalous rumours' to distract 'our loving people' from 'that glorious work'. Charles pressured the reluctant, warning Mary More, a rich widow, who refused to give her mite, that she did so 'upon peril of our utmost displeasure'.[43] He sent letters to the justices and sheriffs of some thirty-six large towns urging them to collect. He directed that fines levied in ecclesiastical cases should go to the cathedral. He reminded the lawyers of the Middle Temple that their pledges hardly matched the prestige and profits of their profession.[44] Charles brooked no obstacle to the completion of his goals. He ordered a wall of the adjacent St Gregory's church, that had been built a few feet across the border on ground belonging to St Paul's, pulled down, because it obstructed the view of the cathedral, notwithstanding the objections of the parishioners (the same fractious bunch who were to place their altar in the middle) that doing so would cause the rest of the church to collapse. The case dragged on until 1638, when the privy council ordered the whole of St Gregory's pulled down.[45] Charles pursued the project of repairing St Paul's with untypical zeal, managing to raise perhaps as much as £40,000 to refurbish the west end (which he adorned with statues of himself and his father), to put in stained glass windows, and strengthen the roof beams. Quite simply – and this is how he saw it – Charles drew a parallel between the state of the church as a building and as an institution. He explained to the Lord Mayor of London in a letter requesting donations for St Paul's:[46]

> It has also been our care since we came to the throne not only to defend the true faith that we profess, but also to maintain the Church and clergy in their proper jurisdiction, and dignity and professions; and with all to encourage and enable our loving subjects, in all places to reedify, repair and beautify their churches, that respect and outward appearance being a good effect and clear evidence of their zeal.

John Bastwicke, MD, saw Charles's efforts in a very different light. He complained that the king was 'making a seat for a Priest's arse to sit in'. To Dr Bastwicke, who like most Puritans had an exceptionally sensitive theological nose, repairing St Paul's reeked of Rome. Although Charles was not, of course, a Catholic, the restoration was the corner stone of religious policies which had, even for far less sensitive nostrils, a distinctly papist effluvium. Charles tried to narrow the boundaries of conformity within the Church of England, forcing many Anglicans who did not agree with him, and who, since Elizabeth's day had found shelter within the church, out into the rain. He was a little like a man who partly lowers his umbrella during a storm. Those who stand closest to him remain dry, especially if they are conservatives, for as he lessened the umbrella's diameter, Charles shifted it from the Calvinist left, where James and Elizabeth had held it, to his Arminian right. Quite naturally those excluded felt resentful, especially the ministers whose careers were jeopardized. To them the current joke, wherein a stranger inquiring about their religious views asks 'What do the Arminians hold?' is told, 'All the best livings in England,' must have left a bitter taste. They would have been just as upset to learn that Charles lumped them, God's Elect, with the Whore of Babylon. 'The neglect of punishing Puritans', he believed, 'breeds papists.'[47]

Neither Charles's toleration of Catholics at court, nor his propensity to side with the church against secular authorities, helped win him favour with the mass of his Protestant lay subjects. The king sustained vicars in parish disputes over tithes, the ecclesiastical authorities in arguments about ship-money assessments, and the deans and chapters of Chichester, Norwich, Exeter and York in quarrels with the city authorities, once telling the lord mayor of the latter that he could not bring his mace, proud symbol of an ancient office, into the Minster.[48] Charles frequently dropped cases against recusants and released Jesuits from prison, because, as he told Father Panzani, he wanted to ensure that no Catholic 'blood shall be spilt during his reign.' Paradoxically, while tolerating Catholics at court, Charles's need for money meant he was less lenient on recusants in the country. Thus as many Protestants became convinced he was soft on papists, most Catholics felt the full weight of the financial exactions of the penal laws.[49] Charles realized the emigration of Puritans to Holland or New England was a useful safety valve. When Laud reported that one Bridges, a notorious separatist from Norwich, had fled to the Netherlands, he replied, 'Let him go. We are well rid of him.'[50]

Charles first attempted to define a comprehensive ecclesiastical policy in January 1630 with the issue of injunctions to Archbishop Abbot for the better governance of the church.[51] Unless required for the king's service, or at court, all bishops were to reside in their dioceses, ordain only worthy candidates to the priesthood, ensure that the liturgy was properly said by priests wearing the correct vestments, and check that privately endowed lectureships did not become the mouth-pieces for Puritan propaganda. To execute these reforms, and maintain the quality of church life, Charles employed bishops, the usual chain of command. He did so not just because he believed in the hierarchy that his father had summed up with the epigram 'No bishops, no kings', but because he had no other alternative. Until 1640 at the earliest the power of the bishops was widely accepted in England. Because bishops were Charles's chief instrument for the reform and government of the church, he made strenuous efforts to augment their incomes. In 1632 and 1643 he commanded all bishops not to lease their property for more than twenty-one years, so sacrificing long-term income for ready cash.[52] 'What great inconveniences must arise in both church and commonwealth,' Charles told the Bishop of St David's, forbidding the sale of diocesan lands in Radnorshire, 'if the authority of bishops be not supported.'[53] Charles did more than prop up episcopal authority to govern the church. After Weston's death, by relying so heavily on Laud, Juxon, and Wren that one royalist complained bishops now 'swarm mightily about this court,' Charles inextricably bound episcopacy with the whole of his personal rule. And when that rule failed, they, like Wolsey a century before, became convenient scapegoats.[54]

In church affairs, Charles and Laud set great store on uniformity of worship. The king ordered English churches abroad to use the Anglican liturgy. He was especially concerned with the state of affairs at the Merchant Adventurers' church at Delft, which he believed was run by 'refractory preachers'. The prelate drew up sets of canons to ensure that the Church of Ireland, that minute established church in an overwhelmingly Catholic country, conformed to Anglican practices, and was equally insistent that no Englishman be allowed to worship in the churches that Dutch and Walloon merchants had established in England.[55]

So long as Laud and Charles confined their pursuit of religious uniformity to foreign churches, Irish Anglicans, or even colonists thousands of miles across the Atlantic, it hardly mattered, causing little dissension. This pleased the king, who wanted peace and quiet in the country as much as he did at court. He told Bishop Bridgeman not to stir up 'controversy which may disturb the union and peace of the church ... or by anything which may perplex and trouble the minds of the people.'[56] Yet, when pushed to the brink in religious matters, Charles did not shrink from the good fight. 'You are in the Right,' he told Laud, 'for if fair means will not, power must resolve it.'[57]

Charles found the restrictions on his power in foreign policy far easier to accept than those in religious matters. After all in the former he was not dealing with the absolutes of faith that could jeopardize his soul, nor with subjects, who by definition should remain subject to his will, but with fellow monarchs, equals, whom he addressed as 'my dear cousin'. If any cousin was inclined to give himself airs, Charles followed suit, dating, for instance, his letters to the Emperor Michael of Russia 'from our imperial city of London', as if that metropolis beside the Thames was not a jot inferior to the one astride of the Moskva.[58] At the same time foreign policy did not have the limitations of domestic affairs. It could be conducted with great secrecy, through ambassadors, who were far more beholden to the king's good will than, say, justices of the peace. No writ from a meddling attorney could say a diplomatic dispatch. No parliamentary petition could protest against a secret treaty. Indeed so long as Charles did not want to go to war, he did not need that body and its taxes. The checks that foreign policy imposed upon the king were both slighter and more acceptable than those of domestic affairs, allowing his ambitions considerable freedom and scope. Charles frequently stated his main foreign policy goal was 'The entire restitution of his brother and nephew to their dignities and patrimony.'[59] Thus no matter how many treaties he broke, allies he betrayed, and blunders he made in the complex world of early seventeenth-century European diplomacy that he hardly understood, to this commitment he remained constant.

Even though on several occasions the king admitted that he was 'too lazy' to write, or read, diplomatic dispatches, in fact he spent more time and effort on foreign affairs than any other type of business: it was, after all, a fit occupation for a sovereign. Many more letters drafted in the king's hand may be found in the foreign state papers than the domestic. They range from important missives of Louis XIII to petty notes concerning the appointment of colonels in the Russian army.[60]

In the four years after Buckingham's death Charles relied heavily for advice in handling foreign affairs on Sir Dudley Carleton, whom he made Secretary of State in 1628. Carleton was an experienced diplomat, who rather than initiating policies carried them out for the king. After his death in 1632 Laud's influence increased. Often he restrained the king, pointing out that England could not afford expensive adventures abroad without calling parliament. But in spite of the allegations of his enemies that he was the Richelieu of England, the archbishop's influence on foreign affairs was not all that great, partly because he was not interested in them, and partly because Charles wished to retain control of them in his own hands – a frustrating location since circumstances at home and abroad allowed him so little latitude of action that, in reality, often all Charles did, or could do, was twiddle his thumbs.[61]

The king's decision never again to call parliament meant that he could not afford an active foreign policy that depended on the use of force, or a convincing threat to do so. This quickly became apparent as his relations with the Commons started to deteriorate. Five days before Buckingham's assassination the Marquis de Chateauneuf, the French ambassador, wrote home that the government's financial weakness made it one 'from which its friends can hope for no assistance, and its enemies need fear no harm.'[62]

By and large Charles's foreign policy was inept: apart from the desire to restore the Palatinate, it lacked a sense of direction and had little impact in world affairs. Yet from these failings came its main virtue. During the 1630s, according to one foreign traveller, throughout England 'the people, both rich and poor, did look cheerful.' Whilst the Thirty Years War ravaged Europe, the inefficacy of Charles's foreign policy brought England a period of peace and prosperity that was, another observer concluded, the envy 'of all other parts of Christendom'.[63]

Charles's foreign policy may be divided into five main periods, with a motif through two of them. The first started before his accession, with Buckingham's series of foreign adventures that included the Mansfeld expedition, the attacks on Cadiz and Ré, and the undeclared wars with Spain and France. Although the origins of the second period of peace-making may be discerned before the duke's death, Felton's dagger greatly accelerated the process that culminated in 1629 with the French treaty, and the Spanish a year later. It produced what the author of *The Practice of Princes* (who wisely hid behind the pseudonym 'A. Ar.') called 'a Hispanol-ished, Frenchified, Romanised or Neutralised' foreign policy.[64] Charles played an active part in bringing this about, as he did in the third phase, that lasted roughly from 1630 to 1634, when he tried to restore the Palatin-ate, first by sending Hamilton to Germany with a military force, and second through a series of rather ineffective negotiations with Gustavus

Adolphus. In addition, during most of the 1630s a sub-theme ran through British foreign policy – the attempt by the queen and her court set, aided by their Puritan allies, to join England to France against Spain. By 1634, at the latest, Charles who at this stage was not greatly swayed by pressure from his wife and her friends, came to realize that English influence in continental affairs was very limited, and started, by compensation, as it were, to build a large fleet. After the Scots Rebellion, the fifth, and final, phase began. Apart from a few attempts to win support from abroad, England ceased to count much in the world, being too preoccupied with the civil war at home.

Towards the end of his life Buckingham seemed to have realized that he must change his foreign policy by returning to a more traditional pattern. On several occasions in 1628 he declared his intention 'to walk new ways', and during the summer, using the Venetians as an intermediary, opened highly secret talks with France and Spain, sending Endymion Porter to Madrid.[65] Buckingham's murder prompted Charles, who was unfamiliar with these initiatives, to continue the duke's old bellicose policies. He launched a naval attack against La Rochelle, in part to honour his slain friend, while at the same time dropping hints to Henrietta Maria and the Venetian ambassador that he was willing to talk peace with France. Since serious negotiations were impossible whilst English troops fought to support a rebellion against Louis XIII, discussions quickly got snagged on the old thorny issue of the queen's French household. Charles described a set of peace proposals from Paris as being 'like the people from whence they came, of no weight and not to be trusted.'[66] After the surrender of La Rochelle Charles changed his tune, his tempo by January becoming decidedly up-beat. He told a deputation of militia officers from the Isle of Wight, who were concerned about the state of their coastal defences, that they need not worry since he was 'on very good terms' with Louis XIII.[67] In fact he exaggerated the progress of discussions, which were still bogged down on petty details, such as the fate of the French privateer, *L'Esprit*. When Father Weston, a Scots Jesuit acting for the French, raised the matter, saying that Marie de Medici was adamant that her son-in-law return the vessel, Charles replied with a pun – that was as rare as it was appalling – 'Let them talk of the Father and the Son, but not of the St Esprit.'[68]

More than anything else, the dismissal of Charles's third parliament forced him to make peace, for, as he had to confess to his Huguenot allies six months later, 'he was not in a position to contribute much further aid.'[69] Under Venetian sponsorship the talks began in earnest at Susa, a French town on the Italian border, where Richelieu was camped with his army. Charles approved the draft treaty the Lord Treasurer's son, Jerome Weston, brought back to London, signing the final version on 10 May.[70] Basically it altered nothing. Both sides agreed to release captured ships and men, and exchange ambassadors. None the less Anglo-French relations remained strained. By September Charles was complaining that Paris had failed to fulfil its side of the bargain: Sir Thomas Dishington, for instance, was still in the Bastille.[71] Yet while continuing to find fault with Louis XIII, and at the same time writing him and his family friendly letters lauding the benefits of peace, Charles was equally tardy in carrying out his side of the bargain. He did not evacuate British troops from Quebec until July 1631.[72]

The Spanish treaty took longer to complete than the French. Convinced that the dons had insulted him in Madrid, Charles felt his honour was at stake, while his sister, and his Dutch allies, were sure something far more tangible was at risk. The negotiations with Spain formally opened in June 1629, when Charles received Rubens, the painter, at Greenwich Palace as an envoy officially accredited to the Spanish Netherlands. Personally the two got along so famously that in November the king sent Sir Francis Cottington to Madrid to discuss peace. At first Charles insisted on the restoration of the Palatinate, but by April of the next year it became obvious that the Spanish would never agree. Even though his hopes that they might change their minds rose briefly during the summer, by September they fell so precipitiously that on 27 September he accepted Cottington's draft treaty, which he officially signed on Guy Fawkes Day 1630 – not the most auspicious date for Protestant England to make friends with Catholic Spain. Charles's choice of a Latin Bible for the ceremony was equally tactless, and helps explain why the public welcomed the treaty with scant enthusiasm: like that with France it settled nothing, going back to the *status quo ante bellum*.[73]

Although the Spanish treaty had little effect on England's enemies, it did harm her friends. When Buckingham sent Porter to Madrid in 1628 to raise the question of negotiations, Charles wrote to Dudley Carleton, British ambassador in The Hague, telling him to reassure the Prince of Orange that negotiations were at a very early stage, and that Dutch interests would be fully protected. Charles's fair words had the opposite effect. Prince William immediately had his ambassador in London seek an audience with the king, whose additional promise, 'I will not treat or abandon my friends', did little to reassure the Dutch.[74] They were right to be concerned. In December Charles ordered Carlisle, ambassador extraordinary in The Hague, not to tell them how far the negotiations with Madrid had progressed.[75] Early the following year he sent another ambassador, Sir Henry Vane, to Holland, and once more pressed the Dutch for troops to recover the Palatinate. When they were unable to agree to this impossible request, Charles convinced himself that his obligations to his allies were now over. By 7 September he was so willing to jettison them that a vague promise of help from Spain was all that was needed to persuade him sign the Treaty of Madrid twenty days later.[76] Relations between England and the Netherlands deteriorated so precipitiously that eight weeks later Cottington and Olivares initialled a secret treaty agreeing to jointly attack and partition Holland.[77] Almost by accident and certainly from ineptitude, Charles set the pattern of Anglo-Dutch relations for half a century. In spite of the marriage in 1640 of his daughter, Mary, to William of Orange, not until the Glorious Revolution were the two nations that a common religious heritage linked and trade rivalries divided, to become friends again.

When in the summer of 1628 Charles promised the Dutch to protect their interests, he made a similar commitment to Frederick and Elizabeth. They did not react with the same suspicion as William of Orange – lacking his military might, they could not afford to do so. In March 1629 Charles once again assured his sister, who had just lost her husband, that 'one of my chiefest ambitions is to do you real service'. As if to prove the point, a little later he asked the French to help her and her family.[78] As the possibility of an agreement with Madrid increased, so did the frantic letters Elizabeth wrote her brother. On 16 August Charles wrote back that while he was sorry to have upset her, he was convinced that a peace with Spain would in fact enhance her sons' chances of regaining their patrimony. Even though Charles did not explain how it would do so, Elizabeth had to be content with vague promises. To be sure he gave them with greater sincerity than any he proffered the Dutch, because the restoration of the Palatinate remained the active goal of his foreign policy for the next three or four years. In 1632, using the Dutch-born painter, Balthazar Gerbier, as an intermediary, he tried to stir up a rebellion in the Spanish Netherlands. Apparently Charles's commitments to the Palatinate overruled any he might have had for consistency, for this plot, which depended on Dutch help, was the complete antithesis of the secret agreement he had made with Spain two years earlier. Anyway, the subterfuge came to naught, largely because Gerbier betrayed it to the Infanta Isabella for 20,000 crowns. The painter played Judas with such skill, signing his letters 'your majesty's most humble, most obedient, most loyal and most zealous servant', that Charles, who had done much to further his career and was always susceptible to the blandishments of an artist, retained him as British ambassador in Brussels for another four years.[79]

Even before the king signed the Spanish treaty, he realized he needed the help of another great power to assist his sister and her sons. So when in the summer of 1630 Gustavus Adolphus, who, like a rocket from the north, had suddenly burst in to the war-torn European scene, asked him for a subsidy of 25,000 ducats a month, Charles did the best he could (short of recalling parliament) to oblige. He sent the Swedish king the Order of the Garter, and let Hamilton raise volunteers for Swedish service.[80] In spite of Charles's strenuous efforts to attract recruits, and his gift of £25,000 towards the expedition's expenses, Hamilton's 6,000 men were not ready to sail until August 1631. The king went down to Portsmouth to wish them godspeed. They needed it. At first all seemed to go well. As they landed at Stralsund on the Baltic coast, Charles sent Sir Robert Anstruther to Vienna, who reported back that both the emperor and the Spanish seemed favourably inclined to help the Palatinate.[81] 'If this opportunity be neglected,' Elizabeth wrote to her brother, after Gustavus's victory of 7 September at Breitenfeld, 'we may be in despair of ever recovering anything.'[82] Her nagging irritated Charles, who complained to Dudley Carleton that she did not appreciate all he had done for her: had he not sent Vane to Germany to negotiate with Gustavus Adolphus? But Charles failed to mention that he told Vane to haggle with that Protestant hero, trying to buy the Swedish king's proven military genius with vague, short-term promises of support. By early 1632 he could no longer offer Hamilton's expeditionary force, for during the winter it had degenerated into a bunch of starving refugees. After his victory at Donauworth in April when Tilly, the great Catholic general, was killed, Gustavus had even less need of English assistance: he broke off negotiations, telling Hamilton in September to take his rabble home.

Ironically Charles's inability to make an alliance with the Swedish king turned out to be a blessing in disguise. In November Gustavus was killed at the Battle of Lutzen, his cause shattered. But it took a year or two for Charles to realize his good fortune and that he no longer had any real hope of influencing European affairs. In 1634 he admitted as much to the Dutch, telling them he was 'resolved to live at peace with everyone'.[83] Such aspirations prompted Charles into sending John Taylor, a minor though experienced diplomat, to Germany to discuss the restoration of the Palatine with the Holy Roman Emperor. From Vienna Taylor wrote wildly optimistic reports that persuaded the king to send out the Earl of Arundel as ambassador extraordinary. Arundel had no illusions about the chances of succeeding in what he described as 'a desperate mission', for he, like most astute observers of European affairs, had long recognized that outside Britain his master had scant influence. None the less, the king's bumbling foreign policy, limited by a failure to define goals, a lack of consistency, and the absence of parliamentary taxes, served his people well. Perhaps Charles was right to commission artists and poets to laud his pacific policies, for all his nation lost in the awful carnage of the Thirty Years War, the most horrible European conflict until the world wars of the twentieth century, were three or four thousand men, and the mirage that some day its sovereign would be able to restore his nephew's patrimony.

As Elizabeth's influence over Charles's foreign policy declined, that of his wife increased, although not so significantly. After her marriage improved following Buckingham's death, Henrietta Maria allied herself with a group led by Dudley Carleton and the Earl of Pembroke that wanted a more aggressive war against Spain. In so doing she was continuing the tradition of an anti-Spanish faction led by someone close to the monarch, that may be traced back through Prince Henry to Queen Elizabeth's Leicester, though, in this case, the leader was motivated not by a radical Protestant hatred of popery, but by the patriotic desire to aid her native land. The Marquis de Chateauneuf, the French ambassador, encouraged the queen's ambitions, employing as his go-between Le Chevalier de Jars, a tennis partner of the king. The three of them formed an alliance with the Puritan Earl of Holland, one of the leaders of the Providence Island Company, which wanted to establish a base of godly privateers astride the Spanish Main.

In 1633 these strange Puritan-papist bedfellows suffered two crushing blows: Richelieu imprisoned Chateuneuf and de Jars for plotting to depose him, and Charles arrested Holland for challenging Jerome Weston to a duel. The queen's links with the anti-Spanish Puritans remained in abeyance until 1635, when, following Lord Treasurer Weston's death, Louis XIII sent a new ambassador to London, the Marquis de Senterre, whom one colleague described as 'the perfect courtier of ladies'.[84] For the next couple of years Senterre, Henrietta Maria and their Puritan allies, as well as Elizabeth's adherents in England, led by Sir Thomas Roe, and her sons, Charles Louis and Rupert, joined to persuade Charles to use his growing naval strength to attack Spain. The pressure on the king was intense: by February 1637 it seemed that he was about to give way, for he wrote, 'I have perceived the impossibility of restoring my sister and nephews by fair means. This has made me fall in with France.' But at the last moment Charles did not stumble. Instead of providing sufficient support to risk a war with Spain, the French continued to build up their own navy in response to the growth of the English ship-money fleet. Although he had sent the Earl of Leicester to Paris in 1636 as British ambassador charged with obtaining French help for the recovery of the Palatinate, all the earl got from five years in Paris was a little insincere sympathy. Furthermore the uninvited arrival in England in 1638 of his mother-in-law, Marie de Medici, with 600 hungry French followers, did nothing to endear Charles to the Gallic cause.

Although the alliance between Henrietta Maria and the Puritan faction had little effect on Charles's foreign policy, it does suggest first that the people who surrounded the king were a far less monolithic group than their critics (then and later), have thought; and second, that the ultra-royalist Catholic party, whose machinations were to prove so damaging to Charles's cause in the early 1640s, did not fully develop until after the outbreak of the Scots Rebellion. Before that time the intrigues of the queen and her set had been little more than petticoat politics – all lace and frills, without the promise of consummation. The barrenness of Her Majesty's games became evident after 1633, with the king's realization that he could no longer intervene with force on the Continent, and his subsequent loss of interest in events abroad. 'To tell the truth,' ambassador Gussoni wrote home to Venice that year, 'this government, just at present, devotes scant attention to foreign affairs.' Two years later his colleague from France confirmed the impression that the king's ministers 'think only of internal affairs'. Later that year, whilst walking one summer's evening with the king in a country garden in Bradford, Somerset, Gussoni tried to raise the question of Italian developments. Charles stalled, skillfully shifting the conversation to hunting and art; but just in case he had offended the diplomat, the next day sent him some venison.[85] In reality a few dead deer and stags were not enough to salve the king's sense of resentment about his inability to pursue an effective foreign policy.

Rebuffed on land, Charles tried to compensate at sea by building up a powerful navy. Because he used ship-money to achieve this foreign policy goal, the repercussions were, however, felt more at home than abroad. Although the gradual growth of the French fleet in the 1630s did pose some threat to England's security, Charles expanded the Royal Navy more for reasons of personal pride than defence. Of course Britain needed a strong navy. She was a growing trading power, with expanding colonies both in the New World and Ireland. She managed to persuade more Dutch boats than has been thought to buy licences to fish in the North Sea. Piracy was a serious problem, the state papers being full of their ourtrages: thirty Sallee ships took 200 captives from Cornwall; Yarmouth was bombarded by Dunkirkers; King's Lynn lost twenty-five boats worth £9,000; Ipswich five valued at £5,000; and the queen's dwarf and midwife were captured in the Channel. Perhaps the most pathetic instance of Britannia's impotence came in a report that Henry Hendy, master of the Dover mail packet, wrote in August 1635. During the past seven weeks pirates had boarded his ship, robbed and beaten him up five times. On the last occasion, the long suffering matelot showed his *laissez passer*, signed by the Secretary of State Coke, to the pirates who told him 'to keep it to wipe his breech'.[86]

In view of such insolence it is no wonder that Charles tried to stamp out piracy. The plight of those men and women captured by North African and Turkish marauders and sold into slavery, concubinage and Islam particularly affected Charles. As a prince of twenty-two, in one of his first acts of public business, he tried to comfort a deputation of grieving women, whose husbands were held in bondage in Algiers.[87] As king he wrote to the pirate chief Sidi Hamlet Laiashi to persuade him to free English captives, and issued a proclamation endorsing the collection of ransom money for their release. Such efforts did little good. In 1635 the king received a petition purportedly from over a thousand women whose menfolk were still slaves of the Infidel.[88] A mighty navy, it appeared, was the only thing that these insolent heretics understood.

A strong navy, too, did nothing to diminish the king's prestige at home. As Edmund Waller told him:[89]

Wherever the navy spreads her canvas wings,
Homage to thee and peace to all she brings.

Robert Powell dedicated his *Life of Alfred* (1635) to Charles because both kings had built up the navy. Charles doubtless relished the comparison for that year he explained he was expanding British sea power to curb the impertinence of foreign warships. The most grandiose claims that the Royal Navy had absolute jurisdiction at sea, could arbitrate maritime disputes between other nations, and secure free trade for all, came a few months afterwards, when Charles issued John Selden's *Mare Clausum*, a bombastic legal treatise that proved to the satisfaction of most English lawyers – though not many foreign ship captains – that Britannia had always, now did, and should for ever rule the waves.[90]

Charles was much involved personally with building up the navy. After collecting art it was his second most important hobby, or, to use his own phrase, 'his proper vanity'. Once when a group of nobles asked him why he spent so much money constructing the *Sovereign of the Seas*, he replied 'Why should he not be admitted to build that ship for his own pleasure?' It was, after all, far more beneficial than the squandering of 'their patrimony on riot and ungodly living' that so many of the aristocracy seemed to go in for.[91] During the 1630s the king spent far more time on the navy than the army. Once he ordered soldiers to march in the traditional English fashion and not the new-fangled continental style, and his government sent out training circulars and drill instructors, which did much to improve the militia.[92] In contrast Charles personally went through many naval papers, especially promotion lists, and often altered the Admiralty's recommendations.[93] Frequently he inspected ships and the royal dockyards. In 1631, for instance, he went to Woolwich in April to see the *Vanguard* launched, to Chatham in June to review the fleet and watch them at gunnery, and in August did the same at Portsmouth.[94] In 1633 Charles had his master shipwright, Pett, build two large vessels at a cost of £3,500 which he christened the *Charles* and the *Henrietta Maria*. The king watched them at their trials. Both were fine sailers, though – quite properly – the former was a little faster than the latter.[95]

In the summer of 1634 Charles embarked on his most ambitious shipbuilding project. During an inspection of the *Leopard* he asked Pett if he could build a super ship of some 1,500 tons. Pett agreed it was technologically possible, and in October sent the king a model of his proposed design. The two spent the following spring selecting oaks for the craft, the keel of which was laid at Woolwich on 21 December 1636. When Pett suggested that they delay the launching until the spring of 1638, there being no point in having the ship in the water for her timbers to rot and grow barnacles and weeds on her hull during the winter, when normally she would be out of commission, Charles disagreed. 'The sooner the better,' he ordered, fixing the launching for 25 September. Unfortunately the tide was not high enough to float the vessel free, and she had to remain aground until the October leap-tide. Charles christened her the *Sovereign of the Seas*. She was the naval wonder of the age, with 100 cannons, a crew of at least 1,000 men, and a high stern magnificently gilded and carved, all costing more than £65,000. Balladeers prophesied that she would:

> Curb the Pope and scourge the Turk,
> And ferret those that thieving lurk.

In fact her career was most undistinguished, and she turned out to be, in the words of the Royal Navy's foremost historian, 'the largest, most ornate and most useless ship afloat'.[96]

The *Sovereign of the Seas* was also an apt symbol of Charles's navy. Apart from the significance of the flagship's name both in terms of Charles's self-image and his ambitions, and its highly decorated stern, which was, in many respects, a floating art gallery (see Plate 9) the navy it led proved to be a particularly inept force. In 1635 the king ordered his first ship-money fleet of some twenty-five vessels under the command of Admiral Lindsey (by now restored in rank though not ability) to patrol the Channel, sweeping it clean of pirates. After an ineffectual attempt to convoy a Spanish treasure fleet (an unusual occupation for the navy of Drake and Hawkins), Lindsey anchored off Spithead, consuming food and cordage, and knighting his captains (all to the king's annoyance), whilst pirates ravaged the south coast, waylaying the cod fleet on its way back from Newfoundland. Even had they tried to chase the buccaneers, the Royal Navy would have had little success for the ships Charles built were too slow and large. Unlike the nimble ferret, the *Sovereign of the Seas* was too large to chase lurking thieves through shoals or up shallow creeks. The only navy capable of dealing with pirates was the Dutch, whose fast small, shallow draft vessels once cut out three privateers from under the Royal Navy's guns, and on another occasion seized a Dunkirker holed up in Yarmouth harbour. Charles, of course, protested about these infringements of English neutrality. Yet two inescapable facts remained: that curbing pirates was as much in England's interests as it was in Holland's, and that Charles's pro-Spanish foreign policy was at odds with his naval pretensions.[97]

Charles decided to build up the Royal Navy in much the same accidental way that he had to rule without parliament: he did not consider the financial ramifications. As far as he was concerned kings set policies, and their ministers found ways to pay for them. In 1635 Sir Francis Windebank wrote him a long letter explaining that the treasury was in bad shape, its commissioners meeting but twice a quarter, with ambassadors rarely paid. 'If your majesty continue in this way,' the Secretary of State concluded, 'your service will infinitely suffer.' Not bothering to write a formal reply

Charles annotated Windebank's letter, 'Haste the Balance & then you shall know more of my mind.'[98]

One reason why Windebank brought the financial crisis to the king's attention was the recent death of the minister who had overseen the crown's revenues with such skill for the past six years. Ever since Clarendon called him 'a man of big looks and a mean and abject spirit', Sir Richard Weston, first Earl of Portland, has had a bad press.[99] Like all financial ministers intent on making economies, Weston was not short of enemies. He tightened up the administration of the treasury by reinstituting the weekly accounts of financial transactions, exposed embezzlement in the royal stables, tried to keep household departments within their budgets, and cut expenditures on pensions from £125,000 to £80,000 a year. On the other side of the ledger he increased the crown's income: knighthood fines produced £190,000, while money from recusants rose fivefold – quite an achievement for a minister wildly suspected of being soft on Catholics.[100] Even though Weston's cheeseparing displeased the queen, he knew how to retain the king's favour. For instance, he always promptly paid the pensions due Elizabeth and her family. Within the limits of not being able to call parliament to vote taxes set by the king's policies and by his own desire to avoid impeachment, Weston was an effective and realistic financial manager, who kept his master under control, and provided him with enough money to pursue his limited goals. After the Lord Treasurer's death no one could curb the king. Charles first replaced Weston with a commission headed by Archbishop Laud, and then by Bishop Juxson as treasurer in his own right, both of whom were, quite naturally, less committed to books of account than those of Common Prayer.

As far as the education of his subjects was concerned, Charles's chief interest lay with the universities, which he insisted should be run in an orderly, uniform and seemly way. At Oxford he had some shacks pulled down between All Souls and Brasenose because they were eye-sores, and was greatly perturbed lest anyone, or anything – be they the city's 300 ale-houses, a couple of radical preachers, hordes of hot-headed undergraduates, or even dons made cantankerous by overwork – disturb the university's peace and decorum. He even let it be known that he found one of the exam questions the university set (on the plague) distasteful. If schism seemed a problem at Oxford, sex agitated Cambridge.[101] In 1630 Charles issued a proclamation that if any scholar was in danger of marrying the daughter of an innkeeper, or any such insalubrious trade, the university authorities could banish the wench at least four miles from town, apparently in the belief that the cold walk across the Fens to Dry Drayton or Westley Waterless would cure even the most unsuitable academic infatuation.[102] The king had a special fondness for the universities. 'Of our Princely affection to learning and care of the good Government of our University,' Charles told Cambridge, he was 'willing to reform whatsoever we find amiss, and reduce all extremities to their proper course.'[103] Charles even let Cambridge question one of his orders. The vice-chancellor and senate wrote to him that they had given degrees to the people he had nominated during his 1632 visit even though several of them had not fulfilled all the requirements. Charles replied that 'out of the special care for the advancement of learning and the honour of our said university,' he would not ask them to do so again – which was about the closest he could ever come to an apology.[104] The king's interest in education was confined to the universities. He visited only Oxford and Cambridge, his single trip to the Inns of Court being to attend a masque. He neither founded grammar schools nor endowed legal lectureships at the Inns of Court, although he ordered that the Company of Barber Surgeons continue their weekly lectures.[105]

The personal rule's most significant piece of social policy was the *Book of Orders* that the privy council issued in January 1631.[106] According to these regulations every month at least two justices of the peace, meeting in petty sessions, should supervise local officers such as constables, church-wardens and overseers of the poor, to see that they curbed mendicants, placed poor children in apprenticeships, punished delinquents, put the idle to work, kept roads repaired and maintained local law and order. Four times a year the justices were to report to their colleagues for the shire, the sheriffs and the itinerant judges, meeting in quarter sessions.

Although there has been some debate over the effectiveness of the *Book of Orders*, its introduction sheds light on the king's role in government, and the formation of policy.[107] The genesis for the idea came from Sir Edward Cecil, Viscount Wimbledon, who after much effort to find suitable employment following the Cadiz expedition was made Governor of Portsmouth. In 1630, he sent the king a memorandum suggesting ways of dealing with the poor, either to demonstrate he could do more than lead his men to Spanish wine warehouses, or else he was genuinely concerned with the plight of demobilized soldiers. Charles passed the proposal to Carleton, who, being much more involved with foreign policy, sat on it until Henry Montagu, the Earl of Manchester, took up the idea, and turned it into the basis for the *Book of Orders*. He did so partly because he had failed to introduce a similar programme a decade earlier, and partly because many members of the government were deeply worried by the immediate economic crisis, in which poor harvests threatened widespread starvation and social dislocation. Even though there is no evidence that Charles helped draft or revise the orders they bear the stamp of his belief (doubtless because the authors knew his predilections, and needed his approval) in a regimented, paternal society, based on Elizabethan precedents, and an idyllic image of the past, in which local elites solved local problems. For this reason Charles wanted gentlemen to leave London to return to their country estates and look after their lands, their tenants, their livestock and their people, because he was sure their ancestors had done so since time immemorial.[108] Similarly Charles granted John Smith a monopoly to inspect lambskins to see that they were properly cured, not because his government desperately needed the £50 Smith paid for the privilege, but because he believed that was the way the economy had always been ordered and standards maintained.[109]

In sum the king set the style of his government's policies – build on the past, regulate in the present, order for the future. The *Book of Orders*, for instance, came in reaction to Wimbledon's memorandum, Manchester's thwarted ambition, and the depression of 1630–2, while monopolies were invariably granted in response to petitioners. Like its predecessors, Charles's government rarely went out to find people to enforce its policies. For example, when it tightened up the procedures of the Court of Wards, an odious institution that preyed on families ravaged by the death of a father with minor children, it relied more on informing for reward than the police action of its own officials. Charles rarely bothered himself with details. There is no evidence, for example, that he drafted or amended any of the letters sent in his name concerning the ambitious schemes to drain the Fens. Rather, by choosing men who were both dependent on him and sympathetic to his own sense of an ordered hierarchy wherein everyone knew and accepted their place, Charles tried to extend the world he created within his court into the country beyond. The success of the crown's social policies during the personal rule was greater than many would credit. Such should not be surprising, for the vast majority of Englishmen shared the king's belief in the absolute necessity of order and hierarchy. 'God Almighty in his most high and wise providence,' preached John Winthrop aboard the *Arabella* just before he and his party were about to land to create a New England, 'hath so disposed of the condition of mankind, as in all times some must be rich, some poor, some high and eminent in power and dignity; others mean and subject.'[110] Had Charles been in the congregation he would have surely agreed with a profound 'Amen!'

The king's practice of either directly or indirectly setting the broad outlines of policy, and then leaving the details and repercussions for his ministers to settle can perhaps be best seen in his dealings with local governments. Relations between the crown and regional executives were not subject to the same judicial review as, say, the levying of taxes. Neither did they take place in the public arena accorded to paliamentary affairs, especially when confined to dealings between the crown and branches of the royal executive, such as the north, Wales, Ireland and Scotland. Attorney General Heath summed up Charles's views of local administration: 'The government of the whole stands upon the well ordering of the parts.'[111]

Heath wrote concerning the bailiffs and alderman of Yarmouth, a particularly troublesome bunch that the king spent much energy trying to coerce.[112] He was a little more successful with their colleagues twenty miles to the west. When in 1635 two aldermen from Norwich questioned the crown's right to appoint lord lieutenants, Charles silenced their impertinence by issuing a writ of *quo warranto* challenging the legality of the city's charter, and, for good measure, summoned the mayor and aldermen to appear before Star Chamber.[113] Two years earlier some dissidents in Newcastle got equally short shrift. He brushed aside their petition accusing the mayor and camberlain of nepotism and embezzlement, as a 'pretence of grievances'.[114]

Complaints from London could not be dismissed so cavalierly, since the capital was both powerful, and the crown's chief source of loans. Even so Charles tried to meddle with the city's affairs. He told the lord mayor to cooperate with the commission he appointed to ensure that the streets were swept and the Thames cleared of wrecks. Believing that hospitality came cheaper than hygiene the city authorities treated the commissioners to a sumptuous banquet, that produced the royal reprimand that they 'were not appointed to be feasted by you, but to see that service effected.'[115] Charles told London not to trespass on the jurisdiction of admiralty courts, and to respect the privileges of Dutch and Huguenot merchants, who were exempt from the city's ship-money assessments, and its regulations that only freemen, who had completed an apprenticeship, could ply a trade within its bounds.[116] He upset the city's pride by failing to make the accustomed entries into London replete with pomp and circumstance, presents from, and knighthoods for, the city fathers. Charles tried to have his candidates appointed as sea-coal metres (a profitable post supervising London's growing trade with Newcastle), and, without success, attempted to interfere with the running of London's court of orphans.[117] King and city quarrelled over more substantial matters. Charles annoyed London by selling pardons to those who had built in the suburbs contrary to statute, and thus outside the city's jurisdiction and tax base. He fined London £12,000 for failing to fulfil its commitments to colonize Ulster, an act that several have cited as a typical piece of highhandedness, even though most Londoners thought it a small price to pay to be rid of that pestilent province. In spite of conflicts over matters both great and small, with the brief exception of 1639 to 1640, Charles retained the support of the capital's ruling oligarchy, not so much for the effectiveness of his policies, but because they needed him to preserve their hegemony, just as much as he needed them to maintain his.[118]

In dealing with the branches of the executive that ruled the north and Wales theoretically Charles had considerable freedom of action. When he appointed Wentworth president of the Council of the North in 1629, and the Earl of Bridgewater president of the Council of Wales in 1633, the king gave them long and elaborate sets of instructions, running to some fifty-three sections of twenty-seven folios for the former, and fifty-five sections for the latter.[119] While there is no evidence that Charles personally drafted or revised these long instructions, it is unlikely that he did not read, or skim, or, at least, was briefed on them. Both sets share common objectives: the lord president was to prevent libels and prosecute traitors; he was to obey the privy council and the king's proclamations. The instructions laid down the fees he and his officers might charge, the expenses they could claim, the accounts books they must keep, and the salaries they were to receive. Other problems were peculiar to each locale: that the king was especially concerned by retainers and recusants in the north is understandable; that the prevention of adultery, incest and fornication in Wales should particularly agitate him, remains something of a puzzle. In many ways these instructions represent the quintessence of the personal rule which was, as Bridgewater learnt, 'His Majesty's much desiring the continuation of good and quiet government.' It was instructive that Charles's definition of good government was quiet government: he did not want the boat rocked because, ultimately, he did not want to be bothered. Yet Charles established no effective machinery to fill the void left by his decision to rule without parliament. Rather than establish new policies he tried to strengthen and refine existing procedures. None the less since Wales and the north during the civil war remained bastions of royalism, the tactics summarized in his instructions were not without success.

The same cannot be said about Charles's policies towards the other two great areas of regional government, Scotland and Ireland, which were, in fact and law, not part of one united kingdom, but separate kingdoms sharing the same sovereign.

Charles took very little direct interest in the government of Ireland. He never visited that country, and before 1633 rarely wrote letters on its affairs.[120] The massive correspondence in the king's name with Sir Henry Cary, Viscount Falkland and Lord Deputy of Ireland, consists almost entirely of minor matters, too petty for Charles's interest or energies. His subsequent lack of knowledge about Ireland proves that at the most the king had very little hand in drafting these letters.[121] Like his father, Charles's chief concern was to ensure that English imperialism in Ireland paid for itself, or, better still, returned a profit. With this end in view, and faced by the threat of a Spanish invasion of Ireland, the king had Falkland open negotiations with Irish landowners in the summer of 1625 that eventually concluded with the 'Graces' of November 1628. In the 'Graces' the crown guaranteed certain Irish land titles, lessened the powers of the court of wards, and let Catholics take a loyalty oath rather than the old oath of supremacy that abjured the temporal powers of the pope. In return the crown received a contribution of £10,000 a year for three years. Following Buckingham's death, Falkland's enemies in England persuaded Charles to dismiss the Lord Deputy, whom he replaced with a duumvirate of Adam Loftus, Viscount Ely, and Richard Boyle, Earl of Cork, two very able men, whose administration was damaged by a deep-rooted hatred of each other, and the end of the contributions agreed upon in the 'Graces'. So in 1633 Charles appointed Sir Thomas Wentworth Lord Deputy of Ireland.

Although Wentworth's administration was a significant one, some have credited him with abilities greater than he actually possessed. In many respects, he has been luckier after death in his biographer than he was in life with his king. True, Wentworth brought law and order to Ireland, even managing to produce a tidy financial profit for the crown. But he did so at a terrible price. He alienated every group in Ireland so severely that less than two years after he left Dublin the island was engulfed in a civil war that swept every one of his master's realms. But like English statesman ever since, Charles assumed that so long as Ireland was quiet all must be well there. The survival of Wentworth's papers enable us to assess the king's part in the government of Ireland during the years from 1633 to 1640. The basic and routine level was via the roughly four hundred letters written in the king's name by his secretaries of state on such petty matters as delinquent taxpayers, or appointments to the Irish bar, about which Charles knew little and cared even less. The forty letters in the king's hand reveal that he was more interested in protecting the Duchess of Buckingham's Irish lands, making sure that London lived up to its obligations in the Derry plantations, and with patronage – over half his letters deal with appointments in the Church of Ireland and at Trinity College, Dublin. Notwithstanding Charles's initial promise 'to servants of your quality . . . I allow no Mediator,' in fact the king's most significant communications with his Lord Deputy came through Sir George Radcliffe and Laud. The archbishop used to read Wentworth's letters to Charles, and then relay the king's wishes and comments to his dear friend and ally. Although Charles refused the Lord Deputy the earldom he wanted so desperately, he fully supported him in Ireland's Byzantine politics. For instance, Charles ordered Viscount Loftus, Wentworth's bitter enemy, 'to submit himself and acknowledge his fault before you, and to petition for pardon.'

On balance Charles supported Wentworth not because he trusted or liked him, but because he provided 'good and quiet government', persuading the Irish parliament to vote taxes, as the people peacefully went about their business neither murdering British soldiers nor boycotting alien landlords. Wentworth confirmed the opinion that all was well in England's other isle by assuring the king that the Irish were 'well satisfied, if not delighted, with His Majesty's gracious government and protection.' The illusion was mutual. 'His Majesty and all that serve him,' Wentworth learnt, 'both approve and commend your judicious and constant procedures on all things concerning His Majesty's service and the good of that kingdom.' Thus when Ireland exploded in rebellion in 1641, the English government and people (just as in more recent times) reacted with the outraged surprise possible only from those who have for years assiduously ignored the fact that they were exploiting another people of a different faith.[122]

About a year after the monarch who had united the two parts of Great Britain died, the Venetian ambassador wrote, 'King James made much of the Scots,' while his son 'is close fisted with them. He has never been crowned, a necessary thing, he has never summoned their parliament.'[123] Unlike his father, Charles neither understood, nor really liked the Scots. And therein lay his undoing. As a prince he concerned himself with Scottish affairs, frequently sending instructions to the privy council in Edinburgh, and sometimes drafting letters for his father's signature. Yet he never completely trusted the Scots, believing that they hid their deviousness behind a façade of plain dealing. He was particularly suspicious of Highlanders, calling them 'that race of people which in former times hath bred so many troubles.' He felt they should be encouraged to emigrate to Nova Scotia.[124] Because England no longer had an ambassador in Scotland, Charles did not receive regular reports on events north of the border. He did not much concern himself with the thousands of communications between his two governments in London and Edinburgh, which – to add to the confusion – shared several institutions, such as parliament, that had the same name, but very different functions and procedures. Basically Charles was an anglicized Scot, who assumed that his fellow countrymen should be the same.

In itself the fact that Charles neither liked, nor understood the Scots was not so serious an impediment. He was not the first, nor last, Englishman to exhibit such traits which, it could be argued, might explain centuries of English hegemony. The real danger was that Charles thought that he knew that nation: after all he had been born there, brought up by them, and many of his best friends, such as Lennox and Hamilton, were Scots.

Soon after becoming King of England, James VI of Scotland tried to strengthen the links between his two realms. He failed. The English parliament objected to giving Scotland freed trade or common citizenship, preferring the two countries to remain linked only by a common monarch.[125] After coming to the throne Charles wisely did not revive his father's attempts at union. Foolishly, however, his neglect destroyed the remarkably effective system by which James had been able to rule Scotland at a distance through powerful local councillors, and put nothing in place of this conciliar form of government. Instead he attempted to institute two major reforms north of the border which anticipated by half a decade the personal rule in England.

First he ordered that no member of the privy council in Edinburgh could also be a judge of the Court of Sessions, Scotland's supreme court. This greatly upset many Scots, including the seventeen men who sat on both. In addition the king failed to appoint powerful magnates, such as the Earl of Montrose, to the privy council. He further weakened the council by setting an awkwardly high quorum for its meetings, and, in 1633, by doubling the number of bishops on its roster, and adding nine Englishmen, all non-residents.

Charles separated the Court of Sessions from the council to enhance the latter's power. As a sign of its new importance he ordered the judges to ride to hearings, betraying an ignorance of Edinburgh's hilly topography, which favoured a dignified procession on foot, rather than a dangerous scramble on horseback. By choosing judges more for their loyalty than their influence, Charles displayed a far more damaging lack of knowledge about the land of his birth. The Court of Sessions (which had no English equivalent) derived its authority from that of its powerful members, rather than any constitutional position. Once they departed, so went the court's influence. To compensate Charles used the prerogative to create alternatives. But the Court of Exchequer, set up to hear matters concerning the royal revenue, never amounted to much, nor did the Commission of Grievances, even though it had proclamations read at every market place that it was open for general business.

These reforms were as unpopular as they were ineffective. Sir James Balfour thought that the new Court of Sessions was 'nothing but the Star Chamber Court of England come down there to play the tyrant.' In late 1626 a deputation of leading Scots nobles and ministers set off south with a petition for the withdrawal of the changes, but before they could reach London the king curtly ordered them home. 'Since our desires be so just and fair, and the means we use so lawful,' he told them, how could any Scot in good faith possibly question what he had done.[126]

The opposition to Charles's second major set of reforms was not so readily silenced, since it threatened the land titles of many Scots. On 14 July 1625 he issued the Revocation Edict cancelling all grants of land made by the crown since 1540, which would include property that had belonged to the church before the Reformation. Although he promised compensation, few landowners surrendered their property, and so in February 1627 Charles issued a second proclamation permitting them to continue to enjoy their lands on crown leases which he could buy back at a 10–year purchase, the profits going to subsidize the stipends of the ministers of the kirk. Even though the Revocation Edict did not result in the wholesale loss of land that many landlords feared, and, on the positive side, helped produce a scheme for supplementing church livings so effective that it lasted up to 1925, none the less Charles got the worst of all worlds: the kirk was ungrateful, the privy council ineffective in enforcing the edict, and the nobility, who were frightened far more than they were fleeced, were alienated from the crown.[127]

From about 1628 to 1633 – more from luck than judgement – the impact of Charles's neglect of Scottish affairs was benign. He left the government of Scotland in the hands of the Earl of Menteith, an extremely competent administrator, who managed to undo much of the damage wrought in Scotland during the first three years of his reign. But when the earl's enemies at court persuaded the king that Menteith's quixotic, and certainly antiquarian, claim to the Earldom of Strathearn was in fact an infringement of the royal prerogative, Charles dismissed him, placing him under house arrest. He was not released until 1637, by which time the king's policies north of the border were beginning to unravel.

Until the crisis of the Scots Prayer Book, Charles demonstrated little effort in either implementing policy in the land of his birth, or satisfying the concerns of its inhabitants. He turned down Sir Archibald Napier's offer to set up a network of correspondents to keep the king fully informed of Scottish affairs.

Having set the broad lines of Scots policy Charles lost interest in both the details of its implementation and the concerns of his Scots subjects. Occasionally he wrote a letter dealing with Scottish matters: he ordered border violence curbed; he told John Stewart, Earl of Traquair and Lord Treasurer of Scotland, to pay the arrears on the pension due his nanny and wet nurse, and his palace servants their wages, which were so behind that they were pawning the tapestries at Holyrood for food. Charles became very interested in Sir William Alexander's scheme for the colonization of Novia Scotia, selling some 114 baronetcies to raise money for the project.[128] But in all, the king's involvement did not amount to much.

A sure sign of his lack of concern with the land of his birth (and one noted by many on both sides of the border) was his reluctance to go to Edinburgh to be crowned. Within a year after his accession the omission caused adverse comment. It was even rumoured that Charles wanted a deputation of leading Scots to come to London with that nation's crown so it could be placed on his head without the bother of leaving home. In July 1628 Charles first announced that he was going to Scotland to open parliament in September. Buckingham's death and the La Rochelle expedition postponed the trip until the spring of the following year, when he put it off to the autumn, and then again to June of 1630, though, as if to demonstrate his good intentions, this time he told his servants to spring clean the Scots palaces.[129] They swept in vain. In November 1631 Charles told the privy council in Edinburgh that he intended coming there to open parliament the following 13 April, but a month before he was due to leave called off his visit to 1633, when, to the surprise of the many Scots, whom his procrastination had both offended and inconvenienced, he actually arrived.[130]

The king took his time riding north. He left London on 8 May, lingered at Theobalds for a few days hunting, before setting off via Royston, Huntingdon, Althorp, Stamford and Grantham. At Welbeck Castle the Earl of Newcastle entertained the royal party so lavishly that he had to drop out of public life for several years to recoup his fortunes. Charles stayed at York from 24–26 May. He knighted the mayor and aldermen, attended divine service at the minster, and ate roast heron at a banquet given by the archbishop. The next day at Richmond he gave £4 to a woman who had had quadruplets. A couple of days later, 200 men, liveried in ash-coloured coats, trimmed with red baize, escorted him into Durham, where he touched the sick for the king's evil. 'The gloomy cloud of our pressures and wants,' Mr Recorder Widdrington told Charles as he welcomed him to Berwick, 'is suddenly banished by the radiant beams of your Sun-like appearance.' In all Charles's progress was a great success; it tapped the reservoirs of his people's loyalty that years of indifference had not evaporated.

North of the border the well seemed equally gushing. After a triumphant progress through the Lowlands, Charles entered Edinburgh on the afternoon of 15 June. All the city magistrates were waiting at the Westgate to welcome him with an elaborate reception: a fifty-four gun salute, the inspection of portraits of all 107 of his Scots predecessors, tableaux, triumphant arches, the presentation s of wreaths and a gold bowl. In the finale, a short dramatic presentation about the power of kings, wherein Justice trampled down Oppression, a nymph concluded, 'The old forget their age and look fresh and young at the sight of so gracious a Prince.' Charles spent the next day resting and at prayer. The morrow he ennobled several Scots, dining that evening in public.

The climax of his visit came on 18 June with his coronation as King of Scotland. John Spottiswood, Archbishop of St Andrews, presided over the service, which lasted for four hours. At about ten in the morning a deputation of nobles escorted the king to Holyrood Abbey, Lennox riding on his right, Hamilton on the left, followed by the Earl of Angus carrying the sword of state, and the Earl of Rothes the sceptre. At the abbey Dr David Lindsay, Bishop of Brechin, gave the sermon, and as Charles was crowned John Guthrie, Bishop of Moray, threw specially minted crowns to the crowds who responded with traditional enthusiasm.[131]

Charles remained in Scotland for only a fortnight longer. He reviewed the militia, attended parliament, and gave the nobles a banquet at which some of the wilder Highland lairds drank far too many toasts, hurling their glasses to the floor after each, with an unrestrained devotion that must have pained its recipient. This might perhaps explain why Charles confined his Scots tour to the Lowlands, travelling to Linlithgow, Stirling, Dunfermline, Falkland and St Johnston. While crossing the Leith a sudden summer storm sprang up, taking twenty-eight lives and nearly drowning the king.[132] Happily Charles's journey home was much less eventful. His wife came from Greenwich to meet him at Stratford, where, according to Windebank, the infant Prince Charles welcomed his father back 'with the prettiest innocent mirth that can be imagined.' Abraham Cowley marked the occasion:[133]

Welcome Great Sir, and with all the joy that's due
To the return of Peace and You. . . .
Others by War their conquests gain,
You like a God your ends obtain. . . .
How could the Scots and we be enemies Grown?
That, and its Master Charles made us One
No Blood so loud as that of Civil War;
It calls for dangers from afar.

If a decade later Cowley reread his lines, they must surely have left a bitter taste. In retrospect, at least, signs of the impending crisis may be discerned even in Charles's triumphant trip to Scotland when at his coronation the bishops upset many God-fearing Presbyterians by wearing surplices, and using the Anglican prayer book. But at the time Charles and his advisers had no reason to worry. Cowley's words seemed to ring true, for his government of Scotland appeared to be making excellent progress. In many ways it prefaced that in England by half a decade, because, apart from patronage, Buckingham was not very interested in affairs north of the border. In Scotland, as he was afterwards to do in England, Charles initiated broad policies and then left their implementation, and the solution of the problems they engendered, to others. He treated his two kingdoms as separate entities, doing little (except for a fishing association that failed) to establish joint Anglo-Scottish ventures.[134] Because he essentially disliked Scots, Charles chose anglicized nobles more for their wit and friendship, than their knowledge and sagacity, to advise him on Scots affairs. Because the style and execution of the personal monarchy in Scotland became not so much a mirror, as a prototype for that in England, the failure of the former led, more than anything else, to the latter's collapse. A small vignette may illustrate this point. In 1637 Charles appointed Laud, Juxon, Montagu, Finch, Windebank and Coke to a committee to revise the Latin grammar used in most English schools. Eight years earlier in 1629 Charles had first proposed revising the rather obtuse Latin grammar, written by Alexander Hume, that was standard throughout Scotland. He told the privy council in Edinburgh to appoint a committee to draft a new grammar, with authority to *subpoena* schoolmasters to give evidence 'on pain of rebellion' if they refused.[135] If Charles was heavy-handed enough to punish reluctant pedants as rebels and traitors, then it is no surprise that when the king's attention turned to books of greater consequence, he was even more intolerant of opposition, and that many of his subjects, first in Scotland, and then in other parts of his realms, reluctantly concluded that rebellion was a pain that must be borne. Ultimately the roots of the failure of the personal monarchy lay not so much in impersonal forces that may have been building up over decades, or even centuries, but in the personality of the monarch himself.

# XII

# 'THAT FATAL BOOK'

When Dr Hannah, Dean of St Giles's Cathedral, Edinburgh, started morning service on Sunday, 23 July 1637, he also began the end of the personal rule. Immediately 'the inferior multitude' in the congregation heckled the dean. When the Bishop of Edinburgh entered the pulpit to try and quieten them, they pelted him with cudgels and stools. The Archbishop of St Andrews slipped out through a side door to enlist the aid of the city authorities, who with some difficulty managed to clear the church. As the crowd howled outside, beating at the doors and throwing stones through the cathedral windows, the ministers within finished the service, and then ran the gauntlet back to the safety of their homes.[1]

The reason for the mob's anger was obvious. They were protesting against the introduction of the new anglicized prayer book that Charles insisted the kirk adopt. The king's decision to do this, and, even more significant, his refusal to heed Scots protests against the new liturgy were no accident; both were central to his personality and policies. With his passion for uniformity, harmony and order, Charles was determined that his subjects on both sides of the border worship in the same fashion. With that inability to compromise that had been engendered in his early years, he quickly convinced himself that St Giles's riot, and the ensuing protests were more than a liturgical brawl, but were a mortal threat against monarchy itself. So he decided to force the new prayer book down the Scots' gullets, no matter the cost.

And the cost proved fatal.

Twenty months after the St Giles's riot the Scots forced Charles to call an English parliament, and thus ended the personal rule. Four years after the incident a civil war broke out in England, complementing and fuelling those in Scotland and Ireland. On a winter's afternoon a dozen years after that fatal summer morning Charles lost his life. Since all these events, as well as the confused and bloody history in between, may be traced back to the liturgy's introduction, Henrietta Maria, whilst a widow exiled in France, was quite right to call it 'that fatal book'.[2]

It has been suggested that the king had to die because his attempt to

189

rule without parliament was so ineffective and unpopular that it was bound to fail, producing a confrontation that Charles could neither win nor settle through negotiations. Being in legal theory – if not in financial reality – revivals of medieval rights, the expedients the crown used to compensate for the loss of parliamentary taxation have become known as 'fiscal feudalism'. These methods took a number of forms, two of the most annoying of which were forest and knighthood fines. By the early seventeenth-century most of the vast tracts of forests that medieval monarchs had established as hunting preserves had been cut down, built on, or farmed. Although such encroachments were technically illegal, they had been tolerated for hundreds of years until 1630, when the Earl of Holland (in his capacity as the Chief Justice of the Royal Forests south of the River Trent), and Attorney General Noy revived the three-centuries-old forest courts to fine all who had trespassed on crown lands.[3] Knighthood fines were another means of raising money through the revival of what one victim bitterly called 'an old skulking statute long since out of use, though not out of force'.[4] According to an act passed in 1227 all commoners worth more than £40 a year were obliged to attend the king's coronation to be knighted: after all, it was only proper that the king honour his wealthiest subjects. By the seventeenth-century inflation had eroded the exclusiveness of this £40 limit, though, perhaps not as severely as one balladeer complained:

> Come all you farmers out of the country
> Carters, ploughmen, hedgers and all.
> Honour invites you to delights,
> Come to Court and be all made knights.

So in 1630 Charles ordered the Attorney General to fine all men worth over £40 who had neglected to attend his coronation. Within five years the crown collected £173,537 from this source.[5]

Monopolies were another annoying, but lucrative way, of raising revenue. Although Elizabeth had given up many monopolies during the 1601 parliament, they were soon revived under the guise of patents which (like their modern namesake) were in theory intended to reward the ingenuity of inventors. In practice, however, they lined the pockets of the crown and its favourites. For Charles they had the additional attraction of maintaining standards and providing stability in the uncertain world of the market place. Nothing seemed too trivial for a royal monopoly. In 1637 the king granted one for the making of beaver hats, and a year later another to organize London's painters, and a third to purge the city of 'lewd and dissolute professors' of music.[6] Some monopolies applied to more vital activities. In 1633 the crown granted one for the manufacture of salt in return for a royalty of 10 shillings per way, greatly upsetting the traditional importers of Biscay salt. Three years later the crown established a saltpetre monopoly, and to ensure adequate supplies of a key raw material of gunpowder, authorized its agents to raid pigeon lofts for hoarded supplies of this obnoxious, but efficacious, compound.

The government appeared just as ridiculous when it used the Royal Navy to stop smugglers avoiding the monopoly the king granted the Company of Soapmakers of Westminster. They were a front for a group of the queen's Catholic friends, authorized in 1631 to use domestic raw materials such as lard, rather than imported fish or whale oil to make soap, which they would sell at 3d a pound, paying the crown a royalty of £4 per ton. This monopoly upset many people: the old makers, who could either come to terms with the new, go out of business, or make bootleg soap; housewives, who claimed that the new soap did not wash as well as the old; and the many Protestants, who found the monopolist's faith even more impure than their product. So the government put on a public display at the Guildhall, wherein two washerwomen, watched by the Lord Mayor of London, the aldermen, the Lord Lieutenant of the Tower, and their ladies, scrubbed and rubbed in two tubs to convince the public that the new (and improved) papist soap washed as well, and lathered better, than the Protestant brand. However, the public remained sceptical, preferring to use cakes made illicitly by the old soap manufacturers. Neither a testimonial signed by eighty prominent ladies, including four countesses and an equal number of viscountesses, affirming that their maids preferred the new product, nor another twin-tub demonstration in Bristol that it washed 'as white . . . and as sweet, or rather sweeter' than the old, convinced many. However in 1637 – too late, alas, to prevent a civil war – the washerwomen of England were allowed to return to the foam of their fathers when the Archbishop of Canterbury persuaded the king to take the monopoly away from the queen's Catholic friends, and return it to the old Protestant company, albeit at double the royalty of £8 a ton.[7]

Less frivolous, more famous, and without doubt the most productive form of fiscal feudalism was ship money. Like parliamentary taxes it was assessed on land and property, being intended to support the Royal Navy. Its origins and legality went back centuries to the time when coastal counties and towns clubbed together to provide ships to defend themselves against amphibious raids. In 1634 the crown decided to extend the shop-money tax to inland counties, turning it into a national tax. When Lord Treasurer Weston suggested that the legality of this extension might first be tested in the courts, Charles brushed aside his advice saying that no man of good will could possibly object, since 'the precedents are so clear.'[8] At first Charles's self-confidence seemed well confirmed. Of the first ship-money assessment in 1635 only £1,023, or 1.13 per cent, was in arrears, and of the much increased 1636 assessment totalling £217,184, only 2.23 per cent remained unpaid. Even though arrears rose during the decade from 3.3 per cent in 1637, 9.9 per cent in 1638, 16.7 per cent in 1639, to

77.3 per cent in 1640, these figures are in many ways misleading. The sheriffs collected the tax a year after it had been assessed, and towards the end of the decade they diverted much of the revenue brought in to pay coat and conduct money for the drafts levied to fight the Scots, thus exaggerating the arrears listed in the treasury accounts.[9]

Like all taxes, ship money was far from popular. Yet the vast majority of the complaints levied against it were administrative, rather than constitutional. For example, in Bedfordshire, a county that later became a parliamentary stronghold, there was not a single constitutional objection to the 1635 ship-money collection, and arrears amounted to a minuscule .014 per cent.[10] The following year in Oxford the sheriff reported, 'I find no one refractory, excepting Mr Markham,' a notorious miser and bedridden bachelor whose only expenses were a couple of illegitimate off-spring. Disputes over ship money resulted from the considerable latitude the crown gave sheriffs in making assessments, and which they used to reward their friends and punish their enemies. Thus the town of Cambridge tried to have the university taxed, and the city of Worcester worked to have the county's assessment raised.[11] John Hampden made the expected challenge in the courts against the new imposition. Yet Hampden lost his case and thus validated the tax's legality. Sir Francis Seymour's protest of 1639 that he could not, in conscience, pay ship money was unusual: far more typical was the attitude of a group of London merchants, who, two months later, told the crown 'they would be most willing to pay the ship money, if they might have your seas free.'[12]

Coming from a group of London merchants – supposedly the van of the rising middle class – such sentiments are surprising. Yet the degree of opposition to the fiscal feudalism in the 1630s was infinitely less than that voiced by the crown's enemies in the 1640s. Merchants might worry about the ineffectiveness of the Royal Navy, washerwomen might wring their calloused hands at the harshness of papist soap, consumers might agree with the contemporary opinion that monopolists were 'canker worms, harpies . . . and latent knaves,' but none was driven to the point of rebellion.[13] Indeed in Northamptonshire those whom the crown fined for breaking the forest laws tended to fight for it in the civil war.[14] What happened was that in 1641 and 1642 Charles's opponents used fiscal feudalism as an explanation – an excuse – for the widening rift between themselves and the king, the real causes of which came so close to the sovereign himself, that to enunciate them openly verged uncomfortably near treason.

Historians have seen fiscal feudalism as the last desperate efforts of a medieval monarchy to escape a deep-rooted crisis that was in part caused by the sale of crown lands over the previous century, and the stubborn refusal of parliament to vote taxes needed to run a modern state. Yet there was nothing new about this. Sir Edward Coke's assertion of 1625 that the 'ordinary charges the king should bear,' echoed the promise Edward IV had made 150 years earlier 'to live on mine own' and seek parliamentary taxes 'but in great and urgent causes'.[15] Although the crown had sold lands worth some £2,100,000 since the Armada, it does not necessarily follow that its financial problems produced its military defeats.[16] The Cadiz expedition failed because of bad planning, bad leadership, bad luck and because it was too large. The assault of St Martin's in the Ré campaign was repulsed because the scaling ladders were too short, surely the result of ineptitude, rather than the lack of a couple of shillings for a few more feet of lumber. During the 1639 Scots campaign, in which the king mobilized some 30,000 men, his short-fall was only £15,000. 'The truth is,' Charles wrote from the front in May, 'that I find my state on money to be such that I shall be able (by the grace of God) to maintain all the men I have afoot for the summer.'[17]

Neither fiscal feudalism, nor the crown's shortages of cash brought down the personal government. Neither did that impersonal tide in which, according to C. H. Firth, 'the individual actor, even when he seems to direct the cause of events is in reality their creature.'[18] Firth was the first of a couple of generations of historians who saw the origins of the English Revolution 'in society not men'.[19] A new middle class, gorged on monastic lands, and satiated with the profits from efficient farming, used parliament as the forum to demand political power commensurate with their newly won economic wealth. When the crown would not give them what they believed was rightfully theirs, they took it by force. On the other side of the coin the aristocracy was in a deep state of crisis, due to the helter-skelter creation of peers by James I, and the aristocracy's need to spend wildly to cut a figure in a world where their incomes were being whittled away by the diseconomies of scale of large hereditary estates.[20] The problem with this essentially Marxist interpretation of the origins of the English revolution is that an examination of a sample of individuals reveals that when the war broke out they did not in aggregate behave in the way that they were supposed to.[21]

Another long-term explanation of the bourgeois – or rather Puritan – revolution – has been radical religion. Yet just because religion became the most significant determinant of the side on which men fought it does not necessarily follow that it produced that fight in the first place. As Monsieur Brienne, the French minister, noted, 'It is a great evil that a political feud should be made into a religious war.'[22] To be sure religion (augmented by nationalism) was a key element in the Scots Rebellion, but in England it was as much a source of stability as conflict.

In sum, the problem of these long-term explanations is that they depend on reading events backwards. What an event became is not necessarily what started it. For instance, the civil war in England and Wales was an east versus west, and a north against south conflict, and yet such fundamental divisions are very hard to discern in the years before the outbreak of hostilities. Long-term explanations tend to impose on the confusion of short-term events a sense of order and planning that they lack in reality. Few men are as far-sighted as posterity (or their enemies) would have us believe. With hindsight it is too easy to telescope the centuries and decades. Clarendon, the greatest historian of the rebellion, did not fall into this error. 'I am not so sharp sighted,' he admitted, 'as those who discern the rebellion contriving from, if not before, the death of Queen Elizabeth.'[23] His myopia should be emulated.

Even in the short term it is hard to see how events in England during the 1630s necessitated a war. In fact, the first fifteen years of Charles's reign were remarkably peaceful. His regime did not leave the impression that it believed 'it was sitting on a powder keg'. Unlike the Tudors he did not have to suppress a Pilgrimage of Grace, Wyatt's rebellion, or the revolt of the northern earls. Towards the end of the personal rule Secretary Windebank boasted that his sovereign had not executed a single aristocrat for treason. He might also have mentioned that during the eleven-years tyranny Charles ordered only one person put to the rack, as compared to sixty-three poor souls tortured during the enlightened days of Good Queen Bess.[24] Perhaps the success of the 1630s explains why members of the Long Parliament who came of age during this period tended to support the crown.[25] Certainly it suggests that if we want to find the long-term causes of the war we should first look outside England.

The idea of introducing an anglicized prayer book to Scotland was not new. In 1619 James had considered a draft version drawn up by John Spottiswood, Archbishop of St Andrews, and Patrick Young, Dean of Winchester, but dropped the idea in the face of objections from the Scots. A decade later John Maxwell, an Edinburgh minister, sent Charles a copy of the draft that James had amended, arguing that so long as it appeared to come from their bishops the Scots would readily accept a new liturgy. With all their ardour for uniformity, Charles and Laud welcomed the idea, although the latter sensed that Scottish enthusiasms were not as wild as Maxwell would have him believe and so delayed the eventual introduction of the prayer book for nearly a decade. Charles used an English service book during his trip to Scotland and coronation in 1633. After his return, and Laud's elevation to the Archbishopric of Canterbury, he ordered the English prayer book used in the Chapel Royal at Edinburgh 'for example's sake', and he told the Scots bishops to 'draw up a liturgy as near that of England as might be.' At their request he sent them an English prayer book annotated with his suggestions, to use as the basis for the draft they sent him six months later. He returned to the bishops with further additions in May 1635. By the end of the year, with much of the type set, Charles even let them make changes in the proofs, and a little later accepted their suggestion to delay publication so as to allow the Scots time to get used to the idea of a new prayer book. In all, Charles took uncharacteristic pains to consult others, and accommodate their suggestions, and was convinced that he had conducted the whole business in 'a fair and legal way'.[26]

The king's careful considerations only delayed the introduction of the prayer book, giving the already formidable opposition north of the border time to grow. One minister called it English 'trash', replete with popish rites that would cause folk to break out into 'vile adulteries'.[27] Although the latter was one of the few calamities spared Scotland over the next generation, the prayer book was perceived as the next stage of a consistent policy set in motion in January 1636 when Charles issued canons ordering that members of the kirk take communion kneeling and remove their hats in church, and that bishops must license all schoolmasters, and permit oral confessions.

That Charles neither liked nor understood the Scots, and yet thought that he did so, was apparent in his dealings with them long before the introduction of the prayer book. His revocation edict made many fear for their lands; his attempts to reform Scotland's government made others worry for their offices; his persecution of Lord Balmerino (who was sentenced to death though not executed) in 1634 for possessing a copy of a petition against changes in the kirk, made still more scared for their lives. In forming his Scottish policies, Charles relied on anglicized Scots, such as the Marquis of Hamilton and the Earl of Lennox. He worked very closely with Archbishop Laud. Both of them had long-standing commitments to bringing Scottish worship in line with English practices. In about 1619 James had rejected 'the frivolous draft' for a new Scots prayer book which Laud, still an ambitious academic, sent him. In 1625 Charles ordered Archbishop Spottiswood to wear an English surplice for his father's funeral; but rather than doing so Scotland's primate refused to attend the burial of one of her foremost kings. While it is difficult to distinguish between Charles's and Laud's roles in devising the new prayer book, and without doubt both encouraged the other in their endeavours, Laud was right to assert, as he did a prisoner in the Tower a decade later, that the ultimate responsibility for that fatal book was the king's. While both were of course responsible, as Kevin Sharpe has correctly observed, 'it was the king who led and the archbishop who followed.'[28]

Very quickly after its first use the new form of service became known as 'Laud's prayer book'. In fact this was a misnomer, for the king gave the Scots bishops a large say in revising the liturgy. In doing so he fatally damaged the already weak institution of Scottish episcopacy by yoking it to a hated alien form of worship. Ironically Charles thought that his consultations and revision would have the opposite effect. Never before had he taken so much trouble consulting representative opinion. His mistake was that the Scots bishops were not really representative of the Scots people. North of the border episcopacy had been planted in stony ground, uneasily coexisting with the tares of Presbyterianism. Charles sowed his seed in a field about which he knew little; it sprang up overnight, not, however, to quickly wither away. To say that he should have been better informed is, perhaps, too harsh a judgment. As Clarendon, a most perceptive observer, recalled, 'there were very few in England who heard of any disorder there, or anything done there that might produce any.'[29] If Scotland were not a distant country, it was at least one about which most Englishmen knew little. On the other hand, Charles did not fall into the Scots crisis by accident. For a man who prized uniformity and the maintenance of royal authority above all else, and saw these values primarily in religious terms, the introduction of an English prayer book into the land of his fathers was as characteristic as his insistence that, come what may, the Scots accept it.

Charles's first reaction to the St Giles's riot was to blame his council in Edinburgh for letting the fracas take place, and allowing the ringleaders to escape unpunished. He wrote ordering the council to enforce the new service without further delay. Confident the problem was solved he returned to his hunting vacation, apparently more bothered by an unusually cold and wet August.[30] By the end of the month, Charles began to realize that the Scots problem was something more than one of those bad English summers that, while irritating at the time, eventually go away and are best forgotten. So he told his Lord Treasurer, the Earl of Traquair, to stay in Edinburgh and sort things out. In September Charles sent the Duke of Lennox to Scotland to find out what was going on, while continuing to blame the St Giles's riot on 'a very slack Council or very bad subjects'.[31] In part the king was correct, for the council's support for the new liturgy was far from wholehearted, several of its members being prominent by their absence when it was first used in St Giles's Cathedral. Like most Scots they saw the prayer book as part of a Catholic conspiracy, and thus allowed dozens of pamphlets to pour off the presses endorsing this view. The king was so annoyed that on 10 October he ordered one polemic, G. Gillespie's *A Dispute Against English Popish Ceremonies*, to be burnt publicly. Whether its reasonable complaint that the liturgy had been 'pressed upon us by naked will and authority, without giving any reason to satisfy our consciences,' or its absurd charge that Richard Hooker and Lancelot Andrewes – two of the king's favourite theologians – were Catholics, upset him the more one cannot say. But banning subversive pamphlets convinced so few Scots that on 1 December Charles had to issue a public declaration that 'he abhoreth all superstitions of Popery.'[32]

On the same day that he banned Gillespie's pamphlet Charles issued a proclamation ordering the crowds that had flocked to Edinburgh in protest against the liturgy to go home. Even though they did so, following a demonstration that turned into a riot that the king described as 'barbarous', they left behind elective representatives, known as The Tables, to continue the struggle.[33] In retaliation Charles told the privy council and the Court of Sessions to leave Edinburgh first for Linlithgow, and then Dundee. Although the loss of the government's business pushed the burghers of Edinburgh more firmly to the other side, Charles continued to believe that firm action would soon resolve the problem. It was, he was sure, not one of substance or principle, but merely 'a needless noise'.[34] Laud agreed, telling the king to 'risk everything rather than yield a jot.' Charles ignored Traquair's frantic warnings that the Scots had become so angry that no longer could they be peacefully stilled.[35] Even when the Lord Treasurer came to London to warn his monarch in person, Charles brushed aside his fears, telling him to return north and enforce the hard line that he was sure would eventually bring the Scots to their senses.

It was in this mood that on 9 February 1638 the king forced matters to a head. Five days after protecting his southern flank by telling the Court of High Commission to investigate religious dissidents in England, he sent his Scots council a proclamation. 'We find our royal authority much impaired,' it ran; thus all protests against the new prayer book must stop on pain of treason. At the same time as he publicly announced a new crime, Charles privately wrote to his legal advisers in Edinburgh asking how he might enforce it, and prosecute those who interrupted divine service or insulted bishops.[36] Once more he raised the stakes without bothering to check what cards he held. In response the leaders of the anti-prayer book movement called his bluff. Immediately after the proclamation had been read in Edinburgh on 19 February, they revised the 1581 Confession of Faith that had been used to oppose the young James VI to draft a national covenant, which they signed after a solemn service in Greyfriars kirk. The covenant touched off a firestorm of national sectarian outrage. On 1 March Edinburgh's ministers and gentlemen swore to uphold the covenant; on 2 March its citizens did the same, and within a few weeks all over Scotland hundreds of thousands of folk from all regions and walks of life pledged to die rather than accept the hated new liturgy. Realizing that the game was lost the Scots bishops fled to England, their leader Archbishop Spottiswood lamenting, 'all that we have done these thirty years past is now down at once.'[37]

The conflagration the proclamation of 9 February touched off caught the king and his advisers unawares, sorely frightening them. When Archie, the royal fool, babbled over his cups in some Westminster tavern that Laud was a rogue and a traitor, the privy council, with the king in the chair, solemnly voted that the jester be thrown out of court with his coat pulled over his head.[38] Apparently their sense of proportion was as much a casualty of the Scots crisis as their sense of humour. They had just received Traquair's warning that the 'height of evils that are like to fall upon us' were so catastrophic that if the prayer book was not withdrawn, he could do no more in Scotland, and that the Marquis of Hamilton be sent north to take the Lord Treasurer's place.

Incapable of the former, the king chose the latter. He and Hamilton spent the second week in May discussing the marquis's mission to Edinburgh. On 16 May Charles gave his friend his written orders. Hamilton was to dismiss any member of the Scots council who refused to sign the December proclamation that the king was not a Catholic. At his discretion he was to issue either of the two proclamations that Charles gave him, one harsh in tone and the other conciliatory, ordering the covenanters to return to their obedience. For his part, the king promised to introduce the prayer book in 'a fair and legal way', and never let the Court of High Commission become 'a just grievance to our loyal subjects'. He left himself loopholes wide enough to drive a cartload of bishops through. Much time and effort went into drawing up Hamilton's instructions, which reveal that the king was involved intimately in the policy for Scotland. He drafted replies to the thirty-three questions about policy that Hamilton sent him, read Traquair's and Spottiswood's drafts, rejecting the latter's suggestion that he accept the covenant with the terse annotation that to do so would leave him as impotent as the Doge of Venice. In other words Charles's first – and last – reaction to the covenant was that it was incompatible with monarchy, and that he was, as he told Hamilton, 'resolved to hazard my Life, rather than suffer authority to be condemned.'[39]

After they had agreed on the instructions, Charles called in Archbishops Laud and Spottiswood, and Bishops Sydserf of Galloway, Whitford of Brechin, and Maxwell of Ross, to tell them that he was sending Hamilton to Scotland to establish religious peace. 'Canterbury desired by way of questions of his Majesty for what he was called,' remembered Hamilton, 'His Majesty answered to hear and bear witness what passed.'[40] Clearly Laud was no longer Charles's chief adviser on religious affairs north of the border.

The death of Hamilton's wife delayed his departure until 26 May. Perhaps it was this loss, or else the recognition that his mission was hopeless that made the marquis pessimistic, for soon after crossing into Scotland, but before opening talks with the covenanters, he wrote to the king urging him to prepare the fleet and militia. When Sir Thomas Hope, the king's advocate in Scotland, confirmed Hamilton's worst fears by refusing to rule that the covenanters were legally traitors, Charles accepted his emissary's appreciation of the situation. 'I expect not anything can reduce that people to obedience, but only force,' he wrote to Hamilton on 11 June. 'In the mean time your care must be dissolve the multitude; and, if it be possible, to possess yourself of my castles of Edinburgh and Stirling (which I do not expect) and to this end, I give you leave to flatter them with what hopes you please.'[41]

The third theme of the king's treatment of the Scots now became apparent. Once he convinced himself that monarchy itself was at stake, and had thus to be defended to the death, then bargaining in bad faith easily followed.

Two days later Charles attacked. The news from Scotland seemed to have improved. Hamilton appeared to be getting events sufficiently under control for the king to order him to persuade as many members as possible of the Court of Sessions, Scotland's supreme court, to rule that the covenant 'is at least against the law, if not treasonable'. At the same time he took the marquis's advice to start military preparations. He also put the Royal Navy on alert 'under pretence', Charles wrote, 'to defend our fishermen', but in truth to convey 6,000 troops to the Firth of Forth. From Ireland Wentworth pledged that the Dublin parliament would vote generous taxes. In England Lord Treasurer Juxon and Chancellor of the Exchequer Cottington promised to raise £200,000. Charles was not worried that the war-like preparations, which did not remain secret for long, might provoke the Scots. Indeed he hoped that they would prompt them into calling a parliament, or general assembly of the church, without his permission, which he believed, 'would the more loudly declare them traitors and the more justify my actions'.[42]

The king's sudden announcement three days later on 30 June that he was suspending the Court of High Commission, and would call a parliament and general assembly to discuss the prayer book is understandable only in the context of his secret advice to Hamilton 'to flatter them'. Anyway, the next day, on 1 July, Charles had second thoughts, telling the marquis that while he could negotiate with the covenanters, he must not promise them anything the king could not concede.[43] By 3 July the king was sufficiently concerned about the Scots crisis to bring it formally to the attention of the English privy council, who appointed a committee to handle the matter.[44]

When Hamilton returned to London a fortnight later he brought the king and his councillors little joy. 'The Scots business is extremely ill indeed,' wrote Laud, 'and what will become of it God knows, but certainly no good.' Laud blamed it all on subversives. 'His Majesty had been notoriously betrayed,' he declared, and to prove the point investigated some treasonable remarks made by one Captain Morris, a Scots soldier, staying in London.[45] Charles's response was more relevant. With that over-cleverness that is so often the spawn of desperation, he told Hamilton to return to Scotland and try to out-wit the covenanters. First he was to promote the more moderate 1560 covenant (with an addendum pledging loyalty to the crown) as an alternative to the current one that was sweeping the land. Yet only 28,000 people signed 'the king's covenant'. Its propagation only fuelled the anger of the people which, Traquair noted, seemed 'rather to increase than diminish'.[46] Charles's second instruction was equally unsuccessful. When Hamilton opened the general assembly in Glasgow cathedral on 21 November he reminded them how graciously the king had withdrawn the prayer book and High Commission, and they were not to display their ingratitude by refusing to let the bishops take their seats. Then, on the king's advice, he tried to distract the general assembly with trivialities. Refusing Charles's red herrings, they forced Hamilton, after a week of acrimonious debate on the king's religious policies, to dissolve the assembly. He stormed out of the chamber in what would have been a dramatic demonstration of vice-regal power, had it not degenerated into a comic interlude when he found the door locked and had to wait fuming for several minutes until the keys were produced. The humiliation rubbed home the painful lesson that negotiations had failed. That night Hamilton wrote to Charles, 'I have done my best.' Now the king must blockade the east coast of Scotland to bring the rebels to their knees. 'Though next to hell I hate this place,' Hamilton concluded, he would still lead an army against the Scots, so long as Charles promised that if he died in battle he would ensure his sons 'be bred in England' and 'my daughters never married in Scotland.'[47]

With his chief adviser on Scots affairs so alienated, and Laud convinced that the covenant was a personal conspiracy against him, Charles became even more certain that firm action was vital. He ordered the general assembly to go home. When they refused, and even abolished episcopacy, Charles's reaction was surprising vapid. Ignoring Laud's warnings that he should not delay a moment, he waited four days before telling Hamilton that he should decide for himself if he wanted to stay or remain in Scotland.[48] During December Charles attended four of the twelve privy council meetings held to discuss the crisis, a sign of England's growing involvement. By the end of the month the king had decided to launch an ambitious four-pronged attack on the rebels. Come the spring he was to lead the main thrust from York, as Hamilton landed on the east coast near Aberdeen, and troops from Ulster and Ireland launched raids on the Highlands and Western Isles.

Putting this complex plan into effect proved way beyond the crown's capabilities. In January 1639 Charles appointed a committee to take overall charge of operations, and a few days later accepted all their initial dozen recommendations, writing 'fit' beside each, as if the details of grand strategy were beneath his dignity.[49] His lieutenants quickly complained about a lack of leadership. 'We daily meet in council, but to little purpose,' the Earl of Northumberland told a friend, adding that the king had given them no idea how money might be found to support the 30,000 troops he wanted.[50]

To this end Charles's first step was to put the militia in the thirteen northern-most English counties on stand-by, and to send Sir Jacob Astley, a veteran of the Thirty Years War, to supervise their training. A couple of weeks afterwards Charles commanded all nobles and gentry with estates in the north to return home immediately to defend their counties, and the following month ordered the lord lieutenants of the remaining southern counties to bring a specified number of troops to a rendezvous at York on 1 April.[51] In addition to this traditional way of mobilizing soldiers for home defence, Charles resorted to a device as archaic as fiscal feudalism. He told his tenants-in-chief to meet him in York with their retainers. In all, the king hoped to raise a host of some 50,000 men, ample enough to crush the Scots. Yet at all levels this army lacked leadership. In the whole of England there were only four master gunners who understood the use of artillery.[52] Charles appointed the Earl of Arundel (who was widely, though wrongly, believed to be a Catholic) commander-in-chief, with the more experienced (and profoundly Protestant) Earl of Essex as his assistant, and made the dispirited Hamilton, rather than the Earl of Northumberland, who was a veteran sailor, admiral of the fleet. Charles gave way to the wishes of his wife – who had just lost a baby – by appointing several of her friends, such as the Earls of Holland and Newport, to critically important senior commands. Henrietta Maria did her husband another disservice by starting a campaign to persuade recusants to support the royal cause. She wrote an open letter to all English Catholics seeking contributions of men and money, whilst her friends, such as Kenelm Digby and Walter Montague, sent fellow Catholics circulars pointing out that the covenanters were a mortal threat to 'the happy moderation we live under.'[53]

Notwithstanding such impolitic tactics which encouraged Catholics, such as those in Berkshire, to demand a greater degree of toleration, initially the crown's efforts to win support in England went well.[54] Charles ordered dozens of houses in London searched for Presbyterian pamphlets, which he had burnt.[55] He wrote letters to leading peers seeking their support, and the following month issued a proclamation explaining to his people why they must fight. 'The disorders and tumults,' he declared, were 'raised in Scotland & Formented by factious Spirits, and those traitorously effected, began on pretence of Religion, the common cloak of Disobedience.' No longer was the prayer book, or episcopacy, or even religion at stake, 'but whether we be their king or not.'[56] Charles even had Secretary Windebank write to all his many friends explaining the king's position, whilst other royalists, such as the poet Suckling, either at the king's behest, or on their own initiative, circulated private pieces arguing that monarchy was in jeopardy.[57] By the following month the royalist line had become less subtle and more shrill, reminding Englishmen what 'the rage and fury' of the Scots might do to 'their wives, children and goods'.[58]

To support his military assault against the covenanters on 25 January Charles instructed Wentworth to land 500 Irish troops at Carlisle by 1 April, and, even though the Earl of Antrim was a Catholic, arm him and his followers to threaten the covenanters from Ulster.[59] To win friends in Scotland, and to ensure the success of Hamilton's seaborne attack, Charles wrote to a number of wavering Scots nobles that he did 'exceedingly value the honour of your friendship'. To punish Scots merchants (whose support he had already lost) he impounded all their ships in English harbours, and asked the Dutch to stop trading with them.[60] At the same time the king began negotiating for the loan of Spanish troops, oblivious to the devastating political repercussions of the introduction of Catholic mercenaries into England.[61] On the contrary, Charles felt confident at the progress of his preparations. He told one courtier that 'he intended, God Willing, to be a short time in Edinburgh to settle that disordered government.'[62] On 26 March he appointed a commission that included Laud, Juxon, Coventry, Windebank, and Northumberland to govern England, warning them to take special precautions to ensure that a rebellion did not break out in the south in his absence. Then, after leaving Windebank eight blank signed commissions, and telling the privy council to attend the queen each Sunday, the Lord Lieutenant of Wales to return to his post, and the gentry to their estates, Charles went off to war for the first time in his life.[63]

No hunting excursions, banquets, or tedious speeches of welcome from municipal worthies delayed the king's ride to York. He covered the 194 miles in five days. On his arrival he immediately briefed his senior officers, becoming caught up in what he described as 'very much business'.[64] He was angry to learn that Traquair had surrendered Dalkeith without firing a shot and placed Scotland's Lord Treasurer under house arrest. He was even more distressed to hear that the city of Aberdeen, the bastion of Scots royalism, had fallen to the rebels with almost as little resistance. So in necessity and out of friendship he pinned his hopes on Hamilton, to whom he sent a string of orders: the marquis was to devise a loyalty oath for the Scots; he was to circulate a petition among them asserting that the king was determined to protect their ancient religion and liberties; he was to forbid the covenanters to come within ten miles of the border; he was to advance towards the Firth of Forth; he was not to advance towards the Firth; he was not to advance towards anywhere; he was to capture Holy Island. Quite obviously Charles did not know what to do next. Even he had to admit that he had not 'expressed ourselves as clearly as we might'.[65]

In sum there had been a failure of leadership. Admittedly the quality of Charles's troops left much to be desired. Those from East Anglia were notoriously undisciplined, one company being so timid that their officers were frightened of being attacked as they marched through Sherwood Forest. When the men arrived at the royalist camp at Berwick they often shot at their officers; a bullet hole was even found in the fabric of the king's tent.[66] To try and restore order Charles instituted a loyalty oath wherein all his troops had to promise to serve him to 'the utmost hazard of my life'.[67] However solemn pledges did little good. They did not, for instance, help Hamilton's fleet of thirty-eight ships, carrying 5,000 soldiers, establish a bridgehead in Scotland (where even the marquis's mother vowed to shoot him if he ever landed). Nor did they further the trade blockade of which Charles had such high hopes.[68] More than anything Charles needed money.

'My Lord Cottington is very industrious about this business,' Windebank told the king, 'and has the best way of worming a citizen that I observed.' Still when the king asked the City of London for a £100,000 loan, and even called the lord mayor and aldermen before the privy council, not even Windebank could 'worm' them. 'The Mayor is such a beast, and his Brethren such cattle,' complained the thwarted Secretary of State, 'they will neither be driven or go of themselves.'[69]

Lack of money, bovine citizens, or mutinous levies were not, however, the true causes of Charles's failure to win the First Bishops' War. As in the past he neglected to define his goals and take the initiative. Thus the morale of his troops fell. A raid across the border in late May that found only women and children did nothing to revive the soldiers' spirits, but instead prompted Sir Edmund Verney to write to his son, 'Our army is but weak, our purse weaker, and if we fight we shall have our throats cut.'[70]

Matters came to a head in early June, when Hamilton led 3,000 cavalry into Scotland to discover the main covenanter army, under General Leslie, encamped at Kelso. Charles forced the marquis to attack the Scots, since he was afraid that his army would refuse to fight if Leslie marched south towards the River Tweed.[71] However the Scots general was as loath to cross the river as were Charles's troops to fight – he believed it might be his Rubicon, and they their Styx. So on 6 June Leslie sent the king a request for negotiations, to which Charles agreed with some prevarication, and far less grace, telling the Scots to send their commissioners to his tent outside Berwick on the morning of 11 June.[72] They came on time. The king was late, taking no notice of them as he entered because the commissioners omitted the customary courtesy of kneeling in his presence.[73] Straightaway he announced that since his honour was at stake he expected them to behave like loyal subjects. If they did, he would not be found wanting. Yet when the Earl of Rothes, the leading commissioner, tried to justify the covenant Charles cut him off, saying they must submit to his judgment. After this inauspicious start the commissioners withdrew for five minutes to set their 'humble desires' down on paper. They wanted parliament to confirm the acts of the Glasgow Assembly, the kirk to have full freedom to determine religious matters, and the king to cancel all hostile moves against Scotland. Charles replied that even though he found their terms 'a little too rude', he would none the less consider them. They had, however, to bear in mind that it was far harder for him to make concessions than they, because as a king he was honour bound to keep his word.

The second day's negotiations opened on as sour a note as the first's. It quickly became ensnared in a discussion over royal authority that was as abstract as it was divisive. Thus it was probably for the best that the king and the commissioners did not meet for the next four days, but left discussions to their juniors, who managed to hammer out an agreement by 17 June. Basically Charles accepted the Scots' demands for a parliament to ratify the acts of the Glasgow Assembly, and both sides promised to start demobilizing within forty-eight hours.[74]

Initially the agreement pleased everyone. Bloodshed had been avoided: the awful prospect of civil war averted. Yet on reflection the euphoria soon disappeared. The covenanters had been so flattered by the king's willingness to talk to them in so 'sober, meek, and patient a fashion', that they were taken in by his promises.[75] John Suckling, the royalist poet, was more realistic: 'Necessity, not good nature,' produced this treaty he wrote from the king's camp, 'and that same necessity which made them wish for Peace, will make them desperate for war, if it succeed not suddenly.[76] Two days after agreeing to the treaty, Charles told Wentworth that 'public affairs . . . are so unpleasing' he could not bear to write about them. On 22 June he sounded even more despondent. 'There is a Scots proverb that bids you to put two locks on your door after you have made peace with a foe.' By the end of the month the king's depression had become nigh desperate. In spite of his advisers' objections he was determined to go in person to Edinburgh to open parliament. 'Believe me, nothing but my presence at this time in that country can save it from irreparable confusion.'[77]

In truth it was not Charles's failure to go to Edinburgh, but the refusal of the Scots commissioners to obey his summons to come to Berwick that led to the treaty's collapse. It did so for the same reason as it had been signed. Both sides were at first eager to avert carnage, and then disappointed that they had given up the opportunity of achieving a more definite resolution on the field of battle. Charles touched on this dilemma – that was to become a crucial issue for at least a generation of conflict – at the treaty's opening session, by asking, 'But when I say one thing and you another, who shall judge?' Only the king's execution, and the revolution of 1688 managed to answer that question.

At the time, however, a far more pertinent question was why did the king behave over the prayer book as he did? Why, in spite of Traquair's warning that it would take a permanent garrison of 40,000 troops – an impossible burden – to force the Scots to accept the liturgy, or why, despite the example of Bishop Whitford, who read the new service with a brace of pistols laid on the lectern and his wife and servants standing before with loaded blunderbusses, only to have his church burnt down that afternoon, did Charles insist on 'that fatal book'?[78]

One answer – and the one that his opponents wanted to believe – was that the king was misled by wicked counsellors. Without doubt the crown was badly informed. Coke told the king that the proclamation ordering the covenanters to lay down their arms was received in Edinburgh 'with humility and joy'. Charles's advisers on Scots affairs favoured a hard line. Hamilton was bitterly alienated from his native land. Laud was sure that the covenanters were in cahoots with English Puritans 'to destroy me'. Windebank, a timid man, was easily frightened that the Scots were 'a people enraged, weary of Monarchical government', hell bent on republicanism.[79] Wentworth agreed, either from conviction or – more likely – out of desire to escape his Irish backwater. He wrote the king a series of letters that the covenanters intended to destroy 'Monarchy itself'. Archbishop Spottiswood warned Charles not to appease the Scots 'because he found upon the sad experience of sixty years that generally they were a people of so gross a grain, they were not gained by punishments and lost by Favours.'[80] All this advice fell on welcome ears, for Charles much preferred the counsel of those who told him what he wanted to hear.

Now, more than ever, the king was getting involved in the daily details of government. He started deciding petitions that previously he had referred to a minister, and began annotating, and even drafting a number of domestic state papers. In a sense he was an inexperienced king who, after fourteen years on the throne, was suddenly sucked into a major crisis, to which he reacted with the superficial overconfidence that only insecurity can induce. Having quickly convinced himself that the Scots were using religion as a pretence for destroying monarchy, he devised a policy as sound, reasonable, and consistent, as any built on sand.

When the troubles in Edinburgh first broke out Charles was sure that firm action would soon end them. When the next year he decided to use military force he was equally convinced that decisive action would rapidly force the Scots back to their senses. When the Treaty of Berwick postponed hostilities, he had no doubt that only his personal presence in Edinburgh could bring back sanity. In sum, when Charles was forced out of the comfortable world of the court that he had made for himself, he refused to accept unpleasant realities, hoping that they could be dispelled as easily as the Fury in a Twelfth Night masque. For instance, in October 1638 Hamilton warned the king that 'the malignancy of the covenanters is greater than ever.' Charles rejected his friend's warning; 'as for the danger that episcopal government is in, I do not hold it so much as you.' And yet in the very same sentence he went on to exaggerate the danger: for I believe that the number of those that are against episcopacy who are not in their hearts against the monarchy, is not so inconsiderable as you take it.'[81]

The myth that the Scots were out to destroy monarchy and establish a republic – a particularly odious form of government – almost certainly came from the king. As early as October 1637 he privately told a friend that the Scots wanted to destroy 'the true state of monarchical government'. Advisers merely reinforced this misapprehension, which by being repeated in royal proclamations gained a life of its own. Once the view that 'a few factious spirits' had 'begun in pretence of religion' a conspiracy 'to shake off all monarchical government' had taken root, the crown's actions became as logical as say those of a president who convinces himself that a matter is no longer a third-rate burglary, but a mortal threat to the office of which he holds the stewardship. Charles turned the Scots Rebellion into one of 'No prayer book – no kings,' agreeing with the poet who told him that now 'the bonds of Nations and of Nature too' hung in the balance. He could not appease the Scots since the matter at stake was far more important than a new liturgy.[82] 'So long as the covenant is in force,' he told Hamilton in June 1638, 'I am no more in Scotland than as a Duke of Venice, which I will rather die than suffer.' Charles had first turned the prayer book into a mortal issue two weeks earlier, letting his friend know on 11 June, 'I <u>will rather die</u> than yield to their <u>impertinent</u> and <u>damnable</u> demands.' To show the depth of his commitment, he underlined his words. The only other time, but one, he did so in well over a thousand letters, came a few days later when he castigated '<u>those traitors</u>, the covenanters'.[83] To yield was quite literally damnable: as Charles eventually proved he preferred to lose his life rather than jeopardize his soul.

Charles was thirty-seven when he started to talk about death and dying. At roughly the same age Dante wrote, 'In the middle of our journey in life, I came to myself within a dark wood, wherein the straight way was lost.' In their late thirties men often experience a profound change: their bodies start to age; death becomes more real (Charles lost a daughter in 1639); life no longer seems an endless road stretching ahead further than the eye can see. Such thoughts may make men depressed, and feel persecuted. For Charles the covenanters were attacking far more than the prayer book: they were out to destroy him personally; he was wholly innocent: 'If this madness of our subjects is such that they will not rest satisfied,' he wrote, 'then the blame for the consequences is theirs.'[84]

For the next decade events seemed to dominate Charles's life. He was far busier in middle age than he had ever been before. At the same time as he exercised more control of his nation's affairs, he became, paradoxically, more their creature. As he entered centre-stage his movements became easier to follow, and his motives and emotions harder to discern. Perhaps the press of business hid them better from himself and others, or else the burning of so many of his private papers lost them to posterity. Compared to the thirties, during the king's last decade there was little court culture to shed light on his innermost feelings. Yet in a curious way the artistic myth turned into the political reality. Figuratively and literally Charles became a man on horseback. He adopted the role of the actor given him in masques, which before had portrayed the monarch as the passive symbol of virtues. Action, even war, gave Charles certainty, satisfying the cavalier thirst for honour that court culture had whetted, and Puritanism could never quench.[85]

1 *far left* Charles, Duke of York. This portrait was painted when he was about eight or nine years old by an unknown artist

2 *left* Charles, Prince of Wales by Daniel Mytens, painted in 1623 after Charles had returned from his abortive attempt to woo the Spanish Infanta

3  Charles I and Henrietta Maria with their two eldest children – a family group by Van Dyck. *c.* 1632

4  Gerard Houckgeest's painting shows Charles I and Henrietta Maria dining in public at Whitehall

5  Charles I with Henrietta Maria and the Prince of Wales, by Hendrick Gerritsz Pot, 1632

6 Rubens completed this lavish ceiling for the Banqueting House in Whitehall in 1635

7 Rubens's 'St George and the Dragon', c. 1630, in which Charles is portrayed as England's patron saint. He has just slain the dragon of war to rescue the fair maiden (Henrietta Maria) and bring peace to his realm

8 'Charles I on horseback' by Van Dyck, *c*. 1636, depicts the king as both warrior and philosopher

9 Peter Pett and the *Sovereign of the Seas*. Charles I's flagship was designed by Phineas Pett and built by his son, Peter, 1634–7

10 This cartoon from a contemporary satirical pamphlet shows Prince Rupert hiding in the bean field following the rout of his army after the battle of Marston Moor. His pet dog, Boy, a standard poodle, lies dead on the field while the roundheads search Rupert's 'private Cabinet' for documents and crucifixes

11 Charles I dictating orders to Sir Edward Walker. By an unknown artist

12 This is thought to be a drawing of Charles I done in later life. The artist is not known

13 Charles is portrayed as a martyr by William Marshall in the frontispiece of *Eikon Basilike*, 1648–9

But as always in life such complicated needs as action, aspirations, fantasy and brave hopes, had to coexist with the immediate demands of prosaic considerations.

For instance in October 1638, at the height of a personal and political crisis, Charles's mother-in-law arrived uninvited in England for a lengthy stay. Marie de Medici was a meddlesome woman, whose son, Louis XIII, had driven her out of France into exile in Brussels. When Charles first heard that she wanted to come and live with him in England he offered the resources of the Royal Navy to take her to Italy or Spain. After a year in Brussels Marie de Medici realized that she had overstayed her welcome, so moved on to Holland, where the authorities were far less patient, making it clear that she must quickly leave. Rather than slam the gates of England in his wife's mother's face, Charles acted the dutiful son-in-law, riding out to Sir Henry Mildmay's house in Marsham, Essex, to meet his unwelcome guest. Their encounter was correct, even superficially cordial. Henrietta's reunion a few days later at Whitehall with the mother she had not seen for thirteen years was ecstatic. Yet Charles never liked his mother-in-law. 'She surrounded herself with busibodies,' he complained, was a constant expense, a flagrant Catholic, and a barrier between himself and his wife.

With the crisis in Scotland, and the disruption of his own domestic tranquillity, Charles turned to some strong figure to solve his problems, just as he had used the Duke of Buckingham. On 23 July 1639 the king ordered Wentworth to return to England. 'The Scots covenant begins to spread too far,' he explained, telling Wentworth to let it be known that he was coming to London to attend to some personal business, such as a Chancery suit.[86] The decision to recall Wentworth seemed to embolden the king, who took a harder line against the Scots. In August he ordered the public hangman to burn one of their propaganda sheets as 'full of falsehood, Dishonour, and Scandal'.[87] A couple of weeks afterwards he proclaimed the Scots who had invaded England and all Englishmen who helped them, arrant traitors, pardonable only if they acknowledged their crimes and begged his forgiveness.[88] Initially he was a little more conciliatory towards the general assembly promised by the Treaty of Berwick, allowing them to exclude the Scots bishops from taking their seats. This concession (which was not made in the best of faith, as the king had privately assured the prelates that he would restore them as soon as feasible) won few votes, since it was given with little grace, and much carping over semantics. Unable to control the general assembly, Traquair dissolved it, all to the king's satisfaction. 'They must not imagine that our granting of a free Assembly and Parliament obliges us to ratify all their fancies,' he warned, adding that if parliament proved as obstreperous as the assembly, it would suffer the same fate as he would dismiss it as well. The king's threats had little effect, except perhaps to augment the covenanters' determination, and encourage them on 8 November to seize control of the Lords of the Articles, parliament's executive committee. One of the king's most loyal supporters lamented, 'The Scotch business is in ill Terms.'[89]

Charles welcomed Wentworth back to England as the only man who could save him. Yet when the Lord Deputy landed at Chester on 13 September he was horrified to find that he was expected to perform miracles, an impression only confirmed by the extraordinarily warm welcome the king gave him on his arrival in London.[90] Charles immediately became dependent on Wentworth, whom he elevated to the peerage that the Lord Deputy had so long sought, and been so often denied. The new Earl of Strafford was still the same old Thomas Wentworth, the man who a quarter century before had been taught the power of the crown, when, in the middle of a trial someone handed him the new list of Yorkshire justices of the peace, and he had to step down from the bench. This public humiliation was the result of his failure to have influential friends at court. It should not be seen as part of a crown versus parliament struggle which prompted Wentworth to first become a leader of the 1628 parliament, and then in a *volte face* a minister of the crown in the 1630s. Wentworth saw parliament as a mechanism for solving county, and then country-wide, problems, and only after he concluded that it was incapable of doing so served his sovereign first as Lord President of the North and then Lord Deputy of Ireland.

To his enemies (of whom he easily made many, all ready to believe the worst of him) Wentworth could appear like a dog, who after a public whipping, came crawling back to lick his master's hand. Even Charles felt uneasy about him, preferring to keep Wentworth away from court, dealing with him indirectly through Laud. Wentworth's personality engendered equally strong feelings. He was a man of great energy and ability, a true believer who gave his all for whatever cause he adopted (or adopted him) with an enthusiasm that left little room for moderation, and none at all for tact. He made enemies needlessly, once urging that John Hampden, an English gentleman, be whipped as if he were a peasant from the bogs of Donegal. Even though he brought law and order to Ireland, he alienated all shades of opinion there so implacably that eighteen months after his death English rule in that island collapsed into a most terrible civil war. On his return to England his friends and enemies saw him as the decisive figure who would either save the day or encompass their ruin. Both were wrong, for by 1639 Wentworth was past his prime. He was pained with gout, his eyes bothered him greatly, his judgment was much impaired, and at times he was so sick that he could not walk or ride, having to be carried in a litter.

Before the ailing Earl of Strafford could make his presence felt the king suffered a humiliating foreign policy reverse. On 6 October a Spanish fleet took refuge in the Downs off Dover from a pursuing Dutch squadron.

Charles told Admiral Pennington to intervene to protect the Spaniards, but on 9 October the Dutch cut out and sank the enemy as the Royal Navy stood idly by. The king was outraged. He vented his anger on the unfortunate Dutch ambassador. His offer to repair the Spanish ships that had been driven ashore near Dover, and replace Secretary Coke with the more sympathetic Windebank did not satisfy the Spanish, while upsetting the Dutch and many Englishmen. To show their contempt for the king's ineffectiveness the French arrested his nephew, Prince Charles Louis, on his way to England, prompting one ambassador to conclude that as far as foreign policy was concerned Charles 'is in no condition to undertake anything'.[91]

Humiliation abroad, plus Strafford's return, prompted the king to take action at home. On 5 December, after weeks of meetings, he told the privy council that he would call a parliament for the following April. Wentworth assured the king that he could manage one in Westminster just as well as he had in Dublin. His council colleagues were less sure, and it took a lot of pressure to persuade them to pledge the king 'their lives and fortunes'. Having been in England during the 1630s they agreed with the Venetian ambassador that 'the long rusted gates of parliament cannot be opened without difficulty.'[92]

In the weeks between his decision to call parliament and its opening, a curious combination of arrogance, action and irrelevance seemed to characterize the king's behaviour. He and his court were caught up with staging that great orgy of self-congratulation (or whistling in the dark), the masque *Salmacida Spoila*). He bought his wife Wimbledon Manor for £16,789 simply because she had taken a fancy to it, or perhaps to cheer her after the loss of a baby, or during the pregnancy of another. Both events seemed to bring the two closer together, as they schemed to have Abbé Ludovic Stuart, Charles's cousin, made a cardinal.[93] Early in 1640 the king rudely received the commissioners the covenanters sent to London in accordance with the Treaty of Berwick. Having kept them waiting he told them that in war he would teach the Scots the lessons they had scorned to learn in peace, and then tried to have the commissioners arrested.[94] Charles sent Strafford back to Ireland to raise 8,000 soldiers, plus £850,000 in taxes and loans, sent out new ship-money assessments, and approached the City of London for a loan.

As others handled the details of these broad policies, Charles's personal attention concentrated on one almost symbolic issue – the defence of Edinburgh castle.[95] When in June 1638 he originally decided to use force to crush the covenanters, he ordered Hamilton to try and seize Edinburgh and Stirling castles, both of which stood on commanding rocky heights, one controlling the capital and the other the entrance to the Highlands. In November 1638 Charles appointed Patrick, Lord Ruthven, governor of Edinburgh castle. He was a distinguished soldier, who had risen to the rank of major general in the service of Gustavus Adolphus. A hard man and harder drinker, Ruthven had been known to drink the Swedish king under the table. Even though he could not persuade the covenanters to hand over Edinburgh castle, Charles was pleased enough with his services to keep him on as governor after it was returned under the terms of the Treaty of Berwick.[96] The king urged Ruthven to improve its defences as fast as he could, and promised to send him reinforcements disguised as common seamen, who would leave their ships at Leith and stroll through the covenanters' lines to the castle. Charles warned the provost and magistrates of Edinburgh that their threat to stop his infiltrators was treasonable, and to show his trust gave Ruthven an allowance of 40 marks a day, sent him more supplies in February, with the authorization to destroy any defences that the covenanters might erect that threatened the castle. As the siege tightened Charles told the garrison, 'Your glory will be great in venturing rather than ... lying still and suffering the yoke to be put on you quietly and without opposition by a company of seditious burghers.' His words inspired Ruthven. On being asked if he would surrender, the governor replied 'Never': even if they tore down the castle's walls he vowed to defend its craggy rock. True to his words, Ruthven held on for four months, until devoid of supplies, too ill to walk, and having lost all his teeth as a result of scurvy, he had to surrender.[97]

While magnificent, the defence of Edinburgh was in fact much less important than Strafford's efforts to raise money in Ireland, where parliament voted hefty tax increases, and the Protestant clergy levied themselves one-sixth of their livings. Charles was most pleased, solicitously telling Strafford not to overtax his failing health on his behalf. Thus when the Lord Deputy returned to England in the spring for the first parliament at Westminster for over a decade, the fact that he took ship on a vessel called the *Confidence* seemed an omen as appropriate as it was auspicious.[98] Certainly balladeers thought so. As Charles was being rowed to the opening of the new parliament on 13 April in the state barge (which had been refurbished for the occasion at a cost of £620), hawkers sold the song:[99]

> We may be assured of this,
> If anything hath been amiss,
> Our king and state will all redress,
> In this good parliament.

But the era of good feelings did not last for long. After the king's opening remarks, Lord Keeper Finch gave parliament a long rambling speech, outlining the government's proposals, and concluding with a warning that 'the king did not require their advice, but an immediate vote of supplies.' Once more the crown spoke loudly and carried a little stick. It let it be known that the covenanters had been engaged in a treasonable correspondence with Louis XIII addressing the French king as 'Au Roi', a salutation which Charles, quite wrongly, asserted was only used by subjects to their lawful king. Parliament was not impressed, vents in both Houses drifting for four days, until on 17 April John Pym rose to speak.[100]

Pym was born in 1584 of an ancient Somerset family. He was four when the Armada threatened his home and its religion, and came to manhood during the last years of Elizabeth's reign, being educated at Oxford and the Middle Temple. First elected to parliament in 1614, he became an important radical in the 1620s, being briefly imprisoned in 1621, and managing the attempt to have Buckingham impeached six years later. During the personal rule Pym returned to his country estates, occasionally visiting London to help run the Providence Island Company, a Puritan privateering venture. At first glance Pym was an unlikely candidate for the man who, after Charles, did more than anyone else to bring about the civil war. He started his parliamentary career as a rabid papist-baiter from the backwoods, and then slowly grew to develop a radical political philosophy that combined the traditional privileges of parliament with *avant-garde* theories of liberty. If he lacked Sir John Eliot's stubbornness, he had his determination. If he had Wentworth's senses of commitment and ability to compromise, he could not turn his coat. Although he did not possess Coke's legal erudition, he could dress up his arguments as ancient and long-lost freedoms. From his Elizabethan roots John Pym matured, until at the age of sixty he emerged as the leader of the House of Commons. It was his sense of cohesion and purpose, his consistency and dangerous determination which transformed that ancient institution.[101]

On 17 April 1640 Pym rose in the Commons' chamber to try and smite the personal rule. He berated the growth of popery and monopolies (all familiar grievances), castigated the collection of tonnage and poundage contrary to the Petition of Right (a controversial point that had produced the tumultuous ending of the 1629 parliament), before breaking new ground by lambasting the growing powers of church courts, the abuse of knighthood fines, and the tyranny of Star Chamber.[102] The initial reaction to this speech was remarkably muted. It might well have passed by unnoticed except by the most determined antiquarians had not Charles decided on 24 April to try and by-pass the Commons and go straight to the Lords to ask them for money to fight the Scots. Their approval, with only eleven negative votes, outraged the Commons far more than Pym's speech. It broke a long-standing convention that the Commons, as representatives of the people, should initiate money bills. Charles misinterpreted their insistence that the Lords back down as a case of wounded pride over a minor breach of etiquette, telling the peers that if the 'Commons would not first trust him, his officers would be disordered, and his business lost.'[103]

None the less eight days later the crown compromised by offering to abolish ship money in return for twelve subsidies. Although generous, the terms had no time to get anywhere, because on 5 May Charles dissolved parliament. He did this so suddenly that the speaker had to be woken at dawn to be told that the king would that day address parliament. 'There can be no occasion of my coming to his House,' the king declared, 'so unpleasing to me as this is, at this time.' He placed the entire blame for the dissolution of the Short Parliament squarely on 'the malicious cunning of some seditiously affected men'.[104]

In itself the Short Parliament was not all that important, and deserved the current epithet 'the still-born parliament', but in its consequences it was profoundly significant. It was a warning, a harbinger. While many of the issues raised in the Short Parliament harked back to the 1620s, Pym's speech of 17 April set the agenda for the forties, just as Charles's sudden dissolution taught many members that if they wanted to heal the body politic they must find some way to remain in session.[105]

Charles's reasons for ending the Short Parliament are hard to discern. Perhaps Sir Henry Vane the senior persuaded him to do so in order to thwart Strafford, who was growing so fast in the king's favour that he threatened to displace all Charles's old counsellors. The king could have been scared that the Commons might start debating his Scots policies. Or else he had high hopes that the negotiations that he was currently conducting with three Spanish ambassadors sent to London to arrange Royal Navy protection for their ships in the Channel, would also produce thousands of Spanish veterans, as well as papal gold, to crush the Scots without parliament's permission.[106]

While deploring the Commons' readiness to take the initiative in criticizing his policies Charles expected from them a higher degree of cohesion than they really possessed. Throughout the Short Parliament he felt an intense sense of urgency; English soldiers were facing the enemy, and must be supported with weapons – not words. Thus he asked the Commons to define their grievances and answer his offer to surrender ship money for the passage of twelve subsidies with a speed that was beyond the capacity of a purely legislative body, particularly when the crown had failed to provide any management, leaving the initiative to members such as Pym.

The precipitate dissolution of the Short Parliament was greeted throughout the land with a sense of foreboding. One diplomat was sure that England would never see another parliament for a very long while. 'Death's harbinger, the sword,' Sir Thomas Peyton told a friend, 'was ready to swallow up this wicked age.' In contrast the king seemed confident and energetic – as he always did after sending a parliament packing. In mid-May he told the Lord Mayor of London that he would not call the next parliament until the Scots had been defeated.[107] Hours after dismissing the Short Parliament he embarked on vigorous plans for their conquest. Strafford privately advised that a naval blockade would bring the covenanters to their knees in weeks, and Henrietta Maria publicly nagged him to take firm action; Charles went looking for money. Still smarting under the humiliation of the Dutch victory off Dover,[108] he agreed to let the navy convoy Spanish ships to the Netherlands in return for 1,200,000 crowns.[109] He tried to speed up the collection of ship money, and asked courtiers and the City of London for loans. The king was in no mood to brook opposition at home. He was outraged when a mob of soldiers stormed the White Lion prison in the capital to rescue their drummer boy. He personally signed the warrant to have John Archer, an apprentice, tortured on the rack to discover the names of his accomplices during the May Day riots, when a mob stormed Archbishop Laud's palace at Lambeth.[110] One rioter, Thomas Bensted, was hung, drawn and quartered for trying to open the palace gates with a crowbar, in what was, without doubt, one of the broadest definitions of high treason ever known in English law.

Prompted less by gratitude for the stern defence of his palace than by the firm conviction that church and state must help each other, Laud used convocation to support the king's hard line. In doing so he further linked the church with the crown's rapidly growing unpopularity: because it was agreed that the king could do no wrong, bishops became scapegoats instead. Convocation was the ecclesiastical equivalent of parliament. Since the Reformation whenever the former dissolved, it ended business. But in May 1640, notwithstanding Laud's reservations, Charles insisted that it continue sitting, since he wanted the passage of the £20,000 in clerical taxes already promised. In addition Laud took the opportunity to adopt an uncompromising set of canons. They ordered altars placed at the east end, communion taken kneeling, all ministers, doctors, even students, to take a loyalty oath to 'the doctrine, discipline and government established in the Church of England', and sermons preached in every parish each quarter that subjects must obey the king since he ruled by divine right.[111]

Neither the prayers of the church nor the racking of apprentices did much to solve the real problems facing the king – raising and paying for a disciplined army to fight the Scots. Stories of his levies' mutinous behaviour were rife. Charles called those from Hertfordshire 'refractory and disobedient'. In Somerset conscripts wore sheets over their uniforms parodying bishops' surplices. In Essex they smashed communion rails and stained-glass windows. In Cambridge, Beccles and Royston they rioted. In Dorset they murdered a subaltern suspected of being a papist. In Oxford they attacked their officers as they were dining upstairs in a tavern, forcing them out on to the beam that held the pub sign, where they were pelted with stones, until one lieutenant fell off into the cesspit below, his skull being smashed as he tried to climb out. Sir Jacob Astley understandably described the men he had been appointed to train as 'all the arch knaves of the kingdom'. They were, Lord Conway added, more 'fit for Bedlam or Bridwell' than the king's service.[112] Even though Charles issued a proclamation threatening mutineers with dire punishments, he was in fact more concerned with a lack of money than a dearth of discipline. On 23 July he wrote asking the Lord Mayor of London for a loan of £200,000, adding with a distinct lack of subtlety that if the money were not forthcoming he would have no alternative but to debase the coinage, despite seriously disrupting the city's trade.[113]

By mid-summer the king was buoyant, particularly compared to the ailing Strafford, who confessed to a friend 'that never had a business been so lost.' If Charles chose the name Henry for the son he had on 8 July to win support by reminding people of his heroic brother, Henrietta Maria thwarted his efforts by persuading her husband to pardon all imprisoned recusants in celebration. Next the king spent ten days hunting at Hampton Court, Oatlands and the New Forest, before returning to London to tell the privy council that he had decided to lead his army in person. Sir Henry Vane applauded the decision, saying that the king's presence was always worth 20,000 troops.[114] Two days later the Scots invaded England, and on 20 July Charles set out from London to stop them. At first the invaders met with scant resistance, managing to take Newcastle without firing a shot. The news prompted the king to write home that he desperately needed £40,000 without which 'the rebels will beat us without striking a stroke'.[115] Initially the king was full of energy. He alerted the militia south of the Trent, formed a band of gentlemen pensioners to protect his wife and children, and reproved the privy council for its lack of spirit: 'I see that you are so frightened that you can resolve on nothing.'[116] On 7 September he determined on the new – or rather archaic – expedient of calling a grand council of peers to York on 24 September to seek their advice. Then he seemed to lose interest in the idea, leaving the details of its procedures to others. The success of a large cavalry raiding force under Captain John Smith stiffened the king's resolve. He ordered the arrest of a group of London citizens who were coming to present him with a petition for a new parliament, sending the Lord Mayor an angry letter of displeasure. A few days later, on learning that Ruthven had at last surrendered Edinburgh castle, Charles backed down, commanding that the petitioners 'are to be flattered, not threatened'.[117]

The opening session of the great council went well, as did those of all of Charles's previous parliaments. He told the peers that he planned to call a parliament for 3 November, but in the meantime needed their advice on the best way to deal with the Scots, and raise enough money to keep his army in the field. Although Secretary Vane thought that the king had never given a better speech, he managed to sway but few peers.[118] Apart from endorsing a new loan from the city, they refused to commit themselves about taxes, remembering the uproar when they initiated a finance bill during the Short Parliament.

The great council did, however, support the decision to open talks with the Scots at Ripon, which on 26 October produced a truce that let the covenanters occupy Northumberland and Durham, and be paid a subsidy of £860 a day.[119] Charles took little part in the negotiations at Ripon to end the Second Bishops' War. Preoccupied with the coming parliamentary session, he did not realize that the Scots' subsidy, and the agreement to adjourn negotiations from Ripon to London meant that parliament could no longer be easily dismissed. So Charles rode south to enter the capital on 30 October in what in retrospect must have seemed like the last day of an Indian summer before a long hard winter. 'I saw His Majesty,' John Evelyn wrote in his diary, 'ride in pomp and a kind of Oration, with all the marks of a happy Peace, restored to the affections of his people.' Four days later – and twenty and a half months after the prayer book's introduction – what Evelyn was to call 'that long, ungrateful, foolish and fatal parliament' began.[120]

# XIII

# 'THE GOVERNMENT ALL IN PIECES'

The Long Parliament opened on 3 November 1640 in much the same fashion as had the Short Parliament six months before. Instead of the usual progress through the streets of London, that the citizens expected, Charles had himself rowed down the Thames the few hundred yards from White-hall to Westminster Steps, walking through the privacy of the Hall to the Lords' chamber, He had little stomach for another parliament. The omens looked bad. A few days earlier a mob screaming 'No bishops' stormed the Court of High Commission as it sat at St Paul's. Laud's portrait unac-countably fell from his study wall, just as Buckingham's had a few days before his murder. At Cambridge, that most sober university, it was reported that the River Cam ran red as blood, and angels were seen fighting over the college roof-tops.[1]

Far more serious, however, were the set-backs the crown received in the general election. The king neglected Windebank's advice to do all he could to ensure the return of his friends.[2] Perhaps feeling against the crown was so strong that there was little he could have done to stem the rout. Of the 493 members of the Commons, the king could count on eighty at the most, and more likely only on sixty-four. The number fell later with the expul-sion of sixteen of his allies for election fraud or being monopolists, and the flight of others, such as Windebank to the Continent.[3] In London Charles suffered an especially serious defeat. Having failed to get his candidate elected Lord Mayor, he was unable to control the return of the city's five members, and thus could not appoint Sir Thomas Gardiner, the city recorder and a capable royalist, speaking of the Lower House. With much haste and scant foresight he selected instead William Lenthall, a lawyer 'of very timorous nature', whose only qualification for the job, thought Clarendon, was the use of 'the drudgery of his profession to make himself rich.'[4]

Recognizing their desperate straits many royalist hardliners urged a cautious approach. John Suckling advised the queen to persuade her hus-band that the only way to obtain 'union with his people' was to satisfy their just demands. She must, he went on, do so with great subtlety because

216

'to kings, as to some kind of patients, it is not always proper to tell them how ill they are.'[5]

In the short speech that he gave at the opening of parliament Charles seemed in fine political health. He could not understand why the Scots had fomented 'so great a sedition . . . on so little grounds'. There were two items on parliament's agenda. First, the absolute necessity of raising money to maintain his army and pay the covenanters their £860 a day subsidy, and second, the need to redress his good people's grievances. 'It should not be my fault if this be not a happy and good parliament,' concluded the king. His jibe was as tactless as it was self-fulfilling, for within ten weeks he was to rebuke the Commons, 'You have taken the Government all in pieces, and, I must say, almost off the hinges.'[6]

Although the opening ceremonies concluded with the traditional service in which Laud asked the Almighty to 'bless this assembly and their counsels', as well as 'a good, a just, and pious and prudent king', it quickly became apparent to many royalists that without their assistance He was unlikely to do either.[7] From the first parliament was unusually united in its opposition to the crown's policies. Yet as the king's extreme opponents became more radical, moderates came over to the crown. During the next fourteen months each side used a series of crises to win over those in the middle, who strove to retain their neutrality.

On all sides there was a widespread conviction that the crisis facing the realm was the work of a conspiracy of papists and 'malignants'. The vagueness of such fears made subversion all the more terrifying and dangerous, adding to a sense of panic. Once two fat MPs happened to step on the same floor-board which broke with a noise like a musket shot, sending the rest of the House rushing for cover. Periodic revelations of papist plots made the wildest seem even more credible, and men more desperate for any solution – one member of parliament even suggested gelding Jesuits. Something obviously was sorely wrong. Someone must be to blame. It could not be the king. Therefore it had to be the bishops, and all the king's other evil advisers such as Strafford. So the opposition concluded that the only way to save the Commonwealth was to purge the government and make sure that the king accepted only the advice of good men (such as themselves).

Not surprisingly Charles did not agree with this analysis. While accepting that something was seriously wrong, he was convinced that it was all the fault of a few wicked conspirators, who like a cancer should be cut out of the body politic. He made surprisingly little effort to save the ministers parliament purged, but neither liked nor trusted the men they put in their place, if for no other reason than they were not of his choosing. Instead he turned to depend more and more on his wife and her inexperienced petticoat politicians. Being Catholics, with a bent for secret intrigue, they confirmed his opponents' worst fears about a papist plot.

But Charles saw the body politic as a fine watch, that had run down because it needed a little cleaning. Only by enhancing his authority, and not through parliament's drastic surgery, could it be made to tick as sweetly as before. The attitudes that he brought to Westminster in December 1640 had been shaped by the parliaments of the 1620s just as much as those of his opponents. Yet the issues they faced were largely the product of a short term crisis, to which they both responded and contributed until the crisis climaxed with the declaration of war.[8]

The Long Parliament spent its first week dealing with routine matters. It decided disputed elections (none in the king's favour), and granted Mrs Burton's and Mrs Bastwick's petitions for the release of their husbands. The only incident of note was the king's retraction on 5 November of his assertion two days earlier that the Scots were arrant rebels.

On 10 November Pym fired the opening salvo. His timing was perfect. Strafford had just returned to London, where the Scots commissioners had been warmly welcomed to resume the talks adjourned from Ripon. Pym started by declaring that the arrest of members for speaking freely was a threat to the ancient privileges of parliament, that prerogative courts, such as Star Chamber and High Commission, had eroded subjects' liberties, that true religion was in peril, and that England was threatened by invasions from Ireland and the Continent. Other members, such as Sir John Colepeper and George Digby, Lord Bristol's son, joined in. Balladeers caught the mood of the house:[9]

> Like silly sheep that did us daily shear
> Like asses strong our backs were made to bear
> Intolerable burdens, year by year,
> No hope, no help, no comfort did appear . . .

Then Sir John Clotworthy shifted the assault from the general to the specific, by attacking Strafford, whom the Commons impeached that day. The earl returned to Westminster that evening to find James Marshall, Gentleman Usher of the Black Rod, waiting to take him to the Tower. Charles's first reaction to his friend's arrest was to try and conciliate his opponents. On 11 November he issued two proclamations. The first ordered all recusants to leave London and his court, and instructed all justices of the peace to confiscate their weapons. The second appointed 8 December as a day of national prayer and fasting. But these tit-bits were not enough to satisfy the widespread hunger for change. 'And now reformation goes on as hot as toast,' Thomas Knyvett wrote to a friend, adding, 'I pray God that the violent turning of the tide do not make an inundation.'[10]

The whirlpool that Knyvett noticed less than three weeks after the Long Parliament opened caught both the king and his senior advisers off-guard. On 4 December Charles let the Commons' committee charged with Strafford's prosecution examine members of the privy council. They promptly accused Sir Frances Windebank of selling recusants' pardons, not collecting their fines and being in the pay of the Spanish. Rather than face these charges (which were not without substance), Windebank eluded the messenger the Commons sent to arrest him by hiding under his bedclothes, before escaping through a foggy night to France. Laud and his henchman, Bishop Wren of Ely, were not so nimble. On 18 December the Commons impeached the pair, ordering them to the Tower. Three days later they instructed Lord Keeper Finch to appear before the bar of the House to answer charges that he had been bribed to rule ship money legal. The night after he brilliantly defended himself, Finch fled to Holland.

Assuming that those who purged his ministers did so in the hope of preferment and not from principle, Charles tried to buy them off, making Lords Hertford, Essex, Bristol, Warwick, Bedford, Saye, Savile and Kimbolton privy councillors.[11] Such a pay-off was too blatant to work. Rather than serving their new master, these men insisted that they could act only according to the wishes of a parliament, which it was becoming apparent to all, was there to stay. As if to symbolize this new fact of political life, on 4 January the Commons ordered the repair of the windows of their chamber, which had been smashed during the days of the personal rule, when it had remained empty and irrelevant.

At this point Henrietta Maria and her friends precipitated a crisis that revealed how rapidly they managed to fill the void left in the king's councils by his purged ministers, and substantiated his enemies' fears. At the queen's instigation Charles reprieved John Goodman, a Douai-educated Jesuit, who had been sentenced to the bloody death an Elizabethan statute prescribed for all Catholic priests found within the realm. This outraged the City of London, which refused to lend the money the king desperately needed to pay his troops and the occupying Scots army. Calling both Houses to Whitehall Charles reminded them there was an emergency in which taxes were desperately needed. Although opposed to any 'alteration' of government, he was by no means adverse to 'reformation'. While he was willing to return to Elizabeth's religious settlement, and cede 'what part of my revenue that shall be found illegal or grievous to the public,' he would not grant the request endorsed by a recent deluge of petitions to deprive the bishops of their votes in the House of Lords. Even though he favoured frequent parliaments, he could not accept the Triennial Bill that would call them automatically every three years. The same day he sent the Lords a message arguing that Father Goodman did not deserve to die: although the jury had convicted him of being a priest they had acquitted him of the far more serious charge of trying to convert Protestants, and in similar instances James and Elizabeth had granted pardons to the condemned.[12] But the Commons were implacable: the Jesuit must die. When Charles countered that this would jeopardize the lives of all Englishmen living abroad in Catholic countries, they demanded that Count Rossetti be sent back to Rome. Neither the king's explanation that the count was not a papal nuncio accredited to the Court of St James, but a private emissary sent to his wife according to her marriage treaty, nor yet one more affirmation that he was not a Catholic, resolved the crisis. Instead Goodman's courage got both sides off the hook: by volunteering to die rather than divide the king from his people he won so much public sympathy that Charles was able to release him into exile.

Closely associated with the fear of popish plots was a widespread distrust of bishops. On 11 December 1,500 Londoners presented parliament with a petition signed by ten times as many, demanding the abolition of bishops, root and branch. Within two months it was followed by similar petitions from eleven other countries. On 25 January 1641 Charles gave his reply. He told parliament that while he was willing to reform the church (having already dropped Bishops Laud and Wren, and restored Williams to favour), he would not countenance the abolition of bishops.

Although Charles was not prepared to see his prerogative whittled away, he was willing to make some concessions. But the grace with which he did so belied his sincerity. When in February he assented to a bill granting him four subsidies and to the Triennial Bill, he told parliament that while they had rarely passed a better piece of legislation than the former the less said about the latter the better. And then Charles went on to ignore his own advice, saying that he disliked the Triennial Bill so much that if he did not enforce it on one could possibly blame him, because, 'to speak freely I have no great encouragement to do it.'[13]

Outright bribery won as few friends as transparent concessions. Charles tried to buy Pym with a place in the privy council. The parliamentarian refused, his shibboleth of the king's good faith being the complete dissolution of the Irish army. Charles's promises to do so eventually were not enough, particularly after he reinforced the Tower of London with a hundred men.[14] This provocation may have been the product of the king's muddled thinking (for at the time he was toying with the idea of reviving the forest laws), or else came from a conscious decision to protect his base in London as he went looking for friends elsewhere.[15]

For some time the Scots had been an obvious choice. On 19 November 1640 the king had attempted to attend the first session of the talks that had been adjourned from Ripon, sweeping aside the protest of Lord Rothes, leader of the Scots delegation, 'Away with trifles, but let us go on to business.' When Rothes insisted, Charles backed down. On 3 December he agreed to the abolition of episcopacy in Scotland. A few days later he accepted that his Scots castles were only to be used to defend the realm from foreign invaders, and not to harass his subjects, and that Scots and Irish citizens living in England should not be forced to abjure the covenant. Charles stalled over the covenanters' last demand that his most ardent supporters in Scotland be exempted from a general pardon, until Hamilton (whose concern for his considerable lands north of the border far exceeded that for his few friends there) persuaded the king to give way. Peace with the covenanters, the marquis urged, would pave the way for an alliance which would enable the king to crush the English parliament, and then turn on his faithless allies to restore the land of his birth to true religion and obedience.

Although an alliance with the Dutch did not promise the same attractions that Hamilton saw in one with the covenanters, Charles was sure that it would be far more acceptable to his English subjects, particularly if it led to the recovery of the Palatinate. Immediately after the dissolution of the Short Parliament Charles had agreed to help the Spanish recover the Low Countries by using Royal Navy vessels to convoy their ships through the Channel in return for a considerable subsidy. Madrid promised much more than it could deliver, and following the expulsion of the Duchess of Chevreuse, together with Windebank's flight (both of them being Hispanophiles), all chances of an alliance with Spain ended. Henrietta Maria urged a French alliance, which Richelieu curtly rejected, forcing her husband to turn to Holland. In January 1641 Charles and Baron de Heenvliet, the Netherland's ambassador, concluded a marriage treaty between the nine-year-old Princess Mary and William of Orange, the Stadholder's son, who was three years her senior. The Dutch gained a useful counter-weight – for by now England was too divided to be counted anyone ally – against Spain. In return Charles obtained the promise that the Hollanders would not help the covenanters, and the prestige of a union with a longstanding Protestant friend. Charles milked the agreement for all it was worth. On 10 February he summoned the House of Lords to ask their advice. Would the treaty benefit religion? England? Might it not help restore the Palatine?[16]

The following month William of Orange landed at Whitehall Steps to be greeted by Prince Charles and James, Duke of York, who escorted him to meet his future father- and mother-in-law. The encounter was strained. Still sulking about the failure of a French alliance, Henrietta Maria refused to kiss William. A fortnight later he and Mary were married in a ceremony noted for its lack of show.

In early July Charles continued his ploy of using foreign policy to win domestic support by publishing a declaration that the restoration of the Palatine had always been and would always be his prime goal. To this end he sent Sir Thomas Roe on an embassy to seek the assistance of the German Diet, and asked parliament to do all it could to help the Protestant cause, 'whereby I hope all the World shall see that there is a good understanding between Me and My people.'[17] No stone seemed too far-fetched for the king to turn. He even wrote to the Polish parliament seeking their support; but unlike their colleagues in Westminster, where both Houses promptly passed motions endorsing Roe's mission, the Poles have yet to reply.[18]

These schemes could not divert parliament from the item that virtually monopolized the nation's attention – Strafford's impeachment. All could unite *against* the earl, which is always much easier than uniting *for* someone. 'Black Tom' as he was widely known, became a useful hate-figure, a bogey man, deflecting discontent away from the king whom it was fervently believed, or at least hoped, could do no wrong.[19] Not just the naive believed that once the earl was out of the way king and people would live happily ever after. Robert Baillie, one of the Scots commissioners who attended Strafford's trial, was sure that 'when we get his head off all things run smooth.' Pym agreed, telling the earl, 'I will never leave you while your head is on your shoulders.'[20]

Ironically this much-feared leviathan was well past his prime. Strafford was a tried, ageing scapegoat, aptly chosen to carry the sins of the past, as well as an excuse for those of the future. Neither his arrest, nor the thirty-one item indictment the Commons sent the Lords seemed to worry the king or his minister. Charles attended the Lords for the formal reading of the charges, chatting to the accused beforehand, and waving to him during the hearing. The trial itself formally opened on 22 Match. It was to occupy England for the next seven weeks, and haunt the king's conscience for the rest of his life. The Lords heard the case in Westminster Hall. Although a throne had been placed for the king's use on the stage built in the centre of the Hall, Charles preferred to eavesdrop in an adjacent room with his wife, family and friends. The most serious charge against Strafford concerned a remark that the earl allegedly made at a meeting of the privy council held on 5 May 1640. According to Sir Henry Vane's notes (which his son had purloined), Strafford advised the king to use Irish troops against 'this kingdom'. However, if the phrase 'this kingdom' referred to Scotland and not England, as Strafford asserted, and Cottington and Juxon testified, then the English House of Lords had no jurisdiction over the matter. Strafford made the most of this point, defending himself with such skill that one member of the audience wrote to a friend 'Tis worth a hundred miles riding to see.'[21] On 10 April Pym's case collapsed. Charles did not have long to savour his friend's victory, for the parliamentary leader immediately had introduced into the Commons a bill of attainder that simply stated that Strafford was guilty, and should be put to death. The opposition did all they could to get the bill through, turning for the first time in two centuries an instrument the crown used to punish its enemies against the king. Mobs swirled around the parliament house heckling the bill's opponents as 'betrayers of their country'. Charles ordered the Lord Mayor to disperse them, but he had neither the heart nor capability to do so. When the Commons passed the attainder on 21 April by 204 votes to 59, Charles straightaway wrote to his minister, 'Upon the word of a king you shall not suffer in life, honour and fortune.' He signed himself, 'your constant, faithful friend, Charles R'.[22]

Having rammed the attainder through the Commons Pym faced two higher hurdles – the Lords and the king. The mob kept up their pressure. They attempted to sack the Spanish ambassador's residence as he was celebrating Easter Mass, and heckled peers as they left and entered the House. Charles attempted to counter such blatant intimidation by coming in person to address the Upper House on 30 April. He said he had heard the evidence against Strafford and 'in my conscience I cannot condemn him of High Treason. . . . I must tell you the Great Truth, which I am sure nobody can know so well as myself,' that he never intended to use the Irish troops in England. Charles, however, missed the point. What was on trial were not the king's intentions, but rather Strafford's advice, a point about which Charles was damningly vague. Instead of basing his defence of his minister on the law, which the Lords' previous rejection of the impeachment case showed supported the accused, Charles accentuated the negative by ending his statement with the request that if they did indeed find Strafford guilty he would be sentenced to a lesser punishment than death.[23]

It could have ben the inherent legal weakness of his case that prompted Pym at this point to release details of a conspiracy hatched by several of the queen's friends, including Sir Henry Jermyn, Sir John Suckling, Sir William D'Avenant, and Sir George Goring, to seize London and the Tower. Sir William Balfour, Lieutenant of the Tower, seemed to confirm the growing belief that subversives threatened England, when he testified that Strafford had offered £20,000 to let him escape and raise a royalist army. As the mob outside bayed for the earl's head, the Lords gave way; they passed the attainder 48 to 11, many faint-hearted peers taking comfort in the thought that Charles's promise to reprieve Strafford let them off the hook. In a panic he sought the advice of his judges, who were of little help. Neither was his wife, who was upset by the revelation of her friend's conspiracies, and her own backstairs midnight meeting with the parliamentary leaders to try and save Strafford.[24] Hoping to repeat Father Goodman's ploy, the earl released Charles from his promise. So the king called on his bishops to see if the Almighty might so the same. Archbishop Ussher, Primate of Ireland, said that Charles must first do his duty to God before that as sovereign – an absolute stand that in more normal times the king would have readily accepted. Now he found Bishop Williams's sophistry more congenial. His dismissal as Lord Keeper, his conviction by Star Chamber and his exile to the diocese of Lincoln had – if that were possible – further blunted the bishop's scruples, while sharpening his ambition. He advised the king that as a private man signing the attainder would be against his conscience, but as a public man, responsible for the public good, he could do so in good faith. Whether Williams's soothing words, or the howling from the mob outside that made the king terrified for his family's safety had the most effect on him, one cannot tell. At any rate Charles signed, consoling himself with the thought that Strafford's lot 'is happier than mine'. In a last desperate attempt Charles, who throughout the affair maintained that his first duty was to protect his family, sent his ten-year-old son, Prince Charles, to beg the Lords to let the earl 'spend the rest of his life in prison'. In return, however, the king offered nothing but a vague promise to be 'more willing' and 'more cheerful' in granting parliaments its desires. Once again Charles ended by letting their lordships off the hook: 'if he must die it were a charity to reprieve him until Saturday.'

The earl was not even given this small boon. On Tuesday, 12 May he was executed on Tower Hill, dying, he told the crowd of well over a hundred thousand, 'with a contented and quiet mind'.[25] As he was being marched out of the Tower on his last journey Wentworth passed under the gate-house in which his dear friend Laud, was confined. The archbishop stretched out a hand through the bars of his cell window, to bless his friend and give 'Thorough' the last rites, before fainting. A few days later Laud bitterly observed that they had both devoted their lives to serving a master 'who knew not how to be or be made great.'[26]

Whether Laud, Strafford, or anyone else could have ever made Charles great is a matter for speculation. What is sure is that there was little grandeur about his betrayal. The king recognized that fact. The evening before the earl's execution he had Juxon tell him that if only his life, and not that of the royal family were in danger, Charles would have pardoned him gladly. The sincerity of the king's anguish is apparent in the prayer (now in Strafford's papers) that he wrote in his own hand:[27]

Gracious Father: the life of man being a warfare upon earth and his life invaded by divers dangers. And none so obnoxious to those dangers as those whom thou hast set to keep thy People from them. I humbly beseech thee to assist me in all the course of my life performing the duty of a King. Suffer no malaise to hurt, no cunning to circumvent, no violence to oppress, no falsehood to betray me. I beseech thee to prevent what I cannot foresee, to master what I cannot withstand, & to unmask & frustrate what I do fear: So I may govern thy People to thy honour, their safety and my comfort.

The king kept at least one promise by looking after the earl's family. Four days after the execution he ordered the Lord Justice of Ireland to pay Lady Strafford £500, and eight months later told him to see she continued to receive the income from her husband's estates.[28] Although the earl's death greatly pained the king, immediately afterwards he seems to have set the matter aside; or else it remained dormant in his conscience for a couple of years, until he was faced with the problem of having to explain why

God had allowed a civil war to break out in England. Like Saint Peter, denying his friend eventually became an impetus to martyrdom.

In the weeks after Strafford's death Charles played for time, graciously accepting the reforms parliament foisted on him, confident that an alliance with the Scots would allow him to regain all be conceded. On 22 June he assented to the act abolishing tonnage and poundage with a generosity that contrasted with the surliness with which he had accepted the Triennial Bill three months before, telling both houses of parliament, 'I never had any design, but to win the affections of my people by any Justice in my government.'[29] He dismissed Count Rossetti (although he and Henrietta Maria did give the emissary a formal farewell). He let Father Ward, and other Jesuits, suffer the bloody death Goodman escaped. He made the Earl of Essex, a moderate peer whose reputation far outshone his accomplishments, Lord Chamberlain in Pembroke's place. He replaced Brian Duppa with the Rev. John Earl as his heir's tutor, and the Earl of Newcastle with Lord Hertford (Essex's brother-in-law) as the boy's governor. Charles even tried to buy the radical Lord Saye and Sele with the very lucrative position of master of the court of wards. The king had become so obliging that it was said he accidentally knighted some fellow who happened to be kneeling beside his path to present a petition.

Charles's new-found benevolence was obvious in the speech he gave parliament on 5 July when he assented to legislation abolishing the prerogative courts, such as Star Chamber and Requests. He ended by announcing he was going to Scotland because he desired 'nothing more than your happiness'. In truth, the king wanted to make them exceedingly unhappy. He made his plan of using the Scots to crush the English parliament clear in a letter he wrote to Argyle in May, wherein he promised to give 'full contentment and satisfaction to my people', in return for 'that retribution of thankfulness that becomes grateful and devoted subjects.' Montrose urged him to come to Edinburgh, arguing that only the king's presence could solve the Scots problem. Charles agreed. With all the superficial self-confidence of the truly insecure, he was convinced that had he followed his own inclinations twelve months before and gone to Scotland after the Treaty of Berwick, affairs there would have been mended long ago: now he must exploit the rift that had just become apparent when the Scots commissioners walked out of their discussions with parliament.

After inspecting the navy, and writing a cordial letter to the Lord President of Wales, whose support he badly needed, Charles left London on 9 August.[30] At Newcastle he inspected the Scots army, as if it were his own rather than one of occupation, and graciously entertained General Leslie at dinner, telling him he approved of all he saw. At six on the evening of 14 August the king entered Edinburgh, escorted by the Elector Palatine, and Lords Hamilton, Lennox and Willoughby. The next day he heard a long sermon from Alexander Henderson, and after another of Henderson's marathon homilies on 17 August went to the Scots parliament.[31] At first the king tried to woo the Scots with flattery, rewards and concessions. He heard divine service according to the rites of the Presbyterian kirk, and entertained old adversaries, such as Argyle and Balmerino, with a show of cordiality.[32] On 19 August he told parliament that nothing had distressed him more than the disagreement between them, and nothing would please him more than settling 'these unhappy mistakings', by cheerfully giving the people of his native land satisfaction in all they desired. According to a leading covenanter, 'the king spoke very graciously.'[33] The next day he approved the covenant. On 25 August he signed the Treaty of London, concluding the negotiations begun at Ripon. He implicitly approved the legislation the Scots parliament had passed the previous year by permitting its publication and not, as he wanted, by touching the acts with his sceptre. By mid-September he even agreed to let parliament approve the appointment of all senior crown officials in Scotland, and made Sir Thomas Hope, Lord Advocate, and Lord Loudoun, Argyle's kinsman, Lord Treasurer. As if that were not enough to win Scottish hearts and minds, the king spent hours playing golf on the links at Leith.

The shallowness of his efforts became apparent in mid-October with the revelation of a conspiracy known as 'The Incident'. Its details were as obscure as they were suspicious. They included an attempt to kidnap and murder Hamilton, Lanark (his brother) and Argyle – supposedly by the king and Montrose, who, to add to the confusion, was in prison, as well as a plot to suborn the loyalty of mercenaries in covenanting employ, which included a late night clandestine meeting with their commander in the king's bedchamber. Charles may have know more about this whole mysterious business than he admitted, for he was always willing to scheme one side off against several others. But if posterity is not clear about Charles's part, few covenanters had any doubts, particularly after he started appearing in parliament with an armed bodyguard. Relations between the king and the Scots quickly deteriorated until not even a marquisate for Argyle nor an earldom for Leslie could rescue them. After the Scots refused to send troops to help him crush the Irish Rebellion, Charles decided to go home. He took his formal farewell of their parliament on 17 November, when Sir Thomas Hope, faithless till the end, replied that 'a contented king is to depart from a contented people.'

Charles returned to London to face problems that had been building up during his absence, and to take advantage of what he sensed was a tide of public turning in his favour. While he was in Scotland he wrote to his wife at least once every three days, sending her letters so secret that he told Edward Nicholas to ensure that she opened them only when she was alone. It is particularly unfortunate that all his letters to his wife from this period have been lost, because Charles often told Nicholas to refer questions to Henrietta Maria, 'for she knows my mind fully.'[34] Although Nicholas fully followed the king's instructions to 'keep me informed about events in England,' and gave his master such candid advice that Charles knighted him on his return from Edinburgh, he treated Nicholas's reports most casually. Often he did not bother to write a letter back to Nicholas, merely scribbling a note on the original which he returned without even making a copy. Perhaps he did so from indolence, or else from reasons of security, for Nicholas wrote he was petrified that his advice would become public and that he would share Strafford's fate. Six months after the calling of the Long Parliament, the regular routines of government were in disarray.

Charles's warm reception in Edinburgh in August had prompted him to take a hard line with the Westminster parliament. When they voted to set up a commission to confirm the Treaty of London, the king told them that it was not really necessary: he would ratify the treaty in the same fashion as his predecessors, and if they wanted to discuss the matter further they should come and see him in Edinburgh.[35] Beside the news in Nicholas's letter of 19 September that the two Houses were falling out, Charles wrote, 'I am not much sorry for it.' A little further on, next to the Secretary of State's observation that if he could settle Scotland he would easily be able to solve England's problems, the king noted that he was sure that he had already done the former. A few days later, on hearing that Pym and his friends were meeting at Lord Mandeville's house to plot strategy for the coming parliamentary session, he told the queen to see that his supporters made similar plans. This was as far as Charles was prepared to go. To Nicholas's suggestion that he give the English parliament the concessions he had just ceded to the Scots he annotated, 'I assure you I do not mean to grant it.'[36] Quite clearly the only justification for making concessions in Scotland was to recover those granted in England.

The swing of English public opinion made this more feasible, and the king more anxious to return to London. 'My long absence is beyond my expectations, so it is against my Desires,' he told Lord Keeper Littleton in a letter to be read aloud to parliament. Charles assiduously courted the City of London. When he noticed that the legislation abolishing tonnage and poundage had accidentally omitted the usual clauses guaranteeing London's traditional privileges and liberties, without being asked to he wrote to the aldermen promising to remedy the neglect. The Lord Mayor and aldermen were getting increasingly concerned about the growth of radicalism in the city, and asked the king if they might organize a civic reception on his return. Charles readily agreed. Convinced that the public still supported episcopacy he appointed several new bishops, all anti-Laudians, and publicly denied the rumours that in Edinburgh he had become a Presbyterian and had promised the covenanters to convert England. 'I am constant for the doctrine and discipline of the Church of England as it was established by Queen Elizabeth and my father, and resolve, by the grace of God, to live and die in the maintenance of it.'[37] In the House of Lords he used the bishops, and even Catholic peers, to modify legislation coming up from the Commons, where he was sure that sentiments were swinging his way. For instance, moderates, such as Edward Hyde, now believed that their erstwhile ally Pym had gone too far by insisting that parliament approve the appointment of the king's ministers. So Charles issued a proclamation that all members return to Westminster, sure that this would flush out his supporters from the more distant shires.[38]

If the king left Scotland on 18 November disappointed by the result of his visit, he set off south with the same confidence with which he had started north but three months before. His optimism at first seemed well-founded. After spending the night of 24 November at Theobalds, he, Princes Charles and James, Princess Mary, the Prince Elector, and a gaggle of dukes rode in their coaches to Stamford Hill, where the sheriffs of London and Middlesex waited to escort them to Moorgate, the road having been smoothed for the occasion by planks laid over the ruts. They reached the city walls about eleven in the morning to find the Lord Mayor, aldermen, and 500 members of the livery companies waiting. As tradition dictated, the Lord Mayor surrendered the keys of the city to the king, who returned them to his safekeeping. As political expediency required, Charles promised that the city would continue to enjoy its ancient liberties, and that he would do all he could to revive trade, and ensure that they regained their Londonderry estates. Thereupon he knighted the Lord Mayor and recorder, and rode to the Guildhall, as the fountains in Cheapside and Cornhill flowed with wine, and the bells pealed from a hundred and twenty churches. A few days later London's Common Council voted to instruct the Lord Mayor and recorder to go to Whitehall to tell the king how happy they all were he was back. On 3 December a second deputation journeyed to Hampton Court to ask him if he and his family would return to spend Christmas in the capital (their civic loyalty being further augmented by the desire to have the court's Yule Tide custom). In both cases Charles readily agreed, knighting the leaders of the deputation, and giving all the members a banquet. The king's supporters were delighted with the progress of events. Edward Hyde, with all the hyperbole of the recent convert, described Charles's entry into London as 'the greatest acclamation of joy that had been known upon any occasion.' Royalist propagandists talked of this 'mutual act of love between his Majesty and the City', and hoped that the rest of the realm might follow the capital's example.[39]

In the most western of Charles's kingdoms such exhortations had a distinctly hollow ring, for by now the rebellion in Ireland was well out of control. Four years earlier Strafford had recognized its basic causes (and, for that matter, the roots of Anglo-Irish conflict ever since) when he wrote, 'I see plainly that, so long as this kingdom continue popish, they are not a people for the crown of England to appear confident of.'[40] Usually, however, the Lord Deputy's advice was not so penetrating. He consistently reported that the Irish were very happy under the crown, and that 'Ireland was a conquered territory, and the king could do with it as he liked.'[41] Taking his own advice at its face value, Strafford managed to alienate all shades of Irish opinion. Perhaps no English ruler could have won the loyalty of the Catholic peasantry, but Strafford did not have to upset the Scots settlers of Ulster by forcing them to take the Black Oath abjuring the covenant, nor make enemies of the Old English, those pre-Reformation and thus Catholic settlers, by threatening their land titles which they loved as dearly as their faith.[42] Strafford tried to control the Protestant New English settlers and and civil servants in Dublin castle by exploiting the rivalries and pursuing his own vendettas. 'We must,' Strafford summed up his tactics, 'govern the natives by the planters and the planters by the natives.'[43] In the short run his policy of dividing to rule worked: in the long run it was catastrophic.

The earl's successors had neither his heavy hand, nor his delicate touch. His trial had put his administration on public view, eroding the crown's authority, while the Scots Rebellion reminded Irish Catholics that England's weakness was their opportunity. When Christopher Wandesford, Strafford's ineffectual successor, died suddenly in December 1640, Charles refused to appoint the Earl of Ormonde, an able and loyal magnate, Lord Deputy. Instead he bowed to pressure from the Dublin parliament, commissioning two ciphers, Sir John Borlase and Sir William Parsons, to rule jointly. Only a mutual antipathy so intense that the two never talked to each other mitigated the malignancy of this decision. Soon Charles became almost as involved with Irish affairs as those of England and Scotland. Bowing to the resentment at the taxes Strafford had forced the Dublin parliament to pass, in April 1641 the king lowered the peer's assessment by a quarter.[44] Claiming that they were entitled to concessions similar to those granted the Scots and English parliaments, the Irish House demanded the repeal of Poynings' Law, reforms in their land laws, and tariff changes. In July, after negotiations in London, Charles agreed to most of their demands: trade was to be encouraged, the acts forbidding the export of Irish wool repealed, an Irish mint established, government officials forbidden to serve as customs farmers, and the Court of High Commission abolished. On one point Charles was adamant; he would not surrender Poynings' Law and thus the privy council's right to veto acts passed by the Irish parliament.[45]

Confident that he had done more than enough to win the loyalty of the Irish, the king attempted to re-enlist the 8,000 troops whom he had been forced to disband the previous May, and started to court Irish opinion. At the same time as he was trying to make an alliance with the covenanters, Charles approached Sir Phelim O'Neil for the aid of the Catholic peasantry against Ulster's Protestant settlers, and Ormonde for the assistance of the

Old Irish landlords.[46] That these secret overtures contradicted each other almost to the point of duplicity, and that Ormonde refused to have any part in them, did not seem to worry the king in the least. To the contrary for the rest of his life Charles continued to hold two inconsistent views of the Irish: they were both papist rebels worthy of the harshest punishment, and a source of loyal soldiers who would scourge his Protestant enemies and rescue their Anglican monarch. So when time – as it had to – proved the impossibility of such contradictory beliefs the king was bitterly disappointed, and Ireland condemned to a civil war as bloody as anything that unhappy land had ever known.

The war started on 23 October 1641, when the Old English, fearful that the growth of radical Protestantism in Westminster would destroy their power in Ireland, launched a pre-emptive strike. Even though an informer betrayed Hugh MacMahon's plot to seize Dublin castle, the British headquarters, all over Ireland men and women rose in revolt with the spontaneity that has always been the tragedy and heroism of Ireland's quest for freedom. 'The crisis has burst upon us with the suddenness of a violent torrent,' Sir William Temple wrote to the king as he cowered inside Dublin castle, adding 'the rebels march on furiously destroying all the English, sparing neither sex nor age, most barbarously murdering them, and that with greater cruelty that was ever used amongst Turks and infidels.' Heading his letter 'late at night', a terrified settler told the king, 'all the papists in the kingdom are conspired against us . . . we cannot resist such a force.[47]

It is hard to overestimate the effect the Irish rebellion had on Protestant England. The tens of thousands of refugees who flooded into the western ports, and the dozens of pamphlets that poured from the presses, provided grossly exaggerated details of Catholic atrocities so horrible that today they can still turn stomachs hardened by Belsen or My Lai.[48] In sum the Irish rebellion raised the political climate to boiling point. Without it an English civil war is inconceivable. Unlike Ireland, or even Scotland, early seventeenth-century England was basically a stable and homogeneous society. It took a great deal to make Englishmen fight Englishmen – tales of babies cut from mother's wombs, gunpowder plots, debauched Protestants left naked to perish in the cold, the conviction that the Irish Rebellion was part of an international Catholic conspiracy already manifest on the Continent with the Thirty Years War, and finally a growing distrust of the king, which seemed to be confirmed by the 'royal commision' (later found to be forged) that the rebels flaunted authorizing their most dastardly deeds. In such a climate the only thing about which all true subjects could agree was that an army must be raised to stamp out the Catholic vermin. Even Lord Balmerino, a leading covenanter who had little cause to love the king, told him that 'these malicious papists' threatened England and Scotland's security.[49] The mayor of Stamford was even more direct.

'Rome's hens,' he told the king on his way south to London, 'daily hatch of its preposterous eggs – crocodile chickens.'[50]

The Irish Rebellion caught Charles, like everyone else, unawares. He heard the news on the links at Leith but, with the *sang froid* of a second Sir Francis Drake, or the addition of the true golfer, finished the round. The king's initial reaction was that the rebellion would help his cause. 'I hope the ill news of Ireland may hinder some of the follies in England,' he wrote to Nicholas on 30 October.[51] The next day he sent Ormonde, his commander-in-chief in Ireland, authority to raise as many troops as necessary.[52] Sure that Protestant horror at the news from across the Irish sea would benefit him by augmenting the widespread royalist reaction, the king went on the attack. 'I have such good success that I will confidently affirm to you,' he told parliament on 2 December, 'that I have left that Nation a most peaceable and contented people.' Much to his dismay, the king continued, instead of finding his English subjects enjoying the concessions he had granted before he left, he came back to discover 'Jealousies, Fights, and Alarms of dangerous designs and plots.'[53]

Charles was referring to the Grand Remonstrance that parliament had passed on 2 November, and which a deputation had presented to him the previous night. He heard them with his usual grace, until the remonstrance alleged a royalist conspiracy to alter the church. 'The devil take him, whosoever he be,' interrupted the king, 'that had a design to change religion.'[54] Charles rapidly regained his composure and asked them to delay publication of the remonstrance for a few days. In fact he almost became jovial, jokingly saying, 'We must not dispose of the bear's skin,' when the deputation read the part of the Grand Remonstrance dealing with the sale of land to be confiscated from Irish rebels.[55] The king's formal reply, delivered to the Commons a few days later, was equally moderate. While he could not accept the remonstrance's charge that 'malignants' had taken over his government, nor parliament's demand that they choose his advisers, he shared their view that there was 'no church . . . upon the earth that professeth the true religion with more purity of doctrine than the Church of England,' and was willing to grant toleration to those 'of tender con science'.[56] To show that he was as concerned as was parliament about events in Ireland, he offered to raise an army of 10,000 men.

The Grand Remonstrance was too long and tedious a recital of the personal rule's real and imagined sins to counter the growing royalist sentiment. In part this came from the inherent conservatism of English society. 'When women preach and cobblers pray the fiends in Hell make holiday,' fulminated a contemporary pamphlet, *Lucifer's Lacky*. Even London's apprentices, usually ready to chant 'No bishops!' at the drop of a mitre, voiced such concerns when they beat up Praise God Barebones, a leather seller by trade and a Puritan by christening and conviction, as he preached to his congregation. The backlash was apparent in the Commons, particularly following the outbreak of the Irish Rebellion. Many members agreed when the king warned them that, 'Deeds not declarations must suppress this great insolency.' Now was the time for all true subjects to support their sovereign, not debate him. Thus in late 1641 Edward Hyde, Sir John Colepeper and Lucius Cary, Lord Falkland, came over to Charles, who in return appointed Colepeper Chancellor of the Exchequer, and Falkland Secretary of State.

The two had less than twenty-four hours to savour the triumph of moderation. On the morning of 3 January Attorney General Sir Edward Herbert rose in parliament to indict five members, John Pym, John Hampden, Arthur Haselrigg, William Strode, and Denzil Holles, plus one peer, Lord Kimbolton, whose name the king personally inserted in the indictment as if to balance the ticket.[57] The attorney general charged them with attempting to deprive the king of his powers, alienating his subjects, subverting the rights of parliament, seducing the people into treason, and designing war against the crown. Therefore His Majesty asked the House to appoint a committee, which should not include disloyal peers, such as Essex, Warwick, Holland, Saye, Brooke and Wharton, secretly to investigate these most serious charges.[58] After Herbert sat down the king's coup came off the rails. For some unexplained reason George Digby failed, as agreed, to follow by up demanding the accused's immediate impeachment.

The psychological moment was lost. The five escaped. The battle lines were drawn.

That evening Charles published charges against the five and sounded out the Dutch ambassador to discover what help he might expect from his son-in-law's country. At midnight he sent a messenger who got the Lord Mayor out of bed to tell him not to send the London militia to guard parliament, which was now under the protection of the Westminster militia commanded by the Marquis of Dorset. Because many of the Westminster troops' livelihood depended on court business the king felt more sure of their loyalty. He also sent another messenger to the Inns of Court, to tell the gentlemen volunteers to stand by.[59]

Once Charles pulled back the spring, Pym baited the trap. After lunch on 4 January he and the other accused MPs ostentatiously went to the Commons confident that their spies at court would quickly let the king know that the cheese was securely in place. At about three in the afternoon Charles set out from Whitehall with a party of soldiers, losing some time on the way to deal with several petitioners.[60] As he passed through Westminster Yard Captain Langrish rushed to the Commons to warn the accused, who straightaway slipped out through a backdoor to the water-gate, where a waiting boat took them to hide-outs in the city. A few minutes later Charles, accompanied by the Elector Palatine, entered the House of Commons. The king strode to the Speaker's chair, glancing around, paying particular attention to the place on the right of the House, near the bar, where Pym usually sat.

'By your leave, Mr Speaker, I must borrow your chair,' the intruder requested with his accustomed politeness. From this vantage point he looked in vain for his opponents.

> I am sorry for this occasion of coming unto you. . . . I must declare unto you here that albeit no king that ever was in England shall be more careful of your privileges . . . yet you must know that in cases of Treason, no person hath a privilege . . . since I see all the birds have flown, I do expect from you that you will send them into me as soon as they return here. But I assure you, on the word of a king, I never did intend any force, but shall proceed against them in a legal and fair way.

Once again, and for the last time in his life, Charles looked around the House. He asked Lenthall if he knew where the five members were. The Speaker fell to his knees and with masterful equivocation replied, 'I have neither eye to see nor tongue to speak in this place but as the house is pleased to direct me.'

So Charles left the House of Commons in defeat, the birds all flown, and with shouts of 'privilege! privilege!' ringing in his ears.

That evening the king ordered the ports closed in case Pym and his cronies tried to leave the country, and instructed the Lord Mayor to search the city, purportedly for caches of stolen arms.[61] He told John Rushworth, clerk of the Commons, to bring him the journal of the day's proceedings. Rushworth, who was to become one of the most important contemporary historians, reported that Charles seemed especially calm.

The mood in London, when Charles rode to the Tower the following morning was very different. 'Sir, let us have our liberties, we desire no more,' someone shouted from the crowd, while another tossed a copy of a sermon given on the text 'To thy tents, O Israel!' into the royal coach.[62] From the Tower, a clear reminder of the crown's naked military power, the king sent word to the Lord Mayor that he wanted to talk to the aldermen and Common Council. At about three he entered the Guildhall. It was very crowded. Charles demanded the immediate return of the five members, denied that he was a papist, and promised rigorously to enforce the law against recusants. 'Parliament, Privileges of Parliament,' some common councillors chanted, as others shouted back, 'God bless the king!' When the hubbub died away Charles asked them what they wanted. 'To hear the advice of your parliament.'

'Who says I do not take the advice of my parliament?' the king answered. 'I do take their advice, and will, but I must distinguish between the parliament and some traitors in it.'

But all this allegation of a parliamentary plot produced were more chants of 'The privileges of Parliament.'

'I have and will observe all the privileges of parliament, but no privilege will protect a traitor from a legal trial,' insisted the king.[63]

This exchange, together with the proclamation issued the same day that the five members were so overwhelmed with guilt that they dared not come out of hiding, convinced few citizens. Two days later Common Council passed a resolution endorsing parliamentary privilege.

Charles seemed confused as to what to do next. On 7 January he ordered a ship carrying ammunition moved downstream from the Tower, lest it provoke the city. The next day he told the Lord Mayor and aldermen to investigate who was responsible for the recent disturbances. Then, without warning, and a little like a driver walking away from the scene of an accident, Charles fled London. On the afternoon of 10 January the royal family left Whitehall Palace, arriving in Hampton Court so suddenly that it was said that they all had to sleep the night in the same bed.

Even though his advisers warned him not to give up the capital Charles never regretted doing so, nor appreciated the political repercussions. London was the centre of trade, law, business, finance, and communications. It was a vast reservoir of talent and manpower, that contained the paraphernalia of government: the courts, records, seals, ledgers, civil servants, palaces and even parliament – all the trade marks of legitimacy. By running away from his problems, Charles surrendered the key to England's government. He was to spend the rest of his life trying to rebuild that government, and regain his capital, only to return nine years later to London as a prisoner, on his way to trial, execution and the establishment of a republic. The civil war did not cause the collapse of monarchical government. Rather the king's dissolution of the traditional forms of government produced the war in 1642, just as eighteen years later the bankruptcy of war engendered the restoration of monarchical rule.

Contemporaries immediately recognized the botched attempt to arrest the five members as a turning point. 'These violent proceedings of the king give much discontent,' one noted, whilst another reported, 'I do find all here full of fears and void of hopes.'[64] The coup was the culmination of policies that had been building for several months: it was the logical consequence of the growing influence of the queen and her Catholic friends.

Court politics were not, of course, new phenomena. During the 1630s they had taken up much of the king's time. With brief exceptions, such as the proposed French Alliance, they amounted to little more than amusing games, played in the closed world of the court, and rarely bothered the king's ministers who handled the substantive business of the personal rule. However, in 1640 and 1641, parliament purged those ministers, forcing the king to accept men he never trusted. So, like a medieval monarch threatened by baronial appointees, Charles brought his government back into his household – or to put it another way, unleashed his household upon government.

This development greatly pleased the queen and her set. To urge her to take an active part in politics Jermyn and Suckling gave Henrietta Maria a copy of D'Avenant's lines:[65]

> Madam, so much peculiar and alone are kings
> To cure this high obnoxious singleness were Queens ordained.

She was far too ready to take their advice. The revelations of the army plot of the following spring showed how willing – indeed anxious – the queen's friends were to use force, possessing all the enthusiasm for war that only those innocent of its horrors can display. As the king's troubles grew he became as politically dependent on Henrietta Maria as he was emotionally. 'Let my wife's direction guide you,' he told Nicholas.[66] To be sure the queen and her friends did not utterly dominate the crown's policies. She was unable, for instance, to prevent Mary's marriage in May 1641 to William of Orange, nor the admission of moderates, such as Hyde, Falkland, Colepeper and (to a lesser extent) Bristol and Digby, into her husband's counsels. Still her influence tended to prevail during moments of crisis. She managed to persuade Charles to arrest the five members by telling him that if he let them get away with treason she could never respect him again.

In retrospect some confrontation between Charles and Pym seemed inevitable. To counter the latter's influence, Charles courted the covenanters, wooed the City of London, flirted with Irish rebels, and on 19 December even offered to balance the budget and slash his household expenses. He was convinced that moderate opinion, particularly in the provinces, agreed with him that events in London had gone too far. Thus he ordered his supporters to return from their country estates to retake their seats in the Commons and issued a proclamation that the prayer book be used in all services. 'God Bless his Majesty, we shall have our religion back again,' shouted the crowd when it was read out in Dover. Encouraged by such support Charles attempted to replace the City of London militia that guarded parliament with the more loyal Westminster companies, and put his own man, Colonel Lunsford, in command of the Tower. Lunsford, who had been convicted of the attempted murder of a neighbour, was typical of the new group of fanatically loyal desperadoes who now surrounded the king, terrifying many moderate citizens.

Behind all these steps loomed a new and vital question that brooked no compromise – who should control the army that was to be levied to fight the Irish. Charles realized this was 'the fittest subject for a king's quarrel', because 'power is but a shadow without the command of militia.'[67] Pym recognized this truism just as readily. On 23 December he consolidated his hold over the city by packing the elections to the Common Council, and a week later had eight bishops impeached. Through his informants at court, Lady Carlisle and William Murray, he let the king know that Henrietta Maria was his next victim. With their help he played Charles with the skill of a fisherman able to see under water. That Charles took the bait is understandable: what is not, however, is that he went in person to the Commons at the head of his troops, to be hauled gasping and twitching on to the bank.

Perhaps Digby's failure to follow up Attorney General Herbert's indictment of the previous day prompted Charles into the not uncommon fallacy of thinking that if you want a job done properly you have to do it yourself. Or else Charles viewed going in person to the Commons as a highly symbolic act, for as Henry VIII had told the members of his last parliament, a king stood no higher than when he stood amongst them. For many the symbols of politics are more important than the substance.[68] While professional politicians may pursue power or profit, most people see politics in symbolic terms, such as law and order, national honour, the queen, the flag, the party. Obviously the king was not a professional who used politics to win wealth or status. If he relished power as a compensation for the insecurity of his early days, then he did so unconsciously. Like most men Charles saw the great political issues in symbolic terms – his coronation oath, the exact form of assent to the Petition of Right, his reaction to the 2 March 1629 fracas, the Scots prayer book, the recurring figure of the emasculated Doge of Venice, and the importance of bishops. All these were as crucial and real to Charles as the symbolism of the art he collected or the masques he performed. As in play the attempt to arrest the five members in person was a highly dramatic gesture, having that quixotic sense of theatre (as well as the same disastrous consequences) as his trip to Madrid. On 4 January 1642 Charles seized centre stage by sitting in Mr Speaker's throne, only to discover that the birds had flown. Eight months later, at Nottingham, in an equally dramatic and symbolic act, he raised his standard, and declared war on his rebellious subjects.

For months after the royal family left London, Whitehall Palace remained vacant. No guards kept out the curious, who wandered around the state apartments gawking at the pictures, and even sat on the throne to try it out for size.[69] A short time before such behaviour would have been unthinkable, even treasonable. Now it showed the drastic change that had taken place in England's government. Having deserted the old forms, the king had to create new ones.

On leaving London, Charles and his family spent the night at Hampton Court, and two days later withdrew to more secure quarters at Windsor castle. On 20 January the king sent parliament a moderate request to state its position regarding royal authority, religion, and its privileges as the basis for discussion. Parliament's answer disappointed the king who replied that he had already conceded them more than had any of his predecessors.[70] Yet – superficially at least – Charles continued to strive for a compromise. On 13 February he told the Lords that he assented to the bills raising troops for Ireland and abolishing the right of the bishops to vote in the Upper House because he was most anxious 'to find a Full Remedy to compose the present distempers.' Even though his letter arrived on St Valentine's Day, it won few hearts. Worse still, it caused many royalists to fear that if the king could desert bishops who then of his friends were safe? The day Charles heard that parliament had rejected his modest proposal of 17 January, he wrote to the leaders of all shades of opinion in Scotland, to Argyle, Loudoun, Lanerick and Montrose, seeking their support, notwithstanding the fact that a week earlier he had told his council in Edinburgh to 'in no way engage themselves in these present differences.'[71]

Whilst Charles talked peace he prepared for war. About four days after the abortive arrest of the five members he ordered the Marquis of Newcastle to try and secure the crucially important arsenal at Hull. When Newcastle failed to do so he determined to send his wife to Holland to buy ammunition and weapons. On 7 February the royal family left Windsor. Having skirted London they reached Dover on 16 February, where Charles and Henrietta Maria lingered for a week, loath to part. After an emotional scene, and promising that he would never make terms with the rebels without her approval, Charles kissed his wife and daughter Mary goodbye. As their ship the *Lion*, and its small escorting flotilla sailed east, ever growing smaller, he galloped after them along the White Cliffs, a forlorn figure desperately waving farewell.

From Dover Charles returned to Canterbury, where, as he promised parliament a few weeks before, he answered their request to sign the militia bill.[72] Hyde's influence was obvious in the king's letter which tried to side step the crucial issue, by declaring that His Majesty would rule according to law, protect his people's property, and had no intention of using force against the Commons. But the militia issue would not go away. Two days later Charles had to tell the messengers the Commons sent to him at Theobalds that he would never sign the bill. So parliament went ahead, passing it as an ordinance which they claimed did not require the royal assent. When Charles heard of this blatantly unconstitutional act his initial response was surprisingly moderate; he dropped the treason charges against the five members, largely in the hope of helping Attorney General Herbert, whom the Commons had just impeached.[73] The arrival of a distinguished delegation at Newmarket on 6 March with the request that he cease his endless perambulations and return to London, goaded the king into denouncing all parliament's complaints as 'trivial and groundless'. Speaking with 'great vehemence', he replied that the flood of seditious pamphlets that parliament had let spew from London's presses had forced him to leave his capital; parliament had broken the law: the judgement of heaven was on his side. Feelings had not cooled a degree when the next day Pembroke, who had once been the king's friend, begged him to yield the right to appoint senior army officers. 'By God not for an hour,' Charles retorted. 'You have asked that of me that was never asked of a king, and with which I would not trust my wife and children.'[74]

Thereupon he left for Cambridge, where his eldest son Prince Charles had preceded him ten days before and had been warmly received by the university, who gave the eleven-year-old boy an honorary MA. While gown cheered the king with an enthusiasm the like of which, one don noted, he had never before heard, town was far less raucous. Several women ran alongside his coach, begging him to return to London or else England would be undone. The failure of the country's gentry to escort him along the Huntingdon Road further irritated Charles, who was so pleased to find the sheriff of Huntingdonshire waiting to welcome him at the county line that he knighted him on the spot.[75] That evening at Hinchingbrooke House Charles wrote to parliament explaining that he was going to York to be in a better position to crush the Irish, and for the last time repeated his request of 20 January for a general statement of their position. As his coach rattled over the ice-hardened ruts of the Great North Road, through Stamford, Newark, and Doncaster, arriving at York on 19 March, he received no reply.[76] So on 2 April he sent parliament a bitter and angry complaint that they were trying to take away 'the freedom of our vote, which were we but a subject were high injustice; but being your king . . .'[77]

If the impasse over the militia bill involved the *de jure* control of the armed forces, Charles's attempt to seize Hull first begged the question *de facto*.[78] On 9 April parliament asked the king to ship the vast arsenal of weapons and ammunition from Hull to the Tower of London from whence, they argued, it could more readily be transferred to Ireland. Charles refused, saying that parliament had no authority to make such a request. He was further angered when they ordered troops under Sir John Hotham to garrison the town. So Charles sent his second son James to Hull to force Hotham to show his hand. The governor let the boy and his attendants in. The next day, 23 April, Charles arrived before the city gates, demanding admission. Had the Lord Mayor of Hull managed to throw the keys of the city's gates down from the wall, had not James's party been preoccupied with eating dinner, or had Charles accepted Hotham's offer that he enter with a dozen, and not the thirty bodyguards on which he insisted, the garrison might have returned to its allegiance. It did not. And so, left fuming outside the main gate, Charles had to slink off to spend the night in Beverley, where all he could do was proclaim Hotham a traitor, and send parliament an irate letter of complaint.[79] He dispatched Sir Lewis Dyve to Holland to tell the queen his side of the story. She was unsympathetic. Equally galling, his nephew, the Prince Elector, was ungrateful, for even though Charles had just sent Sir Thomas Roe on yet one more mission to the Continent on his behalf, the humiliation at Hull convinced him that the Palatine could expect no more from the King of England.[80]

As the first open military act of defiance, Hotham's refusal to admit the king into part of his realm troubled the Scots greatly enough to send Loudon to York to try and heal the widening breach. Since they were occupying two northern English countries the king's response, telling them to mind their own business, is understandable. He wanted action, not adjudication. 'Argyle, this is a time,' Charles wrote, 'wherein my servants that are able and willing to have occasion to show themselves, and (according as they now appear) will prove themselves worthy or not of my favour.'[81] However, this plea, coupled with personal ones he sent to several leading Scots, including the council, elicited no support. In such a frosty climate Charles's choice of Hamilton as his emissary to Edinburgh was nearly as inept as the marquis's suggestion that Henrietta Maria mediate the rift between her husband and parliament.[82]

Charles's efforts to win Irish support were just as fanciful. After sending Ormonde's plans in February 'for reducing the Rebels' so secret that he could not commit them to paper, the following month the king suggested that he go in person to Ireland to put down the rebellion. Luckily both Ormonde's victory at Killsaith and his warning dissuaded the king from this foolish idea, although Charles's appetite for Irish troops remained as keen as ever.[83]

Even though he neglected his wife's suggestions to cultivate the Welsh, they more than any other of the king's subjects satisfied this hunger, serving the king with a loyalty that may be traced through the rising flood of anti-Cymric tirades that poured from parliament's presses.[84]

While the king won the loyalty of Wales without much effort, he spent considerable time trying to gain that of the north. On 12 May he told a small carefully chosen group of Yorkshire gentlemen that, 'Since treason is countenanced so near to me it is time to look to me safety.'[85] Because the audience was not large enough and too exclusive to have much effect on the opinion of England's largest county, the king called all of Yorkshire's freeholders to an assembly at Heyworth Moor on 3 June. Even had he not stuttered badly, he could not have addressed the estimated 100,000 Yorkshiremen who attended, and instead distributed copies of a manifesto reiterating his case. A small incident marred the impact of this assembly. As Sir Thomas Fairfax, one of Lord Savile's many adherents, tried to present the king with a petition, Charles insulted him by quite literally brushing him aside. To consolidate his position in the north, Charles ordered Lord Keeper Littleton to bring the courts and the Great Seal from London to York. After much hesitation – for both sides were trying to force key men off the fence – Littleton complied, mindful no doubt of the implications of the threat Charles added in his own hand, 'I expect your obedience.'[86]

During the summer of 1642 king and parliament waged a propaganda campaign, publishing vast numbers of manifestoes setting forth their cases. This persuaded the converted of the righteousness of their cause rather than dislodging neutrals from an overcrowded fence. To show that he enjoyed widespread support throughout the land, Charles printed loyal addresses from Yorkshire, Hereford, Cornwall, Cumberland, Westmoreland, Kent, Flint, Lincoln, Newark and Lancaster.[87] To define their goals on 21 June parliament published the Nineteen propositions.[88] In his first response, a declaration made to a group of nobles at York, Charles made the crucial error of talking about a 'war against parliament'.[89] Even though his opponents were a minority of those elected to the Commons in 1640, he handed them the inestimable advantage of retaining the venerable and legitimizing name of parliament. In much the same way, by accepting legislation that required him to call parliament at least every three years he gave that ancient body an institutional permanency it had never before known. The crown's reply, drafted by Colepeper and Falkland, to the Nineteen Propositions was long and complex. It argued that if the king accepted parliament's demands he would become 'a prisoner', and 'in effect at once depose himself and his prosperity.' Accepting the propositions was not merely impossible, it was unnecessary, for if parliament disapproved of the actions of the king's ministers, they could always impeach them.[90]

While the targets of such propaganda were the uncommitted, those from whom Charles sought men and money were the convinced. Oxford and Cambridge Universities generously responded to the king's appeals by donating their college plate, the former doing so with such zeal that Charles printed his personal letter of thanks to the vice-chancellor.[91] Courtiers were equally generous. Inigo Jones lent £500. In Holland Henrietta Maria managed to raise 300,000 guilders by pawning the crown jewels.[92] Like a modern politician on the stump Charles learnt to oblige his contributors, promising Lord Herbert, for instance, to reward his sister and cousin and give him the Order of the Garter in return for a £10,000 loan.[93] The king ordered surplus crown land, such as parks and forests sold off, and asked the customs farmers to pay their rents as soon as possible.[94] When Charles heard that parliament had forbidden the sale of the crown jewels, he threatened the City with the loss of its charter if it lent the rebels a penny.'[95]

To raise troops Charles wrote dozens of personal letters to local men of influence, and resorted to the commission of array, a fourteenth-century instrument, that allowed its recipients in each country to levy men and money. Although John Seldenm, the distinguished jurist, promptly ruled these commissions illegal, they were in fact an effective constitutional foundation upon which the royalist army was recruited.[96] Charles botched his attempt to win over the Royal Navy, that service on which he had lavished so much care, attention and money during the personal rule. Acting under powers it had just given itself in the militia ordinance, parliament instructed Admiral Penington, an old sea dog, whose career had been marked more by a canine loyalty to his master than enterprise, to haul down his flag. Countermanding this order Charles forbade the navy to transport ordnance from Hull to London. In late June, following the attempt by some Royal Navy ships who had gone over to parliament to capture the *Providence*, which was running gunpowder to the king from Holland, Charles revoked the Earl of Northumberland's commission as Lord High Admiral. He ordered the Earl of Warwick, a leading parliamentarian, off his flagship, the *James*, and appointed Penington to command the fleet, with instructions to rendezvous with all his ships at Bridlington Bay, off the Yorkshire coast. The king's attempt to force his sailors to show their hands failed, because Penington procrastinated, and the men stayed loyal to their parliamentary commanders.[97] Thus the navy ceased to be royal. By siding with parliament it isolated the British Isles, sparing them the horrors, so graphically shown by the Thirty Years War, of foreign intervention.

The navy's defection prompted Charles's second attempt of early July to seize Hull. A few weeks before a parliamentary ship had captured a ketch carrying a passenger, assumed to be French, for that was the only tongue he appeared to understand. He was taken to Hull where he secretly revealed himself as George Digby to Hotham whom he managed to persuade to surrender the town, so long as Charles invested it with a force large enough for him to do so honourably. Charles and his troops surrounded Hull, confident of an easy victory. The defenders, led by Sir James Meldrum, a Scots mercenary parliament had sent to help – and keep an eye on – Hotham, sallied out driving the royalists from their trenches.

Once more Charles had struck too soon, and had to retreat north to the less glamorous, though more important task, of winning support. He gave a speech to the gentry and freeholders of Lincolnshire. To those of Northamptonshire he declared he was fighting to preserve the law – that very same law that protected their property, and without which no man could safely enjoy his own.[98] At Lancaster he inspected the county militia, spoke to local leading citizens, and attended Sunday worship with the mayor and council, before setting back to once more address Yorkshire's gentry.[99]

In early August, having (one must assume more from habit than hope) despatched another appeal to the emperor to restore the Palatinate, Charles cleared the decks for action. He sent his mother-in-law abroad. (It was a tribute to the force of that lady's character that it was the only thing left about which king and parliament could still agree, the later rapidly voting £3,000 for Marie de Medici's expenses.)[100] Charles ordered the Earl of Essex and his senior officers to surrender their commissions in the rebel army on pain of treason.[101] On 12 August he issued a proclamation charging all subjects, good and true, to meet him at Nottingham for the formal declaration of war.[102]

It had been so long since a King of England had ceremonially proscribed his subjects in rebellion that the heralds were not quite sure of the proper form.[103] Charles turned down their suggestion that the royal standard be hung from a turret window within the castle walls. It should, he insisted, be planted on Eastcroft Common for all to see. The ceremony was not as impressive as the king hoped. As three cavalry troops, and an infantry battalion stood miserably in a down-pour, the herald tried to read out the king's declaration, a task made more difficult by the rain which blotched the ink of the several last minute additions Charles himself had made. As the men dutifully shouted 'God save the King!' the standard was planted in a shallow hole hastily dug with knives and bare hands – only to be blown down into the mud that night by a sudden storm.

Initially few responded to their sovereign's call. His army remained so pitifully weak that a few days later Sir Jacob Astley had to warn, 'he could not give any assurance against his majesty being taken out of bed if the rebels make a brisk attempt.' In Nottingham the cost of entertaining the king and his senior officers, as well as the damage his troops did to the grazing on Eastcroft Common, upset many citizens. Throughout England men were more concerned with bringing in the harvest, many agreeing with John Taylor, 'Me thinks the proverb should not be forgot / That wars are sweet to those that know them not.'[104] And so they tried to remain on the fence.

But for some time Charles had been striving to push them off.

Rather than an inevitable, even accidental drift into civil war, during the first eight months of 1642 Charles forced the pace. In February his wife urged that 'to settle affairs it was necessary to unsettle them first.'[105] On 7 June Charles announced that it was 'his last and absolute determination to set up his standard,' and he was only delayed from doing so for seven weeks by his advisers.[106] Even though the vast majority of his subjects wanted peace, declaring war gave the king the inestimable advantage of turning fractious parliamentarians into foul traitors, and appealing to the habits of obedience ingrained in Englishmen for a millennium. As his amendments to the propaganda that the crown put out in the intensive campaign that both sides waged in the months before the war reveal, Charles personalized the conflict.[107] Ultimately Charles found war a simple answer to a complex problem; it brought the relief that always seemed to come from action. Just as war with the covenanters cut through the complications of the debate over the prayer book, so war with the rebels south of the border resolved the complications of debate with parliament. One royalist standard seemed to capture this message. It showed a cavalier using a sword to cut a knot – presumably the Gordian Knot of Peace. War was direct; it did not engender the sense of guilt that compromise produced; it was a matter of black and white, of friend and foe. Thus a few days after raising the royal standard Charles wrote to Traquair, 'The time is now come for my faithful friends to show themselves.'[108]

After the complexities of the Prayer Book Rebellion, the frustrations of the two Bishops' Wars, the still-birth of the Short Parliament, the cussedness of the Long, the betrayal of Strafford, the attempt to win back the covenanters, the hope and threat of the Irish Rebellion, and the long propaganda campaign of the summer of 1642, for Charles his cause became remarkably clear. 'GIVE CAESAR HIS DUE' declared the slogan he had emblazoned on the battle flag that was to be carried throughout a complex series of British civil wars, wherein for the next generation Englishmen, Scotsmen, Irishmen and Welshmen fought each other, and amongst themselves, to decide what in fact should be rendered unto Caesar and what should be left, if not to God then, at least, to their consciences.

# XIV

# 'TO FIGHT FOR MY CROWN
# AND MY DIGNITY'

For three years and eight months after Charles raised his standard at Nottingham, England, Scotland, Ireland and Wales were engaged in the first of a series of civil wars. For Charles this was a time of great strain and involvement. He worked very diligently on state papers, trying to oversee the war; yet he left the all-important strategic and administrative details to others. He rode long and hard, relishing the rigours of the campaign as much as he had the pleasure of the chase. The war broke up his family. For much of it his wife was abroad, trying to raise the men and material that he needed almost as desperately as he missed her. For months he was away from his children, or had to try and bring them up in Oxford, which was no longer a university town of dreaming spires, but an overcrowded, bawdy city under siege. Yet there were compensations. Charles enjoyed the soldier's life, with its directness, its simple answers, its comradeship. Moments, such as the picnic lunch at Lostwithiel with his front-line troops, just before his greatest personal victory, gave him a sense of belonging that only those who have loved soldering can fully appreciate, and those who have known the full depths of loneliness can completely savour.

While all wars are confused affairs, civil wars are especially chaotic, and that which afflicted the British Isles during the 1640s more than most. It was hard to tell one side from the other. More often than not they wore the same uniforms. Often they spoke the same language: sometimes the same dialect. There were no clear-cut battle lines; men could, and did, change sides. Brother fought brother, father battled son, parent disowned child, and exemptions to any general attempt to classify each side can be readily found. There were, in effect, three main civil wars: one in England, where Charles held the north, Wales, the borders, and the West Country; the second in Scotland that was part of a far older struggle between the Highlands and Lowlands, that started as a reaction to the Tudor conquest and Jacobean colonization, was precipitated by fears of a Puritan parliament at Westminster, and soon became a Catholic demand for religious and political freedom.

In retrospect it may be possible to make sense of this labyrinthine conflict without doing too much harm to the chaos that is reality. Some have credited the king with the grand strategy of trying to use the north, Wales and the west as a base to capture London, parliament's jugular. In fact Charles never had any such clear and consistent overall strategy. His efforts to obtain help from Ireland, Scotland, Wales, France, Portugal, Denmark and Spain, from Catholic and covenanter, from Arminians and Independents, show how he made desperate, and frequently disparate, efforts to win men and money wherever conceivable. For Charles, as with most participants in any major conflict, the civil war was a long and indistinctly delineated process, divided more by the seasons than the swing of the strategic pendulum from one side to the other. Only with the artificial clarity of hindsight is it possible to divide the war into sections: an opening phase in 1642, when the first blood was shed and innocence lost; royalist victories in 1643; a parliamentary triumph in the north and a defeat in the west in 1644; and finally the decisive defeat of Naseby and the craven loss of Bristol in 1645, which forced the king to surrender to the Scots the following year.

Some geographic, strategic or chronological order is possible only in retrospect, and although it is the historian's duty to impose such a system, in doing so he may make the past understandable only by distorting it. For those who lived through the civil war the conflict was hard to comprehend. There were no clear lines in red and blue crayon on the map, on which flags could be moved in orderly array: only confused reports of major battles that stood as signposts pointing to the realization of eventual defeat, along a road littered by countless skirmishes, forced marches, hurried councils of war, hours of boredom and moments of pure fear. If we analyse the options open to the king, we imply that he recognized that he did indeed have choices, and sat down to carefully select them. On the other hand by telescoping events that took months, even years, into a few pages that may be read in as many minutes, we run the risk of making deliberate decisions, taken agonizingly over a long period, seem like snap judgements.

In spite of the complexities of the war, the confusion of men's motives in fighting it, the king's failure to work out an overall strategy, or even pause to see where he had come from and whither he might go, for Charles the essential issue remained quite clear. The day before the Battle of Edgehill, while out hunting, he came across a local gentleman, Richard Shuckburgh, who asked him why he was marching at the head of an army to fight so many of his subjects. Charles's reply was as simple as it was sincere. 'I am going to fight for my crown and my dignity.'[1]

Hours after Charles proclaimed a rebellion, his advisers had second thoughts. On 25 August the council urged him to propose peace talks to parliament. For hours he refused until late that night, worn down by their unanimous voice, he gave way. Afterwards Charles was so upset that he burst into tears, and that night slept hardly a wink.[2] The next morning a fairly conciliatory message was on its way from Nottingham to Westminster. Parliament rejected it out of hand on the grounds that they could not treat with the king so long as he proclaimed them traitors. So three days later Charles offered to withdraw the proclamation if they would withdrew theirs condemning his most loyal followers. He added that he was very willing to consider 'a thorough reformation of religion' and was 'ready to grant anything that shall be really for the good of our subjects.' In reply parliament asked for the power to confiscate the estates of those they deemed delinquent. By October the peace overtures that Charles had reluctantly initiated degenerated into a billingsgate, with each side accusing the other of treason.

The crown's efforts to make peace did, however, have one valuable result. By goading parliament into declaring the land of all royalists potentially liable to forefeiture, they persuaded thousands to flock to the royal standard. During the second week in September recruits poured in, particularly from Yorkshire, Staffordshire and Lincolnshire. To equip them the universities donated silver plate, and Shropshire's recusants paid their fines three years in advance. 'No neutrality is admitted,' observed Sir Thomas Roe, 'both parts resolve that those who are not with them are against them.'[3] Suspecting Nottingham's trained bands, the king disarmed them, giving their weapons to more loyal troops. Charles told the Earl of Newcastle that since 'the rebellion is grown to that height,' he must use all men, regardless of their religion or nationality so long as they 'are willing and able to serve me.'[4] Some helped quietly. Charles asked the Earl of Kingston to lend him £5,000 'without any noise'.[5] Others assisted the king in the hope of future recognition. The Earl of Worcester lent £10,000 in return for the promise of the Order of the Garter.[6] A few came reluctantly out of a sense of duty. 'I have eaten his bread and served him near thirty years,' declared Sir Edmund Verney, 'and will not do so base a thing as forsake him, and choose rather to lose my life (which I am sure to do) to preserve those things that are against my conscience.'[7] More volunteered with alacrity. The king's nephew, Prince Rupert, galloped to Nottingham so fast that his horse slipped, throwing him and dislocating his shoulder; the accident delayed his arrival for all of three hours. At Nottingham Rupert quickly proved his worth, explaining to the king's officers martial skills, such as the use of a petard. In addition to being a member of the royal family, Rupert was an experienced soldier. At twenty-three, already a veteran of the Thirty Years War, the prince had the expertise and energy to turn the king's cavalry into a formidable fighting force.[8]

Growing with every mile, and with the king at its head, the royal army marched from Nottingham, via Derby, to Stafford. Just outside the town, on the Wellington road, Charles called his men together on 19 September for a speech. He reminded them of the importance of military discipline. They were fighting for true religion, their king and the laws of the land. Their enemies were 'but traitors, most of them Brownists, Anabaptists, and atheists'. Finally Charles promised 'to the utmost of his powers to defend and maintain the true Protestant religion,' to preserve his subjects' property, and 'the privileges and Freedoms of Parliament.' It was all stirring stuff! A ringing declaration from a soft-spoken, stuttering monarch that sounded better when read in the ghost-written and widely circulated broadsheets.[9]

On marched the royal army. 'The king's condition is much improved of late, his condition increases daily,' Lord Spencer told his wife on 21 September, 'the king of late is much adverse to peace.' Passing through Shrewsbury the army reached Chester two days later, where the king had ordered the trained bands to be ready to welcome him. 'Long live King Charles, Victorious over all his enemies,' declaimed the recorder in his official greeting. As welcome as such a reception might be, more valued was the news that the same day Rupert had won the first cavalier battle – or rather skirmish – at Powick Bridge. Charles ordered his address of the 19th read from the city's pulpits, and Chester searched for parliamentary sympathizers.[10]

The following Tuesday Charles set out for Shrewsbury, seeking and finding support along the way. At Wrexham on 27 September he told the inhabitants of Denbigh and Flint that by seizing the Royal Navy parliament had left them vulnerable to seaborne attacks from Irish pirates. The next day, at Shrewsbury, he repeated his charge to the people of Shropshire, an inland county protected to the west by the mountains of Snowdonia.[11]

Charles was in fine form. One courtier wrote home, 'I never saw the king look better, he is very cheerful.'[12] The prospect of action stimulated the king, who had been very upset by the council's insistence on peace overtures. Intellectually war suited his concept of a hierarchical order of deference and obligations, of which an army is the classic example. He told the Scots,[13]

And as it ought to be the continual study of all good and pious princes to preserve their people, so certainly it is the duty of all loyal and faithful subjects to maintain the greatness and just authority of their princes, so without this reciprocal endeavour there can be no happiness for the prince nor security for the people.

In this intellectual framework, amounting almost to a contractual philosophy, Charles revealed an emotional involvement by concluding that his enemies' main objective was 'making us nothing.' For Charles going to war satisfied both head and heart; politically confrontation worked to his advantage by appealing to Englishmen's centuries-old ingrained habits of obedience. In addition Charles quite simply believed that as rebels his enemies deserved war, treason being a crime that must never prosper. Going to war banished self-doubt, past failures, gave him a cause as worthy as the Palatinate for which he had struggled since adolescence, and endowed him with a sense of belonging, of being needed, of having someone to hate and something to love. Writing to his Lucasta, Richard Lovelace spoke for every cavalier from the king down:[14]

> True; a new mistress now I chase,
> The first foe in the field,
> And with a stronger faith embrace
> A sword, a horse, a shield

Charles felt much the same way. 'Expecting daily a battle,' he wrote less than a week before Edgehill, 'I think the rebels want either courage or strength to fight.'[15]

After shadow-boxing for weeks (for it takes a lot of courage to cast the first blow in a war between brothers), the two armies met at Edgehill, half a dozen miles northwest of Banbury, on 23 October 1642. On learning that the parliamentary forces commanded by the Earl of Essex were at Kineton, Rupert mustered his men atop the ridge at Edgehill, a first-rate defensive position, being clear of obstacles. Essex wisely held his ground forcing Rupert to move down to the level fields below. Led by the prince, the royalist cavalry attacked, smashing through four infantry regiments. But in the excitement of the chase, they charged too fast and too far. As they plundered the parliamentary baggage train at Kineton, back at Edgehill Essex's infantry regrouped, to hold their ground for a draw.

Charles's role at Edgehill came before and after the battle, which he watched from the safety of the ridge, leaving tactical command to Rupert.[16] At five in the morning of the battle he called a meeting of his senior officers, and accepted Rupert's advice to draw the men up in the Dutch formation, and not the Swedish, as his commander-in-chief, Robert Bertie, Earl of Lindsey, urged. A little later Charles summoned his officers for a pep-talk and then, dressed in a black ermine-lined cape, rode along his lines to encourage the men. After the battle the king seemed stunned, almost shell-shocked, with that lethargy that so often besets those who have survived combat for the first time. He curtly rejected Sir John Colepeper's suggestion that he withdraw to the ridge, preferring to pass the night near his wounded, whose screams an early frost turned into mortal moans. On the field of battle Sir Edmund Verney lay dead, killed while carrying his master's standard with the same loyalty with which a generation before he had defended him from Jesuits in Madrid. Perhaps Charles recalled their youthful adventures; certainly he was very upset by the death of Lord Lindsey, who on having his advice rejected, resigned as commander-in-chief to lead his regiment into battle. Charles wrote to Lindsey's son, who had been wounded and taken prisoner, 'you cannot be more sensible (as I believe) of your father's loss than myself, his death confirming the estimation I ever had of him.'[17] As the king later confessed to Rupert the carnage and loss of life left him 'exceedingly and deeply grieved.'[18] So much so that he turned down Rupert's idea of an immediate attack on London by 3,000 cavalry. Edgehill showed Charles – and for that matter all England – that the face of battle was really not as pretty as Lovelace would have his Lucasta believe.

Slowly, and still numbed, the king and his army moved to the sanctuary of Oxford, which for three and a half years was to be their main base. Charles made arrangements for the care of the wounded, using money borrowed from the colleges. After assuring the inhabitants of the county that he had no intention of forsaking them, and greatly appreciated their loyalty, on 3 November he set out for Reading. This move, combined with an offer to pardon all subjects who returned to their allegiance, threw London into such a panic that the following day a deputation from the city arrived to discuss peace. Charles waited four days before formally responding that he was always ready to receive petitions from all his subjects, so long as he had not proscribed them traitors. So on 11 November a more senior delegation, headed by the Earls of Northumberland and Pembroke entered Charles's forward positions at Colnbrook to start talks.

On Rupert's advice, however, the king continued advancing, and thus laid himself open to the charge of negotiating in bad faith. The point became moot the following day when the prince and his cavalry sacked Brentford. By continental standards it was a pretty tame affair: some looting, a little plundering, but not a single murder. None the less the capture of Brentford terrified London into mobilizing its militia, which it sent out to Turnham Green, four miles west of the suburbs.[19]

At Turnham Green, on 13 November, one of the decisive military confrontations (for it was not bloody enough to be called a battle) of the civil war took place: here Charles lost the only chance of a speedy victory. Because parliament's strength was concentrated in London, taking the capital would have destroyed their ability to fight. By contrast, since the crown's support was dispersed in less populated and peripheral areas such as Wales, the west, the north and the Highlands, any parliamentary victory would, as events proved, take years.

Twenty-four thousand London militia faced six thousand cavaliers at Turnham Green. 'Remember the cause is for God and for the defence of yourself and your children,' their general, Philip Skippon, reminded them, with the admonition to 'Pray hearty and fight hearty'.[20] That evening, after a lot of praying and little fighting from both sides, Charles ordered his men to withdraw. Most observers agree that to continue to attack London would have been 'madness'. However, if the king's soldiers were outnumbered, cold, and short of supplies, then he should never have left Colnbrook, two days before, and paid the political cost of laying himself open to charges of duplicity, without any compensatory military gain. His subsequent explanation that he had retreated from. Turnham Green to lower tensions in London, convinced only the most ardent royalists.[21] On 23 November Charles returned to Oxford to spend the winter preparing to continue the war the following year, negotiate for its end, and recover from the ordeal of the past few weeks.

Although the slaughter at Edgehill, and the reverse at Turnham Green depressed him, he was as determined as ever. 'I cannot but tell you,' Charles confided to Hamilton, 'I have set my rest on the Justice of my case, being resolved that no Extremity or Misfortune shall make me yield. For either I will be a Glorious King or a patient Martyr.'[22] He went on to explain why the Almighty had brought him so low. 'The failure of one friend hath indeed gone very near to me,' he wrote, alluding to Strafford. 'I am certain that God hath either totally forgiven me, and that he will bless this good greater cause in my hands, or that all my punishment shall be in this world.' A greater part of his punishment, Charles concluded was an inability to reward his friends. He tried to take his frustrations out on his enemies, ordering that the prisoners captured at Brentford (including Captain John Lilburne) be tried for treason, and could have hung a few had not parliament threatened to execute twice as many cavaliers in retaliation.[23]

To wage war the king needed an effective organization. The problem was that he never sat down with his advisers to draw up a chain of command, but allowed one to evolve haphazardly. The privy council, that venerable and prestigious committee which had run England's day-to-day government for well over a century, lost influence to the council of war, on which only two privy councillors, Digby and Colepeper, sat. The council of war was an informal group. The king chose its members, the number of whom fluctuated between ten and seventeen, built around a core that consisted of Hyde, Nicholas, Ruthven, Rupert and Digby.[24] Since the council of war's records have been destroyed it is hard to say much about its deliberations, or even how often it met. It has clear, however, that it failed to coordinate and plan the crown's war effort. It lacked a staff to handle detail, and its secretary, Sir Edward Walker, was a pompous little fellow, whom a colleague called 'an ambitious and foolish man, that studies nothing but his own ends.'[25] Most fatal was the king's neglect of the council. He did not use it to control the factions among his advisers; although represented on the council, they frequently by-passed it, in the hope of getting the king's ear.

The first faction consisted of the professional soldiers: men such as Ruthven, whom Charles appointed to succeed Lindsey. A veteran of Gustavus Adolphus's army, and the heroic defender of Edinburgh castle, by 1643 Ruthven was too old, too tired, and too willing to let Rupert have his way to amount to much, which may explain why Charles made him Earl of Brentford the following year. The sergeant major in command of the infantry was Sir Jacob Astley, another veteran of Gustavus's service. He was a first-rate soldier, and a brave field commander, with an unusual gift for words, who before the Battle of Edgehill led his men in the prayer, 'O Lord! thou knowest how busy I must be this day. If I forget thee do not thou forget me.'[26] Sir Arthur Aston, another veteran of Swedish service, commanded the dragoons, who were mounted infantry used as scouts and skirmishers.

There were two groups of civilians on the council of war. The hardliners, who until the bitter end wanted to continue fighting even after the professionals told them it was all over, came from the court circle centred around Henrietta Maria. George Digby's influence grew as he told the king what he wanted to hear; that of Henry Jermyn depended on an intimacy with the queen so strong that some gossiped they must be lovers.

By and large the loyalty of the moderates to the king's cause was based on the conviction that by the end of 1641 the Long Parliament had gone too far, and that during a crisis, such as the Irish revolt, a subject's duty was to his sovereign. For these reasons Lucius Cary, Lord Falkland, accepted the Secretaryship of State, albeit with a reluctance that his performance of that office readily demonstrated. He was loath to dirty his hands with intelligence, build a spy network, or even intercept and read the enemies' mail. He failed to control the generals, once telling Rupert, in neglecting me you neglect the king. By late 1643 Falkland had become so disillusioned, or so impatient, that he lost his life in a desperate charge at Newbury. From his office in Pembroke College Sir Edward Nicholas, the other Secretary of State, effectively handled the vast mass of routine business, remaining in Oxford and minding the store, whilst others went off to fight the war.[27]

Of the moderates on the council the most important was Sir Edward Hyde, later the Earl of Clarendon, and one of the most influential historians of the period. He was a diligent, perceptive man, with the historian's ability to digest large amounts of material, and the politician's knack of judging men. 'Ned Hyde must be secretary,' Charles confided to his wife, 'for indeed I can trust no other.'[28] During 1642 and early 1643 Hyde, more than anyone else, defined the royalist cause in a series of manifestoes, which he drafted and Charles annotated.[29] The king's input can be readily traced by analysing the parenthetical statements which were highly characteristic of his style. For instance, the text of the manifesto issued in the king's name on 6 December 1642, accusing parliament of lawlessness, used a debating trick familiar to any House of Commons' man: Clarendon turned Pym's own words that, 'If you take away law, all things will be confusion,' against him. In contrast, the parenthetical statements adopt a very different point of view. There are ten in the first half of the manifesto, as compared to three in the second, which would suggest that as the king read through the draft Hyde gave him, he lost interest. Rather than underscoring the manifesto's main legal arguments, Charles's additions are highly personal – even paranoidal – in their defence of a king who had consistently behaved with patience in the face of unmatched provocations. The same difference between the text and the parentheses is obvious in the manifesto published in the summer of 1642 condemning Hotham's resistance at Hull. The text declared that 'no rule of law or justice' could possibly justify such a deed, which the parenthetical statements blamed on 'the private practice and subtle insinuations of some few malignant persons', whom the king promised 'to speedily discover and punish'. The insertions in the manifesto issued on 30 July 1643 which denied that Charles intended altering established religion were just as shrill, maintaining that 'such scandalous imputations' were made 'falsely, scandalously, and against the conscience of the contrivors'.

Charles's part in defining the crown's goals was typical of the way in which he conducted the war. Lacking confidence in his abilities, he convinced himself that the war was a baseless attack on him personally by a gang of wicked men. Since his conscience was clear, theirs must be stained. So he annotated from the sidelines, often leaving major decisions to others, whose self-confidence, if not their judgment, was greater than his. He ignored the council of war, preferring to defer to his generals, some of whom, such as Newcastle in the north, Montrose in the Highlands, and Ormonde and Glamorgan in Ireland, were in effect theatre commanders. He allowed them to by-pass his rudimentary chain of command, frequently taking the advice, so Clarendon complained, of the man who talked to him last. Thus the crown's war effort was poorly coordinated. Charles enjoyed being a soldier, with its comradeship of shared discomfort and danger, but he disliked being a general, having to send men into battle to die. Even more he hated the petty intrigues of command: the need to make appointments, and the incessant suits for office. 'I am persecuted regarding places,' he complained to his wife.[30] Not surprisingly Charles's wartime government displayed many of the defects it had in peace.

A lack of central direction was paramount in the efforts the crown made during the winter of 1642/3 to prepare the next summer's campaign. While issuing orders to try and curb the indiscipline that had cost him so much public support after the sack of Brentford, Charles did nothing to control the exuberance of his cavalry that had lost him the Battle of Edgehill.[31] He did try, however, to build up support in the West Country by opening up their trade and telling them not to pay customs duties to parliament.[32] Once more he asked the Oxford colleges for the loan of their plate, of which he received 1,834 lbs.[33] He told George Cooke, Bishop of Hereford, to collect money in his diocese, and purge it all of parliamentary ministers. The king ordered Rupert to ship cloth for uniforms from the newly captured town of Cirencester to Oxford. He told the Earl of Northampton to raid Banbury for food and supplies, and the sheriffs of Gloucester to disband the county's militia, so their weapons could be given to more reliable men.[34] Everywhere – to Monmouthshire, to Newcastle, to Shropshire – the king sent for troops.[35]

The greatest expectations the king had for reinforcements was from Ireland, so during the first few months of 1643 he sent Ormonde a stream of letters telling him to make a truce with the Catholic rebels. The Lord Deputy's talks with them got nowhere largely because the terms that the king offered were far less generous than his military weakness in Ireland, and his desperate need to transfer troops to England would warrant, and because he was at the same time trying to negotiate with the rebels' most obdurate enemies – the English parliament, the City of London, and the Scots-Irish covenanters.[36]

Even before Charles raised his standard in August 1642, the worsening relations between him and parliament greatly worried the Scots, who tried to use their good offices to reconcile the two. Since at the time they were also charging Charles £860 a day for the privilege of occupying England's two most northerly counties, he quite naturally felt their offices were far from impeccable. So Charles brushed aside their peace overtures with platitudes and manifestoes. Eventually he could no longer ignore the petition the general assembly of the kirk passed in early 1643, and which a deputation presented him in Oxford in February.[37] Charles curtly told the Scots to mind their own business: 'the differences between his majesty and the Houses of Parliament had not the least relation to peace between the two kingdoms.' But within a couple of months the king realized that the barrage of personal letters that he sent to friends, local worthies, and boroughs in Scotland would not keep that nation neutral, and the best he could hope for was goading them into the heinous crime of declaring war against their sovereign. The ensuing confusion in Scotland would be so great that Charles was confident that 'no forces would come from hence this summer into England.'

Charles could not, of course, tell the City of London to keep its nose out of English affairs. The war had hurt the city, widening its internal political divisions and damaging the trade of an entrepot whose hinterland lay under royalist control. To exploit these troubles Charles publicly authorized the trained bands (those veterans who had stood up to him at Turnham Green but a month before) to shoot the mob. Five days later he received a deputation from the city authorities petitioning for peace. Instead of exploiting this feeling, and widening the gap between London and the more bellicose members of parliament with a conciliatory gesture, Charles's reply, read before Common Council on 13 January, demanded the arrest of the Lord Mayor and three aldermen. His attempt three days later to circumvent the corporation's traditional government by appealing directly to the sheriffs and city companies met with an equally chilly reception: the city returned to the rebel camp where it remained for the rest of the war. The next month Charles recognized that London was lost, and ordered a total economic blockade of the city, which he called the 'seat of rebellion'.[38]

To a large degree Charles's negotiations with the capital and the covenanters were attempts to outflank his most immediate enemy, parliament. He had dismissed the peace overtures they sent him after Turnham Green as insults from a few desperate renegades.[39] He was hardly more receptive to those read on him on 1 February, continually interrupting the commissioners. When, on 3 February, he formally turned down their terms, Charles explained that to accept parliament's demand for the abolition of bishops, and control of the militia, would destroy the prerogative and the church.[40] The following Sunday, after taking communion in Christ Church cathedral to dispel canards that he was a papist the king made a public declaration, which he had widely circulated, denying that he was a Catholic, and affirming his faith in the Church of England.[41] Paradoxically this hard public stance facilitated rather than hampered the opening of serious negotiations, for it helped purge the guilt that Charles always felt when he talked to those whom he believed to be beyond the pale. Even so, his refusal to meet Lord Saye delayed the arrival of the parliamentary commissioners at Oxford until 21 March.[42]

Although Charles welcomed them with surprising warmth, it soon became obvious that the two sides were drifting even farther apart. The king was irritated to learn that parliament had given the commissioners almost no discretion, and so insisted that all bargaining be carried out through the exchange of written proposals.[43] On 4 April he opened a fresh can of worms by demanding the right to appoint naval captains, and quibbled about the details of truce lines, the punishment of deserters and the naval blockades.[44] Eight days afterwards in what Charles claimed was his last desperate demonstration of a most sincere desire for peace, he offered to demobilize all his troops if parliament did the same, restored his rights and revenues, and allowed all the members they had expelled to resume their seats. Two days later talks finally collapsed. As far as the king was concerned the talks, that became known as the Treaty of Oxford, never had much of a chance of succeeding, and military victories in early 1643 convinced him that he did not have to end the war through negotiations.

Rupert's capture of Cirencester in early February, and the subsequent parade of booty and prisoners through the streets of Oxford greatly heartened the king. He told his nephew to continue pressing the enemy, first by threatening Bristol and then besieging Lichfield.[45] The prince did so with such ferocity that on 18 April Charles had to write to him that, while he was distressed his people had been so misguided 'that we must use so sharp a medicine as the sword to cure their malady,' he nevertheless wanted to recapture their affections more than their towns, desiring not 'their destruction but conversion'.[46] This long, and rather rambling letter, written two days after he broke off talks with Oxford, and the same day as he issued a proclamation promising a free pardon and a 5-shilling bonus to all rebels who deserted and swore an oath of allegiance, suggests a certain degree of ambivalence on the king's part about going back to war.[47] The series of letters he sent to friends in Scotland over the next few weeks confirm this suspicion. In them Charles repeated his conciliatory theme, saying that nothing was dearer to him than the preservation of his native people's love.[48]

If Charles had some slight nagging doubts about breaking off peace talks, he knew full well that his wife had none at all. During the year Henrietta Maria spent in Holland raising men and munitions for him, Charles wrote her weekly descriptions of his hopes and fears, his plans, of his friends and enemies. He blamed himself for her sufferings: 'I think it not the least of my misfortune that for my sake you have seen so much hazard.'[49] He told her how much he loved and missed her, and how his loneliness was aggravated by lameness and failing sight. From Henrietta Maria he sought love, understanding, and approval. Instead she scolded, 'Do not lose courage, and continue to act with resolution.' Indeed her nagging became so vehement that during the Treaty of Oxford a breach developed between them wider than any they had known since Buckingham's murder.[50]

During her return to England Henrietta Maria displayed the full depth of her resolution and courage. After a terrible storm in the North Sea, in which she was almost the only person who was not convinced they would drown, the queen landed at Bridlington, Yorkshire, on 22 February. The next day a parliamentary naval squadron bombarded the royal party, which had to take cover in a ditch. 'The balls were whistling about me in such a style that you may easily believe that I loved not such noise,' she wrote to her husband with brave aplomb, adding, 'a sergeant was killed not within twenty paces of me.'[51] After this ordeal she spent the next four months rallying the north.

Even though part of Charles hankered for peace, and another feared his wife's scorn if he did not continue the war, overall he found compromise and conciliation painful. He had never really been committed to the Treaty of Oxford, consenting to talks only to humour his moderate advisers, and avoid the exprobration of being a warmonger who refused to countenance peace. 'I promise you to be wary of a Treaty,' he assured Newcastle in November, 'as you deserve.'[52] The day after he rejected parliament's initial proposals he confided to Ormonde that only God 'can draw peace out of these articles'.[53] Parliament's modified terms impressed him even less: they were 'so unreasonable that I cannot grant them.'[54] Charles was convinced that divine right monarchs should not – could not – haggle with traitors.

255

With my own power my majesty they wound
In the king's name the king himself they uncrown
So doest the dust destroy the diamond.

So ran some lines attributed to the king's pen at this time. That his enemies paid lip service to such sentiments greatly aggravated him and his friends. Parliament struck medals showing Charles seated on the throne surrounded by his faithful Lords and Commons. Their propaganda claimed that they were actually fighting to rescue the king from his evil advisers. All this was, of course, patently absurd. In a poem celebrating Henrietta Maria's survival at Bridlington, William Cartwright sarcastically wondered if parliament had bombarded the queen *'for the king's Own Good'*?[55]

Before Charles could open up a corridor to enable his wife to safely join him in Oxford he had to secure the south. His main concern was Reading. In a single week in mid-April he wrote to his nephew four times to leave the siege of Lichfield.[56] 'If Rupert come not speedily,' lamented Nicholas, 'Reading will be lost.'[57] Instructing the prince to rendezvous with him at Abingdon, Charles left Oxford on 24 April at the head of a relief column. But a small parliamentary force held him up at Caversham Bridge, until Colonel Richard Fielding surrendered Reading on 27 April.[58]

The failure of Charles's first independent command, and Fielding's subsequent court martial, did nothing to discourage the recruits who poured in from the north; nor did it dishearten the king. On 20 May he formally rejected parliament's peace terms with such scorn that they threatened to hang the royal messenger. In retaliation Charles announced that since parliament had been taken over by a few desperadoes, 'who have sacrificed the Peace and Prosperity of their country to their own Pride, Malice and Ambition,' his true subjects need no longer obey its edicts.[59]

More than anything else the possibility of seeing his wife stiffened the king's resolve. On 7 July he told Henry Wilmot to stage a feint on the Welsh borders to draw off Sir William Waller's parliamentary army, and instructed Rupert (who had just captured Lichfield, having disregarded his uncle's frenzied entreaties to relieve Reading) to meet the queen at Stratford-upon-Avon (where she was being entertained by Shakespeare's daughter, Susanna).[60] Together Rupert and Henrietta's escort of 6,000 troops commanded by Sir Henry Jermyn, withdrew southeast to Kineton. Here, within yards of the field of Edgehill, and at the same hour that Wilmot was routing Waller's troops at Roundway Down, Charles and Henrietta Maria were reunited. The following day, to the pealing of church and college bells, the happy couple entered Oxford. That summer, the last they ever spent together, they conceived their youngest child.

Fortified by his wife's presence Charles told Rupert to capture Bristol: he would remain at Oxford ready to block any parliamentary move from London, or East Anglia, to relieve England's second city. The king's plan was a complete success. He was ecstatic to learn of Bristol's surrender on 26 July, sending Rupert fulsome congratulations.[61] His appreciation extended even to Prince Charles Louis.[62] Although his oldest nephew had just come out publicly for parliament, the king sent an ambassador to Munster, and personal letters to France, Sweden, Denmark, Cologne and Mainz requesting their help in recovering the Palatinate.

As the ink dried on his letters, disputes over the spoils of victory confronted the king. After the surrender of Bristol the Marquis of Hertford made Ralph Hopton its governor, much to the annoyance of Rupert who, as the successful commander, felt he had the right to make the appointment. Charles agreed with his nephew, but managed to placate Hopton with a gracious letter plus a baronetcy, and Hertford by telling him he could no longer be spared at the front, his advice being too badly needed in Oxford. To further soothe ruffled feelings, and pay tribute to his victorious troops, Charles paid a state visit to Bristol.[63]

It was to have consequences that none could have foreseen. Learning that the king was in Bristol, Colonel Massey, governor of Gloucester, offered to surrender the city if Charles rode the thirty-five miles along the River Severn to claim it in person. When Charles arrived outside the gates, Massey reneged on his promise. The king was outraged, and determined to capture personally the parliamentary garrison to punish its perfidious commander rather than for its strategic worth. He rejected Rupert's plan for a frontal assault, preferring the less costly, though slower, tactic of mining the walls. Just before the charge was due to be fired, however, it rained (not unusual in an English summer), flooding the mine. Undismayed the king opted for Rupert's plan, which had a good chance of success since the defenders were down to their last three barrels of powder, had not their heroism galvanized parliament into action. The Earl of Essex marched his relief force west so fast that he forced the king to lift the siege on 5 September, and withdraw to Sudely castle. Charles had rejected his advisers' urgings to stand and fight on the grounds that the small fields and thick hedgerows around Gloucester would negate his superiority in cavalry. The news that Prince Maurice had won a victory at Barnstaple a few days before augmented Charles's sense of failure without raising his morale. He wrote to Ormonde blaming parliament for unnecessarily pro- longing the war, adding that he was in such desperate straits that he needed Irish troops more than ever. According to local legend, as the king was withdrawing from Gloucester, one of his sons asked if they were going home: 'We have no home,' the king replied. Whether true or not, it is a good tale for at Gloucester Charles met the beginning of his end.[64]

Yet the 1643 campaign season was by no means over. Essex had to get safely back to London. Charles pursued him, desperately trying to coordi- nate the various parts of his army in a mad race east, which he won at Newbury, fifty miles from London, by cutting off the parliamentary forces.

The following day, 20 September, Essex tried to outflank the town, but ended up in the thickly hedged country to the south, where his infantry's predominance gave him an advantage. Refusing Rupert's advice to wait until reinforcements of dragoons (who could fight much better than cavalry behind hedges and along narrow sunken lanes) arrived from Oxford, and failing to occupy the high ground of Round Hill, Charles promptly attacked. By nightfall, with the battle stalemated, he felt he had to withdraw towards Oxford, and allow the enemy to return safely home. Thus London remained as elusive a prize as ever. All Charles could do was unleash his privateers (based in Dartmouth) to ravage the city's seaborne trade.[65]

During his first full campaign season Charles displayed two fatal weaknesses as a military commander. In battle he failed to follow up his advantages, or press home the attack, while in the council of war he was unable to co-ordinate the crown's efforts or restrain its factions. Having allowed a smaller rebel force to stop his attempt to relieve Reading, he became sucked into the siege of Gloucester, and then lifted that siege instead of facing Essex's army. He pleaded for Rupert's advice and help to save Reading then ignored his nephew's suggestions at Gloucester and Newbury. Last – and far from least – he failed to follow up the first day's fighting at Newbury, when with a little luck, and a lot of determination he might have been able to destroy the main parliamentary army, and even capture London. Quite simply Charles lacked the self-confidence, the arrogance, which is the hallmark of a successful military commander. 'His gentleness and princely affability to all men,' Clarendon recalled, not only hampered him on the field of battle, but added to dissension and jealousy of it. Colonel Fielding's surrender of Reading, his court martial condemnation and his later reprieve, precipitated a bitter quarrel between soldiers and civilians over the conduct of the war. Military victories, like the capture of Bristol, made the former more confident (and demanding), whilst the return of the queen (who, as a Frenchwoman, opposed the growing influence of her German nephews, Rupert and Maurice) encouraged the latter. Although Charles ably settled the dispute over the appointment of Bristol's governor, his handling of a major quarrel in August 1643 was, even Clarendon had to admit, 'a great error'. In the summer Lords Bedford, Holland and Clare came to Oxford to offer to return to the crown. Holland, at least, hoped to be restored to the royal offices he had previously enjoyed. In her husband's absence Henrietta Maria received the peers so coldly that Charles had to leave the siege of Gloucester for a couple of days to return to Oxford. He was nearly as frigid as his wife, particularly towards Holland, who long ago had been the dear friend who had gone to Paris to woo Henrietta Maria on his behalf, and insisted that Holland apologize for all his transgressions. The proud peer refused to submit. Eventually he, and the other two lords, returned to London, creating the distinct impression that Charles was implacable, and that his offers of peace and pardon to all who returned to their allegiance were not worth the paper on which they were circulated.[66]

While all this was going on two agreements turned the English civil war into a struggle that involved all three of Charles's kingdoms: Ormonde agreed to a year's truce with the Irish rebels on 15 September, and parliament signed the Solemn League and Covenant with the Scots on 25 September. In ten days the war had widened so chasmatically that it took decades to close the gap.

Since the outbreak of the Prayer Book Rebellion Charles expected much of the Irish troops: they were loyal, fierce, fast, and eager to serve him. Recognizing that government had broken down in Ireland, on 11 January 1643 Charles authorized Ormonde to open peace talks with the rebels, and categorically ordered him to do so on 23 April. So keen was the king to have a truce that in July he offered to repeal Poynings' Law, and told the council in Dublin to apply the great seal to whatever Ormonde signed his name.[67] The articles agreed upon in September established a year's truce, with each side staying in their present positions, freed all prisoners, and gained the king £20,000 in money and cattle from the rebels.[68]

If Charles was pleased by these terms his chief agent in Ireland was not. James Butler, twelfth Earl and first Duke of Ormonde, was born in 1610, the scion of one of Ireland's leading Catholic families. Because his father died when he was nine he became a ward of the crown and was brought up a Protestant. During the 1630s he and Wentworth worked well together, and he would have been his successor had it not been for the objections of the Dublin parliament. Ormonde was a handsome man; moderate in private, he was determined in public to be second to none other than his sovereign. Trusted and loyal, powerful and energetic, brave and obedient, the king had no better friend and adviser on the other side of the Irish sea; it was a tragedy for them both – as well as their two lands – that Charles did not rely on Ormonde more. He should never, for example, have ignored Ormonde's warning that an accommodation with the Catholic rebels would do him untold damage in England. After all Strafford had lost his head for suggesting that Irish troops be brought to England. This does not mean that Charles was unaware of the problem. In his private letters and public pronouncements he projected the blame on the other side: if only parliament had voted enough money in 1641 to crush the rebellion at its inception he would never have had to come to terms with the rebels.[69] The only sop he threw to hard-line English Protestant opinion was to order a fast day held each month in support of their beleaguered co-religionists. It did no one much good. The truce worsened relations between king and parliament so badly that in November they hung one of his messengers as a spy. Quite simply the Irish terrified most Englishmen: by land and by sea those fearsome figments of so many Protestant nightmares were coming. In fact, the part Irish soldiers played in the English civil war was slight: in fantasy it was enormous.[70]

Parliament's alliance with the Scots was in many respects the corollary of the king's Irish truce. Following the rejection of their peace initiative in March 1643, the covenanters called a convention that drafted a Solemn League and Covenant. Although this document loyally pledged 'to preserve and defend the King's Majesty's person and authority' its real implications were very different.[71] In return for their military help, the covenanters thought parliament agreed to make England Presbyterian. All along the king consistently tried to thwart the alliance. Calling their leaders not 'persons of quality, place or trust', he ordered the members of the convention home. The covenanters so infuriated Charles that he declared, 'we believe they have forgot they have a king.'[72] After describing those English MPs who voted for the covenant as 'our most malicious enemies', he prayed, 'God will punish such undutiful thoughts.' Just in case His chastisement was insufficient, the king put his armies on alert, told Newcastle to raise the siege of Hull and prepare to receive reinforcements from Holland (which never came), and ordered the city of Chester to protect the earl's left flank. Charles was so confident 'the pride and tyranny of a Scots invasion would rally all true Englishmen to his cause,' that he turned down Montrose's suggestion of a Highland rising in the covenanter rear. Instead he took the advice of the Marquis of Hamilton, a man whose friendship for the king had become more a matter of memory than substance, not to unduly provoke the covenanters.[73]

The Solemn League and Covenant and the Irish truce were turning points in the British civil wars. The first was the product of the king's insistence that the Scots accept an English form of prayer, the second of his frustrations. If to Charles the Irish were St George, to most of his English and Scots subjects they were the dragons. No single act did the king more political harm than the landing of troops from Ireland at Chester in early 1644, and less military benefit, for they were readily beaten, with many of those captured going over to parliament.[74] So long as parliament controlled the seas the king had great difficulty shipping troops over from Ireland, while parliamentary aid from Scotland was readily available across a common land-border. In addition the Presbyterian Scots were neither so feared nor detested as the Catholic Irish. Yet the political price parliament paid for the help was nearly as great as that extracted from the king for Irish assistance.

As early as December 1643 Charles recognized that the Solemn League and Covenant could well split his enemies; he started to exploit the rift, which eventually was to grow so serious that it bedevilled the peace and helped produce two more civil wars. That all lay well in the future. For Charles, as 1644 opened the second full year of fighting, the invasion from the north was both his chief concern and the key to success. As his dear friend, the Earl of Newcastle, told him, 'If your majesty beat the Scots, your game is absolutely won.'[75]

# XV

# 'THESE TIMES ARE ONES OF PUBLIC DANGER'

In many respects the scene was familiar. On Tuesday, 22 January 1644, Charles went in state to address both houses of parliament. He spoke very graciously to them saying that he knew he could count of their help because as the natural leaders of society, they were fully aware how reluctant he had been to take up arms against the rebels – men so desperate that they had even invited a foreign army, the Scots, to invade England. Now that the rights, liberties and property· of all true Englishmen, such as themselves, were in jeopardy, he needed their advice more than ever before.[1]

In other respects the scene was very different. The king was not giving his speech in parliament's usual chamber, but in the great hall at Christ Church, Oxford. He did not address the whole company, but a minority of royalists and moderates. Fifty-seven miles to the east, the other body, whom Charles called 'those rebels at Westminster' still sat in the chamber from which two years before he had stormed in defeat. Indeed, for Charles to summon a parliament when he was at war with those who claimed to be the true representatives of the people, was a desperate step. It was, as the king privately admitted, a sign that 'These times are ones of public danger.'[2]

As usual parliament's initial reaction to the king's opening speech was favourable. On 26 January the Oxford assembly voted that all loyal Englishmen must resist the Scots invasion on penalty of treason. Yet their support for the war was not limitless. The following day 118 members of the Commons and thirty-four peers (which was probably most of those who came to Oxford, and nearly as many as those who sat at Westminster) signed a letter asking the king to send a message to Essex requesting negotiations.[3] Disturbed by what he and his advisers saw as a lack of action, Charles addressed the Oxford parliament for the second time on 7 February. While he appreciated their condemnation of the Scots invaders and their collaborators, he now desperately needed money to give teeth to such fine sentiments. To ensure that 'these enemies of peace shall have their just reward,' he asked parliament to pass a forced loan, which he promised to repay the moment he won the war. If he did not live long enough to see that happy day, 'here is one,' declared the king pushing forward his eldest son Charles, 'I hope will.' This dramatic gesture, the first time Charles publicly talked of not living to see the crown's inevitable victory, had the required effect. Parliament voted forced loans of £100,000, and a little later excise taxes. Next they became entangled in a rather undignified squabble with their estranged colleagues at Westminster. When the latter refused to accept the peace proposals they sent them, on the grounds that the members at Oxford were not a true parliament, the king's parliament voted their rivals at Westminster traitors.

After this unseemly exchange, Charles decided to be rid of his parliament. All they did was eat badly needed food and take up room in a city that was becoming daily more crowded, as the campaign season drew closer. So on 16 April the king called both Houses to announce he was adjourning them until 8 October. He thanked them for their help. Now they were to return to their counties and raise the money that had been voted, and more importantly, 'inform my subjects of the barbarity and Odiousness of this rebellion [and] how solicitous I have been for peace.'[4]

In truth Charles never really liked nor trusted parliaments, neither had he ever been able to work with them. He would have dissolved parliament in March 1642 had not Hyde persuaded him that such a flagrant breach of the recently passed act which stated that parliament could not be dissolved without its own consent would harm his cause more than help it. In January the next year the king issued a proclamation that since the Westminster parliament was no longer free his subjects need not obey it. But Charles made a serious mistake by continuing to refer to the body that sat in Westminster as 'the English parliament'. He preferred to accept the privy council's advice rather than his wife's shrill reprimands.[5] His main reason for calling a parliament to Oxford was not to work effectively with a representative body, but to upstage those members who remained in London. In public he was willing to let the Oxford parliament legitimize his war effort, telling the sheriffs of Montgomery, for instance, that his orders to levy men for Rupert's army came, 'By the Advice of the Lords and Commons assembled in Oxford.'[6] But in private he contemptuously dismissed the House as 'the mongrel parliament'.[7] Oxford was best rid of them.

War-torn Oxford was a lively place. A city under siege, a beautiful university town where raucous drill sergeants had displaced speculative dons. Through its peaceful gardens and contemplative quadrangles the royal family strolled with their spaniels. Past the colleges cavalry trotted, trying to catch the eyes of the pretty women whom the court, no matter where, seemed to attract. Through the streets infantry marched, and cattle were driven, both on their way to the slaughter. The town was packed with troops, camp followers, ladies, doxies, court officials and flunkeys. There was hardly room for them all to be jammed into lodging houses and colleges. The great quad of Christ Church was a stockyard for captured beasts. Inside the college the king tried to maintain the splendour of what had once been the most formal court in Europe. The master of the revels put on entertainments, William D'Avenant continued to write verse, and William Dobson went on painting court portraits. A beagle pack had even been smuggled through the blockade. Charles ordered all government officials, pensioners and patentees to come to Oxford on pain of losing their incomes. Still, try as he might, there was something artificial about life at Oxford. The decorum of the king's rooms at Christ's Church and the queen's at Merton could not hide the fact that Oxford was a brave, brawling, licentious, often bored, occasionally, frightened, garrison town. The soldiers' behaviour became so intolerable that Charles issued a proclamation ordering all men to attend church regularly, and be fined a shilling for each obscenity – a threat, which even partially enforced, would have gone a long way to end the crown's perennial financial problems.[8]

Dissension at court climaxed after the king's failure to take Gloucester. While Rupert was off recruiting men in Wales, or fighting in the Midlands, his enemies plotted with and against each other, so vigorously that Arthur Trevor, the prince's agent in Oxford, warned him, 'Persuasion avails little at Court, where always the orator convinces sooner than the argument.' Even Henrietta Maria, Rupert's opponent, agreed, telling her husband; 'if a person speaks to you boldly, you refuse nothing.'[9]

The queen found life at Oxford increasingly distasteful. Being with her husband was insufficient compensation for the perils and uncouthness of war. At thirty-four pregnancy was more burdensome than ever, the morning sickness of the first few months of her term sapping her strength. Each day seemed to bring a new danger. As parliament's armies tightened their hold around the city, their threat to impeach her seemed to bring a new danger. As parliament's armies tightened their hold around the city, their threat to impeach her seemed to grow more likely. So by the spring of 1644 she decided she must leave her husband and have her baby in a more peaceful and secure place. Charles tried hard to dissuade her, but for the first time since Buckingham's death she would not obey him. On 17 April a sad little party set out through the city's south gate. The king, his two eldest sons and his wife, with an escort of cavalry, rode together the five miles to Abindgon, where they parted; Henrietta Maria to continue to the West Country, and Charles and the boys back to Oxford. The king never saw his wife again.

Two military threats, the Scots invasion of the north and a parliamentary thrust towards the Midlands, forced Henrietta Maria to flee from Oxford. Rupert's brilliant recapture of Newark on 21 March rebuffed the first. Even though his delighted uncle told him that it 'is no less than the saving of the North,' desperate pleas for help from the Yorkshire gentry soon convinced the king that unaided the Earl of Newcastle could not hold the covenanters back for long, and that 'The safety of not only the City of York and the whole North but even of ourselves and the kingdom,' depended on beating the Scots and their allies.[10] But Charles did not know how he was to achieve this most immediate priority. One day he urged Rupert to follow General Manchester's parliamentary forces north, and the next told him that Manchester was really marching south on Oxford.[11] Nothing less than the prince's presence enabled the council of war held in Oxford in late April to work out a cohesive strategy for the coming season. With the bulk of the king's army, including Newcastle's forces, Rupert was to destroy the Scots, while Charles, having strengthened Oxford's outlying garrisons at Reading, Banbury, Abindgon and Wallingford, conducted an essentially passive campaign tying up the parliamentary forces in the south. No sooner had Rupert left than Digby persuaded the king to deviate from their carefully agreed-upon strategy, by transferring soldiers from Abindgon and Reading to Oxford to fight a more aggressive defence.[12] Weakening the city's outer defences enabled Essex to move his troops in closer to blockade Oxford, where it seemed that the royalist forces would become trapped. After spending the day hunting at Woodstock trying to decide what to do next, the king extricated his troops from Oxford on 3 June, marching first south and then west towards Bristol. Here he ordered Prince Maurice, who had just failed to take Lyme Regis, to rendezvous with his men.[13] At Worcester on 7 June the king realized that he had made a serious error. 'I must observe that the chief hope of my resource is, under God from you,' he admitted to Rupert, 'and I believe that if you had been with me I would not have been put to the straights that I am now in. I confess the best had been to have followed your advice . . . but we too easily quitted Abingdon.'[14]

Galvanized, perhaps, by this unusual display of penitence, Charles moved with remarkable alacrity – one might almost say panic. In the letter he wrote Rupert from Tichenhill House, near Worcester, on 14 June he described himself as being 'in extreme necessity.' After congratulating his nephew for capturing Stockton, Bolton and Liverpool, the king ordered him to take York. If he could not do so. Rupert was to return to Worcester to join forces with the king. So vague were Charles's orders, which in effect gave Rupert discretion to cancel the strategy that had been agreed upon in April (which the king had already breached by weakening Oxford's outposts and then moving west instead of staying in the south), that they amounted almost to a *carte blanche*. Colepeper realized as much, telling the king, 'You are undone for upon this peremptory order he will fight whatever comes on it.'[15] Colepeper's censure, plus the awful realization that he should have never deviated from the council of war's plans, prompted the king to hurry back to Oxford, where he picked up fresh troops, and then marched northeast twenty-four miles to Buckingham. At this strategically placed market town the council of war met on 22 June to discuss their options: they could go north and join Rupert and New-castle to defeat Manchester and the Scots; they could sally east and ravage the Eastern Association's base in East Anglia which was unprotected, as most of the men from this parliamentary heartland were off in the north; or third they could thrust southeast and take the biggest prize of them all, London. At this critical juncture Charles hesitated. By sending Digby and Colepeper to Oxford to sound out opinion there he lost momentum, and allowed London's trained bands time to position themselves between him and the city, and Sir William Waller the opportunity to threaten his rear. So Charles had to pull back.

Marching west, his and Waller's armies converged at Cropredy Bridge on 28 June. Noticing that the king had allowed his columns to straggle Waller attacked them across the bridge, which he easily took by pushing aside the piquet Charles had posted, and thus imperilled the royal van-guard. At this point Lord Cleveland, who commanded the crown's rear, attacked Waller. By threatening to regain the bridge, Cleveland forced the parliamentary general to extricate his men back over it lest half his army be cut off on far side of the River Cherwell. By evening both armies were back on their respective banks. Although Cropredy Bridge was a messy battle in which there was no clear-cut victor, overall the king came out of it the better, since afterwards Waller was plagued with mutiny and deser-tion. So the king had cause enough to spend 29 June at an open-air service of thanksgiving, hanging a parliamentary spy, and writing to the queen of his victory.[16]

Henrietta Maria was in Exeter where, on 14 June, she had given birth to a daughter. It was a painful confinement that left the mother very weak, and the baby with one shoulder permanently lower than the other. 'Here is the woefullest spectacle my eyes yet ever looked upon,' an attendant wrote home, 'the most worn and weak pitiful creature in the world, the poor Queen.'[17] Charles did what little he could to help. Before the birth he begged the royal family's doctor, Mayerne, 'for the love of me go to my wife, C.R.' Afterwards he wrote how delighted he was at the birth of 'my youngest, and as they say, prettiest daughter,' telling Henrietta Maria to chose whatever name she wished for the child (she chose her own), so long as the baby was safely christened an Anglican in Exeter cathedral. Finally the king suggested she use this happy event to offer Essex a free pardon if he surrendered and returned to his allegiance. Far from doing so, the parliamentary general would not even grant the ailing queen a safe conduct to go to Bath to take is healing waters. Sick, helpless, and hated, the queen boarded ship at Falmouth on 14 July and after being fired upon by a parliamentary vessel landed at Brest, so ill that doctors agreed that 'her days will not be many'.

Meanwhile Rupert was trying to contain the most serious threat to the crown – the invading Scots who had been joined by Fairfax's infantry and

Cromwell's cavalry. The two generals were typical of the new leaders who were beginning to take command of the army, rising to power not because, like the Earls of Essex or Manchester, they had honourable names that lent distinction to a dubious cause, but because of their abilities. They were, to borrow Cromwell's adage, plain russet-coated captains, who knew what they fought for and loved what they knew, rather than what you would call gentlemen, and were nothing else.[18]

The first wicket, however, did not fall to the players. Acting on the strength of the king's *carte blanche* of 14 June (the original of which he carried on him till his dying day), Rupert relieved York on 21 June. Overruling the Earl of Newcastle's advice to wait since the enemy outnumbered them by 10,000 men, Rupert led his troops eight miles east of the city to Marston Moor. It was seven on the long summer evening of 2 July 1644, before the two sides, in all some 46,000, were ready to fight the civil war's biggest battle. At first all went well for Rupert. His infantry held in the centre, while on the left his cavalry seemed to be gaining an edge. Then suddenly on the right Cromwell's horse charged, smashing through Lord Byron's foot soldiers. 'God made them as stubble to our swords,' exulted the jubilant Cromwell with his characteristic certainty of the Almighty's doings. By nine the battle had become a rout. Thousands were slain. Rupert only managed to escape by vaulting over a fence to hide in a bean field, an ignominious symbol of the crown's utter rout, which its enemies gleefully recorded in unflattering cartoons (see Plate 10).

A few days after the battle Newcastle went into exile on the Continent. 'He was a gentleman of grandeur, generosity, loyalty and steady and forward courage,' recalled Sir Philip Warwick, who served with him, 'but his edge had too much of a razor to it.'[19] An aristocrat of great wealth and influence, Newcastle had defended the king's interests in the north since the outbreak of war, for which Charles was most grateful. 'I cannot but thank you over again for the daily care, pain and good account you give me of my affairs in your parts,' he wrote to Newcastle in October 1642. When, tired of the incessant bickering and back-biting that bedevilled the royalist high command, Newcastle threatened to resign Charles implored him, 'If you leave my service I am sure all the North is lost. Remember all courage is not in fighting, constancy in a good cause being the chief and the despising of slanderous tongues and pens being not the least ingredient.'[20] Thus Charles was able to retain the marquis's loyalty. Even after Rupert – a foreigner, and years his junior – overruled his suggestion that they wait for reinforcements, or for the enemy's three armies to break up, before venturing out of York, Newcastle kept the faith, declaring before the Battle of Marston Moor, 'I have no other ambition than to live and die a loyal subject of his Majesty.' Afterwards Charles wrote to him that his self-imposed exile was not really necessary, for he greatly appreciated the marquis's gallant defence of York.[21] When Newcastle refused to return, the king sent him another most gracious letter in November thanking him for his services, sacrifices and sufferings: he must not blame himself or the loss of the north, added the king, but take comfort that, 'one day, God willing, peace will return and he will be able to reward his friends as is their due.'[22] It was a moving letter full of kindness and concern, showing a capacity for friendship that, if not new, had remained largely dormant for many years. For the king civil war was – as for anyone else who fought in it – a radical experience, but combat did not make him more extreme in his objectives; instead it taught him the worth of true friendship. By showing him countless examples of heroic loyalty from both peers and commoners, the war made the king more constant to both his principles and friends, as well as a more human and more likeable man.

Immediately after the defeat at Marston Moor and the partial victory of Cropredy Bridge, Charles sent out peace feelers to parliament. The terms he offered on 4 July were much the same as before: the maintenance of the true Protestant religion, guarantees for the just privileges of parliament, safeguards for his subjects' liberties and property, a general pardon, and religious toleration for those of 'tender consciences'.[23]

While waiting for a reply to these proposals the king withdrew from Cropredy west to Evesham for a fortnight's rest before deciding to pursue the Earl of Essex and his army to Devon and Cornwall, where they had marched in the hope of capturing the queen. Henrietta Maria, who had sailed to France in mid-July, did her husband one last service by luring the parliamentary army into the Devon and Cornwall peninsula, which, with Wales, was the great reservoir of royalist manpower. After marching through Somerset, where few men responded to his blandishments, Charles reached Exeter on 26 July. Pausing long enough to see his youngest child for the first time, and inspect the 4,600 troops Maurice brought in, Charles crossed the River Tamar on 1 August. Essex was trapped by the sea in the south and the wastes of Bodmin Moor to the north. Slowly Charles forced him back into the Lostwithiel peninsula. On 6 August the king sent the Earl an artfully contrived invitation to give up. Few subjects had ever had the opportunity now granted Essex for doing 'their king's, their country's and their own good'. This was the moment for the two of them to complete 'that blessed work', and make peace. Although Charles did not draft this letter he did add the parenthetic clauses which personalized its main argument. Surrender, Essex was told, would bring about 'The happy settlement of this miserable kingdom (Which all good men desire)', and 'oblige your king in the highest degree (an action certainly of the greatest piety, prudence and honour).'[24]

The king's invitation to yield was not the only message that Essex received on 6 August. Sir Henry Wilmot, general of the Royal Horse, also sent him a letter proposing that they both unite to purge Digby and Rupert from the king's councils – the two apparently being the wicked advisers of parliamentary myth. Disappointment spawned Wilmot's treason. Even though Charles had made him a baron for his services at Roundway Down and Cropredy Bridge and even arranged his marriage to a rich widow, Wilmot was still not happy. He felt (quite correctly) that Charles did not like him personally, and tried to use Rupert's defeat at Marston Moor to turn the king against his nephew and ingratiate himself in the royal favour. With his sense of intrigue that was to become even more byzantine as the war got more desperate, Digby wanted no one to supplant him as Rupert's chief adversary, and thus betrayed Wilmot's plot to the king. Two days later Charles arrested Wilmot, replacing him with Digby's friend, George Goring. Surprisingly the revelation of Wilmot's perfidy did not appear to particularly trouble Charles who generously allowed him to go into exile, and expressed the hope that such leniency might make Rupert and Digby friends.[25]

Slowly the king tightened the noose about Essex's army. On 21 August he took the town of Lostwithiel, cutting off Essex's escape to the north and east. He drove the enemy back south down the peninsula, as he sent troops along his right front to harass them from the west. Charles's capture of Castle Dore on 31 August convinced Essex that further resistance was hopeless. That night, as his cavalry under Sir William Balfour slipped through the king's lines to safety (even though Charles had intelligence of the plan), Essex escaped on a fishing boat, leaving Philip Skippon to negotiate terms.

Skippon surrendered on 3 September. Lostwithiel was, Essex admitted, 'the greatest blow we have ever suffered.' It was as remarkable a feat of generalship as Marston Moor. But instead of pursuing the routed foe whilst their trembling commander skulked in a bean patch, Charles failed to follow up his victory. He permitted Skippon's 6,000 infantry to pile up their arms, and march out of the trap he had so astutely set them, their bands playing, standards flying, officers retaining their swords, and with nothing more than the promise not to fight him again until they reached Southampton. Thus the king let success slip through the arms of misplaced magnanimity.

Essex's escape, Balfour's breakout, and the generous terms granted Skippon meant that the western campaign was far from won. On 4 September Charles ordered Goring's cavalry to cover his march across Dartmoor to Tavistock. Arriving there Charles told Rupert to move his troops south to Oxford to stand by 'for another blow which may end our business.' Two days later the king sent parliament his terms of 4 July, and once again received no reply. After failing to quickly take Plymouth, on 11 September he left Sir Richard Grenville blockading that important port, and marched to Chard. Here the royal army spent a week resting and receiving reinforcements: the king authorized Goring to make terms with the garrison at Barnstaple, and issued another call for a speedily negotiated peace.[26] Then he and his men were ready for the kill. 'We are now marching eastwards, victorious and strong,' crowed Digby, 'so that you may confidently esteem his Majesty's affairs here in the best part they have been at any time since these unhappy wars.'[27]

At the head of his troops, Charles advanced through Salisbury, reaching Newbury on 22 October, where he established his headquarters. He knighted Colonel John Boys, governor of Donnington Castle, two miles to the north, and told Rupert to join him with as many infantry as he could bring. He sent 800 cavalry under the Earl of Northampton to relieve Banbury castle and thus secure his northern flank, leaving himself with a little over 9,000 men for the main battle. All the parliamentary armies, Essex's from the west, Manchester's from the north, and the London-trained bands, came together at Newbury, where at a council of war held on 26 October their roundhead leaders decided on a two-pronged attack: Waller's troops were to outflank Donnington Castle with a fourteen-mile forced march at night to attack Speen on the king's left, at the same time as Manchester assaulted his right at Shaw House. The plan nearly worked. Had the timing of the two attacks on the afternoon of 27 October been closer, had Manchester pressed his home with more than his usual lack of spirit, or had Cromwell on the left followed up the capture of Speen with his accustomed élan, then parliament might have won a noted victory. As it was, the king, after personally failing to rally his men when they ran in panic from Speen, decided to withdraw that night. Detaching his wounded, cannon and baggage with Sir John Boys, Charles quietly infiltrated his forces through the 1,500 yard gap between Donnington Castle and Shaw House, crossing the Thames at Wallingford before the enemy realized the birds had flown.[28]

Leaving his troops to make their own way back to Oxford, Charles rode with only a small escort and without stopping during the seventy-five miles to Bristol, where he met Rupert on the afternoon of the next day. For the next forty-eight hours the king and prince discussed their options. Then they returned to Oxford where Charles ordered every available man on parade. After inspecting the troops, which included fresh Welsh levies under Sir Charles Gerard, and appointing Rupert commander-in-chief in place of Ruthven, who had been wounded at Newbury, the king ordered the advance. He relieved Colonel Boys at Donnington Castle without much trouble, and the next day challenged the main parliamentary forces to fight at Speenhamland. They declined. Even though the roundheads made it back to the safety of London, their tails were between their legs. The cavaliers fully deserved the triumphant entry they received on 23 November, when they returned to their winter quarters in Oxford.

Charles had cause enough to feel pleased. The year that began with the Scots invasion and continued with the disaster at Marston Moor, ended with a gratifying victory at Lostwithiel and a creditable rematch at Newbury. Indeed the king's performance so worried parliament that after much debate the following April they passed the self-denying ordinance purging their army of incompetent aristocratic officers, and establishing a well-trained, well-paid and well-equipped new model army. Ironically Charles's personal victories laid the groundwork for his eventual defeat.

As a battlefield commander the king was unquestionably brave, almost to the point of foolhardiness. He shrugged off his narrow escape from capture at Woodstock by declaring that, 'Possibly he might be found in the hands of the Earl of Essex, but he would be dead first.' At Edgehill he was cool under fire. At Naseby he wanted to lead a last desperate charge against Cromwell's cavalry. Once, when a canon ball smashed to pulp a man standing a few paces from him, Charles seemed unmoved.[29] Yet the king's personal courage won him neither victory nor his men's unbounded admiration. There was something cold-hearted about it. He could not shrug off a near miss with a coarse jest. After evading capture at Woodstock he talked about dying, something about which most soldiers do not like to be reminded. After combat the king fell into that lethargy that is so common among troops who realize they have actually survived, and so disastrous in their officers since it prevents them from continuing to hit the enemy while they suffer the same post-combat fatigue. Between battles the king had an aura of patient suffering. For instance, a few days after Cropredy Bridge, as he was in hot pursuit of Essex, his coach broke down during a thunderstorm. Some of his officers offered to cut through the thick hedgerows so he could shelter in an adjacent cottage. Charles refused; when they congratulated him on his forbearance, he replied, 'That as God had given afflictions to exercise his patience, so he had given him patience to bear his afflictions.'[30]

Of such stuff are martyrs made. It might impress his chaplain (who told the story), but not his troopers, for it lacked the common touch. Even though he shared his men's dangers and discomforts, sleeping under a hedge with his vanguard at Lostwithiel, he was unable to rally the defeated soldiers at the second battle of Newbury. Charles could not win his men's trust as a likeable human being, nor frighten them as a god-like figure whose wrath was more terrible than that of his enemy's. The king was a poor disciplinarian, unable to curb his cavalier's appetite for loot and plunder which grew as the war turned against them and defeats became common and pay-days rarer. In sum Charles was too mild a man to be a great, or even an effective, general. As one officer recalled, 'I never observed any great severity in the King either toward the enemy when he had him in his power, or to the soldiers in his own army, except at Wing, a house of my Lord Carnarvon where he commanded to be hanged on a sign post, a soldier, for stealing the chalice out of the church.'[31] Most likely Charles punished the looter less for breaking that code of military discipline – by

which battles are won – and more for transgressing against the church –
for which the king had begun a war that he was now starting to lose.

The royalist rank and file neither particularly liked nor feared Charles
as a man. But as King of England, Scotland, Ireland and Wales he was still
a potent force. It mattered not if his mistakes 'break his army never so
often',[32] a roundhead ruefully noted, for 'his person will raise another.'
Indeed the king won the greatest loyalty from those subjects who culturally
differed from him the most. The Cornish were still highly Celtic, with
their own language, ways and clannishness. Even more alien were the
Welsh and the Scots Highlanders, who continued to fight and die for him
long after everyone else believed his cause was lost. His intimacy with the
Earls of Newcastle and Glamorgan, and the Marquis of Worcester showed
how war helped Charles develop a capacity for friendship. Yet he found
it very hard to communicate this feeling towards the soldiers and officers
who risked their lives in his cause. This does not mean that he felt no
obligation towards them. To the contrary their loyalty touched him as
deeply as the perfidy of turncoats hurt.[33] A restrained man, he tried to
show his appreciation for his troops' sufferings by spending the night near
them after Edgehill or by bivouacking with them at Lostwithiel. At Oxford
he appointed John Bissel commissary for the sick and wounded, authorized
a collection taken for their care, and turned Sir William Spenser's house
into a military hospital. After the first battle at Newbury the king ordered
the mayor to do all he could to save the wounded from both sides.[34]

As the war progressed Charles learnt much as a battlefield commander.
Although he played little part in the Battle of Cropredy Bridge, his conduct
of the Lostwithiel campaign was masterful. The king's pursuit of Essex
was remorseless, his tactical grasp during the capture of the town of
Lostwithiel first rate, his co-ordination of the dispersed forces surrounding
Essex's army remarkable, especially as small fields and thick hedges hampered communications on a perimeter of over twenty miles. Perhaps the
secret of the king's success during the Cornish campaign was that he
developed enough self-confidence to trust his own judgment: he may have
done so from desperation, since his wife was sending him a stream of
hysterical letters saying she was about to breathe her last, or else he no
longer felt that sense of repressed inferiority towards his nephew since
Rupert had just lost Marston Moor. Yet if Lostwithiel was almost a perfect
campaign, the king must be faulted for throwing away its fruits: worried
by a lack of supplies he lost his nerve. 'It hath pleased God to have given
me an unexpected Victory,' Charles wrote to Rupert the following day,
'and you will find the particulars (which I leave to others) that God's
protection of a just cause was never more apparent than this time, for had
our success been either deferred or of another kind, nothing but a direct
miracle could have saved us.'[35] Charles dismissed what could have been a
decisive triumph as a closely run and fortunate fluke.

At Newbury the king managed to escape the fate that he was able to inflict on the enemy at Lostwithiel. The credit for spotting the gap in the parliamentary lines, and then using his strongpoint at Donnington Castle as a conduit for a night withdrawal (one of the most difficult of military operations) was undoubtedly the king's. So too must be that for the rapid regrouping and recapture of Newbury which worried his adversaries enough to create the new model army. Yet while the king grew tactically as a military commander strategy remained a major weakness. Even though he quickly recognized his error in failing to adhere to the plans agreed upon by the April council of war, he worsened the situation by giving Rupert the vague orders of 14 June, which were a mistake, although not as fatal as the prince would have posterity believe. What were Charles's overall intentions in the second Newbury campaign? To regain the outposts around Oxford he had lost by deviating from the council of war's master plan?[36] To destroy the parliamentary forces and take London? If the answer is the former, then Charles ably succeeded: if the latter, he totally failed. The trouble was that he never really asked such questions. Only rarely did Charles sit down (as at Buckingham) to list the options, and even then he failed to choose between them. The king squandered the chief advantage he had – that of being king. As commander-in-chief he had the inherent capacity of defining his goals and co-ordinating their execution.

Charles's strategic flaws filtered over into the way in which he organized his army. For instance he never had an effective intelligence system. While delighting in the minutiae and romance of ciphers, secret codes, and smuggled messages, the king sent far too many letters for his own security.[37] His army had too many officers, especially aristocrats, and not enough food. According to one story, during the siege of Oxford, a royalist trooper shouted down from the walls, 'Roundhead, fling me up half a mutton, and I will fling you down a Lord.'[38] Charles never overcame his shortage of infantry. He allowed his stag-hunting squires to raise too many cavalry. Especially wasteful of resources were the many royalist garrisons (of which there were twenty-five in Shropshire alone). Usually based on some fortified country house they were as vulnerable to capture as slight to the other side.[39] Since the parts of England that Charles controlled were the poorest and least populated, he could not afford to waste a single man. Instead of hoping that the will of the wisp from Ireland would save him, the king would have been better employed in raising more infantry to win his battles, and more money to pay his men and so curb their ever growing dependence on loot and plunder, which as the months dragged by cost him public support. Charles's explanation to the inhabitants of Somerset (who refused to join him, even when he seemed to have the upper hand against the Earl of Essex) that his men's indiscipline was really their fault convinced few, particularly those whose property had been stolen.[40]

Charles was slow to wage total war. At first he was loath to seize and sell rebels' property to pay his own troops. In 1643 he ordered that this be done only with his specific approval, not granting a *carte blanche* for sequestrations until 1544. He started the war by using local magnates, such as Dorset, Hertford and Newcastle, as his theatre commanders. He was used to working with them: he liked them: as the traditional leaders of a hierarchical society they represented the England for which he was fighting. But when the gentlemen failed in battle the players stepped in. Quickly professionals such as Princes Rupert and Maurice, or Sir Richard Grenville took over, to wage the war, collect taxes, and raise troops with a rigour that became counter-productive, alienating many of the crown's natural supporters.[41]

In assessing Charles's role as a military commander a paradox emerges. While the imprint of the king's hand directing the war is hard to see from the records, a lot of footprints are discernible. During the war Charles was far more active than he had ever been in the years of peace, reading papers, riding incessantly, attending councils, signing orders and seeking advice. Yet he spent comparatively little time on details. There is a portrait of Charles standing near Sir Edward Walker, secretary to the council of war, who has a piece of paper on a drum (rather a difficult place on which to write), pen poised ready for the king's commands (see Plate 11). A glance at the four volumes of Walker's papers shows that the king had very little direct input into them, there being only one order in Charles's hand.[42] In war the king was content to let his artists perpetuate the same myths about him as they had in peace.

All this the year 1644 most amply demonstrated.

# XVI

# 'THE BATTLE OF ALL FOR ALL'

Charles seemed optimistic as he spent the winter at Oxford preparing for the 1645 campaign. 'I thank God my affairs begin to smile on me again,' he boasted to his wife in May.[1] The arrival of a peace overture from parliament soon after he returned to Oxford convinced him that the rebels were weakening. For the coming fight the king trained strenuously, energetically recruiting men, raising money at home and abroad, scrounging supplies wherever he could, and writing orders. The news of Montrose's victories were most heartening. The mirage of help from Ireland seemed so real that Charles tried to purchase it at any price. As her health improved Henrietta Maria did all she could in France to assist her husband, while at sea royalist privateers won the king's gratitude (and their own fortunes) by ravaging London's maritime trade. Yet the enemy was no less energetic. They remodelled the army, replacing aristocratic leaders with plain russet-coated captains. Although Charles did not recognize the danger of these reforms, dismissing Fairfax as 'the rebels' new brutish general', he did realize that the struggle was approaching its crisis. Convinced that 'This summer will be the hottest for war of any that has been yet,' he decided to fight 'the battle of all for all.'[2]

Charles's confidence explains why he treated the parliamentary emissaries, who arrived in Oxford on 27 November 1644, with marked frigidity. After being kept waiting a couple of hours outside the city gates, and then being lodged in mean quarters, he received them after dinner, as he, Maurice and Rupert strolled through Christ Church gardens. As soon as they told him they had come to present terms which they had no authority to modify, Charles dismissed them, saying that his time was too valuable to waste with postilions. The king's contempt was obvious in the handwritten note he gave them three days later to take back to Westminster. Because parliament's terms were too complex and far reaching, and their emissaries had no authority to vary them, His Majesty could not, of course, give an immediate answer. He would do so in due course, and thus requested safe conducts for the Earls of Southampton and Richmond so that they might take his reply to London.[3] The king may have assumed that a message conveyed by such high-born ambassadors would have a greater chance of success; certainly he preferred to deal with earls, even if they were on the other side. He sent a trumpeter to Essex to ask for the safe conducts and as usual, Essex passed the request on to parliament, which granted it reluctantly. On 14 December Richmond and Southampton rode to London, where three days later they presented the king's proposals to a joint session of Lords, Commons and Scots commissioners. On 3 January parliament nominated sixteen commissioners who, with four Scots, were to meet the king at Uxbridge, eight miles west of the capital. Two weeks later Charles accepted their terms.

Even though in doing so the king expressed the hope that they would be able to reach 'a safe and well grounded peace', disagreements arose between the two sides even before the talks got under way. Parliament refused to accept the validity of the patents of nobility that Charles had granted several of his commissioners on the grounds that they had been issued after Lord Keeper Littleton's defection from London with the Great Seal. Although not serious enough to prevent negotiations – being resolved by that Puritan bromide, a day of prayer and thanksgiving – this quibble, together with the king's confession to his wife of 'the impossibility of this present treaty should produce a peace', shows that neither side entered Sir John Bennet's house (the royalists by the front door, and the parliamentarians by the back) at Uxbridge on 30 January for the first day's talks, replete with either confidence or conciliation.[4]

Initially the negotiators agreed to a twenty-day deadline, to concentrate on religion first, and to use the six points proposed by the crown on 21 January as their basic agenda. These suggested that all forts, towns, and ships captured from the king be restored; all illegal acts revoked; all prisoners of war released; everyone exempted from a general pardon to be tried according to law; legislation to be passed protecting the church and men of tender conscience; and the establishment of an immediate ceasefire while final details of the peace were worked out.[5] Although, as Charles admitted, his proposals contained few new concessions or ideas, the negotiators worked long and hard, sometimes until two in the morning, to try and turn them into the basis for a lasting agreement.[6] Until the other side refused to let his negotiators use the Anglican prayer book, parliament having just passed an ordinance replacing it with a Directory, Charles approved the general direction of the first few days' negotiations. Telling Secretary of State Nicholas that the rebels had acted 'barbarously', he let his anger cloud his judgment.[7] He advised his commissioners to remind the other side they were arrant rebels and their end must be damnation, ruin and infamy, unless they repented.[8] Charles was convinced that this stern warning would soon bring the rebels to their senses. Fortunately, his commissioners knew better, and ignored the king's advice. A week later he told them that while he supported their general conduct of negotiations, they had gone too far in offering to surrender control of the militia for three years; parliament would have taken less once they realized they were losing public support. When the parliamentary commissioners first raised the issue of Scotland, the king maintained that he could not discuss that nation's affairs without consulting Montrose. Parliament insisted, Charles gave way, and within a few days a tentative agreement was reached on both religion and Scotland, that Charles liked enough to tell Nicholas not to 'vary a jot', unless it was to improve the terms still further.[9]

Forty-eight hours later, on 17 February, Charles drastically hardened his stance, warning Nicholas, 'I will not go one jot further.' While he might make a few more minor concessions regarding the militia, the king must control the committee that was to be established to supervise the armed forces. Although he was willing to let parliament nominate some royal officials, these were to be ones 'not of great trust ... but as much profit as you will.'[10] More because of its transparency than the probity of its potential recipients, this bribe found no takers. Charles, of course, saw it differently, telling his wife that 'the unreasonable stubbornness of the rebels daily make the treaty less likely.'[11] The king's offer to come to London in person was met with an equally chilling response. On 24 February, negotiations finally ended.

The immediate explanations for the collapse of the Uxbridge talks are not hard to find. The passage by the House of Lords on 15 February of the ordinance establishing the new model army and the news, a few days later, of Montrose's victory over Argyle at Tippermuir, convinced both sides that their chances of winning the war militarily had greatly increased.

Charles – it is true – did not need much convincing. Always reluctant to deal with rebels he had no great commitment to a negotiated end of hostilities. In private he admitted that his reply to parliament's initial overtures was 'at most a ceremonial'.[12] But he could not openly dismiss them out of hand, having to conciliate public opinion which every day grew more weary of bloodshed, and his own moderate counsellors, such as Hyde, Nicholas and Colepeper. At the same time as he allowed the moderates to set the pace at Uxbridge, he revealed his true feelings to Ormonde and Henrietta Maria. To the former he wrote on 9 January never to make peace abandoning his friends, honour or safety.

Even though the king ended this letter by adding that he was amazed anyone could stoop so low as to spread rumours of discord between him and his wife, in fact the tattle-tellers told the truth.[13] In private, and with a vehemence that would have shocked the troubadours, who less than a half-dozen years before waxed lyrical about the perfection of courtly love, Henrietta Maria had taken her husband to task. 'For the honour of God, trust not yourself to these people,' she chastised him. 'If you consent to this you are lost.'[14] Charles's reply that he was surprised she should think he would be as silly to act 'so cheaply or foolishly' seems not a little strained, particularly when compared to the undisguised glee with which a little later he told her he had ended negotiations: he could see nothing but good coming from breaking them off: he had been most reasonable: all men of fair judgment must blame the rebels for their intransigence.[15] On the morrow Charles seemed even more pleased to inform the queen that he had sent the Oxford parliament packing.[16]

All the time that Charles was talking of peace, he (like the other side) was getting ready for war. At Oxford he would get up early. Twice a week he inspected the city's defences and artillery with such regularity that an enemy sniper could have set his watch by it. In the afternoons he walked in a college garden, attended chapel, had dinner, and passed the evenings in conversation, playing chess or real tennis, and writing letters and orders.[17] He appealed to the people of Oxfordshire for recruits, ordered the governor of Bath to send supplies, and Sir Thomas Campion to scout the countryside for grain, hemp and flax.[18] He organized a cavalry force to raid Buckinghamshire for sixty cart horses to pull his artillery train, and tried to settle a complex and tedious squabble involving Sir John Wintour.[19] By spring time Charles had every right to boast to Rupert that he had been far from idle in getting ready for the coming campaign.[20]

The preparations that most concerned the king involved the creation in March 1645 of a separate command in the west under the titular charge of the Prince of Wales. The king sent out a stream of orders – to collect £5,000 in Oxford, to sequester saltpetre and brimstone, to send ordnance to Monmouth, to confiscate rebel lands in Somerset, to appoint captains in the West Country.[21] Because the western command had been set up more for political than military reasons, the king's efforts were of limited value, sometimes producing the worst of both worlds. When the Prince of Wales tried to exercise independent authority by, for example, appointing Sir Henry Greenfield gentleman of his bedchamber, the king got most irritated, insisting that such decisions were still rightfully his; but at the same time, as military defeats worsened communications between him and the west, the king could not handle such routine matters.[22] In fact, the only person who gained from the establishment of the new command was Digby, who managed to get his rival, Hyde, shunted off as the prince's chief adviser.

The execution of Charles's old friend and counsellor, Archbishop Laud, on 10 January, did not appear to have much effect on the king. Although the Commons had impeached Laud back in December 1640, they kept him in cold storage in the Tower for nearly four years until the Lords brought him to trial. Time had muted the feelings Charles had for the archbishop. He was almost like a bit of broken old furniture, stored long ago in the attic, that parliament decided to throw out during a spring cleaning. To his credit, Charles sent Laud a blanket pardon for any treasons he might have committed, and when the archbishop pointed out a legal flaw in it, promptly sent an amended draft. That was all Charles could do, for he could never have prevented the execution of an old, broken, harmless man of seventy-two, a symbol whom the enemies of the Church of England hated with the same exaggerated passion as his partisans in later years would accord reverence. At the time, however, Charles managed to derive some personal comfort from this vindictive act, which was symptomatic of the growing hatreds engendered by four years of civil war. A few days after the archbishop's death he wrote to his wife, 'nothing can be more evident than that Strafford's innocent blood has been one of the great causes of God's judgments upon this nation by a furious civil war.' So far God had been punishing both sides since they were equally guilty: but now parliament had committed so heinous a crime as murdering an Archbishop of Canterbury he was sure that the Almighty's 'hand of justice must be heavier upon them and lighter upon us.'[23]

As Charles's old friends faded from his affections, new ones, such as Montrose, took their place. James Graham, Fifth Earl and First Marquis of Montrose, was one of those truly romantic Highland heroes that the Stuart cause produced. He was born in 1612, scion of one of Scotland's leading families, was educated at St Andrews University, married at seventeen, and departed on a three-year grand tour of Europe. On his return in 1636 Charles treated him coolly, perhaps because Hamilton, the king's friend, feared another Scots rival. Not surprisingly Montrose reacted by supporting the covenanters, his unit being one of the first to cross the River Tweed in 1640. The following year, during the royal visit to Edinburgh, Hamilton may have managed to persuade Charles to arrest Montrose for treason. None the less Montrose slowly came over to the king. In part this was a reaction to Hamilton's defection, the erstwhile favourite becoming more concerned with preserving his ancestral lands north of the border than his monarch's friendship. Montrose also fell out with the Earl of Argyle, the great covenanting chief, whom he suspected of planing to turn the king into a mere cipher. Charles, as always, initially treated the convert cautiously. He refused Montrose's offer of early 1643 to raise a Highland revolt but the covenanter invasion of England the following January forced him to change his mind, and appoint Montrose his Lieutenant-General in Scotland. The marquis's first attempt to stir up a revolt failed, and within a few weeks he had to flee to England. In August, disguised, and with only two companions, Montrose returned to the Highlands to begin one of the most remarkable military campaigns that Great Britain has ever known. Within a year he won six major battles, moving his small forces with great speed across the mountains and through the glens. Personally brave, a great tactician and a fine leader of some of the fiercest soldiers in the king's cause, Montrose set the north ablaze. The flames warmed Charles's hopes, becoming 'one of the most essential parts in my affairs'.[24] Once he was so delighted to learn of yet another victory that he knighted the messenger on the spot. Montrose's triumph at the Battle of Inverlochy played a large part in persuading Charles to break off the Treaty of Uxbridge. 'The more your majesty grants,' the marquis warned, 'the more will be asked.'[25] Concessions were unnecessary, Montrose went on, because by summer's end, having vanquished the convenanters, he would join Charles with 20,000 Highlanders to extract vengeance (and even more plunder), from the king's English enemies.[26] But Montrose's brave promises were founded on sand. Even though it kept some covenanting troops from taking an active part in the war in England, his campaign was less a struggle between loyal Highlanders and Lowland rebels than a clan feud between the Campbells, led by Archibald Campbell, the Earl of Argyle, and the MacDonalds, many of whom were Ulstermen loyal to the Earl of Antrim.

As he lost ground in England Charles became fatally dependent on the Celtic fringe.

The Glamorgan affair dramatically demonstrated this deterioration. Ever since the outbreak of the rebellion against the prayer book Charles had pinned his hopes on Irish troops. He continually wrote to Wentworth, and then Ormonde, telling them to send him reinforcements.[27] Some, but not enough, troops arrived, and so in January 1645 the king adopted a new and more perilous scheme to get Irish aid. He gave Edward Somerset, the Earl of Glamorgan, a virtual *carte blanche* to go to Ireland and make peace with the rebels.[28] Charles chose Glamorgan for a number of reasons. Both he and his father, with extensive lands and influence in South Wales, where Irish troops could land. Through his second wife, an Irishwoman, the earl had good connections with the Catholic nobility.[29] However, by dispatching Glamorgan to Ireland, Charles was by-passing his own Lord Lieutenant, the Marquis of Ormonde, who was so adamantly opposed to a sell-out to the rebels that the previous November he had threatened to resign, a political gesture almost unheard of in the seventeenth century. Charles tried to mollify Ormonde by authorizing Glamorgan to offer the Lord Lieutenant the Order of the Garter (if he felt that a sweetener was necessary), and bombarded him with unequivocal commands 'to conclude a peace with the Irish whatever it cost'. Even if the price included the repeal of Poynings' Law and punitive legislation against Catholics 'we shall not think it a hard bargain', since the benefits would be even greater. By the end of March the king told his wife, 'I am confidently assured of considerable and sudden supply of men from Ireland.'[30]

Henrietta Maria was in Paris trying to persuade the French, Dutch, Irish, Danes, Scots, Swedes, and the pope – in fact anyone who would listen – to try and help her husband. This policy of seeking foreign help, which went back to Princess Mary's marriage to William of Orange in 1640, had scant success. Most European powers were secretly happy to see England embroiled in a civil war which prevented her from interfering on the Continent. The crown's conflicting suits tended to cancel each other out. Far more skilled diplomats than Charles or Henrietta Maria would have found it impossible to persuade the Dutch and French, traditional enemies, to unite and help a rival, England, or to cultivate Montrose and his Highlanders while promising to cede the Shetland Islands and Orkneys in return for Swedish assistance. Even Charles started to have doubts about the efficacy of help from abroad, especially when he became convinced that Cardinal Mazarin was secretly communicating with Speaker Lenthall of the Commons. Henrietta Maria persisted, even to the point of sending an emissary to Holland to propose a marriage between Prince Charles and a daughter of the House of Orange. 'I do not cease to labour for your affairs, and I hope well,' she castigated her husband, 'provided you do not spoil what I do.'[31]

Psychologically incapable of attacking their divinely anointed – if not appointed – sovereign the king's enemies went for his wife, who as a foreigner and a papist neatly fitted the bill as the wicked adviser who corrupted a basically good sovereign. Their suspicions were not without substance. Henrietta Maria always urged Charles to take a hard line, and 'to continue in your constant resolution to die rather than to submit basely.' She even warned him to be careful of the Oxford parliament.[32] The queen became so hated that she had to flee England for her life. She and her husband wrote to each other often of their innermost fears, feelings and loneliness. 'Without thy company,' Charles confided, 'I can neither have peace nor comfort with my self.' But letters give a distorted view of their relationship. After all separation is not the norm of marriage. Charles was very concerned about his wife's health, and that someone might intercept their letters. He was worried that he might press her too hard to obtain French help, and thus precipitate a quarrel that with uncertain and slow communications would take months to patch up, further adding to his misery. So he tended to sound confident.[33] In March 1645 he told her, 'The general face of my affairs, me thinks, begins to mend'; in May, 'we all here think to be very hopeful'; in June, 'my affairs were never in so fair or hopeful a way.'[34] One reason why Charles struck an assured tone was to try and persuade the French that with only a little help from them the rebels 'would be easily brought to reason'.[35] Another was that he still loved his wife. As he grew more dependent on her, and increasingly missed her, he became not a little frightened of her growing stridency. 'Believe me, sweet heart, thy kindness is as necessary to comfort my heart as this assistance is for my affairs.'[36] In such assurances was that element of fear which is implicit in the gift of love, particularly from one so insecure as Charles to a woman with Henrietta Maria's narrow determination. When she reprimanded her husband for offering too much at Uxbridge, he quickly backed down, and went on to volunteer to abolish all recusancy laws as soon as possible. Even though this concession would facilitate the negotiations the queen was conducting with the Vatican, Charles explained that his real reason for making it was his regret that during their marriage religion had always come between them.[37]

To a degree, in writing to his wife, Charles shaped his nuances to tell her what she wanted to hear. For instance, after the collapse of the Treaty of Uxbridge, while the king seemed most depressed to Hyde, one of its leading proponents, his letters to his wife sound distinctly cheerful.

In the long run the queen's influence on the king was neither as great or malign as either her enemies or his apologists would have us believe. She might badger him, concern him, make him feel guilty, and worry him with long descriptions of her ill-health, but she could not make him do what at heart he did not want to do. Paradoxically it was her hold over him, the intensity of his love, that eventually gave him the rationale for opposing her. 'I pray thee consider, since I love thee above all earthly things, and that my contentment is inseparably conjoined with thee, must not all my actions tend to serve and please thee.'[38] In essence Charles was convinced that his feelings towards Henrietta Maria were (like those to his people) so pure no reasonable person could ever question his acts. They did, and in the end he lost both his wife and his life.

Such an outcome was, naturally, far from Charles's mind when he, Rupert and Maurice rode out of Oxford on 7 May at the head of an army of 11,000 men to start the 1645 campaign. An astrologer's forecast that, having won 'the battle of all for all', they would readily capture London, bolstered their confidence. The next day, after reviewing his troops at Stow-on-the-Wold, the king held a council of war to discuss how to make good the seer's prediction. His advisers were divided. Most urged going west to attack Fairfax, who was threatening Taunton. Rupert favoured marching north to either relieve Chester, an *entrepôt* for Irish help, or to link up with Montrose. Charles compromised. He sent Goring west with part of his army, while he moved north with the main body. Dividing his limited forces was a mistake that he may have recognized, for the following day he wrote to Ormonde that he needed Irish troops so badly he would abolish Poynings' Law.[39] 'My first work will be the relief of Chester, which I am confident will be easily and speedily done.' Afterwards he would either attack East Anglia, or back-track to join Goring in wiping out Fairfax.[40] As he marched from Stow through the Welsh Borders, recruits flocked to the colours replacing those men sent off with Goring. They encouraged the king, particularly after they beat off a couple of minor attacks. 'We are (God be thanked), all well and in heart,' he exulted.[41] Then, at Market Drayton, on hearing that Fairfax had started to invest Oxford, and that Sir William Brereton had lifted his siege of the royalist garrison of Chester, Charles accepted Rupert's advice to strike east and take Leicester. He could use this as a spring-board for an assault on East Anglia, the new model army's heartland, which would force Fairfax to leave Oxford. All Charles's advisers accepted the plan. It would, boasted Digby, ensure a decisive victory 'for never had the king such good men.'[42] The royalists' sudden shift caught Leicester's garrison off-guard. When they imprisoned the herald who demanded they surrender the city without further ado, Rupert opened fire against the south wall, which he breached and through which he launched a night assault. Within an hour Leicester was the king's and its plunder his soldiers'. Over the next few days 140 cart-loads of booty left the city, and it was a rare royalist trooper who did not have his share of the prize money in gold and silver.

> This Day is Yours Great CHARLES! and in the War
> Your Fate, and Ours, alike Victorious are.

So the poet Robert Herrick told the king, whose letters to the queen revealed complete agreement.[43]

Charles procrastinated. He failed to kick the enemy when they were down. Instead of adhering to the original plan to use Leicester to threaten East Anglia, or even following Rupert's advice of joining Montrose (which would have prevented his Yorkshire cavalry from returning to their base at Newark-on-Trent), Charles decided to move south. 'I am now hastening to the relief of Oxford,' he informed Henrietta Maria, 'when, if it pleases God to bless me according to these beginnings, it may make us see London the next winter.'[44] A few days later Charles sounded less hopeful, telling William Legge, Oxford's governor, that the city must hold out for at least six more months on its own. He could do nothing to help them until Goring had captured Taunton, and brought his troops back to rejoin the main army.[45] When the king heard, as Rupert forecast, that the capture of Leicester had forced Fairfax away from Oxford, he was delighted enough to 'expect probably a merry winter'.[46]

Forewarned, but not forearmed, Charles let himself be caught napping. The king was hunting near Daventry when he heard that Fairfax's forces were only five miles away, and hurried back to Leicester to summon the council of war. Rupert begged him to withdraw to join the Yorkshire cavalry at Newark. Digby and Ashburnham opposed such a shameful retreat: instead they must confront Fairfax, utterly destroy him, and return in triumph to Oxford. Charles agreed. Rejecting even Rupert's suggestion that they wait for Goring and his men to join them, the king ordered the army to stand and fight just north of the obscure Northamptonshire village of Naseby.

Early on the morning of 14 June the royalist forces of some 7,500 men took up their positions on a mile-long front astride the road leading from Naseby to Sibbertoft. When the sun burned away the dawn mist, they saw facing them a parliamentary army of as many as 13,600 soldiers. Straightaway battle commenced. Rupert's cavalry attacked on the right, sweeping past the dragoons Fairfax had posted in the hedgerows to harass them.

They routed Ireton's horse, and then charged pellmell to plunder the parliamentary baggage train half a mile in the rear. Once more Charles's deer-hunting squires had tally-hoed too fast and too far. Meanwhile, as the infantry battled in the centre, with neither side seeming to gain the edge in some of the fiercest hand-to-hand combat the war had seen, Cromwell's cavalry attacked the king's left, pushing back Sir Marmaduke Langdale's horse. With Rupert out trying to regroup his forces and the battle hanging in the balance, Charles wanted to lead his cavalry reserve in a last desperate charge against the Ironsides. However the civil war was not to end in a personal fight to the finish between Cromwell and Charles because the Earl of Carnwath pulled the king back, begging him not to hazard his life in a futile gesture.

Thus the royal army collapsed. As their sovereign and his bodyguard rode in silent defeat back to Leicester, 5,000 men surrendered leaving 1,000 of their comrades dead or dying on the field. It was neither an honourable defeat nor a gracious victory. The roundheads murdered 100 Irish prisoners on the spot, and slashed the faces of the royalist camp-followers, whom they mistook for whores, either to deter them from that profession, or else, like true Puritans, to make its practice less pleasing for all concerned.

Naseby was 'the battle of all for all': it was the decisive moment that the king sought – and lost. His part in the campaign had been crucial. In early May he had split his army; in early June he had failed to follow up his victory at Leicester, telling the council that he must wait for Goring before acting. Yet nine days later, at the council held on 13 June, Charles rejected Rupert's suggestion not to seek a decisive engagement. There is no doubt that just before Naseby Charles was most confused, for earlier on the 13th he appeared to have accepted the prince's plan to withdraw to Newark, telling Nicholas that they were about to march to Belvoir, and then a few hours later he determined to stand and fight. Digby urged Charles to do so, not because he thought it the best military policy (having in letter to Jermyn confided he thought it advisable to wait for Goring), but because he wanted to oppose his rival, Rupert.[47]

None the less, the final decision was the king's. So too must be the blame. Had Charles ordered Goring to leave Taunton (where he got bogged down, and was eventually destroyed at the Battle of Langport on 10 July) to join him, the king might have won the decisive battle. As it was, even though outnumbered two to one, Naseby was a close run affair. Had Rupert been able to control his horse, and they regrouped sooner, had the king's infantry held a little longer, had Langdale's cavalry been more dogged in defence, or had Charles led that last desperate charge, the outcome could have been different.

Such speculations must have been bitter had the king and his advisers indulged in them, as they rode back through Leicester to spend the night of their defeat at Ashby-de-la-Zouch. Then they travelled through Lichfield to Wolverhampton, where they stayed at the Widow Burnsford's house, passing the next night at the Angel Inn, Bewdley, before arriving at Hereford for supper on 19 June. Yet neither the king, nor his counsellors, seemed dismayed. 'The consequence of this disaster will have not great extent,' wrote Digby on 20 June. Three days later Charles informed the Earl of Glamorgan, who had just landed in Ireland, that he was 'no wise disheartened by our late Misfortune . . . I hope shortly to recover my late loss with advantage, if such succour come to me from that Kingdom.'[48] To a degree the king was putting on the best possible face so as not to scare away the last chance of being rescued by Irish troops, for the same day he sent his son a letter so secret that he was to show it to no one, not even Hyde:[49]

> My later Misfortunes remember me to command you that which I hope you will never have to obey, it is thus: if I should at any time be taken prisoner by the rebels, I command you (upon my blessing), never to yield to any conditions that are dishonourable, unsafe to your person, or derogatory to royal authority, upon any considerations whatsoever, though it were for the saving of my life; which in such case (I am most confident) is in the greatest security by your constant resolution, and not a whit the more in danger for their threatening, unless thereby you should yield to their desires. But let their resolutions be never so barbarous, the saving of my life by complying with them, would make me end my days with torture and disquiet of mind, not giving you my blessing, and cursing all the rest who are consenting to it. But your constancy will make me die cheerfully, praising God for giving me so gallant a son, and heaping my blessing on you.

For the first time Charles recognized that he might well lose both the civil war, and his life, and thus took care to safeguard the reversionary interest. Within a few days such gloomy clouds cleared, only to be darkened by one more blow from Naseby field.

Among the 200 royalist wagons parliament captured after the battle was one carrying a prize worth far more than chests of gold and silver.[50] Quickly realizing the value of the large cache of the king's most private papers that fell into its hands, parliament published an annotated title, *The King's Cabinet Opened*. The effect was, as John Milton recalled, of 'the greatest importance'. Charles's schemes to bring French and Irish troops to England, his offer of the Orkneys and Shetland Isles to Sweden, the queen's double, even treble dealings, the king's bad faith were all revealed to public gaze. On reading them Sir Trevor Williams, a leading royalist from South Wales, went over to parliament, while Robert Baillie, the Presbyterian divine, and Colonel Hutchinson, the regicide, agreed they could never again trust the king. It would be difficult to exaggerate the impact of the publication of the king's letters captured at Naseby, together with Digby's papers taken at Sherborne, and the queen's correspondence fished from the sea off Dartmouth, after the messenger threw them overboard, forgetting to weight the pouch, just before his ship surrendered. They revealed the ruler's sordid secrets: they turned his professions of good faith into hypocrisy, his sincerity into deceit, his sacred oath into a casual lie. And yet Charles never appreciated the incalculable damage they did him. While admitting that *The King's Cabinet Opened* was an accurate transcript 'with only some words here and there mistaken, and some commands misplaced', and regretting the phrase 'mongrel parliament' to describe the members who answered his call to Oxford, the king refused 'as a Good Protestant, or honest man, to blush for any of those papers.'[51] A month after they appeared he ordered Nicholas to publish a manifesto denying that he had ever attempted to introduce Irish soldiers into the English civil war. It was too late. If Charles believed such a disavowal he was one of the few men in England who did.

In Wales the situation was different. The principality was the cradle of the king's infantry. From Agincourt to Normandy her foot soldiers have been the finest in the British army, combining the élan of the Scots or Irish in attack with the stolid determination of the English in defence. All along the Welsh had been the most loyal, the bravest, of the king's soldiers. The first heroes of the crown's cause were two Welsh privates who died fighting the covenanters in August 1640, as their English comrades ran. Throughout the war the Welsh remained loyal to the memory of these men, whom their bards praised, and parliamentary hacks vilified in cheap broadsheets.[52] Why Wales kept faith right up to the end has never been satisfactorily explained. Powerful magnates such as Archbishop Williams and the Marquis of Worcester may have been able to keep the north and south loyal, while Charles's protection of the border's wool trade from the encroachments of the London merchant adventurers held the centre.[53] The principality's recently anglicized gentry may have been afraid of losing the loyalty of their Welsh-speaking tenants. Or else the ordinary Welsh soldier saw the war as a simple matter of tribal fealty – of 'Gwell angau na Chwilydd' – of 'death before dishonour'.[54]

After Naseby Charles retreated to Wales spending the first two weeks in July at Raglan castle with the Marquis of Worcester, recovering from his ordeals. As he played bowls, went to church, and enjoyed fascinating conversations about poetry and politics, Charles planned the future. 'I have such good hope of my Welsh levies,' he wrote, 'that I doubt not (by the Grace of God) to be in the head of a greater Army within this two months than I have seen this year.'[55] The king's plans were founded more on hope than reality. Rupert warned him that he had no chance of persuading Montrose and the covenanters to ally against parliament. Charles seemed to agree with him when they met at Blackrock, Monmouthshire, on 22

July, but two days later changed his mind, and, as if to soften the blow, sent the prince two infantry regiments to help his defence of Bristol.[56] Rupert wrote back with the professional soldier's brutal sense of realism: 'His Majesty hath no way left to preserve his posterity, kingdom and nobility but by a treaty. I believe it a more prudent way to retain something than to lose all.'[57] Such distasteful advice stung Charles to reply: 'Speaking as a mere soldier or statesman, I must say that there is no probability but of my ruin; yet as a Christian, I must tell you that God will not suffer rebels or traitors to prosper.' The king had spoken. The matter was closed. Therefore 'I earnestly desire you no ways to hanker after treaties.'[58]

To obtain a victory based on faith rather than reason, Charles resorted to a number of expedients. First he sent Ormonde yet another desperate request for Irish troops, without whom, he declared, 'I am likely to be reduced to great extremities.'[59] Second to retain – or recover – Rupert's trust, he wrote his nephew a most affectionate note.[60] Third, he sent his eldest son a very sombre warning. 'Charles it is very fit for me now to prepare for the worst . . . wherefore I know that my pleasure is, whensoever you find yourself in apparent danger of falling into the Rebel's hand, that you convey yourself into France.'[61] Then, to counter such defeatist thoughts Charles ordered 'all melancholy men' banished from his presence, much preferring the company of congenial optimists, like George Digby.[62]

Digby was born in 1612 in Madrid where his father (later the Earl of Bristol) was the British ambassador. As a boy he impressed the House of Lords with a moving defence of his father during the earl's impeachment. As a young man on his first visit to court Charles harshly punished him for becoming involved in a brawl. That Digby became a leading member of the opposition during the early days of the Long Parliament is not surprising. What is surprising was that the son of the ambassador whom the Earl of Stamford gleefully told the king had once been as 'loathsome to your majesty as a dog's vomit', suddenly became one of his most loyal adherents.[63] In early 1641 he defended the Earl of Strafford so effectively that parliament ordered the public hangman to burn the printed copy of his speech. By the following year his advice that the king turn London inside out to find the Five Members made him so unpopular that he had to escape to Holland, days before the Commons impeached him for high treason. Digby did not, however, remain abroad for long. On his way back to England he was captured and taken to Hull, where he persuaded Sir John Hotham to betray the city. Later Digby fought with distinction at Edgehill, but resigned his command after falling out with Rupert, and was later wounded at the siege of Lichfield. Charles appointed him Secretary of State in 1643. Digby rose to become one of his most influential advisers.

He has had a bad press. Digby has been portrayed as the *eminence grise* who urged his leader on to Götterdämmerung. Perhaps his worst mistake was incurring Clarendon's enmity, which was in the long run even more damaging to one's historical reputation than letting the enemy capture and publish one's letters – which anyway happened to Digby after the Battle of Sherborne.[64] Admittedly he was neither an oily diplomat telling no one but his master what they wanted to hear, nor was he a great administrator. But he was as brave in battle as he was determined in intrigue. After persuading Charles to ignore Rupert's advice not to stand and fight at Naseby he blamed the prince for the king's defeat.[65] After privately admitting that the king would have to accept whatever terms the rebels offered, he publicly assured the Prince of Wales that God would surely give them victory, and that the news of Montrose's successes made him 'a better Christian'.[66] None the less, Clarendon's harsh condemnation that his rival, Digby, was the unfittest man to advise Charles was both unfair and self-serving: by making Digby a scapegoat Clarendon was protecting his own and the king's reputations.[67]

For instance, it was Charles's idea – not Digby's – to leave South Wales on 5 August and march north towards Montrose. On arriving in Doncaster on 18 August the king buoyantly described the state of his affairs as 'miraculously good'. The local gentry were loyal, and he had plenty of provisions, and enough recruits to make 'a lusty stock for next year's army'.[68] Within a few hours, on learning that General Leslie and his covenanters were but ten miles away, the king's confidence evaporated. He pulled his men back through Retford, Newark, Belvoir, and Stamford. At Huntingdon, Cromwell's home town, he paused long enough to issue a jaunty manifesto to 'resolve by the grace of God, never to yield up the church to the government of Papists, Presbyterians, or Independents.'[69] Then he resumed a brutal forced march via Oxford back to the Welsh borders. 'No dinner ... a cruel day,' recalled one attendant of the final twenty-four miles to Worcester.[70]

Once back in his Welsh bastion Charles's most immediate goal was the relief of Bristol. Fairfax had been besieging England's second city since mid-August, when its governor, Rupert, assured the king he could easily hold out for at least four months. On 9 September Charles wrote to his nephew that relief was on its way. The same day he told Montrose that he would not be able to join him until he had destroyed Fairfax.[71] The king's strategy was simple. Goring would march on Bristol with his levies from the south and west country. After securing his rear by clearing Herefordshire of rebels, the king would ferry 3,000 infantry across the River Severn to Berkeley castle, where they would link up with an equal number of cavalry who had ridden in a left hook through Gloucestershire. Convinced that his last desperate throw of the dice would win back all he had lost, Charles was crushed when Rupert surrendered Bristol on 10 September. Outnumbered seven to one, with Fort Prior, a key bastion, lost and it garrison massacred, and with little support from the citizens, and good terms from Fairfax, the prince saw no point in further resistance. It was entirely a professional decision. As he had told his uncle before the siege started the war was already lost. Continuing to fight a hopeless siege that according to the rules of war was bound to end in the sack of the city and the annihilation of its garrison, was not part of the soldiers' contract. Always willing to fight the good fight, Rupert was glad when the bad one was over. As Colonel Butler, the prince's escort after the surrender, reported, 'I find him a man much inclined to a happy peace.'[72]

Charles's inclinations could not have been more different. Six weeks before he had admitted that as a 'mere soldier or statesman' he could not expect to win, yet as 'a Christian' he knew that God would not let rebels prevail, and thus ordered Rupert to end all defeatist talk. The king was at Raglan on 11 September when a messenger told him of his nephew's treachery. It 'hath given me more grief than any misfortune since this damnable Rebellion,' confessed the king.[73] The news paralysed him. He could do nothing for three days, but turn in upon himself to try and explain this 'strange and inexcusable behaviour'.[74] All the time Digby played on the distraught king's fears. Had not Rupert and his henchman, Colonel Legge, governor of Oxford, been seen talking intimately as they walked through Christ Church gardens? Could they be plotting to surrender yet another royalist stronghold? Might they not conspire to replace the House of Stuart with the House of Palatine? Indeed had not parliament just voted Rupert's eldest brother, Charles Louis, an £8,000 pension, just before the surrender of Bristol? Surely it was more than a coincidence.

Three days after learning of his nephew's betrayal Charles took action. On 14 September he dismissed Rupert, ordered Nicholas to arrest Legge, and to use force if Rupert did not use the enclosed passport (gallingly signed by Digby) to immediately leave the realm.[75] The king's letter revealed the utter depth of his anguish:[76]

> Nephew:
> though the loss of Bristol be a great blow to me, yet your surrendering it as you did, is of so much affliction to me that it makes me forget not only the consideration of that place, but is likewise the greatest trial of my constancy that has befallen me; for what is to be done after one who is so near me both in blood and friendship submits himself to so mean an action? (I give it the easiest term). Such – I have so much more to say that I will say no more of it: only lest rashness of judgement be laid to my charge . . . My conclusion is to desire you to seek your subsistence (until it pleases God) to determine my condition, somewhere beyond the seas . . .
> Your loving uncle and most faithful friend
> Charles R.

Why did Charles discharge the man 'who is so near to me in both blood and friendship'? The explanation that Rupert, his friends, and the king's defenders preferred was that Digby's insinuations poisoned Charles against his nephew. This would suggest that when kings fail, ardent royalists need the excuse of wicked advisers as much, if not more, than rabid parliamentarians. Yet Charles's anger was so hot that it did not require Digby's jealousy to fan it. It was Charles, not Digby, who had Legge arrested, and after Digby left the king to go north in October, the animosity remained as burning as before.[77] Try as he might to convince himself that 'the great error proceeded not from any change of affection, but merely from his judgement seduced by some rotten hearted villains,' Charles found the wicked counsellor theory unconvincing, and had to accept that Rupert had disobeyed his most direct commands. Thus when Lord Charles Gerard reproached him for being too dependent on Digby, Charles irritatedly asked if he though, 'I am but a child? Digby can lead me where he list? What can the most desolate rebels say more?'[78] The king was upset because Rupert had promised to hold Bristol for at least four months so long as his men remained loyal. 'Did you keep it four days?' Charles scornfully asked, 'was there anything like mutiny? If you be not resolved to carry yourself according to my resolution, you are no fit company for me.'[79] When Rupert surrendered, dashing the king's last chance of entrapping Fairfax and snatching victory from the jaws of defeat, Charles banished him from his company. Most painful of all Charles felt he had been let down by his own flesh and blood, the son of the sister whose cause he had championed for so long, and the close friend of a man who found friendship so hard to make.

In several ways Charles saw himself as Rupert's father. When Frederick died suddenly at the age of thirty-six in 1632, he promised the orphaned children, 'I will now occupy the place of the deceased.'[80] He faithfully sent Elizabeth money to raise her family. During Rupert's visit to England in 1636 his swashbuckling charm, enthusiasm, and love of music delighted his uncle. The feeling was mutual. Whilst out hunting the day before he had to sail back to Holland, the young prince told the king that sometimes he wished his horse might throw him so he would break his neck and leave his bones in England.[81] The following year, acting *in loco parentis* for the boy, Charles tried to persuade Richelieu to let Rupert marry the Duke of Rohan's daughter, one of the richest heiresses in France.[82]

At the outbreak of civil war Rupert rushed to his uncle's aid. He brought badly needed military skills, tactical knowledge, strategical insights, the energy of youth, and the caution of a veteran who had seen both battle and the inside of his enemies' prisons. Rupert was a brilliant administrator: his genius was an ability to raise, train and lead cavalry, to turn them into a force that might well have won the civil war. Whenever Charles rejected his nephew's sound advice he did so at his peril. 'I must observe that the chief hope of my resource is, under God, from you,' the king told him in 1644. Charles came to feel most confident of the general who ultimately betrayed him. 'I mean not to trust you by halves,' wrote the king, 'an earnest desire to you is as much as a peremptory command to others.'[83] Until Naseby nothing serious came between the two. The desertion of Rupert's brother, Charles Louis and his mother, Elizabeth of Bohemia, did not sour their friendship. Occasionally they disagreed over tactics. For instance, Charles told his nephew not to sink to the continental practice of executing a rebel prisoner in retaliation for the royalist who was hung from the walls of Lichfield Cathedral Close.[84] Yet most of the time their differences complemented each other. Charles knew what he wanted from the war, and that Rupert, with his killer instinct, was the man best able to obtain it.

The war brought the two closer together. 'Though Mars be now most in vogue, yet Hymen may be times remembered,' Charles once wrote supporting his nephew's suit for Mme Rohan.[85] When Rupert was away fighting he liaised with the king through the Duke of Richmond, whose wife, Mary Villiers, was Buckingham's daughter, a reminder of lost happiness. At least twice in writing, and unknown times in person, Charles promised to protect Rupert 'as one of my children', the second letter being written only two weeks before the capitulation of Bristol.[86] 'Tell my son,' the king wrote to Nicholas, who had custody of Prince James, the same day he dismissed his nephew, 'that I should be less grieved to hear that he is knocked on the Head, than that he should do so mean an action.'[87] After Naseby Charles warned Prince Charles he would disown him if he sold out to the enemy.[88] When Rupert surrendered Bristol, that is what Charles did. The king told the prince 'as he is your uncle, he is in nature a parent to you and swears that if Prince Charles had done as you did he would do the same.'[89]

For Charles the loss of Bristol was as traumatic as Henry's death or Buckingham's murder. He spent the day after he dismissed Rupert riding around in one large circle halfway to Bromyard, and back again to Hereford. Seven days later he told Maurice that thinking about 'this great error' was almost unbearable. One cavalier described his master as 'in a most low and despicable condition': another added, 'the king knows not whither to go.'[90]

Basically Charles had two options: march south to confront the main parliamentary forces, or go north to protect Chester and possibly join Montrose. He chose the second, leaving Hereford on 18 September. After an arduous ride, once continually in the saddle from six in the morning to midnight, he entered Chester on 23 September, managing to slip through the parliamentary lines west of the city. The following day the king's cavalry under Sir Marmaduke Langdale sallied out, but losing the advantage of surprise, were decimated at the Battle of Rowton Heath. 'O Lord, O Lord, what have I done that should cause my people to deal thus with me?' the king was supposed to have cried out (in a suspiciously calvary-like phrase) as he watched the battle from the Phoenix Tower.

This time, however, no new army was to rise from the ashes of defeat. The next day the king had to flee from Chester, feinting west to throw his enemies off the trail, before back-tracking for Newark, the only major garrison in the north still in his hands. At Denbigh on 28 September the king received another crushing blow. He learnt that Leslie had just decisively defeated Montrose at Philiphaugh. Reeling, he told Goring to break out of Oxford with his cavalry to join him, ordered Prince Charles to sail from the West Country for France, commanded that Prince James be brought to him, and told Nicholas to be careful that Oxford did not fall from treason within. 'It is the fashion to yield towns basely,' he bitterly added.[91] For almost a week after he reached Newark on 4 October, Charles seemed undecided and confused. He told Ormonde that the death of Lord Lichfield with so many good men at Rowton Heath, and the reports that Montrose had perished at Philiphaugh had 'put me into a fit of deep melancholy and despair that I have never been subject unto.'[92] Now he needed Irish soldiers so badly, the king went on, that he was willing to return to Chester if that would facilitate their landing. Yet by the same post he sent Nicholas a letter that he was about to march north, and in fact did do so, reaching the Marquis of Worcester's house at Welbeck on 13 October. The day after he left Welbeck Charles held a council of war, which recommended that he split his forces, sending Digby with the bulk of the cavalry to continue northwards while he returned to Newark with the rest of the army.

Three years before at Nottingham Charles and his cavaliers had gone to the wars full of romantic self-confidence and youthful vigour. As Richard Lovelace explained to his Lucasta he would never have left her 'Loved I not honour more.' Now, at Newark, a dozen miles away from where the cavaliers had so hopefully raised their standard, defeat blew down their fine aspirations into the mire of petty squabbles.

Following his dismissal Rupert immediately sent his uncle a verbosely apologetic letter – of the sort that the king usually loved – begging to be allowed to come and explain why he had ceded Bristol.[93] He received no reply. Charles was concerned that the prince might use the visit to persuade his supporters to stage a coup and force a negotiated peace on any terms. Such fears might have been behind the king's decision to detach Gerard with 300 hot-headed cavaliers to Belvoir Castle, twelve miles south of Newark. Charles normally did not bother to explain the rationale for such routine orders, but this time he told Gerard that it was part of a wider plan (of which no other examples may be found) of dispersing his forces.[94] On 15 October Rupert arrived at Belvoir with 100 supporters, and in defiance of the king's express commands rode the next day to Newark to demand that the council of war judge his conduct.[95] Unable to resist this request for a court martial – which is almost a prerogative of all who hold the king's commission, particularly when they have 100 heavily armed and excitable friends with them – Charles agreed. On 21 October he accepted the court's findings that while Rupert was not guilty of 'the least want of courage or Fidelity', he could have held Bristol a little longer, especially as relief was on the way.[96]

A split verdict pleased no one. Charles remained fearful of Rupert, whose followers were as belligerent at ever. Matters came to a head on 26 October when the king told Sir Richard Willis, one of the prince's hottest heads, that he was replacing him as governor of Newark with Lord Belasyse. The offer of the command of the royal bodyguard failed to placate Willis, but rather than soothe his wounded pride, Charles walked out of the room. A little later, Willis, Rupert, Maurice, Gerard, with some thirty cavaliers burst in as the king was about to have dinner. Willis's dismissal was, Gerard complained, all Digby's doing. Digby was a traitor who had misled the king. With barely suppressed rage Charles got up from the table, ordering Willis to follow him to his room. Sir Richard refused; he almost challenged his sovereign to a duel, saying that a public insult demanded public satisfaction. Such insolence produced a backlash among the king's other officers and persuaded Charles to leave the matter alone, sure that Rupert and his friends would 'be punished by their own reflections'. The next afternoon, after stewing in their own juices, they returned to request Willis's reinstatement, adding that they hoped that His Majesty would not consider the previous day's exuberance a mutiny. With that self-mocking irony that he was learning to cope with adversity, Charles replied 'he would not christen it, but it looked very like one.'[97]

Having been given the choice of returning to their obedience or departing Newark, Rupert and his followers left the city on 28 October. Deeply hurt the prince complained to the king that 'the meanest subject that you have could not be so unkind and unnaturally treated.'[98] In December Rupert once again tried to be reconciled with the king, and after sending Charles an abject apology he was allowed back to Oxford, where in an emotional scene the two publicly embraced. Although he was restored to the king's favour, the prince never regained Charles's trust.[99]

The king still had a war to fight. After sending out cavalry patrols to cover his withdrawal, and alerting the troops at Belvoir to be ready for a rear-guard action, Charles slipped out of Newark at eleven on the night of 3 November. With only a couple of hours sleep, he galloped the ninety miles to Oxford, where he arrived in time for supper on 5 November. And so, exactly forty years after the Almighty had saved his father from the Gunpowder Plot, Charles came back from the wars, to try in defeat to resolve the seemingly unsolvable problem that Matthew Parker's popular ballad summed up so neatly: 'Let's hope for a peace, for the wars will not cease/Till the king enjoys his own again.'[100]

The four months after the Battle of Naseby had brought the king little joy. Charles had suffered a series of crushing military reverses – Naseby, Langport, the surrenders of Leicester and Bristol, Legge's supposed treason at Oxford, Lord Lichfield's death at Rowton, the mutiny at Newark, the rout at Philiphaugh, the loss of the Highlands – they were all devastating blows that might have forced another man into capitulation or (according to one's point of view) into recognizing reality. During this period the king was constantly on the move, riding some 1,200 miles, often through the most rugged terrain. The longest that Charles ever stayed in one place was eighteen days at Newark, and that could hardly be considered a rest stop.[101] During the winter of 1645–6 conditions at Oxford were most uncomfortable. Charles had to scrounge £30 a month to pay his household expenses.[102] His soldiers had to eat horsemeat. Communications became so bad that runners had to carry their messages in hollow bullets that they swallowed if apprehended. No wonder Charles described this as an 'extra-ordinary way of conveyancing' and prayed that it might 'please God to enable us to endure things to better conditions.'[103]

The long war had taken its toll on both king and country. Charles had been involved in eight major battles: the civil war killed a higher proportion of his subjects than any other conflict except that of 1914–18. At the start Charles had viewed the Prayer Book Rebellion as a challenge against monarchical order. By the end of the war, while still stressing the need to preserve secular authority, he shifted his emphasis to protecting the Church of England. The war deepened the intensity of the king's religious faith. It became a crusade, in which compromise was as necessary as it was difficult. Another force that stood in the way of conciliation was Charles's loyalty to his followers. At one level both parties recognized this as a form of paternalism. 'I die, I take it, for maintaining the Fifth Commandment,' said Lord Capel just before parliament executed him for being a royalist.[104]

At another level the comradeship of battle much intensified Charles's feelings towards his supporters. The civil war radicalized all who fought and survived it, be they Anglican, Puritan, papist, Highlander, Ironside or Irish rebel. It was a crucible that taught lace-covered cavaliers to love what they fought for as intensely as plain russet-coated captains. During three years of war Charles never doubted what he fought for, although his love for it increased. He remained steadfastly – stubbornly – faithful to his goals. 'You will meet with no enemies but traitors, most of them Brownists, Anabaptists, and Atheists, such as who desire to destroy both Church and State,' Charles warned his army in September 1642 just before their first major battle.[105] In August 1645, soon after their last one, he told them, 'I resolve, by the Grace of God, never to yield up the church to this govern-ment of Papists, Presbyterians or Independents, not to injure my successors by lessening the crown of that ecclesiastical or military power which my predecessors left me.'[106] By the last winter of the war the king was no closer to making this resolve good than he had been in the first. He could either continue to fight, escape into exile, negotiate with parliament, go over to the Scots, or obtain help from Ireland.

Every day his first option, continuing the war, became less feasible. Almost every messenger who managed to slip into Oxford through the enemy lines brought bad tidings: the Cornish militia would not leave their county and Prince Charles had arrested their leader, Sir Richard Grenville, for insubordination; Goring was constantly drunk, he had failed to take Plymouth; Wales was denuded of recruits; Archbishop Williams could not hold Conway castle for much longer; Carmarthen, Chepstow, Hereford, and Monmouth had fallen; down to its last slice of turkey pie and uneaten peacock, Beeston castle was starved into submission. As a royalist poet lamented:[107]

> Another city Lost! Alas poor king!
> Still future griefs from former griefs do spring!

Trying to raise money and men from a ravaged land further alienated people from the crown. After three hard years of war groups of neutrals, known as Clubmen, who wanted both sides to leave them alone to live as best they might, became a potent force. 'If you offer to plunder or take our cattle,' threatened one of their banners, 'be assured we will give you battle.'[108] Charles was fully aware of their feelings, having been warned by Rupert of Clubmen discontent in the West Country and by Sir Richard Campion, his governor in Buckinghamshire and Bedfordshire, that the arrest of delinquent taxpayers would result in the loss of the parts of the counties where the king's writ still ran. Charles ignored what he dismissed as 'the troubles and dangers of these times', insisting that money must still be collected, troops levied and the war to on no matter what the cost.

Charles's second option, exile, had little appeal. He was afraid that if he left the realm the rebels would declare he had abdicated (as was to happen to James II), capture his heir and make him a puppet monarch. To prevent this he sent the Prince of Wales to the West Country, whose many harbours and creeks provided dozens of bolt holes for the Continent. As the war turned against him, Charles wrote with increasing frequency to his son of the dangers of being taken. He must look after himself so if the rebels captured the king the heir could continue the fight.[109]

In a sense his son's safety was the long spoon Charles felt he must have before supping with the devil. On 5 December he asked parliament for safe conducts to let Richmond, Southampton, Ashburnham and Jeffrey Palmer go to London to start talks. After parliament ignored five similar requests, Charles published them in mid-January as *A Collection of His Majesties Most Generous Messsages for Peace*. This appeal to public opinion failed to sway parliament, which rightly suspected the king really intended dividing, and thus ruling his enemies. 'Cajole the Independents and Scots,' Charles secretly advised Richmond.[110] At the same time, lest reports of negotiations damage the morale of his few remaining beleaguered garrisons, Charles wrote to Lord Belasyse, governor of Newark, that he would sign only an honourable and lasting peace that would protect his soldiers' interests.[111]

The arrival of Jean de Montreuil, the French ambassador, in Oxford in the New Year opened up Charles's fourth option, going to join the covenanters. Henrietta Maria's entreaties, as well as the possibility that a parliamentary triumph would free the new model army to intervene on the Continent, concerned Cardinal Mazarin enough to send Montreuil to England to mediate. At their first meeting on 2 January Charles declared that he would never abandon his friends and conscience, nor go into exile, but warmed to the ambassador's suggestion he join the Scots. He cautioned, however, that while he would tolerate Presbyterianism in England, he could never make it the established church: 'He would rather lose his crown than his soul.'[112]

Charles never had such obdurate principles when dealing with the Irish. Apart from the fact that he neither hated nor feared them with the venom most Englishmen felt, he still clung to the hope that waves of loyal Irish troops would storm ashore at Bristol, Chester, Cardiff or Liverpool, and – like the Seventh Cavalry – charge, bugles blowing, to rescue him in the nick of time. Thus in January 1645 Charles had sent the Earl of Glamorgan to Ireland to make a treaty with the Catholic rebels (known as the Confederation of Kilkenny from the place where they had first organized).[113] Although Glamorgan took his time getting to Ireland, being shipwrecked in his first attempt to sail from Caenarvon, once he arrived in mid-summer he quickly opened talks, signing a secret treaty with the confederation on 25 August. In return for 10,000 Irish troops Charles agreed to tolerate the Catholic church in Ireland, exempt it from the jurisdiction of Protestant ministers, and restore most of its lands. These sweeping concessions did not, however, satisfy Giovanni Battista Rinuccini, Archbishop of Fermoy, whom Pope Innocent X sent to Ireland to win complete freedom for the church.[114] On his arrival in Dublin in November, Rinuccini insisted that the secret treaty be renegotiated. Glamorgan readily agreed, and on 20 December signed a second treaty by which the Irish promised to send 3,000 troops to Chester in return for a Catholic university, a Catholic Lord Lieutenant, and Catholic bishops in the Irish House of Lords – in effect for Roman Catholicism to become Ireland's established faith.

A few weeks earlier in one of those incidents that had become an unhappy commonplace in Ireland, Sir Charles Coote ambushed and killed the Catholic Archbishop of Tuam near Sligo. Searching the prelate's baggage he found a document far more valuable than any silver chalice or bejewelled crozier – a copy of the earlier, and less incriminating, treaty.

This Ulster's Protestants promptly published, raising a firestorm. Ormonde immediately arrested Glamorgan for treason. When the earl tried to defend himself by showing the commissions Charles has sent him the previous March, Ormonde and Digby (now a refugee in Dublin as he could no longer continue to fight in the North of England) dismissed it as a forgery: their sovereign would have never been so foolish as to grant anyone such sweeping powers.[115] Yet had they reread the series of letters that the king had sent to Dublin over the past twelve months urging a peace 'what ever it cost' they would not have been so shocked.[116] The king's enemies were outraged. It confirmed the worst suspicions the Naseby letters aroused, revealing, the king's public denials of plotting to bring Irish troops to England, and his assertion but days before the Glamorgan treaty became public that 'all men who pretend any goodness must desire peace,' as rank hypocrisy.[117] Even Digby – the king's sycophant – had to admit to Nicholas (who reluctantly agreed), that the treaty 'caused a revolt from him of all good Protestants' because it lent credence to the rebels' claim that all along the king had instigated the Irish rebellions, had the blood of thousands of innocent settlers on his hands, and was himself a secret papist.[118]

Charles was not unaware of the risk of sending a man as inexperienced and zealous as Glamorgan to negotiate behind the Lord Lieutenant's back. He even advised Ormonde of Glamorgan's faults: 'His honesty and affection to my service will not deceive you,' warned the king, 'but I will not answer for his judgement.'[119] All the time, however, Charles dismissed Ormonde's objections to a peace with the confederates as the reluctance of a timid man afraid to take responsibility for so controversial a step. So long as the treaty remained secret, Charles convinced himself that Ormonde would go along, and all would work out for the best.[120] When it became public, even Charles realized that its effects were so damaging and his own position had become so perilous that someone else had to take the blame. Immediately he wrote to parliament on 29 January disavowing the treaty as repugnant to his honour and prejudicial to his church; Glamorgan was to be arrested for exceeding his authority. If parliament would only let him come in person to London to discuss ending the war, the king went on, he would give them a free hand to do what they wished with the Irish, let them appoint senior army and navy commanders and officers of state, permit judges to hold office for life, allow all Protestants freedom of worship, and grant a general pardon.

In the Machiavellian underworld of high politcs there may be nothing wrong for a prince to allow a subordinate to take the rap. Indeed had Charles been more inclined to sell out his friends he might well have died in bed. Still, having assured Glamorgan in secret orders 'to perfect what he shall promise in our name,' Charles's open disavowal was unconvincing, particularly when he signed his letters to the pope on the same subject as 'your very humble and obedient servant'.[121] The King's public explanation of some of the treaty's most damaging clauses, 'His majesty saitheth that he remembers it not,' seemed as hollow as the news that arrived in London a few days later that to conciliate the rebels Ormonde had freed Glamorgan.[122] In private the king, who always found friendships as hard to break as to make, was more honest. 'Both you and I have been abused in this business,' he wrote to Glamorgan.[123] Even though the earl had exceeded his commission, the king consoled him that this was water under the bridge: what now mattered was the future. Soon afterwards Charles promised him that the shabby treatment they had endured following the treaty's publication 'begets in me a desire of Revenge & Reparation to us both'.[124]

Towards the Irish confederates Charles displayed all the anger of a spurned suitor, who had never been given much encouragement in the first place. 'I am as little obliged to the Irish as I can be to any nation,' he wrote, 'for all this last year they have only fed me with vain hopes, looking upon my daily ruin.'[125] Notwithstanding the fact that it was he who had pressed for a treaty, given Glamorgan a *carte blanche*, and even had Ormonde sign a third treaty in March 1646, as far as Charles was concerned his affair with the Irish was over.[126]

The king's response to the Glamorgan treaty's publication reflected a wider confusion in his thinking, which is obvious in the memorandum he wrote for himself at about this time trying to define his options.[127] While an anlaysis of the king's policies during the winter of 1645-6 might enable us to see them more clearly, it also hides the fact that they were interrelated, and that under tremendous pressure the king flitted from one to the other, convinced that if he dropped but one of the balls he was juggling – the war, parliament, the Scots, the Irish, Montrose – there 'would be no church'.[128] On the other hand he was equally aware of his opponents' problems. 'Knowing assuredly the great animosity which is between the Independents and Presbyterians, I have great reason to hope that one of the factions would so address themselves to me that I might without great difficulty obtain my so just ends,' he wrote to his wife on 18 January, adding that if parliament was too divided to make terms with him, the Scots would.[129] At the time such confidence seemed well founded, for a couple of weeks later parliament instructed the common hangman to publicly burn the newly published papers of the Scots commissioners.[130] Charles sent a note to Montreuil, who had just left to negotiate on his behalf with the covenanters, 'I will foretell their ruin, except they agree with me.'[131] Two months after the disclosure of the Glamorgan treaty Charles was sure he had repaired the damage, and told Henrietta Maria, 'Now men have more reason to trust to my promises, finding me constant to my grounds.'[132]

Far from being widened by a ground swell of public trust, the options available to the king were rapidly narrowing. His only chance of continuing to fight was an invasion of 5,000 French troops, who were to land at

Hastings – not the most felicitous spot. If they failed to come, 'all is lost,' he implored his wife, 'for God's sake if thou lovest me see what may be done for the landing of the 5,000.'[133] There was to be no second Battle of Hastings, only a skirmish at Stow-on-the-Wold, where on 21 March the king lost the remnants of his last army. The next month the West Country collapsed with the surrender of Exeter, St Michael's Mount, and Barnstaple, exacerbating Charles's fears that the rebels would take his son.[134] By May all that remained were a few isolated strong points such as Woodstock, Newark and North Wales.

Negotiations with parliament became equally forlorn. Their refusal to acknowledge his overtures convinced Charles that 'nothing will satisfy them but the ruin, not only of us, our Posterity, and friends, but even monarchy itself.'[135] His last ditch attempt to form a coalition with the Independents on the grounds that if the Presbyterians won that would stamp out radical sects as readily as they would Anglicans, elicited no response.[136]

Charles believed the most formidable obstacle to an alliance with the Scots was their insistence that he and England became Presbyterians. He lectured Henrietta Maria that Calvinism was just as bad as papism, being contrary to scripture, born in rebellion, and designed 'to steal or force the crown from the king's head'.[137] This tactless confusion of Rome with Geneva provoked a quarrel with his wife. 'I am blamed for granting too much and not yielding enough,' he remonstrated with her, 'but I plead Not Guilty to both.'[138]

If Charles believed he was innocent, having offered the convenanters generous terms, notwithstanding what he saw as a growing movement in parliament to exterminate him and his family, the verdict of the Scots was non-proven.[139] They saw his promises to take instruction in Presbyterianism and 'to strive to content them in anything that shall not be against my conscience,' as a slight concession qualified by a large loophole.[140] So on 1 April they replied via Montreuil in equally vague terms that they would receive him with the honours due their monarch and assist 'in the procuring of a happy and well grounded peace'.[141] The date was appropriate. Charles believed what he wanted to believe. He talked of leaving for Scotland on Monday or Tuesday, and then put off his departure till Wednesday, all along brushing aside the thorny issue of religion. 'As for the church business, I hope to manage it so as not to give them distaste, and yet do nothing against my conscience.'[142] He planned to make the Scots and parliament 'irreconcilable enemies', and thus forge an unlikely alliance of covenanters, Ulstermen and Highlanders to win 'an honourable and speedy peace'.[143] Even when he heard nothing from Montreuil for several days his expectations did not dim. 'I am ready to go at an hour's warning,' he wrote on 13 April. Yet wishing to hedge his bets, the same day he gave Gilbert Sheldon, Warden of All Souls College, a secret signed vow that if

'God restore me to my just kingly rights', he would return to the Church of England all impropriations held by the crown.[144] The following day, having heard nothing from either the ambassador or the Almighty, Charles admitted that he was in 'very great straits'. With the least encouragement from the Scots, he told Montreuil on 19 April, 'I have resolved to run any risks to go to them.'[145]

Charles had to wait another seven days before the covenanters' reply arrived. It was so discouraging that he angrily called them 'abominable retracted rogues, for Montreuil himself is ashamed of them, they having retracted almost everything which they made him promise me.'[146] In desperation the following day he sent Fairfax a vague offer to accept whatever conditions parliament wanted, so long as they let him live and continue as king. Its prompt rejection convinced Charles that he could no longer safely remain in Oxford, but must slip through the parliamentary lines perhaps to go to King's Lynn, where he might take ship for Ireland, France, Denmark, the Highlands, in fact anywhere but to the 'perfidious' covenanters.[147] So, after laying a couple of smoke screens by telling the council of war that he was going to London, and sending Lords Lindsey and Southampton to Colonel Rainsborough to discuss surrender terms, Charles left Oxford. His departure was pathetically secret. At three on the morning of 27 April Sir Thomas Glenham, the governor, opened the east gate for Michael Hudson, the king's chaplain, and John Ashburnham, his friend. 'Farewell Harry!' someone called out from the wall to their servant, who rode a few paces behind with the baggage. Having risked the battle of all, Charles Stuart lost nearly everything, including the freedom to acknowledge his own name.

# XVII

# 'WHAT WAY TO WALK'

When Charles rode over Magdalen Bridge and up Headington Hill before dawn on 27 April, he began a journey that ended thirty-three months later outside the Banqueting Hall at Whitehall. The path he took was not, however, a high road running, with detours, or exits, inevitably to its destination. For most of the time the crown sat on Charles's head, and his head rested on his shoulders as securely as ever, the decision to depose and execute him being taken but a couple of months before his death. During this period there were several options open to the king, who knew what he wanted but became increasngly confused as how to get it. Thus he slithered and slid with the inconsistency of a man with flexible means and constant goals. Recognizing that as the monarch he was the most potent force for stability in an unstable land, he overplayed this ace, and so lost his stake, to produce a dozen years of instability so intractable that the restoration of monarchy became the only solution. With a foresight that owed more to the king's emotional needs than his political sagacity, Charles foresaw this outcome as 'through a glass darkly'. The last two years of his life were ones of temendous personal development. Like the hero of a classic tragedy, whose fatal flaw produced his dénouement, from suffering he learnt much wisdom until by the end ripeness was all. His letters revealed a more likeable man, the prisoner who treated laundresses or cooks' wives with a kindness and concern that as king he rarely showed to lords or their ladies.

Such growth should not be exaggerated. For much of his time, as his escape from Oxford shows, Charles was running away from problems, not towards their solution. Having fled the scene he became passive, as if the escape was enough in itself, and waited for others to take the initiative. Thus the push of intolerable situations, rather than the pull of viable solutions determined his actions until, at the end, with nowhere else to run, and all his options foreclosed, Charles let others decide how his journey should finish. But the start of the complex road from Oxford plunged both the king and his subjects into confusion. As Sir Charles Erskine told his wife, 'We are in no less expectations of troubles than when you left us, every hour producing strong effects and changes in our affairs, so that honest men can hardly know what way to walk.'[1]

Beyond the fact that he was leaving a city that was about to fall, Charles followed Ashburnham and Hudson out of Oxford with little clear idea of where he was headed. Michael Hudson was dressed appropriately enough as a minister, having received his doctor of divinity degree from Oxford in 1643. He was a plain outspoken fellow, whose bluntness surpisingly won the king's friendship and a royal chaplaincy, perhaps because of his intense loyalty. The following year Hudson died heroically fighting for his master. John Ashburnham was equally devoted, though not as headstrong. He first entered royal service in 1628 through a connection with the Duke of Buckingham, a distant cousin. Following his old servant and new disciple the king rode through a patrol of dragoons at Dorchester, and another of cavalry at Benson.[2] At Henley-on-Thames the corporal of the guard asked Charles if his master was a member of the House of Commons. No, the king replied, he served one of the Lords. At Hillingdon the royal party stopped at an inn for a meal, and then waited for three or four hours, as Charles pondered. Perhaps he entertained some fantastic hope that the Lord Mayor would ride out the ten miles from London to escort him in triumph into the city, as he had in November 1642, or that he might slip into the capital *incognito* to hide, and at the right moment emerge to lead the growing number of citizens who feared the army's rising power. Hudson and Ashburnham advised him against such fantastic plans, saying that the king was too well known to survive in disguise in London for long; he should try King's Lynn, a town he had never visited, and where a boat for the Continent could readily be had.

So about two in the afternoon of 27 April the small party left Hillingdon, riding in a wide sweep around the capital to St Albans. What Charles thought of if he looked back from Harrow-on-the-Hill towards the city that had been the scene of so much happiness in the thirties and the root of rebellion in the forties, that had been the prize he had never been able to take in war, and the financial stronghold whose support he had failed to win in peace, one cannot say. But we do know that when Sir Philip Warwick, the king's confidant at Carisbrooke castle tried to discuss this period with him Charles refused to talk. Perhaps the memory of the fear, uncertainty, the crushed hopes and strain of being on the run still pained him. Without doubt an incident at St Albans badly frightened the royal party. An old man armed with a halberd demanded who they were; 'From parliament,' they answered, throwing the fellow a sixpenny tip. A few minutes later a horseman galloped up. They were greatly relieved to discover he was not the van of a parliamentary posse, but a lonely drunk, desperate for company and conversation, whom they had to shake off before spending the night at Wheathampstead.

The following day they set off at dawn. Charles told Hudson to go and find Montreuil to see if he had managed to make a more satisfactory deal with the Scots; they would rendezvous at Downham Market, ten miles south of King's Lynn. Charles and Ashburnham rode through Baldock, along the ridge with its distant glimpses of Ashwell steeple, and through the hunting fields that had been James's passion to Royston, where Steenie and Baby Charles had been rapturously reunited with their 'Dear Dad'. By now the news of their escape had spread, and they had to slip past Cambridge by night, through back roads across the Fens, arriving at Downham Market on 30 April. They stayed four days at the Swan Inn, alerting the landlord's suspicions by asking for a fire in their room (it was May) in which they burnt papers, and those of the town barber whom they summoned to repair the damage done by using knives to cut and disguise their hair. When Hudson returned with a vague promise from Montreuil that the Scots would treat the king honourably and not make him act against his conscience, and after Charles recognized he had no chance of finding passage from King's Lynn, he set out for Newark. The king did not take the direct route, but in a wide detour he revisited places he had loved in more peaceful times, riding past Hinchingbrooke House at Huntingdon, scene of many a glorious hunt, and through Little Gidding, where Nicholas Ferrar had had his idyllic Anglican community. Charles passed the night on the floor of an ale house at Coppingford with the keeper and his family, and the morning of the next day arrived at Montreuil's lodgings in Southwell. Then, after a few hours rest, the King of England, Scotland, Ireland and Wales rode the half-dozen miles to Newark to surrender to his covenanting subjects.

Charles's people were sorely divided.

His opponents in England may be categorized in two ways, one according to religion and the other by institution. First there were the Presbyterians who advocated the Scots form of church government by elders, and the Independents who preferred the more radical system of self-governing congregations. Second there were the remnants of the Long Parliament, who still considered themselves the legitimate representatives of the nation, and the army, whose officers and men were determined to win what they knew, loved and had fought for in the name of God's people. While these groups tended to coincide, and one can find exceptions to the generalization that the Presbyterians dominated parliament (and the City of London), and the Independents were powerful in the army, they are useful categories if only because Charles and his advisers used them to make policy, and attempted to exploit their differences.[3]

The King's supporters who had flex into exile on the Continent may be divided into two factions. One centred about the queen, being a continuation of her court set of the 1630s, and the other, a more moderate group, around the heir. The royalists left in England were even more fragmented and demoralized, having to come to terms with the victors over the fines they had to pay in order to keep their property. Recusants had the particularly painful job of trying to compound for their estates without mortgaging their souls.

The situation in Scotland was just as muddled. The most powerful group was the covenanters, whose leader was the Marquis of Argyle, and whose strength lay in the Lowlands, towns, gentry, ministers and the Clan Campbell. The Earl of Callander led a party of neutrals, who were not as significant as those in England, while Hamilton headed a bevy of moderate royalist aristocrats. Following their defeat at Philiphaugh in September 1645, Montrose's ulta-royalist Highlanders were a spent force.

Ireland's ultras, the Confederation of Kilkenny, were far from beaten, continuing to defeat the Protestant forces sent to crush them, and excite the king's most improbable hopes and his enemies' wildest fears that they might directly intervene in England's affairs.

Amid all the uncertainty of what Oliver Cromwell called 'a quarrelsome age', the monarchy seemed the only rock on which stability could ever be rebuilt.[4] As a contemporary ballad put it.[5]

> If now you would know what remedy
> There may for all these mischieves be,
> Then may King Charles alone,
> Be sat upon the throne.

Charles recognized this advantage. 'You cannot be without me,' he told the army commanders, 'you will fall to ruin if I do not sustain you.'[6] However, the king completely misunderstood the nature of his support. During the war Charles found it hard to persuade ordinary Englishmen to serve in his infantry, having to rely on Welsh, Irish and Scots troops. After the war, as a result of which as many as 300,000 or 6 per cent of all his subjects died, people wanted to return to the normalcy that monarchy symbolized.[7] For instance, those who rioted at Canterbury on 25 December 1647 following the abolition of Christmas wanted the restoration of their traditional roast goose and plum pudding far more than recusants, courtiers or plump prelates. While Charles publicly declared that all he longed for was 'a happy and well grounded peace' and that 'all men who pretended any goodness must desire peace,' in private he tried to divide in order to rule.[8] 'I am endeavouring', he wrote to Digby in March, 'to draw either the Presbyterians or Independents to side with me for extirpating the other so I shall be really king again.'[9] In addition Charles tried to exploit the internal Scots divisions, those between parliament and the army, dissension within the army between the officers and the rank and file, and (as he confided to his wife) 'to make the English rebels and Scots irreconcilable enemies.'[10]

Charles convinced himself that he could pursue what might otherwise be considered a dishonourable and contradictory policy since his own motives were so good and those of his enemies so bad. Presbyterianism was, to use his own favourite adjective, 'damnable'.[11] He felt very guilty of having let his friends down.[12] Even though he had promised to 'never abandon Ireland', by 1646 he persuaded himself that because the Irish had forsaken him he could break his word to a nation, 'which is as a reed, and the more you rely on it, will run into your hand the deeper.'[13] Thus when the king moved from trying to win a solution by war to reaching one at the conference table, he brought with him the worse possible psychological framework – a constancy of ends that justified the most flexible means.

The king's arrival at Newark pleased and astounded the Scots. Immediately they told parliament that it was a golden opportunity to bring peace and security to both kingdoms.[14] Such, Charles assured them, was his heartfelt desire – so long, of course, as it did not go against his conscience. And to demonstrate his good intentions he ordered Lord Belasyse to surrender the royalist garison to Newark.[15] The era of good feeling lasted for but a few days. The Scots removed the king to Newcastle, which he entered on 13 May, without the ceremonial honours due a monarch, being lodged in the mayor's house, and guarded by a detachment of musketeers.[16] He quickly realized that he was in fact a prisoner, and advised Ashburnham and Hudson to flee before the Scots handed them over to parliament.

Four days after the king's arrival in Newcastle, Robert Douglas, a minister of the kirk, began his instruction in the virtues of Presbyterianism with the first of a long series of even longer sermons. In late May and early June Charles and Alexander Henderson, Rector of Edinburgh University and a leading Presbyterian theologian, publicly debated religion.[17] The king opened with a profession of faith in the Anglican church and the need for bishops. The vital importance of both doctrines, he artfully explained to his audience, having been taught him by that great King of Scotland James the Sixth. Henderson replied in like coin that there was no shame in changing one's mind: after all an equally illustrious ancestor, Henry VIII, had done so. Presbyterianism completed the Henrician Reformation by purging the church of its papist residue – bishops. When Henderson said he was sure that James VI would have heartily approved of this reform, Charles sharply disagreed, reminding the minister, 'I had the happiness to know him much better than you.' So the argument continued. Each side exchanged a total of eight papers: neither made any significant concessions. On their knees the covenanters begged Charles to convert: he was obdurate. Although he managed to impress Henderson that he was 'the most intelligent man I spoke with,' the minister and his fellows caused the king so much anguish that he may be forgiven if he felt some relief to learn of Henderson's death a couple of months later.[18] 'I never knew what it was to be barbarously baited before,' Charles lamented to Henrietta Maria, 'there was never man so alone as I.'[19] He worried about the future, his crown, his children, and his own safety. He toyed with the idea of escape, reproached himself for going over to the Scots, fulminated against his captors, and all the time wallowed in self-pitying affection. 'Thy love preserves my life,' he told his wife in the special cipher he kept hidden under his pillow, her kindness 'upholds my courage'.[20]

After the covenanters failed to come to terms with the king, it was the turn of the Presbyterians who dominated the English parliament. The victory of the confederate leader, Owen Roe O'Neil, over a convenanter army at Benburb on 5 June reminded Presbyterians on both sides of the border how much they needed an accommodation with the king in England to free them to do God's work in Ireland.[21] Charles's vague offer to surrender his garrisons at Dublin and Drogheda encouraged parliament a little, though not enough, to accept his request to come to London to talk peace in person.[22] Instead they sent him a deputation. Their terms, known as the Newcastle Propositions, demanded sweeping concessions: the king was to confirm all of parliament's ordinances, become a Presbyterian, abolish bishops, reform the universities, persecute recusants and Independents, give up command of the militia for twenty years, and exempt a large number of named royalists from pardon.[23] Even before the delegation reached Newcastle, Charles declared he would not yield 'one jot'.[24] He was just as obdurate when, on 30 July, after a particularly harrowing journey up the Great North Road, they formally presented parliament's propositions. Had they power to negotiate? No, they answered, only authority to convey the king's answers back to Westminster. 'An honest trumpeter might have done as much,' Charles retorted. Quite understandably the Earl of Loudoun, the covenanter leader, took umbrage, and warned the king that if he continued his intransigence 'all England will join against you as one man and . . . depose you, and set up another government.'[25] In the formal reply Charles sent parliament the next day, he seemed to have taken the earl's advice, having softened his tone. Since parliament's proposals envisaged such a radical change in the way the two kingdoms were governed, Charles wrote, he needed time to consider them, or better still, requested a safe conduct to come to London to discuss their ideas face to face. While naturally he could not accept anything that might prejudice the royal prerogative, he would 'cheerfully grant' all things 'which shall be really for the good and peace of his people.'[26]

In private the king was far less obliging. He refused to desert the church, or jeopardize his conscience. Had not his father, 'the wisest king since Solomon', Charles wrote to his own heir, coined the maxim, 'No bishops, no kings'? Presbyterians were really republican revolutionaries acting under pretence of religion. They would never stop him passing his son the full patrimony that James left him.[27]

In public the king had to hide his true feelings. Instead of rejecting the Newcastle Propositions out of hand he stalled. In early September he blamed the Scots for failing to set an example by refusing to make the slightest concessions. Their lapse was especially reprehensible since further talks would be most fruitful. A couple of weeks later Charles went on to warn the covenanters that if he could not reach agreement with them, he might be forced to do so with the Independents.[28] To underscore the threat at the end of the month Charles had discussions with a committee of some sixty leading Independent divines. All along he was under intense pressure from both his friends abroad, as well as his enemies at home, to make some sort of agreement. 'I am daily more and more threatened from London,' he complained to his wife in August. A week later Colepeper, Jermyn and Ashburnham wrote from France begging him to make concessions. If he refused, they warned, he would have to choose between being king in a Presbyterian country or losing the crown. 'How can you think it possible for me to find joy in anything after this'?[29] he complained. In early November he vented his hurt and anger on Sir William D'Avenant, who came to Newcastle with a message from the queen and her counsellors that he must become a Presbyterian so as to retain control of the militia. When D'Avenant added that all his friends favoured giving up episcopacy, Charles asked which ones? Colepeper and Jermyn, the poet replied. Jermyn knew nothing about religion, counterblasted the king, Colepeper had none, and D'Avenant must never again enter his presence. Still deeply hurt the poet a few weeks later recounted the incident to the queen. She felt 'more fear than hope'.[30]

The split between Charles and Henrietta Maria, which had first surfaced over the Treaty of Uxbridge, now widened. After two decades of marraige to a devout Anglican, Henrietta Maria could not comprehend what was now perhaps, the most important thing in her husband's life – his religion. With the insensitivity of the zealot who had come to England twenty-one years before, more as a Catholic missionary than a bride, she still thought that one Protestant heresy was just as bad as any other. With a Machiavellian sense of the reality of power (that was a credit to the daughter of the king who said Paris was worth a mass), she begged her husband to 'grant nothing more and suffer anything than give up the militia.'[31] But as Charles told Bishop Juxon, religion was 'everything'.[32] If the pulpits teach not obedience,' he wrote, 'the king will have but small comfort of the militia.'[33] With an insensitivity that matched his wife's, Charles told her that accepting Presbyterianism was nearly as bad as becoming a papist, for 'it is less ill in many respects to submit to one than many popes.'[34] The imbroglio between the two became increasngly acrimonious. 'I shall not set my foot in England,' the queen threatened if he made any more concessions, because 'you have cut your throat' with those already granted.[35] 'For God's sake leave off threatening me with thy desire to meddle,' the king replied, 'as thou lovest me give me so much comfort (and God knows I have but little, and that little must come from thee).'[36]

Cajoled by those he loved, and bullied by men he hated, the king became slightly paranoiac. He aplogized to Hamilton for not writing at length by explaining, 'that the letter will be suitable to the times, without Method or reason, and yet you will find some lasting truths in it, which again puts me out of fashion.'[37] On other occasions Charles was able to get his own back. Once at divine service a particularly offensive minister called for the singing of Psalm 52: 'why boastest thou thyself, thou tyrant, that thou can'st do mischief.' Charles managed to divert the congregation into reciting Psalm 56: 'Be merciful unto me, O God, for man goeth about to devour me.'[38] Aside from humour and despair there was little for the king. Telling Montrose to stay in the Highlands would not rekindle his fortunes in Scotland. No assistance could be expected from the Confederation of Kilkenny.[39] 'Indeed the business of Ireland is a very bad business,' Hyde lamented in December. The possibility of royalist risings in England and Wales that Charles discussed with Michael Hudson that month appeared equally futile.[40]

Escape therefore seemed the only way out of an intolerable situation. Charles first raised the idea of fleeing to the Continent in early June, less than a month after he had joined the Scots. By July he was convinced, 'I am lost if I go not unto France by the end of August,' and implored his wife to make the necessary arrangements.[41] In August he admitted to Ormonde that he was 'an honourable prisoner'. The following month he asked his daughter, Mary, to have her husband, William of Orange, send a Dutch ship to Newcastle, ostensibly to carry messages, but in fact to stand by to spirit him to Holland, in case his second attempt to reach agreement on the basis of the Newcastle Propositions failed.

As part of this second initiative the king offered to surrender the militia for ten years – even life – and become a Presbyterian for five, rather than three as before, so long as the Anglican church would eventually be restored as England's established religion. When the Scots adamantly rejected these concessions, Charles hardened his stance, vowing, 'I will never quit my right to the militia, abandon my friends . . . or authorise the covenant.' After the Earl of Lanark, Hamilton's brother, urged him to be more cooperative, Charles came up with his final reply to the Newcastle Propositions: although equally uncompromising in substance, it was perhaps a little more conciliatory in tone. By now it was too late.[42] So on Christmas Day 1646, Charles made a confused and half-hearted attempt to escape on the Dutch ship his daughter sent, and which had spent the past months in Newcastle harbour pretendingto clean its hull. The wind proved as feeble as the king's resolve, the attempt got nowhere, and the next day Charles found his guard doubled and three parliamentary frigates patrolling outside the harbour. He lost hope of ever being free. 'For now, it is only the question I shall be a prisoner in England or Scotland,' he wrote on 15 January, 'I think to be better used in England, though I have more friends in Scotland.'[43]

Since September at least the king had recognized that if he did not come to terms with the covenanters they would probably hand him over to parliament.[44] Yet he treated the parliamentary delegation that reached Newcastle in mid-January to take him back as if he had some choice in the matter, receiving them like petitioners in his presence chamber, graciously hearing their message, and dismissing them with the promise they would have their answer in a day or two.[45] Five days later the Scots rather sheepishly told the king that they were going to return home and leave him behind in parliamentary custody. As their army marched out of the city, bands playing and pipes swirling, Newcastle's fishwives screamed 'Judas! Judas!' taunting the Scots for agreeing to leave Charles behind in England in return for payment of debts worth £400,000. Charles contributed to the legend that they had betrayed their master (albeit for a lot more than thirty pieces of silver) by taunting they had sold him 'at too cheap a rate'.[46]

After seven months of being harangued by Presbyterian ministers, nagged by his wife, berated by her advisers, rejected by both parliament and the army, and thwarted in escape, the journey back to Holdenby seemed like a holiday. When he was a prisoner a change of venue always cheered the king as much as it had in freer times when he had moved from one hunting lodge to another. He left Newcastle on 3 February, riding via Durham to Richmond, where he touched the sick for the king's evil. For two miles outside Leeds the roads were lined with cheering crowds. General Fairfax welcome him to Nottingham. At Holdenby House the gentry of Northamptonshire, a notoriously Puritan county, waited to greet him. Clement Kinnersley, a trusted servant, had got the house ready for his master. Charles's table was as well served as during the happier days of peace, with an allowance of twenty-eight dishes at £30 per diem. A household staff of 120 servants brought the king everything he wanted except for his freedom, which he was denied by a garrison commanded by Major General Browne and Colonel Graves, and large enough to cost parliament £282 a day.[47] In contrast to such lavish hospitality and extensive precautions, parliament's refusal to allow the king his own Anglican chaplains was most petty. It produced several unseemly incidents. After the Presbyterian ministers, the Reverends Marshall and Carrill, said grace, Charles would say his own Anglican blessing. On Sundays he refused to attend their church services, preferring to send the day alone in his room in prayer, study and contemplation.[48] During the week the king would take vigorous walks in the gardens with the Earl of Pembroke and General Browne. Sometimes he rode over to Harrowden or Althorp, Lord Spencer's lovely house on the other side of the valley, to play bowls, a game to which he was becoming increasingly addicted.

The refusal of parliament's commissioners to let him have his own chaplains, or make any concessions regarding religion in return for his on practically everything else, greatly upset the king.[49] Less than three weeks after coming to Holdenby he wrote to the French ambassador, 'never was a prisoner more strictly guarded than I am. I must tell you I see nothing but ruin to my person through the behaviour of their commissioners.'[50] Even though Charles went on to declare, 'I am resolved the rather to perish than ... act against my conscience,' he made a dramatic offer on 20 May. He would become a Presbyterian for three years, cede the militia for ten, and be even more generous if parliament let him come to London to negotiate the final details in person.[51] Once again it was too late.

Charles was playing bowls at Althorp, on the afternoon of 2 June when he heard that a party of cavalry was headed to Holdenby. Immediately he returned there to discuss the threat with General Browne and Colonel Graves. All agreed to stand their ground. Browne called his men together to explain the situation, and doubled the guard. Late that night 500 troopers led by Cornet George Joyce arrived. They were a tough bunch, all volunteers from different units, commanded not by a colonel as was usual for a cavalry regiment, but by an ensign, the most junior commissioned rank. Joyce had been a tailor's apprentice, served with distinction in Cromwell's regiment, and had been commissioned by Fairfax, who once described him as 'an Arch-Agitator'.[52] On entering Holdenby House he demanded to see the king. Graves and Browne asked him on whose authority. His own, the ensign replied. As the argument continued, with the king's servants joining in, becoming louder by the minute, the parliamentary garrison went over to Joyce's side, whether swayed by their arguments or numbers, one cannot tell. The noise woke the king. Ringing the little silver bell he always kept beside his bed, he called a servant, James Maxwell, who told him what had happened. Charles agreed to admit the cornet who, with a drawn sword in one hand and an unholstered pistol in the other, entered the royal bedroom. He apologized for disturbing His Majesty at so late an hour. 'No matter if you mean no harm,' interrupted the king. 'If you permit me I shall have no hurt. You may take away my life if you will, having the sword in your hand.' All parliament wanted, Joyce explained, was the king's protection. Would he be made to do anything against his conscience, Charles asked. Certainly not, the cornet replied, 'he would be unwilling to force anyone against his conscience, much less your Majesty.' After Joyce promised he could bring his servants, Charles agreed to leave Holdenby with him at six that morning.[53]

At the appointed hour Charles walked out of the house, to the adjacent place of flat land (now a delightful lawn) around which 500 troopers were drawn up in full battle order, their horses impatiently stamping in the cold early morning light. Charles asked Joyce what commission – what authority – he had to take him away. The cornet replied he was doing so to prevent another civil war, and further needless bloodshed. What commission did he have, asked the king. Again Joyce stalled. A letter from General Fairfax? Joyce told Charles not to keep on asking such questions: he had already given a good enough answer.

'I Pray you, Mr Joyce, deal ingenuously with me, and tell me what commission you have.'

'Here is my commission.'

'Where?'

'Behind me,' explained the cornet, pointing to his regiment of volunteers.

'It is as fair a commission, and as well written as I have seen a commission written in my life: a company of handsome proper gentlemen as I have seen in a great while. But if I should refuse yet to go with you, I hope you will not force me? I am your King and you ought not to lay violent hands upon your King, for I acknowledge none here to be above me but God.'

'Our desires are not to force Your Majesty but humbly entreat your Majesty to go with us.'

When the parliamentary commissioners moved to stop Joyce, he signalled his men to use force if necessary. Charles mounted his horse.

'Now Gentlemen, for the place you intend to have me?'

'If it please your Majesty to Oxford.'

'That is no good air.'

'Then to Cambridge.'

Replying that he liked neither university town, the king suggested Newmarket. Joyce agreed. Charles asked how far they must travel that day:

'As far as your Majesty can ride.'

'I can ride as far as you or anyone else,' retorted the king, trying rather pathetically to snatch a morsel of self-respect from a humiliating defeat.

The responsibility for the king's seizure at Holdenby is hard to ascertain. For some weeks the idea of arresting him had been bruited around the radical Leveller regiments. It was one with which Joyce fully agreed, having vowed a few weeks earlier 'to do things as were never yet done on earth.'[54] It seems certain that Cromwell used the conversations he had with Joyce in London in late May to suggest that he seize the king, while warning that if the mission failed he would be disowned.[55] Although Cromwell adhered to this cover story, personally telling Charles two weeks after the abduction that Joyce had acted entirely on his own initiative, the fact that Cromwell eventually promoted the cornet, and gave him a £100 pension, confirmed Charles's retort, 'I'll not believe you unless you hang him.'[56]

Hanging Joyce would have been rank ingratitude. His coup greatly strengthened the position of the army radicals, with whom Cromwell had just thrown in his lot. Now they held a trump in a game where the cards that remained unplayed daily became fewer as the stakes increased. 'They must either sink us or we sink them,' declared one protagonist of the increasingly bitter struggle over how, and by whom, the realm should be ruled. Seldom have the alternatives been so dramatically displayed as on the lawn outside Holdenby House. On one side were Joyce's cavalry, 'as good a law as now I can see executed by any judge in England,' thought John Lilburne: on the other stood Charles insisting, as he would till the end, 'I am your King.'[57]

From Holdenby prisoner and escort rode to Huntingdon, where they spent the night of 3 June at Hichingbrooke House. They would have passed the next night at Newmarket, had not Fairfax sent his aide, Major Robert Huntington, to intercept them four miles from Cambridge. Fairfax was afraid that if they went through the university town, the dons and undergraduates might demonstrate their support. At Childersley Charles stayed at Sir John Cutt's house, to which the scholars and tutors journeyed to shout appropriately learned 'Vivat Rex's!' Senior army officers also came in nearly as large a crowd – Generals Fairfax, Cromwell, Ireton, and Colonels Whalley, Rich and Dean – to inspect their guest. He received them all gracefully, taking advantage of Fairfax's embarrassed denials that Joyce acted on anyone's authority but his own, to obtain the promise that he could have his own chaplains back. In return Charles gave the army the impression he would accept whatever terms they pleased.[58]

By-passing Cambridge, the royal party reached Newmarket on 9 June, where the king stayed in his father's hunting lodge for a fortnight. The army replaced Joyce with a more senior and congenial officer, and let the Duke of Richmond, Sir William Fleetwood, and the Reverend Doctors Sheldon, Hammond and Holdsworth attend the king. All this heartened Charles. He hunted in the same fields as he had as a young man with his father and Buckingham, went out in his coach, and was 'at home' to the gentry of Cambridgeshire, Suffolk and Essex, who flocked to Newmarket with their families to pay their respects.[59] Less welcome were the overtures from the Scots, which Charles roundly rejected, saying he had not the slightest desire to join the kirk. He was quite happy where he was. 'This army speaks to me very fair,' he confided to a friend, 'which makes me hope well.'[60]

The army's decision to move the king to Hampton Court raised his expectations even higher, for he was sure that the closer he got to London the easier it would be to play parliament and the Scots commissioners at Westminster off against each other. Charles reached Royston on 24 June. The townspeople's warm welcome, and the army's courtesy more than compensated for the decay into which the hunting lodge that contained so many memories of happier times had fallen. When a colonel barged into the solemn ceremony during which, according to ancient custom, an emblem of the Garter was being returned to the king on the death of its recipient, and not even Charles's scowls could persuade the fellow to leave, the king's barber told him to clear off.[61] Having been captured by a tailor's apprentice, the sovereign of England's most ancient and honourable order of chivalry had to be rescued by the man who cut his hair. Truly had Charles's world turned upside-down!

The next day on his arrival at Hatfield House the army let the king publicly use the Anglican prayer book. This concession, the first time he had been allowed to do so in over a year, much pleased him. on 3 July he reached Caversham, where he wrote, 'I am at much more freedom than I were, for my friends have free access to me, my chaplains wait upon me according to their vocation, and I have free intelligence with my wife and anybody else whom I please.'[62] The army even let him see his children, who had fallen into their hands after the royalist surrender. Charles's two-day reunion with James and Elizabeth in August was so moving that it brought tears even to Cromwell's eyes (he, Fairfax, and Charles, the Elector Palatine, having come to Windsor to prepare the ground for the army's formal peace proposals).[63]

A deputation of senior officers formally presented these proposals to Charles in late July. Known as the Heads of the Proposals, they went much further than the Newcastle Propositions suggested a year earlier:[64] parliament was to meet at least 120 and no more than 240 days a year, committees of both Houses were to handle business during recesses, the franchise was to be expanded, constituencies reformed according to tax assessments, parliament allowed to raise money without the king's approval for ten years, a council of state, dominated by senior officers, to control the militia for seven, bishops were to be stripped of their temporal author-ity, and use of the prayer book was to be made optional.

Even before he formally received these terms Charles decided to reject them. He attempted to buy off the military commanders with promises of peerages and promotion, and was surprised to find no one would take the bait. Even so he convinced himself that once they understood their real interests they would readily grant him, parliament and the people 'what is their own'.[65] Charles felt confident enough to ignore General Ireton's warning, 'Sir, you have the intention of being the arbitrator between Parlia-ment and us, and we mean it to be between your Majesty and the Par-liament.' He immediately turned down the Heads of the Proposals, curtly reminding the military delegation that they needed him far more than he needed them. Sir John Berkeley was horrified. Standing beside the king he whispered that if his majesty had some secret weapon to win the war, he wished to God he had kept it as well concealed from the army as he had from his own advisers.[66] Although Charles's abrupt rejection of theHeads of the Proposals did not terminate discussions between theking and the army, the future implications of his stand were grave. By offering to negotiate with the king the senior officers had gone out on a limb: their position became increasingly precarious as the rank and file daily grew more radical, and the king, confident that royalist support amongst the

Scots, London and parliament was growing, became more obdurate. After sending General Fairfax a less than honest promise denying the rumours that he was trying to cultivate the Presbyterians, Charles moved to Oatlands Palance, where his mood was described as 'very merry'.[67] He wrote encouragingly to Ormonde and Digby in Dublin, to the covenanters in Scotland, and Hyde on the Continent, while continuing to string the army along with the carrot of agreement.[68]

Following his arrival on 24 August at Hampton Court, which Clement Kinnersley had prepared for his comfort, it seemed as if the court enjoyed a brief Indian summer before the storms and cold of winter. Those were 'halcyon days', Sir Thomas Herbert remembered: his chaplains attended the king, his nobles waited on him, his children came over for visits, and lords and ladies, generals and aldermen rode every day from London to pay their respects. Just as toughness made Charles stubborn, so appeasement made him confident, particularly when both parliament and the army competed for his favour. In September he turned down parliament's peace terms (which were in effect a rehash of the Newcastle Propositions) explaining that the Heads of the Proposals 'were much more conducive to the Satisfaction of all interests, and may be a better Foundation for a lasting Peace.' By failing to follow such honeyed words with hard concessions, Charles produced an impasse that the growing influence of the radical Levellers in the army (who vowed to make the king 'a dead dog') daily became more perilous: the realm drifted towards anarchy. 'I hear all things in England are in very great confusion still,' wrote Sir Edward Nicholas from the Continent. 'As the king at first called a Parliament he could not rule, and afterwards the Parliament raised an army it could not rule, so the army have agitators they cannot rule,' Sir Edward continued in one of the most succinct contemporary analyses of the course of the English civil war. 'What will the end be,' he, like thousands of the king's subjects, fearfully wondered, 'God only knows.'[69]

# XVIII

# 'REMEMBER THY END'

Charles fully shared Sir Edward Nicholas's concerns for the future of his crown and country. From the greening of the summer, when the army treated him with unwanted respect, and parliamentarians, colonels and covenanters courted him with such deference that Charles persuaded himself that they could not survive without him, the king's hopes browned and fell with the leaves of autumn. Once again he decided to escape from the unbearable conditions of his captivity at Hampton Court.[1] Having reached the decision in late October, he complained to Colonel Edward Whalley, the commander of the Hampton Court garrison, that the noise of his guards walking their beats at night disturbed his daughter, Elizabeth, who had come to stay with him for a few days. Whalley promised to tell the soldiers not to make so much noise, but the next morning Charles said it had made no difference. So the colonel agreed to post his men further away from the king's rooms. A few days afterwards Charles told his servant, John Ashburnham, to withdraw his parole, which prompted Whalley to dismiss him, and gave the king an excuse to retract his own promise not to escape in protest. Whalley did not, however, return the sentries to their original beats. A little later, on about 3 November, Charles told Sir William Legge, a gentleman of the bedchamber, to go and tell John Ashburnham and Sir John Berkeley to arrange the king's flight. After a couple of sessions at an inn in Thames Ditton, and a late night meeting with the king himself in the Long Gallery at Hampton Court, they agreed to make the break on Thursday, 11 November to take advantage of Charles's practice of retiring early to his room on Mondays and Thursdays to write letters. Leaving by a back stairway Charles slipped out of Hampton Court, through the gloom and rain of an early winter evening to Thames Ditton, where a boat waited to row him across the Thames. On the south bank Ashburnham and Berkeley were ready with horses; together they disappeared into the night.

The next morning, sensing that something was amiss, Whalley demanded to see the king. Patrick Mawl, a groom of the bedchamber, tried to put him off, saying that his master must not be woken. Eventually Whalley prevailed; he entered the king's room to find the bed empty, Charles's pet greyhound whimpering in the corner, and two letters left on the desk. The first thanked Whalley and his assistant, Major Harrington, for their kind treatment, and requested them to deliver various items, including a Van Dyck portrait of the queen and the wretched dog, to the Duke of Richmond. In the second, addressed to parliament, Charles explained his reasons for leaving Hampton Court. After the army had doubled his guard, and dismissed his trusted servants he had to find more freedom to satisfy the different needs of the Presbyterians and Independents, the army and parliament, the English and Scots. 'Let me be heard with Freedom, Honour and Safety, and I shall instantly break through the clouds of retirement, and show myself ready to be *Pater Patria*,' promised the king.[2]

Because Charles feared being poisoned if he remained at Hampton Court he concentrated his efforts on breaking out of confinement, giving little thought to his ultimate destination.[3] On this his advisers could not agree. At their first secret planning session Legge (who had just escaped from parliamentary custody) favoured the Isle of Jersey, where the king would still be within his dominions, and have a ready escape route to France. Berkeley thought that Charles should go directly to the Continent, while Ashburnham urged the dramatic gesture of riding into London to place himself at the head of moderate opinion, which Ashburnham maintained, was growing by the hour. Unable to reach consensus at their second meeting on 7 November they vaguely accepted that the king should stay in the south of England, whilst they sounded out royalists in the Isle of Wight to see if they would receive him, and arrange for several ships to be standing by in various secluded harbours to take him to the Continent in case the first plan miscarried.

Charles had not ridden many miles from Hampton Court when he asked Berkeley about these vessels. He gave Sir John the distinct impression that he intended taking one of them abroad. Berkeley replied that he had never been told to make such arrangements. Why then, Charles asked, had Ashburnham said he had? Sir John suggested that perhaps Ashburnham wanted to increase his own influence with the king at the expense of other equally trusted counsellors. 'I think that thou art in the right,' Charles answered, placing his hand on Berkeley's shoulder.'[4]

The immediate problem of putting distance between himself and Hampton Court postponed further discussion about their destination for several hours. As they got lost in Windsor Forest it was daylight before they reached the inn at Bishop's Sutton, where fresh horses had been arranged. Because it was no longer dark, and the local parliamentary committee hapened to be meeting in the inn, they had to be most careful making the exchange. They rode off as fast as possible. A few hours later, Charles stopped on the brow of a hill near Southampton, and told his servants to dismount so they might rest their horses and discuss what to do next. He turned down Berkeley's idea of going to the West Country to find a vessel to take them abroad, perhaps because Sir John had been urging him to accept the Heads of the Proposals. Instead he agreed with Ashburnham, who had been his constant friend and loyal servant ever since they had slipped out of Oxford nineteen months before, that they should sound out Colonel Robert Hammond, whom parliament had just appointed governor of the Isle of Wight. Ashburnham had recently met Hammond and found him surprisingly favourable to the king's cause. So Charles told Ashburnham and Berkeley to go and ask the governor if he would give the king sanctuary on the island. He and Legge would ride to the Earl of Southampton's house at Titchfield where they would all rendez-vous. As the party split up, Berkeley shouted back to the king that if they did not return to Titchfield within twenty-four hours he should assume they had been taken and flee without them. After spending the night at Lymington, Ashburnham and Berkeley crossed over to the Isle of Wight on 13 November, and a few hours later were ushered in to see Hammond at his headquarters, Carisbrooke castle.

The castle is situated a mile southwest of Newport, the island's capital, built at the navigable head of the River Medina. Carisbrooke had originally been a Norman keep, constructed on top of a man-made mound, about which were more recent buildings, including the governor's house, guard quarters, and a chapel. Around them all ran a high wall with a battlement, along which sentries marched to and from the guard-house which was built into the massive main west gate. During the sixteenth century the Tudors had raised a three-quarter mile outer earthen bank with slits for cannon. In all Carisbrooke was an imposing stronghold, with walls capable of keeping attckers out and uninvited guests in.

The castle's governor was equally formidable. At the age of twenty-six Colonel Robert Hammond was a seasoned veteran. A protége of the Earl of Essex, he had survived three years of hard combat to command his own regiment. By 1647 the army had become too radical for Hammond who arranged to be transferred to a remote spot such as the Isle of Wight to escape the turmoil he was sure must follow the civil war.

On discovering that his backwater had suddenly become a maelstrom Hammond was mightily upset. 'Oh Gentlemen,' he reproached Ash-burnham and Berkeley, when they told him the king wanted to come to the Isle of Wight, 'you have undone me.' Even though Charles's emissaries immediately realized they had erred in telling Hammond too much, they did not resort to the contingency plan of failing to rendezvous within the set time. Instead they agreed to take Hammond to Tichfield, mortgaging the king's options in return for the vague promise that the colonel would treat him with 'honour and honesty'.

Hammond, Ashburnham and Berkeley rode to Cowes, where they joined the castle's captain and a couple of soldiers, and sailed up Southampton

Water to Titchfield. On landing Ashburnham hurried upstairs to the king's room. 'What! Have you brought Hammond with you?' cried Charles. 'Oh you have undone me: for I am by this means made fast from stirring.' Telling the king that the ship he had arranged to take him to France should arrive any moment from Southampton (it proved as ephemeral as the rest of Ashburnham's armada), the distraught servant asked his master if he should creep downstairs and kill the governor and his escort. Charles walked to and fro for a while pondering. 'The world would not excuse me,' he concluded. 'For if I should follow that counsel it should be said (and believed) that [Hammond] had ventured his life for me, and I had unworthily taken it.'[5] As Ashburnham stood by weeping copiously, Charles called Hammond up to say that he accepted the governor's promise, and would come quietly to the Isle of Wight.

The king soon came to regret this decision. At Carisbrooke, Charles frequently said that after escaping from Hampton Court he had never intended coming to the island. The trouble was that Charles never intended going anywhere definite, for like a prisoner of war he could see little further than beyond the other side of the barbed wire. Once over it, hunted, on the run, and faced with finding a destination, he let events and others make the decision for him. At Titchfield he behaved with all lethargy of a recaptured prisoner. 'No it is too late to think of anything but going the way you have forced upon me,' he told Ashburnham, when he suggested one last desperate bid for freedom, 'but leave the issue to God.'

Some might say that He did not tarry in giving His answer. After sailing back to Cowes, to spend the night at the Feathers Inn, Charles was very disturbed to read the text carved above the bed: 'Remember thy end.'[6]

The next morning a small incident restored the king's spirits. As he rode through Newport a gentlewoman plucked a damask rose, the last flower left in her garden, and gave it to him saying that she would pray for him.[7] After lunch at Carisbrooke castle the king received gentry from all over the island who came to pay their respects. He let them kiss his hand, and told them that threats from the Levellers had forced him to leave Hampton Court. The king's initial reception impressed Sir John Oglander, an astute observer, and one of the staunchest royalists on the island. Even though the king's choice of the Isle of Wight worried Sir John, who rightly feared that it would become a trap from which the king could never wriggle, a few days later he was proudly entertaining his sovereign at Nunwell, his country house near Sandown.[8] The king's coach was shipped to the island in early December, much to the delight of the inhabitants, who had never seen such a splendid vehicle rattle along their rutted roads. Charles used the coach for trips to the Needles, the spectacular line of rocks that jut out to sea from a bay of many coloured sands at the extreme west of the island, and to Yarmouth, with its fine harbour. According to one story, he came across a funeral procession, and asked whose it was. Sir James

Chamberlain, was the reply, a royalist who had just died of wounds suffered in the war. Charles dismounted and joined the mourners. His first few days on the island seemed to confirm the king's initial elation and that Oglander's fears were groundless. 'I am daily more and more satisfied with this governor,' he wrote, 'and feel these islanders very good, peaceable and quiet people.'[9]

The afternoon he arrived at Carisbrooke Charles publicly announced that he had come seeking freedom to make peace. 'I desire not a drop of Christian blood should be spilt.' In private he started negotiations, confident that his escape had both strengthened his position and widened his options.

Reports that one of Fairfax's regiments in Hertfordshire had demonstrated in his favour may have emboldened Charles to send Berkeley to see the general, purportedly to ask for protection for his chaplains, Doctors Sheldon, Holdsworth, and Haywood, who had just landed on the island, but really to sound Fairfax out about a parley. Sir John quickly discovered that the army was far from favourably disposed towards his master. Happening to bump into George Joyce he learned that many officers wanted to put the king on trial.[10] The vehemence of their hatred so frightened Berkeley that he hurried back to Carisbrooke to warn Charles that he must flee before it was too late. The king assured him that things were not as bad as Sir John thought, and anyway if escape became necessary, he would have no trouble leaving the island.[11] First they must exhaust all chances of a negotiated settlement, because, as Ashburnham warned and Charles knew full well, he would be burning his boats if he took a ship to France. 'It is less ill for my affairs,' he told his wife, 'that I should be a prisoner within my dominions than at liberty anywhere else.'[12]

During his first evening at Carisbrooke Charles sat down to draft the letter that was read out in parliament on 17 November. In it the king suggested reopening talks since 'he conceives himself to be at more freedom and security than formerly.' Characteristically he put his demands before his concessions: he would not abolish bishops, nor allow the alienation of their lands since such was both contrary to his conscience and Magna Carta, Chapter I of which protected the church, and which he had sworn to uphold. This bit of sophistry hung a few parliamentary radicals on their own constitutional petards, and may well have disguised the very real concessions the king offered; he would permit a Presbyterian form of government for three years, surrender the militia and the right to appoint all senior officers of state for life, and grant a universal pardon.[13] Hearing nothing more from Westminster he once again, on 6 December, asked parliament for a reply: agreement was so close, and he had made so many magnanimous concessions, that surely they must be willing to make the small effort to bring peace to his 'miserable distracted kingdom'.[14]

Parliament reacted by passing four bills containing their terms, which included the surrender of the militia for twenty years, abolition of bishops completely, settlement of the soldiers' arrears in pay, and the punishment of leading royalists.[15] The four bills were not proposals on the basis of which an agreement could be hammered out, but an ultimatum that the king could accept by giving the traditional royal assent. To obtain it, parliament sent a deputation headed by the Earl of Denbigh to the king, with the warning that he had four days to accept their terms. On the day the deadline expired, Charles called the delegation to his room. Sitting surrounded by his worried looking advisers, he asked if they had authority to negotiate. When Denbigh answered they had not, Charles handed him a sealed letter. Confused, the earl withdrew for a hurried conference with his colleagues, before returning to say that parliament wanted them to take back an answer, and since the letter was sealed they could not tell if it really contained one. Whenever he had served His Majesty as an ambassador to foreign princes, Denbigh continued, he had never delivered a message without knowing its contents. Charles acerbically answered that none of the two score ambassadors he had sent abroad ever had the impertinence to break his seal. To this insult (Berkeley recalled), Denbigh replied 'in harsher terms than one Gentleman ought to use to another.'[16] Eventually Charles broke the seals and handed Ashburnham the letter to read aloud. As Denbigh suspected, the king unilaterally turned down the four bills because they would 'not only divest himself of all sovereignty', but would jeopardize his subjects' rights 'by making parliament omnipotent'. The reply concluded, 'His Majesty is very much at ease with himself having fulfilled the offices of both a Christian and a King.'[17]

Charles's inner peace almost certainly came from another source – the secret alliance he had made a couple of days previously with the covenanters. But the discourteous way in which he rejected parliament's terms is hard to explain. Usually Charles was a polite man, who let others have their say so long as they did the same. Yet on several occasions in the past sixteen months he had dismissed peace overtures with unwarranted and untypical rudeness. In August 1646 he turned down the Newcastle Propositions by telling the distinguished delegation that parliament might as well send an 'honest trumpeter'. In the previous July he rejected the Heads of the Proposals by informing the senior army officers they needed him far more than he needed them. He tried to slough off the four bills with the same transparent deviousness with which he had first attempted to agree to the Petition of Right. On all these occasions the setting in which the king operated underscored the authority and majesty of his office. For centuries petitioners had on bended knee humbly presented their requests to the sovereign, as he sat on the throne surrounded by his great officers. Now they came with non-negotiable demands: now men who once served the crown as ambassadors abroad brought messags from his enemies at home. Thus even though Charles had decided to reject their terms, the contradiction between the setting and the new realities of power was so painful that it may have prompted him to speak more harshly than gentlemen are wont one with another.

Charles had conducted his talks with the Scots commissioners first at Hampton Court, and then a few weeks later at Carisbrooke in much more gracious tones. He let them know that he was very willing to be flexible. 'Many things may be offered to obtain a treaty,' he told the Earl of Lanark, 'that may be altered when one comes to treat.'[18] To his old nemesis Charles wrote in equally conciliatory terms; 'Argyle, howsoever heretofore you and I have differed in judgement, I believe now that the present state of affairs are such as will make you heartily embrace my cause, it being grounded on those particulars that were never in question between you and me.'[19] Charles had meetings with the Scots commissioners, Lanark, Loudoun, and Lauderdale on Christmas day (such being the necessity of those unmerry times), and signed an agreement with them on 26 December. The terms the covenanters gave were far better than those parliament proffered: Presbyterianism for only three years with exceptions for the king and his household, after which a convention of sixty divines should be called to settle religion. In return the Scots confirmed the king's right to control the militia, veto legislation, appoint officers of state and, most pertinent of all, promised to invade England.[20]

At Ashburnham's suggestion the secret treaty was sealed in lead and buried in the grounds of Berkeley's house; none the less news of the agreement soon leaked out.[21] Charles's curt rejection of the four bills may have given the game away, since immediately afterwards parliament tightened security at Carisbrooke. Realizing that he was a prisoner once more, Charles started to plan his escape. Notwithstanding his parole to Hammond, he wrote to his wife to send a French ship to Southampton, and had Ashburnham secretly stable four or five horses on the mainland. According to one story, Charles was booted and spurred, all ready to go, when he looked out of the window and saw the castle's weather vane suddenly shift north, the new wind preventing him from sailing down the Medina to Cowes.[22] Why he did not opt for the much faster means of riding, or even walking to Cowes, one cannot say, particularly as a northerly wind would have facilitated his getaway to the Continent. Anyway by the time the wind had changed six days later parliament had increased his guard with 200 veterans from Hammond's old regiment, expelled the king's advisers, and appointed Thomas Herbert, Captain Anthony Mildmay, Silus Titus, and Robert Persons, his conservators. They had special responsibility for the king's security, having to stay with him all day. When he was asleep they were required to spend the night standing outside his bedroom door. All these changes upset both Charles and his partisans on the island. One of them, Captain Burly, a veteran of the royal army, became so outraged that he staged a one-man (plus drummer boy) rising in Newport, marching on the castle with his musket and a few sympathetic women to try and rescue their monarch.[23]

For this romantically ridiculous affair parliament had Burley hung, drawn and quartered for treason. They over-reacted because they felt they were losing control of events. The alliance with the Scots and the encouragement it gave English royalists frighened them enough to vote on 3 January 1648 that anyone attempting to negotiate with the king without their permission was guilty of high treason.[24]

Relations between Charles and Hammond reflected parliament's new harshness. In mid-January Charles formally complained to the governor about worsening conditions at Carisbrooke. Was he now in fact a prisoner? Why, and at whose command? Hammond roundly answered that His Majesty knew the reasons full well, and that he was acting on the orders of both Houses of Parliament.[25] Five weeks later they had another altercation, when Hammond informed the king that his servants would have to be reduced to no more than thirty.

'Why do you use me thus?' asked the king. 'Did you not engage your honour you would take no advantage from thence against me?'[26]

'I said nothing,' replied Hammond, forgetting the vague promise he had given Ashburnham and Berkeley.

'You are an equivocating gentleman,' the king snapped back, the closest he ever came to calling anyone a liar. If the army was really in favour of liberty, as it claimed, Charles asked, then why should he not be allowed his chaplains? To Hammond's explanation that this was not possible, the king countered, 'You use me neither like a gentleman nor a Christian.'

'I'll speak with you when you are in better terms,' the governor replied, trying to break off the argument before it went too far.

'I have slept well tonight,' retorted the king, implying that he was not the one in a bad mood.

'I have used you very civilly.'

'Why do you not so now, then?'

Sensing that things had indeed gone too far, Charles tried to deflect Hammond's angry jibe that he had become too big for his boots into a reference about his own height. He replied that the royal cobbler was to blame for making him seem taller than he really was, by cutting the soles of his shoes too thick. In the hope that wit might have prevailed where indignation had failed, Charles asked, 'Shall I have liberty to go about to take the air?'

'No,' the colonel concluded, 'I cannot grant it.'

This exchange, which was recorded verbatim, illustrated the tensions Charles experienced as he came to accept that Carisbrooke, where he had been welcomed as a refugee, was now a prison. To lull his gaolers he called his servants together to tell them that there was 'no remedy but patience.' In private he was less sanguine, confiding to his friend (and clerk of the kitchen), Abraham Dowcett, 'My condition is not so ill as I expect it will be.'[27]

Once more escape seemed the only way out.

It took Sir Henry Firebrace but a week to make the plans. The hallmark of Sir Henry's career was loyalty. He had served the king as a page of the bedchamber during the balmy days of peace, and during the winter of defeat returned to attend his master, first at Newcastle, then Holdenby, and finally the Isle of Wight. He arranged for the king to squeeze through the bars of his bedroom window and drop to the castle lawn. There he would meet Charles with a rope to lower him down the wall, so he could clamber over the outer bank to join Richard Osborne, a gentleman usher, and Edward Worsley, a local royalist, who were waiting with fast horses to take him to a fishing boat anchored at some secluded beach. Charles liked the plan. During an afternoon walk he reconnoitred his climb over the castle wall. He was so confident of success that he postponed his escape for two weeks, thus increasing the chances of discovery. On the other hand, he refused to file through the bars of his bedroom window on grounds of security. The risk was unnecessary, the king insisted. Having already managed to squeeze his head through the bars he was sure that the rest of his body could follow.

On the evening of 27 March Firebrace threw a pebble up against Charles's window to signal that all was ready. He heard the window open, and the king puff and strain as he tried to get through. For a terrible moment Firebrace feared that His Majesty might be ignominiously stuck, until he saw him place a candle on the sill, the signal to call off the attempt.

Cutting the bars without being caught proved harder than anyone anticipated. Charles suggested using an endless screw which, rather like a modern scissors car-jack, would force them open. While spectacularly fast, and dramatically noisy, this was not as feasible as the slow, but surer, method of filing.[28]

Meanwhile Firebrace suggested another plan. He would bring a servant, Henry Chapman, to Carisbrooke dressed as a country bumpkin with a false beard, wig, white cap, grey coat, white stockings, and broad hat. This outlandish garb would impress itself so surely on the guards' minds that when Charles walked out of the castle in Chapman's place, similarly attired, they would only notice the dress and ignore his features. Charles liked the cunning plan, calling it 'unquestionably the most practicable'. Unfortunately Chapman could not get in past the guards.[29]

This failure convinced the king that his need to escape increased daily. Whilst walking in the grounds in late April the weather suddenly turned chilly. Having sent Herbert back to his room for a cloak, he was outraged when his servant found Hammond searching his desk for secret papers.[30] As a result Charles stopped keeping copies of all his letters. That Hammond spent hours sitting outside his room further added to the king's unease. The news that his son James had successfully escaped to France from parliamentary custody in London, disguised as a woman, deepened his resolve, while augmenting his sense of failure.[31]

William Lilly, the astrologer, and Jane Whorwood, an ardent royalist, revived Firebrace's original plan by obtaining files and nitric acid in London, which they managed to pass to the king as he was playing bowls. They also sent him hard wax, which mixed with readily available ink could be used to fill the cuts filed in the bars, and long grey socks to place over his boots, thus quietening his exit through the castle grounds. Charles accepted Firebrace's suggestion not to cut through the bars on his own windows, since they were more likely to be tested, but to use the adjacent stairway to exit through a groundfloor window, the bars on which Richard Osborne would previously sever.[32] I do extremely like your newest way,' Charles congratulated Firebrace on 24 April. Two days later he seemed to have changed his mind, telling the page the purpose of all his preparations was not immediate escape, but 'that I might leave as I see occasions.'[33]

Whether motivated by the wish to widen his options, or simply cold feet, Charles's reservations soon became academic. At the end of the month Hammond moved the king to new quarters on the north side of the castle, adjacent to the walls. From these rooms Charles tired to break out in early May. As his accomplices waited outside with horses he once again failed to squeeze between the bars.[34] Getting wind of the attempt, Hammond built a raised wooden sentry walk beside the wall and beneath the king's window. This forced the king's accessories to find three guards who would accept £100 to look the other way as Charles climbed out of the window, the bars of which he eroded almost all the way through with nitric acid. A last-minute change in the duty roster postponed the escape from 24 May to the 28th, when all three bribed guards were assigned to the walkway. Everything was ready. Outside the castle Osborne and Worsley hid with horses. In a remote cove John Newland, a Newport merchant, waited with a small boat to take the king to another secluded landing near Portsmouth where Captain Titus had been standing by every night for ten days to take Charles across southern England to the Medway, where Jane Whorwood was ready aboard the ship she had chartered.[35]

At the last moment two of the bribed soldiers told Hammond, who promptly increased the guard, and posted ambushes around the castle. As he walked through the grounds Abraham Dowcett stumbled across a piquet. When Osborne and Worsley saw him being marched off to the guardhouse, panic stricken they galloped through an ambush, without being hit, to hide in some woods for several days. Elated that he had foiled the plot Hammond entered the king's rooms to test the bars. Charles asked him his business. 'May it please your Majesty,' the governor crowed, 'I am come to take my leave of you, for I hear you are going away.'[36]

In addition to Hammond's diligence (for which parliament sent him a

£100 bonus), Charles's escape attempts failed because of a deplorable lack of security.[37] Every time the king sent or received a letter he ran the risk of its interception, but he still insisted on writing with promiscuous frequency, sometimes twice a day to the same person. For 1648 alone 159 of his secret letters have survived, and since many of them were cover letters for packets of correspondence, and because Charles burnt all his 'in' letters and stopped keeping copies of the 'outs', his correspondence that year may have run to almost a thousand items.[38] Charles remained placidly confident that his communications were secure, that his ciphers could not be broken, that no one could recognize his disguised hand-writing, and that his 'letter boxes', such as piles of laundry, spaces under the carpets, or the back pockets of servant's breeches, remained undetected. The king constantly broke the golden rule of intelligence, the need to know, letting almost anyone into his secrets. Since the Derby House committee of peers and M. P.s had a spy in the king's household, as well as outside informants, such as Lady Carlisle, and Mr Lowe, a London merchant, they had no difficulty in learning about escape attempts. For instance, they warned Hammond of the country bumpkin caper a few days after it was hatched. None the less, apart from one scare, which he quickly convinced himself was groundless, the king refused to believe that his communications had been compromised. 'I cannot think anyone so great a Devil,' he wrote, 'as to betray me.'[39]

Charles took outlandish risks because letters were vitally important to him. He read smuggled newsletters with an avidity he had never given diplomatic reports. He sent his secretary, Nicholas Oudart, to Prince James in exile with much more enthusiasm than he ever dispatched proud aristo-crats as ambassadors extraordinary to the Holy Roman Emperor. Through secret letters Charles could still play the king: he could encourage royalist resistance, propose rewards for his followers, urge his children not to give in, whilst he declared how much he missed and loved them. As he admitted to one clandestine messenger there was 'no greater service' that could be rendered the crown, 'but to get a letter conveyed to my wife for me, and to take care that I may have the answer returned.'[40]

To Charles his days at Carisbrooke increasingly became 'these damnable times'. After morning prayer he would walk the quarter-mile circuit of the castle wall, often with Hammond, before retiring to his room to read and write letters. Dinner was a pleasant occasion. For the first time in his life Charles developed an interest in food and, as always, enjoyed table talk on such topics as morality, ethics, history, and the royal prerogative. When the discussion became heated, he would end it with a touch of humour. Charles became especially fond of Mr Troughton, the governor's chaplain, who had just come down from university. The two spent hours debating theology, the younger man still with an undergraduate's vigour, the older with the wisdom and self-certainty of the don his father had always wanted to be.[41] In the afternoons Charles enjoyed playing bowls on the green Hammond built for him on the parade ground west of the castle with the governor, Major Cromwell (Oliver's nephew and name sake), Herbert, and Anthony Mildmay. Because the summer of 1648 was the wettest for forty years, with less than three dry days from May Day to mid-September, Hammond even built a small pavilion for that most dismal of English summer diversions – taking shelter as rain stops play.[42]

Reading and writing were the king's main intellectual recreations. The Bible was his favourite, followed closely by devotional works, such as Bishop Andrewes's *Sermons*, Richard Hooker's *Laws of Ecclesiastical Polity*, George Sandys's *Paraphrases on the Psalms of David*, and George Herbert's *Divine Poems*. He found such books a great consolation. 'Dum spero spiro,' he annotated one, 'While I hope I live.' For light reading he enjoyed Spenser's *Faerie Queene*, Shakespeare's plays (which he annotated), and Sir John Harrington's translation of Ludovico Ariosto's *Orlando Furioso*. Charles even did some translation for his own amusement, including *De Juramento* by Robert Sanderson, whom parliament had just deprived of the Regius Professorship of Theology at Oxford.

Although a prisoner Charles did not lack visitors. Some came to be touched for the king's evil, others to gawk as God's anointed walked the battlements or played bowls. Some visitors, such as Sir John Oglander, who rode over from Nunwell once a week with books from his library, were always most welcome. Others were not. For instance, Obadiah Sedgewick, an army chaplain, not only insisted that Charles read his recently published *Leaves on the Tree of Life*, but went on to the late hours elaborating on this 120–page exposition of a single – admittedly obstruse – verse of the Bible. Charles's tactful suggestion that the author needed some sleep sent the Reverend Obadiah happily to bed, convinced that his treatment of Revelations XXII, 2 was exhaustive, rather than exhausting.[43]

From such impositions Charles, like all prisoners, had to take comfort in small victories. When parliament dismissed his barber, he refused to let their man shave him, growing a beard and his hair long in protest. After Hammond slipped and hurt his back, Charles crowed with delight that it was divine punishment for 'incivility'.[44] As the days dragged he made the governor the lightning rod for his mounting frustrations. In July he wrote that Hammond had always treated him well and with respect; by late August that he was a barbarian, 'a pox ... for I think the Devil cannot out-go him neither in Malice nor Cunning.'[45]

During the last year of his life Charles found much pleasure in the company of ordinary people, realizing his own humanity from their simple loyalty. Like his son, Charles II, after the Battle of Worcester, or his great-grandson Bonnie Prince Charlie after Culloden Moor, in adversity he came to know his subjects in a way that few monarchs can. 'Let not cautiousness beget fear and be confident of me,' he encouraged Mrs Dowcett, the wife of his kitchen clerk, who was petrified lest parliament find out she had been smuggling letters to the queen. Charles was deeply touched when she eventually overcame her fears enough to send him a cheerful note.[46] He was especially grateful when his laundress, Mary Wheeler, and her daughter left and picked up messages under the rug in his room, telling them, 'I know that nothing will come amiss when it comes in thy hand.'[47] He deeply appreciated the loyalty of Captain Titus, originally one of the conservators parliament appointed to watch the king, who had come over to his side. At nights he and Henry Firebrace used to talk through a slit cut in his bedroom wall, hidden during the day by a tapestry. Charles responded to the ordinary kindness of all these humble folk with that sense of equality and mutual respect that in the past he had found so hard to show, and that is the hallmark of true friendship. 'All I have to say,' he told Titus, 'is that I see you well satisfied with me, so I am with you.' After the army dismissed Titus and Firebrace he wrote saying how much he valued their fealty as 'true Englishmen'.[48]

To fill the void left by their departure Charles's intimacy with William Hopkins grew. Hopkins, a friend of Sir John Oglander, was headmaster of Newport Grammar School. His royalism went back to August 1642, when a parliamentary mob sacked his house for signing a loyal manifesto. At first Charles and Hopkins plotted a rising of local royalists, in which Hammond was to be taken hostage to ensure the king's escape to France. Since this intrigue was nearly as hare brained as Captain Burley's, the king fortunately discarded it. When talks with parliament started in the autumn, Charles came to rely on the schoolmaster as a trusted counsellor. He treated Mrs Hopkins with a solicitude he had rarely shown the wives of his great officers of state, and even humoured their son who took offence at some unintended slight with that surliness painfully familiar to the parents of adolescents. 'As for yourself, be sure,' Charles promised the Hopkins family, 'when I keep house again there will be those, who shall think themselves happy & yet sit lower at the table than you.'[49]

Without doubt the most curious and, maybe, the most significant of Charles's friendships with ordinary people was that with Jane Whorwood. The exact nature of their relationship will never be fully known, not just because very little of their correspondence has survived, and most that remains being oblique notes through third parties in which Jane and Charles were very guarded, but because one gets the impression that neither really understood what was developing between them; and if they did, it both intrigued and frightened them.

Jane was the daughter of William Ryder of Kingston upon Thames, a surveyor of James I's stables. In 1634 at the age of nineteen she married Brome, the eldest son of Sir Thomas Whorwood, of Holton, Oxfordshire. By the end of the civil war it seems their marriage had broken down, or else Brome was an extraordinarily accommodating man who allowed his wife unusual freedom. In late 1647 Alderman Thomas Adams, leader of the City of London's royalists, sent her to Hampton Court with half of the £1,000 in gold he had collected for the king's use. Apparently the courier impressed both Charles and his powerful city friends. He asked her where he should go once he had got out from Hampton Court; Adams trusted her with the balance of the money, some of which she had Mrs Dowcett smuggle to the king, and the rest she used to buy files and nitric acid, and hire the get-away vessel on which she waited on the Medway in May. By July Jane was in the Isle of Wight, probably staying with the Hopkinses, with whom she soon became close friends. On 26 July Charles wrote to 'Sweet Jane Whorwood' suggesting that she might circumvent the Derby House rule that only those with their permission could visit him, by having Captain Anthony Mildmay invite her to his room, into which the king could come, thus supposedly meeting her by accident. He signed this letter 'your most loving Charles', and was soon describing himself as 'her best Platonic Lover or Servant'.[50] Over the next few months he sent her at least sixteen messages and met her several more times.[51] At the start of August he begged her not to leave the island. One can only guess why on 13 August he asked Hopkins to 'Tell Jane Whorwood ... her Platonic Way doth much spoil the taste of my mind.'[52] He chaffed when she and Mrs Hopkins could not come and see him, and then looked forward inordinately to their visits. When Jane did not reply to his letters, the king became testy. When she suffered some unspecified 'barbarity' from 'a pretended ... gentleman', he sent her a 'consoliatory letter'. The next day he followed with another hoping that it would bring 'her Contentment ... for her's to me gave me much.' By September Jane seemed to have mended her platonic ways, calling him 'my dear friend' and signing herself with the *nom de plume*, 'Your Most affectionate Helen'.[53]

What can – or should – be made of all this? While a life of the second Charles might briefly dismiss such a relationship as one more notch on that merry monarch's well-notched bed-post, for the first Charles the situation was very different. Although there is absolutely no evidence that they had an affair in the physical sense of the word, emotionally their relationship was important. For a man whose uxorious fidelity had become a byword, to call someone else's wife 'Sweet Jane Whorwood' and sign himself her 'loving Charles' would suggest he was more than the 'best Platonic Lover' to which he admitted. Jane was an attractive thirty-year-old woman, with a fine head of red hair, whom a parliamentary intelligence report described as 'a tall well fashioned and well languaged gentlewoman, with a round Visage and pock holes in her face.'[54] Although he showed his years Charles had grown personally, showing a capacity to give himself, make friends, and win the loyalty of ordinary people. If his fortunes had fallen, he was still king, and retained the aphrodisiac of power. He had not seen his wife for four years, during which the two had increasingly quar-

relled over fundamental issues, as communications between them deteriorated. Indeed Charles seemed not a little guilty about his feelings towards
Jane. Although he once assured her that if his wife found out about their
friendship he knew she would surely approve, Charles never once mentioned Jane to Henrietta Maria. Thus while we can never be sure of the
exact place Jane held in the king's affections, there is no doubt that it was
a very special one. In their last letter he told her that she gave him 'great
contentment'.[55] And as Charles had to face the consequences of starting –
and then losing – the second civil war he needed all the happiness he could
possibly get.

The immediate origins of the second civil war went back to the accord
Charles made with the Scots on Boxing Day 1647. His curt rejection of
parliament's overtures two days later prompted them into passing the vote
of 'no address' which forbade any further dealings with the king on pain of
treason. So Charles responded by justifying the alliance with a declaration
addressed 'To all my subjects, of whatsoever Nature, Quality or Condition'. In it the king maintained that although he had been wretchedly
treated his only goal was to protect his good people from the arbitrary
acts of a parliament that had long ceased to represent them. If parliament
had signed the Solemn League and Covenant in 1643 why should he not
make a similar agreement with the Scots? Such, after all, was the only way
peace could be restored to both kingdoms. This declaration was a clever
and effective piece of propaganda; unlike those that preceded the first civil
war, it was largely Charles's work. In its opening question, 'Am I to be
left alone,' Charles set Britain's agenda for the next six months by asking
if the realm should continue a monarchy.[56] Nevertheless the royalist revolts
that erupted following the declaration's publication were not specifically
intended to bring back the pre-1640 monarchy that Charles wanted. They
were rather the product of agitation in a war-weary land, when many were
coming to the reluctant conclusion that until the king should enjoy his
own again, they would never enjoy theirs.

Although in late 1646 Charles had been plotting a rising with Michael
Hudson, and in 1647 intriguing with Lord Capel, there is no evidence
from surviving letters that he directly stirred up the revolts that broke out
in the first five months of 1648.[57] They were basically spontaneous and
uncoordinated. In May an army mutiny, which royalists rapidly took over,
sparked the first in South Wales. Although Thomas Horton easily managed
to crush the royalists' main forces at St Fagan's near Cardiff before
Cromwell and his army arrived, the survivors' spirited defence of Pembroke castle tied him up for two months, leaving Fairfax to deal with
risings in Kent and Essex. The capture of Pembroke castle in July 1648
enabled Cromwell to move his forces northeast to counter the Scots who
had invaded England a week earlier, and had been formally welcomed by
the king's announcement that, 'it is no small' comfort to me that my native

country has so true a sense of my present condition.'[58] The covenanters had not long to savour His Majesty's favour, for at Preston on 17–19 August Cromwell brilliantly routed their much larger army. The second civil war was over, and with it died the king's hopes of gaining his goals by force of arms.

It had been a far more brutal fight than the first civil war. One veteran sardonically observed that Englishmen now treated their captured compatriots with the cruelty usually reserved for the Irish. For instance, after Michael Hudson agreed in return for quarter to surrender Woodcroft House in Northamptonshire, which he had raised in one of those hopeless gestures that were becoming a royalist forte, the roundheads threw him over the battlements. As he hung on to a drainage spout they hacked off his hands. He plummeted to the moat, where they finished him off with a musket blow to the head. Finally they cut out his tongue, an act of mutilation unheard of in England.[59] Again in late August 1648 following his capture of Colchester,the last royalist stronghold, General Fairfax shot two of the garrison's senior officers. Six months later Lord Capel was executed for his part in the siege.

The army's attitude to the king reflected this new spirit of vindictiveness. Many soldiers believed that he, and his supporters, were war criminals for refusing to accept the verdict of the first civil war. Rather like the defenders of a fortress who held out long beyond reason, they deserved no quarter. Lucy Hutchinson, whose husband was a leading army officer, put it this way: 'We found he had no intention to the people's good but to proceed by our factions to regain by art what he had lost in fight.'[60] So at a tearful and prayer-ridden three-day meeting of the council of war at Windsor castle in April the army resolved 'to call Charles Stuart, that man of blood, to an account for the blood he had shed and mischief he had done to his utmost against the Lord's causes and people.'[61]

The second civil war frightened the army and parliament in very different ways – the former got angry, and the latter got cold feet. On 29 July, three weeks after the scots had crossed the border, parliament once more voted to negotiate with the king. 'I have not great hope that much good will come of it,' Charles reacted initially, 'because I do not believe that those who come to Treat will have Power to debate, but only to propose.' The terms that the parliamentary commissioners, the Earl of Middlesex, Sir John Hippesley and John Bulkeley (the local MP for Yarmouth) presented at Carisbrooke on 7 August came as a pleasant surprise. Three days later Charles formally congratulated them that they had brought 'a fair beginning to a happy peace', particularly in view of the army's growing power.[62] Because he lacked advisers and thus 'I can no more treat than blind men judge colours,' the king requested that they might be allowd to rejoin him, and that the Scots be permitted to take part in the talks.[63] Although Charles convinced himself that the commissioners had returned to Westminster

'very well satisfied,' it took parliament nearly two weeks to repeal the vote
of 'no address' and open the way to formal talks, doing so, the king
sadly noted, by 'not so full a majority as I could have wished.'[64] Neither
parliament's reservations nor their refusal to let the Scots take part damp-
ened the king's spirits. 'For God forbid that either my two houses or I
should carp at circumstances to give the least impediment to this treaty,
much less the happy finding of it.'[65]

In agreeing to open talks parliament also let Charles leave Carisbrooke
Castle, with its unhappy memories of failed escape attempts and petty
harassments, for more congenial quarters in Newport. As he was taking a
last walk about the castle grounds he met the master gunner's nine-year-
old son, who was marching up and down a battlement. What was he doing,
asked the king. Defending your majesty, the lad replied. Smiling, Charles
patted his head. 'I am going away from here and do not expect to return,'
he confided, giving the boy the ruby ring which he used to hold his
cravat.[66]

In Newport Charles stayed with his friend, William Hopkins. Once
more faithful servants, Will Murray, Ashburnham, Firebrace, Mrs Wheeler,
and trusted advisers, Richmond, Hertford, Southampton and Lindsey, and
sober chaplains, Sanderson, Sheldon, Hammond, and even his old secretary,
Sir Edward Walker, attended the king.[67] Allowed out riding again, he
showed his old skills had not gone rusty; when going down the steep hill
to Newport the bridle broke, but he was able to stop his horse without
reins or breaking his neck.[68] Charles seemed to be acting as if he were a
real king once more. His coachmen were issued new livery, he encouraged
efforts to discover silver in Somerset, requested a favour from the governor
of Newfoundland, a pardon from the sheriffs of London, granted safe
conducts to John Kerckhoven and Lady Stanhope to return to England,
and appointed Sir Simonds D'Ewes, keeper of the royal libraries and medal
collection.[69] Happy days really seemed here again when Elizabeth Steben,
a sixteen-year-old gentlewoman from Winchester, claimed her sight had
been much improved after being touched by the king.[70] Although this
seemed a good omen for the start of talks, Charles hedged his bets. 'If the
guilt of our great sins cause this Treaty to break off in vain,' he publicly
prayed, 'let the truth clearly appear whom those men are which under
pretence of the public good do preserve their private ends.'[71]

On Monday morning, 18 September, talks opened at Newport Grammar
School. Charles sat under the canopy of state, at the head of a large
table, with his advisers behind him, facing the parliamentary delegation.
Negotiations were conducted by exchange of notes. If either party wanted
to discuss a point amongst themselves, they retired to adjacent rooms.

At first the talks went well. After once more raising the issue of partici-
pation of the Scots – a question so dead that Charles's infatuation with it
amounted almost to necrophilia – he quickly agreed to parliament's first

major demand for the revocation of all his wartime acts and ordinances, on the condition that no concession from either side be binding until the whole treaty had been signed.[72] On 25 September the commissioners presented their second major set of proposals: the abolition of the prayer book and of bishops, the sale of their lands, and the establishment of Presbyterianism. For Charles these were the key issues. As the commissioners spent the next day relaxing with Hammond at Carisbrooke, playing bowls and firing off the cannon, he wrestled with that mighty opponent, his conscience. After another day of prayer and fasting brought no answer, he asked one of his chaplains, Dr Hammond (the governor's uncle) to draft a reply. Since Hammond's answer failed to satisfy the king's scruples, he resorted to the familiar tactic of delay, suggesting that they first deal with less controversial matters.[73] The commissioners would have none of it: neither would parliament, to whom he tried to appeal behind their commissioners' backs. So both sides had to spend the first week of October debating the thorny issue of church government. On 8 October the king made a major concession. He would accept all parliament's demands so long as they did not include the total abolition of bishops. After eight more weeks' debate (and the exchange of countless biblical citations), the commissioners eventually accepted the king's proposals for an agreement that bishops should be abrogated for three years, after which a committee of sixty divines should settle church government.[74]

Concessions on other areas came more easily. On 9 October the king agreed to surrender the militia for twenty years, and two days later, did the same for the government of Ireland, Consent was soon reached on minor matters, including the abolition of the court of wards, the disenfranchisement of peers created since 1642, the appointment of chief officers of state, and the confirmation of London's rights and privileges. On the last sticky issue, pardon for royalists, Charles managed to get the number excluded much reduced. Just before the initial forty-day limit expired on 6 November, parliament extended it for another fourteen days, and when that ran out, and the commissioners were actually waiting in Cowes for the ferry to take them back to the mainland, parliament sent another four-day extension, at the end of which agreement was reached.[75]

In coming to terms, the first time he ever did so with parliamentary commissioners, Charles conceded thirty-eight of their demands in return for four of his own.[76] He agreed to restrictions on the power of the monarchy and modifications to the Church of England far greater than any proposed in 1641, or even in the years immediately after the first civil war. Some royalists at Newport thought the treaty a sell-out and in protest barricaded themselves in the George Inn, from which it took four files of musketeers to dislodge them. The treaty did not impress Sir John Oglander. Sardonically he wondered if it would usher in a utopia, the fulfilment of everyone's wildest wish, and – after the worst summer he could remember – 'fair weather'?

Why then did Charles give up so much – even if it did turn out to be too little and too late?

A simple answer was that he was frightened by the growing power of the army, and was as desperate to come to terms with parliament as they were with him. Yet the process through which the king operated at Newport was a little more complicated. When talks started, he seemed confident. 'The king is wonderfully improved,' noted the Earl of Salisbury.[77] Every evening he would discuss the day's talks with his advisers, before dictating summaries (all since lost) for his son. Quickly, however, Charles realized that parliament was obdurate. After he gave way on the church, he had second thoughts, and tried to run from a situation that was becoming increasingly intolerable. 'I pray you be quick and diligent in freeing me,' he begged Hopkins on the night of 9 October, having just ceded the militia for twenty years, the one point his wife had berated him not to give up. Two days later he implored Hopkins, 'as you Love my Safety, go on cheerfully with your preparations, for I cannot make good what I now put them in hope of . . .' The following night he confessed that he had granted, and would continue to grant concessions 'which will directly make me no king,' adding, 'I am lost if I do not escape.' A week afterwards he confessed he could only stall for a couple more days at the most.[78] Charles's desperation was as intense as his chances of successfully getting away were hopeless. Details of the king's plans were common gossip in Newport. The Derby House Committee alerted Hammond about Charles's final effort of 12 November within twenty-four hours of its suggestion.[79]

Realizing that he could no longer flee, and must make a peace that was daily becoming as odious as it was unrealistic, Charles nearly broke down, confessing to his son of a 'great trouble of mind'.[80] One evening Sir Philip Warwick remembered the king had to turn his back to his advisers lest they notice his tears. Another evening, as they were going over the day's business, Gipsy, Charles's greyhound, scratched against the door. As he let him in Warwick asked his sovereign if he preferred greyhounds to spaniels. 'Yes,' came the reply, 'for they equally love their masters, yet they do not flatter them so much.' Frequently the king took refuge in misery. 'Rebus in adversis facile est contemnere vitam: Fortiter ille facit qui miser esse potest,' he annotated a book, expressing his melancholy that, 'In hard times it is easy to despise life; he acts bravely who is able to be unhappy.'[81] On another occasion Charles compared himself to the commander of a fort ordered to hold to the last man and so turn his defences into his own tomb. Sometimes Charles blamed his advisers. 'I wish I had consulted nobody but my own self, for then, when in honour or conscience I could not have complied I could have easily been positive; for with Job I would have willingly have chosen misery than ruin.'[82]

333

The king's anguish was apparent in the speech he gave the commissioners when they left Newport on 27 November to return to Westminster to have parliament accept the terms they had worked out.[83]

> 'My Lords, you are come to take your leave of me, and I believe that we shall surely never see one another again. But God's will be done. I thank God I shall make my peace with him, and shall not fear whatsoever he shall suffer men to do unto me. You cannot but know that in my fall and ruin you see your own, and that also of those near unto you. I pray you God send you better friends than I have found.'

Two days later Charles wrote to his son, 'The Commissioners are gone; the corn is now in the ground; we expect the harvest.'[84] Planted in stony soil, the seed sprang up to be reaped two nights later.

Although the origins of the army's decision to arrest and try the king may be traced back months, even years, to the growth of radicalism among the rank and file, and to the council of war's meeting at Windsor in April 1648 that vowed revenge on 'Charles Stuart, that man of blood', in fact the decision to bring him to justice was not taken until 16 November. The following day Henry Ireton, Thomas Harrison, and John Desborough ordered Hammond to imprison Charles at Carisbrooke. When Hammond refused without written orders from parliament, they recalled him to the army's headquarters at Farnham, where he was arrested.

On 29 November Colonel Ralph Cobbet and Captain John Merriman arrived in the Isle of Wight with instructions from the army council to seize the king. Suspecting some coup Charles spent the day in prayer, and heard his chaplain, Dr Henry Ferne, preach on the text: 'Though it tarry, wait for it, because it will surely come, it will not tarry.'[85] Afterwards Charles wrote his son a tearful letter: 'We know not but this may be the last time we may speak to you, or the world publicly. We are sensible into whose hands we are fallen.'[86]

A little before eight the next evening Firebrace came to the king's room to pick up some letters. He told Charles that the situation was desperate: the castle was surrounded by the van of the 2,000 infantry which had landed on the island that morning. When Charles replied there was no need to be so worried, since Hammond had only gone to London on personal business, Firebrace explained that the army had arrested the governor. However, there was still just enough time to slip through the chaos of the troop take-over in the November gloom to take John Newland's boat for freedom.[87] Charles hesitated. He called Richmond and Lindsey to inquire if they knew what was going on. They asked Captain Edward Cooke, an officer from Hammond's regiment, who had secretly come over to the king. He replied he did not know what was taking place: so they sent him to Newport to ask Major Rolph. This ex-shoemaker, and ardent

Leveller, who had just been acquitted by a court martial for threatening to kill the king, ominously replied that Charles would be safe for 'that night'. Disregarding his warning, and Lindsey and Southampton's entreaties, Charles would not try and escape, saying it was impossible. When they argued that he could slip through the confusion caused by the army's take-over and even sent Cooke out through the milling soldiers to prove the assertion, Charles still refused. The army would be angry. He might fail. He could not break his parole. When Lindsey reminded him that his escape from Hampton Court had worked, Charles agreed to let Cooke, who by now had learnt the password, walk through the sentries disguised in a thick cloak. Even though once again he managed to pass in and out without alerting their suspicions, Charles refused to escape. It could not – it would not work. Cooke, Lindsey and Southampton all pleaded with him to try, arguing that his parole was no longer binding since the army had broken theirs by arresting Hammond and reinforcing the garrison. Charles was obdurate. Before going to bed at one in the morning he wrote himself a note explaining his reasons for staying.[88]

By the time a violent knocking at the door woke the king early the next morning, it was too late. Sir Henry Mildmay went to see who was there. An army officer shouted that he must see the king immediately. Charles told Mildmay to open up. The soldiers barged in. They ordered the king to get dressed: they were going to take him away.

'Where?' Charles asked.

'To the castle.'

'What castle?'

'The castle.'

'What castle,' the exasperated monarch noted, 'is no castle at all.'

So, after hurried whispers, the officers told him, 'Hurst castle.'

'You could not have chosen a worse,' the king replied.

There was worse to come. Colonel Cobbet, whom by now Charles realized was the leader of the new troops, refused to show him his orders from General Fairfax. Instead he forced the king into his coach so quickly that he did not have time to eat the hot breakfast that Firebrace had arranged. Cobbet posted troops about the coach to stop the royal servants from kissing their master's hand farewell. Major Rolph tried to join the king inside, but Charles managed to literally boot the Leveller out saying, 'It is not come to that yet.' Accompanied only by Sir Thomas Herbert, who had dragged himself from his sick-bed, and James Harrington, Charles was driven to Worsley Tower, a bleak spot a little beyond Yarmouth to wait for the boat that eventually took him the choppy three-hour sail to Hurst castle.[89]

Hurst castle was a dismal place. Built by Henry VIII, its thick damp walls had all the charm of a modern pillbox. Its governor, a fierce swarthy fellow treated the king so rudely that even Major Rolph had to reprimand him, whereupon the fellow displayed all the obsequiousness of the fallen bully. Charles's room was small and poky. It was so dark that he needed candles to read at noon. Often he would walk along the beach, the pebbles crunching under foot, talking with Herbert and Harrington, as he looked across the Solent at the patrolling parliamentary squadron, and the low grey outline of the Isle of Wight beyond.

Rapidly the king's predicament got worse. In London on 6 December the army purged parliament of its opponents. Colonel Pride stood at parliament's door turning away those listed by his seniors, and throwing the recalcitrants into a cold room (misleadingly known as 'Hell'). Now parliament was a rubber stamp, ready to do whatever the soldiers wished: and what they wanted, more than anything else, was to try Charles Stuart.

Back at Hurst castle the army expelled Harrington from the king's service for vigorously defending his master when some officers accused him of perfidy. Charles used the faithful servant's departure to smuggle a new cipher to Nicholas Oudart, and a note to Firebrace that although he had 'little or no news', he was to forward his best wishes to his friends, including Titus, Lady Carlisle, and Jane Whorwood.[90] After a couple of weeks of being (to use the king's own description) 'closely kept & civily used,' he was woken one night by the noise of the drawbridge being operated at midnight. The next morning he called Herbert to ask what it meant. From Captain Reynolds, the servant learned that Colonel Thomas Harrison, one of Fairfax's aides, and a leading advocate of trying the king, had arrived. The news upset Charles so much, for he was sure that Harrison had come to murder him secretly, that Herbert burst into tears. The king told Herbert to cease, and go and find out the reason for Harrison's visit: he was doubtless relieved to learn the colonel brought orders to move him to Windsor castle.

As usual, the prospect of a journey, particularly to one of his own castles, cheered the king. On 19 December he and Cobbet walked the couple of miles along the shingle spit to the mainland where they mounted horses to ride through the New Forest, scene of many a happier gallop, to Winchester. Here the mayor and local gentry warmly welcomed Charles. The next day outside Alresford a cavalry squadron lined the road, its commander smartly saluting his sovereign. Charles asked the colonel's name, and on being told it was Harrison, said he was surprised that so odious a man should be so handsome. At Farnham, just before supper Charles noticed Harrison at the other end of the room. Beckoning the colonel over, he told him that he suspected he had come to Hurst castle to murder him. Harrison denied such had ever been the military's intentions, for 'the law was equally obliging to great and small.' The next day at Bagshot Charles's faint hopes of escape evaporated, when the horse, supposedly the swiftest in England, Oudart had waiting at Lord Newbury's house, where the king stopped for dinner, suddenly went lame.

Arriving at Windsor castle on 22 December, the king was lodged in his usual rooms. He spent the next few mornings in prayer, and the afternoons strolling with Colonel Whichot along the battlements. He attended church in St George's Chapel, which now seemed naked without the banners of the Knights of the Garter that used to hang above the stalls. When Hugh Peter, the ranting Puritan, tried to preach, the king walked out. At Windsor trivial details preoccupied Charles and his last personal servant, Sir Thomas Herbert. After an exciting career travelling in India and the Middle East, parliament appointed Herbert to the king's service at Holdenby. Gradually he came over to his master, serving him with efficient civility, rather than the devotion he emphasized in his *Memoirs of the Last Years of the Reign of King Charles I*, first published in 1678. One day he lost and then found his master's diamond seal. One night Herbert placed his pallet bed so close to the fire that it caught alight, and the king had to put it out, adamantly refusing the help of his guards who hammered at the door demanding to know what was going on. Another morning Herbert overslept, allowing his master to wake first. When he apologized, for the strain was beginning to show on the normally impeccable valet, Charles told him not to worry, promising to give him an alarm clock (which he did). Sir John Temple reported that the king seemed not to take any notice of the preparations to put him on trial for his life. He ordered some melon seeds kept so they could be planted in the spring for his enjoyment at harvest tide. The king clung to old long dead hopes. 'He hath a strange conceit of my Lord of Ormond working for him in Ireland,' Temple noticed on 3 January 1649, 'he hangs still upon that twig.'[91] But even that twig had to snap after a surprise search of the king's rooms turned up some secret correspondence, and the army increased the guard so tightly that they severed all communications with his wife and friends.

Only the parody of pomp remained. On 19 January the king's coach, drawn by six horses, waited outside the castle. Below the keep the roads were lined with musketeers and pike men, not as a guard of honour but to foil any rescue. Harrison's squadron waited to escort His Majesty to London. He was silent as his coach bumped and rolled over the ice-rutted road through Brentford and Hammersmith, retracing the way he had taken just over seven years before when he fled London after failing to arrest the Five Members. As he entered his capital, unnoticed, and a prisoner, he had a good idea what was to be his fate. 'I do expect the worst,' Charles wrote at Hurst castle, anticipating the moment for which the past few months – perhaps indeed much of his life – had been but a prologue.[92]

A decade earlier in 1638 Charles had threatened, 'I will rather die than yield to the <u>impertinent</u> and damnable demands ... of <u>these traitors</u>, the covenanters.'[93] After two wars against the Scots, the calling of the Long and Short Parliaments, the fiasco of the Five Members, one Irish Rebellion, two civil wars, fighting five major battles and countless skirmishes, after at least half a dozen attempts to negotiate a peace, and nigh as many to effect an escape, Charles found his rhetoric becoming reality. Of course, not until very late in the day did killing the king seem anything more than a heinous fantasy. Although such groups as the Levellers wanted him tried, the army commanders, Ireton and Cromwell, did not accept the idea until November 1648; as late as Christmas they would have let Charles live if he had agreed to become a figurehead like the Doge of Venice. Even though his enemies decided to execute him and turn England into a republic only three months before they did so, for a decade before Charles was convinced that this was their intention all along. His original rationale for vowing to die rather than give in to the covenanters was that their real aim was not the abolition of the prayer book, but of monarchy itself. Eight years later, following his defeat in war, he confided to the French ambassador that many of his opponents wanted 'the extirpation of Monarchy, and particularly of my Family'.[94] Building on an erroneous premise, Charles refused to make realistic concessions, and thus self-fulfilled his own false prophecies.

In a way things would have been easier for the king and his cause if he had always refused to give an inch. The possibility of compromise needlessly prolonged the fighting, making it far more bitter. The process of compromise laid the king open to charges of negotiating in bad faith, and caused him intense guilt. Invariably he conceded at great psychological cost for a negligible political return, the former always ensuring the latter was too little and came too late. All this came from the king's unyielding and authoritarian personality. During this process one part of the king's personality emerged to dominate the rest. What we might call his super-ego, and what Charles knew as his conscience, became so mighty a force that a few days before his execution he wrote to his son that his conscience, 'I thank God, is dearer to me than a thousand kingdoms.'[95]

The psychological climate in which monarchs grew up and ruled made it hard for them to compromise. Even Elizabeth and James (who would never have come to the English throne had they not been devious negotiators) had to camouflage their concessions with the trappings of divine right. According to this widely accepted theory – which was a most welcome salve to so weak an ego as Charles's – a monarch should neither answer to, nor bargain with, his people. Those who surrounded the king during the balmy days of peace confirmed this view with their plays, masques and paintings. Paradoxically in the awful days after the war the king's companions, ordinary folk, such as Titus, Firebrace, the Hopkinses, the Wheelers, Jane Whorwood, Ashburnham and Herbert, all did the same. It was as if the 1636 masque had been right all along: even if a flunkey had shooed away the simple peasants who wanted to see Charles and Henrietta Maria to present them with some baked pumpkins, when given the chance the real people truly loved their king.

The conditions in which Charles was asked to compromise were particularly trying. Although he was still king (albeit beaten nine and ninety times), and was treated as the sovereign, being served his food on bended knee right up until two days before his trial, for most of the twenty months after the Scots took him to Newcastle he recognized he was in reality a prisoner. The tensions between being a monarch and a captive sometimes produced the uncharacteristic rudeness with which he rejected peace overtures, forcing him into a new painful image of himself, particularly when the chasm between form and reality became unbearably wide. 'You use me neither like a gentleman nor a Christian,' he cried out to Colonel Hammond.[96] At the same time,. however, suffering made him realize his own worth as a man rather than a monarch, which the loyalty and friendship of ordinary men and women confirmed.

Compromise also increased his guilty feelings, adding to that burden he bore for betraying Wentworth. Time and time again Charles dwelt on this agony. During the negotiations for the Treaty of Newport, when he was already upset for having conceded so much, he called the betrayal 'the greatest sin he had ever committed.'[97] Although in the long run denying his friends led Charles (like St Peter or St Paul) to martyrdom, in the short term it pushed him towards escape.[98]

Bolting is one response to any human dilemma. Although Charles was not a physical coward, he did run away from Oxford and Hampton Court, and was only too happy to leave Newcastle, Holdenby and Carisbrooke. He left the first two and tried to escape from Carisbrooke without any clear idea of where he was headed, the push of an intolerable situation being far stronger than the pull of a workable solution. Perhaps this explains an ambivalence towards escape that sometimes seemed so strong that it appeared he was courting failure.

Like the hero in classic Greek tragedy, Charles learned wisdom through suffering. And suffer he did. Even though his health remained surprisingly good, he soon lost the hardness that four years of campaigning had produced.[99] Signs of strain were obvious (see Plate 12): the veins on his hands became more prominent; his hair got thinner and turned grey; his face seemed more haggard; the Scots barbarously baited him; ensigns kidnapped him; sanctimonious divines bored him; soldiers searched his rooms. To deal with these tribulations Charles developed a droll sense of humour. 'Madam: if my condition were according to your wishes for me,' he wrote to Lady Worcester in October 1648, 'I should not have been long in answering your letter.'[100] Sometimes the sardonic shell collapsed to reveal maudlin self-pity:

> My life they prize at such a slender rate
> That in my absence they draw bills of hate
> To prove the king a traitor to the State.

None the less Charles realized his sufferings not only helped redeem his guilt, but brought wisdom. 'We bless God we have those inward refreshments that the malice of our enemies cannot disturb. We have learnt to own ourself by retiring unto ourself and therefore can the better digest what befalls us,' he observed in November 1648.[101] Less than two months later he wrote to his son, 'It is some kind of deceiving and lessening the injury of long restraint, when I find my leisure and solitude have produced something worthy of myself and useful to you.'[102]

The new role as a parent that Charles had been forced to adopt after the war divided his family brought him both happiness and despair, self-knowledge and hope for the future. He enjoyed seeing James, Henry and Elizabeth, relishing a sense of intimacy with them he had never before known with any of his children. The contrast between the stern distant figure whom Hendrick Pot had painted stolidly standing at the other end of a long table from his wife and heir (see Plate 5), and the father worrying about his children's safety or trying to explain why he could not come and see them as he promised is moving. 'Dear Daughter,' he wrote to Elizabeth in 1647, 'this is to assure you that it is not through forgetfulness or want of kindness that I have not all this time sent for you, but for reasons as is fitter for you to imagine.' A year later he had to explain why she had not heard from him. 'Dear Daughter, it is not from want of Affection that makes me write so seldom to you, but want of matter such as I could wish; and indeed I am loath to write to those I love when I am out of humour (as I have been these days past) lest my letters should trouble those I desire to please.'[103] This new love for his children, which was warmly reciprocated, helped make the prospect of his own death a little easier: they were pledges of both his own immortality and that the crown of England might continue. So in his last years Charles shifted his aspirations from his wife to his eldest son to ensure that the king would not die in vain.

Through his death, the ultimate human act, Charles managed to resolve the tensions between compromise and conscience that went back to his earliest years. Charles disliked ambiguity. Thus he often took seemingly decisive actions in moments of great anxiety. He dissolved parliament in March 1629 and again in May 1640. He found a great relief in raising the royal standard in August 1642, and gained a sense of great inner peace in seeking martyrdom – death being the least ambiguous moment in our lives. Although martyrdom might engender the suspicion that one was in fact committing the sin of suicide, or else might be doing the right deed for the wrong reason, it was the most complete act of redemption – martyrdom was the great escape, the only way one can win by losing.

A quarter of a century before, on 3 April 1625, John Donne preached his first court sermon of the new reign on the text, 'If the foundations be destroyed what can the righteous do.' He told Charles that, 'The Holy

Church of God, ever delighted herself in a holy officiousness in the Com-
memoration of Martyrs.' Eight months later at his coronation Charles
heard a sermon preached on the text, 'Be faithful unto death and I will
give you the crown of life.'[104] As he grew older Christ's question, 'What
profiteth a man if he gain the whole world and lose his soul,' had great
meaning for the king. At Holdenby he asked for a copy of *The Crown of
Thornes*.[105] The shouts of 'Judas! Judas!' the Newcastle fishwives shouted
at the Scots as they handed him over to parliament for far more than thirty
pieces of silver, did not displease the king. Neither did the image of the
patient Christ-like martyr that his disciples created in *Eikon Basilike* (see
Plate 13).

*Eikon Basilike*, or the *King's Book*, is a remarkable work.[106] Published
immediately after Charles's death, it went into thirty-five English editions
within a year. Purportedly written by the king during his captivity, *Eikon
Basilike* was in fact the work of John Gauden, Dean of Bocking in Essex.
It portrayed Charles as a noble martyr dying for the sins of his people.
The book is in many ways a caricature of the king. Charles says many of
the sorts of things that he might have said, or wished he had indeed said.
As evidence for his character it is unreliable not because it distorts the
truth but because it parodies it. Yet as a broadly drawn model to which
the king could aspire, and by which his followers could remember him,
*Eikon Basilike* was a potent force. Gauden wrote from Charles's notes,
and since the king reviewed his drafts he was fully aware of the larger
than life picture of himself that he was helping create, and which only his
death could fully realize. Like John Foxe's *Book of Martyrs*, which Charles
also read during the long hours at Carisbrooke, *Eikon Basilike* was a text-
book on the right way to die. In it Charles helped write the script for his
last – and greatest – role which he described as 'the honour of a kind of
martyrdom'.[107]

Just as in the last act of court masques fantasy and reality became one,
Charles truly seemed to find that inner serenity that *Eikon Basilike*
accorded him. 'I thank God that I shall make my peace with him,' he told
the parliamentary commissioners as they left Newport speaking, one present remembered, 'with much cheerfulness and serene contentment and
courage free from disturbances.'[108] Two days later, when the army arrested
him, another eyewitness recalled, 'he showed no discomposure at all.' If
he had been asked how he felt on being taken to London for his trial, and
anticipated execution, he might well have answered with the words of the
poem 'On a quiet conscience,' that many believed he had just written.[109]

Close thine eyes and sleep secure,
Thy soul is safe, thy body sure.
He that guards thee, he that keeps
Never slumbers, never sleeps.

## CHARLES I

A quiet conscience on thy breast
Has only peace, has only rest.

# XIX

# 'AN INCORRUPTIBLE CROWN'

So when this corruptible shall have put on incorruption and this mortal shall have put on immortality, then shall be brought to pass the saying that is written, Death is swallowed up in victory.

1 Corinthians 15, 54

The last act in Charles's life opened in an appropriate theatre.[1] On Saturday, 20 January 1649, the king's trial began in Westminster Hall. It was the biggest room in the kingdom, 300 feet long with massive hammer-roof beams, having been originally built by William Rufus in 1097, three years before his own violent death. Here Edward II had been forced to abdicate in 1327. Here, in the palace he had rebuilt, Richard II was deposed in 1399 in a dramatic confrontation whose essence Shakespeare captured with the Bishop of Carlisle's question, 'What subject can pass sentence on his king?'[2] Here Sir Thomas More had been condemned in an equally powerful dramatic piece. Here it was that Guy Fawkes and the Earl of Strafford had been tried. However, the hall was not just the theatre for exceptional cases. Everyday it was the apex of England's court system, where Common Pleas, King's Bench, Chancery, and Exchequer sat, divided with chest-high partitions, and surrounded by stationers' booths, coffee shops, and taverns.

Perhaps the army leaders chose Westminster Hall for the king's trial in the hope that its ordinariness might help legitimize their proceedings. Even though Algernon Sidney had warned Cromwell that, 'First the king can be tried by no court and secondly no man can be tried by this court,' they were determined that some court must try the king.[3] So on 6 January, two days after passing a motion claiming to represent all the people of England, the army's puppet Rump Parliament voted to establish a high court of some 135 named judges to hear the case against Charles Stuart. Only fifty-three of those nominated turned up on 8 January for the court's first session held in the Painted Chamber, adjacent to the House of Lords. They appointed John Ashe, Anthony Steele, Isaac Dorislaus and John Cook prosecutors, of whom the latter quickly emerged as leader. Cook was a barrister from Gray's Inn, a republican and religious enthusiast. He had some advanced ideas about temperance, and a national health and legal aid service, but was a solid enough fellow; a dedicated prosecutor, with the cutting edge that only complete self-righteousness can bestow. Two days later the court elected another Gray's Inn barrister, John Bradshaw, their Lord President. He too was a competent jurist, who after a successful career in London became Chief Justice of Cheshire. To his new appointment Bradshaw brought some prestige, more legal learning, and the abundant certainty that he was doing his duty.

On the morning of 20 January the army moved Charles in an enclosed sedan chair from St James's Palace to Whitehall Steps, where he boarded a heavily curtained barge. They were taking no chances. Two hundred soldiers guarded the inside of Westminster Hall, another two companies stood by outside, and boat loads of musketeers escorted the king's barge as it was rowed the half mile to the steps near Sir Robert Cotton's house, which was one of several private residences between Westminster Palace and the Thames. Here he was lodged in a bedroom next to Sir Robert's study, where the antiquarian had kept the library and papers that Charles had seized two decades before. At Cotton's house the guards treated the king with scant respect, smoking and keeping their hats on in his presence and barging into his room without knocking, as his servants vainly tried to maintain some semblance of royal dignity.

About a quarter of an hour after the court had come to order, with 68 out of the 135 judges answering the roll call, a dozen halberdiers under Colonel Tomlinson marched Charles into Westminster Hall. He would hardly have recognized the place. The stalls and partitions of the old law courts were gone. At the north end of the hall was a stage where Lord President Bradshaw sat on a velvet chair, with a desk in front and his fellow judges seated on benches behind. In the middle of the stage two clerks sat, pens poised to take notes on a table covered with a Turkish carpet, whereon also rested the Lord President's sword and mace of office. In the enclosed dock facing the judges, was a red velvet chair, and on its right a small table with pen and ink and paper. Behind the dock a high partition ran almost the whole width of the hall, cutting off all but the top of the prisoner's head from the view of the audience who stood in the well behind the line of pikemen. Around the wall and in the corners of the hall workmen had erected special stands, from which fee paying spectators could see the king march in. The sergeant of arms gestured him to enter the dock. Charles looked sternly around, first at the judges, then at the people in the galleries, before sitting down. He got up, turned round once more to gaze at the audience, and guards, and sat down. To his friends the king appeared calm: to his enemies he seemed insolent for having refused to remove his hat in the judges' presence. Calling for silence Bradshaw told Cook to read the charges. Being 'trusted with a limited power to govern by and according to the Law of the Land ... for the benefit of the people,' the indictment accused the king of having 'traitor-ously and maliciously waged war against his people'.[4]

Cook had read only a few words before Charles tried to get his attention. 'Hold a little,' he said, tapping the prosecutor on the shoulder with the silver-headed cane that he invariably carried, and which in happier days he had often had himself painted holding as a symbol of his rank.[5] The attorney took no notice. Charles tapped again, and again. On the third occasion the silver tip of the cane fell off, and rolled noisily across the hastily constructed wooden floor. It was a dramatic moment; one that every observer in the hushed hall clearly recalled. No one dared move to pick up the tip. Charles waited for a servant to do so, before realizing that for the first time in his life there was no minion ready to attend to his slightest need, and that he was utterly alone to fend for himself. 'It really made a great impression on me,' he confessed a few days later.[6] Still the king quickly regained his composure. As Cook droned on reading the charge, Charles got up, looked around, sat down again, and when the indictment called him 'a tyrant and traitor', laughed out aloud. After the charges were finished Bradshaw asked the king to plead: 'The court expects an answer.'

'I would know by what power I am called hither,' the king replied. Pointing out that he had been arrested in the midst of negotiations with parliament and forcibly brought to London, he demanded, 'Now I would know by what authority, I mean lawful; there are many unlawful authori-ties in the world, there are robbers and highwaymen.' After this telling dig, Charles shifted from a legal to an absolutist defence. 'Remember I am your king, your lawful king, and what sins you bring upon your hand, and the judgement of God upon his land.' Then he returned to the legal argument. 'Let me know by what lawful authority am I seated here, and I shall not be unwilling to answer.'

Bradshaw explained that he had been brought to trial 'in the name of the people of England, of which you are elected king.'

'England was never an elective kingdom, but a hereditary kingdom for these thousand years,' Charles crushingly replied. 'I do stand more for the liberty of my people than any here that come to be my pretended Judges,' he went on, adding that he would be betraying 'that duty I owe to God, and my country,' if he were 'to submit to a tyrannical or any other ways unlawful authority.'

Realizing that the king was getting the better of the fight, Bradshaw ordered the court adjourned until Monday, saying that the judges were fully satisfied their authority was legitimate. Their satisfaction, the prisoner retorted, was immaterial: what counted was the law. As he was being led out some in the crowd heckled him, 'Justice! Justice!' and others 'God save the King!' Charles seemed confident. Having won the first round with dignity and some devastating punches, he had cause enough to say as he walked past the sword of justice that lay on the clerk's table, 'I have no fear of that.'

In many ways the second day's trial on 22 January was a repeat of the first. Cook asked Charles how did he plead, explaining that a refusal would be taken *pro confesso* as an automatic plea of guilty according to the well-established legal precedent.

'I know as much law as any gentleman in England,' Charles frigidly answered, and thus wanted to know by what law he was being tried. 'It is not my case alone, it is the Freedom and the Liberty of the people of England,' for which he claimed to be standing. 'For if power without law may make laws, may alter the fundamental law of the Kingdom, I do not know what subject he is in England that can be sure of his life.'

Thus the argument went around and around for perhaps another half an hour, with the king refusing to plead and Bradshaw insisting he must.

'Sir, you are not to dispute our authority.'

'I do not know how a king can become a delinquent.'

'Sir, neither you, nor any man are permitted to dispute that point,' Bradshaw replied, arguing that the court's mandate came from the Commons of England.

'I deny that. Show me one precedent.'

'Sir, you are not to interrupt while the Court is speaking to you.'

'I say, Sir, by your favour,' answered the king, with sarcastic politeness, 'that the Commons of England was never a Court of Judicature. I would know how that can be so?'

Eventually Bradshaw managed to silence the king. The clerk re-read the charges. Charles refused to plead. The Lord President ordered him taken away.

'I do require that you give me my Reasons . . .'

'Sir, 'tis not for prisoners to require.'

'*Prisoner, Sir*! *I am not an ordinary prisoner,*' replied the king in so devastating a tone that even the hacks of parliament allowed to record the trial printed it in italics.

Having lost round two, Bradshaw ordered the king taken back to Sir Robert Cotton's house. One trooper called out 'God bless you, Sir' as the king walked past. His officer hit him on the head with a cane, prompting Charles to observe, 'The punishment exceeded the offence.' Back in his room Charles prayed for a while. Refreshed, he told Herbert he was sure that the ordinary soldiers bore him no malice, their officers having commanded them to shout 'Justice! Justice!' as he was taken out of court. His judges were no better. They were such an insignificant group of men he could only recognize eight of them.[7]

The following day the king continued his successful tactic of refusing to plead. When Bradshaw tried to have him answer the indictment that Cook once more read out in full, Charles replied, 'For the charge I value it not a Rush. It is the liberty of the People of England I stand for.' Half an hour later, and not a moment too soon for the prosecution, Bradshaw ordered the king removed and the court adjourned to meet the next day in the Painted Hall. Here, without the prisoner, the court heard evidence that added little to the case against the king, though it may have done something to soothe the judges' tattered nerves. John Bennet of Harwood, Yorkshire, testified he saw Charles Stuart raise the royal standard at Nottingham. Arthur Young, barber-surgeon of London, swore that he had seen him at Edgehill. David Evans of Abergavenny remembered the accused being at Naseby. John Moore from Cork recalled him at both Newbury and at the sack of Leicester. Michael Potts of Sharperton, Northumberland, placed the accused at Cropredy Bridge and again at Lostwithiel. And so on they prattled, a total of thirty-three witnesses underscoring the fact that the prosecution's case was as long in facts as it was short in law.

Such deficiencies did not deter the sixty-seven judges, who assembled privately at ten in the morning of 27 January in the Painted Chamber. They voted that 'Charles Stuart, as a Tyrant, Traitor, Murderer, and Public Enemy to the good people of this nation, shall be put to death by the severing of his Head from his body.' After adjourning for lunch the court reassembled in Westminster Hall for sentencing. As the escort marched Charles in the troops in the hall shouted, 'Execution! Justice! Execution!' Bradshaw was wearing his full scarlet judicial robes, to show the seriousness of what he had to do (as well as a black hat with steel plates sewn inside to acknowledge the danger of doing it). Guessing his fate Charles took the initiative, for he knew as well as any gentleman in England that according to law a man sentenced to death could no longer address the court.

'I desire a word to be heard a little, and I hope I shall give no cause of interruption.'

'You may answer in your time, hear the court first.'

'If it please you, Sir, I desire to be heard.'

'Sir, you shall be heard in due time, but you are to hear the Court first,' Bradshaw insisted. He eventually shut the prisoner up with the promise to let him speak before passing sentence. Once more the charges against the king were read out, and once more Charles refused to plead. This time he broke new ground. Arguing that as the consequences of the 'ugly sentence, which I believe will pass upon me,' would be so horrendous and could not be undone, he proposed that his case be transferred to a joint session of parliament.

Although Bradshaw would have none of it, others liked the idea. As the Lord President announced that justice had been delayed long enough already, a heated argument broke out among the judges who sat behind him. In spite of Cromwell's hissed reproof, 'Art thou mad?' Can'st thou not sit still and be quiet?' one of the judges, John Downes, insisted that the court adjourn to consider the king's proposal. All Downes's stubbornness did was to put off the inevitable for half an hour. When the court reconvened, Bradshaw cited Magna Carta's provision against denying justice to reject the king's motion, and the prisoner's protests notwithstanding begun summing up. He made a good defence of a bad case. Replete with precedents for deposing tyrants that went back to Caligula, Bradshaw concluded that Charles Stuart had broken the contract between ruler and ruled. Having spoken for forty minutes he told the clerk to read the sentence, after which all his fellow judges rose to signify their assent.

'Will you hear me a word, Sir?' the condemned man asked.

'Sir, you are not to be heard after sentence,' Bradshaw answered.

'No, Sir.'

'No, Sir; by your favour, Sir,' replied the Lord President, 'Guard, withdraw your prisoner.'

'I may speak after the sentence. By your favour, Sir. I may speak after the sentence ever.' It was too late. The guard started to hustle him out. Some of the soldiers blew pipe smoke on his face, one even spat at him as Charles shouted back, 'By your Favour, Hold! The sentence, Sir – I say, Sir, I do – I am not suffered to speak. Expect what justice other People will have.' As the clamour screaming for justice reached a crescendo, Charles had to defend himself with that ironic humour that was his shield against adversity. 'Poor souls,' he observed, 'for a piece of money they would do so for their commanders.'

The trial of Charles I was over. It had been one of those great dramatic moments in English history worthy of a playwright as skilled as those who captured the trials of Richard II or Sir Thomas More held in the same theatre. The drama had its hero – a dignified king, whom one member of the audience recalled 'spoke excellently well, and majestically without impediment in the least'.[8] In Bradshaw, Cook and Cromwell the performance had villains whose villainy could be mitigated – or even augmented – by the sincere belief that they were doing the greater right. The piece had its fool, the ineffectual John Downes. It had bit parts, such as the masked figure (surely Lady Fairfax), who shouted out from the audience, 'he has more wit than to be here,' when the clerk read the absent general's name from the roll of judges, and the brave trooper hit for blessing his fallen sovereign. There was a chorus of soldiers, barracking the people's will. There were moments of exciting dialogue. There were two incompatible ideologies clashing head on. The prosecution claimed the government was answerable to the people, and anticipating John Locke and Thomas Jefferson, maintained that if the king broke the contract then the people had the right to punish him. Charles's contrasting argument that by trying the king the state was setting itself above the law, also looked forward, anticipating those totalitarian governments wherein power unchecked by law meant no man's life, liberty, or property were safely his own.

Yet in many respects the arguments that both sides advanced were artificial. While they might become signposts for the future, in truth at the time they were window-dressing for decisions already taken.

Two civil wars, a catholic rebellion, countless broken promises, and nearly as many dead friends, had convinced the army leaders that the king must die. His execution would not only prevent him from continuing to wage a third, even fourth, civil war, while seducing the faint-hearted with false promises of peace, but was justly deserved. They were so sure that God wanted Charles to be punished that they did not secretly murder him in some dank cell of Hurst castle, but openly so all could see and learn from his guilt. 'It was not a thing,' explained a regicide a dozen years later at his own treason trial, 'done in a corner.'[9]

The problem was doing it in some legitimate court of law. Although there had been precedents in Strafford and Laud's cases, these at best provided a poor justification for trying the king.[10] Recognizing this dilemma, one roundhead officer declared that although he was sure putting the king on trial was 'a just thing yet I know not how it may be justly done.'[11] Voicing the certainty common to all winners Oliver Cromwell crushed John Downes's legalistic quibbles by retorting that only a madman could not see that justice must be done in spite of the law.

The case that Charles made to defend himself during his trial was as artificial as the prosecution's. On the first day he put forward two main arguments. First, a legal one that the court had no jurisdiction, and second, a divine right one that putting the Lord's anointed on trial was a sacrilege for which those guilty must answer at the day of judgment. Recognizing that even – or particularly – in an illegal court a legal defence carried more weight, Charles quickly dropped the second argument and elaborated on the first until he claimed to be standing up for the rights of all freeborn Englishmen. For instance, all three of the defences he sketched out in a speech he drafted (though never gave), on the second evening of his trial were essentially legal.[12] Yet apart from the four days of his trial (and a brief mention on the scaffold), Charles never attached much significance to legal defences. While he did ask Cornet Joyce and Colonel Cobbet for their warrants, more typical of the king's attitude to legalisms was that shown towards Lord Bristol, who in 1626 replied that, 'it will be impossible for any man to be safe' if the House of Lords accepted Charles's contention that if an impeached man defended himself it impugned 'the king's honour'.[13] In private conversations and letters Charles never defended his actions in legal terms. He insisted he was dying to protect England's church, its bishops, his friends and his conscience.[14] Thus the change at his trial when he adopted a new and very effective legal defence delighted his friends and outraged his enemies. 'The king's deportment was very majestic and steady,' recalled Sir Philip Warwick, 'and though his tongue usually hesitated, yet he was very free at this time, for he was never discomposed in mind.'[15] On the other hand the spectacle of a man who before had always maintained that he was above the law now hiding behind it goaded Bradshaw into telling the king that he could not have it both ways: 'You disavow us as a court, and therefore for you to address yourself to us is not to be permitted.'[16]

After the trial was over Charles was taken from Westminster Hall in an enclosed sedan chair the few hundred yards down King Street, through the privy garden to his old room in Whitehall Palace.[17] From the windows, shops and pavement people peered through the winter afternoon's gloom at the chair carrying the condemned sovereign, some crying, others merely curious. At Whitehall Charles told Herbert that he would see no one but his children and chaplain, Bishop Juxon. When his faithful friends, Richmond, Hertford, Southampton and Lindsey, and his perfidious nephew, the Elector Palatine, asked for an audience, he gracefully turned them down, brushing aside their desperate eleventh-hour to attempt to find some way to save his life.[18] Though Charles did not know when he was to die, he did know it would not be long, and he needed all his time and energy to prepare for this last great act.

That evening, Colonel Matthew Tomlinson, commander of the king's guard, let Edward Seymour deliver a letter from Prince Charles written but four days before. The messenger was so overcome with grief that he swooned wailing to the floor, grasping his sovereign's knees, and had to be prised off. Following this distressing exhibition, Charles took an emerald and diamond ring from his hand and gave it to Herbert, telling him to slip past the guard and deliver it to Mary Wheeler, his laundress, who now lived in Channel Row. In return she gave him a small cabinet, which Herbert brought back to the king. He opened the box. When all he found were several diamonds and precious stones, mainly bits from broken-up badges of the Garter and St George, Charles sadly told his servant, 'You see all the wealth now in my power.' For most of that Sunday he remained in Whitehall, until about five in the afternoon, when the army moved him to St James's Palace, perhaps to spare him the noise of the carpenters erecting a scaffold outside the Banqueting Hall. The rest of the day he spent in prayer and listening to a sermon from Bishop Juxon. William Juxon, Bishop of London, had been a protégé of Archbishop Laud, succeeding him as President of St John's College, Oxford. Juxon lacked his mentor's gall. A gentle man, who never aroused his opponents' hatred, he was the perfect comforter for the king's Gethsemane.

Charles passed Monday morning in burning his papers and ciphers, before saying goodbye to his children, Elizabeth, a sickly thirteen-year-old who died of consumption the following year at Carisbrooke Castle, and Henry, who at nine already displayed the pugnacious determination that was to make him a formidable soldier.[19] The children, crying, were ushered into their father's room to receive his blessing. Charles raised them to their feet. He told them not to grieve: they must obey their mother, and their eldest brother, Charles, as their lawful sovereign. Then the king became agitated. When Elizabeth, who was old enough to realize that she would never again see her father, grew hysterical, he vehemently told her, 'Sweet heart, you will forget this.'

'No,' she insisted, 'I shall never forget it whilst I live,' promising to write down all the details as soon as she could (which she did that evening). Her father said he was going 'to a Glorious Death . . . for the laws of the Land and for maintaining the true Protestant religion.' He urged her to read Richard Hooker's *Lawes of Ecclesiastical Politie*, Bishop Andrewes's *Sermons*, and Laud's Anglican apologia, *A Relation of the Conference Between W. Laud and Mr Fisher, the Jesuit*. She was to tell her mother that his thoughts had never strayed from his wife. She must not cry, he was to be a martyr, and one day 'the Lord should settle his throne on his son, and that we shall all be happier than we could have expected to have been had he lived.'

Charles took his youngest son on his lap. 'Now they will cut off thy father's head. Mark, Child, what I say. They will cut off my head and perhaps make thee king. But mark what I say, you must not be a king, so long as your brothers Charles and James so live, for they will cut off your brothers' heads (when they catch them), and cut off thy head too at last. And therefore I charge you do not be made a king by them.' Charles was painfully concerned that a puppet monarch might turn his martyrdom into an empty gesture, so when his son vowed, 'I will be torn in pieces first,' he was very relieved. The boy's courage touched even the most stern-hearted witnesses, reducing the hardened veterans who stood guard beside the king to tears. By now both children were crying too, and unable to bear the emotion any longer Charles turned his back to them, before suddenly spinning round for one last, long hug.

Later that day – all passion spent – Juxon preached to the king on the text, 'I am not ashamed on the gospel of Christ: for it is the power of God unto salvation for everyone that believeth.' The king took communion, ate and drank a little and then retired to his room. Juxon managed to persuade Colonel Francis Hacker, the officer commanding the king's guard, to withdraw the two sentries posted inside Charles's bedroom outside the door, so after the bishop left, the king was able to continue praying and reading devotional works for a couple more hours undisturbed. He told Herbert to bring his pallet bed beside his own, and to lay out his best clothes, since he must be up early in the morning having important work to do. At about two in the morning Charles at last fell asleep.[20]

He slept soundly for about four hours, unlike Herbert, who was troubled by a nightmare, his tossing waking the king a couple of hours before dawn. What was the matter, Charles asked. Herbert answered that he dreamt that Laud, dressed in all his episcopal finery, entered the room, and had a long conversation with the king over by the window. As the archbishop left Charles fell face to the ground, but before Herbert could raise his master, he woke up. Charles agreed it was a remarkable dream. Perhaps his friend, the archbishop, was trying to tell him something. 'Herbert,' the king continued, as he got out of bed, 'this is my second Marriage Day. I will be as trim today as may be: for before night I hope to be espoused to my blessed Jesus.' The king dressed with great care, telling Herbert to give him an extra shirt in case he shivered in the cold, and the rabble think him quaking with cowardice. 'I fear not death! Death is not terrible to me, bless my God, I am prepared.'[21]

Soon afterwards Juxon entered with a message that the court had nominated five Puritan preachers to minister to Charles's last needs. Curtly he rejected this insensitive gesture. 'Tell them plainly that they have so often and causelessly prayed against me, shall never pray with me in this agony.'[22] The protective shield of the patient martyr who had just declared he did not fear death was beginning to crack. Perhaps it was not as strong as Thomas Herbert, whose *Memoirs* are the chief source of the king's last days, would have us believe. Yet Charles did manage to die with dignity, 'his faith,' Herbert concluded, 'overcoming his fear.'[23]

Charles spent the next few hours alone with Juxon, who gave him communion, and read Matthew XXVII, the story of Christ's crucifixion. Afterwards Charles asked him if he had chosen it specially. No, Juxon replied, it happened to be the lesson the prayer book appointed for the day, a coincidence that cheered Charles greatly.

After some more prayer, and Herbert's return, someone knocked on the door. Fearful it was Colonel Hacker with the last summons, Herbert refused to answer, until a second knock came and Charles told him to open the door. He asked the colonel to wait outside for a few more minutes which the king spent in silent meditation. Taking Juxon's hand, he said, 'Come let us go,' before turning to ask Herbert to bring the silver clock he always kept beside his bed. What was the time, he asked. About ten, Herbert replied, and Charles told him to keep the clock as a memento.

Several companies of infantry were waiting outside St James's Palace. Juxon fell in on the kings' right, Colonel Tomlinson on his left, with Herbert behind as they were marched across St James's Park, the cacophony of the soldiers' drums making conversation almost impossible. They entered Whitehall Palace by the Tiltyard Steps, went along the gallery over the Holbein Gate, past the privy council chamber, to the king's bedroom. Here once had hung portraits of his wife, his brother, his sister, his brother-in-law, Buckingham and his family. Now the walls were bare, his pictures sold off, his palace a run-down barracks. For some time the royal party waited, as parliament passed an ordinance against proclaiming a new monarch, and asserting its own sovereignty. The king rested a while on his bed, prayed a little and at Juxon's urging that he would not want to faint for lack of nourishment ate a small loaf of bread and drank a glass of claret. Charles asked Herbert for his white satin nightcap. Herbert whispered to Juxon that he be excused, for he could go no further, and must be spared the sight of his master's execution. And so they waited, the silver clock ticking away the last day-long minutes of Charles's life.

A little after two, Colonel Hacker came to the bedroom door to tell Charles Stuart that it was time. As he got up, Juxon and Herbert fell to their knees. He gave them his hand to kiss, and then raised the venerable prelate to his feet. Through the preaching place, with the stone pulpit symbolizing Charles's commitment to the church and its influence, prisoner and escort marched. His last servant was a bishop, episcopacy being as loyal to him as he had been to it. His last view of the art that had meant so much to him came as he walked through the Banqueting Hall. The cold January light must have intensified the lushness of Rubens's glorious ceiling celebrating both the majesty of monarchy, for which Charles was dying, and his father's union of the crowns of England and Scotland, from which so many of his troubles had come. At last what one observer called the 'saddest sight that England ever saw,' came through one of the Banqueting Hall's first floor windows (or else a hole cut in the wall) out to the scaffold built into the street.[24]

The scaffold was draped in black. On it stood the executioner and his assistant, so well-disguised that no one has ever discovered their identity for sure. On the middle of it was the block, so short that the condemned man could not kneel, but had to lie face down on the floor. Nailed to it were large staples to which he could be tied in case he struggled. In front of the scaffold pikemen stood, stamping their feet in a cold so bitter that the Thames had frozen. At either end of the street cavalry were stationed, their mounts' breath turning to vapour, whinnying as if they sensed some great moment. Everywhere about the scaffold, in the street, behind windows, and even on icy rooftops, crowds waited for the king's last speech.

They were to be disappointed. Although the army realized they could not deprive Charles of the privilege accorded the most notorious felon, by using the guards as a barrier to keep the people back, they ensured that few could catch his words. After trying to make himself heard Charles gave up, and addressed Colonel Tomlinson, Juxon and a nearby shorthand writer.

He did not want the people to take his submission to punishment as an admission of guilt. When they examined the record, they would clearly see that it was parliament who had started the war, not he.

'I will only say this. That an unjust sentence that I suffered to take effect is punished now by an unjust sentence on me. That is . . .' But Charles could not continue this painful allusion to Strafford's death, and had to return to a more comfortable topic. 'You must give God his due,' he exhorted, before losing the train of his thought when someone on the scaffold bent down to try the sharpness of the closely honed axe. 'Hurt not the Axe that may hurt me,' Charles begged. Recovering his composure the king turned to his most potent argument. He was dying for the liberty and freedom of his people. 'A subject and sovereign,' he maintained, as he had for the whole of his life, 'are clear different things.' He repeated his legal defence saying he was giving up his life to defy arbitrary power: 'I am a Martyr to the People.'

The strain of the occasion seemed too much for the king, whose thoughts started to wander, and Juxon had to remind him to make the traditional declaration of faith. 'I die a Christian according to the Profession of the Church of England,' Charles affirmed, 'I have a good cause and a gracious God. I will say no more.' Frightened that the headsman might take several tries to hack his head from his body he requested Colonel Hacker, 'Take care they do not put me in pain.' Extending his hands as he lay face down – rather like a man submitting to crucifixion – was to be the signal for the executioner to do his duty. He asked Juxon to tuck his hair under his white cap leaving his neck free of obstructions, and once more declared that his cause was good and that God was on his side. Juxon agreed, Soon, the prelate assured him, he would be in heaven. 'And there you will find to your great Joy, the prize you hasten to – a crown of glory.'

'I go from a corruptible to an incorruptible crown, where no disturbances can be, no disturbances, in the world,' answered the king. He spoke, as he had throughout the ordeal of both his trial and scaffold confession, without hesitation. At last he had lost his stutter – so often the symptom of some intense inner psychological conflict – that had tormented him for the whole of his life.

Charles handed Juxon the Badge of the Order of Saint George and the cloak he wore, took off his doublet, put his cloak on again, asked if the block could be raised, reminded the headsman of the signal, cryptically told Juxon 'Remember!' and prayed a while, looking up to what he was sure would be his immediate destination.

Then, a little after two in the afternoon of 30 January 1649, having been on the scaffold for no more than fifteen minutes, Charles fell to the floor and placed his head on the block. Thinking the headsman, who bent to remove some strands of hair upon his nape, was about to strike, Charles told him to wait for the signal. It soon came. The axe swung down. It severed his neck in one clean blow at the third vertebra and sent Charles to the 'incorruptible crown' and lack of disturbance that he was sure would be his in the next world, and that had eluded him for so much of his time in this life.[25]

# ABBREVIATIONS

All dates are old style, with the year starting on 1 January. Citations are given as follows: (1) date, given in the English fashion with the day, not month first; when the reference is to the seventeenth century, the first two digits of the year have been omitted; (2) then author; (3) addressee; (4) the reference. Manuscripts are usually cited by call number. To save space notes have often been combined, with a full stop between each. Place of publication not given if London.

| | |
|---|---|
| Add. MSS | Additional manuscripts in British Library |
| *APC* | J. R. Dasent, *Acts of the Privy Council of England*, 32 vols (1890–1907) |
| Ash. MSS | Ashmolean manuscripts in Bodleian Library |
| Ashburnham, *Narrative* | John Ashburnham, *A Narrative . . . of his attendance on King Charles*, 2 vols (1830) |
| Baillie, *Letters* | *The Letters and Journals of Robert Baillie*, ed., D. Laing (Edinburgh, 1841–2) |
| Bankes MSS | Manuscripts of Attorney General Sir John Bankes, Bodleian Library |
| Berkeley, *Memoirs* | Sir John Berkeley's 'Memoirs', in appendix to John Ashburnham, *Narrative* |
| *Bib. Regia* | Charles, *Bibliotheca Regia or The Royal Library* (The Hague, 1649) |
| *BIHR* | *Bulletin of the Institute of Historical Research* |
| Birch, *Court* | Thomas Birch, *Court and Times of Charles I*, ed., R. F. Williams, 2 vols (1848) |
| BL | British Library |
| Bod. | Bodleian Library |
| Burnet, *Hamilton* | *Memoirs of the Lives and Actions of James and William, Dukes of Hamilton and Castlehead* (1852) |
| *CCSP* | O. Ogle, W. H. Bliss and W. D. MacGray, eds, *Calendar of Clarendon State Papers*, 3 vols (Oxford, 1867–76) |
| *CSP* | R. Scrope and T. Monkhouse, eds, *State Papers Collected by Edward, Earl of Clarendon*, 3 vols (Oxford, 1767–86) |
| *CSPD* | *Calendar of State Papers, Domestic* |
| *CSPI* | *Calendar of State Papers, Ireland* |
| *CSPV* | *Calendar of State Papers, Venetian* |
| CUL | Cambridge University Library |
| *Cabala* | *Cabala sive scrinia sacra* (1691) |

| | |
|---|---|
| Carte, *Ormonde* | Thomas Carte, *The Life of James Duke of Ormonde containing . . . a collection of letters*, 6 vols (Oxford, 1851) |
| Chamberlain, *Letters* | *The Letters of John Chamberlain*, ed., N. E. McClure (Philadelphia, 1939), 2 vols, cited by date |
| Charles, *Letters* | *The Letters, Speeches, and Proclamations of King Charles I* (1935) |
| Charles, *Works* | *The Works of Charles I* (1687) |
| Clarendon, *History* | Edward Hyde, Earl of Clarendon, *The History of the Rebellion and Civil Wars in England*. Unless otherwise stated reference is to 1888 edition |
| *Commons Debates, 1621* | W. Notestein, F. H. Relf and H. Simpson, eds, *Commons Debates, 1621*, 7 vols (New Haven, 1935) |
| *Commons Debates, 1625* | S. R. Gardiner, ed., *Debates in the House of Commons in 1625* (Camden Soc., 1873) |
| *Commons Debates, 1628* | R. C. Johnson *et al.*, *Commons Debates in 1628*, 6 vols (New Haven, 1977–83) |
| *Commons Debates, 1629* | W. Notestein and F. H. Relf, *The Commons Debates for 1629* (Minneapolis, 1921) |
| *Concilia* | *Concilia Magnae Britanniae et Hibernae* (1737) |
| *DNB* | *The Dictionary of National Biography*, eds, L. Stephen and S. Lee, 66 vols (1885–1901) |
| *EHR* | *English Historical Review* |
| Eg. MSS | Egerton manuscripts in British Library |
| Ellis, *Letters* | Sir Henry Ellis, *Original Letters Illustrative of English History*, 11 vols (1824–46) |
| Evelyn, *Memoirs* | *Memoirs illustrative of the Life and Writing of John Evelyn, comprising his Diary . . . and . . . Letters*, ed., E. S. Beer, 6 vols (1955) |
| Folger MSS | Manuscripts in Folger Shakespeare Library, Washington, DC |
| Foster MSS | Foster manuscripts in Victoria and Albert Museum |
| Gardiner, *Civil War* | S. R. Gardiner, *History of the Great Civil War, 1642–9*, 4 vols (1893) |
| Gardiner, *History* | S. R. Gardiner, *History of England, 1603–42*, 10 vols (1893) |
| Gardiner, *Constitutional Documents* | S. R. Gardiner, *The Constitutional Documents of the Puritan Revolution, 1625–60* (1906) |
| Hacket, *Scrinia* | John Hacket, *Scrinia Reserata: A memorial offered to the great deserving of John Williams D. D. . . . containing a series of the most remarkable occurrences and transactions of his life*, 2 parts (1693) |
| Halliwell, *Letters* | J. O. Halliwell, ed., *Letters of the Kings of England*, 2 vols (1846) |
| Hardwicke, *SP* | Earl of Hardwicke, *Miscellaneous State Papers, 1501–1726*, 2 vols (1778) |
| Herbert, *Memoirs* | Sir Thomas Herbert, *Memoirs of the last years of the reign of King Charles* (1678; and 1959 edition by Roger Lockyer) |
| Harl. MSS | Harleian manuscripts in British Library |
| HMC | Historical Manuscripts Commission |
| Hunt, MSS | Manuscripts in Huntington Library, California |

| | |
|---|---|
| *King's Peace* | C. V. Wedgwood, *The King's Peace* (1971) |
| *King's War* | C. V. Wedgwood, *The King's War* (1971) |
| Lands. MSS | Landsdowne manuscripts in British Library |
| Laud, *Works* | *The Works of the most Reverend father in God, William Laud*, eds, W. Scot and J. Bliss, 7 vols (Oxford, 1847–60) |
| *Lords Journal* | *Journal of the House of Lords, 1578–1714* (1767 +) |
| Nalson, *Collections* | John Nalson, *An Impartial Collection of the Great Affairs of State*, 2 vols (1682–3) |
| NRA | National Register of Archives, Chancery Lane |
| *P & P* | *Past and Present* |
| PRO | Public Record Office |
| *Parliamentary History* | *The Parliamentary... History of England*, 12 vols (1763) |
| Rawl. MSS | Rawlinson manuscripts in Bodleian Library |
| *Reliquiae* | *Reliquiae Sacrae Carolina*, 2 parts (Hague, 1649) |
| *Remembrancia* | W. H. and H. C. Overall, *The Remembrancia, Preserved Among the Archives of London* (1878) |
| Rushworth, *Collections* | John Rushworth, *Historical Collections of Private Passages of State*, 8 vols (1659–1701) |
| Rymer, *Foedera* | T. Rymer and R. Sanderson, eds, *Foedera*, 20 vols (1704–32) |
| Sloane MSS | Sloane manuscripts in British Library |
| SP 14–15 | State Papers, James I, in Public Records Office (PRO) |
| SP 16 | State Papers, Charles I |
| SP 71 | State Papers, Barbary States |
| SP 75 | State Papers, Denmark |
| SP 78 | State Papers, France |
| SP 80 | State Papers, Germany and Empire |
| SP 81 | State Papers, German States |
| SP 82 | State Papers, Hanseatic and Hamburg |
| SP 84 | State Papers, Holland |
| SP 88 | State Papers, Poland |
| SP 91 | State Papers, Russia |
| SP 92 | State Papers, Savoy |
| SP 94 | State Papers, Spain |
| SP 95 | State Papers, Sweden |
| SP 99 | State Papers, Venice |
| Str. P. | Strafford Papers in Sheffield Public Library |
| Steele, *Proclamations* | *A Bibliography of Royal Proclamations*, ed., R. R. Steele (Oxford, 1910) |
| *STC* | A. W. Pollard and G. R. Redgrave, *A Short-title Catalogue of Books printed in England, Scotland and Ireland* (1969) |
| Stowe MSS | Stowe manuscripts in British Library |
| Tanner MSS | Tanner manuscripts in Bodleian Library |
| *TRHS* | *Transactions of the Royal Historical Society* |
| Warburton, *Cavaliers* | E. Warburton, *Memoirs of Prince Rupert and the Cavaliers*, 3 vols (1849) |

Warwick, *Memoirs*    Sir Philip Warwick, *Memoirs of the Reigne of King Charles* (Edinburgh, 1813)

Wentworth, *Letters*    *The Earl of Strafford's Letters and Dispatches*, 2 vols, ed., W. Knowler (1739)

# NOTES

## PREFACE 'THAT MEMORABLE SCENE'

1 *Contarini Fleming*, pt I, ch. 23.
2 For example see William Lilly, *Life and Death of Charles I* (1774).
3 For example see Gertrude Himmelfarb, 'The new history', *Commentary*, LIX (1 January 1975) 72–80, and Jacques Barzun, *Clio and the Doctors* (Chicago, 1974).
4 Laud, *Works*, III, 147.
5 John Nelson, *A True copy of the Journal of . . . the Trial of King Charles I* (1684) 92.
6 Walter Mischel, 'Reconsidering conceptions of personality: a cognitive social learning perspective', *Psychological Review*, LXXX (1977) 252 ff, and 'The interface of person and situation', in David Magnusson and N. Endler, eds, *Personality at the Crosslands* (Hilldale, NJ, 1977) 333–52, and 'On the interface of cognition and personality', *American Psychologist*, XXXIV, 9 (September 1979) 740–52. Albert Bandura, *Social Learning Theory* (Engelwood Cliffs, NJ, 1977). Julian B. Rotter, *Social Learning and Clinical Psychology* (Englewood Cliffs, NJ, 1977). Martin Seligman, *Learned Helplessness* (New York, 1975), and 'General expectations for external versus internal control of reinforcement', *Psychological Monographs*, LXXX (1965).
7 For an example see L. Kohlburg's comparative study of the US, Taiwan, Turkey, Mexico and the Yucatan in 'The child as a moral philosopher', in *Readings in Developmental Psychology Today* (Del Mar, California, 1970), 105–15

## PREFACE TO THE SECOND EDITION

1 C. Hibbert, *Charles I* (1968); Margaret Toynbee, *King Charles I* (1968); D. R. Watson, *The Life and Times of Charles I* (1972); John Bowle, *Charles I* (1975); Pauline Gregg, *King Charles I* (1981).
2 Conrad Russell, *The Fall of the British Monarchies, 1637–42* (Oxford, 1991); J. Morrill, *The Scottish National Covenant in its British Context* (1990); Peter Donald, *An Uncounselled King: Charles I and the Scottish Troubles, 1637–1641* (1990); Maurice Lee, *The Road to Revolution: Scotland Under Charles I* (1985); Steven Ellis, ' "Not mere English": The British Perspective, 1400–1650,' in *History Today*, xxxviii (1988), 4–49; N. Canny, *Colonial Identity in the Atlantic World* (Princeton, N.J., 1987).
3 George M. Kren, 'Psychohistory Today', in *The Journal of Psychohistory*, 17 / 4 (Spring 1990), 386–8. For a good discussion of the recent state of

psychohistory see W. E. Runyon, ed., *Psychohistory and Historical Interpretation* (New York, 1988); for a brilliant defense see Peter Gay, *Freud and the Historians* (New York, 1985).
4 Quoted by Gay, *op. cit.*, 41.
5 Kevin Sharpe, *The Personal Rule of Charles I* (1993), 192.
6 R. Cust, *The Forced Loan*, (1987), 17.
7 *Ibid.*, 88.
8 L. J. Reeve, *Charles I and the Road to Personal Rule* (1989), 103.
9 Thomas Cogswell, *The Blessed Revolution: English Politics and the Coming of the War, 1621–24* (Cambridge, 1989).
10 BL: Harl. MSS, 6988, 109–10.
11 Robert Shephard, 'Court Factions in Early Modern England', in *Journal of Modern History*, 64 (December 1992), 720ff, is an excellent survey of the recent works. Neil Cuddy's essay, 'The Revival of the Entourage: the Bedchamber of James I, 1603–25', in D. Starkey, ed., *The English Court* (1987), 173–225 is interesting.
12 R. M. Smuts, *Court Culture and the Origin of a Royalist Tradition in Early Stuart England* (1987), 190–5.
13 K. Sharpe, *Politics and Ideas in Early Stuart England* (1989), 107.
14 Reeve, op. cit., 3–4.
15 Flashback Television, *The Civil War*; Lee, *op. cit.*, 243–4.
16 The best known work is *Criticism and Compliment: The Politics of Literature in the England of Charles I* (1987).
17 Reeve, *op. cit.*, 198.
18 *Ibid.*, 263.
19 Sharpe (1993), *op. cit.*, 202.
20 Cust, *op. cit.*, 42, 323.
21 Donald, *op. cit.*, 78.
22 C. Russell, *Parliaments and English Politics, 1621–29* (1979), 422.
23 *Ibid.*, 57, 120–5.

## I THE DUKE 'FAR OUT OF ORDER'

1 BL: Sloane MSS, 1788, 10.
2 John Blinsele, 'An account of the birth and baptism of Prince Charles', Folger MSS, Na. 102.
3 Alexander MacDonald, *Letters to James VI of Scotland* (Maitland Club, XXXV, 1835) lxxxvi. J. H. Burton, D. Mason, P. H. Brown and H. Paton, eds, *The Register of the Privy Council of Scotland* (Edinburgh 1877 +) 2nd Series, I, 90 (a). One mark equals a third of a pound. All sums in Scots pounds. Charles to Traquair, HMC *9th Report*, appendix 2, 245.
4 J. J. Keevil, 'The illness of Charles, Duke of Albany from 1600 to 1612', *Journal of the History of Medicine*, IX (October 1954) 407–19, and 'Charles I and rickets', *Lancet* (20 March 1954) 631. My thanks for medical advice on Charles are due to Dr D'Akok and Dr John Carlton.
5 Atkins to James, 13/5/04. Hertfordshire Record Office, MSS, 65447, SP 14/14/8.
6 Adam Anderson, ed., *Letters and State Papers of the Reign of James VI* (1838) 46–7. George Seton, *Memoirs of Alexander Seton* (1882) 56.
7 HMC, *Salisbury*, XVI, 137–8, 163.
8 *Ibid.*, 176, 195, 227; XIX, 27.
9 Helen Stocks, *Records of the Borough of Leicester, 1603–88* (Cambridge, 1923) 20–1, 31.

10 T. Rymer and R. Sanderson, eds, *Foedera* (1704–32) XVI, 611–12, SP 15/37/37 and 21.

11 SP 15/37/13.

12 Robert Carey, *The Memoirs of R. Carey, Earl of Monmouth* (Oxford, 1972) 25–6, 66–9. Daniel Price, *Spiritual Odours to the Memory of Prince Henry* (1613).

13 SP 14/14/24. HMC, *Salisbury*, XIX, 278, 412–13. *CSPD, 1603–10*, 445, 527, 623. SP 14/58/25.

14 Sir Anthony Weldon, *The Court and Character of King James* (1651) 215–16. Hertfordshire Record Office MSS, 65447, 2.

15 A pair of reinforced boots, purported to be Charles's, are in the London Museum.

16 Frederick Devon, *Issues of the Exchequer* (1836) 17. Hertfordshire Record Office MSS, 65667, 2.

17 Sir Ralph Winwood, *Memorials of Affairs of State*, ed., E. Sawyer (1725) II, 43–4. 10/1/5, Vincent to Benson, SP 14/12/16.

18 My thanks to the Master of St John's College, Cambridge, for allowing me to see this in his lodge.

19 25/11/04, Lake to Cecil, HMC, *Salisbury*, VI, 367. 3/1/05, Coke to Cranborne, *ibid.*, XVII, 4. *Ibid.*, XXIII, 201–2. HMC, *De Lisle*, III, 188. *CSPD 1603–10*, 248.

20 Henry, Charles's elder brother, spent 161 days that year at court: SP 14/53/58–9.

21 27/2/07, Guistinian to Doge, *CSPV, 1603–7*, 691. See also *CSPV, 1607–10*, 362, 792, and *CSPV, 1610–13*, 175, 181.

22 HMC, *Devonshire*, II, 317.

23 15/5/11, Foscarini and Correr to Doge, *CSPV, 1610–13*, 236.

24 Sir John Harrington, *Nugae Antiquae* (1804) I, 348.

25 Agnes Strickland, *Lives of the Queens of England* (1840–8) IV, 44–5.

26 Sir Anthony Weldon, 'Observations upon the King from his Childhood', in Sir Walter Scott, ed., *Secret History of the Court of James I* (1811) II, 63. 21/7/11, Foscarini to Doge, *CSPV, 1610–13*, 280.

27 Sigmund Freud, *Collected Papers* (1952) IV, 367.

28 Sir Anthony Weldon, 'Court and Character of King James (1650)' in Scott, *op. cit.*, II, 1–2.

29 *Ibid.*, II, 75.

30 Phineas Pett, *Autobiography* (Naval Records Society, LI, 1918) 80.

31 BL: Add. MSS, 19402, 43. MacDonald, *op. cit.*, npg, three letters.

32 Sir Henry Wotton, 'A Panegyrick to King Charles', in *Reliquiae Wottonianae* (1654) 142.

33 PRO: LS 13/280/304.

34 12/11/12, Beaulieu to Trumbell, Scott, *op. cit.*, I, 429.

35 23/7/07, 11/10/07, 26/5/08, Le Boderie to King, Frederick Von Raumer, *History of the 16th and 17th Centuries Illustrated by Original Documents* (1838) II, 223.

36 4/5/11, Correr to Doge, *CSPV, 1610–13*, 217. Jerry W. Williamson, *The Myth of the Conqueror: Henry Stuart: A Study in Seventeenth-Century Personation* (New York, 1978).

37 Moulin to Doge, report for 1607, *CSPV, 1603–7*, 737.

38 10/1/05, Vincent to Benson, SP 14/12/16. For other versions see William Lily, *Life and Death of Charles I* (1774, first published 1651) 177–8; Peter Heylin,

*A Short View of the Life and Reign of King Charles* (1658) 6–7, and *CSPV, 1603–7*, 739.

39  28/2/11, BL: Harl. MSS, 6986, 174.

40  10/3/11, Correr to Doge, *CSPV, 1610–13*, 186.

41  MacDonald, *op. cit.*, xxxviii, nd. BL: Harl. MSS, 6986, 156.

42  G. Goodman, *The Court of King James the First* (1839) I, 247. Chamberlain, *Letters*, I, 388–9. Norman Moore, *The Illness and Death of Henry Prince of Wales in 1612: A Historical Case of Typhoid Fever* (1882). Francis Osborne, 'Some Traditionall Memoryes of the Raigne of King James' (1658) in Scott, *op. cit.*, I, 269.

## II 'THE ILLUSTRIOUS HOPE OF GREAT BRITAIN'

1  Thomas Middleton, *Civitatis Amor* (1616).

2  6/11/12, Dorset to Edmondes, Alexander MacDonald, *Letters to James VI of Scotland* (Maitland Club, XXXV, 1835) xxxix.

3  29/12/12, Foscarini to Doge, *CSPV, 1610–13*, 727.

4  C. V. Wedgwood, *Poetry and Politics under the Stuarts* (Cambridge, 1960) 20–1. Henry King, *The English Poems of Henry King*, ed. Margaret Crum (Oxford, 1965) 65. 'Elegies and other tracts issued on the death of Henry, Prince of Wales, 1612,' *Publications of the Edinburgh Bibliographical Society*, VI (1906) 132–58.

5  SP 78/61/21.

6  *CSPD, 1610–18*, 189. Sir Henry Wotton, *Life and Letters*, ed. L. P. Smith (Oxford, 1907) II, 115–16, 131–2. 'A Politique Dispute about the Happiest Marriage for the Most Noble Prince', Bod: MSS Eng. Hist. c. 28, 75. 3/12/12, Bondi to Doge, *CSPV, 1610–13*. 31/12/12, Chamberlain, *Letters*, I, 399. 31/12/12, Wake to Carleton, *CSPD, 1610–18*, 163.

7  R. Dallington, *Aphorismes* (1612) dedication. William Lily, *Life and Death of Charles I* (1774, first published 1651) 2.

8  Franklin B. Williams, *Index of Dedications and Commendatory Verses in English books before 1641* (1962).

9  M. A. E. Green, *Elizabeth, Electress Palatine and Queen of Bohemia* (1909) 47.

10  *The Marriage of the Two Great Princes, Frederick Count Palatine and the Lady Elizabeth* (1613). Shakespeare may have been alluding to this wedding in *The Tempest*, when a wise old man's beautiful daughter falls for a handsome man from overseas.

11  John Donne, *The Complete English Poems*, ed. A. J. Smith (1971) 137–8.

12  J. Nichols, *The Progresses, Processions and Magnificent Festivals of James the First* (1828) II, 607. CUL: MSS Mn IV 57, no. 11, 869.

13  16/2/13, Foscarini, *CSPV, 1610–13*, 767.

14  29/4/13, Chamberlain, *Letters* I, 442.

15  *Archaeologia*, XV (1806) 1–12. *CSPD, 1610–18*, 28. BL: Add. MSS, 28621, 13.

16  SP 14/72/107–11. *Grants of Manors and Lands in Wales and England from James I to his son Prince Charles* (1866). *CSPD, 1610–18*, 206. 30/11/12, Foscarini to Doge, *CSPV, 1610–13*, 698. Peter Heylin, *A Short View of the Life and Reign of King Charles* (1658) 9–10.

17  2/12/12, Wake to Carleton, SP 99/11/1513.

18  BL: Harl. MSS, 6986, 182.

19  *CSPV, 1610–13*, 172 et seq. *La declaration de notre Souverain touchant les pretentions du fils de sa majeste Charles au Duche de Cornouaille* (1613). 29/6/

13, Holles to Digby, HMC, *Portland*, IX, 14. 30/6/13, 15/7/13, Lorkin to Puckering, T. Birch, *Court and Times of James I* (1849) 252, 255–8.

20 Frederick Devon, *Issues of the Exchequer . . . James I* (1836) 17 and 34. *CSPD, 1610–18*, 64. HMC, *Salisbury*, XXI, 36. SP 14/53/13.

21 Richard Perrinchief, *The Royal Martyr* (1676) 261–2.

22 *CSPD, 1610–18*, 368, 382, 395, 397 and 414. *APC, 1615–16*, 508. 30/10/16, Roe to Charles, BL: Add. MSS, 6115, 125. Ben Jonson, *Works*, eds, C. H. Herford and P. and E. M. Simpson (Oxford, 1925–52) 232–5.

23 26/2/14, Foscarini to Doge, *CSPV, 1613–15*, 203. 18/9/14, 1/5/17, Lionello to Doge, *CSPV, 1615–17*, 483, 754.

24 For example see 8/12/13, Suffolk to Lake, SP 14/75/37, and 'Commission of Prince Charles's Household', SP 14/141/105. *CSPD, 1603–10*, 226, 327, 340, 346. SP 16/47/106.

25 24/11/13 and 8/12/13, Suffolk to Lake, SP 14/75/24 and 37. Commission of 20/12/13 in SP 14/11/4 Grant book, 105. Chamberlain, *Letters*, I, 585 and II, 58. 20/3/17, Gerard to Carleton, SP 14/90/135.

26 1/10/17, Charles to Sir Richard Smith, CUL: MSS Ee, IV, 2, 229. BL: Add. MSS, 6027 and 28621, 13.

27 Nichols, *op. cit.*, II, 626–7.

28 *CSPD, 1580–1625*, 539–40.

29 16/3/15, Chamberlain, *Letters*, I, 58609. 26/9/15, Foscarini to Doge, *CSPV, 1615–17*, 54.

30 22/4/16, James to Charles, Bod: Ash. MSS, 109, 18. 24/3/15, Chamberlain, *Letters*, I, 611. 25/7/16, Sherburn to Carleton, SP 14/88/30.

31 Nichols, *op. cit.*, III, 207. 9/11/16, Beecher to Carleton, SP 14/89/15. Daniel Powell, *The Love of Wales to their Soveraigne Prince* (1616, reprinted 1827). Lionello to Doge, *CSPV, 1615–17*, 512. 9/11/16, Chamberlain, *Letters*, II, 31–4. Publishers echoed these sentiments, binding descriptions of Charles's installation with Henry's, presumably to help sales.

32 28/5/17, Charles to James, MacDonald, *op. cit.*, npg. 30/3/17, Lionello to Doge, *CSPV, 1615–17*, 710.

33 The theoretical basis for this section is from Sigmund Freud, 'Mourning and melancholia', *Collected Papers*, IV (1925) 152–72; Erik Erikson, *Identity, Youth and Crisis* (New York, 1968) 178–9, and Martha Wolfenstein, 'How is mourning possible?' *Psychoanalytic Study of the Child*, XXI (1966) 93–123.

34 20/10/16, Elizabeth to Charles, HMC, *Bath*, II, 64.

35 Homosexuality is a difficult, even controversial, term to define. It may be seen as a physical act, or a psychological state. In the seventeenth-century statute law (25 Henry VIII, c. 6), defined homosexuality in terms of buggery, while more recently the Kinsey report listed three degrees, the least serious being physical contact leading to orgasm. On the other hand many authorities see homosexuality in a broader context. Freud observed that 'every human being oscillates all through his life between heterosexual and homosexual feelings,' while Dr Clifford Allen simply defines homosexuality as 'the attraction towards someone of the same sex'. While trying when possible to differentiate between the physical act and the psychological state (the two can, of course, be combined), I have used the term in its broadest sense to describe the direction of the libido to a member of the same sex. S. Freud, 'Psycho-analytic notes upon an autobiographical account of a case of paranoia,' *Collected Papers*, III (1925) 429–30. A. C. Kinsey *et al.*, *Sexual Behaviour of the Human Male* (1948). Clifford E. Allen, *Homosexuality: its nature, causation and treatment*

(1958) 10. D. J. West, *Homosexuality (1968)*. *Irving Bieber et al., Homosexuality: a psychoanalytic study* (New York, 1962).

36 Antonia Fraser, *King James VI of Scotland, I of England* (1974) 36–9.
37 Sir John Oglander, *A Royalist Notebook*, ed. F. Bamford (1936). A. L. Rowe, *Homosexuals in History* (1977) 58–65. G. Taylor, *Sex in History* (1953) 150.
38 Francis Osborne, *Secret History of King James I and King Charles I* (1690) 22–3.
39 West, *op. cit.*, 207–8. Freud, *Collected Papers*, III (1925) 445.
40 Sir Anthony Weldon, 'Court and character of King James', in *The Secret History of the Court of King James*, ed., Sir Walter Scott (Edinburgh, 1811) I, 374–7.
41 1611, Howard to Harington, Sir John Harington, *Nugae Antiquae* (1804) 390–1.
42 James, *Basilikon Doron* (1944 ed.) 109.
43 James, *Works* (1616) 529.
44 16/3/15, Chamberlain, *Letters*, I, 586–9.
45 S. Freud, *The Ego and the Id* (1923).
46 Quoted by W. G. Murdock, *The Royal Stuarts in their connection with Arts and Letters* (1908) 163.
47 Charles, *Letters*, 272. For other statements on the power of Charles's conscience see his letters to his wife in J. Bruce, *Charles I in 1646* (Camden Society, LXIII, 1856) 79–82, and the poem attributed to him in George Chalmers, ed., *The PoeticRemains of some of the Scottish Kings* (1824) 203.
48 Robert Wilkinson, *A Paire of Sermons* (1614).
49 Perrinchief, *op. cit.*, 728.

## III 'BABY CHARLES,' 'STEENIE' AND THEIR 'DEAR DAD'

1 Dudley Digges to Parliament, *Lords Journal, 596*, quoted in C. Russell, *Parliament and English Politics, 1621–9* (1979) 10.
2 Clarendon, *History* I, 42. Arthur Wilson, *The History of Great Britain being the Life and Reign of King James the First* (1653) 147.
3 Halliwell, *Letters*, II, 131.
4 G. Goodman, *The Court of King James the First* (1839) I, 225–6. Sir John Oglander, *A Royalist's Notebook* (1936) 41.
5 Gardiner, *History*, III, 98. Roger Lockyer, *Buckingham: The Life and Political Career of George Villiers, First Duke of Buckingham* (1981) 22.
6 Busino's description of England, *CSPV, 1617–19*, 188. Ellis, *Letters*, 101.
7 Sir Anthony Weldon, 'Court and character of King James', in *The Secret History of the Court of James I*, ed., Sir Walter Scott (Edinburgh, 1811) I, 443.
8 4/3/16 & 31/5/16, Sherburn to Carleton, SP 14/86/95 and SP 14/87/40.
9 7/4/77, Bennet to Winwood, HMC, *Buccleuch*, I, 195.
10 Sir Francis Bacon, *Works*, ed., James Speeding *et al.*, (1858) XIII, 55. 31/5/16, Sherburn to Carleton, SP 14/87/40.
11 23/6/18, Lorkin to ?, HMC, *Bath*, II, 68.
12 30/6/18, Lorkin to Puckering, BL: Add. MSS, 4176, 71.
13 16/10/18, Carey to Carleton, *CSPD, 1610–18*, 585. BL: Harl. MSS, 6986, 83. 15/5/19, Brent to Carleton, SP 14/109/34.
14 D. J. West, *Homosexuality* (1968) 116.
15 Richard Perrinchief, *The Royal Martyr* (1676) 9.
16 30/3/19 & 4/5/19, Harwood to Carleton, *CPSD, 1619–23*, 28. 10/5/19, Chamberlain, *Letters*, II, 227.
17 Peter Heylin, *A Short View of the Life and Reign of King Charles* (1658) 11.

18  12/6/19, Harwood to Carleton, SP 14/109/89. 17/1/20, Lando to Doge, *CSPV*, *1619–21*, 201.

19  Nd, Charles to Buckingham, Halliwell, *Letters*, II, 153–5.

20  11/3/20, Chamberlain, *Letters*, II, 293.

21  'The Manner of the first coming into the tiltyard of the High and Mighty Prince Charles', Bod: Ash. MSS, 837, 129–32. 27/3/20, Younge to Zouch, SP 14/113/42.

22  *The Magnificent, Princely and most Royal Entertainment given to the high and Mighty Prince and Princess Frederick ... Elizabeth ... after their landing on the shores of Germany* (1613).

23  Quoted, C. V. Wedgwood, *The Thirty Years War* (New York, 1961), 69.

24  SP 81/17/127.

25  S. R. Gardiner, *Letters and other documents illustrating the relations between England and Germany at the commencement of the Thirty Years War, 1618–20* (Camden Soc., XC and XCVIII, 1865–8) 149. 15/9/20, BL: Sloane MSS, 4161, 122. SP 14/117/94.

26  'Karen Horney', *International Encyclopedia of the Social Sciences* (New York, 1968) VI, 1513–15. J. G. Flugel, *Man, Morals and Society* (1945) 302–11.

27  John and Virginia Demos, 'Adolescence in a historical perspective', *Journal of Marriage and the Family*, XXXI, 3 (August 1969) 632–8.

28  2/6/16, Lionello to Doge, *CSPV, 1615–17*, 340. 19/11/16, Brent to Carleton, *CSPD, 1610–18*, 407.

29  15/3/20, Gondomar to Philip IV, in Fray Francisco de Jesus, *Narrative of the Spanish Marriage Treaty*, ed., S. R. Gardiner (Camden Soc., 1869) 321. 12/8/21, Bristol to Charles, *CCSP*, I, 22.

30  J. H. Burton *et al.*, *Register of the Privy Council of Scotland, 1619–22* (Edinburgh, 1877+) 246–9, and *Register of the Privy Council of Scotland, 1622–5*, 41–3.

31  Freud, 'Three essays on the theory of sexuality', *Collected Works* (1953) 227. Erik Erikson, *The Challenge of Youth* (New York, 1965) 10.

32  Peter Blos, *On Adolescence: A Psychoanalytic Interpretation* (New York, 1962) 224.

33  27/6/19, Charles to Hay, SP 81/16/127. 1/1/21, Lando to Doge, *CSPV, 1619–21*, 688.

34  Peter Loewenburg, 'The unsuccessful adolescence of Heinrich Himmler', *American Historical Review*, LXXVI, 3 (June, 1971) 630, charts this process in another context.

35  Rushworth, *Collections*, I, 12.

36  Thomas Scott, 'Sir Walter Raleigh's Ghost is England's Forewarner' (1626) in *Somer's Tracts*, II, 508–23, 555–608. Nehemiah Wallington, *Historical Notes of the Reign of Charles I*, ed., R. Webb (1869) I, 12.

37  11/10/20 and 1/12/20, Lando to Doge, *CSPV, 1619–20*, 57, 65.

38  12/9/19, Tilliers to Louis XIII, Frederick Von Raumer, *History of the 16th and 17th Centuries Illustrated by Original Documents* (1838) III, 237. 8/6/20, Lando to Doge, *CSPV, 1619–21*, 399. C. Avery and K. Watson, 'Medici and Stuarts: A Grand Ducal Gift of Giovanni Bologna Bronzes for Henry, Prince of Wales,' in C. Avery, *Studies in European Sculpture* (1981), 103.

39  Robert Zaller, *The Parliament of 1621: A Study in Constitutional Conflict* (Berkeley, 1971) 4.

40  3 and 5/3/21, *Lords Journals*, III, 34, 37. 26/2/21 and 20/4/21, Lando to Doge, *CSPV, 1619–21*, 748, and *CSPV, 1621–3*, 40. *Commons Debates, 1621*, II, 231; IV, 158; V, 43.

41 *APC, 1619–21*, 352–3. While Charles often attended privy council meetings he was not formally made a member until 26 March 1622; *CSPD, 1621–3*, 363.
42 *Commons Debates, 1621*, II, 231; VI, 71. 28/3/21, Chamberlain, *Letters*, II, 357–8.
43 *Commons Debates, 1621*, II, 426; II, 806; V, 196, 394.
44 *Ibid*, I, 518.
45 *Ibid*, V, 27.
46 Folger, MSS, X, d, 232.
47 Bacon, *Works*, XVI, 268–71, 288.
48 Hacket, *Scrinia*.
49 Yelverton soon apologized, so James set him free in July 1624, and in May of the next year Charles made him a judge of common pleas. Chamberlain, *Letters*, II, 369. Zaller, *op. cit.*, 116 ff. DNB.
50 Zaller, *op. cit.*, 112–14. *Commons Debates, 1621*, II, 405–6.
51 28/10/21, Charles to Buckingham, BL: Harl. MSS, 6487, 96.
52 Rushworth, *Collections*, I, 30. Goodman, *op. cit.*, 209–10.
53 BL: Sloane MSS, 1828, 82. 7/12/21, Calvert to Buckingham, *Commons Debates, 1621*, VII, 624–5. Russell, *op. cit.*, 137.

## IV 'THE VOYAGE OF THE KINGHTS OF ADVENTURE'

1 Sir Henry Wotton, *A Short View of the Life and Death of George Villiers, Duke of Buckingham* (orig. 1642), *Harleian Miscellany*, VII, 5–10.
2 22/2/23, Mainwaring to Zouch, SP 14/138/58.
3 3/3/23, Conway to Brooke, SP 14/139/26.
4 Fray Francisco de Jesus, *Narrative of the Spanish Marriage Treaty*, ed., S. R. Gardiner (Camden Soc., 1869) 103. SP 94/29/108–11.
5 10/1/08, Gustinian to Doge, *CSPV, 1607–10*, 146. 23/8/20, Philip III to Gondomar, Jesus, *op. cit.*, p. 323. 5/11/22, Philip IV to Olivares, Bod: MSS Eng. Hist. e. 28, 103.
6 30/1/21, James to Parliament, *CSPV, 1619–23*, 271. 28/11/21 Pym to House of Commons, Sir Edward Nicholas, *Proceedings of the House of Commons, 1621*, II, 237. 22/12/20, Chamberlain, *Letters*, II, 331.
7 22/2/22, Digby to Charles, SP 94/26/38.
8 20/1/19, 29/12/19, 14/1/20, 13/4/21, 3/8/21, 5 and 19/10/21, Lando to Doge, *CSPV, 1619–21*, 210, 218, 279; *CSPV, 1621–3*, 34, 130, 193, 205. Jesus, *op. cit.*, 153–4. 25/8/21, Locke to Carleton, *CSPD, 1619–23*, 285. A. L. Loomie, 'Gondomar's selection of English officers in 1622', *EHR*, 88 (348) 574–81.
9 14/2/12, Digby to James, BL: Harl. MSS, 7002, 178. 22/11/13, Digby to James, *CSPD, 1610–18*, 199. 2/6/17, Gondomar to Philip IV, Jesus, *op. cit.*, 134–6, and comments of John Bennet, an English Jesuit, Jesus, *op. cit.*, 169.
10 21/10/22, 22/2/22, 31/8/22 and 3/12/22, Digby to Charles, SP 94/25/261, SP 94/26/38, SP 94/25/205 and 310.
11 *Considerations upon the Treaty of Marriage between England and Spain* (1623) 12.
12 Clarendon, *History*, I, 14–22.
13 1/2/23, Valaresso to Doge, *CSPV, 1621–3*, 761.
14 24/3/17, Lionello to Doge, *CSPV, 1615–17*, 718. 25/4/17, Danvers to Carleton, *CSPD, 1610–18*, 461. 29/3/17, Chamberlain, *Letters*, II, 67. Jesus, *op. cit.*, 153–4.
15 14/3/21, Charles to Philip IV, Rushworth, *Collections*, I, 59. 27/2/23, Calvert to Carleton, SP 84/11/148–9. 7/3/23, Valaresso to Doge, *CSPV, 1621–3*, 804. 25/2/23, Kellie to Mar, HMC, *Mar and Kellie*, 153.

16 3/3/23, Surian to Doge, *CSPV, 1621–3*, 800. 4/3/23, Morsini to Doge, *ibid.*, 803. 19/4/23, Antelini to Doge, *ibid.*, 843.

17 27/2/23, Dudley Carleton to Sir Dudley Carleton, SP 14/138/99. Sir Robert Carey, *Memoirs* (Oxford, 1972) 77. 20/2/23, Kellie to Mar, HMC, *Mar and Kellie*, 151–2.

18 *CSPD, 1619–23*, 498–9. 18/3/23, Edmondes to Carleton, SP 14/139/125.

19 22/2/23, Charles and Buckingham to James, BL: Harl. MSS, 6987, 6, 10. Wotton, *op. cit.*, 5. 15/3/23, Chamberlain to Carleton, SP 84/111/159.

20 2 and 4/3/23, Pesaro to Doge, *CSPV, 1621–3*, 796, 801. SP 94/26/249.

21 13/3/23, Kellie to Mar, HMC, *Mar and Kellie*, 155. Wotton, *op. cit.*, 5–10. *Life of Edward, Lord Herbert of Cherbury written by Himself*, ed., Sir Walter Scott (1826) 238–42.

22 Charles and Buckingham to James, BL: Harl. MSS, 6987, 10.

23 Sir Richard Wynne, 'A brief relation of what was observed by the Prince's servants on their journey into Spain in the year 1623', printed in Simonds D'Ewes, *Autobiography* (1845) II, 441. SP 94/26/117.

24 SP 94/26/121. BL: Add. MSS, 5832, 195 ff. 17/3/23, Howell to Savage, James Howell, *Epistolae-Ho-Elianae*, ed., Joseph Jacobs (1890, orig. 1645) I, 164.

25 *A True Relation and Journal of the Manner and Arrival and Magnificent Entertainment given to the High and Mighty Prince Charles* (1623). 'Newes From Spain . . .', BL: Eg. MSS, 2884, 17. Jesus, *op. cit.*, 325.

26 18/3/23, ? to ? Birch, *Court and Times of James I*, ed., R. F. Williams (1849) II, 278–9; Wynne, *op. cit.*, II, 432.

27 8/3/23, Kellie to Mar, HMC, *Mar and Kellie*, 158. 26/3/23, Sir Charles Montague to Edward Lord Montague, HMC, *Buccleuch*, I, 256. 14/3/23, Valaresso to Doge, *CSPV, 1621–3*, 819.

28 10/3/23, Porter to wife, SP 14/139/81. 10/3/23, Charles and Buckingham to James, BL: Harl. MSS, 6987, 21.

29 16/4/23, Kellie to Mar, HMC, *Mar and Kellie*, 7.

30 18 and 25/3/23, 4/4/23, Charles and Buckingham to James, BL: Harl. MSS, 6987, 35, 44, 46, 48. 4/4/23, Conway to Wentworth, SP 14/142/34.

31 14 and 27/4/23, Corner to Doge, *CSPV, 1623–5*, 34, 38. Jesus, *op. cit.*, 234–40. 10/7/23, Howell to Porter, Howell, *op. cit.*, I, 168–70.

32 Sir Anthony Weldon, 'Court and Character to King James', in *The Secret History of the Court of James I*, ed. Sir Walter Scott (Edinburgh, 1811) I, 456–7.

33 For examples see 8/8/23, Mathew to Duchess of Buckingham, in G. Goodman, *The Court of King James the First* (1839) 306, and Rushworth, *Collections*, I, 188. For Olivares's reaction to Buckingham's death see *CSPV, 1628–9*, 331.

34 2/5/23, Williams to Buckingham, Hacket, *Scrinia*, 124–5.

35 3/4/23, Vane to Conway, *CSPD, 1619–23*, 550. 1/4/23, James to Charles and Buckingham, J. Nichols, *The Progresses, Processions and Magnificent Festivals of James the First* (1828) IV, 840.

36 3/5/23, Chamberlain, *Letters*, II, 494.

37 3/6/23, Corner to Doge, *CSPV, 1623–5*, 54.

38 25/3/23, 22, 25 and 29/4/23, Charles and Buckingham to James, BL: Harl. MSS, 6987, 73, 82, 90; and J. O. Halliwell, ed., *Letters of the Kings of England* (1846) I, 187–8.

39 10/7/23, Howell to Porter, Howell, *op. cit.*, I, 168–70.

40 SP 94/27/173.

41 SP 94/27/87.

42 14/6/23, James to Charles and Buckingham, Earl of Hardwicke, *Miscellaneous*

*State Papers* (1778) I, 421. 26, 27 and 29/6/23, Charles and Buckingham to James, BL: Harl. MSS, 6987, 107, 109 and 113.

43 23/7/23, Younge to Zouch, *CSPD, 1623–5*, 27. 26/7/23, Chamberlain, *Letters*, II, 508–12.

44 Jesus, *op. cit.*, 340–2. Rushworth, *Collections*, I, 87.

45 29/7/23 and 9/8/23, Charles and Buckingham to James, BL: Harl. MSS, 6987, 126–7, 159. Gardiner, *History*, V, 126.

46 20/8/23, Charles to James, BL: Harl. MSS, 6987, 19.

47 18/8/23, Howell to Savage, Howell, *op. cit.*, I, 182.

48 Wynne, *op. cit.*, II, 380, 405–6. 15/8/23, Howell to North, Howell, *op. cit.*, I, 171–3. 10/9/23, Corner to Doge, *CSPV, 1623–5*, 147.

49 Juan Pena, *A Relation of the Royal Festivals made by the King of Spain* (1623). Andres Almansa, *The Joyful Returne of the Most Illustrious Prince, Charles* (1623). Anon, 'Relation to the Departure', in *Somer's Tracts*, II, 540–9.

50 SP 94/28/117.

51 6/10/23, Corner to Doge, *CSPV, 1623–5*, 133.

52 Halliwell, *op. cit.*, II, 229. SP 94/28/73. 28/11/23, Olivares to Philip IV, Jesus, *op. cit.*, 192–3. 14/9/23, Charles to Bristol, SP 94/28/93.

53 Mossini to Doge, *CSPV, 1623–5*, 172.

54 6/9/23, Carleton to Carleton, *CPSD, 1623–5*, 74. Andres de Almansa y Mendoza, *The Joyful Returne of the Most Illustrious Prince, Charles* (1623) 41. Sir John Finett, *Finetti Philoxensis* (1656) 121. Phineas Pett, *Autobiography* (Naval Records Society, LI, 1918) 128–33.

55 Clarendon, *History*, I, 22. Cecil T. Davies, 'Wandsworth Church Wardens' Accounts, 1620–30', *Surrey Archaeological Collections*, XX (1907) 189. Charles Drew, *Lambeth Churchwardens Accounts* (Surrey Record Society, 1950) II, 40, 100. 6/10/23, Chamberlain, *Letters*, II, 55–7.

56 For example: 'His Former toyes (I Believe) he now disdains/as much as Calvin or the Puritaines,' SP 14/153/112–14. Bod: Tanner MSS, 306, 258. Richard Perrinchief, *The Royal Martyr* (1676) 14.

57 11/11/23, Mead to Stuteville, Birch, *op. cit.*, II, 420. Oxford University, *Carolus Redux* (1623).

58 *CSPD, 1623–5*, 503.

59 Hacket, *Scrinia*, I, 165. Laud, *Works*, III, 143.

60 6/10/23, Valaresso to Doge, *CSPV, 1623–5*, 160. 22/9/23, Kellie to Mar, HMC, *Mar and Kellie*, 179.

61 Quoted by Charles H. Carter, *Secret Diplomacy of the Hapsburgs, 1598–1625*, (New York, 1964) 41.

## V 'THE YOUNG FOLKS SHALL HAVE THEIR WORLD'

1 4/11/23, Kellie to Mar, HMC, *Mar and Kellie*, 183.

2 20/10/23, Younge to Zouch, SP 14/153/81.

3 9/11/23, Conway to Calvert, SP 14/153/313.

4 4/11/23, Kellie to Mar, HMC, *Mar and Kellie*, 183.

5 Hacket, *Scrinia*, I, 165. See also 8/10/23, Charles to Bristol, HMC, *8th Report*, I, 215, and 8/10/23, James to Bristol, SP 94/23/134.

6 8/10/23, Charles to Aston, SP 94/28/138. 9/10/23, Conway to Carleton, *CSPD, 1623–5*, 91. 8/10/23, Charles to Philip IV: Fray Francisco de Jesus, *Narrative of the Spanish Marriage Treaty*, 251.

7 1/11/23, Valaresso to Doge, *CSPV, 1623–5*, 201. Laud, *Works*, I, 144. 21/11/23, Chamberlain, *Letters*, II, 527.

8 24/10/23, Bristol to Calvert, J. Nichols, *Progresses, Processions and Magnificent Festivals of James the First* (1828) IV, 933.

9 8/10/23, Chamberlain, *Letters*, II, 522. Gardiner, *History*, V, 143 gives date as 1 November and *CSPV* as the 5th.

10 14–15/11/23, Charles to Bristol, HMC, *8th Report*, I, 216. 21 and 29/11/23, Valaresso to Doge, *CSPV, 1623–5*, 207 and 216. J. Q. Adams, *The Dramatic Records of Sir Henry Herbert, Master of the Revels* (New Haven, 1917) 51. G. Parry, *The Golden Age Restor'd* (Manchester, 1981) 138.

11 Adams, *op. cit.*, 50. Gardiner, *History*, 159–60, gives 28 December as date of summons, but F. M. Powicke and E. P. Fryde, *Handbook of British Chronology* (1961) 337, say 20 December.

12 Hacket, *Scrinia*, I, 169. 31/1/24, Chamberlain, *Letters*, II, 541–2.

13 Rushworth, *Collections*, I, 115–17.

14 *Ibid.*, 119–26. Kellie to Mar, HMC, *Mar and Kellie*, 193. SP 14/160/64.

15 5/3/24, Valaresso to Doge, *CSPV, 1623–5*, 299. 29/2/24, Locke to Carleton, SP 14/159/94. 1/3/24, Carleton to Carleton, SP 84/114/186. *Commons Journals*, I, 733.

16 18/3/24, Chamberlain, *Letters*, II, 549–50. Valaresso wrote home that Charles's action was the gossip of London, 19/3/24, *CSPV, 1623–5*, 318.

17 25/3/24, SP 14/161/37.

18 Sir Robert Cotton, *Cottoni Posthuma*, ed., Edward Goldsmith (Edinburgh, 1884, first ed. 1651) 7.

19 Robert Ruigh, *The Parliament of 1624* (Cambridge, Mass., 1971) 270–301. 25/4/24, Nethersole to Carleton, SP 14/163/50–1. 3/5/24, Maestro to James, SP 14/164/8.

20 Hacket, *Scrinia*.

21 26/4/24, Charles to Buckingham, BL: Harl. MSS, 6987, 211.

22 Bod: Tanner MSS, 250, 14. Gardiner, *History*, V, 229.

23 12/5/24, Locke to Carlton, *CSPD, 1623–5*, 242.

24 2/6/24, Charles to Carlisle, SP 78/72/275.

25 Nd, Countess of Bedford to Elizabeth of Bohemia, William Seward, *Anecdotes of some distinguished persons* (1798), I, 215–16. 23/4/24, Tilliers to Louis XIII, Frederick Von Raumer, *History of the 16th and 17th Centuries Illustrated from Original Documents* (1838) II, 287. SP 14/160/9. 20/3/24, Chamberlain, *Letters*, II, 55.

26 Clarendon, *History*, I, 28, may here have let hindsight overrule history. But it's a good story ...

27 13/5/26, Mar to Kellie, HMC, *Mar and Kellie*, 200. C. Russell, *Parliament and English Politics, 1621–9* (1979) 190–5.

28 20/8/23, Bristol to Williams, *Cabala*, 21. 29/8/23, Bristol to James, SP 94/27/231. 24/10/23, *ibid.*, SP 94/28/192–6. Howell to North, Nichols, *op. cit.*, IV, 941. 6/12/23, Bristol to Buckingham, *Cabala*, 28. 28/1/24, Bristol to Charles, SP 94/26/17. Howell to Clifford, James Howell, *Epistolae-Ho-Elianae*, ed. Joseph Jacobs (1892) 189.

29 Bristol to Charles, *The Earl of Bristol's defence of his negotiations in Spain* (1871) vii-viii. 1/6/24, Charles to Buckingham, BL: Harl. MSS, 6987. 10/7/24, Bristol to Charles, HMC, *8th Report*, I, 216. 15/7/24 Bristol to Conway, *CSPD, 1623–5*, 303.

30 Charles to Aston, SP 94/28/138. 13/12/23?, Buckingham to Aston, *Cabala*, 36. 22/13/23, Aston to Buckingham, *ibid.*, 36–8.

31 17/2/24 and 14/3/24, Carlisle to Buckingham, *ibid.*, 274–6, 282–4. 26/2/24, Rich to Charles, *ibid.*, 276–7.

32 23/6/24, Kellie to Mar, HMC, *Mar and Kellie*, 206.
33 Charles to Carlisle, SP 78/73/40. Charles to Rich, *CSP*, II, ix.
34 15/8/24, SP 78/72/170 and SP 78/73/50. 8/10/24, Charles to Carlisle, SP78/73/139.
35 *CSP*, I, 501.
36 George Marcelline, *Epithalium Gallo-Britannicum* (1624), 4 and 18/12/24, Chamberlain, *Letters*, II, 588–93. 18/12/24, Carleton to Carleton, SP 14/176/67.
37 19/4/24, Carleton to Carleton, *CSPD, 1623–5*, 219. 18/12/24, Carleton to Nethersole, SP 14/176/66. 8/1/25, Chamberlain, *Letters*, II, 596. 28/1/25, Anon to anon, T. Birch, *Court and Times of James I* (1849) II, 492. 25/1/6, Cromwell to Council of War, SP 14/181/23. For the relationship between MPs and those who elected them see D. Hirst, *The Representative of the People?* (1975).
38 2/3/25, Cromwell to Carleton, SP 84/126/3.
39 11 or 12/24, James to Buckingham, G. Goodman, *The Court of King James I* (1839) II, 379. 24/1/24, Charles to Buckingham, BL: Harl. MSS, 6987, 203.
40 *Memoires de Brienne*, I, 399, quoted Gardiner, *History*, V, 317.
41 30/7/23, J. P. Cooper, *Wentworth Papers, 1597–1628* (1973) 190–1.
42 19/10–24, Charles to Carlisle, SP 78/73/250.
43 BL: Harl. MSS, 6987, 211.
44 *CSPD, 1623–5*, 113.
45 31/9/22, Lando to Doge, *CSP.V, 1621–3*, 450–4, has a long description of Prince Charles.
46 Dr Murray Snyder of the Speech Rehabilitation Institute of New York City has stated that 'Underneath the cloak of inhibition and mild manners, the stutterer often seethes with anger,' quoted *Time* (24 August 1970), 42.
47 Richard Perrinchief, *The Royal Martyr* (1676) 247–8.
48 Lando to Doge, *CSPV, 1621–3*, 450–4.
49 6/9/22, Valaresso to Doge, *CSPV, 1621–3*, 592.

## VI 'OUR ONLY LAWFUL, LINEAL AND RIGHTFUL LIEGE LORD'

1 Rushworth, *Collections*, I, 155.
2 27/3/25, Pesaro to Doge, *CSPV, 1623–5*, 879. 27/3/25, Chamberlain to Elizabeth, SP 16/1/2.
3 John Rous, *the Diary of John Rous*, ed., M. A. E. Green (Camden Soc., 1856) 1. CUL: Mn IV, 57, no. 12, 280. *Great Britaine's sorrow at the death of King James . . . and the peoples joy at the proclaiming of . . . Charles* (1625).
4 31/3/25, Pesaro to Doge, *CSPV, 1625–6*, 4. 5/4/25, Neve to Holland, Birch, *Court*, I, 3. E. Simpson and G. Pottes, *The Sermons of John Donne* (Berkeley, 1953) VI, 241–2.
5 31/3/25, HMC, *Skrine*, 15–17. Knyvett to wife, *The Knyvett Letters*, ed., B. Schofield (1949) 66. 14 and 21/5/25, Chamberlain, *Letters*, II, 616, 619.
6 7/4/25 Kellie to Mar, HMC, *Mar and Kellie*, 227. T. Rymer and R. Sanderson, eds, *Foedera* (1704–32) XVIII, 18.
7 SP 16/1/43. Rymer and Sanderson, *op. cit.*, XVIII, 25–6. *CSPD, 1625–6*, 12. SP 16/2/25. Charles commissioned Ley, Pembroke and Weston to investigate the Isle of Wight's defences in June; Add. MSS 24064, 7.
8 D. Hirst, 'The Privy Council and the problems of enforcement in the 1620's', *Journal of British Studies*, XVIII, 1 (Fall 1978) 46–66. 17/4/25, Mathew to Carleton, SP 16/1/67.

9 Laud, *Works*, III, 159. Bod. MSS, Eng. Hist., e. 28, 549–67.

10 Rawl. MSS, D 392, 356 ff. Nicholas Tyacke dates Charles's Arminianism from 1623: *Antic-Calvinists: the Rise of English Arminianism, c. 1590–1640* (Oxford, 1987), 114.

11 3/1/26, Bod. MSS, Eng. Hist., e. 28, 549–67. For more on Charles's religion see Chapter XI.

12 Simonds D'Ewes, *The Autobiography and Correspondence of Simonds D'Ewes*, ed., J. O. Halliwell (1845) III, 65.

13 J. Cosin, *Works* (Oxford, 1834–55) II, 74, quoted by N. Tyacke, 'Arminianism in England in Religion and Politics, 1604 to 1640,' D. Phil, Oxford (1968). This dissertation is fundamental for understanding Arminianism. J. S. McCauley, 'Richard Montague: Caroline Bishop, 1557–1641', Cambridge, PhD (1964), argues that Charles did not fully support Arminianism until 1628.

14 *A Relation of the Glorious Triumphs and the Order of the Ceremonies observed at the Marriage of... Charles... and... Henrietta Maria* (1625). 6/5/25, Morsini to Doge, *CSPV, 1625–6*, 61.

15 22/4/25, *APC, 1625–6*, 31.

16 17/6/25, Meddus to Stuteville, Birch, *Court*, I, 29–32. Phineas Pett, *Autobiography* (Naval Records Society, LI, 1918).

17 17 and 20/6/25, 8 and 21/7/25, Pesaro to Doge, *CSPV, 1625–6*, 126, 163, 187–8. 1/6/25, Meddus to Mead, Birch, *Court*, I, 38–9.

18 17/6/25, Meddus to Stuteville, Birch, *Court*, I, 29–32. Sir John Finett, *Finetti Philoxensis* (1656) 152. 14/6/25, Charles to Louis XIII, SP 78/75/76.

19 2/7/25, Mead to Stuteville, Birch, *Court*, I, 40.

20 Carola Oman, *Henrietta Maria* (1936) 25. Quentin Bone, *Henrietta Maria: Queen of the Cavaliers* (Urbana, 1972) 29–30. Contarini to Doge, *CSPV, 1625–6*, 607 and 614. 29/6/25, Salvetti to Florence, HMC, *Skrine*, 27.

21 SP 16/2/1–5. 15/12/25, Charles to Abbot, *Bib. Regia*, 13–15. Charles to Judges, Add. MSS. 34324, 242.

22 Quoted C. H. Firth, 'Ballad History of the Reigns of James I and Charles I', *TRHS* (3rd Series, 5 and 6, 1911–12) 19.

23 17/6/25, Cromwell to Conway, SP 84/127/242.

24 21/7/25, Pesaro to Doge, *CSPV, 1625–6*, 187–8. 1/7/25, Salvetti to Florence, HMC, *Skrine*, 25. 26/11/25, Charles to Buckingham, Harl. MSS, 6988, 1. 12/7/26, Charles to Carleton, *Bib. Regia*, 219–22. 7/2/6, Contarini to Doge, *CSPV, 1625–6*, 604. Clarendon, *History*, I, 69.

25 8/4/25, Charles to Buckingham, *CSPD, 1625–6*, 7. 20/4/25, Meddus to Mead, Birch, *Court*, I, 11–12.

26 SP 81/33/63. This paper is now in the PRO.

27 Quoted by C. V. Wedgwood, *Poetry and Politics under the Stuarts*, (Cambridge, 1960) 36.

28 *APC, 1625–6*, 14. Hacket, *Scrinia*, II, 4.

29 Rushworth, *Collections*, I, 172.

30 S. R. Gardiner, *Debates in the House of Commons in 1625* (Camden Soc., 1873) 67.

31 *Ibid.*, 106–7.

32 Rushworth, *Collections*, I, 177–9, 181–6. 11/8/25, Nethersole to Carleton, SP 16/5/33.

33 HMC, *Mar and Kellie*, II, 281.

34 Conrad Russell, 'Parliamentary History in Perspective, 1604–1629', *History*, LXI, 201 (February, 1976) 1–27.

35 Pesaro to Doge, *CSPV, 1625–6*, 217.

36 William Lilly, *The Life and Death of Charles I* (1774) 25, 193.
37 Mende to Louis XIII, Frederick Von Raumer, *History of the 16th and 17th Centuries Illustrated from Original Documents* (1838) II, 292–3.
38 16/8/25, Pesaro to Doge, *CSPV, 1625–6*, 217.
39 Hacket, *Scrinia*, 65–6.
40 *Ibid.*, II, 27.
41 30/7/25, Charles to Lord Lieutenants, Tanner MSS, 177, 188. *APC, 1626*, 322–3. SP 16/6/70 and 128–9. Huntington MSS: HA 1335–7. In his important book *The Forced Loan and English Politics, 1626–28* (Oxford, 1987), Richard Cust disagrees with those who emphasize consensus during the 1620s and suggests that there was much more 'potential for conflict within the English political system'. While agreeing that Charles and Buckingham worked closely together, he suggests that from the start the king was the senior partner. Dr Cust, however, interprets the king's sentiments from his public documents, such as proclamations, rather than his private statements, such as letters or conversations with friends.
42 8/9/25, St Leger to Conway, SP 16/6/101. 30/8/25, Pesaro to Doge, *CSPV, 1625–6*, 330.
43 4/10/25, Harl. MSS, 3638, 107.
44 13/9/25, Pesaro to Doge, *CSPV, 1625–6*, 244.
45 SP 16/5/86–7. Harl. MSS 1584, 17, 375–8.
46 13/7/25, Pesaro to Doge, *CSPV, 1625–6*, 245. Salvetti's estimate was eighty-one ships with 15,726 men, HMC, *Skrine*, 35.
47 8/9/25, Locke to Carleton, SP 16/6/34. John Glanville, *The Voyage to Cadiz*, ed., A. Grosart (Camden Soc., 1883) 3–4.
48 8/11/25, Wimbledon to Buckingham, SP 16/9/30. Glanville, *op. cit.*, 59.
49 19/1/26, Chamberlain, *Letters*, II, 628.
50 22/11/25, Delaware to Edmondes, BL: Stowe MSS, 176, 268. 29/10/25, St Leger to Buckingham, SP 16/8/59.

## VII 'A SHAMEFUL RETURN'

1 John Rous, *The Diary of John Rous*, ed., M. A. E. Green (Camden Soc., 1856) 1.
2 *CSPD, 1625–6*, 222. John Glanville, *The Voyage to Cadiz*, ed., Alexander Grant (Camden Soc., 1883) 120.
3 *CSPD, 1625–6*, 177, 184, 214, 216, 227, 306–7, and 350.
4 19/12/25, St Leger to Buckingham, SP 16/12/18. John Young, *Diary*, ed., F. R. Goodman (1928) 87.
5 15/4/26, Birch, *Court*, I, 95.
6 *Proclamation: By the King: touching his Coronation* (1626). 19/1/26, Chamberlain, *Letters*, II, 627. HMC, *Skrine*, 43.
7 The description of the coronation is from the eye-witness accounts of Bradshaw, Herald of Arms, in SP 16/20/12, and Simonds D'Ewes, *The Autobiography and Correspondence of Sir Simonds D'Ewes*, ed., J. O. Halliwell (1845) I, 292–3, and II, 174. Laud, *Works*, III, 181–2.
8 Sir William Sanderson, *A Compleat History of the Life and Raigne of King Charles* (1658) 25.
9 4/2/25, D'Ewes, *op. cit.*, II, 174.
10 Gardiner, *History*, VI, 48–9.
11 10/2/26, Pesaro to Doge, *CSPV, 1625–6*, 474.
12 Laud, *Works*, I, 63.
13 7/3/26, Chamberlain, *Letters*, 629.

14 Gardiner, *History*, VI, 56.
15 10/6/26, Charles to Bristol, SP 16/18/34. S. R. Gardiner, *Documents illustrating the Impeachment of Buckingham in 1626* (Camden Soc., 1889) xxv-xxxvi, 174.
16 *Ibid.*
17 12/5/26, Meddus to Mead, Birch, *Court*, I, 101–2. Rushworth, *Collections*, I, 357. C. Russell, *Parliament and English Politics, 1621–9* (1979) 311.
18 'The manner of the Duke of Buckingham's Election', by Anon (almost certainly a don, most likely on the losing side) Sloane MSS, 1775, 23 ff. 1/6/26, Mead to Stuteville, Birch, *Court*, I, 107.
19 Charles to Suffolk, CUL: MSS Mn 1, 52, 6, 157–9.
20 6 and 7/6/26, Charles to Commons, and 7/6/26, Commons to Charles, Sloane MSS, 1755, 44 ff.
21 Rushworth, *Collections*, I, 390–1.
22 Birch, *Court*, I, 111–12.
23 3/5/26, Charles to the Council of War, SP 16/26/33. The council's minutes are in SP 16/28. 6/5/26, Charles to Totness, SP 16/25/103.
24 Gardiner, *History*, VI, 83.
25 *Bib. Regia*, 210–12.
26 Add. MSS, 9806, 1. For more on this see Michael B. Young, 'Charles I and the Erosion of Trust, 1625–28', in *Albion*, 22/2 (Summer 1990), 217–35.
27 Quoted by C. Russell, *Crisis of Parliaments* (1971) 310.
28 Quoted by Gardiner, *History*, VI, 110.
29 9/2/27, Charles to Lord Lieutenants, *CSPD, 1627–8*,49.
30 1/7/26, 13/10/26, *CSPV, 1625–6*, 645, 780. 8 and 11/12/27, *CSPV, 1626–8*, 71. *APC, 1616*, 306. *CSPD, 1624–5*, 494–5. Phineas Pett, *Autobiography* (Naval Records Society, LI, 1918) 137.
31 *APC, 1626*, 51, 63–5, 164, 180–2, 197, 215.
32 14/8/27, Charles to Privy Council, SP 16/33/1–2. 31/8/27, Charles to Peers, SP 16/34/65. 9/27? Charles to Lord Lieutenants, SP 16/3/116. *Proclamation: For the Restraint of Mariners and Souldiers* (1626). 7/7/26, Charles to JPs, Hunt. MSS, HA 1340.
33 *APC, 1626*, 186. Birch, *Court*, II, 190. 19/7/26, SP 16/71/43.
34 *CSPD, 1627–8*, 86, 117, 437. *Bib. Regia*, 249–50. 1/10/27, Charles to Buckingham, Harl. MSS, 6988, 42–3.
35 Harl. MSS, 6988, 1.
36 18/12/25, Rudyard to Nethersole, SP 16/12/4.
37 'A true relation of the affair outside Durham House', SP 78/77/300. 10/3/26, Charles to Louis XIII, SP 78/78/87. 'Relation of a brawl', *Catholic Record Society Publications*, I, Miscellanea, V.
38 12/7/26, Charles to Buckingham, Halliwell, *Letters*, 266–70. SP 78/79/291, article 5.
39 12/7/26, Charles to Carleton, *Bib. Regia*, 219–22.
40 My thanks to Roy Schrieber for this point about Lady Carlisle's ambitions. 21/6/26, Rossi to Doge, *CSPV, 1625–6*, 680.
41 11/8/26, Rossi to Doge, *CSPV, 1625–6*, 704. 16/7/26, Charles to Louis XIII, SP 78/79/13–14: the fact that there are four drafts of this letter suggests that it was not an easy one to write.
42 Accounts of the expulsion taken from *CSPV, 1625–6*, 696, and Pory to Mead, William Powell, *John Pory* (Chapel Hill, 1976) appendix of microfiche letters, 105–7.
43 11/8/26, Mead to Stuteville, Birch, *Court*, I 136–7. *APC, 1626*, 165–6. List of Debts in SP 16/34/94, 417. 7/8/26, Charles to Buckingham, Harl. MSS, 6988, 11.

44 25/8/26, Contarini, *CSPV, 1625–6*, 718–9. HMC, *Skrine*, 82–3.
45 François de Bassompiere, *Memoirs of the Embassy of François de Bassompiere* (1819) 25–68. 29/9/26, and 3, 10 & 24/11/26, Contarini to Doge, *CSPV, 1626–8*, 17, 34, 58. 6 and 20/10/26, and 3/11/26, HMC, *Skrine*, 85–7.
46 SP 78/79/115. Charles repeated these sentiments in a letter of 27/7/26 to Louis XIII, SP 78/79/162.
47 SP 78/79/130–4.
48 13/8/26, Alleyne to Buckingham, *CSPD, 1625–6*, 403. 8/9/26, Carleton to Charles, SP 78/80/6.
49 30/12/26, Pesaro to Doge, *CSPV, 1625–6*, 412, 4/27, Charles to Frederick, SP 81/34/189.
50 3/4/26 and 1/5/26, Charles to Buckingham, *CSPD, 1627–8*, 154, 159. 15/6/27, HMC, *Skrine*, 119. 15/6/27, ? to Mead, Birch, *Court*, I, 240–1.
51 C. H. Firth, 'Ballad history of the reigns of James I and Charles I', *Transactions of the Royal Historical Society*, 3rd series, 5 and 6 (1911–12) 20.
52 In the seventeenth century a sergeant major was not a non-commissioned officer but a senior office of field or even general rank. For instance his rough equivalent in a modern British brigade would be the brigade major and in a US regiment the S1: 1/5/27, Blundell to Buckingham, *CSPD, 1627–8*, 1.
53 T. Rymer and R. Sanderson, eds, *Foedera* (1704–32) XVIII, 892–5.
54 16/5/27, ? to Mead, Birch, *Court*, I, 226. 22/5/27, HMC, *Skrine*, 118.
55 Since Conway, who suffered badly from sea-sickness, enjoyed his meal it is safe to assume the day was fine: 11/6/27, Mason to Nicholas, SP 16/66/67, and various letters to Mead, Birch, *Court*, I, 240–8.
56 Henry Vane's letters to Conway were passed on to the king, sometimes within minutes of their arrival: Hardwicke, *SP*, II, 23–6, 31–4, 41–3. Buckingham's friends arranged the publication of *A Journal of all the proceedings of the Duke of Buckingham*, *A Continued Journal of all the proceedings of the Duke of Buckingham*, and *A True Report of all the special Passages of note lately happened in the Island of Ré. . . .*
57 SP 16/78/71/
58 5/11/27, SP 16/84/24.
59 *CSPD, 1627–8*, 454. James Howell, *Epistolae-Ho-Elianae*, ed., Joseph Jacobs (1892) 201.
60 23/2/27, Charles to Buckingham, Hardwicke, *SP*, II, 22. 29/7/27, Charles to Carlisle, *CSPD, 1627–8*, x–xi.
61 Henrietta Maria to Lord Treasurer, *CSPD, 1627–8*, 283.
62 Harl. MSS, 6988, 33.
63 17/8/27, Contarini to Doge, *CSPV, 1626–8*, 424.
64 25/6/27, Goring to Buckingham, SP 16/67/105. 20/8/27, *APC, 1627*, 492–3. 11/8/27, Charles to Poulett, SP 16/73/68.
65 17 and 27/7/27, and 1/8/27, *CSPD, 1627–8*, viii–ix. 21/7/27, Conway to Privy Council, SP 16/71/63.
66 11/5/27, Charles to Salisbury, HMC, *Salisbury*, XXI, 228. 28/6/27 and 19/9/27, Charles to Buckingham, Harl. MSS, 6988, 42–3.
67 27 and 30/9/27, Buckingham to Conway, Hardwicke, *SP*, II, 46, 48–51. 13/10/27, Charles to Holland, *CSPD, 1627–8*, 385. 24/10/27, Wilmot to Conway, SP 16/84/65.
68 Rous, *op. cit.*, 12.

## VIII TO 'TAKE THAT SLIME AWAY'

1 28/11/27, Denbigh to Buckingham, 29/11/27, Bagg to Buckingham, *CSPD, 1627–8*, 449–50, 454.
2 Attributed to Alexander Gill, *CSPD, 1628–9*, 240.
3 16/11/27, ? to Mead, Birch, *Court*, I, 285.
4 John Rous, *The Diary of John Rous*, ed., M. A. E. Green (Camden Soc., 1856) 13.
5 C. V. Wedgwood, *Poetry and Politics under the Stuarts* (Cambridge, 1960) 37.
6 Harl. MSS, 6988, 76, 80. 13/11/27, Conway to son, SP 16/84/67.
7 13/11/27, Conway to son, SP 16/84/67.
8 *CSPD, 1627–8*, xiv-xv.
9 3/11/27, Exeter to Buckingham, SP 16/81/16. 15/11/27, Manchester to Buckingham, SP 16/84/81.
10 14/11/27, Beaulieu to Puckering, Birch, *Court*, I, 284. 12/12/27, HMC, *Skrine*, 132–3. 22/11/27, Contarini to Doge, *CSPV, 1626–8*, 622.
11 20/11/27, Conway to son, *CSPD, 1627–8*, 442.
12 *CSPV, 1626–8*, 650.
13 Harl. MSS, 6988, 78.
14 Mead to Stuteville, Birch, *Court*, I, 305.
15 12/11/27, Nicholas to Charles, *CSPD, 1627–8*, 431. 6/11/27, Charles to Buckingam, Harl. MSS, 6988, 57. 23/2/28, Charles to Buckingham, Halliwell, *Letters*, II, 281–2.
16 Charles met with the privy council ten times in December as compared to his average of once every three weeks for the rest of 1628. *APC, 1627–8*, 227–9, 246. *CSPD, 1627–8*, 481, 506. SP 16/28.
17 *CSPD, 1627–8*, 506, 555, 560, 574.
18 *Ibid.*, 491.
19 *APC, 1627–8*, 163, 167, 232, 455, 462, 463–6. *CSPD, 1627–8*, 555, 563.
20 8/3/28, Mead to Stuteville, Birch, *Court*, I, 327.
21 5/2/28, Contarini to Doge, *CSPV, 1628–9*, 21.
22 Rushworth, *Collections*, I, 447.
23 10 and 24/3/28, *Bib. Regia*, 25–6, 37–9. *Commons Debates, 1628*, II, 3.
24 *CSPV, 1628–9*, 66–7. *Commons Debates, 1628*, II, 316.
25 L. Boynton, 'Billeting: the example of the Isle of Wight', *English Historical Revue*, LXXIV, 290 (1959) 23–40; VIII, 24. 2/6/28, Mayor and Aldermen of Canterbury to Privy Council, *CSPD, 1628–9*, 145. Petition of Walloon congregation, Canterbury, SP 16/104/32 II. 10/2/28, Maldon petition, SP 16/92/85. *Commons Debates, 1628*, II, 282, 297, 325.
26 *CSPD, 1627–8*, 551–2. *APC, 1627–8*, 276, 282, 296.
27 19/4/28, Mead to Stuteville, Birch, *Court*, I, 344–6. *Commons Debates, 1628*, II, 430–2.
28 2/5/28, Charles to Commons, SP 16/103/5. *Commons Debates, 1628*, II, 213.
29 12/5/28, Charles to Lords, Rushworth, *Collections*, I, 560–1. *Commons Debates, 1628*, II, 372–3.
30 17/5/28, Charles to Denbigh, SP 16/104/8. 19/5/28, Charles to Coke, SO 16/104/21. 9/5/28, Denbigh to Buckingham, SP 16/103/50. 21/5/28, Woodward to Windebank, SP 16/104/27. 2/6/28, Zorizi to Doge, *CSPV, 1628–9*, 118. *CSPD, 1628–9*, 141/
31 F. H. Relf, *The Petition of Right* (Minneapolis, 1917) 49–57. Rushworth, *Collections*, I, 588–91. E. R. Forster, 'Petitions and the Petition of Right', *Journal of British Studies*, XIV, 1 (November, 1974) 21–45. Stephen White, *Sir Edward Coke and the 'Grievances of the Commonwealth'* (Chapel Hill, 1979) 227–72.

Conrad Russell, *Parliaments and English Politics, 1621–29* (Oxford, 1982) 323–89. My thanks to J. A. Guy for letter me read his unpublished paper 'The origins of the Petition of Right reconsidered'. *Commons Debates, 1628*, III, 125.

32 Rushworth, *Collections*, I, 607. *Commons Debates, 1628*, IV, 54–5.
33 Gardiner, *History*, VI, 309–10. *Commons Debates, 1628*, IV, 182.
34 7/6/28, *CSPD, 1628–9*, 153. 9.6.28, Conway to Coke, *CSPD, 1628–9*, 156. *Commons Debates, 1628*, III, 614.
35 5/28?, memo in Charles's hand, *CSPD, 1628–9*, 142. 6/6/28, Charles to Buckingham, Harl. MSS, 6988, 87. E. R. Forster, 'Printing the Petition of Right', *Huntington Library Quarterly*, XXXVIII, 1 (Nov., 1974) 81–3. 7/6/28, Nethersole to Elizabeth, SP 16/106/55.
36 19/6/28, Nethersole to Elizabeth, *CSPD, 1628–9*, 169. 20/6/28, Contarini to Doge, *CSPV, 1628–9*, 156. *Commons Debates, 1628*, IV, 311–17, gives a slightly different version of Charles's insult.
37 Aston to Carlisle, *CSPD, 1628–9*, 218. *CSPV, 1628–9*, 173. Rushworth, *Collections*, I, 626–7. Harl. MSS, 390, 420–1.
38 *CSVP, 1628–9*, 126–7, 154.
39 *CSPD, 1628–9*, 179, 198, 217. *DNB*.
40 21/6/28, Mead to Stuteville, Birch, *Court*, I, 364. *CSPD, 1628–9*, 278.
41 In spite of it all the robbers didn't get away. SP 16/114/231. 29/6/28, Mead to Stuteville, Birch, *Court*, I, 368–9. William Powell, *John Pory* (Chapel Hill, 1976) microfiche addenda, 126. Clarendon, *History*, I, 74–9. Rous, *op. cit.*, 19.
42 Rushworth, *Colections*, I, 618.
43 21/6/28, Mead to Stuteville, Birch, *Court*, I, 365.
44 18/5/28, Charles to Pennington, SP 16/104/14.
45 *CSPD, 1628–9*, 149–50, 177.
46 23/7/2, Charles to Buckingham, Harl. MSS, 6988, 32.
47 27/7/28, Conway to Buckingham, *CSPD, 1628–9*, 234. Sir John Oglander, *Memoirs*, ed., W. H. Long (1936) 44–5.
48 *CSPD, 1625–6*, 47. Sir Henry Wotton, *Sort View of the Life and Death of George Villiers, Duke of Buckingham* (1642) 20–2. Hamon L'Estrange, *The Reign of King Charles* (1655) 106–7.
49 Eye-witness accounts of a Mr Birford in HMC, *Skrine*, 244–5, and Dudley Carleton in SP 16/114/20.
50 Hacket, *Scrinia*, II, 5.
51 Sir Thomas Phillipps, ed., *Sir Dudley Carleton's State Letters during his Embassy to the Hague* (1841) 10–11.
52 23/2/28, Harl. MSS, 6988, 60.
53 6/11/27, Harl. MSS, 6988, 53.
54 SP 16/22/51.
55 29/6/28, Mead to Stuteville, Birch, *Court*, I, 368–9.
56 Eg. MSS, 2816.
57 SP 16/52/1–2/
58 John Milton recorded gossip that Charles 'was known to have committed all manner of lewdness with his confidant, the duke.' F. W. Fairholt, ed., *Poems and Songs relating to George Villiers* (1850) 9. See Chapter II, note 35, for more on this.
59 Rushworth, *Collections*, I, 345.
60 24/5/28, Bagg to Buckingham, SP 16/105/5: for another example see SP 16/84/93/
61 *CSPD, 1627–8*, 87, 91. 27/8/28, Carleton to Elizabeth, SP 16/114/17.

62 The following table calculated from T. E. Tomlins *et al.*, eds, *Statutes of the Realm* (1810–28), illustrates this point. 'Public-national' is defined as legislation effecting the interests of the crown, e.g. foreign policy or taxation. 'Public-local' are acts which are clearly of private interest but are labelled 'public', e.g. one for the repair of Chepstow bridge which, in spite of being a notorious bottle-neck in the seventeenth as well as the twentieth century, was clearly a local matter. 'Private' is self-explanatory. The process was repeated in 1640/1: see Bankes MSS 22/18/2.

| Parliaments: | Public-national | Public-local | Private |
|---|---|---|---|
| 1603–4 | 4 | 29 | 39 |
| 1605–6 | 4 | 23 | 29 |
| 1606–7 | 1 | 12 | 20 |
| 1609–10 | 3 | 21 | 43 |
| 1614 | 0 | 0 | 0 |
| 1621 | 2 | 0 | 0 |
| 1624 | 0 | 35 | 38 |
| 1625 | 6 | 1 | 0 |
| 1627 | 8 | 0 | 0 |

63 R. L. Armstrong, ed., *Poems of James Shirley* (New York, 1941) 5. For a different view of Charles I and Buckingham, and for the 1620s as a whole, see Thomas Cogswell's provocative work, *The Blessed Revolution: English Politics and the Coming of the War, 1621–24* (Cambridge, 1989).

## IX 'SOVEREIGNTY MAINTAINED ABOVE ALL'

1 10/29, Earl of Banbury to Carleton, SP 16/150/114.
2 2/9/28, Contarini to Doge, *CSPV, 1628–9*, 283. 23/8/28. Conway to Coke, HMC, *Cowper*, I, 364. 23/8/28, Carleton to Conway, *CSPD, 1628–9*, 265. 24/8/28, Charles to Privy Council, *APC, 1628–9*, 36.
3 28/8/28, Carleton to Coke, SP 16/114/27.
4 Birch, *Court*, I, 390–1. Hamon L'Estrange, *The Reign of King Charles* (1655) 91–2.
5 *CSPD, 1628–9*, 277, 310, 314, 319, 325, 326. Birch, *Court*, I, 423, 431.
6 26/8/28, Carleton to Coke, *CSPD, 1628–9*, 269.
7 27/8/28, Charles to Elizabeth, SP 16/114/17. *CSPD, 1628–9*, 274, 349. W. H. Long, ed., *The Oglander Memoirs* (1888) 51.
8 1/9/28, Hay to Carlisle, SP 16/116/4. F. W. Fairholt, ed., *Poems and Songs Relating to George Villiers* (Percy Soc., 1850) 35. 20/9/26, Mead to Stuteville, Birch, *Court*, I, 396.
9 27/8/28, SP 16/114/17.
10 Charles to Cambridge University, CUL MSS, Patrick Papers, XXIII, 24. 20/9/28, Mead to Stuteville, Birch, *Court*, I, 396–9.
11 28/7/28, Contarini to Doge, *CSPV, 1628–9*, 213.
12 3/10/28, *CSPD, 1628–9*, 310, 343.
13 24/11/28, SP 16/121/47.
14 22/12/28, Goring to Carlisle, SP 16/123/8.
15 20/5/29, Beaulieu to Puckering, Birch, *Court*, I, 328.
16 Henrietta Maria, *Letters*, 15–16.
17 14/9/28 and 8/10/28, Mead to Stuteville, Birch, *Court*, II, 50.
18 24/8/28, Conway to Laud, SP 16/114/3/
19 3 and 4/9/28, Carleton to Coke, *CSPD, 1628–9*, 315.
20 13/9/28, Mead to Stuteville, Birch, *Court*, I, 394.

21 3.10.28, Lindsey to Charles, SP 16/118/8. 5/11/28, report of Capt. Button, SP 16/120/17, I. Rushworth, *Collections*, I, 636. Reports of Ambassador Zorzi who was with Louis XIII at La Rochelle, *CSPV, 1628–9*, 133, 169, 182, 201, 250, 325, 360, 425.

22 14/10/28, Charles to Lindsey, SP 16/118/66. 13/11/28, Conway to Lindsey, *CSPD, 1628–9*, 375. 15/11/28, Plumleigh to Nicholas, SP 16/120/72.

23 Steele, *Proclamations*, 1563. 11/28 and 12/1/29, Charles to Rohan, SP 78/83/195 and SP 78/84/3.

24 27/8/28, Algenon to Salisbury, HMC, *Salisbury*, XXI, 24. 24/8/28 and 1/9/28, Sussex to Conway, SP 16/114/5 and SP 16/116/3. 24/8/28, Holland to Charles, SP 16/14/1.

25 28/8/28. Hippisley to Conway, *CSPD, 1628–9*, 272. 28.8.28, Bagg to Conway, SP 16/114/26.

26 *CSPD, 1628–9*, 276–7.

27 20/9/28, Birch, *Court*, I, 396–9.

28 CUL, MSS, Patrick Papers, XXIII, 24–7.

29 19/12/28, Pory to Mead, W. S. Powell, *John Pory*, microfiche appendix, 141–2.

30 24/8/28, Conway to Laud, SP 16/114/3.

31 Clarendon, *History*, I, 84.

32 D. Alexander, *Charles I's Lord Treasurer* (Chapel Hill, 1975) 126–30. 2/12/28, Contarini to Doge, *CSPV, 1628–9*, 432.

33 20/9/28, Mead to Stuteville, Birch, *Court*, I, 396.

34 *CSPD, 1628–9*, 333, 407. SP 75/9/217. 16/10/28, Salvetti to Florence, HMC, *Skrine*, 166–7.

35 22/12/28, Murray to Carlisle, SP 16/123/87–8. Sir Robert Ashton sent Carlisle a similar letter on 19 September, SP 16/122/58.

36 30/9/28, Carleton to Carlisle, Birch, *Court*, I, 403–4. Steele, *Proclamations*, 1559.

37 11/9/28, Duppa's report, SP 16/116/101/ 28/8/28 Willoughby's examination, SP 16/114/31.

38 'Against the opposing of the Duke in Parliament', Richard Corbet, *Poems*, eds, J. A. W. Bennett and H. R. Trevor-Roper (Oxford, 1955) 82.

39 11/12/28, Steele, *Proclamations*, 1566. Rushworth, *Collections*, I, 642.

40 6/12/28, Salvetti to Florence, HMC, *Skrine*, 173. 19/12/28, Pory to Mead, Powell, *op. cit.*, 142.

41 SP 92/15/87.

42 Rushworth, *Collections*, I, 664–5. W. Notestein and F. Relf, eds, *Commons Debates for 1629* (Minneapolis, 1921) 11.

43 26/1/29, Contarini to Doge, *CSPV, 1628–9*, 530.

44 Steele, *Proclamations*, 1572. Rushworth, *Collections*, I, 651–4. Notestein, *op. cit.*, 28.

45 *APC, 1628–9*, 331.

46 Instructions to Vane, SP 84/139/60, and to Roe in S. R. Gardiner, *Sir Thomas Roe's Mission to Gustavus Adolphus* (Camden Soc., 1875) 5. Minutes of Council of War, SP 16/28.

47 28/2/29, Contarini to Doge, *CSPV, 1628–9*, 566.

48 Gardiner, *Constitutional Documents*, 82–3. Notestein, *op. cit.*, 252–7.

49 Simonds D'Ewes, *Autobiography*, (1845) I, 402.

50 6 & 13/3/29, Contarini to Doge, *CSPV, 1628–9*, 579–81, 589. *APC, 1628–9*, 356. Charles to Elizabeth, SP 81/35/161. I. H. C. Fraser, 'Agitation in the Commons, 2 March 1629', *BIHR*, XXX (1957) 86–95.

51 Rushworth, *Collections*, I, 662.

52 Gardiner, *Constitutional Documents*, 83–99.

53 SP 16/14/42–52.

54 T. Rymer and R. Sanderson, eds, *Foedera*, (1704–32) XIX, 62. SP 16/154/34. 25/10/32, 13 and 24/10/32, Powell, *op. cit.*, 19, 312, 342.

55 13/3/29, *CSPV, 1628–9*, 589.


## X A FAMILY AT 'FULL PEACE AND TRANQUILITY'

1 4/7/35, Charles to Bankes, SP 16/293/26. My definition of the court is very different from G. R. Elton's, which is implicit in the title of his article, 'The Tudor Government: The Points of Control, III, the "Court" ', *TRHS* (1976) 211–28. R. M. Smuts, *Court Culture and the Origin of a Royalist Tradition in Early Stuart England* (1987), 190–5, defines a court in a far broader fashion than I do.

2 *The Duchess of Malfi*, Act I, scene 1, lines 6–9.

3 2/7/33, HMC, *Cowper*, II, 25.

4 5/6/19, Rubens to Olivares, quoted C. V. Wedgwood, *The Political Career of Peter Paul Rubens* (1976) 47.

5 G. E. Aylmer, *The King's Servants* (New York, 1961) 26 ff.

6 SP 16/178/6 and 7.

7 G. E. Aylmer, 'Attempts at administrative reform, 1625–40', *EHR* (1957) LXXII, 229–59.

8 20/12/31, Edmondes to Vane, SP 16/204/80.

9 24/3/30, the privy council ordered them torn down, *APC, 1629–30*, 327, 339.

10 G. P. Akrigg, *Jacobean Pageant* (New York, 1967).

11 Itinerary from *CSPD, 1634–5*, 149. W. H. Stevenson, ed., *Records of the Borough of Nottingham* (1882–1956) V, 166–8. Str. P. 15/156 shows similar pattern during the following summer. Rushworth, *Collections*, II, 283.

12 Taken from *CSPD, CSPV*, and itinerary in Str. P. 17/148.

13 *CSPV, 1632–6*, 279, 515. *CSPV, 1636–9*, 64. *APC, 1630–1*, 352. *CSPD, 1631–3*, 394–5.

14 Lucy Hutchinson, *Memoirs of the Life of Colonel Hutchinson* (1965) 67. No date, PRO LC5/180. 9/1/31, SP 16/182/31. 21/8/31, HMC, *Cowper*, I, 281.

15 2/8/34, Anon to Phelips, HMC, *Phelips, 3rd Report*, 283.

16 13/8/29 and 11/6/30, *CSPD, 1629–31*, 37, 279.

17 9/9/31, *CSPV, 1629–32*, 544. 5/8/29, Cottington to Wentworth, *Wentworth Letters*, I, 51.

18 18/5/33 and 3/6/33, Goring to Coke, HMC, *Cowper*, I, 11, 17.

19 22/9/36, Correr to Doge, *CSPV, 1636–9*, 77. 28/9/36, Rossingham to Puckering, Birch, *Court*, II, 250.

20 Quoted by M. Ashley, *The Stuarts in Love* (1963).

21 15/8/35, Con to Barbarini, Add. MSS 15389, 196, quoted by Gardiner, *History*, VI, 336.

22 Quoted by Margaret Pickel, *Charles I as a Patron of Poetry and Drama* (1936) 36.

23 H. Moller, 'The meaning of courtly love', *Journal of American Folklore*, LXXIII (1960), 39–49. Richard A. Koenigsburg, 'Culture and unconscious fantasy: observations on courtly love', *Psychoanalytic Review*, LIV (1967) 36–50.

24 Ben Jonson, *Works*, eds., C. H. Hereford and E. M. Simpson (1925–52) VII, 739–40. Jonson did not believe all this silliness.

25 Thomas Carew, 'To the Queen', quoted, Pickel, *op. cit.*, 57. Erica Veevers, *Images of Love and Religion: Queen Henrietta Maria and Court Entertainment*

(Cambridge, 1989), 3–5. M. Butler, *Theatre and Crisis, 1632–42* (Cambridge, 1984), 40 ff.

26 Melvin W. Askew, 'Courtly love: neurosis as an institution', *Psychoanalytic Review*, LII (1965) 19–29.
27 4/1/30, *CSPV, 1629–32*, 350.
28 *CSPD, 1629–31*, 314.
29 Birch, *Court*, II, 308.
30 Richard Corbet, *Poems*, eds, J. A. W. Bennett and H. R. Trevor-Roper (Oxford, 1955) 84–6.
31 Live children from Sir M. Powicke and E. B. Fryde, *Handbook of British Chronology* (1961) 40–1. Still-births from *CSPV, 1636–9*, 174; *CSPD, 1638–9*, 362. Julia Dobson, *The Children of Charles I* (1975).
32 For example, see SP 16/147/7.
33 SP 16/186/19 and SP 81/36/149.
34 Quoted by M. A. E. Green, *Elizabeth of Bohemia* (1849–55) 303.
35 26/4/38, Charles to Leicester, SP 78/105/277.
36 Harl. MSS, 6988, 1. 4/9/39, Add. MSS, 19832, 48v.
37 20/5/35, Charles to Bath, *CSPD, 1633–4*, 864. 26/5/35, Bath to Holland, HMC, *Cowper*, II, 14.
38 For example, see *CSPD, 1629–31*, 217. *CSPD, 1633–4*, 119. SP 16/298/95. Bankes MSS, 15/10.
39 Hacket, *Scrinia*, II, 26.
40 L. M. Venuti, 'The Cavaliers in Love: Erotic Poetry in the Court of Charles I', Columbia, PhD (1980) 243.
41 23/10/37, Conway to Wentworth, Wentworth, *Letters*, II, 124.
42 R. M. Smuts, 'The culture of absolutism at the court of Charles I', Princeton, PhD, (1976) 302 ff. The phrase the 'queen's set' is mine.
43 Clarendon, *History*, I, 111. Smuts, *op. cit.*, 308.
44 R. F. Williams, ed., *Memoirs of . . . the Capuchin Friars* (1848) II, 308–9.
45 Gregorio Panzani, *Memoirs*, ed., J. Berington (1793) 186, 148–52.
46 Gordon Albion, *Charles I and the Court of Rome* (1935) 164. This is an excellent study. For a summary, see Albion, *Charles and the Papacy* (Royal Stuart Papers, VI, 1974).
47 21/8/35, *CSPV, 1632–6*, 443. A check of the *CSPD* shows no further action.
48 10/5/38, Garrard to Wentworth, Wentworth, *Letters*, II, 165.
49 *CSPD, 1631–3*, 142. *CSVP, 1632–6*, 309.
50 Clarendon, *History*, I, 91.
51 Simonds D'Ewes, *Autobiography* (1845) II, 100.
52 Albion, *op. cit.*, 15.
53 Smuts, *op. cit.*, 302, and his excellent article, 'The Puritan followers of Henrietta Maria in the 1630's', *EHR*, XCIII (1978) 26–45.
54 11/4/30, Charles to Keeper of Southwark Clink, *Bib. Regia*, 257. See also *CSPD, 1631–3*, 218.
55 Bod. MSS, Eng. Hist. e 28, 549–67.
56 Albion, *op. cit.*, 235.
57 SP 16/211/91: on exhibit in Museum Wall, Case XV, 6.
58 Panzani, *op. cit.*, 135. Albion, *op. cit.*, 187 & 233.?/6/31, SP 16/195/32.
59 Panzani, *op. cit.*, 170.
60 *Ibid.*, 134.
61 *APC, 1629–30*, 303–4, 307. 3/11/37, Correr to Doge, 12/1/38, Zonca to Doge, *CSPV, 1636–9*, 319, 358.
62 *CSP*, I, 153–4.

63 Rushworth, *Collections*, II, 32.
64 Sir Henry Wotton, 'A Panegyrick to King Charles', in *Reliquiae Wottonianae* (1654) 145.
65 Horace Walpole, *Ancedotes of Painting* (1762–71) II, 93 ff.
66 Sir Claude Phillips, *The Picture Gallery of Charles I* (1896). Margaret Whinney and Oliver Millar, *English Art, 1625–1714* (Oxford, 1957). Ursula Hoff, *Charles I, Patron of Artists* (1942).
67 Francis C. Springwell, *Connoisseur & Diplomat: The Earl of Arundel's Embassy to Germany in 1636* (1963).
68 R. Davies, 'An inventory of the Duke of Buckingham's pictures', *Burlington Magazine*, X (1907). D. Howarth 'Lord Arundel and the English collection', (Cambridge, PhD, 1977).
69 3/9/21, Rubens to Trumbell, W. N. Sainsbury, *Original unpublished papers illustrative of the life of Sir Peter Paul Rubens* (1859) 59–61.
70 Nys quoted in G. Parry, *The Golden Age Restor'd* (Manchester, 1981) 216. Memo of 8/7/34, Halliwell, *Letters*, II, 288–9.
71 George Vertue, *Catalogue of Pictures of Charles I* (1757). Henry G. Hewlett, 'Charles I as a picture collector', *Nineteenth Century*, XXVIII (August, 1890) 201–11.
72 Walpole, *op. cit.*, II, 142–3. William G. B. Murdock, *The Royal Stuarts in their Connection with Art and Letters* (1908) 183–6.
73 Vertue, *op. cit.*, 6. Walpole, *op. cit.*, I, 136, says collection fetched £38,025, while Phillips, *op. cit.*, 47–51, says that by 1653 they reached £118,081.
74 'The non-such Charles, his character extracted out of diverse transactions', quoted by C. Oman, *Henrietta Maria* (1936) 79.
75 *CSPD, 1633–4*, 43. D. Alexander, *Charles I's Lord Treasurer* (Chapel Hill, 1975) 179.
76 Oman, *op. cit.*, 92.
77 30/1/36, Panzani to Rome, PRO, Roman Transcripts, quoted Smuts, *op. cit.*
78 Albion, *op. cit.*, 394–8.
79 S. Freud, 'The reaction of the poet to day dreaming', *Collected Works* (1925) IV, 173–83. T. W. Adorno *et al.*, *The Authoritarian Personality* (1950).
80 Edmund Waller, *Poetical Works*, ed., I Bell (1777) 67.
81 Wotton, *op. cit.*, 194–5. Murdock, *op. cit.*, 164–5.
82 Roy Strong, *Van Dyck's 'Charles I on Horseback'* (1972) 25.
83 Vertue, *op. cit.*, 123–4.
84 Oliver Millar, *Rubens and the Whitehall Ceiling* (1958).
85 P. Bjurstrom, 'Rubens "St George and the Dragon"', *Art Quarterly* (Spring 1955), 27–42.
86 Strong, *op. cit.* Instructions to Le Sueur in SP 16/156/154.
87 M. S. Steele, *Plays and Masques at Court* (New Haven, 1926).
88 Pickel, *op. cit.*, 104 ff.
89 10/1/31, Mead to Stuteville, Birch, *Court*, II, 89.
90 CUL MSS, Mn IV, 57, #22, 304. Pickel, *op. cit.*, 116–19.
91 Bacon, 'Of masques and triumphs', quoted Per Palme, *The Triumph of Peace* (1956) 135. Jones quoted by Steven Orgel, *The Jonsonian Masque* (Cambridge, Mass., 1965) 3. M. Butler, 'The English drama and its political setting, 1632–42' (Cambridge, PhD, 1981) 274.
92 M. McGowan, 'As through a looking glass: Donne's Epithalamia in their courtly context', in *John Donne, Essays*, ed., A. J. Smith (1972) 175–218.
93 *CSPV, 1617–19*, 188.

94 Steven Orgel and Roy Strong, *Inigo Jones: The Theatre of the Stuart Court* (1973) 43.
96 E. Mercer, 'The houses of the gentry', *Past and Present*, 5 (1954) 11–32.
97 Jonson, *op. cit.*, VII, 735.
98 Strong, *Splendour at Court*, 217–18.
99 Quoted in Steven Orgel, *The Illusion of Power*, 56. M. C. Bradbrook, *The Living Monument: Shakespeare and the Theatre of His Time* (Cambridge, 1976) 245–57.
100 Oliver Millar, 'Charles I, Honthurst and Van Dyck', *Burlington Magazine* (1954) 36–42. Butler, *op. cit.*, 3–4, does not accept the view that during the 1630s the theatre was 'a mouthpiece of the court, subservient, helpless, dependent, toadying'. He argues instead that 'The best court players were vehicles of criticism rather than compliment.'
101 Sir William D'Avenant, *Dramatic Works*, eds, J. Maidment and W. H. Logan (1872–4) II, 312–26.
102 Strong, *Illusions*, 79.

## XI 'HIS OWN DIRECTION AND COMMANDMENT'

1 Rushworth, *Collections*, I, 659.
2 Kevin Sharpe, *The Personal Rule of Charles I* (1992) is a work of great diligence, full of useful information. Its view of Charles I and his role in the 1630s is, I believe, deeply flawed.
3 Bankes MSS, 37/54. G. R. Elton, *Policy and Police* (1971) 134.
4 I am grateful to Father James Larkin for allowing me to see the proofs of his forthcoming edition of Charles's proclamations.
5 Gardiner, *Constitutional Documents*, 83–99. Steele, *Proclamations*. 11/8/33, Netdersole to Charles, *CSP*, I, 60. 22/5/29 and 30/12/31, *CSPV, 1629–32*, 73, 573–5. 15/3/33 and 10/6/35, *CSPV, 1632–6*, 87, 401, 444, 500. 20/12/31, Edmondes to Vane, SP 16/206/80, substantiates the Venetian reports.
6 SP 16/150/3 and 10. SP 16/141/44–52. SP 16/154/34.
7 22/1/35, Charles to Wentworth, Halliwell, *Letters*, II, 287.
8 *APC, 1629–30*, 177. 7/11/29, Harsnett to Vane, Birch, *Court*, II, 37. Perry Simpson, 'Charles I as a drama critic', *Bodleian Quarterly Review*, VIII, 92 (1936–7) 257–62.
9 Bankes MSS, 63/39.
10 5/5/29, Williams to Carleton, SP 16/142/19.
11 CUL: Lett. 12, A 18. Bankes MSS, 37/61/2.
12 Bankes MSS, Bundle 17.
13 3/8/31, Falkland to Carleton, SP 16/198/9).
14 24/1/36, SP 16/312/12.
15 9/8/35, *CSP*, I, 302.
16 See 21/9/31 and 31/12/31, Burnet, *Hamilton*, 24, 27.
17 C. Rogers, ed., *The Earl of Stirling's Register of Royal Letters Relating to Affairs of Scotland and Nova Scotia from 1615 to 1635* (1885) 2 vols.
18 Hacket, *Scrinia*, II, 8.
19 P. Haskell, 'Sir Francis Windebank, and the personal rule of Charles I', (Southampton, PhD, 1978) II, 585.
20 PRO: PC2/43/247.
21 Our knowledge of Carleton will be greatly enhanced by John Reeve's forthcoming Cambridge PhD. Clarendon, *History*, I, 81, 113–15. Quoted by D. Coke, *The Last Elizabethan: Sir John Coke, 1563–1644* (1937) 199.

22 31/5/32, Charles to Abbot, Tanner MSS, 71, 42.

23 21/9/26, Charles I, *Instructions unto all Bishops* (1626) 1–2.

24 Rushworth, *Collections*, I, 445.

25 Hugh Trevor-Roper's *Archbishop Laud* (1960); and C. Carlton, *Archbishop William Laud* (1987). Christopher Hill's *The Economic Problems of the Church* (1971) has some valuable insights. E. R. Adair, 'Laud and the Church of England', *Church History*, V (1936) is also useful. C. F. Pritchard, *Reading, Charter Acts and Orders, 1253–1911* (1913), 76–7. J. M. Building, *Reading Records* (1892) III, 136–7, 418.

26 Quoted in *King's Peace*, 103.

27 Laud, *Works*, III, 170.

28 For Strafford see the report of Sir Nathaniel Brent, Vicar General, for 1635, SP 16/293/128. For more on Laud's reforms, see Carlton, *op. cit.*, 132–43.

29 T. Fuller, *Church History of Britain* (1656) X, 218–19.

30 Rushworth, *Collections*, II, 191–3. L. A. Govett, *The King's Book of Sports* (1890). PRO: PC2/44/272.

31 This story was associated with so many incidents that it may be worth telling more than it is worth believing: 6/12/34, Gerald to Wentworth, Wentworth, *Letters*, I, 166.

32 1/8/34, Laud, *Works*, VI, 388. C. H. Cooper, *Annals of Cambridge* (1842–53) III, 279–83. *Concilia*, IV, 525.

33 William Cobbet, *State Trials*, IV, 359.

34 Laud, *Works*, V, 323. *Concilia*, IV, 574.

35 Laud, *Works*, V, 324–70.

36 11/9/35, SP 16/297/33.

37 3/11/33, SP 16/250/12.

38 11/10/29, Rushworth, *Collections*, II, 28.

39 *CSPD, 1634–5*, 432. *CSPD, 1635–6*, 164–5.

40 26/6/35, *CSPD, 1635*, 234. SP 16/229/116. For a case of urinating in the cathedral see S. R. Gardiner, *Reports of . . . High Commission* (1886) 240.

41 Charles, *His Majesty's Commission . . . St Paul's* (1631, STC 9254).

42 23/5/34, Charles to Laud, *Concilia*, IV, 492.

43 SP 16/281/36.

44 15/7/34, Commissioners to Sheriffs and JPs, SP 16/213/35a. Charles to Dean and Chapter of St Paul's, SP 16/281/34. 30/5/37, Charles to Juxon, *CSPD, 1637*, 158. 28/5/38, Charles to Littleton, Add. MSS, 21505, 20.

45 Rushworth, *Collections*, II, 90–3, 402–3. Sanderson, *Reign of Charles I*, 175 ff.

46 ?/6/31, SP 16/195/32.

47 Sanderson, *op. cit.*, 178. *CSPD, 1633–4*, 444.

48 *CSPD, 1631–3*, 189. *CSPD, 1635–6*, 166 ff, 538–9. *CSPD, 1637*, 277. Lands. MSS, 973, 110–14. Tanner MSS, 220, 151.

49 Gregorio Panzani, *Memoirs* (1793) ed. J. Berington, 206. K. L. Lindley, 'Lay Catholics in the reign of Charles I', *Journal of Ecclesiastical History*, 22 (1971) 119–121.

50 Laud, *Works*, V, 340.

51 Sloane MSS, 1775, 74, no date. Stowe MSS, 119, 13, dated 12/1/30. There is a letter from Abbot to Laud relating to the king's instructions dated 30/12/29 in SP 16/143/100–5.

52 22/6/34 and 6/10/34, Charles to Laud, SP 16/270/6, and *Concilia*, IV, 493–4. Charles to Bishop of Bath and Wells, Charles, *Letters*, 88–9. 8 and 17/7/32, Charles to Abbot, SP 16/220/36 and 79. For examples of implementation see CUL MSS, Mn, I, 49, 33, 13. 13/8/35, Charles to Lord Keeper, SP 16/295/58.

53  9/7/37, *Concilia*, IV, 535–6.

54  5/4/36, Gerrard to Wentworth, Wentworth, *Letters*, I, 2.

55  SP 16/239/64. SP 16/247/3. SP 16/270/3. SP 16/289/4. *Concilia*, V, 496–516.

56  SP 16/211/87.

57  Laud, *Works*, V, 366.

58  For example see 30/5/31, 1/1/32, 5/1/35, in SP 91/2/164, 206 and SP 91/3/5.

59  SP 78/85/236. Reprinted in HMC, *De Lisle*, IV, xxii. Sharpe, *op. cit.*, 507–601, 825–48; and J. Reeve, *Charles I and the Road to Personal Rule* (1989), 227–88, are excellent recent contributions to our understanding of foreign policy during the 1630s.

60  SP 91/2/187–8. SP 84/144/54.

61  Roe to Elizabeth, SP 16/286/34 and SP 16/300/22.

62  *CSPV, 1629–32*, 176–80. Windebank agreed, SP 16/239/71.

63  Clarendon, *History*, I, 118, 131. John Aubrey, *Brief Lives* (1957 ed.) quoted by G. Huxley, *Endymion Porter* (1959) 164.

64  *Ibid.*, 64. There is no good survey of Charles's foreign policy.

65  27/8/28, Carleton to Elizabeth, SP 16/114/17.

66  1/10/28, Charles to Carlisle, W. N. Sainsbury, *Original unpublished papers illustrative of the life of Sir Peter Paul Rubens* (1859) 118n.

67  W. H. Long, ed., *The Oglander Memoirs* (1888) 51–2.

68  8/5/29, *CSPV, 1629–32*, 19.

69  Rushworth, *Collections*, II, 6.

70  *The Articles of Peace agreed upon betwixt Great Britaine and France* (STC 9250).

71  17/9/29, Charles to Elizabeth, SP 78/84/303.

72  SP 78/85/48. SP 78/88/75, 79, 244. SP 78/89/209. SP 78/91/197. Stowe MSS, 132, 290–3. Rogers, *op. cit.*, xxxviii.

73  1/10/29, Charles to Heath, SP 16/150/1. 19/11/29 and 5/12/29, Charles to Cottington, Sainsbury, *op. cit.*, 139–41.?/12/29, 4/2/30, 7/4/30, 27/9/30, Charles to Cottington, SP 94/34/129, 169, 212 and SP 94/35/43. Rushworth, *Collections*, II, 75.

74  *CSPV, 1628–9*, 194, 237–8.

75  16/12/28, Charles to Carlisle, Sainsbury, *op. cit.*, 199n.

76  24/10/29, SP 84/140/112. 5/1/30, 1/3/30, 5/7/30, 7/9/30, 15/12/30, SP 84/141/5, 100, 284, SP 84/142/66, 238. 32/8/30, Charles to States General, SP 84/142/61.

77  *CSP*, I, 49.

78  2/3/29, 16/8/30, Charles to Elizabeth, SP 81/35/161 and SP 81/36/81. Charles's memo on the French proposals, SP 78/85/236. 7/9/30, Charles to Vane, SP 84/142/66.

79  Hardwicke, *SP*, II, 79–93. *DNB*, Gerbier. 28/8/38, Gerbier to Charles, SP 77/28/497/

80  19/6/30, Charles to Lord Lieutenants, HMC, *3rd Report*, 60. 30/6/32, Charles to Spence, SP 95/2/120–1. Charles to Waterman, SP 16/195/15. For recruiting see SP 95/3/85.

81  5/3/31 and 21/3/31, Charles to Anstruther, SP 80/7/202 and 230.

82  7/10/31, SP 81/37/77. Burnet, *Hamilton*, 20–31. 20/9/31, Charles to Vane, SP 88/8/50.?/10/31, Charles to Gustavus, Rushworth, *Collections*, II, 172–3.

83  3/10/34, *CSPV, 1632–6*, 288.

84  Wentworth, *Letters*, II, 53, quoted by R. M. Smuts, 'The Puritan followers of Henrietta Maria in the 1630s', *English History Review*, XCIII, 366 (1978) 26–45, on which much of this section is based.

85  24/5/33, *CSPV, 1632–6*, 110. 7/8/36, *CSPV, 1636–9*, 44–6.

86 My thanks to Robin Swales for the point about licences. *CSPV, 1625–6*, 83, 89, 218. *CSPD, 1625–6*, 274, 288. *CSPD, 1627–8*, 84–5, 151. SP 16/295/44 II.

87 9/8/22, *CSPV, 1621–3*, 561.

88 SP 71/12/136. Steele, *Proclamations*, 1637. *CSPD, 1635–6*, 15.

89 G. Thorn-Drury, ed., *The Poems of Edmund Waller* (1893) I, 15.

90 *STC* 20161. SP 16/291/58.

91 W, Lilly, *Life and Death of Charles I* (1774) 190. All Souls College, Oxford, MSS 301, 20.

92 *Remembrancia, 1599–1664*, 254. Charles to Suffolk, Charles, *Letters*, 83–4. Privy Council to Lord Lieutenants, *CSPD, 1635*, 46. L. Boynton, *The Elizabethan Militia* (1967). D. P. Carter, 'The Exact Militia in Lancashire, 1625–40', *Northern History*, X (1975) 87–106.

93 For examples see SP 16/16/64 and SP 16/286/17.

94 Phineas Pett, *Autobiography* (1910) 146–7. *CSPD, 1631–3*, 90–119.

95 *CSPD, 1631–3*, 422, Pett, *op. cit.*, 149.

96 *CSPD, 1634–5*, 153, 232, 237, 338, 456, 499. *CSPD, 1637*, 212. C. H. Firth, *Naval Songs and Ballads* (1908) 38–46. M. Oppenheim, *A History of the Administration of the Royal Navy* (1896) 252. Pett, *op. cit.*, 156–67.

97 *CSPD, 1633–4*, 24, 117, 118, 173, 222–3. *CSPD, 1635*, 55, 389. *CSPV, 1632–6*, 398, 401, 475.

98 22/10/35, *CSP*, I, 352–4.

99 Clarendon, *History*, I, 92.

100 M. van C. Alexander, *Charles I's Lord Treasurer* (1976) 158–64.

101 For Charles's letters on this see SP 16/198/53 and 56, SP 16/215/32, and *CSPD, 1629–31*, 46–7. Laud's warning on the king's displeasure, *CSPD, 1629–31*, 360.

102 CUL MSS, Mn., II, 25, #5, 18.

103 272/10/33. Charles to Cambridge University, SP 16/246/83.

104 SP 16/214/83.

105 8/12/32. *CSPD, 1631–3*, 455.

106 *Orders and Directions... for the Better Administration of Justice... and... the Relief of the Poor* (1631).

107 Thomas G. Barnes, *Somerset, 1625–40* (Cambridge, Mass., 1961) chapter VII. P. Slack, 'Books of Orders: the making of English social policy, 1577–1631', *TRHS*, XXX (1980) 1–22 and B. W. Quintrell, 'The Making of Charles I's Book of Orders', *EHR*, XCV, 376 (July 1980) 555–72, disagree.

108 Steele, *Proclamations*, 1647.

109 Bankes MSS, 40/8.

110 Edmund S. Morgan, ed., *The Founding of Massachusetts* (New York, 1964) 190.

111 *CSPD, 1629–31*, 40.

112 *CSPD, 1629–31*, 8, 23, 34, 37, 40, 42, 134. *CSPD, 1637–8*, 171. HMC, *9th Report*, Ap-1, 310.

113 PRO: PC 2/45/101.

114 SP 16/240/52.

115 *CSPD, 1634–5*, 163, SP 16/172/25 and 95. *APC, 1630–1*, 261.

116 3/1/35, *CSPD, 1634–5*. 30/3/35, Charles to Lord Mayor of Lon'on, *CSPD, 1634–5*, 602. 26/5/35, Charles to Judges, SP 16/278/44.

117 Charles to Lord Mayor, SP 16/289/2. Charles Carlton, *The Court of Orphans* (1974). D. M. Bergeron, 'Charles I's royal entries into London', *Guildhall Miscellany*, III (1970) 91–7.

118 Valerie Pearl, *London and the Outbreak of the Puritan Revolution* (1961). Robert Ashton, 'Charles I and the City', in F. J. Fisher, ed., *Essays Presented*

*to R. H. Tawney* (1961) 138–63, and *The City and The Court* (1979) argues for a much greater degree of alienation.

119 18/6/29, Wentworth's instructions in Rawl. MSS, C197 and 12/5/33. Bridgewater's in Huntingdon Library, Ellesmere MSS, 7571.

120 The only letter I have found that Charles wrote on Ireland is 32/8/10 to Coke in HMC, *Cowper*, I, 469, on Scots ministers in Ulster.

121 Falkland correspondence is in Add. MSS, 18824. Aidan Clarke, *The Graces, 1625–41* (Dublin, 1968).

122 15/8/27, Wentworth to Charles, Wentworth, *Letters*, II, 93. 17/6/35, Charles to Wentworth, *Letters*, I, 431. See also 8/12/30, Cork to Carleton, *CSPI, 1625–36*, 589, that in forty-three years he had never known Ireland more content. This section based on Wentworth's papers in Sheffield Public Library, especially Str. P. 3, Str. P. 40/6–10, 12–14, 18–25, Str. P. 15/114, 175, Str. P. 18/100.

123 *CSPV, 1626–8*, 615.

124 17/16/29, Charles to Aith, HMC, *Montrose*, 3rd Report, 401.

125 C. V. Wedgwood, 'Anglo-Scottish relations, 1603–40,' *TRHS*, 4th series, XXXII, (1950) 31–48.

126 J. H. Burton, *et al.*, eds, *Register of the Privy Council of Scotland, 1629–30* (1877–1933) XXXIV–LIV. M. Lee, *Government by Pen: Scotland under James VI and I* (Urbana, 1980).

127 G. Donaldson, *Scotland: James V to James VII* (1965) 269–79. Maurice Lee, *The Road to Revolution: Scotland Under Charles I, 1625–37* (Urbana, 1985); Peter Donald, *An Uncounselled King: Charles I and the Scottish Troubles* (Cambridge, 1990); Alan MacInnes, *Charles I and the Making of the Covenanting Movement* (Edinburgh, 1991).

128 Charles to Traquair, HMC, *9th Report*, 241 ff. HMC, *Montrose* 3rd Report, 401: Steele, *Proclamations*, 1612. D. Laing, *Royal Letters* (1867).

129 5/7/28 and 28/8/28, Charles to Scots Privy Council, Rogers, *op. cit.*, 291, 308–9. H. L'Estrange, *The Reign of King Charles* (1655–6) 125–6.

130 Burton, *op. cit.*, XXXIII. Rogers, *op. cit.*, 427. *CSPD, 1631–3*, 192, 270, 454, 457, 576–7, 585–6.

131 *Fairfax Correspondence*, ed., G. W. Johnson (1848) I, 275–83. Falkland, *Annals*, 429. Rawl. MSS, D49. SP 16/240/53. Harl. MSS, 4707, 3. *Entertainment ... Charles ... Edinburgh* (STC 5023). C. Wordsworth, *The Manner of the Coronation of King Charles I* (1892) XVI–XVII. C. S. Terry, 'Visits of Charles I to Newcastle', *Archaeologia Aeliana*, XXI, 83–94.

132 16/5/34, Pelham to Conway, *CSPD, 1634–5*, 26. Later nineteen witches in Lancashire were condemned for conjuring up the storm.

133 15/7/33. Windebank to Coke, HMC, *Cowper*, II, 26. Abraham Cowley, *Writings*, ed., A. R. Waller (1905–6) I, 22–3.

134 19/11/31, draft of Fishing Association's regulations in king's hand, SP 16/203/54.

135 *CSPD, 1637*, 53. Burton, *op. cit.*, XXXI–XXXII.

## XII 'THAT FATAL BOOK'

1 Rushworth, *Collections*, II, 387 ff. Hamon L'Estrange, *The Reign of King Charles* (1655) 167. D. Stevenson, *The Scots Revolution 1637–44* (Newton Abbot, 1973) 60–5.

2 Quoted in C. W. Cort, *The Royal Martyr* (1924) 166.

3 G. Hammersley, 'The revival of Forest Laws', *History*, LXV (1960) 84–102.

4 L'Estrange, *op. cit.*, 110.

5 H. H. Leonard, 'Distraint of knighthood', *History*, LXIII (1978) 23–37. W. P. Baildon, 'Compositions for not taking knighthood at the coronation of Charles I', *Yorks Arch. Society*, Misc. I (1920). F. C. Dietz, *English Public Finance, 1558–1661* (1932) 262.

6 *CSPD, 1637*, 395. *CSPD, 1637–8*, 319. Bankes MSS, 12/21.

7 H. E. Mathews, *Proceedings... Soapmakers* (Bristol Record Society, 1960) 6–8, 189, 194. Gardiner, *History*, 71 ff.

8 M. van C. Alexander, *Charles I's Lord Treasurer* (1976) 211.

9 M. D. Gordon, 'The collection of ship money in the reign of Charles I', *TRHS*, 3rd Series, 4 (1910) 141–62. R. J. Swales, 'The ship money levy of 1628', *BIHR*, L (1977) 164–76. My thanks to John Morrill for this point.

10 C. G. Bonsey, 'Ship money papers...', *Bucks Record Society* (1965). For more on the continuing debate on Ship Money, see P. Lake, 'The Collection of Ship Money in Cheshire in the 1630s', in *Northern History*, XVII (1981), 71; K. Fincham, 'The Judges' Decision on Ship Money in February 1637: The Reaction of Kent', in *BIHR*, LVII (1984), 236; C. A. Clifford, 'Ship Money in Hampshire, Collection and Collapse', in *Southern History*, V/4 (1982), 92; K. Sharpe, *The Personal Rule of Charles I* (1992), 580–1.

11 CUL: Patrick Papers, 25, 5–6.

12 24/5/39 and 6/7/39, Windebank to Charles, *CSP*, I, 47–8, 60.

13 Hacket, *Scrinia*, I, 49.

14 P. A. Pettit, 'Charles I and forests', *Northamptonshire Past and Present* (1962) 61.

15 *Rotuli Parliamentorum*, V, 573, quoted, A. J. Salvin, *The Precarious Balance* (New York, 1973) 100. C. Russell, *Crisis of Parliaments* (1971) 260.

16 SP 16/178/11. Dietz, *op. cit.*

17 13/5/39, Charles to Hamilton, Burnet, *Hamilton*, 172.

18 C. H. Firth, 'Review of Clarendon's *History*', *EHR*, XIX (1904), 483.

19 C. Hill, *The English Revolution* (1955), 8.

20 L. Stone, *The Causes of the English Revolution* (1972).

21 D. Brunton and D. H. Pennington, *Members of the Long Parliament* (1954). M. F. Keeler, *The Long Parliament, 1640–1* (1954).

22 Frederick Von Raumer, *History of the 16th and 17th Centuries Illustrated from Original Documents* (1838), II, 328.

23 Clarendon, *History*, I, 5. For a penetrating critique, with all the relevant citations of the revisionist interpretation, see the articles by T. K. Rabb and D. Hirst in *P&P* (August, 1981). For a recent summary, see C. Russell, *The Causes of the English Civil War* (Oxford, 1990).

24 J. H. Langbein, *Torture and the Law of Proof* (1978).

25 C. Russell, *The Fall of the British Monarchies, 1637–42* (Oxford, 1991), 1. Brunton, *op. cit.*, 15–16.

26 G. Donaldson, *The Making of the Scottish Prayer Book* (Edinburgh, 1954) 41–2. Laud, *Works*, II, 301–2.

27 Baillie to Spang, Baillie, *Letters*, 4. K. Sharpe, *The Personal Rule of Charles I* (1992), 109. J. Reeve says that Laud was most to blame. In the first edition of this book I agreed with Conrad Russell (*The Fall of the English Monarchies* (1991), 31) that responsibility should be should be divided between the two equally, but since writing *Archbishop Laud* (1987) I am convinced that Charles was both the initiator and guiding force.

28 Clarendon, *History*, I, 145. Hacket, *Scrinia*, 64.

29 7/8/38, Laud to Traquair, Rushworth, Collections, II, 389–90.

30 *CSPD, 1637*, 370.
31 27/8/37, Charles to Traquair, HMC, *9th Report*, 248. Baillie, *Letters*, 453.
32 *Bib. Regia*, 142–4.
33 Rushworth, *Collections*, II, 401–2.
34 10/10/37, Charles to Scots Council, Baillie, *Letters*, I, 453.
35 27/10/37, *CSPV, 1636–9*, 316. 19/10/37, Traquair to Hamilton, Hardwicke, *SP*, 95–7.
36 HMC, *9th Report*, 248. 4/2/38, Charles to High Commission, Harl. MSS, 787, 95. 9/2/38, *Bib. Regia*, 145–7.
37 Quoted in *King's Peace*, 35.
38 Bankes MSS, 18/24. Rushworth, *Collections*, II, 470–1. 20/3/38, Gerrard to Wentworth, Wentworth, *Letters*, II, 154. The story in Sir Walter Scott's *The Secret History in the Court of James I* (1811) II, 401–2, that Archie teased Laud, 'Who is the fool now? Did not your grace hear the news from Stirling?' sounds too good to be true. It is not supported in the Bankes MSS. However Archie had the last laugh. He retired to write a popular book of jokes, which was the most tedious work consulted in my research.
39 Burnet, *Hamilton*, 56–65. Rushworth, *Collections*, II, 746–7.
40 S. R. Gardiner, *Hamilton Papers* (Camden Soc., 1880) 1–2.
41 Burnet, *Hamilton*, 52. 11/6/38, Charles to Hamilton, Charles, *Letters*, 106–7.
42 13, 20, 25/6/37, Charles to Hamilton, Charles, *Letters*, 106–12.
43 Rushworth, *Collections*, II, 754–5. Charles, *Letters*, 110–11.
44 *CSPV, 1636–9*, 435–6. 3/7/38, Gerrard to Wentworth, Wentworth, *Letters*, II, 181.
45 20/7/38, Charles to Wentworth, Wentworth, *Letters*, 184–5. *CSPD, 1637–8*, 591.
46 27/7/38 and 9/10/38, Charles to Hamilton, Rushworth, *Collections*, II, 713–14, 780–1, 841–2. Hardwicke, *SP*, II, 111–12. Stevenson, *op. cit.*, 111.
47 27/11/38, Hamilton to Charles, Hardwicke, *SP*, II, 113–21. 29/11/38, Rushworth, *Collections*, I, 845–9, 857.
48 3 and 7/12/38, Burnet, *Hamilton*, 126, 136.
49 *CSPD, 1638–9*, 340, 345.
50 29/1/39, Northumberland to Conway, SP 16/410/80.
51 *CSPD, 1638–9*, 307, 372, 514–15. Steele, *Proclamations*, 1791. Charles, *Letters*, 111–12. HMC, *Salisbury*, XXI, 299–300. Harl. MSS, 6988, 109–10.
52 *CSPD, 1638–9*, 440, 448, 581–2, 626.
53 Rushworth, *Collections*, II, 820.
54 21/4/39, *CSP*, II, 38.
55 *CSPD, 1638–9*, 489, 497, 517.
56 Harl. MSS, 6988, 109–10. 20/2/39, *Bib. Regia*, 173–80. Steele, *Proclamations*, 1795. *CSPD, 1638–9*, 508. Rushworth, *Collections*, II, 831–3, 841–2. For examples of Charles's letters see: Hunt. MSS, HA 1349–51; Harl. MSS, 6988, 109–10; HMC, *Salisbury*, XXI, 299; Charles, *Letters*, 111–12; *Bib. Regia*, 173–80.
57 24/2/39, Charles to Windebank, *CSPD, 1639*, 75. Suckling's letter to 'a Gentleman of Norfolk', in his *Works*, I, 142, is a model for the anonymous letter in CUL MSS, Gg, IV, 13(D) no. 107, 21–3.
58 18/3/39, Charles to Huntington, Hunt. MSS, HA 1351.
59 Charles, *Letters*, 102.
60 18/1/39, Charles to Lauderdale, Add. MSS, 23113, 5. 18/1/39, Charles to Nithersdale, NRA, 11211, 79, G, 150–2. 16/3/39, Charles to Traquair, HMC, *9th Report*, 244. 9/4/39, Charles to Huntley, John Stuart, 'The Gordon Letters', *Spalding Club Misc.* (1846) 219. 31/3/39, *CSP*, II, 34–6.
61 *CSP*, II, 19–30, 50.

62 26/2/39, Reade to Conway, SP 16/413/92. He sounds equally confident in HMC, *9th Report*, 249.

63 Rushworth, *Collections*, III, 886. *CSPD, 1638–9*, 447, 608.

64 10/4/39, Charles to Wentworth, Str. P., 3, 69.

65 2, 3, 5, 7, 10, 18, 23, 25/4/39 and 8, 17, 22, 29/5/39, Charles to Hamilton, Burnet, *Hamilton*, 151–61, and Rushworth, *Collections*, III, 904–25. *CSPD, 1639*, 77–9.

66 Rawl. MSS, B 210, 36. 4/6/39, Reade to Newgate, *CSPD, 1639*, 272.

67 *Bib. Regia*, 371–3.

68 Burnet, *Hamilton*, 172.

69 Steele, *Proclamations*, 1800. *CSP*, II, 46.

70 Rawl. MSS, B 210, 37 v. J. Bruce, ed., *Letters and Papers of the Verney Family* (Camden Soc., 1853, LVI) 228.

71 4/6/39, Vane to Hamilton, Rushworth, *Collections*, III, 936–7.

72 Harl. MSS, 6851. 7.

73 Sir Edward Walker's description of negotiations in Add. MSS 38847, 1–9, 14. Folger MSS, X, d, 450.

74 *Bib. Regia*, 187–94.

75 28/9/39, Baillie to Spang, Baillie, *Letters*, I, 211–14. Charles emerges as a more conciliatory figure in Baillie's letters than in Sir Edward Walker's description in Add. MSS, 38847.

76 John Suckling, *Works*, ed., A. H. Thompson (New York, 1910) I, 147–8.

77 20, 27, 30/6/39, Charles to Wentworth, Wentworth, *Letters*, II, 361–2.

78 Baillie, *Letters*, I, 41. 40,000 troops would today be equal in relevant terms to 552,000 British and 2,300,000 US soldiers.

79 29/5/39, Coke to Charles, *CSPD, 1639*, 247–8. Laud, 'Diary', *Works*, III, 230. 31/3/39 and 6/39, Windebank to Charles, *CSP*, II, 35, 56–7.

80 Peter Heylin, *Cyprianus Anglicus, or the History of the Life and Death of Laud* (1668) 384–5.

81 20/10/38, Charles to Hamilton, Halliwell, *Letters*, II, 304–6.

82 29/10/38, Charles to Hamilton, Burnet, *Hamilton*, 112. 28/8/38, Charles to Traquair, HMC, *9th Report*, 249 and 25/6/38, Charles, *Letters*, 109–10.

83 11, 20, 25/6/38, Charles to Hamilton, Halliwell, *Letters*, II, 290–303. Elliot Jaques, 'Death and the mid-life crisis', *International Journal of Psychoanalysis*, XLVII (October, 1965) 502–4.

84 G. Parry, *The Golden Age Restor'd* (Manchester, 1981) 268. M. Jones, *English Politics and the Concept of Honour* (1978). J. G. Marston, 'Gentry Honour and Royalism in Early Stuart England', *Journal of British Studies*, XIII (1973–4) 21–43.

85 *CSPD, 1636–9*, 26, 408. *CSP*, II, 59. HMC, *6th Report*, 284.

86 Wentworth, *Letters*, II, 372–3. S. P. Salt, 'Thomas Wentworth and Parliament, 1620–9', *Northern History*, XVI (1980) 131–68.

87 4/8/39, Rushworth, *Collections*, III, 965–6.

88 20/8/39, *Bib Regia*, 195–7.

89 27/7/39 and c21/8/39, Charles to Traquair, Rushworth, *Collections*, III, 949–51, 953–5. 29/3/39, *ibid.*, HMC, *9th Report*, 249. 6/8/39, Charles to Scots bishops, *CSPD, 1639*, 435, and Rushworth, *Collections*, III, 951–2. P. Zagorin, 'Did Stafford Change Sides?', in *EHR*, 101 (1986), 149–63.

90 21/9/39, Charles to Radcliffe, Wentworth, *Letters*, II, 181–3.

91 *CSPV, 1640–2*, 16.

92 *CSPV, 1636–9*, 309–16. 12/12/39, Nicholas to Pennington, SP 16/435/64. 13/12/39, Windebank to Hamilton, *CSP*, II, 81.

93 Gordon Albion, *Charles I and the court of Rome* (1935) 319.
94 *CSPV, 1640–2*, 28, 38.
95 11/3/40, Charles to Norfolk, HMC, *9th Report*, 312. Steele, *Proclamations*, 1814. 14/4/40, Charles to London, *CSPD, 1640*, 41.
96 6/4/39, Charles to Ruthven, Rawl. MSS, A 148, 12.
97 Rawl. MSS, A 148, 17, 21, 38, 47, 66, 70, 102, 148, and SP 16/432/35, SP 16/449/27. *DNB*.
98 Wentworth, *Letters*, II, 391–2, 398. Charles, *Letters*, 105. Rushworth, *Collections*, III, 1097. Aidan Clark, 'The breakdown of authority, 1640–1', in T. W. Moody, ed., *New History of Ireland*, III, 274.
99 *CSPD, 1639–40*, 487. C. H. Firth, 'The reign of Charles I', *TRHS* (1912) 41.
100 Notes for letter in Charles's hand, SP 16/447/71. 11/4/40, Charles to Leicester, SP 16/450/60 and SP 78/109/170. *Lords Journal*, IV, 46–8. For royalist propaganda, see H. E. Rollins, *Cavalier and Puritans* (New York, 1923) 85.
101 Any assessment of Pym must await Conrad Russell's biography: meanwhile see his 'The Parliamentary Career of John Pym, 1621–9', in *The English Commonwealth, 1547–1640*, eds, P. Clark, A. G. R. Smith, and N. Tyacke (Leicester, 1979) 147–64.
102 SP 16/450/108. Esther Cope and W. Coates, *Proceedings of the Short Parliament* (1977).
103 *Bib. Regia*, 341–3.
104 *Bib. Regia*, 344–6, 430–51.
105 E. Cope, 'The king's declaration concerning the dissolution of the Short Parliament', *HLQ*, XL, 4 (1977) 325–31. R. Cust argues that there were strong ideological links between the opposition in parliaments of the 1620s and the 1640s, in 'News and Politics in Early Seventeenth Century England', in *Past and Present* (1986), 60–90.
106 J. H. Elliott, 'The year of the three ambassadors', *History and Imagination*, ed., D. Lloyd-Jones (Oxford, 1981), 165–8.
107 *CSPV, 1640–2*, 67. D. Gardiner, ed., *The Oxinden Letters* (1933) 174. Clarendon, *History*, I, 111. 19/5/40, Charles to London, Tanner MSS, 290, 124.
108 SP 16/452/31. *CSPV, 1640–2*, 70.
109 *CSP*, II, 82. *CCSP*, 194.
110 Hunt. MSS, ELL 7834. SP 16/454/39.
111 *Concilia*, IV, 543. Laud, *Works*, III, 284, V, 607–33. Heylin, *op. cit.*, 429–30.
112 8/7/40, Charles to Salisbury, HMC, *Salisbury*, XXI, 317. *CSPD, 1640*, 366, 477, 490, 580. Steele, *Proclamations*, 1821. Von Raumer, *op. cit.*, II, 316. SP 16/455/No. 38. *CSP*, II, 101.
113 *CSPD, 1640*, 500. SP 16/465/630.
114 Wentworth, *Letters*, II, 398. Carlisle to Bridgewater, Hunt. MSS, ELL 7845. *CSPD, 1640*, 590–1, 630.
115 Vane to Windebank, SP 16/465/50. 27/8/40, Charles to Windebank, *CSP*, II, 91.
116 31/8/40, Charles to Salisbury, HMC, *Salisbury*, XXI, 320. Charles's annotations in *CSP*, II, 112. 31/8/40, Steele, *Proclamations*, 1827.
117 *CSP*, II, 95–7. Rushworth, *Collections*, III, 1257.
118 Rushworth, *Collections*, III, 1275. 24/9/40, Vane to Windebank, *CSPD, 1640–1*, 91–2.
119 26/9/40, Charles to London, Harl. MSS, 1219,7,26.
120 Evelyn, *Memoirs*, II, 26.

## XIII 'THE GOVERNMENT ALL IN PIECES'

1 Laud, *Works*, III, 238. C. H. Cooper, *Annals of Cambridge* (Cambridge, 1904) II, 303.
2 25/9/40, Windebank to Charles, *CSP*, II, 123.
3 Robert Ashton, *The English Civil War* (1978) 129–32.
4 Clarendon, *History*, I, 218 ff.
5 Sir John Suckling, *Works* (New York, 1910) I, 163–7.
6 Rushworth, *Collections*, III, 1335.
7 *CSPD, 1640–1*, 242.
8 Anthony Fletcher, *The Outbreak of the English Civil War* (1981). C. Hibbard, 'Charles I and the popish plot', (Yale PhD, 1975).
9 H. E. Rollins, ed., *Cavalier and Puritan* (New York, 1923) 140.
10 Steele, *Proclamations*, 1831–2. HMC, *Various Collections*, II, 259.
11 Brian Manning, 'The aristocracy and the downfall of Charles I', in *Politics, Religion and the English Civil War*, ed., B. Manning (1973) 36–79. Paul Christianson, 'The peers, the people and parliamentary management in the first six months of the Long Parliament', *Journal of Modern History* (December, 1977) 575–99. Clayton Roberts, 'The Earl of Bedford and the coming of the English Civl War', *ibid.*, 100–15.
12 Tanner MSS, 65, 247.
13 Rushworth, *Collections*, IV, 188.
14 *Ibid.*, IV, 238.
15 18/3/41, Charles to Littleton, Juxon, Holland and Dorset, *CSPD, 1640–1*, 504.
16 *Lords Journal*, IV, 157.
17 Charles, *His Majesty's Manifesto touching the Palatine Cause* (1641). Nalson, *Collections*, II, 383–7.
18 Alex Janta, 'Letter by Charles I', *Polish Review*, XVIII, 3 (1973) 52–7.
19 Elliot Jacques, 'Social systems as defence against persecutory and depressive anxiety', Melanie Klein, ed., *New Directions in Psycho-Analysis* (New York, 1957) 485 ff.
20 James Welwood, *Memoirs* (1700) 52. G. W. Johnson, ed., *Fairfax Memoirs* (1848) I, 127.
21 31/3/41, Knyvett to Burton, HMC, *Various Collections*, II, 261.
22 Wentworth, *Letters*, II, 416.
23 Rushworth, *Collections*, III, 239. Nalson, *Collections*, II, 186.
24 Quinton Bone, *Henrietta Maria* (Urbana, 1972) 123.
25 Hamon L'Estrange, *The Reign of King Charles* (1655) 263–5.
26 Laud, *Works*, III, 443.
27 Str. P., 40/67.
28 29/5/41, *CSPI, 1633–47*, 293. 20/1/42, Str. P., 40/66.
29 Rushworth, *Collections*, IV, 297.
30 3/8/41, HMC, *12th Report*, appendix 9, p. 20. Phineas Pett, *Autobiography*, ed., W. G. Perrin (1918).
31 Robert Baillie, *Letters and Journals*, ed., D. Laing (Edinburgh, 1841–2) I, 385–90.
32 M. Napier, *Memorials of Montrose* (Edinburgh, 1848–50) I, 310–16. Hugh Trevor-Roper, 'Scotland and the Puritan revolution', *Historical Essays* (1957) 87–90.
33 Rushworth, *Collections*, IV, 382. Baillie, *op. cit.*, I, 386.
34 Evelyn, *Memoirs*, I, 14, 36–9, 72.
35 Nalson, *Collections*, II, 468.
36 Evelyn, *Memoirs*, I, 27–8, 36–9, 41–3, 55–6.

37 *King Charles his resolution concerning the Government of the Church of England* (1641). Evelyn, *Memoirs*, I, 44–7.

38 *Ibid.*, I, 81.

39 *Ovatio Carolina* (1641). Rushworth, *Collections* IV, 429. John Taylor, *England's Comfort and London's Joy* (1641). Clarendon, *History*, I, 434–5.

40 Quoted by T. L. Coonan, *The Irish Catholic Confederacy and the Puritan Revolution* (New York, 1954) 49.

41 13/8/37, Wentworth to Charles, Wentworth, *Letters*, II, 93. Nalson, *Collections*, I, 11–12.

42 Wentworth, *Letters*, II, 345, 353.

43 Quoted J. C. Beckett, *The Making of Modern Ireland* (1966) 65.

44 *CSPI, 1633–47*, 279.

45 *CSPI, 1633–47*, 317.

46 Carte, *Ormonde*, III, 31–2. *CSPI, 1633–47*, 281. P. J. Cornish, 'The rising of 1641', in T. W. Moody, F. X. Martin, F. J. Byrne, eds, *A New History of Ireland, 1534–1691* (1976) III, 289–316. A. Clark, *The Old English in Ireland, 1625–42* (1966) 228–9.

47 12/12/41, *CSPI, 1633–47*, 344, 354. A. Clark, 'The Genesis of the Ulster rising of 1641', *Plantation to Partition*, ed., P. Roebuck (Belfast, 1981) 29–45.

48 K. J. Lindley, 'The impact of the Irish Rebellion in England and Wales', *Irish Historical Studies* XVIII (1970). For examples of atrocities on both sides see Charles Carlton, *Bigotry and Blood* (Chicago, 1977) 21–5.

49 Lord Balmerino's speech in the High Court of Parliament, quoted C. L. Hamilton 'Scotland, Ireland, the English Civil War', *Albion*, VII (1975) 121. R. Dunlop, 'The Forged Commission of 1641', *English Historical Review*, II (1887) 338–40, 527–33.

50 Evelyn, *Memoirs*, I, 112.

51 *Ibid.*, I, 64.

52 Add. MSS. 28938, 120. *CSPI, 1633–47*, 353.

53 Nalson, *Collections*, II, 708.

54 *Ibid.*, II, 709–10.

55 Rushworth, *Collections*, IV, 257.

56 Gardiner, *Constitutional Documents*, 233–5.

57 Eg. MSS, 2546, 20. Now in display case in public exhibition area. Gardiner, *Constitutional Documents*, 236–7. Although Charles charged six they are invariably referred to as the Five Members.

58 *CCSP*, I, 222. Clarendon, *History*, II, 545.

59 Rushworth, *Collections*, IV, 477 ff.

60 I have relied on Rushworth for a description of the events of 4 January. As he was clerk to the Commons and talked to Charles that evening he is a first-rate source.

61 HMC, *Cholmondley*, 344. *CSPD, 1641–3*, 231.

62 William Lilly, *Life and Death of Charles I* (1774) 232–4. Lilly was in London at the time.

63 *The King Majesty's Demand to the House of Commons together with the Speech to the Court of Aldermen and Common Council* (1641). *CSPD, 1641–3*, 238, 242–4, 249.

64 5/1/42, Smith to Pennington, SP 16/488/21. 27/1/42, Oxinden to Barham, D. Gardiner, *Oxinden Letters* (1933) 271–2.

65 Suckling, *op. cit.*, I, 163–7.

66 Evelyn, *Memoirs*, I, 14, 54.

67 'The King's cabinet opened', *Harleian Miscellany*, VII, 525. L. G. Schwoerer, *No Standing Armies!* (1973).
68 M. Edelman, *Politics as Symbolic Action* (New York, 1971).
69 *A Deep Sigh Breathed through the Lodgings at Whitehall* (164?).
70 Clarendon, *History*, I, 535–7. CUL MSS, Mn, I, 46, 1.
71 19/1/42, Charles to Lanerick, and 26/1/42, Charles to Argyle and Loudon, Burnet, *Hamilton*, 242. 27/1/42, Charles to Montrose, Napier, *op. cit.*, 366.
72 G. Trease, *Portrait of a Cavalier, William Cavendish, First Duke of Newcastle* (New York, 1979) 90–1.
73 Tanner MSS, 66, 250. Eg. MSS, 2978, 18.
74 Clarendon, *History*, I, 589.
75 CUL MSS, IV, 57, no. 23, 307.
76 15/3/42, Charles to Parliament, Charles, *Works*, 98. Hyde to Charles, *CCSP*, I, 225.
77 B. H. G. Wormald, *Clarendon* (1951) 91–4. Clarendon, *History*, II, 10–12.
78 B. N. Reckitt, *Charles I and Hull* (1952).
79 CUL MSS, Mn, I, 45, 393 has letters dated 22, 24 and 28 April. Rushworth, *Collections*, IV, 567–8, has one of 22 April.
80 27/3/42, Charles to Roe, *CSPD, 1641–3*, 301. He recalled Roe on 17 May 1642, *ibid.*, 324–5.
81 HMC, *Argyle, 6th Report*, 612.
82 7/5 and 26/6/42, Charles to Traquair, HMC, *9th Report*, appendix 2, 243. 20/5/42, Charles to Privy Council, *Reliquiae*, 179. D. Stevenson, *The Scottish Revolution, 1637–44* (Newton Abbot, 1973) 248.
83 18/5/42, Charles to Ormonde, Carte, *Ormonde*, III, 76. 8/2/42, 11/5/42 and 9/7/42, *ibid.*, Add. MSS, 28938, 120. 13/4/42, *ibid.*, *CSPI, 1633–47*, 357. 25/4/42, Charles to Parliament, Charles, *Letters*, 117–22.
84 *Catalogue of the Prints and Drawings in the British Museum*, I.
85 Rushworth, *Collections*, IV, 615–16. Joyce Malcolm, 'A king in search of soldiers: Charles I in 1642', *Historical Journal*, XXI (1978) 251–73.
86 Add. MSS, 18992, np.
87 Rushworth, *Collections*, IV, ch. 6.
88 Gardiner, *Constitutional Documents*, 249–54.
89 Rushworth, *Collections*, IV, 626.
90 Clarendon, *History*, II, 135–64, 172–6.
91 *His Majesties Two Letters* (1641). CUL MSS, Mn, 2, 25, 325–8.
92 *CSPD, 1641–3*, 362.
93 6/3 and 9/5/42, Charles to Herbert, Harl. MSS, 6988, 121, 123. HMC, *Beaufort*, 11–12.
94 *CSPD, 1641–3*, 67, 334.
95 *CCSP*, I, 232. *Reliquae*, 184–6.
96 To Earl of Leicester, *Lords Journal*, V, 232. To Devonshire, Hunt. MSS, HA 1355–6. To Huntington, Hunt. MSS, 1354–8. To F. ffarington, HMC, *F. ffarington, 6th Report*, 447. To Mayor of Boston, Charles, *Letters*, 126. To Mayor of Leicester, H. Stocks, *Records . . . Leicester, 1603–88*, 313. Malcolm, *op. cit.* Gardiner, *Constitutional Documents*, 259–61.
97 Fletcher, *op. cit.*, 322. R. E. Hutton, *The Royalist War Effort, 1642–46* (Oxford, 1981) 6.
98 J. R. Powell and E. K. Timings, eds, *Documents Relating to the Civil War, 1642–48* (1963) 12–21.
99 Tanner MSS, 63, 99. Rushworth, *Collections*, IV, 652–3. Charles to Huntington, Hunt, MSS, HA 1357. Stocks, *op. cit.*, 316–17.

100 *CSPD, 1641–3*, 69, 73–5.
101 Rawl. MSS, IV, 645. CUL MSS, Mn, I, 45, 396.
102 *CSPD, 1641–3*, xlv.
103 Lilly, *op. cit.* (1774), 242. *A True and Exact Relation of the Manner of His Majesties Setting up of His Standard of Nottingham* (1642).
104 Clarendon, *History*, II, 293. W. H. Stevenson, *et al.*, *Records... Nottingham* (1882–1956) V. John Taylor, *Works* (1877) no. 12, 5.
105 *CSPV, 1640–4*, 295.
106 *His Majesty's Resolution concerning the Setting up of His Standard* (1641).
107 Clarendon, *History* (1886) III, 128–9.
108 HMC, *9th Report*, appendix 2, 243.

## XIV 'TO FIGHT FOR MY CROWN AND MY DIGNITY'

1 Gardiner, *Civil War*, I, 41.
2 Clarendon, *History*, II, 300–1. *Parliamentary History*, XI, 411–12, 415–16. Rushworth, *Collections*, V, 2.
3 18/10/42, Harl. MSS, 1901, 486.
4 23/9/42, Charles to Newcastle, Harl. MSS, 6988, 125.
5 9/9/42, Stowe MSS, 154, 10.
6 *Lords Journal*, V, 376. Harl. MSS, 2135, 72. Rushworth, *Collections*, V, 20–1. Clarendon, *History*, II, 312–13. Rawl. MSS, D924, 143. Tanner MSS, 64, 3.
7 Clarendon, *Life* (1761 ed.) I, 134.
8 E. Scott, *Rupert, Prince Palatine* (1899) 59–61.
9 9/9/42, HMC, *Beaufort*, 11–12.
10 *A True and Exact Relation of the King's Entertainment at Chester* (1642). Harl. MSS, 2135, 72. 18 and 26/9/42, Charles to Chester, HMC, *Cholmondley*, 344. Collins, *Sydney Papers* (1746) II, 667.
11 Tanner MSS, 64, 44. Rawl. MSS, V, 21, 23, 52.
12 Quoted *King's War*, 121.
13 Burnet, *Hamilton*, 257.
14 M. H. Abrams, *et al.*, *Norton Anthology of English Literature* (New York, 1974) I, 1547.
15 Burnet, *Hamilton*, 258.
16 23/8/42, Charles to Rupert, Warburton, *Cavaliers*, I, 12.
17 27/10/42, W. D. Fellowes, *Historical Sketches* (1829) 321.
18 18/4/43, Charles to Rupert, Warburton, *Cavaliers*, II, 167–8.
19 Rushworth, *Collections*, V, 53. Clarendon, *History*, II, 388–98.
20 *Parliamentary History*, XII, 38.
21 18/11/42, Charles to Parliament, Clarendon, *History*, II, 398.
22 Rushworth, *Collections*, V, 396–7.
23 Clarendon, *History*, II, 411. *Memoirs of Edmund Ludlow* (Oxford, 1849) I, 35.
24 Ian Roy, 'The Royalist Council of War', *BIHR*, XXXV (1962) 150–69.
25 Sir Edward Walker attacked the ambitious with equal venom in Rawl. MSS, D392, 270–90. He remained loyal to the crown, going into exile. At the restoration Charles II rewarded him amply enough so that he could buy Shakespeare's house at Stratford for his retirement. Sir Edward Nicholas, *Papers*, ed., G. F. Warner (Camden Soc., 1886–1920) II, 11.
26 Warwick, *Memoirs*, I, 229.
27 Warburton, *Cavaliers*, I, 368. D. Henry, a practicing psychiatrist, argues that Falkland became so depressed that he committed suicide at Newbury. See 'The Death of Lord Falkland', in *History Today*, XXI/12 (1971), 842–7.

28 CUL MSS, Mn, I, 45, 398.
29 Clarendon, *History*, II, 390, 420–5, 432–5, and III, 119. John Reeve, *Charles I and the Road to Personal Rule* (1989), 111, shows a similar process taking place during the drafting of the proclamation issued on 27 March 1629 defending the decision to dissolve parliament.
30 23/1/43, Charles to wife, *Reliquiae*, 236–8.
31 Rushworth, *Collections*, V, 67–8, 316–17. 'Some proclamations of Charles I', *Bodleian Quarterly Record*, VIII, 90 (1936) 12. Warburton, *Cavaliers*, II, 70–1.
32 Rushworth, *Collections*, V, 83–4, 87, 146.
33 HMC, *St John's College*, 467. HMC, *Wadham College*, 480.
34 15 and 21/1/43, Charles to Coke, Sloane MSS, 4161, 295. 3/2/43, Charles to Rupert, Warburton, *Cavaliers*, II, 15. 2/1/43, Charles to Northampton, *ibid.*, 91. 12/2/43, Charles to Gloucester, *Reliquiae*, 198–201.
35 5/1/43, Charles to Worcester, HMC, *12th Report*, appendix 1, 12. 12 and 22/1/43, Charles to Newcastle, Harl. MSS, 6988, 123, and Add. MSS, 38847, 28. Corpus Christi College, Oxford, MSS 307, 291.
36 Carte, *Ormonde*, III, 117, 125–6, 135–6. Add. MSS, 28938, 121. Charles, *Letters*, 132–4.
37 Rushworth, *Collections*, V, 393. *Reliquiae*, 203–6.
38 28/12/42, Charles to Lord Mayor, *CSPD, 1641–3*, 214. Clarendon, *History*, II, 432–5. 17/1/43, Charles to Sheriffs, Rushworth, *Collections*, V, 120–2. 18/1/42, Charles to Watermen, Carpenters and Barber Surgeons, CUL MSS, Mn, I, 46, no. 2, 1.
39 Clarendon, *History*, II, 402. Rushworth, *Collections*, IV, 402.
40 Clarendon, *History*, II, 444–5. Gardiner, *Constitutional Documents*, 262–7.
41 Tanner MSS, 60, 584.
42 20/2/43 and 6/3/43, Charles to Lords, Tanner MSS, 64, 173, 181.
43 23/3/43, Charles to Parliament, Rushworth, *Collections*, V, 177–9. Clarendon, *History* II 520–4.
44 4 and 8/4/43, Charles to Parliament, Rushworth, *Collections*, V, 186–93.
45 1 and 3/2/43, 8/3/43, 9/4/43, Warburton, *Cavaliers*, II, 115, 140, 155–6.
46 Warburton, *Cavaliers*, II, 167–8.
47 12/4/43, Charles to Parliament, Rushworth, *Collections*, V, 259–61. Proclamation in *ibid.*, 315.
48 Charles to Lanerick, Burnet, *Hamilton*, 309–10. Charles to Wemyss and Elcho, HMC, *Wemyss*, 423. Charles to Earl of Dunfermline, HMC, *Gordon*, 645.
49 13/2/43, *Reliquiae*, 239–41.
50 M. A. E. Green, *Letters of Queen Henrietta Maria* (1857) 149–63.
51 3/2/43, Charles to Rupert, W. A. Day, ed., *Pythouse Papers* (1879) 1. Green *op. cit,*. 167.
52 29/12/42, Harl. MSS, 6988, 131.
53 Add. MSS, 28938, 121.
54 Charles to wife, 2/3/43, CUL MSS. Mn, I, 45, 397.
55 C. Kantorowicz, *The King's Two Bodies* (Princeton, 1957) 21, 41. William Cartwright, 'On the Queen's return from the low countries', *Poems and Plays* (Madison, 1951) 351.
56 15, 16, 21/4/43, Warburton, *Cavaliers*, II, 166, 171–4.
57 Clarendon, *History*, II, 505–20. Rushworth, *Collections*, V, 398–406. D. Stevenson, *The Scottish Revolution, 1637–44* (Newton Abbot, 1973) 251–74.
58 21/4/43, Charles to Bampfield, Royal Archives Windsor, transcript in NRA #1157, 4.
59 Rushworth, *Collections*, V, 321, 337–40.

60 7/7/43, Charles to Jermyn, C. Petrie, *King Charles, Prince Rupert, and the Civil War* (1974) 41.
61 28/7/43, Warburton, *Cavaliers*, II, 268.
62 Add. MSS, 1901, 1–4.
63 Charles to Hopton, *Bellum Civile*, ed., C. E. H. Chadwyck-Healy (1902) 59. Warburton, *Cavaliers*, II, 269. Clarendon, *History*, III, 120–5.
64 5/9/43, Charles to Rupert, Petrie, *op. cit.*, 111. 5/9/43, Charles to Maurice, Warburton, *Cavaliers*, II, 305. 7/9/43, Charles to Ormonde, Carte, *Ormonde*, III, 172–3. Gardiner, *Civil War*, I, 205–7.
65 1, 13 and 29/12/43, Charles to Governor of Dartmouth, J. R. Powell and E. K. Timings, eds, *Documents Relating to the Civil War, 1642–48* (1963) 107. Charles, *Letters*, 137. Warburton, *Cavaliers*, II, 338–9.
66 Clarendon, *History*, III, 195, 222–4.
67 P. J. Cornish, 'The rising of 1641', in T. W. Moody, F. X. Martin, F. J. Byrne, eds, *New History of Ireland, 1524–1691* (1976) III, 303–7. Carte, *Ormonde*, III, 166–9.
68 Rushworth, *Collections*, V, 549.
69 7/9/43, Charles to Ormonde, Carte, *Ormonde*, III, 172–3. 11/12/43, Charles to Bryon, HMC, *Dod*, 258. 22/5/43, Charles to Hamilton, Burnet, *Hamilton*, 294. 10/6/43, Charles to Scots Convention, *ibid.*, 297.
70 Rushworth, *Collections*, V, 365. Clarendon, *History*, III, 252–3. Joyce L. Malcolm, 'All the king's men', *Irish Historical Studies*, XXI, 83 (March 1979), 239–64, does not accept this view.
71 Gardiner, *Constitutional Documents*, 267–71.
72 26/9/43, Charles to Scots Council, Burnet, *Hamilton*, 312–14.
73 7/11/43, Charles to Chester, Harl. MSS, 2145, 1. 4 and 12/11/43, Charles to Rupert, Day, *op. cit.*, 1–3. 21/11/43, *ibid.*, Petrie, *op. cit.*, 111. 28/9/43, Charles to Hamilton, Burnet, *Hamilton*, 317.
74 Most of them were English soldiers returning from a couple of years service in Ireland.
75 16/2/44, Newcastle to Charles, Warburton, *Cavaliers*, II, 381.

## XV 'THESE TIMES ARE ONES OF PUBLIC DANGER'

1 Rushworth, *Collections*, V, 561. Edward Hyde, *The Life of Edward Hyde, Earl of Clarendon* (Oxford, 1759) 86.
2 2/1/44, Charles to Dean and Chapter of Canterbury, in C. E. Woodruff, 'Some seventeenth-century letters and petitions from the muniments of the Dean and Chapter of Canterbury', *Archaeologia Cantiana* XLII (1930) 118.
3 Rushworth, *Collections*, V, 565, 580–1. Clarendon, *History*, III, 293.
4 Edward Walker, *His Majesty's Progress* (1705) 10: in Rawl. MSS, D 392, 1–110.
5 Evelyn, *Memoirs*, I, 125. 21/4/45, Charles to wife, Rushworth, *Collections*, V, 943.
6 25/5/44, Hunt. MSS, HA 1425. For another example see Rawl. MSS, D 395, 76.
7 *King's Cabinet Opened* (1645) 12. When his enemies published this letter after they captured his correspondence at Naseby, Charles called them 'the mongrel parliament'. 4/8/45, Evelyn, *Memoirs*, I, 139–40.
8 Rushworth, *Collections*, V, 663–7.
9 Add. MSS, 18981. Elizabeth Hamilton, *Henrietta Maria* (New York, 1976).
10 17/4/44, Charles to Nicholas Hunt. MSS, HA 1364.
11 21/4/44, Charles to Rupert, W. A. Day, ed., *Pythouse Papers* (1879).
12 22/4/44, Charles to Rupert, Warburton, *Cavaliers*, I, 514.

13 19/5/44, Charles to Maurice, Rawl. MSS, D 392, 351. 29/5/44, Charles to Maurice, Harl. MSS, 6988, 176.
14 Warburton, *Cavaliers*, II, 415.
15 *Ibid.*, II, 438.
16 30/6/44, Charles to wife, *CSPD, 1644*, 314.
17 3/7/44, Francis Basset to wife, R. Polwhele, *Traditions and Recollections* (1826) I, 17.
18 Thomas Carlyle, *The Letters and Speeches of Oliver Cromwell* (London, 1904) I, 154.
19 Warwick, *Memoirs*, 262.
20 Ellis, *Letters*, III, iii, 298.
21 *CSPD, 1644*, xxxvi.
22 Harl. MSS, 6988, 178.
23 Rushworth, *Collections*, V, 687.
24 Add. MSS, 27402, 79.
25 30/8/44, Charles to Rupert, Warburton, *Cavaliers*, III, 23.
26 4 and 12/9/44, Charles to Goring, Tanner MSS, 61, 112, 128. 6/9/44, Charles to Rupert, Warburton, *Cavaliers*, I, 514. 8/9/44, Charles to Parliament, Rushworth, *Collections*, V, 712.
27 Carte, *Ormonde*, VI, 199, quoted in *King's War*, 347.
28 20/10/44, Charles to Rupert, Foster MSS. 5/7/44, Cromwell to Walton, C. Petrie, *King Charles, Prince Rupert and the Civil War* (1974) 105.
29 Clarendon, *History*, III, 353. Cannon-ball incident took place at Beacon Hill in August 1644.
30 Peter Heylin, *Short View of the Life and reign of King Charles* (1658) 63–4.
31 Sir Henry Slingsby, *Diary* (1836) 161.
32 Gardiner, *Civil War*, I, 354.
33 For Weemes's perfidy see Clarendon, *History* (1876) IV, 503, and Add. MSS, 28938, 123.
34 Margaret Toynbee, *Papers of Captain Henry Stevens* (1962) 18–19.
35 S. R. Gardiner, *Fortescue Papers* (Camden Soc., 1871) 218–19.
36 11/10/44, Warburton, *Cavaliers*, III, 27.
37 For examples of Charles's ciphers see Harl. MSS, 6988, 194 and Eg. MSS, 1788, 51 ff. For attempts to confuse see Evelyn, *Memoirs*, I, 129–31.
38 F. Bamford, ed., *A Royalist's Notebook* (1936) 117.
39 John Morrill, *Revolt of the Provinces* (1976) 82.
40 13/7/44, Speech to inhabitants of Somerset, Rushworth, *Collections* V, 688–90.
41 R. E. Hutton, *The Royalist War Effort, 1642–46* (Oxford, 1981).
42 Harl. MSS, 6802, 52.

## XVI 'THE BATTLE OF ALL FOR ALL'

1 14/5/45, Halliwell, *Letters*, II, 378.
2 25/2/45, Charles to wife, *Reliquiae*, 262–3.
3 30/11/44, in Charles's hand, Tanner MSS, 61, 195.
4 Add. MSS, 21505, 23.
5 Charles, *Letters*, 149–50.
6 22/1/45, Charles to wife, Rushworth, *Collections*, V, 943–4.
7 5/2/45, Charles to Nicholas, *CCSP*, I, 257.
8 Annotation of 6/2/45 on Nicholas to Charles, Evelyn, *Memoirs*, I, 115–17.
9 30/1/45 and 8, 11, 15/2/45, Charles to Nicholas, Evelyn, *Memoirs*, I, 114–15, 118–20.

10 17/2/45, Charles to Nicholas, Evelyn, *Memoirs*, I, 120–1.
11 19/2/45, Charles to wife, Rushworth, *Collections*, V, 947.
12 3/12/44, Charles to wife, *Archaeologia*, LIII (1892) 157–8.?/12/45, Charles to wife, Rushworth, *Collections*, V, 942.
13 Add. MSS, 28938, 123. Rushworth, *Collections*, V, 945.
14 27/1/43, Henrietta Maria to Charles, Halliwell, *Letters*, II, 362. Full text without dates in M. A. E. Green, *Letters of Queen Henrietta Maria* (1857) 282. L. Kaplan, 'Charles I's flights to the Scots', *Albion*, 11/3 (1979) 207–23.
15 19/2/45 and 9/3/45, Charles to wife, *Reliquiae*, 260–5.
16 13/3/45, Charles to wife, Rushworth, *Collections*, V, 948.
17 Henry Slingsby, *Diary* (1836) 140.
18 Rawl. MSS, C 125, 10–11. Tanner MSS, 61, 209.
19 Warburton, *Cavaliers*, I, 527.
20 Add. MSS, 5716, 11. 4 and 7/3/45, and 7/4/45, Charles to Rupert, Warburton, *Cavaliers*, I, 515, 526–7.
21 Rawl. MSS, C 125, 9–12.
22 9/5/45, Charles to wife, *Reliquiae*, 254–6.
23 Halliwell, *Letters*, II, 361.
24 4/1/45, Charles to Ormonde, Carte, *Ormonde*, III, 367.
25 M. Napier, *Memorials of Montrose* (Edinburgh, 1848–50) II, 177–8.
26 9/5/45, Charles to wife, *Reliquiae*, 254–6.
27 9/1/45, Add. MSS, 28938, 123.
28 H. Dircks, *The Life, Times, and Scientific Labours of the Second Marquis of Worcester* (1865) 74–80. For a facsimile in Charles's hand see S. R. Gardiner, 'Charles I and the Earl of Glamorgan', *EHR*, 2 (1887) 687–708.
29 30/4/45, Charles to Rinuccini, T. Birch, *An Inquiry into the Share Which Charles I Had in the Transactions of the Earl of Glamorgan* (1756) 30–1.
30 9/1/45, Add. MSS, 28938, 123. 16/2/45, *CCSP*, I, 258. 27/2/45, Charles *Letters*, 152–3. 20/3/45, Halliwell, *Letters*, II, 371.
31 Green, *op. cit.*, 286, 290.
32 11/10/42 and 14/2/44, *ibid.*, 285.
33 21/5/45, HMC, *1st Report*, appendix 8. 1/1/45, *Reliquiae*, 256–7.
34 27/3/45 and 14/5/45, Halliwell, *Letters*, II, 373, 380. 9/6/45, *Reliquiae*, 256–7.
35 22/1/45, Rushworth, *Collections*, V, 943–4.
36 9/4/45, Halliwell, *Letters*, II, 377–8.
37 5 and 13/3/45, Rushworth, *Collections*, V, 948.
38 9/4/45, Halliwell, *Letters*, II, 377.
39 Add. MSS. 28938, 124.
40 12/5/45, Charles to wife, Harl. MSS, 7379, 42.
41 18/5/45, Evelyn, *Memoirs*, I, 178.
42 25/5/45, Digby to Jermyn, SP 106/10/2
43 Robert Herrick, *Poetical Works* (1956) 271.
44 Harl. MSS, 7379, 41.
45 3/6/45, Digby to Legge, HMC, *1st Report*, appendix 16. 4/6/45, Charles to Nicholas, Evelyn, *Memoirs*, I, 129–31.
46 9/6/45, Evelyn, *Memoirs*, I, 131.2
47 13/6/45, Evelyn, *Memoirs*, I, 134–5.
48 19/6/45, Digby to Ormonde, Carte, *Ormonde*, VI, 301.
49 Clarendon, *History*, IV, 168–9.
50 R. E. Maddison, ' "The King's Cabinet Opened": A case study in pamphlet history', *Notes and Queries* (1966) no. 2142–9.
51 4/8/45, Charles to Nicholas, Evelyn, *Memoirs*, I, 139–40.

52 C. H. Firth, 'The reign of Charles I', *TRHS*, 3rd Series, VI, (1912) 41.
53 1/8/43, Charles to Williams, Hacket, *Scrinia*, II, 210. 2/8/44, Charles to Worcester, HMC, *12th Report*, appendix 9, 13. Clarendon, *History*, I, 100–1
54 This is the motto of the Welch Regiment. The fact that the author served in this regiment may possibly have influenced his conclusions about the stirring virtues of Welsh soldiers.
55 Evelyn, *Memoirs*, I, 135–6.
56 24/7/45, Charles Petrie, ed., *King Charles, Prince Rupert and the Civil War* (1974) 8.
57 28/7/45, Warburton, *Cavaliers*, III, 149.
58 31/7/45, Halliwell, *Letters*, II, 283–5.
59 31/7/45, Charles, *Letters*, 154–6.
60 4/5/45, Warburton, *Cavaliers*, III, 152.
61 5/8/45, Harl. MSS, 6988, 185.
62 Evelyn, *Memoirs*, I, 135–6.
63 4/8/43, *CSP*, II, 151.
64 *Lord George Digby's Cabinet* (1646).
65 5/8/45, Digby to Jermyn, Add. MSS, 3359, 11.
66 27/8/45, Digby to Jermyn, *CSPD, 1645–7*, 86. Gardiner, *Civil War*, II, 313.
67 Clarendon, *History*, (1876), II, 99.
68 25/8/45, Evelyn, *Memoirs*, I, 142.
69 25/8/45, Charles to Nicholas, Halliwell, *Letters*, II, 389.
70 'Iter Carolium', *Somer's Tracts*, V, 272.
71 9/9/45, Charles to Rupert, HMC, *9th Report*, appendix 2, 438. Charles to Montrose, Napier, *op. cit.*, II, 572.
72 Quoted in Gardiner, *Civil War*, II, 317n.
73 20/9/45, Harl. MSS, 6988, 190.
74 14/9/45, Evelyn, *Memoirs*, I, 149. C. V. Wedgwood, 'The Elector Palatine and the Civil War', *History Today*, IV (1954) 3–10. L. Kaplan, 'The "plot" to depose Charles I in 1644', *BIHR* XLIV, 110 (1971) 216–23.
75 Evelyn, *Memoirs*, I, 149.
76 Clarendon, *History*, IV, 93.
77 10/10/45, Evelyn, *Memoirs*, I, 152–3.
78 Gardiner, *Civil War*, II, 375.
79 15/10/45, Charles to Rupert, Harl. MSS, 31022, 68.
80 Quoted in Green, *op. cit.*, 303.
81 24/6/37, Str. P., II, 84.
82 26/4/38, Charles to Leicester, SP 78/105/277.
83 7/6/44, Warburton, *Cavaliers*, II, 415. 12/3/43, W. A. Day, ed., *Pythouse Papers* (1879) 4.
84 18/4/43, Warburton, *Cavaliers*, II, 167–8.
85 Harl. MSS, 6988, 149.
86 15/3/43, Day, *op. cit.*, 5. 4/8/45, Warburton, *Cavaliers*, III, 152.
87 Evelyn, *Memoirs*, I, 149.
88 23/6/45, Clarendon, *History*, IV, 168–9.
89 21/11/45, Legge to Rupert, Petrie, *op. cit.*, 24–5. Charles released Legge in the autumn.
90 21/9/45, Henry Verney to Ralph Verney, HMC, *7th Report*, appendix 452.
91 29/9/45, Charles to Colepeper, *CCSP*, I, 278. 1/10/45, Charles to Nicholas, Evelyn, *Memoirs*, I, 146–7.
92 10/10/45, Harl. MSS, 4231, 14–15. 10/10/45, Evelyn, *Memoirs*, I, 152–3.
93 9/45, Petrie, *op. cit.*, 19–20.

94 6/10/45, Charles to Lucas, *CSPD, 1645–7*, 174.

95 15/10/45, Charles to Rupert, Harl. MSS, 31022, 68.

96 Rushworth, *Collections*, VI, 84–5.

97 Clarendon, *History*, IV, 126.

98 31/10/45, Rupert to Charles, Petrie, *op. cit.*, 23.

99 Tanner, MSS, 60, 348–84. Clarendon, *History*, IV, 154–6. Charles, *Letters*, 163–5.

100 M. B. Pickel, *Charles I as a Patron of Poetry and Drama* (1936) 9.

101 'Iter Carolium', *Somer's Tracts*, V.

102 J. Moore, 'Life of John, Lord Belasyse', Folger MSS, V, a. 216, np.

103 Charles to Willoughby, Sloane, MSS, 856, 83.

104 J. G. Marston, 'Gentry, honour and loyalism in early Stuart England', *Journal of British Studies*, XIII (November 1973) 21–43.

105 Rushworth, *Collections*, V, 20–1.

106 Halliwell, *Letters*, II, 389.

107 Alexander Brome quoted in H. Morley, *King and Commons: Cavalier and Puritan Song* (1868) 104.

108 Quoted, Gardiner, *Civil War*, II, 306.

109 Rushworth, *Collections*, 565. Clarendon, *History*, IV, 109–10, 168–9. Harl. MSS, 6988, 185.

110 1/46, Warburton, *Cavaliers*, III, 218. Although J. H. Hexter has shown the distinction between Presbyterians and Independents was blurred, it is still a useful one, if only because Charles accepted and operated upon it. 'The problem of the Presbyterian Independents', *American Historical Review*, XLIV (1938) 29–49.

111 Folger MSS, V, a. 216, np.

112 1/1/46, Montreuil to Mazarin, Frederick Von Raumer, *History of the 16th and 17th Centuries Illustrated by Original Documents* (1838) II, 340. 15/1/46, Montreuil to Mazarin, J. G. Fotheringham, *Diplomatic Correspondence of Jean Montereul* (Edinburgh, 1898–9) II, 102–10. 10/1/46, *CCSP*, II, 209–10.

113 P. Cornish, chapters in T. Moody, F. X. Martin, and F. J. Byrne, eds, *A New History of Ireland, 1534–1691* (1976) III. John Lowe, 'The Glamorgan mission to Ireland', *Studia Hibernia*, IV (1964) 155–96, and 'Charles I and the Confederation of Kilkenny', *Irish Historical Studies*, XIX, 53 (1954) 1–19.

114 16/3/45, Cardinal Pamphilio's instructions to Rinuccini, Birch, *Court*, 33 ff.

115 Birch, *Court*, 90. Commission of 12/3/45 in Dircks, *op. cit.*, 75–6.

116 9/1/45, 5 and 21/5/45, 18/6/45, 1/12/45, 18/1/46, Add. MSS, 28938, 123–5. 27/2/45, Charles, *Letters*, 152–3. 19/6/45, CUL MSS, Mn I, 45, 403. 5/8/45, G. H. Orphen, 'An unpublished letter from Charles I to the Marquis of Ormonde', *English Historical Review*, XXXVI (1921) 229–34. 2/12/45 and 19/1/45, Carte, *Ormonde*, III, 432–41.

117 Sloane MSS, 4161, 92. Harl. MSS, 787, 67.

118 4/1/46, Digby to Nicholas, Rushworth, *Collections*, IV, 1, 240–2. Nicholas's concurrence of 31/1/45 in Carte, *Ormonde*, III, 447.

119 27/12/44, Dircks, *op. cit.*, 78.

120 12/5/45, Charles to wife, Harl. MSS, 7379, 42. 22/10/45, Charles to Ormonde, Carte, *Ormonde*, III, 43. 14/1/46, J. Bruce, *Charles I in 1646* (Camden Soc., 1856) 9.

121 30/1/45, Charles to Rinuccini, Birch, *Court*, 30–1. 2 and 12/1/45, 12/3/45, Dircks, *op. cit.*, 72–80. 20/10/45, *Letters*, 16, 160: he did not end his other letter to the pope on the Spanish marriage in such a craven fashion.

122 31/1/46, Charles to Irish Council, Carte, *Ormonde*, III, 446.

123 3/2/46, Charles to Glamorgan, Harl. MSS, 6988, 191.

124 6/4/46, Charles to Glamorgan, Harl. MSS, 6988, 195.

125 8/2/46, Charles to wife, Bruce, *op. cit.*, 16–18.

126 17/2/46, Charles to Ormonde, Carte, *Ormonde*, III, 449. 26/3/46, Charles to Digby, *ibid.*, 452. 5/4/46, Charles to Glamorgan, Harl. MSS, 7988, 193.

127 Evelyn, *Memoirs*, I, 171.

128 11/1/46, Charles to wife, Bruce, *op. cit.*, 6–9.

129 14 and 18/1/46, Charles to wife, *ibid.*, 9–11.

130 Robert Ashton, *The English Civil War* (1978) 251.

131 21/1/46, Clarendon, *History*, IV, 165.

132 12/3/46, Bruce, *op. cit.*, 25.

133 1 and 19/2/46, *ibid.*, 14–20. 2/2/46, Charles to Colepeper, *CSP*, II, 206–7.

134 13/4/46, Bruce, *op. cit.*,, 33–5. See also 22/3/46, Charles to Rupert, Charles, *Letters*, 175.

135 3/4/46, Charles to Ormonde, Add. MSS, 28938 126.

136 26/2/45, 23/3/45, Charles to House of Lords, Rushworth, *Collections*, VI, 223–5. 2/3/45, Nicholas to Vane, Evelyn, *Memoirs*, I, 159.

137 19/2/46, 3 and 16/3/46, Bruce, *op. cit.*, 18–20, 22–3, 26–7. Evelyn, *Memoirs*, I, 160–2.

138 3/3/46, Bruce, *op. cit.*, 22.

139 23/3/46, Charles to Montreuil, *CSP*, II, 219.

140 *CSP*, II, 218–22.

141 D. Stevenson, *Revolution and Counter Revolution in Scotland 1644–51* (Newton Abbot, 1977) 60 ff. 1/4/46, Montreuil, Harl. MSS, 6988, 192. 26/2/46, Montreuil to Mazarin, Fotheringham, *op. cit.*, I, 152.

142 6/4/46, Bruce, *op. cit.*, 31–2. 4/4/46, Charles to Ormonde, Add. MSS, 28938, 126.

143 2, 4, and 6/4/46, Bruce, *op. cit.*, 31–2. 4/4/46, Charles to Ormonde, Add. MSS, 28938, 126.

144 Photo in *Archaeologia*, LII (1892) plate VIII. Sheldon immediately buried the promise, and dug it up at the Restoration.

145 13 and 15/4/46, Bruce, *op. cit.*, 33–6. 19.4.46, Fotheringham, *op. cit.*, I, 183.

146 21/4/46, Bruce, *op. cit.*, 36–7.

147 22/4/46, *ibid.*, 37–9.

## XVII 'WHAT WAY TO TALK'

1 10.6.46, HMC, *4th Report*, 522.

2 Rawl. MSS, B 225, 14. Francis Peck, *Desiderata Curiosa* (1779) 21.

3 *CSP*, II, 285–90.

4 27/7/46, W. C. Abbott, ed., *The Writings and Speeches of Oliver Cromwell* (Cambridge, Mass., 1937–47) I, 408.

5 H. Rollins, *Cavalier and Puritans* (New York, 1923) 28.

6 Berkeley, *Memoirs*, cliv.

7 These estimates are rough, based on Sir Edward Walker's 'Short life of Charles I', in Rawl. MSS, D 392, 347. For a more sophisticated estimate of civil war casualties, see Charles Carlton, *Going to the Wars: The Experience of the British Civil Wars, 1638–51* (1992), 201–14.

8 15 and 18/5/46, Charles to Peers, Rawl. MSS, B 225 and Harl. MSS, 787, 67. 18/5/46, Charles to Governor of Oxford, CUL MSS, I, 46, 5.

9 Carte, *Ormonde*, III, 454. Charles wrote the same to his wife, 18/1/46, John Bruce, *Charles I in 1646* (Camden Soc., 1856) 11.

10 17/1/46, Charles to Peers and 19.5.46 to Lord Mayor, Charles, *Letters*, 167,

181. Bruce, *op. cit.*, 11, 48. *CSP*, II, 540. 27/10/46, Charles to Jermyn, Halliwell, *Letters*, II, 428.

11 Bruce, *op. cit.*, 18–20, 22–3, 86. *CSP*, II, 209–10.

12 16/7/46, Mark Napier, *Memorials of Montrose and his Times*, II, 637–8. Charles expressed same sentiments to his garrisons; see Warburton, *Cavaliers*, III, 227, and HMC, *4th Report*, appendix, 341.

13 10/12/46, Charles to Ormonde, Add. MSS, 28938, 127. 47/1/28, Hyde to Berkeley, *CSP*, II, 33. Bruce, *op. cit.*, 16–18.

14 Tanner MSS, 59, 129.

15 Ashburnham, *Narrative*, II, 75–7. Folger MSS, V. a. 216, np.

16 C. S. Terry, *The Life and Campaigns of Alexander Leslie, First Earl of Leven* (1899) 408.

17 Charles, *The Papers Which Passed at Newcastle* (1649).

18 Alexander Henderson, *Character of King Charles* (1692) preface.

19 Bruce, *op. cit.*, 45–6.

20 *Ibid.*, 41–3, 45, 50. Halliwell, *Letters*, II, 439–40. Harl. Mss, 6988, 211.

21 11/7/46, Charles to Peers, Carte, *Ormonde*, III, 487.

22 11/6/46, Charles to Peers, *Lords Journal*, VIII, 374.

23 Gardiner, *Constitutional Documents*, 290–1.

24 22/7/46, *Charles*, Letters, 199–201.

25 Quoted Robert Ashton, *The English Civil War* (1978) 291.

26 Charles, *Letters*, 202–3.

27 31/8/46, Charles to wife, Bruce, *op. cit.*, 62. Charles to Prince Charles, *CSP*, II, 254; see also 274, 277, 313.

28 Burnet, *Hamilton*, 367–70.

29 24/8/46, Charles to wife, Bruce, *op. cit.*, 61. 31/8/46, Charles to Jermyn, *CSP*, II, 255–6, Jermyn and Colepeper to Charles, *CSP*, II, 261.

30 Ashburnham, *Narrative*, II, lxvi. *CSP*, II, 271. M. A. E. Green, ed., *Letters of Queen Henrietta Maria* (1857) 271, 329–31.

31 Green, *op. cit.*, 327–9.

32 30//9/46, Charles, *Letters*, 208–9.

33 Bruce, *op. cit.*, 79–83.

34 *CSP*, II, 264.

35 Green, *op. cit.*, 334–5.

36 Bruce, *op. cit.*, 77.

37 Rushworth, *Collections*, VI, 329.

38 *King's War*, 567.

39 *CSP*, II, 287. Add. MSS, 28938, 126–8. Bruce, *op. cit.*, 60–3. CUL MSS. I, 45, 407.

40 28/11/46, Charles to wife, Bruce *op. cit.*, 77.

41 Halliwell, *Letters*, II, 439–40.

42 Gardiner, *Civil War*, II, 172–88. Bruce, *op. cit.*, 76. Burnet, *Hamilton*, 381, 385–8. Rushworth, *Collections*, VI, 393.

43 *CSP*, II, 329–30.

44 Bruce, *op. cit.*, 66–7.

45 Herbert, *Memoirs*, 42–3.

46 14/1/47, Charles to Scots Commissioners, Rushworth, *Collections*, VI, 394; D. Stevenson, *Revolution and Counter-Revolution in Scotland, 1644–51* (Newton Abbot, 1977) 80.

47 Peck, *op. cit.*, IX, 25. Herbert, *Memoirs*, 44.

48 Clarendon, *History* IV, 214.

NOTES

49 6.3.47, Charles to Peers, Harl. MSS, 787, 97, and Tanner MSS, 59, 800. Folger MSS, Yd 341 dates this letter 17 Feb 1647.
50 6/3/47, Charles to Bellieree, J. G. Fotheringham, *Diplomatic Correspondence of Jean Montereul* (Edinburgh, 1898–9) II, 75.
51 12/5/47, Charles to Peer, Charles, *Letters*, 214–19.
52 G. W. Johnson, *Memorials of the Reign of Charles the First* (1848) I, 112.
53 Description of Holdenby affair including verbatim conversations from Herbert, *Memoirs*, 25–40, and Rushworth, *Collections*, VI, 515–17. Herbert was there, and Rushworth interviewed a parliamentary commissioner.
54 *Commons Journal*, VI, 111.
55 Abbott, *op. cit.*, I, 452–7. Antonia Fraser, *Cromwell: Our Chief of men* (St Albans, 1975) 194–5. C. Hill, *World Turned Upside Down* (1972) 49.
56 Sir Philip Warwick, *Memoirs of the Reigne of King Charles* (Edinburgh, 1803) 331, says this incident took place in Royston on 24–6/6/47. Major Huntington says at Childersley on 5–9/6/47, in 'Narrative' in G. S. Stevenson, ed., *Charles I in Captivity from Contemporary Sources* (1927).
57 John Lilburne, *Two Letters* (1647) quoted Hill, *op. cit.*, 52.
58 17/6/47, Charles to Fairfax, C. H. Firth, ed., *Selections from the Papers of William Clarke* (Camden Soc., 1891–1901, I, 135.
59 21/6/47, Charles to ?, Add. MSS, 5015, 21. Herbert, *Memoirs*, 56–9.
60 Clarendon, *History*, IV, 226–8. 22/6/47, Charles to Lanerick, Burnet, *Hamilton*, 401.
61 Herbert, *Memoirs*, 60–1.
62 12/7/47, Charle to Lanerick, Burnet, *Hamilton*, 402.
63 4/7/47, Charles to James, Charles, *Letters*, 231. Clarendon, *History*, IV, 237.
64 They are dated 1/8/47, Gardiner, *Constitutional Documents*, 316–26.
65 Burnet, *Hamilton*, 402.
66 Berkeley, *Memoirs*, 15, 33–5.
67 3/8/47, *CSP*, II, 373–4, and Rushworth, *Collections*, VII, 753. Clarendon MSS, 2573, quoted by Gardiner, *Civil War*, III, 353.
68 19.8.47, Harl. MSS, 35029, 2. 23/7/47 Add. MSS, 28938, 128. Burnet, *Hamilton*, 404.
69 G. S. Stevenson, *op. cit.*, 71. *CSP*, II, 382.


XVIII 'REMEMBER THY END'

1 This is based on Edward Whalley, *His Departure from Hampton Court* (1847); Berkeley, *Memoirs*, clxvii; Ashburnham, *Narrative*, II, 100–14; Clarendon, *History*, IV, 263–5; Jack D. Jones, *The Royal Prisoner: Charles I at Carisbrooe* (1965) 12–23.
2 *Reliquiae*, 277. Rushworth, *Collections*, VII, 871–2.
3 11/11/47, Cromwell to Whalley, W. C. Abbott, *The Writings and Speeches of Oliver Cromwell* (Cambridge, Mass., 1937–47) I, 551. 13/11/47, CUL MSS, Mn, I, 47, 460. I owe the point about being poisoned to John Adamson.
4 Berkeley, *Memoirs*, clxvii–clxxvi.
5 David Stephenson, *Revolution and Counter-Revolution in Scotland, 1644–51* (1977) 137.
6 Jones, *op. cit.*, 23.
7 Herbert, *Memoirs*, 69.
8 John Oglander, *A Royalist Notebook*, ed., F. Bamford (1936) 113, 127. H. Long, *The Oglander Memoirs* (1888) 64–5.
9 23/11/47, Charles to Lanerick, Burnet, *Hamilton*, 414.

10 26 and 27/11/47, Charles to Firebrace, Eg. MSS, 2618, 21, 23, *CSP*, II, appendix xli.
11 Berkeley, *Memoirs*, clxxxvii.
12 5/12/46, *CSP*, II, 305.
13 Gardiner, *Constitutional Documents*, 328–30.
14 *Lords Journal*, IX, 567.
15 Gardiner, *Constitutional Documents*, 335–47.
16 Berkeley, *Memoirs*, IX, 621.
17 *Lords Journal*, IX, 621.
18 19 and 29/11/47, 6 and 8/12/47, Charles to Lanark, Burnet, *Hamilton*, 412–20.
19 Facsimile in A. MacDonald, *Letters of the Argyle Family* (Edinburgh, 1839) 40.
20 Gardiner, *Constitutional Documents*, 347–53.
21 Ashburnham, *Narrative*, II, 123.
22 Berkeley, *Memoirs* CXCV. Ashburnham, *Narrative*, II, 120. C. H. Firth, ed., *Selections from the Papers of William Clarke* (Camden Soc., 1891–1901) I, 420.
23 Clarendon, *History*, IV, 279–80.
24 Gardiner, *Civil War*, IV, 51.
25 *CSPD, 1648–9*, 3.
26 Quoted Stevenson, *op. cit.*, 88–9.
27 28/2/48, Charles to Dowcett, C. W. Firebrace, *Honest Harry, Being the Biography of Sir Henry Firebrace* (1932) 266.
28 9, 10 and 11/4/48, Eg. MSS, 1533, 9–12.
29 11/4/48, Charles to Firebrace, Eg. MSS, 1788, 4. 12 and 13/4/48, Charles to Titus, Eg. MSS, 1533, 6, 11. John Reeve, *Charles I and the Road to Personal Rule* (1989), 111, shows a similar process taking place during the drafting of the proclamation issued on 27 March 1629 defending the decision to dissolve parliament.
30 Herbert, *Memoirs* (1959) 48–9. Charles to Titus, Eg. MSS, 1533, 4.
31 Charles to Titus, Eg. MSS, 1533, 8. Charles to ?, Add. MSS, 35029, 5.
32 Eg. MSS, 1788, 7, 10, 15, 18, 21.
33 P. Barwick, *The Life of ... John Barwick ... with an appendix of letters from King Charles I* (1724) 387.
34 3/5/47, Charles to Firebrace, Eg. MSS, 1788, 1.
35 14 and 24/5/48, Charles to Titus, Eg. MSS, 1533, 13, 15.
36 Jones, *op. cit.*, 97.
37 G. Hillier, *A Narrative of Attempted Escapes of Charles I* (1852), 189.
38 Charles's cover letter to Firebrace of 26/4/48 contained letters to his wife, Lady Carlisle, Francis Cresset, Legge, and two for both Jane Whorwood and Mr Lowe, Eg. MSS, 1788, 19.
39 Add. MSS, 35029, 3.
40 1/7/48, Charles to Titus, Eg. MSS, 1533, 16.
41 SP 9/246/32, (Newspaper Collections).
42 Bamford, *op. cit.*, 121.
43 Berkeley, *Memoirs*, 91–8.
44 Charles's correspondence with Hopkins is in the royal archives, Windsor, transcripts of which are in NRA file 1157. Firebrace, *op. cit.*, prints most of them. 21/7/48, Firebrace, *op. cit.*, 326.
45 1/8/48, Charles to Firebrace, Eg. MSS, 1788, 41. 1, 21 and 23/8/48, Charles to Hopkins, Firebrace, *op. cit.*, 336.
46 12, 19/1/48, and 27/2/48, Charles to Dowcett, Firebrace, *op. cit.*, 263–4.
47 CUL, Add. MSS, 7311.

48 14/5/48, Charles to Titus, Eg. MSS, 1533, 13. 25/5/48, Charles to Firebrace, Eg. MSS, 1788, 14.

49 8/10/48, 15/8/48 and 16/7/48, Charles to Hopkins, Firebrace, *op. cit.*, 322–3, 333–4, 343.

50 13/2/48, Charles to Walker, CUL, Add. MSS, 7311. 12/8/48, 2 and 3/9/48, Charles to Hopkins, Firebrace, *op. cit.*, 332, 339–40. 23 and 24/7/48, Charles to Whorwood, Eg. MSS, 1788, 24, 35.

51 These totals inferred from his letters to Hopkins and Firebrace.

52 Charles to Hopkins, Firebrace, *op. cit.*, 333.

53 21/9/48, Whorwood to Charles, *ibid.*, 341–2.

54 *Ibid.*, 107.

55 30/12/48, Charles to Hopkins, *ibid.*, 347. See also 27/12/48, Charles to Firebrace, Eg. MSS, 1788, 49.

56 CUL MSS, Mn I, 45, 405–7. Charles, *Works*, 1301.

57 1/7/48, Charles to Titus, Eg. MSS, 1533, 16.

58 31/7/48, Charle to Scots Parliament and Assembly, Harl. MSS, 6988, 210–11.

59 Francis Peck, *Desiderata Curiosa* (1779) ix.

60 Lucy Hutchinson, *Memoirs of the Life of Colonel Hutchinson* (1968) 242.

61 Gardiner, *Civil War*, IV, 119.

62 21/8/48, Charles to Hopkins, Firebrace, *op. cit.*, 329–30. Charle to Firebrace, Eg. MSS, 1788, 42.

63 Harl. MSS, 6988, 212.

64 Rushworth, *Collections*, VII, 1241.

65 Tanner MSS, 57, 280. *Lords Journal*, X, 474, 498, 501. CUL MSS, I, 46, 31–2.

66 The ring may be seen today in the castle museum. Jones, *op. cit.*, 112.

67 Herbert, *Memoirs*, 118.

68 Rushworth, *Collections*, VII, 1264.

69 26/10/48, Charles to Lewis Incladon, NRA, 0279, 2. 11/11/48, Charles to Kirk, Eg. MSS, 2395, 36. 20/9/48, Charles to Sheriffs, Rushworth, *Collections*, VII, 1272. 10/10/48, Charles to Kerckhoven, Rawl. MSS, Letters, 115, 433. 19/10/48, Charles to D'Ewes, Harl. MSS, 6988, 216.

70 Diary of Nicholas Oudart in Peck, *op. cit.*, 392.

71 Rushworth, *Collections*, VII, 1266. Rawl. MSS, D 851, 190.

72 *Lords Journal*, X, 51. John Thurloe, A Collection of State Papers (1742) I, 103.

73 Tanner MSS, 57, B 399.

74 *Lords Journal*, X, 536–7, 583, 603.

75 Tanner MSS, 61, 426. *Lords Journal*, X, 544–9, 562, 566, 577, 589, 597, 603, 618–21.

76 Peck, *op. cit.*, 407.

77 Warwick, *Memoirs*, 366.

78 7, 8, 9, 16, 17/10/48, Charles to Hopkins, Firebrace, *op. cit.*, 344–6.

79 9 and 12/11/48, Charles to Firebrace, *op. cit.*, 346–7. Gardiner, *Civil War*, IV, 242.

80 *CSP*, II, 428.

81 Hillier, *op. cit.*, 233. My thanks to Edward Thompson for this point.

82 Warwick, *Memoirs*, 360–4.

83 Oglander, *op. cit.*, 70–1.

84 Charles, *Letters*, 239–41.

85 Habbakuk, II, 3.

86 Charles, *Letters*, 239.

87 Based on Firebrace's narrative in Stevenson, *op. cit.*, 140–2, and Cooke's in Rushworth, *Collections*, vii, 1344–8.

88 Ash. MSS, 800, 36.
89 Herbert, *Memoirs*, 160.
90 5/12/48, Charles to Oudart, Peck, *op. cit.*, 411. 5/12/48, Charles to Firebrace, Eg. MSS, 1788, 47.
91 Herbert, *Memoirs*, 76–9.
92 Halliwell, *Letters*, II, 457–61.
93 *Ibid.*, II, 457–61.
94 *CSP*, II, 219.
95 Charle,s *Letters*, 272.
96 Stevenson, *op. cit.*, 88–9.
97 Firth, *op. cit.*, II, appendix C, p. 268.
98 For example, see Berkeley, *Memoirs*, cxcv.
99 Herbert, *Memoirs*, 49.
100 HMC, *12th Report*, appendix 9, 33.
101 Charles, *Letters*, 239–41. HMC, *De Lisle*, IV, 578.
102 Charles, *Letters*, 262.
103 14/10/47 and 27/10/48, Sloane MSS, 3299, 145–7.
104 SP 16/20/72. E. Simpson and G. Potter, eds, *The Sermons of John Donne* (Berkeley, 1953) VI, 241–2.
105 *CSP*, II, appendix, xxxvii.
106 F. F. Madam, *A New Bibliography of Eikon Basilike* (Oxford, 1950). Philip Knachel, *Eikon Basilike* (1969). H. R. Trevor-Roper, 'Eikon Basilike', *History Today*, I (1951) 7–12.
107 Charles, *Letters*, 266. In this section the following theoretical books have been useful: Peter Berger, *The Sacred Canopy: Elements of a Sociological Theory of Religion* (New York, 1968); Sigmund Freud, *Moses and Monotheism* (1939); Max Weber, *Essays in Sociology* (New York, 1958); Albert Bandura, *Social Learning Theory* (Englewood Cliffs, 1977); Seymour Bymer, 'Patterns of Tudor Martyrdom', *American History Review*, 83, 3 (June, 1978) and the response by L. M. Hill and Monsell Patterson, *ibid.* (October 1979) 1229–30. I am most grateful to Peter Loewenberg for sending me a copy of his stimulating essay 'Anxiety in History', in *Journal of Preventive Psychiatry and Allied Disciplines*, IV, 2/1 (1990), 141–63.
108 Oglander, *op. cit.*, 70–1.
109 George Chalmers, *Poetic Remains of the Scottish Kings* (1827) 203.

### XIX 'AN INCORRUPTIBLE CROWN'

1 In addition to C. V. Wedgwood's brilliant *Trial of Charles I* (published in US as *A Coffin for King Charles*) I have used the three main contemporary accounts: (1) Gilbert Mabbot, 'A perfect narrative', in H. L. Stephens, ed., *State Trials* (1889) I, 75–122; (2) John Nalson, *A True Copy of the Journal of the High Court of Jutice for the Trial of Charles I* (1684), which contains the notes of John Phelps, Clerk to the Court; (3) 'Bradshaw's Journal', in J. G. Muddiman, *Trial of King Charles I* (1928) appendix A. I have compressed the verbatim record, both sides' arguments were tedious and repetitive, as they often failed to make contact, lacking common ground.
2 Richard II, Act IV, Scene 1.
3 Sydney Papers 237, quoted Gardiner, *Civil War*, IV, 296.
4 Nalson, *op. cit.*, 26.
5 P. Held, 'Roi de la Caise', *Art Bulletin*, XL (1958) 139–48.
6 Warwick, *Memoirs*, 380.

7 W. L. Sachse, 'An analysis of the Regicide Court', *Journal of British Studies*, XIII (1973) 69–85.

8 William Lily, *True History of King James the First and King Charles the First* (1822) 149.

9 Thomas Harrison, quoted Wedgwood, *op. cit.*, 252.

10 A. Hast, 'State treason trials during the Puritan revolution', *Historical Journal*, XV (1972) 49.

11 Major Francis White, quoted, Wedgwood, *op. cit.*, 166.

12 Charles, *Letters*, 259–61.

13 SP 16/23/102.

14 Charles, *Letters*, 261–73.

15 Warwick, *Memoirs*, 379.

16 Nalson, *op. cit.*, 81.

17 Herbert, *Memoirs*, 119–30.

18 The story that Prince Charles sent parliament a signed and sealed blank sheet of paper on which they could write whatever terms were necessary to save his father was an eighteenth-century fabrication. See note by J. P. Gilson in Harl. MSS, 9988.

19 Nalson, *op. cit.*, 84–9. Herbert, *Memoirs*, 247–54.

20 Herbert to Samway, Tanner MSS, 37, 204.

21 Herbert, *Memoirs*, 126.

22 Juxon told Warwick, *Memoirs*, 387.

23 Herbert, *Memoirs*, 181–4.

24 *Ibid.*, 129–30.

25 H. Halford, 'An account of the opening of the tomb of King Charles I at Windsor', in *Essays and Orations* (1831).

# INDEX